Fodor's

P9-CAG-958

48102835 / # Club Med / AA# OWJGNB (handwritten)

SWITZERLAND

45th Edition

Where to Stay and Eat
for All Budgets

Must-See Sights
and Local Secrets

Ratings You Can Trust

Fodor's Travel Publications   New York, Toronto, London, Sydney, Auckland
www.fodors.com

FODOR'S SWITZERLAND
Editor: Robert I. C. Fisher

Editorial Contributors: Nancy Coons, Katrin Gygax, Suzanne Hégelé, Gail Mangold-Vine, Alexis Munier, Sharon-Anne Wilcox, Kay Winzenried

Production Editors: Tom Holton, Jennifer DePrima
Maps & Illustrations: David Lindroth and Mark Stroud, *cartographers*; Bob Blake, Rebecca Baer, *map editors;* William Wu, *information graphics*
Design: Fabrizio LaRocca, *creative director*; Guido Caroti, Siobhan O'Hare, *art directors*; Tina Malaney, Ann McBride, Chie Ushio, Jessica Walsh, *designers*; Melanie Marin, *senior picture editor;* Moon Sun Kim, *cover designer*
Cover Photo (Lake high above the town of Zermatt on the Matterhorn, Valais Alps): PatitucciPhoto/Outdoor Collection/Aurora Photos
Production Manager: Angela L. McLean

COPYRIGHT
Copyright © 2009 by Fodor's Travel, a division of Random House, Inc.

Fodor's is a registered trademark of Random House, Inc.

All rights reserved. Published in the United States by Fodor's Travel, a division of Random House, Inc., and simultaneously in Canada by Random House of Canada, Limited, Toronto. Distributed by Random House, Inc., New York.

No maps, illustrations, or other portions of this book may be reproduced in any form without written permission from the publisher.

45th Edition

ISBN 978-1-4000-0822-3

ISSN 0071-6553

SPECIAL SALES
This book is available at special discounts for bulk purchases for sales promotions or premiums. Special editions, including personalized covers, excerpts of existing books, and corporate imprints, can be created in large quantities for special needs. For more information, write to Special Markets/Premium Sales, 1745 Broadway, MD 6-2, New York, New York 10019, or e-mail specialmarkets@randomhouse.com.

AN IMPORTANT TIP & AN INVITATION
Although all prices, opening times, and other details in this book are based on information supplied to us at press time, changes occur all the time in the travel world, and Fodor's cannot accept responsibility for facts that become outdated or for inadvertent errors or omissions. So **always confirm information when it matters,** especially if you're making a detour to visit a specific place. Your experiences—positive and negative—matter to us. If we have missed or misstated something, **please write to us.** We follow up on all suggestions. Contact the Switzerland editor at editors@fodors.com or c/o Fodor's at 1745 Broadway, New York, NY 10019.

PRINTED IN THE UNITED STATES OF AMERICA

10 9 8 7 6 5 4 3 2

Be a Fodor's Correspondent

Your opinion matters. It matters to us. It matters to your fellow Fodor's travelers, too. And we'd like to hear it. In fact, we need to hear it.

When you share your experiences and opinions, you become an active member of the Fodor's community. That means we'll not only use your feedback to make our books better, but we'll publish your names and comments whenever possible. Throughout our guides, look for "Word of Mouth," excerpts of your unvarnished feedback.

Here's how you can help improve Fodor's for all of us.

Tell us when we're right. We rely on local writers to give you an insider's perspective. But our writers and staff editors—who are the best in the business—depend on you. Your positive feedback is a vote to renew our recommendations for the next edition.

Tell us when we're wrong. We're proud that we update most of our guides every year. But we're not perfect. Things change. Hotels cut services. Museums change hours. Charming cafés lose charm. If our writer didn't quite capture the essence of a place, tell us how you'd do it differently. If any of our descriptions are inaccurate or inadequate, we'll incorporate your changes in the next edition and will correct factual errors at fodors.com immediately.

Tell us what to include. You probably have had fantastic travel experiences that aren't yet in Fodor's. Why not share them with a community of like-minded travelers? Maybe you chanced upon a beach or bistro or B&B that you don't want to keep to yourself. Tell us why we should include it. And share your discoveries and experiences with everyone directly at fodors.com. Your input may lead us to add a new listing or highlight a place we cover with a "Highly Recommended" star or with our highest rating, "Fodor's Choice."

Give us your opinion instantly at our feedback center at www.fodors.com/feedback. You may also e-mail editors@fodors.com with the subject line "Switzerland Editor." Or send your nominations, comments, and complaints by mail to Switzerland Editor, Fodor's, 1745 Broadway, New York, NY 10019.

You and travelers like you are the heart of the Fodor's community. Make our community richer by sharing your experiences. Be a Fodor's correspondent.

Happy Traveling!

Tim Jarrell, Publisher

CONTENTS

MAPS

ABOUT THIS BOOK

Our Ratings

Sometimes you find terrific travel experiences and sometimes they just find you. But usually the burden is on you to select the right combination of experiences. That's where our ratings come in.

As travelers we've all discovered a place so wonderful that its worthiness is obvious. And sometimes that place is so experiential that superlatives don't do it justice: you just have to be there to know. These sights, properties, and experiences get our highest rating, **Fodor's Choice**, indicated by orange stars throughout this book.

Black stars highlight sights and properties we deem **Highly Recommended**, places that our writers, editors, and readers praise again and again for consistency and excellence.

By default, there's another category: any place we include in this book is by definition worth your time, unless we say otherwise. And we will.

Disagree with any of our choices? Care to nominate a place or suggest that we rate one more highly? Visit our feedback center at www. fodors.com/feedback.

Budget Well

Hotel and restaurant price categories from ¢ to $$$$ are defined in the opening pages of each chapter. For attractions, we always give standard adult admission fees; reductions are usually available for children, students, and senior citizens. Want to pay with plastic? **AE, D, DC, MC, V** following restaurant and hotel listings indicate whether American Express, Discover, Diner's Club, MasterCard, and Visa are accepted.

Restaurants

Unless we state otherwise, restaurants are open for lunch and dinner daily. We mention dress only when there's a specific requirement and reservations only when they're essential or not accepted—it's always best to book ahead.

Hotels

Hotels have private bath, phone, TV, and air-conditioning and operate on the European Plan (aka EP, meaning without meals), unless we specify that they use the Continental Plan (CP, with a continental breakfast), Breakfast Plan (BP, with a full breakfast), or Modified American Plan (MAP, with breakfast and dinner), or are all-inclusive (including all meals and most activities). We

always list facilities but not whether you'll be charged an extra fee to use them, so when pricing accommodations, find out what's included.

Many Listings

★	Fodor's Choice
★	Highly recommended
✉	Physical address
✛	Directions
⌂	Mailing address
☎	Telephone
🖷	Fax
⊕	On the Web
✍	E-mail
💳	Admission fee
☉	Open/closed times
Ⓜ	Metro stations
▭	Credit cards

Hotels & Restaurants

🏨	Hotel
🛏	Number of rooms
☌	Facilities
🍽	Meal plans
✗	Restaurant
☕	Reservations
↘	Smoking
🍷	BYOB
✗🏨	Hotel with restaurant that warrants a visit

Outdoors

🏌	Golf
⛺	Camping

Other

☚	Family-friendly
⇨	See also
✉	Branch address
☞	Take note

Experience Switzerland

WORD OF MOUTH

"We felt sad on having left Switzerland, where we had enjoyed a wonderful 7–8 days. Who said that the Swiss were dull and boring? We had found them to be very warm and friendly and they all spoke excellent English. We had rehearsed some key German words and phrases before starting this trip, but never needed to use them. And what a gorgeous country they have."

—indiancouple

WHAT'S WHERE

1 Zürich. Given that it is one of the world's leading financial centers, Zürich is surprisingly small, but its wealth of cultural riches more than makes up for its size. Tour the luxuriously gentrified **Altstadt** (Old Town), then take in the hulking **Grossmünster** cathedral, great modern art at the **Bührle** Museum, and top Old Masters at Winterthur's **Oskar Reinhart Collection.**

2 Eastern Switzerland. East of Zürich the Rhine snakes through some of the most untouched regions of Switzerland; in tiny towns and small cities, amid wood-shingle farmhouses and grand Baroque churches, discover the old Rhine city of **Schaffhausen,** known for its medieval frescoes, **St. Gallen,** a busy textile center with an active Old Town, and princely **Liechtenstein.**

3 Graubünden. The mountains of what used to be called Rhaetia once made the region of Graubünden difficult to rule. Today emperors and kings have been replaced by new conquerors: tourists, who take the gorgeous train ride to **Arosa,** visit "Heidi-Country" in **Maienfeld,** hang out with writers in **Klosters** and billionaires in **Davos,** and ski and be seen in glitzy **St. Moritz.**

Schaffhausen

Rhine

Basel Brugg Baden Winterthur Frauenfeld

Aarau

Olten Zürich

Solothurn Küsnacht

Zug

Luzern Schwyz

BERN Langnau

Sarnen Altdorf

Thun Meiringen

Interlaken Wassen

Grindelwald

Wengen Andermatt

BERNER ALPS Jungfraujoch

LEPONTINE ALPS

Rhône e Rhône Brig Biasca

Sierre Visp

Simplon Pass Locarno

PENNINE ALPS Zermatt Ascona

Matterhorn

ITALY

GERMANY

Kreuzlingen

Bodensee

2

Arbon   Rorschach

Wil

St.Gallen

Appenzell

AUSTRIA

Buchs   Vaduz

LIECHTENSTEIN

Sargans

Glarus

GLARNER ALPS

Chur

Davos

Scuol

3   Zernez

Inn

RHAETIAN ALPS   ENGADINE   ALPS

St. Moritz

4

Bellinzona

gáno

0   40 miles

0   60 km

4 Ticino. With its intoxicating *italianità* (Italian flair), Ticino is an irresistible combination of Mediterranean pleasures and Swiss efficiency. The region's sinuous lakes, perhaps its greatest attraction, beckon with strolls along fashionable waterfront promenades. Concentrate on beauteous **Lugano,** serene **Locarno,** and rustic **Ascona,** set on the shore of Lago Maggiore.

5 Luzern & Central Switzerland. Central Switzerland is the most-visited region in the country. No wonder: you can take a paddleboat steamer on the **Vierwaldstättersee** lake past some of the most beautiful (and bluest) lakeside vistas to the **Rütli Meadow**— "birthplace" of Switzerland— and the fabled Wilhelm Tell chapel. **Luzern** itself has a medieval Old Town so cleanly refurbished it could be mistaken for a museum exhibit.

6 Basel. Set where Switzerland meets Germany and France, Basel's position put it at the very center of Europe. In the 15th century, the city won the right to hold an unlimited number of fairs, which today range from a famous Fasnacht carnival to the chic ArtBasel. A lovely Old Town, a Rhine riverwalk, and great modern art— including the Museum Tinguely and Fondation Beyeler—also make Basel a best bet.

WHAT'S WHERE

7 Fribourg & Neuchâtel.
Largely undiscovered, these
two cantons (states) are
favored for getaways of western Switzerland. Fribourg,
part German and part French,
is divided into a check-
erboard of fields with a
neatness only the Swiss can
achieve—the highlight is the
stunningly picturesque castle
at **Gruyères.** Other treasures:
lakeside **Neuchâtel** and
Gothic-era **Fribourg.**

8 Bern. A city of broad
medieval streets, Switzerland's federal capital sits in
the country's largest canton,
whose size and influence mirror the pride of its citizens.
The famed sandstone arcades,
painted fountains, performing
mechanical clock of the **Zytglogge,** Gothic **Münster,** and
art-filled **Zentrum Paul Klee**
are as ardently protected as
the country's neutrality.

9 Berner Oberland. Kiss
the sky in this hyper-magical
province—a "summit of summits" that includes the peaks
of the **Eiger, Mönch, and
Jungfrau.** From the hub of
Interlaken, journey up to
gorgeous eagle's-nest towns
like **Mürren** and **Wengen**
and down to the "Shangri-la"
valley that is **Lauterbrunnen.**
A taste of the high life awaits
in glam **Gstaad.** The Berner
Oberland is a must-do!

FRANCE

Porrentruy

JURA MOUNTAINS

Doubs

7

Biel

La Chaux-de-Fonds

Neuchâtel

Murten

Lac de Neuchâtel

Payerne

Fribourg

Yverdon

Lausanne

Gruyères

Gstaad

11

Vevey

Nyon

Lac Léman

Montreux

Geneva

12

Sion

FRANCE

Martigny

Verbier

Grand St. Bernard Pass

0   40 miles

0   60 km

10 Valais. This is the Switzerland of raclette eaters, winemakers, yodelers—and, oh, yes, the **Matterhorn.** From the valley of the Rhône explore the citadel of **Sion** and take resort luxury to new heights in **Saas-Fee, Verbier,** and **Crans-Montana.** Of course, you'll feel unsated if you miss Switzerland's most photographed icon, the Matterhorn, so end up in its lovely home, **Zermatt.**

11 Vaud. Centered around **Lac Léman (Lake Geneva),** this French-speaking canton harbors Alpine villages, glamorous lake resorts, and verdant vineyards. But be sure to immerse yourself in the Old Town and hyperactive waterfront of **Lausanne,** harbor-front **Vevey,** Riviera-like **Montreux,** and lakeside **Château de Chillon**—Switzerland's most fabled castle.

12 Geneva. As the birthplace of Calvinism and the International Red Cross, home to the European headquarters of the United Nations, and a stronghold of private banks, Geneva early on established the city's outsize importance. But with its manageable size, it remains a blessing for all visitors. The Palais des Nations, Old City, magical Lac Léman, and the feathery Jet d'Eau—Geneva's "Eiffel Tower"—are the top sights.

SWITZERLAND PLANNER

Getting Here

The two main airports in Geneva (Geneva International Airport (aka Cointrin, ⊕ www. gva.ch) and Zürich (Unique Zürich Airport, ⊕ www.zurich-airport.com) will get you here from anywhere in the world, nonstop from New York, Miami, Los Angeles, Montreal, and London, for example.

The Basel/Mulhouse airport offers flights from European destinations and is less crowded.

The smaller airports at Bern (⊕ www.alpar.ch) and Locarno (Aeroporto Cantonale Locarno, ☎091/7351560, no Web site) host local and short-haul flights as well as private jet traffic.

Public transportation from/ to all airports is excellent (as it is throughout the country) and generally much faster and cheaper than taxis.

And think twice about domestic flights within Switzerland.

If you calculate getting from your hotel to the airport, the flight time including delays, and getting to your next hotel, taking the train is often faster and more comfortable, as trains and buses will take you almost anywhere in Switzerland.

Restaurants: The Basics

Many places close after lunch (as of 3 PM) and reopen for dinner (about 6 PM). In remote regions it may prove difficult to find kitchens open past 9 or 10 PM, so plan ahead. Many restaurants are closed on Sunday, and many close for the month of August or even longer. No matter if you choose a superstar-chef paradise like Philippe Rochat's Restaurant de l'Hôtel de Ville or a Ticinese grotti tavern, you'll discover Swiss food has its roots in earthy peasant cuisine, the kind Heidi enjoyed. Ribsticking mainstays, like the ubiquitous pan-Swiss dish called *Geschnetzeltes Kalbfleisch* (or *emincé de veau*, with its mounds of cut veal wallowing in rich, buttery cream), are often served from chaffing dishes with portions large enough for two healthy farm boys. It must have been all that hiking that kept little Heidi slim and trim. Today, most Swiss natives also get a boost from trendier kitchens that offer light seasonal recipes.

Hotels: The Basics

No matter how many stars they have, there are pretty much two types of hotels in Switzerland: the old-style chintz-and-velvet venues, and the airy, parquet-flooring-and-modular-furniture boutique hotels of the past ten years. The ugly stepsister of the latter species is the one that isn't so much retro as a leftover original from the 1970's. Luckily, many of the grandes dames have kept themselves spry and fresh over the years, from the luxurious palace-hotels that are home to well-off internationals to the comfortable home-style baby-grands with chatty managers at the reception desk. Prices across the board can be lofty: you will pay more for minimal comforts here than in any other European country. And compared to the two double beds and bath-shower combos found in American motels, spaces can be small, bathtubs cost extra, and single rooms may only be big enough for a single bed. What you're paying for is service, reliability, and cleanliness. For the lowdown on such Swiss eccentricities as the standard "double bed" (*lit matrimonial*), the general lack of air-conditioning, and the sometimes requisite demi-pension plan, see our Accommodations section in the Travel Smart chapter.

Gear: Essential Items to Pack

Even in July and August the evening air grows chilly in the mountains, so bring a warm sweater. And bring along a hat or sunscreen, as the atmosphere is thinner at high altitudes. You should wear sunscreen all through the year; many different brands are available at ski shops near the slopes. Glaciers can be blinding in the sun, so be sure to bring sunglasses, which should have side shields especially for high-altitude hiking or skiing. Good walking shoes or hiking boots are a must, whether you're tackling medieval cobblestones or mountain trails.

And if you're heading up into the peaks, remember that the higher you go, the more chance there is for altitude sickness to strike—symptoms include numbness, tingling, nausea, drowsiness, vision problems, but most often head-aches: always have some aspirin on hand. If you plan to spend extended periods in rural areas and natural pre-serves, take precautions against ticks, especially in spring and summer. Wear long sleeves, long pants, and boots, and apply insect repellent containing the powerful repellent DEET. Two vaccines against tick-borne infections are available in Europe: TicoVac (also known as FSME Immun) and Encepur, but neither has been approved in the United States.

The one thing that seems to be the budgetary breaking point for practically every hotel manager in all categories: the washcloth. Seldom seen, bring your own. If you're planning on shopping and cooking, a tote bag will come in handy: most groceries do not provide bags, but sturdy, reusable plastic totes can be bought at checkout. Coin-operated laundries are rare, so laundry soap is useful for hand washing.

Behind the Wheel

As tempting as it is—having your own space, taking off whenever you want, listening to Radiohead (or Wagner) full blast—driving in Switzerland is usually more work than enjoyment. With overloaded freeways (the traffic jam in front of the north end of the Gotthard Tunnel can get you stuck for up to eight hours during the Easter break!), mad locals in the throes of road rage, poverty-inducing parking fees, and city centers a maze of one-way or pedestrian-only streets, Switzerland's excellent public transit network means you can even get to Corippo, Ticino (pop. 17), at least once an hour.

Speaking the Language(s)

The Swiss are champions of multilingualism: at least one foreign language is mandatory in most schools from the primary level.

And lucky you: these days, the foreign language of choice is English.

A large percentage of the population speaks at least a little English, especially in cities and large towns or tourist regions.

Don't forget to be polite: ask first before launching into English.

That small bit of consideration will get you a lot farther, especially with natives suffering from tourist overload.

Local languages are German, French, and Italian.

Although the home-grown variants of German and Italian are difficult to understand by those who speak the standard versions, Swiss Germans and Swiss Italians also speak High German or Standard Italian, which are the official written languages in those parts of the country.

Swiss French differs only slightly from Standard French and won't pose a problem.

Switzerland's fourth official language is Romansh, but is very rarely an individual's only language.

UNDERSTANDING THE SWISS

Up in the hoary, windswept heights and black fir forests of the Alps, an electric eye beams open a glistening all-glass door—and reveals the honey-gold glow of wood, the sheen of copper, the burnt-chocolate tones of ancient wooden rafters.

Candles flicker; Sterno radiates blue-white flames under russet pots of bubbling fondue. The cheery boomp-chick boomp-chick of an accordion filters down from high-tech stereo speakers cleverly concealed behind oversize cowbells.

Waitresses in starched black dirndls and waiters in spotless white ties scuttle briskly from kitchen to table, table to kitchen, while platters of gravy-laden veal, sizzling Rösti (hash brown potatoes), and rosy entrecôte simmer over steel trivets—preheated, electrically controlled—ready to be proudly, seamlessly served.

Coziness under strict control, anachronism versus state-of-the-art technology: strange bedfellows in a storybook land. Nowhere else in Europe can you find a combination as welcoming and as alien, as comfortable and as remote, as engaging and as disengaged as a glass cable car to the clouds.

This is the paradox of the Swiss, whose primary national aesthetic pitches rustic Alpine homeyness against high-tech urban efficiency.

Though they're proud, sober, self-contained, independent culturally and politically, disdainful of the shabby and the slipshod, painfully neat, rigorously prompt—the Swiss have a weakness for cuteness, and they indulge in incongruously coy diminutives: a German Bierstube (pub) becomes a Stübli, Kuchen (cake) becomes Küchli, Wurst becomes Würstli, and a coupe (glass) of champagne becomes a Cüplí.

It is lucky for travelers, this dichotomy of the folksy and the functional.

It means your trains get you to your fire-lit lodge on time. It means the cable car that sweeps you to a mountaintop has been subjected to grueling inspections. It means the handwoven curtains are boiled and starched, and the high-thread-count bed linens are turned back with a chocolate at night.

It means the scarlet geraniums that cascade from window boxes on every carved balcony are tended like prize orchids.

It means the pipe smoke that builds up in the Stübli at night is aired out daily, as sparkling clean double-glazed windows are thrown open on every floor, every morning, to let sharp, cool mountain air course through hallways, bedrooms, and fresh-bleached baths.

Yet there is a stinginess that peeks around the apron of that rosy-cheeked efficiency. Liquor here is measured with scientific precision into glasses marked for one centiliter or two, and the local wines come in carafes reminiscent of laboratory beakers.

Despite the fine linens and puffs of down that adorn each bed, double beds have separate mattresses with sheets tucked primly down the middle, sometimes so tightly you have to lift the mattress to loosen the barrier.

And if you wash out your socks and hang them loosely on the shower rod in the morning, you may return at night and find them straightened, spaced, toes pointing the same direction, as orderly as little lead soldiers.

Nevertheless there is an earthiness about these people, as at ease with the soil as they are appalled by dirt.

A banker in Zürich may rent a postage-stamp parcel of land in a crowded patchwork outside town, sowing tight rows of cabbages and strawberries, weeding bright borders of marigolds, and on Sunday he may visit his miniature estate, pull a chair out from the tidy toolshed, and simply sit and smoke, like Heidi's Alm-Uncle surveying his Alpine realm.

An elderly woman may don knickers and loden hat and board a postbus to the mountains and climb steep, rocky trails at a brisk clip, cheeks glowing, eyes as icy bright as the glaciers above her.

There's a 21st-century counterpoint to this: the high-tech, jet-set glamour that splashes vivid colors across the slopes at St. Moritz, Gstaad, Zermatt, Verbier.

Step out of a bulbous steel-and-glass cable car onto a concrete platform at 6,560 feet and see Switzerland transformed, its workers' blue overalls and good wool suits exchanged for ski suits.

Wholesome, healthy faces disappear behind mirrored goggles and war-paint sunblock, and gaudy skis and poles bristle militarily, like the pikes and halberds in the Battle of Sempach.

The contradictions mount: while fur-clad socialites raise jeweled fingers to bid at Sotheby's on Geneva's quai du Mont-Blanc, the women of Appenzell stand beside the men on the Landsgemeindeplatz and raise their hands to vote locally—a right not won until 1991.

While digital screens tick off beef futures in Zürich, the crude harmony of cowbells echoes in velvet mountain pastures.

While a Mercedes roars down an expressway expertly blasted through solid rock, a horse-drawn plow peels back thin topsoil in an Alpine garden plot, impossibly steep, improbably high.

And on August 1, the Swiss national holiday, while spectacular displays of fireworks explode in sizzling colors over the cities and towns, the mountain folk build the bonfires that glow quietly, splendidly, on every hillside of every Alp, uniting Swiss citizens as they celebrate their proud independence, their cultural wealth, and above all their diversity. It's that diversity and those quirky contradictions that make Switzerland a tourist capital—the folksy, fiercely efficient innkeeper to the world.

Cantons of Switzerland

WHEN TO GO

In July and August, Switzerland's best weather coincides with the heaviest crowds. June and September are still pleasant, and hotel prices can be slightly lower, especially in resorts. In May and June the mountains are at their loveliest, with Alpine flowers blooming and the peaks capped with snow; however, as ski season is over and high summer hasn't begun, this is often considered low season, and many resort hotels close down. Those that remain open reduce their prices considerably. Another low-season disadvantage: some cable car and cogwheel train operations take a break between the midwinter and midsummer rushes; some must wait for snow to clear before reopening. The most prestigious ski resorts charge top prices during the Christmas–New Year holidays but reduce them slightly in early January. February through Easter is prime time again. Late autumn—from mid-October through early December—is the least appealing season for visiting the Alps because there's usually little snow, no foliage, and a tendency toward dampness and fog. If you're sticking to the cities to shop and tour museums, you won't notice the doldrums that take over the resorts. The exception to the above rules of thumb: the Ticino, the only portion of Switzerland south of the Alps, boasts a Mediterranean climate and declares high season from April through October. Many of its hotels close down altogether from November through March.

Climate

Summer in Switzerland generally lasts from July to September and tends to be mild, although night temperatures can be chilly in some locations. At high altitudes, the air remains crisp through the hottest summer days. Beautiful fall foliage begins to lose its grip on the trees by the end of October, when the autumn rains usually sweep through the country. Snow can make its first appearance in November, which is usually foggy. Cold temperatures kick in from January to March, often dropping below freezing.

TOP SWITZERLAND ATTRACTIONS

The Matterhorn

(A) Of course. Alternatively called Il Cervino (Italian) or (Le Cervin), this is Switzerland's trademark, drawing crowds every year. The pedestrian-only town of Zermatt offers a fairy-tale version of the typical Alpine village, with carriage rides, chalet restaurants and hotels, and shops galore, all under the shadow of the world's most recognizable peak. For a grand vista, head to the summit station of Gornergat, where nature's snaggle-toothed masterpiece steals the thunder from all surrounding mountains.

Mürren

(B) A Noah's Ark town that perches on a cliff-face over the southern end of the Lauterbrunnen Valley, this half-earthly, half-heavenly village is pasted like a wasp's nest 3,200 feet up a mountain. Dine on a nearly levitating terrace and it seems you can practically reach out and touch the Eiger and Jungfrau peaks.

Continue on up the mountain via cable-car to reach the spectacular Schilthorn peak, crowned by the Piz Gloria viewing station and restaurant (many will recognize its starring role as Ernst Blofeld's hideout in the James Bond film *On Her Majesty's Secret Service*).

Luzern

(C) The town that's on everyone's list. A mere nine square miles in size, Luzern is many of Switzerland's cities in a nutshell: a well-preserved medieval Old Town, a magnificent lakefront, and a wide variety of shops stuffed with souvenirs. As you stroll along the lakeshore promenade, many Alpine views will look familiar, as this is where all those travel poster photos originate.

The Jungfraujoch

(D) With an altitude of 11,400 feet, and an almost alien landscape slathered in whipped-cream snow all year round, this is the most accessible high-altitude peak in Europe. Don't try to attempt it all in one day—add an overnight or at least a very long lunch mid-way in Grindelwald, say—because the difference in altitude from valley floor to the "Top of Europe" will literally make your head spin.

Lake Geneva's Wine Country

(E) From Nyon to Aigle, the slopes of Lake Geneva are carpeted with vineyards that produce some of Switzerland's best wines. While you'll find a few varieties—mainly chasselas or pinot noir—exported to stores at home, this is the only place to taste the rest. Say "santé" to your new best friends: arvine, gamaret, or humagne rouge, for example.

Lauterbrunnen Valley

(F) The "high" point of any trip to the mountainous Berner Oberland region may turn out to be Europe's most "viewtiful" valley. Sheltered from the world by picture-perfect mountains and threaded by more than 72 cascading waterfalls, Lauterbrunnen makes you feel as if you had stumbled upon a film set for *Lost Horizon*'s Shangri-la.

St. Moritz

(G) Take New York luxury, then Paris fashion, a bit of London and Milan as well, a drop of Munich, a handful of Rome, large swaths of premium ski slopes, add the bubbling "champagne climate" of dry air and sun, mix well and pour onto a few acres in a gorgeous high-altitude valley. How can anything compare with this über-chic resort?

The Tellskapelle, Lake Luzern

(H) Set on one of the most glorious stretches of the Urnersee—the southern leg of Lake Luzern—this High Victorian lakefront chapel honoring the legendary Wilhelm Tell is so magnificently picturesque it will practically click your camera for you.

QUINTESSENTIAL SWITZERLAND

Cheese: The Swiss Cure

It was Swiss cheese that put the apples in the cheeks of the hardy little mountain girl named Heidi, the heroine earth-child who inspired Victorians to leave dark city streets for clear Alpine air; to rise early, work hard, and—first and foremost—eat cheese three times a day. For Heidi and Clara—for whom daily meals of cheese and goat's milk worked a mountain miracle—butterfat was a virtue; cholesterol a concept unborn. Today cheese is still a way of life in Switzerland, so every visitor has to try the famous *fondue* at least once (it may be a winter fixture, but tourists are allowed to eat it year-round). Once the Gruyère, Emmental, or Appenzeller is melted and skillfully mixed with a soupçon of garlic, a teaspoon of flour, and some white wine, the richly aromatic whole is brought to table in the pipkin and placed on a spirit lamp. Guests armed with long-handled forks then spear small squares of bread or meat into the steaming dish. But the eating of fondue is a fine art: each guest who fails to withdraw his morsel is called upon to offer a bottle of wine to the company—a lady, they say, pays with a kiss to whom she chooses. Fondue is rendered all the more convivial by the tradition of downing a shot of 90-proof kirsch halfway through the pot: the *coup du milieu*.

What Makes Them Tick?

It lies on the beveled-glass countertop of Vacheron Constantin's Geneva store: centuries of technology compressed into a miniature of gold and glass, its second hand sweeping to a point within 10 seconds of when it reached the same point last month—Swiss precision in microcosm. The fact that Vacheron is the world's oldest manufacturer of watches (it sold its first sober design in 1755) underscores the fact that these mechanical gems, as

If you want to get a sense of contemporary Swiss culture and indulge in some of its pleasures, start by familiarizing yourself with the rituals of daily life. These are a few highlights—things you can savor with relative ease.

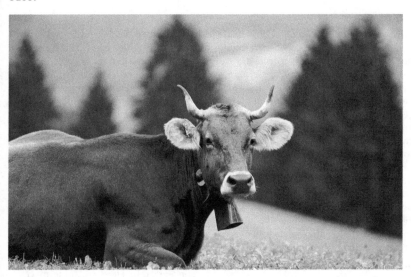

they were, are also Swiss history. During the Reformation, Calvin banned gilded crucifixes and chalices, leaving scores of brilliantly skilled goldsmiths with idle hands. Before long, an industry was launched, which, to this day, makes you believe in national stereotypes: the Swiss are precise and persevering. You can see this when a factory worker neatly drops into place a minute hand the size of an eyelash; or in the gradations of firewood stacked from finest kindling to fattest logs with the geometric complexity of inlay at a country inn; or as you step off a train in Lausanne just as the second hand on the station clock hits the arrival time. Yes, Swiss watchmaking is a science, but visit Geneva's Patek Philippe Museum to be wowed by fantastical creations, brilliant colors, and awe-inspring detail. Clearly, Swiss watchmaking is about much more than time.

How Now, Brown Cow?

Many images leap to mind when you think of Switzerland but surely only one sound: cowbells tinkling in happy indiscipline. This is a sound many travelers often later hear in their dreams, one that many wish could be "photographed." Even city slickers fall under the spell of Switzerland's cows. Get up close to these pretty brown-and-white livestock and you can smell their sweet breath—testament to all the succulent grasses (which also go in many of the world's top perfumes) they've munched. Newspapers recently reported that Switzerland's cows were "stressed," so these days many of them get to go on "vacations" from factories to spend summers up in the hills. After all, without the milk of these cash cows, Swiss cheese and chocolate wouldn't be half as famous. Now if they could only create a breed that produces *chocolate* milk!

IF YOU LIKE

Great Food

La Cuisine? Die Kockkunst? La Cucina? Like the patchwork that is Switzerland, fine Swiss food is a culinary trifecta drawn from three countries: France, Germany, and Italy. French areas like Vaud and Neuchâtel still seduce with *cuisine bourgeoise* and such delights as beef entrecôte and *truite meunière*. Over in German cantons such as Schwyz and Luzern, Teutonic nature conquers Gaul with servings of sausage and schnitzel in nearly Wagnerian proportions. Heading south, Italian risotto and gnocchi appear virtually unscathed in the Ticino. Today, however, a bevy of superstar chefs has begun to strike a diplomatic balance between French, German, and Italian styles.

Restaurant de l'Hôtel de Ville—Phillippe Rochat, Crissier, Vaud. Rochat spent nearly 20 years with legendary chef Freddy Giradet, and he maintains a creative level that vies with the best chefs of Paris.

Petermann's Kunststuben, Zürich. Listed as one of Forbes's most expensive restaurants in the world, set in an 1879 house hung with modern paintings ("Kunststuben" means art studio), this is the stage for Horst Petermann, whose Tuscan dove with pine nuts or salmon in caviar crème are so strikingly arranged on the plate you feel you should hang the main course on the wall, not eat it.

Waldhotel Fletschhorn, Saas-Fee, Valais. Crowned Gault-Millau's "Chef of the Year" in 2007, Markus Neff has been wowing foodies with his lobster dim sum and bison tournedos. To learn how he mixmasters Alpine foods with exotic styles, sign up for one of the cooking classes given by this red-haired wunderkind.

"Peak" Experiences

"Mountains are the beginning and end of all scenery," the great 19th-century writer John Ruskin once observed. And if mountains have a "home" it is truly Switzerland—a summit of summits. View collectors flock to that big schlock candy mountain, the Matterhorn. Adventurers are seduced by the "sheer" excitement of the Jungfrau. "Social climbers" head to the chic villages of Wengen and Mürren, which seem to levitate at either end of the Lauterbrunnen valley, while daredevils worship at the foot of the Eiger's notorious north face. No matter where you head, you'll find hillside footpaths can be almost as crowded as supermarket checkout lines (remember: the higher the trail, the less "conversation"—you need to concentrate!). Here are some places that will leave you with that top-of-the-world feeling.

Matterhorn, Valais. From the summit station of Gernergrat, this snaggle-toothed mountain steals the thunder from all surrounding peaks.

Jungfraujoch, the Berner Oberland. From the top of the 11,395-foot-high Jungfraujoch, the Aletsch Glacier looks like a vast sea of ice.

Neuhausen am Rheinfall, Eastern Switzerland. With its mists, roaring water, jutting rocks, and bushy crags, the Rheinfall, from the Neuhausen side, appears truly Wagnerian.

Lauterbrunnen Valley, the Berner Oberland. Looking more like a painting than real life, the jaw-dropping vista of this Shangri-la valley is spectacularly threaded by 72 waterfalls that plummet from sky-high cliffs.

Traveling Through Time

Wander the slopes of Klewenalp above the Vierwaldstättersee on a still spring day, gaze across the placid waters beneath and it is easy to identify Switzerland as a land of peace. Wander on a mile or so and you are reminded that for much of its time Switzerland has been nothing of the kind. Here is the Rütli, the meadow where legend avers that the men of the three forest cantons, Uri, Schwyz, and Unterwalden, met in 1291 to plot the overthrow of their Habsburg landlords (thereby creating the world's first democracy). But move beyond this spot—hallowed by Wilhelm Tell—and you'll find Switzerland is practically crawling with history from border to border.

Old Town, Basel. When the sound of fife-and-drum music drifts from upstairs windows of guild houses of Basel's Old Town, you'll think the Middle Ages have dawned again.

Tellfreilichtspiele, Interlaken, Berner Oberland. For a festive evening, rent a lap blanket and settle in to watch a grand retelling of the life of Wilhelm Tell, performed under the stars.

Monument de la Rèformation, Geneva. The complex history of the Protestant Reformation as it unfolded across Europe is boldly rendered in granite.

Stiftsbibliothek and Kathedrale, St. Gallen. For Rococo splendor and opulence, nothing beats this complex of Abbey Library and Cathedral, adorned with spectacular excesses of 18th-century wedding-cake trim.

The Most Beautiful Villages

Whatever town or valley you pick, you'll have a battle on your hands insisting that your favorite spot in Switzerland *is* the (only/best/unique) top place in the country. The *whole* of Switzerland is undeniably beautiful. But there are certain places where the needle would fly right off the scale if they were rated on a beauty-measuring gauge. Oozing half-timbered houses and sgraffitoed chapels, these once-upon-a-timefied places have a sense of tranquillity not even tour buses can ruin. Nearly everyone has a mind's-eye view of the perfect Swiss village—and here are some candidates.

Guarda, Graubünden. This federally protected hamlet in the Lower Engandine is full of architectural photo-ops, with cobblestone streets and flower boxes filled with red geraniums.

Stein-am-Rhein, Eastern Switzerland. A nearly perfectly preserved medieval village, Stein is replete with shingled, half-timber town houses boasting ornate oriels and flamboyant frescoes.

Gandria, the Ticino. Clinging vertiginously to a hillside, its flower-filled balconies overlooking Lake Lugano, the tiny town of Gandria retains the ambience of an ancient fishing village.

Mürren, Bernese Oberland. Closer to the sky than the earth, this jewel presides over the majestic Lauterbrunnen Valley and offers a so-close-you-can-touch-it vista of the Eiger.

Gruyères, Fribourg. Right out of a Brothers Grimm fairy tale, this storybook village is crowned with one of the most picture-perfect castles in Switzerland.

SWITZERLAND TODAY

People

After centuries of poverty, with fathers sending sons abroad as mercenaries (resulting in Swiss Guards at the Vatican, for example) and citizens emigrating in hopes of a better life (found in America by families such as the Zellwegers, the Chevrolets, and the Roethlisbergers), today's prosperity has led to a decrease in population growth and a marked increase in immigration.

These days, a large international population (about a fifth of the populace) lives alongside the Meiers, the Favres, and the Bernasconis.

They have arrived on Swiss shores brought here by unrest around the world (especially in the former Yugoslavia), the need for manpower, and that old familiar search for a better life.

The resulting cultural mix has unnerved some, but it also works world-flattening magic—in the traditional town of Brütten there is a "Stars and Stripes" American-style restaurant in an old Swiss farmhouse run by a family from Sri Lanka.

Politics

Quick: can you name the president of Switzerland? Don't feel bad if you can't—the position is refilled once a year.

Every December the Swiss parliament elects or reconfirms seven of its members to make up the executive Federal Council.

These seven are each the heads of an administrative department (Foreign Affairs, Home Affairs, Justice, etc.).

They rotate annually to act as a "first among equals" president who has no individual power of his or her own.

Simply said, the president gets to represent the country in international and domestic matters but still has a day job.

Switzerland is also one of the most democratic countries in the world as far as citizen participation is concerned.

Within this "direct democracy" any citizen can try to change a law—or propose a new one—by collecting at least 50,000 signatures within 100 days and presenting them to the local, regional, or federal government (depending on which level presides over the issue).

The result are referendums and initiatives voted on by the population as many as six times a year.

Economics

With an economy that is stable, thanks mainly to its banking and taxation system (even in these volatile times), Switzerland enjoys a rare prosperity.

It is home to multinational corporations (often drawn here by low and flat-rate taxes) and local companies active in pharmaceuticals, chemicals, precision instruments, insurance, real estate, and, of course, banking.

With a decidedly business-friendly government, one area stands out in this capitalist utopia: agriculture.

Given that there is only so much space in roughly 16,000 square miles of country—much of which is made up of steep mountains that are hard to develop—and that green Alps are an essential draw for the tourism industry, great efforts are made to ensure that what Mark Twain once called "a large, humpy, solid rock, with a thin skin of grass stretched over it" doesn't all get paved over.

Culture

The rural traditions you'd expect—alphorns, yodeling, cows festooned with flowers—are alive and well, and not just a show put on for the tourists (although that's not unheard of either).

Almost every town has some kind of festival at least once a season, where you can sample the local food and do the local dance, with an added Italian, German, or French flavor.

Thanks to full government coffers and charitable businesses, you'll also find a wide variety of art, dance, and musical offerings.

These happily range from the cutting edge to the traditional high-brow.

And not just in the expected urban settings, either, as evidenced by the gallery of surrealist artist H.R. Giger (the designer of the monster in Ridley Scott's 1979 movie *Alien*) in the tiny and quintessentially Swiss town of Gruyères.

The Sexes

Picture it: There's a battle in the streets. Long-haired kids in tie-dyed T-shirts throw rocks at tanks fitted with water cannons, as the establishment wonders what's happened to the youth of today. Chicago, 1968?

Nope: Zürich, 1980. It's no wonder, then, that Switzerland still tends to lag behind in terms of equality of the sexes.

Granted, in most cities and large towns the issue is disappearing, but there is still a surprising number of companies where the corporate culture feels like an episode of *Mad Men*.

There are plenty of villages where an unmarried woman is considered an unnecessary waste.

And mothers sending their children to (extremely hard to find) daycare are treated as if they were letting them be brought up by wolves. Welcome to the 19th century?

Sports

Switzerland is an extremely active country. Hiking, biking, windsurfing, kayaking, hang-gliding, and golf (if you are among the generous who consider golf a sport) are just some of the amusements practiced by young and old.

And then there's this little thing called skiing.

As far as spectator sports go, in summer it's soccer; in winter, hockey.

Both come with fan clubs and, unfortunately, hooligans eager for a fight.

Luckily, there is also this great thing called *Hornussen*: a puck is placed on a ramp and shot into the air with a whip-like staff.

As it comes down, the opposing team members try to swat it down with boards on posts that look like giant picket signs. No, really.

GREAT ITINERARIES

SWISS GASTRONOMY

9 Days. This food-intensive itinerary offers aficionados an opportunity to travel from one great dining experience to another, sampling the very finest *haute gastronomie* at one stop, the most authentic regional classics—even the earthiest peasant cuisines—at another. Incidental pleasures—wandering in the Alps, for example, or strolling through medieval town centers in Switzerland's greatest cities—can be squeezed in between meals. Remember that reservations must be made well in advance.

Geneva

2 nights. Your first night, indulge in a hearty Lyonnaise meal at the Bistrot du Bœuf Rouge. For lunch the next day, head out into the vineyards for exquisite seasonal cuisine at the Domaine de Châteauvieux. Back in Geneva, have a relatively light Ticinese supper at La Favola. Fill the time between meals with a brisk stroll along the quais or a visit to one of the city's many museums. ⇨ *Chapter 13.*

Lausanne

1 night. Testing Philippe Rochat's mettle at Restaurant de l'Hôtel de Ville in nearby Crissier may be the triumph of the trip— but reserve judgment for after Basel and Zürich. At night, head down to the waterfront at Ouchy and have a chic, light supper at the Café Beau-Rivage. ⇨ *La Côte & Lausanne in Chapter 12.*

Basel

1 night. Two hours north, lunch at Bruderholz, which gives Philippe Rochat a run for his money. Then, after visiting, say, the Münster and the history museum, relax in the downstairs bistro at the Teufelhof: the light specialties are prepared by Michael

BY PUBLIC TRANSPORTATION

Each of the stopovers is accessible by train, though some of the restaurants may require cabs or tram rides; a rental car will give you more flexibility for reaching country inns.

Baader, who is chef for the top-notch restaurant upstairs as well. ⇨ *Chapter 7.*

Zürich

2 nights. Have lunch at Petermann's Kunststuben, in the suburb of Küssnacht, where the gastronomy vies for the title "best in Switzerland." Then, after a thorough walking tour of Zürich's Old Town, you can settle in for an atmospheric, old-world evening at the Picasso- and Matisse-lined Kronenhalle. ⇨ *Chapter 2.*

Luzern

1 night. For a total contrast and perhaps the most authentically *Swiss* meal of your tour, head for Galliker and a lunch of real farm food. Having absorbed the Lion Monument, crossed the Kapellbrücke, and toured the history museum, you can think about the evening meal: a light, sophisticated river-fish meal at Rotes Gatter, in Des Balances hotel, affords waterfront views. ⇨ *Chapter 6.*

Saas-Fee

1 night. From Luzern allow for a full day's scenic mountain drive south over the Brünigpass, then on over the Grimselpass and down the Rhône Valley to Brig and the spectacular little resort of Saas-Fee. Once there, retreat to the isolated Waldhotel Fletschhorn for a sophisticated dinner by rising star Markus Neff (Gault-Millau's Chef of the Year 2006) and a bare minimum of one night to take in the mountain air. ⇨ *Zermatt & Saas-Fee in Chapter 11.*

Verbier

1 night. Following the Rhône back west toward Geneva, take one more Alpine side trip up to this famous ski resort to feast and sleep at Rosalp, the popular rustic-chic inn in the village center. ⇨ *Val d'Entremont to the Col du Grand St-Bernard in Chapter 11.*

CASTLES & CATHEDRALS

8 Days. Romantics, history buffs, and architecture fans can circle western Switzerland to take in some of the country's best medieval and Gothic landmarks.

Geneva

1 night. The excavations below the 12th-century Cathédrale St-Pierre, open to the public as the *site archéologique,* have yielded two 4th-century sanctuaries, Roman mosaics, and an 11th-century crypt. ⇨ *Chapter 13.*

Montreux

1 night. The Château de Chillon, partially surrounded by the waters of Lake Geneva, may be the most completely and authentically furnished in Switzerland. Lord Byron signed the pillar where his "Prisoner of Chillon" was manacled. ⇨ *Lavaux Vignobles & Montreux in Chapter 12.*

Gruyères

1 night. This magnificently beautiful castle-village draws crowds to its central street, souvenir shops, quaint inns, and frescoed castle, complete with dungeon and spectacular views. ⇨ *Fribourg in Chapter 8.*

Fribourg

1 night. This bilingual city is the last Catholic stronghold of western Switzerland, rooted in its single-tower Cathédrale St-Nicolas. The cathedral's Last Judgment tympanum and Art Nouveau stained-glass windows deserve attention—but leave time to explore the Old Town, with its multilevel fortifications constructed for the ubiquitous Zähringens. ⇨ *Fribourg in Chapter 8.*

Thun

1 night. If you're driving, cut across Fribourg toward Thun (by train, connect through Bern), where you'll see the Bernese Alps in all their splendor. Schloss Zähringen, which dates from 1191, features a knights' hall, tapestries, local ceramics, and an intimidating collection of weapons. ⇨ *Thunersee in Chapter 10.*

Bern

1 night. The Zähringens fortified this goose-neck in the River Aare; its 15th-century Münster features a restored (full-color, painted) main portal. ⇨ *Chapter 9.*

Basel

1 night. In this historic, cosmopolitan city is a Münster with a lovely Romanesque portal and the tomb of the great humanist Erasmus. ⇨ *Chapter 7.*

BY PUBLIC TRANSPORTATION

The complete itinerary works by rail, with most sites accessible on foot from the station; Gruyères has bus connections to the elevated castle and the Old Town.

Zürich

Zürich's Old Town

WORD OF MOUTH

"Zürich's Old Town is surprisingly charming, with a beautiful lake-front. I had a delicious lunch at the Zeughauskeller—the 'crossbow of William Tell' is mounted on the wall. Certainly the best-defended lunch I have ever eaten!" —Biz

"There is not much to see/do in Zürich? That is s-o-o-o not true! Zürich is very rich in architecture, in history, in museums, and day excursions. Just the city itself can keep you busy for days if you take the trouble to look and ask." —WallyKringen

WELCOME TO ZÜRICH

TOP REASONS TO GO

★ **A dip in the Middle Ages:** Museum-perfect in their leaded-glass and Gothic-wood details, a dozen medieval guildhalls have been transformed into time-burnished restaurants.

★ **Extreme shopping:** Luxury-encrusted with noted shops, the Bahnhofstrasse is also lined with banks to re-fill your empty wallets—the nearby Altstadt has other "Ring bell to enter" bou-tiques, one of which may have that $10,000 belt you've been looking for.

★ **Amazing architec-ture:** The Old Town and the Left Bank's Oberdorf and Niederdorf have barely changed since the 18th century—savor their pedestrian-only cobble-stone streets, medieval churches, and see-and-be-seen outdoor cafés.

★ **The "Great Church":** The Grossmünster lords over the city, both archi-tecturally and psychically, for here Ulrich Zwingli taught the city to buckle down, fear the Lord, and hail the Protestant work ethic in the 15th century.

1 The Altstadt. Zürich's Old Town is the main reason you're here, thanks to Gothic treasures like the Fraumün-ster, more shops than you could shake a tiara at, an amazing collection of res-taurants, and it's all right on the lake.

2 Niederdorf & Oberdorf. Less dignified, more lively, Zürich's east bank is noted for its cultural goodies, including the velvet-and-cherub splendor of the star-studded opera house and the Kunsthaus (Museum of Art).

3 The Zürcher See. It's a bit too narrow for decent waterskiing, but every other activity is on offer on this beautiful lake, from swim-ming to people-watching (every café with even one square foot of sidewalk space puts its tables out-side). This may be the only major city in the world where you can actually swim in the heart of down-town—as hundreds do on hot summer days.

4 Zürich West. For something completely different, head here to check out the latest modern architecture—since the 1990s the area has undergone an extreme makeover, and old factories have made room for trendy lofts and hip clubs.

5 Winterthur. Zürich proper is surprisingly small, given its international cachet, but today the towns surrounding it have become city "suburbs," especially this museum-rich town famed for its art collections.

2

GETTING ORIENTED

Visitors are often surprised by the beauty of Zürich, perhaps imagining it one vast high-tech banking hall, all chrome and computers. But the city's location—straddling the Limmat River and flanked by two mini-mountains, the Zürichberg and the Üetliberg—would tempt any landscape painter. Zürich may be small—it can be crossed in a mere 20 minutes on foot—but it has international cachet.

ZÜRICH PLANNER

How to Get Here

Zürich may not be the geographic center of the country, but in many ways it is the heart. You can get here from anywhere, by car or train, boat, or bus.

The Swiss Federal Railways (SBB, 0900/300300, www.sbb.ch) manage everything—check them out when planning your trip. Trains arrive hourly from Geneva (80 SF one-way), Bern (46 SF one-way), Luzern (23 SF one-way), Lugano (59 SF one-way), St. Gallen (28 SF one-way), and Basel (31 SF one-way). There are also connections from Paris (with or without the TGV), Munich, Frankfurt, and Milan several times a day.

Switzerland's highway system also networks through Zürich: the A1 (from St. Gallen to Geneva and Bern), the A2 (from Lugano connecting through Luzern), and the A3 (from Chur to Basel), the A4 (from Luzern).

Winterthur is a mere 20 minutes to a half-hour away, depending on the type of transportation. By car, take the A1 in the direction of St. Gallen.

By train, take any one of the two to five trains leaving from the Hauptbahnhof or the Bahnhof Stadelhofen every hour (11.40 SF one-way).

Not Everyone's a Millionaire

If restaurant prices are setting your credit card on fire, the local Migros or Coop are great places to load up on picnic food, and take-out stands (mainly called "take-aways" after the British model) can be found all over the city center.

Something's Always Going On

If you see an elephant wandering around the streets of Zürich, don't worry: it just means the circus is in town. In the winter months a series of circuses—with acrobats, fire-eaters, and lion tamers—travel throughout the country in red-and-white caravans, each stopping along the way in Zürich. In addition to the usual opera, theater, and concert seasons, the city holds a variety of events throughout the year.

One of Zürich's most important festivals is Sächsilüüte, a kind of Groundhog Day in which descendents of medieval guild members circle a burning snowman until its head blows off (how long this takes determines whether spring will come early or late).

The annual debate has become almost as interesting as the event itself, as the male-only guilds refuse to let women participate.

When spring finally arrives, so does Jazznojazz, with jazz musicians playing at venues all over town. Summer is time for Christopher Street Day, a huge celebration of gay pride.

Even if you don't speak German, you should still attend the Theater Spektakel, a two-week outdoor theater festival, for the excellent food. Sensuous dancing marks the nine days of Tangowoche, while techno music is the sound track for the lovefest called Street Parade.

Fall arrives with the Lange Nacht der Museen, when museums leave their doors open all night. Knabenschiessen, a country fair held on the outskirts of the city, lets youngsters test their aim at shooting competitions. Toward the end of the year is Expovina, a wine exhibition, held on boats moored at Bürkliplatz—and then there's that elephant again.

Careful!

If Swiss drivers have a reputation throughout Europe for being unnecessarily impolite in their lead-footedness, Zürich must be where they're all hatched and trained.

With a good number of streets in town marked "one-way" or "pedestrian-only" or with a speed limit of only 30 kph (18 mph), many drivers take out their frustrations on their fellow man.

Pedestrian crossings seem to be a great place to line up a target, and God forbid you should hesitate a nanosecond after the light has turned green before flooring it—the red-faced guy behind you in the Alfa will immediately inspire you to move along.

The rate of road rage is unnervingly high in Züurich, although it's still not L.A. Most favor going after the object of their ire with their bare fists or a knife instead of a gun. Reassuring, isn't it?

We should mention here that public transit is excellent throughout the city.

Tour Options

Bus Tours. Cityrama's daily tour covers the main city sights; the trip lasts three hours, leaving at 11 AM; it costs 45 SF. The Zürich Trolley Experience (32 SF) gives a good general idea of the city in two hours; it leaves at 9:45 AM, noon, and 2 PM. The Combo Tour goes farther and includes a train trip to the top of the nearby Üetliberg. This is also a daily tour, given at 9:45 AM, noon, and 2 PM; it takes four hours and costs 40 SF. All tours start from the Hauptbahnhof. In addition, three introductory bus tours with English commentary are offered by Zürich's tourist office. **Tourist information** (✉Hauptbahnhof, Kreis 1, ☎044/2154000).

Walking Tours. Daily from June to October, the tourist office offers two-hour walking tours (20 SF) that start at the Hauptbahnhof. You can join a group with English-language commentary, but the times vary, so call ahead. **Tourist information** (✉Hauptbahnhof, Kreis 1, ☎044/2154000).

Bicycle Tours. From May to September, Friday through Sunday at 10:30 AM, you can take a 2½-hour bike tour from Zürich's opera house for 25 SF. The tour is given in German and English; bikes are supplied. Reservations are necessary only for four or more people. **Zurich by Bike** (☎076/3087016 ⊕www.zurichbybike.ch).

Transportation Basics

Once you're here, it's a good idea to park the car if you have one, since those streets that aren't pedestrian zones are liable to be one-way—you'll get fewer headaches on foot, and the city's public transit system (ZVV, 0840/988988, www.zvv.ch) is excellent, thanks to its trams and trains (buses go only to the suburbs).

The Zürich Card (15 SF) gets you 24 hours of municipal public transportation in the greater Zürich area, plus free entry into more than 40 museums (Tourist Information, Hauptbahnhof; 044/2154000, www.zuerich.com). A network of water taxis services the upper Limmat and the lake (044/7777777).

How's the Weather?

The temperate climate has four distinct seasons. Spring can be a mad mix of brilliant sun and rain, which means colorful blossoms abound. Summers are humid and have been quite hot in the last years, rivaling some Asian nations; evening thunderstorms are frequent.

Fall becomes crisp around the end of October, and winter brings a low fog ceiling (this is when locals head for any nearby peak over 5,000 feet) or light-to-slushy snow that tends to melt after a week or so.

GETTING AROUND

By Air

Unique Zürich Airport is Switzerland's most important airport and the 10th-busiest in the world. Some 60 airlines, including American, United, and, of course, Swiss Air Lines, known as Swiss, serve this airport, located 11 km (7 mi) north of the city. You can also catch domestic and European flights out of Unique on Swiss. It's easy to take a Swiss Federal Railways feeder train directly from the airport to Zürich's Hauptbahnhof (main station). Tickets cost 5.80 SF one-way, and trains run every 10–15 minutes, arriving in 10 minutes. Taxis cost dearly in Zürich. A ride into the center costs 50 to 60 SF and takes around 20 minutes. Most larger hotels have their own shuttles to and from the airport.

Airport Information Unique Zürich Airport (☎ 0900/ 300313).

By Car

The A2 expressway from Basel to Zürich leads directly into the city. A1 continues east to St. Gallen. Approaching from the south and the St. Gotthard route, take A14 from Luzern (Lucerne); after a brief break of highway (E41) it feeds into A3 and approaches the city along the lake's western shore.

By Taxi

Taxis are very expensive, with an 8 SF minimum but no charge for additional passengers. An available taxi is indicated by an illuminated rooftop light. You can order a cab by calling Züri Taxi or Alpha Taxi.

Taxi Companies Alpha Taxi (☎ 044/7777777). **Züri Taxi** (☎ 044/2222222).

By Train

There are straightforward connections and several express routes leading directly into Zürich from Basel, Geneva, Bern, and Lugano. All roads lead to the Hauptbahnhof in the city center.

Train Information Hauptbahnhof (☎ 0900/300300 ⊕ www.rail.ch).

By Tram

ZVV, the tram service in Zürich, is swift and timely. It runs from 5:30 AM to midnight, every six minutes at peak hours, every 12 minutes at other times.

All-day passes cost 7.20 SF and can be purchased from the same vending machines at the stops that post maps and sell one-ride tickets; you must buy your ticket before you board.

Free route plans are available from VBZ Züri-Linie (Zürich Public Transport) offices, located at major crossroads (Paradepl., Bellevue, Central, Limmatpl.). Stops are clearly signposted.

The **Zurich Card** (15 SF) gets you 24 hours of travel in the greater Zürich area on all trams, buses, trains, boats, cable cars and cog-wheel trains, plus free entry into more than 40 museums.

It's available from **Tourist information** (✉ Hauptbahnhof, Kreis 1, ☎ 044/2154000)

Contacts ZVV (☎ 0848/988988 ⊕ www.zvv.ch).

Updated by
Katrin Gygax

WHEN THE POUND STERLING sagged in the 1960s, the wounded English blamed "the gnomes of Zürich," a term that evoked images of elfin Swiss bankers slyly manipulating world currencies behind closed doors. What the English failed to fathom was that the Zürichers' drive comes not from the mists of folkloric forests but from the pulpit of the Grossmünster, and the fiery sermons of Reformation leader Ulrich Zwingli blasting the evils of idle hands and the devil's playthings. The resulting ironclad work ethic is what made Zürich one of the world's leading financial centers. One of Zwingli's lessons stressed the transient nature of wealth, and Zürichers show native caution in enjoying their fabulous gains. Nor have they turned their backs on the humble signposts of their heritage: the city's graceful, shuttered Gothic buildings still outnumber the newer chrome-and-glass towers.

Zürich, which sits astride the Limmat River at the point where it emerges from the Zürcher See (Zürich Lake) is, in fact, a very beautiful city. Its charming *Altstadt* (Old Town), which makes up a substantial part of the city center, is full of beautifully restored historic buildings. In the distance, snowy mountains overlook the lake, whose shores are dominated by centuries-old mansions. Few high-rise buildings disturb the skyline, and even their heights are modest by U.S. standards. In keeping with Zürich's solid bourgeois character, there are no dominating castles to haunt the Züricher with memories of imperialism.

The earliest known Zürichers, circa 4500 BC, lived by the lakeside in small houses perched on stilts. Underwater archaeologists have discovered a wealth of prehistoric artifacts dating back thousands of years, from Stone Age pottery to Bronze Age necklaces, and many such relics are on display at the Schweizerisches Landesmuseum (Swiss National Museum) near the main train station. At last count, the remains of 34 Stone Age and Bronze Age settlements are thought to be scattered around the lake.

In the 1st century BC the Romans, attracted by the city's central location, built a customhouse on a hill overlooking the Limmat River. In time the customhouse became a fortress, remnants of which can be seen on the Lindenhof, a square in the city center. The Romans were also accommodating enough to provide Zürich with its patron saints. Legend has it that the Roman governor beheaded a Christian brother and sister, Felix and Regula, on a small island in the river; the martyred siblings then picked up their heads, waded through the water, and walked up a hill before collapsing where the Grossmünster now stands.

After the Germanic Alemanni, ancestors of the present-day Zürichers, expelled the Romans in the 5th century, the region declined in importance until, four centuries later, the Carolingians built an imperial palace on the Limmat. Louis the German, grandson of Charlemagne, then founded an abbey here, appointing as the first abbess his own daughter. The abbey was built on the site of what is now the Fraumünster, near Bahnhofstrasse.

By the 12th century, Zürich was already renowned as a center for commerce; many of its diligent merchants had made fortunes dealing in silk, wool, linen, and leather goods. By 1336 this privileged class had become too powerful in the view of the newly emerging band of tradesmen and laborers who, allied with a charismatic aristocrat named Rudolf Brun, overthrew the merchants' town council and established Zürich's famous trade guilds. Those 13 original guilds never lost power until the French Revolution—and have yet to lose their prestige. Every year Zürich's leading businessmen dress up in medieval costumes for the guilds' traditional march through the streets, heading for the magnificent guildhalls.

If the guilds defined Zürich's commerce, the Reformation defined its soul. From his pulpit in the Grossmünster, Zwingli galvanized the region, and he ingrained in Zürichers a devotion to thrift and industriousness—so successfully that it ultimately led them into temptation: the temptation to achieve global influence and tremendous wealth. Today the Zürich stock exchange is the fourth-largest in the world, after those of New York, London, and Tokyo.

Nevertheless, Zürich is not your typical cold-hearted business center. In 1916 a group of artists and writers rebelling against the restraints of traditional artistic expression—among them Tristan Tzara, Jean Arp, and Hugo Ball—founded the avant-garde Dadaist movement here. The fertile atmosphere also attracted Irish author James Joyce, who spent years here while re-creating his native Dublin in his *Ulysses* and *A Portrait of the Artist as a Young Man*. Today the city's extraordinary museums and galleries and luxurious shops along Bahnhofstrasse, Zürich's Fifth Avenue, attest to its position as Switzerland's cultural—if not political—capital.

The latest addition to the city's profile is Zürich West, an industrial neighborhood that is rapidly being reinvented, with former factories being turned into spaces for restaurants, bars, art galleries, and dance clubs. This scene of construction and restoration will most likely be ongoing well into 2009.

EXPLORING ZÜRICH

From the northern tip of the Zürcher See, the Limmat River starts its brief journey to the Aare and, ultimately, to the Rhine—and it neatly bisects Zürich at the starting gate. The city is crisscrossed by lovely, low bridges. On the left bank are the Altstadt, the grander, genteel pedestrian zone of the old medieval center; the Hauptbahnhof, the main train station; and Bahnhofplatz, a major urban crossroads and the beginning of the world-famous luxury shopping street, Bahnhofstrasse. The right bank constitutes the livelier old section, divided into the Oberdorf (Upper Village) toward Bellevue, and the Niederdorf (Lower Village), from Marktgasse to Central and along Niederdorfstrasse, which fairly throbs on weekends. Most streets between Central and Bellevue are pedestrian-only zones, as is the Limmatquai from the Rudolf-Brun-Brücke to the Münsterbrücke.

CLOSE UP

Ulrich Zwingli, Freedom Fighter

Visitors to Zürich soon hear about Ulrich Zwingli, the no-nonsense (and, one suspects, humor-free) religious reformer who taught the city to buckle down, work hard, and fear the Lord. But who was this much revered man of the cloth, and why is he depicted holding a huge sword in the statue that stands in front of the Wasserkirche?

In 1484 Zwingli was born in the tiny village of Wildhaus in the canton of St. Gallen. He entered the priesthood, eventually rising to the head position at the Grossmünster in the city of Zürich. He had no problem declaring publicly where he differed with the teachings of the Catholic Church. His first quarrel, around 1512, was over the evils of the Swiss mercenary service propagated by the Pope. A few years later, around 1519, he joined the fight against the church's growing practice of exacting payment for the forgiveness of sins.

Taking a closer look at the New Testament, Zwingli came up with his own very simple theology: if it's not in the Bible, it doesn't apply. This focus on both the Old and New Testaments soon spread throughout the Christian world, affecting Protestant congregations all the way to the English colonies in America. While Martin Luther's form of protest was largely peaceful, Zwingli was not above getting into the fray. As people took up arms over their right to worship as they saw fit, Zwingli suited up and went to battle. He died in 1531, along with 500 of his compatriots, clutching that very big sword at the Battle of Kappel am Albis in the canton of Zürich.

Scattered throughout the town are 13 medieval guildhalls, or *Zunfthäuser*, which once formed the backbone of Zürich's commercial society. Today most of these house atmospheric restaurants, where high ceilings, leaded-glass windows, and coats of arms evoke the mood of merchants at their trade. Often these restaurants are one floor above street level because in the days before flood control the river would rise and inundate the ground floors.

Zürich is officially divided into a dozen numbered *Kreise* (districts), which spiral out clockwise from the center of the city. Kreis 1, covering the historic core, includes the Altstadt, Oberdorf, and Niederdorf. Zürich West is part of Kreis 5. Most areas in the city are commonly known by their Kreis, and a Kreis number is generally the most helpful in giving directions.

Numbers in the text correspond to numbers in the margin and on the Zürich map.

BAHNHOFSTRASSE & THE ALTSTADT

The Altstadt (Old Town) is home to several of Zürich's most important landmarks—the Lindenhof, St. Peters, the Fraumünster, and the Stadthaus—as well as the shop-lined Bahnhofstrasse.

MAIN ATTRACTIONS

Bahnhofstrasse. Reputedly "the most expensive street in the world"—thanks to all its extravagantly priced jewelry shops—Zürich's principal boulevard offers luxury shopping and hulking department stores, whereas much shifting and hoarding of the world's wealth takes place discreetly behind the banks' upstairs windows. You can enjoy your window shopping here in relative peace: the only vehicles allowed are the municipal trams. The long-standing story of a treasure trove hidden below Bahnhofstrasse has been quashed, however—the subterranean vaults that once stored great piles of gold and silver now lie empty. In 1998 a local journalist was allowed access to the vaults; at the end of the dark labyrinths the scribe found nothing but empty rooms, the precious metals having been moved to a site near the airport several years earlier. ⊠ *Runs north–southwest of Limmat River, Kreis 1.*

❻ ★ Fraumünster *(Church of Our Lady).* Of the church spires that are Zürich's signature, the Fraumünster's is the most delicate, a graceful sweep to a narrow spire. It was added to the Gothic structure in 1732; the remains of Louis the German's original 9th-century abbey are below. Its Romanesque choir is a perfect spot for meditation beneath the ocher, sapphire, and ruby glow of the 1970 stained-glass windows by the Russian-born Marc Chagall, who loved Zürich. The Graubünden sculptor Alberto Giacometti's cousin, Augusto Giacometti, executed the fine painted window, made in 1930, in the north transept. ⊠ *Stadthausquai, Kreis 1* ⊙ *Daily 10–4.*

OFF THE BEATEN PATH

Museum Rietberg. Dancing Indian Shivas, contemplative Tibetan thangkas, late-18th-century literary paintings from China, and royal Benin bronzes from Nigeria: these are just a few of the treasures in the prodigious gathering of non-European art on view here. This is the only museum of its kind in Switzerland, with the main focus on Asia, Africa, and Ancient America, and thereby hangs a tale. Back in the 1920s, inspired by the new fashion and status of "exotic" primitive art (just like another person, who happened to be named Picasso), Baron Eduard von der Heydt began traveling to the four corners of the globe. He amassed a vast collection at bargain-basement prices (today, of course, many of these objects would break auction records). The main collection is now on view in the huge underground Smaragd Building. The Villa Wesendonck, the famous Neoclassical jewel that was once a fabled home to Richard Wagner (it was for the lady of the house that he wrote his *Wesendonck Songs*) houses objects from India, the pre-Columbian Americas, Australia, and the Pacific Islands; there's more Indian, Islamic, and Oriental art in an adjacent museum, the Park-Villa Rieter. You will find Cambodian Khmer sculptures, jade Chinese tomb art, Japanese Noh masks, and even ancient Swiss masks—over the years other collections have donated quirky items to the baron's main holdings. From the city center, follow Seestrasse south about 1¾ km (1 mi) until you see signs for the museum; or take Tram 7 to the Rietberg Museum stop. ⊠ *Gablerstr. 15, Kreis 2* ☎ *044/2063131* ⊕ *www.rietberg.ch* 💷 *16 SF* ⊙ *Tues.–Sun. 10–5; open until 8 on Wed. and Thurs.*

A GOOD WALK

Begin at the **Hauptbahnhof**, a massive 19th-century edifice. Directly behind the Hauptbahnhof is the **Schweizerisches Landesmuseum**, housed in an enormous 19th-century neo-Gothic mansion, behind that is a shady green park. Walk northward to the tip of the park, cross on the left-hand side of the bridge, turn north a bit along Sihlquai, and head up Ausstellungsstrasse to the **Museum für Gestaltung**, which holds an impressive collection of 20th-century graphic art. Back at the train station, look across Bahnhofplatz, and you'll see traffic careening around a statue of Alfred Escher, the man who brought Zürich into the modern age.

Cross the square to Bahnhofstrasse, Zürich's principal business and shopping boulevard. A quarter of the way up the street—about five blocks—veer left into Rennweg and left again on Fortunagasse, an atmospheric medieval street well removed from the contemporary elegance of Bahnhofstrasse. Climb up to the **Lindenhof**, a quiet, gravel square with a view across the river to the Niederdorf. From here a maze of medieval alleys leads off to your right. Nestled among them is **St. Peters Kirche**, whose tower has the largest clock face in Europe.

From St. Peters Kirche bear right on Schlüsselgasse and duck into a narrow alley, Thermengasse, which leads left; you'll walk directly over excavated ruins of Roman baths. At Weinplatz, turn right on Storchengasse, where some of the most elite boutiques are concentrated, and head toward the delicate spires of the **Fraumünster**. In the same square you'll see two of Zürich's finest guildhalls, the **Zunfthaus zur Waag** and **Zunfthaus zur Meisen**.

Wind left up Waaggasse past the Hotel Savoy to **Paradeplatz**. From here you can take a quick side trip to the art collection at **Haus Konstruktiv** by going up Talackerstrasse to Sihlstrasse, turning left onto Selnaustrasse. Back at Paradeplatz, continue south on Bahnhofstrasse, which, as it nears the lake, opens onto a vista of boats, wide waters, and (on a clear day) distant peaks. At Bürkliplatz, look to your right: those manicured parks are the front lawn of the Hotel Baur au Lac, the aristocrat of Swiss hotels. Beyond, you'll see the modern structure of the Kongresshaus and the Tonhalle, where the Zürich Tonhalle Orchestra resides. Across General-Guisan-Quai is one of the local swans' favorite hangouts: the boat dock, which is the base for trips around the Zürcher See.

Here you can take General-Guisan-Quai west to Seestrasse to the **Museum Rietberg** (about a 25-minute walk) or turn left and cross the Quaibrücke (Quay Bridge) for one of the finest views in town, especially at night, when the floodlit spires are mirrored in the inky river, whose surface is disturbed only by drifting, sleeping swans.

TIMING

The area is surprisingly compact; half a day is enough time for a cursory visit. If you're planning on museum hopping, the Schweizerisches Landesmuseum and Museum Rietberg merit at least two hours apiece.

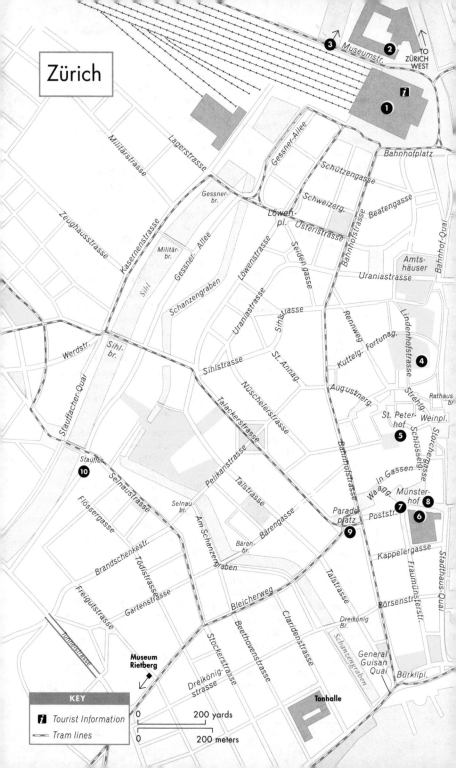

Zürich

TO ZÜRICH WEST

Museumstr.

Bahnhofplatz

Schützengasse

Schweizerg.

Beatengasse

Löwen-pl.

Gessner-br.

Gessner-Allee

Useristrasse

Amts-häuser

Uraniastrasse

Bahnhofstrasse

Militärstrasse

Lagerstrasse

Zeughausstrasse

Kasernenstrasse

Militär-br.

Gessner-Allee

Sihl

Schanzengraben

Löwenstrasse

Seiden gasse

Uraniastrasse

Sihlstrasse

Rennweg

Kuttelg.

Fortunag.

Lindenhofstrasse

Werdstr.

Sihl-br.

Sihlstrasse

St. Annag.

Nüschelerstrasse

Augustinerg.

Strehlg.

Rathaus-br.

Stauffacher-Quai

Talackerstrasse

Bahnhofstrasse

St. Peter-hof

Weinpl.

Schlüsselg.

Storchengasse

Stauffbr.

Selnaustrasse

Pelikanstrasse

Talstrasse

In Gassen

Waag g.

Münster-hof

Flössergasse

Selnau-br.

Am Schanzengraben

Bärengasse

Bären-br.

Parade platz

Poststr.

Kappelergasse

Stadthaus-Quai

Brandschenkestr.

Tödistrasse

Gartenstrasse

Bleicherweg

Talstrasse

Fraumünsterstr.

Börsenstrasse

Freigutstrasse

Tunnelstrasse

Museum Rietberg

Dreikönig-strasse

Stockerstrasse

Beethovenstrasse

Claridenstrasse

Dreikönig Br.

Schanzengraben

General Guisan Quai

Bürklipl.

Tonhalle

KEY

i Tourist Information

Tram lines

0   200 yards

0   200 meters

⑨ Paradeplatz *(Parade Square).* The hub of Bahnhofstrasse and a tram junction, this square is a great place to observe a microcosm of the local upper crust—furrowed-brow bankers striding to work while their fur-trimmed wives struggle with half a dozen bags and the dilemma of where to shop next. While you're at it, spoil your taste buds with incredible chocolate from the Sprüngli café. ⊠ *Intersection of Bahnhofstr. and Poststr., Kreis 1.*

⑤ St. Peters Kirche. Dating from the early 13th century, Zürich's oldest parish church has the largest clock face in Europe. A church has been on this site since the 9th century. The existing building has been considerably expanded over the years: styles range from a Romanesque choir to a Baroque nave. The tower, for example, was extended in 1534, when the clock was added. Keep an eye out for inexpensive or even free classical concerts. ⊠ *St. Peterhofstatt, Kreis 1* 🕿 *No phone* ⊙ *Weekdays 8–6, Sat. 9–4, Sun. noon–7.*

② Schweizerisches Landesmuseum *(Swiss National Museum).* Housed in a gargantuan neo-Gothic building dating from 1889, the Swiss National Museum owns an enormous collection of objects dating from the Stone Age to modern times. There are costumes, furniture, early watches, and a great deal of military history, including thousands of toy soldiers reenacting famous battles. In the hall of arms there's a splendid mural, painted by the late-19th-century Bernese artist Ferdinand Hodler, called *The Retreat of the Swiss Confederates at Marignano.* The work depicts a defeat in 1515 by the French. ⊠ *Museumstr. 2, Kreis 5* 🕿 *044/2186511* ⊕ *www.musee-suisse.ch* 🎫 *10 SF* ⊙ *Tues.–Wed., Sun. 10–5, Thurs. 10–7.*

⑧ Zunfthaus zur Meisen. Set on the bank of the Limmat across the river from the towering Fraumünster is Zürich's most beautiful guildhall, comprising a magnificent suite of reception salons, several of which are topped by extravagant Baroque stucco ceilings. Erected for the city's wine merchants in the 18th century, the Zunfthaus today is a fitting showplace for the Swiss National Museum's ceramics collection. The Kilchberg-Schooren porcelain works flourished in Zürich from 1763 to 1790 and their masterwork—a 300-piece dining service created for the monastery Einsiedeln in 1775—takes center stage, along with exquisite figurines and table decor. Also on view are Nyon porcelains, Swiss pottery, and faience. Enter on the Fraumünster side. ⊠ *Münsterhof 20, Kreis 1* 🕿 *044/2212807* ⊕ *www.musee-suisse.com/e/index2.html* 🎫 *3 SF* ⊙ *Tues.–Sun. 10:30–5.*

⑦ Zunfthaus zur Waag *(Scales Guildhall).* Renaissance in style—note the broad Tuscan columns and decorative strapwork on the grand facade—this circa-1637 guildhall was the meeting place for linen weavers and hatmakers. Today it houses a restaurant of the same name, offering Zürich specialties and "small deliciouses." The main salon is staidly Biedermeier in style, so try to snag a seat in the walnut-lined Zunft-Zaal guildhall, lined with stained-glass windows. Even better are the tables right in front of the building, while an adjacent time-stained, medieval cloister is the evocative setting for a drink. ⊠*Münsterhof 8, Kreis 1* ⊕*www.zunfthaus-zur-waag.ch.*

ALSO WORTH SEEING

Alfred Escher. Leave it to Zürich to have a statue that honors not a saint, not a poet or artist, but rather the financial wizard who single-handedly dragged Zürich into the modern age back in the mid-19th century. Escher (1819–82) established the city as a major banking center, championed the development of the federal railways and the city's university, and pushed through the construction of the tunnel under the St. Gotthard Pass. ⊠*In the middle of Bahnhofpl., Kreis 1.*

❶ **Hauptbahnhof** *(Main Railway Station).* From the bustling main concourse of this immaculate 19th-century edifice you can watch crowds rushing to their famously on-time trains. Beneath lies a shopping mall, open daily from 8 to 8 (an exception to the closed-on-Sunday rule), with everything from grocery stores to clothing boutiques and bookshops. ⊠*Between Museumstr. and Bahnhofpl., Kreis 1.*

❿ **Haus Konstruktiv** *(Museum of Constructivist Art).* Housed in a former electrical substation set by the River Sihl—an impressive 1930s Modernist architectural statement in its own right—this collection traces the history of Constructivist Art, which became one of the vogues of the 1930s–40s and had a big following in Switzerland (especially among its trailblazing graphic-art designers). The showpiece is the Rockefeller Dining Room, a 1963 salon designed by Swiss artist Fritz Glarner and looking very much like a pop-up Mondrian painting. Over the years the collection has broadened to include minimal art, concept art, and neo geo work (a style based on Japanese animation). Featured artists include Sophie Taeuber-Arp, Paul Klee, and Max Bill. During the year there are several temporary shows. ⊠*Selnaustr. 25, Kreis 1* ☎*044/2177080* ⊕*www.hauskonstruktiv.ch* ☉*14 SF* ☉*Tues., Thurs., and Fri. noon–6, Wed. noon–8, weekends 11–6.*

❹ **Lindenhof** *(Linden Court).* On the site of this quiet square, overlooking both sides of the river, a Roman customhouse and fortress and a Carolingian palace once stood. The fountain was erected in 1912, commemorating the day in 1292 when Zürich's women saved the city from the Habsburgs. As the story goes, the town was on the brink of defeat as the Habsburg aggressors moved in. Determined to avoid this humiliation, the town's women donned armor and marched to the Lindenhof. On seeing them, the enemy thought they were faced with another army and promptly beat a strategic retreat. Today, the scene could hardly be less martial, as locals play boccie and chess under the trees. ⊠*Bordered by Fortunag. to the west and intersected by Lindenhofstr., Kreis 1.*

❸ **Museum für Gestaltung** *(Design Museum).* Envisioned as an academy devoted to design and applied arts, this imposing structure—it was designed by Adolf Steger and Karl Egender as a Functionalist manifesto—is today the main repository for Switzerland's important legacy in graphic design, posters, and applied arts. Innovative temporary exhibitions focus on architecture, poster art, graphic design, and photography, and recent shows included such subjects as "Comix!," "Breaking

the Rules," and "Paris, May 68."
✉ *Ausstellungstr. 60, Kreis 5*
☎ *044/4466767* ⊕ *www.museum-gestaltung.ch* 🎟 *9 SF* ⊗ *Tues.–Thurs. 10–8, Fri.–Sun. 10–7.*

NIEDERDORF & OBERDORF

As soon as you step off the Quai Bridge on the right bank of the Limmat River, you'll notice a difference: the atmosphere is more casual. The area is also the center of Zürich's nightlife—both upscale and down, with the city's opera house and its historic theater, as well as plenty of

TOUT SWEET

Zürich's top confiserie, Sprüngli (Paradeplatz., Kreis 1, 044/2244711), the landmark chocolatier and café for wealthy Bahnhofstrasse habitués, concocts heavenly truffles and *Luxemburgerli*, small cream-filled cookies that require immediate eating. Good, plain hot lunches and salads are also served. There are also branches at the Hauptbahnhof and on Löwenplatz.

bars and clubs. As you explore the area along Münstergasse to Marktgasse, parallel to the river, you'll notice a less Calvinistic bent. Each of the narrow streets and alleys that shoot east off Marktgasse (which quickly becomes Niederdorfstrasse) offers its own brand of entertainment. Niederdorfstrasse eventually empties onto the Central tram intersection, across the river from the main train station; from there it's easy to catch a tram along Bahnhofstrasse or the Limmatquai.

MAIN ATTRACTIONS

㉒ Graphische Sammlung *(Graphics Collection)*. The impressive collection of the Federal Institute of Technology includes a vast library of woodcuts, etchings, and engravings by such European masters as Dürer, Rembrandt, Goya, and Picasso. Pieces from the permanent collection are often arranged in thematic exhibitions. Take Tram 6 or 10 from the Bahnhofplatz or Central stops or Tram 9 from Bellevue to the ETH/Universitätsspital stop. ✉ *Rämistr. 101, Kreis 1* ☎ *044/6324046* ⊕ *www.gs.ethz.ch* 🎟 *Free* ⊗ *Mon., Tues., Thurs., and Fri. 10–5, Wed. 10–7.*

⓮ Grossmünster *(Great Church)*. This impressive cathedral is affection-
Fodor's Choice   ately known to English speakers as the "Gross Monster." Executed on
★   the plump twin towers (circa 1781) are classical caricatures of Gothic forms bordering on the comical. The core of the structure was built in the 12th century on the site of a Carolingian church dedicated to the memory of martyrs Felix and Regula, who allegedly carried their severed heads to the spot. Charlemagne is said to have founded the church after his horse stumbled over their burial site. On the side of the south tower an enormous stone Charlemagne sits enthroned; the original statue, carved in the late 15th century, is protected in the crypt. In keeping with what the 16th-century reformer Zwingli preached from the Grossmünster's pulpit, the interior is spare, even forbidding, with all luxurious ornamentation long since stripped away. The only artistic touches are modern: stained-glass windows by Augusto Giacometti, and ornate bronze doors in the north and south portals, dating from the late 1940s. ✉ *Zwinglipl., Kreis 1* ☎ *044/2525949* ⊗ *Daily 9–6; tower weekdays 9:15–5; cloister weekdays 9–6.*

Kunsthaus *(Museum of Art).* With a varied and high-quality permanent collection of paintings—medieval, Dutch and Italian Baroque, and Impressionist—the Kunsthaus is possibly Zürich's best art museum. The collection of Swiss art includes some fascinating works; others might be an acquired taste. Besides works by Ferdinand Hodler, with their mix of realism and stylization, there's a superb room full of Johann

> **FAR-SIGHTED VIEWING**
>
> When Emil-George Bührle toured visitors around his famed collection, he would bounce from Renoir to Rembrandt to Degas, and back again. "That is the way one ought to go around museums," he would say. "It gives you a new angle of vision."

Heinrich Füssli paintings, which hover between the darkly ethereal and the grotesque. And then there's Picasso, Klee, Degas, Matisse, Kandinsky, Chagall, and Munch, all satisfyingly represented. ⊠ *Heimpl. 1, Kreis 1* ☎ *044/2538484* ⊕ *www.kunsthaus.ch* ☞ *Varies with exhibition* ☉ *Wed.–Fri. 10–8, Sat., Sun.,Tues 10–6.*

Rathaus *(Town Hall).* Zürich's striking Baroque government building dates from 1694–98. Its interior remains as well preserved as its facade: there's a richly decorated stucco ceiling in the banquet hall and a fine ceramic stove in the council room. ⊠ *Limmatquai 55, Kreis 1* ☎ *043/2596801* ☞ *Free* ☉ *By appointment only.*

Stiftung Sammlung E.G. Bührle. A stunning array of Cézannes, Manets, Monets, and Degas make this eye-knocking collection one of the best art museums in Europe—unfortunately and tragically, since a spectacular robbery in February 2008, visits are by appointment only. Amazingly, this fabled collection was all put together in the space of a single decade. During the 1950s, Zürich industrialist E.G. Bührle purchased the finest offerings from the world's most prestigious art dealers, winding up with a collection studded with legendary Impressionist and Postimpressionist works, including Cézanne's *Self Portrait with Palette,* Renoir's *Little Irene,* and Degas's *Little Dancer.* The museum also encompasses religious sculptures (with great holdings of medieval wooden Pietà sculptures), as well as Spanish and Italian paintings from the 16th to 18th centuries and gorgeous landscapes by Dutch masters like Meindert Hobbema and Salomon van Ruysdael. Take Tram 11 from Bellevue, then Bus 77 from Hegibachplatz to the Altenhofstrasse stop. ⊠ *Zollikerstr. 172, Kreis 8* ☎ *044/4220086* ⊕ *www.buehrle.ch* ☞ *25 SF* ☉ *By appointment only, first Wed. of each month.*

ALSO WORTH SEEING

Helmhaus. The open court of this museum once served as a linen market. Inside there are changing exhibitions of contemporary, often experimental, art by Zürich-based artists. In spring the museum hosts an exhibition of works from the city's annual competition for young artists. ⊠ *Limmatquai 31, Kreis 1* ☎ *044/2516177* ⊕ *www.helmhaus.org* ☞ *Free* ☉ *Tues., Wed., and Fri.–Sun. 10–6, Thurs. 10–8.*

Kirchgasse. Antiques, art, and book enthusiasts will delight in the shops on this street. No. 13 was Zwingli's last home before he was killed in battle (1531) while defending the Reformation.

Rindermarkt. Fans of Gottfried Keller, commonly considered Switzerland's national poet and novelist, will want to visit this street. The 19th-century writer's former home, at No. 9, became famous thanks to his novel *Der Grüne Heinrich* (*Green Henry*). Opposite is the restaurant, Zur Oepfelchammer, where Keller ate regularly. ⊠*Street between Marktg. and Neumarkt, Kreis 1.*

⓫ **Schauspielhaus Pfauenbühne** *(Peacock Theater).* During World War II this was the only German-language theater in Europe that wasn't muzzled by the Nazis, and it attracted some of the continent's bravest and best artists. It has been presenting plays ever since it was built in 1884; today its productions aren't always so risky, but they are stunningly mounted and performed, in German of course. There are no tours, so to see the interior you must see a show. ⊠*Rämistr. 34, Kreis 1* ☎*044/2587777* ⊕*www.schauspielhaus.ch.*

⓰ **Wasserkirche** *(Water Church).* One of Switzerland's most delicate late-Gothic structures, this church displays stained glass by Augusto Giacometti. Both the church and the Helmhaus once stood on the island on which martyrs Felix and Regula supposedly lost their heads. ⊠*Limmatquai 31, Kreis 1* ☉ *Wed. 2–5, Sat. noon–5.*

㉑ **Zoologisches Museum.** Engaging and high-tech, the Zoological Museum
☯ allows you a close look in its accessible displays on Swiss insects, birds, and amphibians. You can examine butterflies and living water creatures through microscopes and listen to birdcalls as you compare avian markings. ⊠*Karl Schmid-Str. 4, Kreis 1* ☎*044/6343838* ⊕*www.unizh.ch/ zoolmus* ⊠*Free* ☉*Tues.–Fri. 9–5, weekends 10–4.*

⓱ **Zunfthaus zum Rüden.** Now housing one of Zürich's finest restaurants, this 13th-century structure was the noblemen's society tavern. Peek inside at the barrel-vaulted ceiling and 30-foot beams; or better yet, stop for a meal. ⊠*Limmatquai 42, Kreis 1.*

⓲ **Zunfthaus zur Saffran.** Portions of this guildhall for haberdashers date from as early as 1389. The modern restaurant downstairs has outdoor seating underneath medieval arches facing the river. ⊠*Limmatquai 54, Kreis 1.*

DADA DADDY'S CURE-ALL

Several artistic and political figures made their homes on narrow Spiegelgasse—Lenin lived at No. 14, just before the Russian Revolution, and at No. 12 the exiled revolutionary German playwright Georg Büchner (1813–37) wrote *Woyzeck* before dying of typhoid. At the foot of the street a plaque marks the site of the Cabaret Voltaire, where the Dadaist movement took shape, conceived in Zürich by French exile Hans Arp, who in the 1920s proclaimed the new movement one that could "heal mankind from the madness of the age."

ZÜRICH ENVIRONS: ZÜRICH WEST TO WINTERTHUR

Switzerland's grandest collection of old master paintings, Zürich's famous Zoo, the city's snazziest contemporary Kunsthalle, and James Joyce's grave are some of the striking attractions located not far from the city center's borders. They may require a pleasant tram ride or train excursion but they are all worth the trip.

Zürich West is one of the city's most happening districts. Although banking is an important part of Zürich's economy, it's not the only one; starting around 1860, the city was a major center for the machine industry, supplying transportation companies with ball bearings, cables, and the like. With this industry in a decline since the early 1990s, there has been a shift toward information technology and the service industry, leaving a great swath of land downstream from the city center with empty warehouses. Today, some of these cavernous spaces have been renovated, while others were torn down to make room for new glass-and-steel creations. The area is now chock-full of lofts, galleries, bars, restaurants, and dance clubs. The result is a swinging cultural center with a throbbing nightlife. The area is loosely bordered by Hardstrasse, Hardturmstrasse, and Pfingstweidstrasse; to get there by public transportation, take Tram 4 or 13 to Escher Wyss Platz. It's roughly a 10-minute trip from the Hauptbahnhof.

SIGHTS TO SEE

Fodor'sChoice
★ **Am Römerholz—Die Sammlung Oskar Reinhart** *(Oskar Reinhart Collection at Schloss Am Römerholz).* Lucas Cranach's *Portrait of Johannes Cuspinian,* Pieter Breughel the Elder's *Adoration of the Magi in the Snow,* Peter Paul Rubens's *Decius Mus,* Edouard Manet's *Au Café,* Toulouse-Lautrec's *Clownesse Cha-U-Kao*—you get the picture. This is one of the greatest private art collections in Switzerland, perhaps only rivaled by the Sammlung Emil-George Bührle in Zürich. The jewel in the crown of Winterthur's art museums, Am Römerholz is virtually wallpapered with legendary paintings. Located 20 km (12 mi) northeast of Zürich, Winterthur made its fortune through the textile industry, and it blossomed thanks to prosperous merchants who developed a love of art. They bequeathed the town some notable art museums, including the Villa Flora/Sammlung Hahnloser (www.villaflora.ch)—a Sezession-style villa with works by Van Gogh, Redon, Vuillard, and Matisse—and the Museum Oskart Reinhart am Stadtgarten (www.museumoskarreinhart.ch), which focuses on "lesser-known" painters that Reinhart hunted down, such as Caspar David Friedrich and Arnold Böcklin. Reinhart's most magnificent treasures wound up at the villa "Am Römerholz," built in 1915 on the hill overlooking town. The collection ranges across five centuries, with pride of place going to 16th-century German and Early Netherlandish paintings, 17th-century French and Flemish paintings, and Impressionist masterworks. Works by Gerard David, Poussin, Daumier, Van Gogh, and nearly 200 other artists stagger the eye, tributes to the extremely cultured upbringing Reinhart (1885–1965) received. Winterthur is a half-hour from Zürich by train, on the main rail route to St. Gallen; trains depart about every 15 minutes. From the train station's Sektor G, take the "Museumbus"

(5 SF), which travels the 15-minute route (from station: 9:45, 10:45 . . . until 4:45; from museum: 10, 11 . . . until 5). By car, follow the autobahn signs for Winterthur–St. Gallen. Take the Winterthur-Ohringen exit onto Schaffhauserstrasse into town, then left on Rychenbergstrasse to Haldenstrasse. ⊠ *Haldenstr. 95, Winterthur* ☎ *052/2692740* ⊕ *www.roemerholz.ch* ☜ *10 SF* ☉ *Tues.–Sun. 10–5, open until 8 on Wed.*

WORD OF MOUTH

"Our kids (ages 6–11) loved the Zürich Zoo! Hilly but manageable, it makes a great day (rainy or sunny). There's a fun wooden-and-rope net playground. The large indoor 'rain forest' is magnificent with huge bats swooping all around."   —PattyNY

James Joyce's Grave. The inimitable Irish author not only lived and wrote in Zürich, but died here as well. The city's most famous literary resident is buried in the Friedhof Fluntern (Fluntern Cemetery); atop his grave sits a contemplative statue of the writer, complete with cigar. A few steps away is the grave of another renowned author, Nobel Prize–winner Elias Canetti. The cemetery is adjacent to the Tram 6 terminus. ☉ *Mar., Apr., Sept., and Oct., daily 7–7; May–Aug., daily 7 AM–8 PM; Nov.–Feb., daily 8–5.*

Kunsthalle *(Center of Contemporary Art).* Set in West Zürich, this Kunsthalle is one of two major art venues on the top floors of a former brewery. It presents new local and international artists in huge, stark white rooms. A survey of Richard Prince's paintings and Keith Tyson's installations mixing objects, paintings, and photography have drawn large crowds of modern art lovers in the past few years. Works are always cutting-edge: you can say you saw it here first. There are four smaller galleries and a well-stocked art bookstore in the same building. ⊠ *Limmatstr. 270, Kreis 5* ☎ *044/2721515* ⊕ *www.kunsthalle zurich.ch* ☜ *8 SF* ☉ *Tues., Wed., and Fri. noon–6, Thurs. noon–8, weekends 11–5.*

Migros Museum für Gegenwartskunst *(Migros Museum of Contemporary Art).* One floor below the Kunsthalle, this airy, white loft has the same focus—up-and-coming contemporary artists—but is privately funded by Switzerland's largest department store chain, Migros. Shows of recent work are interspersed with exhibitions from the extensive Migros collection, which includes works by Andy Warhol. The museum sponsors regular discussions with the artists, often in English. ⊠ *Limmatstr. 270, Kreis 5* ☎ *044/2772050* ⊕ *www.migrosmuseum.ch* ☜ *8 SF* ☉ *Tues., Wed., and Fri. noon–6, Thurs. noon–8, weekends 11–5.*

♻ **Zürich Zoo.** This is one of Europe's outstanding zoos, with more than 1,500 animals, including Asian elephants, black rhinos, seals, and big cats. One of the more unusual attractions is a huge dome stocked with flora and (luckily small) free-range fauna you might encounter in a jungle in Madagascar. Set in a tree-filled park, the zoo is just east of the city center and easily reached by Trams 5 and 6. ⊠ *Zürichbergstr. 221, Kreis 6* ☎ *044/2542505* ⊕ *www.zoo.ch* ☜ *22 SF* ☉ *Mar.–Oct., daily 9–6; Nov.–Feb., daily 9–5.*

WHERE TO EAT

THE SCENE

Since the mid-1990s, Zürich's restaurant trade has boomed. The new establishments, both Swiss and international, tend to favor lighter, leaner meals served in bright spaces that are often open to the street. The traditional cuisine, no longer ubiquitous but still easily found, is called *nach Zürcher Art,* meaning "cooked in the Zürich style." Think meat, mushrooms, potatoes, butter, cream—an extremely rich cuisine, perfectly suited to the leaded-glass and burnished-oak guildhalls.

In exploring Zürich's core, in fact, you will want to enter at least one of these famous medieval "union clubhouses" scattered along the riverfront neighborhoods; the best way is to dine in one, as all but the Zunfthaus zur Meisen have been converted into restaurants. On your way to the restroom, sneak a peek into their other dining rooms—they are, for the most part, museum-perfect in their leaded-glass and Gothic-wood detail.

Zürich's signature dish, which you'll encounter throughout both French and German Switzerland, is *Geschnetzeltes Kalbfleisch,* or in French *émincé de veau:* bite-size slices of milky veal (and sometimes veal kidneys) sautéed in butter and swimming in a rich brown sauce thick with cream, white wine, shallots, and mushrooms. Its closest cousin is *Geschnetzeltes Kalbsleber* (calves' liver), served much the same way. You may also find *Spätzli,* flour-egg dough fingers, either pressed through a sieve or snipped, gnocchi-style, and served in butter.

Another culinary must is Zürich's favorite portable food, sausage and *Bürli* (a crunchy roll), eaten separately, two-fisted style. The best are to be had at Bellevue at the Sterne-Grill. *Kalbsbratwurst* (veal) is mild, the smaller *Cervelat* (pork) saltier. Join the locals and munch away while waiting for a tram.

Zürichers also have a definite sweet tooth: refined cafés draw crowds for afternoon pastries, and chocolate shops vie for the unofficial honor of making the best chocolate truffles in town.

WHAT IT COSTS IN SWISS FRANCS				
¢	$	$$	$$$	$$$$
AT DINNER under 15 SF	15 SF–25 SF	25 SF–45 SF	45 SF–65 SF	over 65 SF

Prices are per person for a main course at dinner.

$$
SWISS
★
✕**Adler's Swiss Chuchi.** Right on the Niederdorf's main square, Hirschenplatz, this squeaky-clean Swiss-kitsch restaurant has an airy, modern decor, with Alpine-rustic chairs and Big Boy–style plastic menus. It serves good home-cooked national specialties: bratwurst, schnitzel, Geschnetzeltes, Rösti, Leberli, battered fish with french fries and tartar sauce—the gang's all here. An added attraction if you're visiting in summer: fondue and raclette, usually winter dishes, are served year-round. Excellent lunch menus are rock-bottom cheap and served double quick.

There's outside seating on the cobblestone pedestrian square in warm weather. ⊠*Roseng. 10, Kreis 1* ☎*044/2669666* ⊟*AE, DC, MC, V.*

$$
SWISS
✕ **Alpenrose.** It doesn't get more Swiss than this: the ingredients, the recipes, the wines, and the decor are all Helvetian. The interior is elegantly casual, with wainscoting and etched-glass windows, linen tablecloths, a stuffed chamois head, and paintings of the Matterhorn and other well-known landmarks. Enjoy seasonal dishes such as *Engadiner pizokel* (flour dumplings) with ham, or duck breast with dried plum sauce and mashed potatoes. The owners' devotion to local ingredients means the menu often changes daily. ⊠*Fabrikstr. 12, Kreis 5* ☎*044/2713919* ⊕*www.restaurant-alpenrose.ch/* ⊟*MC, V* ☉*Closed Mon. and mid-July–mid-Aug.*

$$
CAMBODIAN
✕ **Angkor.** A bit of Siem Reap in the middle of Zürich West: the lavish interior is full of stone carvings and wood latticework that seem right out of Ta Prohm, but minus the jungle. The menu is huge and heaped with green curry, oyster sauce, and ginger, covering India, Thailand, Vietnam, and Japan. The lunch specials are a good deal for those on a budget, while multicourse meals guarantee to fill you up if you're in search of just a little bit more. Tables double in number with outside summer seating on the square. ⊠*Giessereistr. 18, Kreis 5* ☎*043/2052888* ⊟*AE, DC, MC, V.*

$$$
ECLECTIC
✕ **Baur au Lac Rive Gauche.** Its nondescript entrance off a noisy street-corner belies the light, beige cubist decor inside, which attracts crowds of hip young business executives and expense-account padders open to the concept of dining to thumping chill-out music. Part and parcel of the noted Baur au Lac hotel, this spot offers specialties that are light, trendy, and off-the-grill with names like "Risotto on the Rocks"—risotto with porcini mushrooms—and "Found Nemo"—wild salmon with lime butter. "D for Two" offers mini-samples of the dessert menu. The wine list taps Hotel Baur au Lac's impressive wine cellar. ⊠*Talstr. 1, Kreis 1* ☎*044/2205060* ⌕*Reservations essential* ⊟*AE, DC, MC, V.*

$$
SWISS
Fodor's Choice
★
✕ **Bierhalle Kropf.** Under the mounted boar's head and restored century-old murals depicting gallivanting cherubs, businesspeople, workers, and shoppers share crowded tables to feast on generous hot dishes and a great selection of sausages. The *Leberknödli* (liver dumplings) are tasty, the potato croquettes are filled with farmer's cheese and garnished with a generous fresh salad, and the *Apfelküechli* (fried apple slices) are tender and sweet. The bustle and clatter provide a lively, sociable experience, and you'll more than likely get to know your neighbor. ⊠*In Gassen 16, Kreis 1* ☎*044/2211805* ⊟*AE, DC, MC, V* ☉*Closed Sun.*

$$
SPANISH
✕ **Bodega Española.** The coats of arms of old Spanish provinces and garlands of onions and garlic encircle the dark-paneled interior of this upstairs Niederdorf restaurant. It specializes in big steaks, seafood, omelets, and paella. Be sure to sample the excellent house rioja (a Spanish wine specialty shop adjoins, so the choice is extensive) and crown your meal with a Cuban cigar. Downstairs is a smoky bar that serves amazing tapas. The waiters all come from the old country, so they know what they're talking about. ⊠*Münsterg. 15, Kreis 1* ☎*044/2512310* ⊟*AE, DC, MC, V.*

$$$$
CONTEMPORARY
★

✕**Caduff's Wine Loft.** In a 19th-century whitewashed former warehouse, industrial lighting, parquet floors, and the occasional strategically placed cactus set the minimalist tone for the kitchen's delicious, simple cuisine. The market determines the menu, which could be anything from wild salmon with crepes and wasabi mayonnaise to elk entrecôte with cream sauce, Spätzli, and vegetables. If you can't decide on a wine, you're welcome to browse downstairs in the candlelit cellar—there are only about 1,000 bottles to choose from. ⊠*Kanzleistr. 126, Kreis 4* ☎*044/2402255* ▤*AE, DC, MC, V.*

$$$$
ITALIAN

✕**Casa Ferlin.** Crimson velvet wallhangings, a baronial fireplace, and 19th-century, brocade-covered banquettes add up to one of Zürich's most sumptuous interiors. Happily, the food is even more impressive, and the quality of what may be Zürich's best homemade pasta keeps regulars coming back. This family-run establishment, in business for almost a century, offers excellent traditional Italian dishes such as beef ravioli, veal fillet in lemon-sage sauce, and zabaglione marsala. The lunch crowd is mostly financial bigwigs, while evenings attract entire local families. ⊠*Stampfenbachstr. 38, Kreis 1* ☎*044/3623509* ⊕*www. casaferlin.ch/* ⟨*Reservations essential* ▤*AE, DC, MC, V* ⊙*Closed weekends and mid-July–mid-Aug.*

$$$$
SWISS
★

✕**Haus zum Rüden.** The most culinarily ambitious of Zürich's many Zunfthaus (historic guild hall) dining places, this fine restaurant is also the most architecturally spectacular, combining a wooden barrel-vaulted ceiling and 30-foot beams. Slick modern improvements—including a glassed-in elevator—manage to blend intelligently with the ancient decor and old-world chandeliers. Innovative entrées might include clear beef soup with vegetable strips and black Perigord truffles, or duck breast in honey ginger sauce. The river views are especially impressive at night; ask for a window table. ⊠*Limmatquai 42, Kreis 1* ☎*044/2619566* ▤*AE, DC, MC, V.*

$$
VEGETARIAN

✕**Hiltl.** Founded in 1898, when vegetarians were regarded as "grass eaters," this restaurant has more than proved its staying power. It was taken over in 1904 by Bavarian Ambrosius Hiltl, who married the cook; the current patron, Rolf Hiltl, is their great-grandson. The enormous buffet offers everything from curried chickpeas to stuffed jalapeños, from breaded cheese dumplings to peas with butter and peppermint. The young business crowd stuffs the place full at lunch; DJs provide the ambience on weekend evenings. ⊠*Sihlstr. 28, Kreis 1* ☎*044/2277000* ▤*AE, DC, MC, V.*

$$$
ITALIAN

✕**Kindli.** In compliance with the kitchen's ban on the use of packaged foods, the meals served at this warm, inviting restaurant are prepared with seasonal ingredients. The results are such innovative dishes as homemade gnocchi with pumpkin, arugula, and truffles, or beef fillet with potatoes, sour cream, and horseradish. There is also a five-course meal accompanied by a glass or two of wine preselected for each course. Rich, colorful paintings, dark-wood paneling, elegant bistro furnishings, and linen table settings add to the upscale, warm comfort of the restaurant. ⊠*Pfalzg. 1, Kreis 1* ☎*043/8887678* ▤*AE, DC, MC, V.*

$$ ✕**Kronenhalle.** From Stravinsky, Brecht, and Joyce to Nureyev, Deneuve,
SWISS   and Saint-Laurent, this beloved landmark has always drawn a stellar
Fodor'sChoice crowd. Every panel of gleaming wood wainscoting frames works by
★   Picasso, Braque, Miró, Chagall, or Matisse, collected by patroness-
             hostess Hulda Zumsteg, who owned the restaurant from 1921 until her
             death in 1985. The tradition is carried on by the family trust, and robust
             cooking is still served in hefty portions: fish in sage butter, veal steak
             in morel sauce, duck *à l'orange* with red cabbage, and Spätzli. There's
             no shame in ordering the sausage and Rösti just to take in the ani-
             mated and genial scene. ⊠*Rämistr. 4, Kreis 1* ☎*044/2516669* ⊕*www.
             kronenhalle.com* ⚑*Reservations essential* ⊟*AE, DC, MC, V.*

$$ ✕**La Salle.** This is a favorite haunt of theatergoers heading for the
CONTEMPORARY Schauspielhaus Schiffbauhalle—it conveniently shares the same build-
             ing. The glass, steel, and concrete interior mixes well with the brick
             elements left from the original factory building. Beneath an enormous
             Murano glass chandelier, elegantly dressed patrons enjoy delicate
             dishes such as entrecôte of lamb in rosemary red wine sauce, or cheese
             crepes with mushrooms and seasonal vegetables. The hefty wine list
             can be sampled at the apricot-color bar, where a smaller version of the
             menu is available. ⊠*Schiffbaustr. 4, Kreis 5* ☎*044/2587071* ⊟*AE,
             DC, MC, V.*

$ ✕**Les Halles.** This old warehouse space in Zürich West has not so much
MEDITERRANEAN been renovated as cleaned up and then highlighted with an eclectic mix
             of antiques and '50s collectibles, all of which are for sale. The fare is
             health-conscious—made from organic ingredients sold in the attached
             health food store—and includes couscous with vegetables, chicken with
             peppers, and tomatoes and eggplant. It's famous for mussels during the
             season. In summer, snag a table on the multitiered veranda out back.
             ⊠*Pfingstweidstr. 6, Kreis 5* ☎*044/2731125* ⊟*AE, DC, MC, V.*

$$ ✕**Mère Catherine.** This popular bistro with a Provençal veneer presents
MEDITERRANEAN blackboard specials, with the chef turning out onion soup, snails in
             cream sauce, ravioli with walnuts, a wide range of fish dishes, and
             traditional French meats such as veal kidneys in mustard sauce with
             rice. The young, bohemian clientele also enjoys the restaurant's small,
             hipster-packed Philosophe bar next door. On warm evenings, opt for
             courtyard seating, where the occasional Spanish guitar trio comes
             by for a smooth serenade. ⊠*Nägelihof 3, Kreis 1* ☎*044/2505940*
             ⊟*AE, MC, V.*

$$ ✕**Nooch.** Zürich's first Japanese noodle bar is spacious and uncluttered,
JAPANESE   and tables are large enough for sharing without cramping your style or
             compromising your privacy. Hearty but health-conscious soups made
             with ramen, soba, and udon noodles are the specialty. The kitchen's
             pledge is to use fresh seasonal ingredients without preservatives, MSG,
             cream, or butter, and to add as little animal fat as possible. The res-
             taurant also has what may be the city's largest gastronomic smoke-free
             zone: only 4 tables out of 26 have been set aside for smokers. ⊠*Hein-
             richstr. 267, Kreis 5* ☎*043/3668535* ⊟*AE, DC, MC, V.*

¢–$ ✕**Odéon.** This historic café–restaurant was once frequented by the pre-
CAFÉ   Revolution Lenin, who nursed a coffee while he read the daily papers.
★   These days an air of countercultural chic mixes with the cigarette

smoke. You can nurse a coffee, too, or choose from a menu of burgers, BLTs, and pasta. ⊠*Limmatquai 2, Kreis 1* ☎*044/2511650* ⊟*AE, DC, MC, V.*

$$$$
ECLECTIC
Fodor's Choice
★
✕**Petermann's Kunststuben.** Set in an 1879 house with rooms replete with aubergine-hued walls, gigantic bouquets, Venetian glass lanterns, and modern paintings ("Kunststuben" means art studio), Petermann's is 9 km (5 mi) south of Zürich in Küsnacht, a village near Rapperswil. Though it's south of the city center, this formal restaurant is more than worth the time and effort to get here. Chef Horst Petermann never rests on his laurels: the ever-changing international French menu may include garlic lamb with

EATS ON THE CHEAP

Zürich's inflated cost of living is reflected in its restaurants. There's a shortage of truly budget options, but keep in mind that daily prix-fixe menus are considerably cheaper and that even the glossiest places have business-lunch menus—your best bet for sampling Zürich's highest cuisine at cut rates. If you're on a tight budget, watch for posted *Tagesteller* offerings. These daily specials, with meat, potatoes, and possibly a hot vegetable, can still be found in the Niederdorf for under 25 SF.

jellied vegetables, with presentation so fantastic it looks more like art than food. On the small side, the restaurant nearly doubles in summer thanks to the flower-fragrant outdoor terrace. ⊠*Seestr. 160, Küsnacht,* ☎*044/9100715* ⊕*www.kunststuben.com* ⌁*Reservations essential* ⊟*AE, DC, MC, V* ⊙*Closed Sun. and Mon., 2 wks in Feb., and 3 wks in late summer.*

$$
ECLECTIC
★
✕**Reithalle.** In a downtown theater complex behind Bahnhofstrasse, this old military riding stable now does its duty as a noisy and popular restaurant. Its past is plain to see, as candles are perched on the mangers and beams. Young locals share long tables arranged mess-hall-style to sample international specialties—from curry to spare ribs—many of them vegetarian, as well as an excellent list of open wines from all over the world listed on the blackboard. In summer the courtyard is lined with communal tables. ⊠*Gessnerallee 8, Kreis 1* ☎*044/2120766* ⊟*AE, MC, V.*

$
SWISS
✕**Rheinfelder Bierhaus.** Locals know this dark, smoky Niederdorf institution by its unsettling nickname, "Bluetig Tuume," or the Bloody Thumb. The venue is nonetheless often packed with happy patrons. It is famous locally for its *entrecôte café de Paris* (steak with herb butter), sausage standbys, and the pride of the Spanish/Romansch owners: a freshly homemade paella, which must be ordered in advance. Snag one of the few tables lined up outside in warm weather—a steady stream of passersby in this pedestrian zone makes for good entertainment. ⊠*Marktg. 19, Kreis 1* ☎*044/2512991* ⊟*No credit cards.*

$$$
SWISS
✕**Seerose.** As soon as it even vaguely looks like it'll be warm enough, the hip deck-shoe crowd drives, runs, cycles, powerboats, or even sails to one of the best places on the lake. It not only has its own dock, it *is* its own dock, jutting far out and offering fabulous views. The food isn't bad either: seasonal ingredients make the difference for dishes such as beef tournedos with match-thin french fries, or lemon sole with basmati

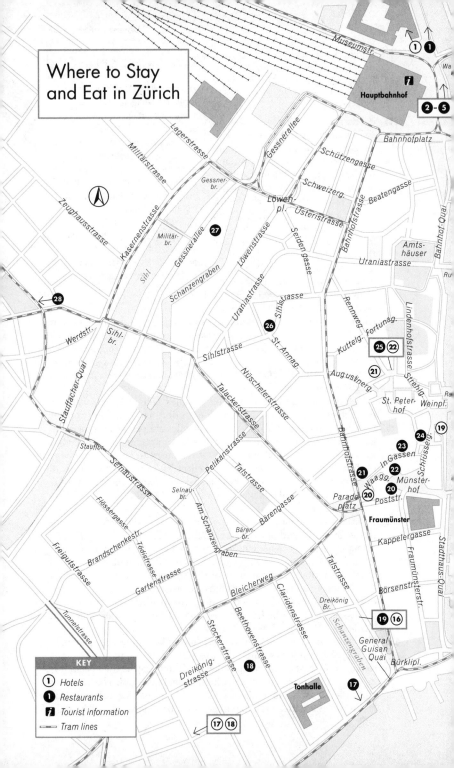

Where to Stay and Eat in Zürich

rice. Sunglasses required. ⊠*Seestr. 493, Kreis 2* ☎*044/4816383* ▤*AE, DC, MC, V.*

$$$ ✕**Veltliner Keller.** Though its rich, carved-wood decor borrows from
SWISS   Graubündner Alpine culture, this dining spot is no tourist trap. The
★   house, built in 1325 and functioning as a restaurant since 1551, has
always stored Italian-Swiss Valtellina wines, which were carried over
the Alps to Zürich. There is a definite emphasis on the heavy and the
meaty, but the kitchen is flexible and reasonably deft with more mod-
ern favorites as well: jumbo shrimp with tomato herb sauce, osso buco
with saffron risotto, and dessert mousses. ⊠*Schlüsselg. 8, Kreis 1*
☎*044/2254040* ▤*AE, DC, MC, V* ⊘*Closed weekends.*

$$$ ✕**Wirtschaft zum Münsterhof.** Upstairs, furnishings are simple, covered
ECLECTIC   in white linens, and medieval walls are exposed (one shows a 13th-
century painting of lovers frolicking in a garden) and scrubbed bare.
But the understated elegance doesn't distract from what's on your plate:
seasonal side dishes complement grilled meats and local fish, such as
prime rib with béarnaise sauce or fillet of perch with rice and spinach.
If you've come just for the daily special or some appetizers with a
bottle of wine, the ground floor is more casual. ⊠*Münsterhof 6, Kreis
1* ☎*044/2114340* ▤*AE, DC, MC, V.*

$-$$ ✕**Zeughauskeller.** Built as an arsenal in 1487, this enormous stone-and-
SWISS   beam hall offers hearty meat platters and a variety of beers and wines
★   in comfortable Germanic chaos. The waitstaff is harried and brisk,
especially at lunchtime, when crowds are thick. Unlike the shabbier
beer halls in Niederdorf, this one is clean and bourgeois, reflecting its
Paradeplatz location. They're not unaccustomed to tourists—menus
are posted in English, Japanese, and at least 10 other languages—but
locals consider this their home away from home. ⊠*Bahnhofstr. 28, at
Paradepl., Kreis 1* ☎*044/2112690* ▤*AE, DC, MC, V.*

$$ ✕**Zum Grünen Glas.** This French-inclined restaurant in a quiet corner
FRENCH   of the Niederdorf is part of the trend toward lighter food and por-
★   tions that don't overflow your plate. You might try handmade spaghetti
with beef slices and ratatouille, or fillet of beef and black tiger shrimp
with bok choy, basmati rice and mango chutney, then finish with a
slice of chocolate cake doused in orange liqueur. Wainscoting, parquet
floors, and crisp white tablecloths make for a comfortable dining room;
an outside courtyard is open in summer. ⊠*Untere Zäune 15, Kreis 1*
☎*044/2516504* ▤*AE, DC, MC, V.*

$$ ✕**Zunfthaus zur Schmiden.** The sense of history should be strong here, as
SWISS   this was the guild house of blacksmiths and barbers, founded in 1412.
While there are time-burnished allurements—wood paneling, leaded
glass, and tile stoves—the historic vibe of the main room is counteracted
by the modern white ceiling and casements. To really channel history,
take a peek at the Zunftsaal, a 19th-century banqueting room extravaganza. At your table, Zürich's meat classics (Geschnetzeltes, liver or
steak with Rösti) come garnished with seasonal vegetables, and there's
a considerable selection of alternatives, fish among them. The guild's
own house-label wine is fine. ⊠*Marktg. 20, Kreis 1* ☎*044/2505848*
⊕*www.zunfthausschmiden.ch* ▤*AE, DC, MC, V.*

$$ ✕**Zunfthaus zur Waag.** With its mag-
SWISS   nificent Renassance-inspired facade,
this airy guildhall, with white-
washed woodwork and leaded-
glass windows looking out to the
Fraumünster, remains a lovely din-
ing spot. The Zunft-Saal (guildhall)
is a pine-wood showpiece, which
greatly outshines the main restau-
rant—a rather dull Biedermeier
room. The kitchen offers light, sea-
sonal dishes such as fillet of perch
in almond butter with spinach, or

ONE SWINGING PLACE
The historic decor at Zur Oepfel-chammer is suprisingly "interac-tive." Any guest who succeeds in swinging around the room's famous wooden rafters three times wins free wine for their table. You'd be amazed at the amount of diners who make the attempt.

glazed lamb cutlets in port sauce with vegetables and potato-dough
pasta. To drink in the impressive architecture, opt for outside tables
on the edge of the cobblestone square in warm weather. ⊠*Münster-
hof 8, Kreis 1* ☎*044/2169966* ⊕*www.zunfthaus-zur-waag.ch* ⊟*AE,
DC, MC, V.*

$$ ✕**Zur Oepfelchammer.** Dating from 1801, this was once the haunt of
SWISS   Zürich's beloved writer Gottfried Keller. One section is a dark and heav-
★   ily graffitied bar, with sagging timbers and slanting floors; there are also
two welcoming little dining rooms with coffered ceilings and plenty of
carved oak and damask—opt for the cozy, charming Gaststube (not the
more staid Stübli). Traditional meat dishes—calves' liver, Geschnetzeltes
Kalbfleisch—are lightened up with fresh seasonal veggies. The place is
always packed, and service can be slow, so stake out a table and plan to
spend the evening. ⊠*Rindermarkt 12, Kreis 1* ☎*044/2512336* ⊕*www.
oepfelchammer.ch/* ⊟*MC, V* ☉*Closed Sun. and Mon.*

WHERE TO STAY

THE SCENE

After years of resting on their laurels, Zurich's hotel directors are airing
out that musty smell, throwing out the chintz, the velvetine, and the
dusty carpet in favor of hardwood floors, sleek 21st-century furnishings,
and modern technology, such as wireless LANs and DVD players.

A string of small boutique hotels has popped up since the turn of the
21st century, all with a strong focus on design, sleeping comfort, and
generous bathrooms—think large bed covered with a fluffy down com-
forter and soft pillows, looking onto an outsized flatscreen TV that
invariably includes video games and a selection of movies, and a white-
tiled bathroom with black slate floors and lots of mirrors. On our
list this includes the hotels Greulich, Seefeld, Widder, and Zürichberg.
Another passion taking over the city—in fact the country—is the trend
toward so-called "wellness" vacations.

Putting a new spin on the 19th- and early-20th-century tradition of the
Swiss sanitorium—where convalescent patients from all over the world
came to Switzerland to cleanse their lungs with Alpine air—hotels here
are, if they have the space, adding pools, saunas, steam rooms, and

special areas for such ministrations as hot stone massage, cosmetic treatment, or body wraps.

Smaller venues like the Hotel Seefeld have simply added a cosmetics studio to cover their customers' skin-care needs, while the upmarket houses cover everything from full-body peels, sports massages, and ice wraps (The Park Hyatt Hotel) all the way through to the comprehensive spa services of the Dolder Grand Hotel, which also includes kotastu footbaths, an aroma pool, indoor and outdoor whirlpools, and, if you're still not feeling like a whole new you, there's even a clinic complete with a team of doctors for cosmetic surgery.

WHAT IT COSTS IN SWISS FRANCS

	¢	$	$$	$$$	$$$$
FOR TWO PEOPLE	under 100 SF	100 SF–200 SF	200 SF–300 SF	300 SF–500 SF	over 500 SF

Prices are for two people in a standard double room, including tax and service.

$$ 🏨 **Adler.** Smack in the middle of Niederdorf, this is a smart, state-of-the-art hotel. From the gleaming lobby to the sleek, modular rooms, the ash-and-granite decor makes the most of tight spaces. Hand-painted murals of city landmarks remind you you're in Zürich. The restaurant off the lobby, Adler's Swiss Chuchi, is known locally as a great year-round place for fondue. **Pros:** no phone call surcharges; clean, bright rooms; hardwood floors. **Cons:** can get noisy on weekends. ⊠ *Roseng. 10, Kreis 1* ☎ *044/2669696* ⊕ *www.hotel-adler.ch* ⇖ *52 rooms* ⟡ *In-room: no a/c, safe, refrigerator, dial-up. In-hotel: restaurant, public Internet, public Wi-Fi* ☐ *AE, DC, MC, V* ⟨○⟩*BP.*

$$$$ 🏨 **Alden Splügenschloss.** Constructed at the turn of the 20th century as luxury apartments, this Relais & Châteaux property consists entirely of suites, all done in beige with chocolate leather accents and filled with such amenities as flat-screen televisions. Each sleek marble bath has its own whirlpool. The lobby retains some alluring fin-de-siècle accents. **Pros:** a very quiet neighborhood; so luxurious even Midas would feel at home. **Cons:** the location—in a spare banking district—may be a little out of the way for sightseeing; very few restaurants or shopping opportunities nearby. ⊠ *Splügenstr. 2, Kreis 1* ☎ *044/2899999* ⊕ *www.alden. ch* ⇖ *22 suites* ⟡ *In-room: refrigerator, Ethernet, dial-up. In-hotel: 2 restaurants, bar* ☐ *AE, DC, MC, V* ⟨○⟩*BP.*

$$$$ 🏨 **Baur au Lac.** Austria's Empress Elisabeth paved the way (spending an
★ entire summer here with a retinue of 60 people). The Russian Tsarina and German Emperor Wilhelm II followed; Richard Wagner arrived and premiered the first act of his *Die Walküre* here, accompanied on the piano by his father-in-law, Franz Liszt. Kings and queens, empresses and dukes took turns visiting (and let's not forget Arthur Rubinstein, Marc Chagall, Henry Moore, and Plácido Domingo), making this hotel a truly upper-crust establishment ever since it opened its doors in 1844. Today there is nary an empress in sight. This is still one highbrow patrician—it even goes so far as to turn its broad back to the commercial center; its front rooms overlook the lake, the canal, and the manicured lawns

2

of its own private park. Le Hall, the vast lobby, has a Jugenstil flavor and is just the place to aperitif the late afternoon away. Upstairs, the signature classic room decor gleams with rich fabrics and Empire mirrors. In summer meals (including breakfast) are served in the glassed-in pavilion along the canal; in winter, in the glowing Restaurant Français. **Pros:** old-world style plus ultramodern comforts such as triple-glazed windows and CD players. **Cons:** service can get a little sniffy. ⊠ *Talstr. 1, Kreis 1* ☎ *044/2205020* ⊕ *www.bauraulac.ch* ⇱ *84 rooms, 42 suites* ⚷ *In-room: safe, refrigerator, dial-up. In-hotel: 2 restaurants, bar, gym, public Wi-Fi* ⊟ *AE, DC, MC, V.*

$$$$ ⬚ **Dolder Grand Hotel.** Zürich has a new pinnacle of hotel luxury—or
★ should we say "new" old: The original 1899 building, resplendent with Disneyesque turrets and timbered balconies, has now been completely refurbished and is now flanked by two glass-and-steel wings that mirror the natural surroundings. Set atop the Zürichberg mountain, this large spa hotel, which began life as a Victorian-era "Kurhaus," has been given a warm mod-minimalist makeover, mixing the Corinthian capitals and crystal chandeliers of the original building with the angular, less-is-more style of the modern wings. The sumptuous guest rooms in creams and pastels, some with hardwood floors, are complemented by an extravagant in-house spa—with everything from good old-fashioned massages to aesthetic dermatology and plastic surgery. While the formal restaurant is very elegant, the stark whiteness and bead curtains of the more casual one downstairs evoke a cafeteria to some eyes. Needless to say, the food is excellent. **Pros:** a destination in itself; gorgeous views; high-end service; very good restaurants. **Cons:** off the beaten track; a bit OTT, pricewise; standard rooms are too small, considering the cost. ⊠ *Kurhausstr. 65, Kreis 7* ☎ *044/4566000* ⊕ *www.thedoldergrand. com* ⇱ *114 rooms, 59 suites* ⚷ *In-room: no a/c (some), safe, refrigerator, Ethernet. In-hotel: 3 restaurants, bar, golf course, 2 tennis courts, pool, gym, spa, bicycles, public Wi-Fi, parking (fee)* ⊟ *AE, DC, MC, V* ⦿*BP.*

¢–$ ⬚ **Etap.** Working on the principle that cheap should only mean inexpensive, this chain hotel is a dependable pick. Every room around the world is exactly the same: violet-and-gray walls and carpeting, one double bed, a single bunk set above it, and shower and toilet in separate, immaculate fiberglass modules. The rate for two is always the same. Take Tram 4 or 13 from the Hauptbahnhof to Escher Wyss Platz; the Etap is within easy walking distance from there. **Pros:** deep in the heart of Zürich West; great value. **Cons:** charmless; one side looks out onto an industrial park. ⊠ *Technoparkstr. 2, Kreis 5* ☎ *044/2762000* ⊕ *www.etaphotel.com* ⇱ *160 rooms* ⚷ *In-room: no a/c, no phone* ⊟ *AE, MC, V.*

$$–$$$ ⬚ **Haus zum Kindli.** This charming little bijou hotel is as artfully styled as a magazine ad, with subtle grays and beiges underscoring the inviting white bed linens and original bath fixtures refurbished to match modern needs. The result is welcoming, intimate, and less contrived than many hotels' cookie-cutter decors. An added attraction is "revitalized" water throughout the hotel–a process said to provide healthier water than the stuff fresh out of the tap. **Pros:** pretend you live in the middle of the Old Town, just steps away from where the town was founded; run home to the bathroom while you're shopping–it's that close! **Cons:** no parking; a little dark during winter. ✉*Pfalzg. 1, Kreis 1* ☏*043/8887676* ⊕*www.kindli.ch* ⇌*16 rooms* &*In-room: no a/c, refrigerator, Ethernet. In-hotel: restaurant, public Wi-Fi, no elevator* ▤*AE, DC, MC, V* ⦿*BP.*

¢–$ **Kafischnaps.** Away from the throb of downtown but still only a 15-minute walk back, this is the best deal in town for those on a budget. Each room has its own color scheme, taken from a local schnapps. Beds are very comfy, with down quilts and soft pillows. The smoky café downstairs doubles as the reception area and breakfast room. Reservations can only be made online. **Pros:** beautifully designed rooms; very hip café; great value. **Cons:** far from the madding crowd; check-in can be annoying if the café is busy. ✉*Kornhausstr. 57, Kreis 6* ☏*043/5388116* ⊕*www.kafischnaps.ch* ⇌*5 rooms* &*In-room: no a/c, no phone, no TV (some), Wi-Fi. In-hotel: restaurant* ▤*AE, DC, MC, V* ⦿*BP.*

$$–$$$ **Lady's First.** Once a rooming house for country girls attending school in the big city, this boutique hotel has two floors that cater exclusively to women—a first in Switzerland. A stylish palette and steel furnishings join the original 1900 parquet floors and high stuccoed ceilings. The extensive wellness center offers saunas, massages, and various treatments, and the use of the facilities is included in the room rate. (Nonguests can also book spa time.) **Pros:** very pro-female, but also respectful of the "modern man." **Cons:** bathrooms were added as niches into each room, so there's less noise insulation. ✉*Mainaustr. 24, Kreis 8* ☏*044/3808010* ⊕*www.ladysfirst.ch* ⇌*28 rooms* &*In-room: no a/c, Ethernet, dial-up. In-hotel: spa, public Wi-Fi* ▤*AE, DC, MC, V* ⦿*BP.*

$–$$ **Leoneck.** From the cowhide-covered front desk to the edelweiss-print curtains, this budget hotel wallows in its Swiss roots, but balances this indulgence with no-nonsense conveniences such as built-in pine furniture and tile baths (albeit with cow-print shower curtains). There isn't much space to stretch out, though, and the furnishings sometimes show their age. The adjoining restaurant, Crazy Cow, slings out its own Swiss kitsch (Rösti-burgers) in an over-the-top decor of milk cans, miniature Matterhorns, and the ubiquitous black-and-white bovines. **Pros:** very friendly service; close to the action but quiet. **Cons:** small rooms; the cow motif gets a little tired after a while. ✉*Leonhardstr. 1, Kreis 1* ☏*044/2542222* ⊕*www.leoneck.ch* ⇌*78 rooms* &*In-room: no a/c, dial-up. In-hotel: restaurant, public Internet, public Wi-Fi* ▤*AE, DC, MC, V* ⦿*BP.*

$ **Limmathof.** This spare but welcoming hotel inhabits a handsome, historic building and is ideally placed on the Limmatquai, minutes from the Hauptbahnhof and steps from the Limmatquai and Central tram stops. All rooms have tile bathrooms and plump down comforters. There's an old-fashioned wood-paneled Weinstube (wine bar) and a bright vegetarian restaurant that doubles as the breakfast room. **Pros:** you won't find it cheaper in this part of town; good service. **Cons:** guest rooms are a bit too 20th century. ✉*Limmatquai 142, Kreis 1*

☎044/2676040 ⊕*www.limmathof.com* ⇆*62 rooms* ⚷*In-room: no a/c, dial-up. In-hotel: restaurant, bar* ☰*AE, DC, MC, V* ❖|*BP.*

$$$$ ⌂ **Park Hyatt.** Just a few blocks from the lake, the wide open spaces
★ of the city's first American-style luxury hotel are accented in black marble, rich maple, and lots of gleaming glass. Rooms have parquet floors with soft carpets, burgundy and beige fabrics on the furnishings, and floor-to-ceiling windows. Bathrooms are so spacious and luxurious you'll want to take one home with you. **Pros:** more space than you'd normally find in a Swiss hotel room; extremely friendly service; an excellent restaurant. **Cons:** neighborhood is business-oriented rather than tourist-oriented; the glass-and-steel style doesn't go with an "old world" experience. ✉*Beethovenstr. 21, Kreis 1* ☎*043/8831234* ⊕*www.hyatt. ch* ⇆*142 rooms, 12 suites* ⚷*In-room: safe, refrigerator, Ethernet, dial-up. In-hotel: restaurant, bar, gym, airport shuttle, public Internet, public Wi-Fi* ☰*AE, DC, MC, V.*

$–$$ ⌂ **Rex.** Its parking-garage architecture brightened up with assertive colors and jazz posters, this foursquare property has some businesspeople's necessities (computer connections, desks big enough to spread out your papers), without the depth of service offered by more expensive hotels. Its restaurant, the Blauer Apfel, draws a loyal, young professional lunch clientele to its cool, blue-halogen-lighted tables. It's three stops from Central heading north on Tram 7 or 15. **Pros:** young and accommodating staff; quiet neighborhood. **Cons:** a bit far from where you want to be. ✉*Weinbergstr. 92, Kreis 6* ☎*044/3602525* ⇆*37 rooms* ⚷*In-room: no a/c, safe, refrigerator. dial-up. In-hotel: restaurant, public Wi-Fi* ☰*AE, DC, MC, V* ❖|*BP.*

$$$$ ⌂ **Romantik Hotel Florhof.** Replete with an away-from-it-all atmosphere,
★ this is a pretty-as-a-picture, protected 17th-century merchant's mansion. In a dreamily quiet residential area by the Kunsthaus (yet just a few tram stops away from the main rail station), this anti-urban hotel is a gentle antidote to the bustle of downtown commerce. Once a bargain option, today the Florhof pampers guests with its polished wood, blue-willow fabric, and wisteria-sheltered garden. The restaurant serves light, seasonal menus. **Pros:** close to everything, yet in a quiet oasis; the terrace with its Neptune fountain alone is worth the trip. **Cons:** terrace restaurant is closed on Sunday, which may be just the day you planned to sit outside. ✉*Florhofg. 4, Kreis 1* ☎*044/2502626* ⊕*www.florhof. ch* ⇆*33 rooms, 2 suites* ⚷*In-room: no a/c (some), safe, refrigerator, Ethernet. In-hotel: restaurant* ☰*AE, DC, MC, V* ❖|*BP.*

$$$ ⌂ **Rössli.** Ultrasmall but friendly, this hotel is in the heart of the Ober-
★ dorf. The chic white-on-white decor mixes stone and wood textures with bold textiles and mosaic tiles. Extras include safes and bathrobes—unusual in this price range. Some singles are tiny, but all have double beds. The suite on the top floor has a roof terrace with a marvelous view of the Limmat and the Altstadt. **Pros:** family-style service; nicely detailed styling. **Cons:** small rooms; can get noisy during local festivals. ✉*Rösslig. 7, Kreis 1* ☎*044/2567050* ⊕*www.hotelroessli.ch* ⇆*16 rooms, 1 suite* ⚷*In-room: no a/c, safe, refrigerator. In-hotel: bar, public Wi-Fi* ☰*AE, DC, MC, V* ❖|*BP.*

$$$$ 🏨 **Savoy Baur en Ville.** Directly on Paradeplatz, at the hub of the banking, shopping, and sightseeing districts, this is one of Zürich's 19th-century landmarks. Despite its venerable age, the hotel perennially improves itself, regularly sprucing up its rooms and amenities to maintain its conservative sleekness. The guest rooms, with gray-stone bathrooms, walk-in closets, and period furniture, typify what the hotel calls its "past-modern" decor. There are two fine restaurants—one French, one Italian—as well as a slick café–bar. **Pros:** you can't get more downtown than this; Sprüngli, the Mecca for chocolate, is right across the street. **Cons:** conservative to the point of stuffiness; more business than tourist hotel. ⊠ *Am Paradepl., Poststr. 12, Kreis 1* 🕾 *044/2152525* ⊕ *www. savoy-baurenville.ch* 🛏 *112 rooms, 8 suites* 🚿 *In-room: refrigerator, no a/c, Ethernet, dial-up. In-hotel: 2 restaurants, bar, public Wi-Fi* ⊟ *AE, DC, MC, V* ⓘⓞⓘ *BP.*

$$$ 🏨 **Seefeld.** In the heart of the lakeside district—close to restaurants, the opera, and movie theaters—this friendly, no-nonsense hotel is a real find. The guest rooms are comfortable, with hardwood floors, sleek furnishings, and sparkling bathrooms. Thanks to double-glazed windows, they are also quite quiet. The king-size beds are a treat not usually found in this country. **Pros:** the in-house restaurant is a local attraction; the roof terrace offers amazing views. **Cons:** on a busy street; directly between tram stops—you'll be doing a lot of walking. ⊠ *Seefeldstr. 63, Kreis 8* 🕾 *044/3874141* ⊕ *www.hotel-seefeld.ch* 🛏 *64 rooms* 🚿 *In-room: no a/c, safe, refrigerator, dial-up. In-hotel: bar, gym, public Internet, public Wi-Fi* ⊟ *AE, DC, MC, V* ⓘⓞⓘ *BP.*

$$–$$$ 🏨 **Seehof.** Offering the best of both worlds, this lodging is in a quiet neighborhood, yet is conveniently close to the opera, movie theaters, and the lake. It's a favorite of hip business executives and travelers looking for seclusion. The interior's leitmotif is modern, minimal; the bright rooms' parquet floors and white walls and furnishings give them a fresh, crisp look. The bar downstairs has a good selection of wines; in summer a garden terrace adds to the charm. **Pros:** small but very nice bathrooms; a good in-house sushi restaurant. **Cons:** on a narrow and charmless side street. ⊠ *Seehofstr. 11, Kreis 1* 🕾 *044/2545757* ⊕ *www. hotelseehof.ch* 🛏 *19 rooms* 🚿 *In-room: no a/c, safe, refrigerator. In-hotel: bar, public Wi-Fi* ⊟ *AE, DC, MC, V* ⓘⓞⓘ *BP.*

$$–$$$ 🏨 **Sheraton Neues Schloss.** Managed by the Sheraton chain, this intimate hotel in the business district, just a few minutes' walk from Paradeplatz and a block from the Tonhalle music hall, offers a warm welcome, good service, and classic decor. Its Le Jardin restaurant (closed Sunday) is popular with theatergoers for its preperformance menu. The hotel is closed during July and August 2009 for renovations. **Pros:** One block from the lake; excellent service. **Cons:** kids are free, but only if they sleep with you in your bed. ⊠ *Stockerstr. 17, Kreis 1* 🕾 *044/2869400* 🛏 *58 rooms* 🚿 *In-room: safe, refrigerator Ethernet. In-hotel: restaurant, public Wi-Fi* ⊟ *AE, DC, MC, V.*

$$$$ 🏨 **Widder.** Zürich's most captivating hotel was created when 10 adjacent medieval houses were gutted and combined—now steel fuses with ancient stone and timeworn wood. Behind every door is a fascinating mix of old and new; a guest room could mix restored 17th-century

Fodor's Choice
★

frescoes and stone floors with a leather bedspread and halogen bell jars. Set in the heart of Zürich's historic quarter, many of the houses look out into a communal courtyard, while others flaunt views of the Rennweg or the Augustinerkirche. Four suites have private roof terraces. **Pros:** the spectacular Room 210; the more modern Room 509. **Cons:** there is no "con," this place is perfect. ⊠ *Rennweg 7, Kreis 1* ☎ *044/2242526* ⊕ *www.widderhotel.ch* ⬦ *42 rooms, 7 suites* ♿ *In-room: safe, refrigerator, Ethernet, dial-up, Wi-Fi. In-hotel: 2 restaurants, bar* ☰ *AE, DC, MC, V.*

$ 🏨 **Zic-Zac Rock Hotel.** Perfectly set in the lively Niederdorf, this hotel lets you indulge your inner groupie. All rooms are named after rock personalities, from Lenny Kravitz to U2, and decorated accordingly. Framed albums, portraits, and gold records hang on the pastel yellow walls. Furnishings are no-frills but comfortable; most rooms share showers and toilets. The American restaurant and bar downstairs draw plenty of nonguests, and on weekends the hotel fairly throbs with bass. **Pros:** frequented by the fun crowd; great in-house Indian restaurant; close to everything. **Cons:** not for light sleepers; some rooms could use an update; the elevator doesn't go to the ground floor. ⊠ *Marktg. 17, Kreis 1* ☎ *044/2612181* ⊕ *www.ziczac.ch* ⬦ *49 rooms, 7 with bath, 2 suites* ♿ *In-room: no a/c. In-hotel: 2 restaurants, bar, airport shuttle* ☰ *AE, DC, MC, V.*

$$$$ 🏨 **Zum Storchen.** The central location of this airy 600-year-old struc-

Fodor's Choice ture—tucked between the Fraumünster and St. Peters Kirche on the

★ gull-studded bank of the Limmat River—is stunning. Rebuilt in 1939 and since renovated, the modern hotel is impeccable and intimately scaled. It has warmly appointed rooms, some with French windows that open over the water. Deluxe corner rooms, with views toward both river and lake, are worth fighting for, as are seats at the terrace café, where dessert is the panaromantic vista of the Altstadt. **Pros:** expert and friendly service; charming Old Town location; the views. **Cons:** mosquitoes in summer (don't sleep with the window open); its proximity to noise during local festivals—and there are many. ⊠ *Weinpl. 2, Kreis 1* ☎ *044/2272727* ⊕ *www.storchen.ch* ⬦ *75 rooms* ♿ *In-room: safe, refrigerator, Ethernet. In-hotel: restaurant, bar, public Wi-Fi* ☰ *AE, DC, MC, V* ⦿ *BP.*

$$$–$$$$ 🏨 **Zürichberg.** You may do a double-take when you walk into the lobby of the Schneckenhaus (Snail House) annex here and discover a miniversion of New York City's Guggenheim Museum's white ramp. Starkly and colorfully modern, this hotel—set about 3 mi outside the city center—is a change-of-pace place. But no one will cough at the crisply minimalistic rooms, all with parquet floors and many hued in deep orangey reds. Tram 6 heads straight to the hotel from the Hauptbahnhof. **Pros:** good restaurant; marvelous view of the city and the Alps from the terrace. **Cons:** a 100-yard schlepp from the tram stop to the hotel. ⊠ *Orellistr. 21, Kreis 7* ☎ *044/2683535* ⊕ *www.zuerichberg.ch* ⬦ *66 rooms* ♿ *In-room: no a/c, safe, refrigerator, dial-up. In-hotel: 2 restaurants, public Internet, public Wi-Fi* ☰ *AE, DC, MC, V* ⦿ *BP.*

NIGHTLIFE & THE ARTS

NIGHTLIFE

Of all the Swiss cities, Zürich has the liveliest nightlife. The Niederdorf is Zürich's nightlife district, with cut-rate hotels, strip joints, and bars crowding along Marktgasse, which becomes Niederdorfstrasse. On Thursday and weekend nights the streets flow with a rowdy crowd of club- and bar-hoppers. In Zürich West, the locales are all a shade hipper. In winter things wind down between midnight and 2 AM, but come summer most places stay open until 4 AM.

> **YOU SAY YOU WANT A REVOLUTION?**
>
> Serving a young, arty crowd until 4 AM, **Odéon** (Limmatquai 2, Kreis 1, 044/2511650) is a cultural icon, a place where Mata Hari danced, Lenin and Trotsky plotted the revolution, and James Joyce scrounged drinks. It gets gayer as the evening wears on, but everyone goes because the place is so chic.

BARS

DOWNTOWN A welcoming bar that tips a wink to Spain's most famous film director, **Almodobar** (⊠*Bleicherweg 68, Kreis 1* ☎*043/8444488*) is as eclectic as its clientele. Sitting on the zebra-skin stools in the bar you'll probably spy young designers in leather pants and faux-fur jackets. **Barfüsser** (⊠*Spitalg. 14, Kreis 1* ☎*044/2514064*), established in 1956, claims to be one of the oldest gay bars in Europe. It has comfortable lounge chairs and space to mix and mingle. There's also excellent sushi. **Barrique** (⊠*Marktg. 17, Kreis 1* ☎*044/2525941*) is a vinotheque featuring a world-renowned wine list. **Café Central Bar** (⊠*Central 1, Kreis 1* ☎*044/2515555*), in the Hotel Central, is a popular neo–Art Deco café by day and a piano bar by night.

Cranberry (⊠*Metzgerg. 3, Kreis 1* ☎*044/2612772*) stocks broad selections of rum and port; it also has an upstairs cigar room. The **James Joyce Pub** (⊠*Pelikanstr. 8, off Bahnhofstr., Kreis 1* ☎*044/2211828*) is a beautifully paneled Irish pub where the wood is as dark as the Guinness. The **Jules Verne Panorama Bar** (⊠*Uraniastr. 9, Kreis 1* ☎*043/8886666*) is a wine bar with a wraparound view of downtown. The narrow bar at the **Kronenhalle** (⊠*Rämistr. 4, Kreis 1* ☎*044/2511597*) draws mobs of well-heeled locals and internationals for its prize-winning cocktails. At **Purpur** (⊠*Seefeldstr. 9, Kreis 2* ☎*044/4192066*), a Moroccan-style lounge, you can take your drinks lying down on a heap of throw pillows while DJs mix ambient sound.

ZÜRICH WEST At **Basilica** (⊠*Heinrichstr. 237, Kreis 5* ☎*043/3669383*), hipsters lounge in an Italianate setting of red velvet and marble statues. Once you get past the name, you'll find that **Hard One** (⊠*Heinrichstr. 269, Kreis 5* ☎*044/4441000*) has great views of Zürich West and a good choice of champagnes.

Not just for intellectuals, **I.Q.** (⊠*Hardstr. 316, Kreis 5* ☎*044/4407440*) has a fully stocked whiskey bar. **Spheres** (⊠*Hardturmstr. 66, Kreis*

5 ☎044/4406622) is a bar and bookstore with a great selection of international magazines.

DANCING

The medieval-theme **Adagio** (✉ *Gotthardstr. 5, Kreis 1* ☎044/2063666) books classic rock, jazz, and tango musicians for well-dressed thirty-somethings. Zürich's exclusive set meets at **Indochine** (✉ *Limmatstr. 275, Kreis 5* ☎044/4481111), whose gorgeous interior evokes Southeast Asia. The music floats between pop, disco, house, and techno. **Kaufleuten** (✉ *Pelikanstr. 18, Kreis 1* ☎044/2253333) is a local landmark that draws a well-dressed, upwardly mobile crowd. It's a popular performance space for established artists such as Prince and Nina Hagen who are looking for an intimate venue. The Rolling Stones once showed up unannounced for an impromptu concert.

Mascotte (✉ *Theaterstr. 10, Kreis 1* ☎044/2524481), blasting everything from funk and soul to house and techno, is popular with all ages. A legendary techno club, **Oxa Dance Hall** (✉ *Andreastr. 70, Oerlikon, Kreis 1* ☎044/3116033) draws thousands of casual young Swiss who dance all night (and often well into the next day). Take Tram 14 from the Hauptbahnhof to the Oerlikon terminus.

THE ARTS

Despite its small population, Zürich is a big city when it comes to the arts; it supports a top-rank orchestra, an opera company, and a theater. Check *Zürich News,* published weekly in English and German, or "Züri-tipp," a German-language supplement to the Friday edition of the daily newspaper *Tages Anzeiger.* The city's annual **Züricher Festspiele**—a celebration of opera, ballet, concerts, theater, and art exhibitions—runs from late June through mid-July. You'll need to book well ahead for this—details are available from the tourist office or **Info- und Ticketoffice** (✉ *Postfach,* ☎044/2063434). Tickets to opera, concert, and theater events can also be bought from the tourist office. Tickets for almost any event can be purchased in advance by telephone from **Ticketcorner** (☎0900/800800). Depending on the event, **Musik Hug** (✉ *Limmatquai 28–30, Kreis 1* ☎044/2694100) makes reservations. The music store **Jecklin** (✉ *Rämistr. 30, Kreis 1* ☎044/2537676) promotes and sells tickets for various music events.

FILM

Movies in Zürich are serious business, with most films presented in the original language. Check newspapers and the ubiquitous posters, and watch for the initials *E/d/f,* which means an English-language version with German (Deutsch) and French subtitles. **Metropol** (✉ *Badenerstr. 16, Kreis 4* ☎0900/556789) has a great sound system and the largest screen in Zürich. The **Zürich Film Festival** (⊕ *www.zurichfilmfestival.org*) takes place every year in early October.

MUSIC

The Zürich Tonhalle Orchestra, named for its concert hall, the **Tonhalle** (⊠*Claridenstr. 7, Kreis 1* ☎*044/2063434* ⊕*www.tonhalle.ch*), which was inaugurated by Brahms in 1895, enjoys international acclaim. There are also solo recitals and chamber programs here. The season runs from September through July; tickets sell out quickly, so book through the Tonhalle.

OPERA

The permanent company at the **Opernhaus** (⊠*Theaterpl., Kreis 1* ☎*044/2686666* ⊕*www.opernhaus.ch*) is widely recognized and difficult to drop in on if you haven't booked well ahead, but single seats can sometimes be secured at the last minute. Performances are held from September through July.

THEATER

The venerable **Schauspielhaus Pfauenbühne** (⊠*Rämistr. 34, Kreis 7* ☎*044/2587777* ⊕*www.schauspielhaus.ch*) has a long history of cutting-edge performances with a strong inventive streak; during World War II this was the only German-language theater in Europe that remained independent. Nowadays its main stage presents finely tuned productions (in German), while experimental works are given in the Keller (cellar). Its sister stage, the **Schauspielhaus Schiffbauhalle** (⊠*Schiffbaustr. 4, Kreis 1* ☎*044/2587777* ⊕*www.schauspielhaus.ch*) is home to large-scale productions, also in German.

During late August and early September the **Theaterspektakel** takes place, with circus tents housing avant-garde theater and experimental performances on the lawns by the lake at Mythenquai.

SHOPPING

Many of Zürich's designer boutiques lie hidden along the narrow streets between Bahnhofstrasse and the Limmat River. Quirky bookstores and antiques shops lurk in the sloping cobblestone alleyways leading off Niedorfstrasse and Oberdorfstrasse. The fabled Bahnhofstrasse—famous because it's reputedly the most expensive street in the world—is dominated by large department stores and extravagantly priced jewelry shops.

The store-lined **Bahnhofstrasse** concentrates much of Zürich's most expensive (from elegant to gaudy) goods at the Paradeplatz end. There's another pocket of good stores around **Löwenstrasse**, southwest of the Hauptbahnhof. The **Niederdorf** offers less expensive, younger fashions, as well as antiques and antiquarian bookshops. The west bank's Altstadt, along **Storchengasse** near the Münsterhof, is a focal point for high-end designer stores.

Many city-center stores are open weekdays 9–8, Saturday 8–4. Most close on Sunday, with the exception of the shops at the Hauptbahnhof and the Stadelhofen train station. Many smaller shops, particularly in the Niederdorf area, open later in the morning or the early afternoon and are closed entirely on Monday.

DEPARTMENT STORES

COOP (✉ *Bellevuepl., Kreis 1* ☎*043/2688700*) is cheap and cheerful. **Globus** (✉ *Bahnhofstr. and Löwenpl., Kreis 1* ☎*044/2266060*) sells men's and women's designer clothes and housewares. There is also a pricey but irresistible delicatessen in the basement. **Jelmoli** (✉ *Bahnhofstr. and Seideng., Kreis 1* ☎*044/2204411* ⊕*www.jelmoli-holding.ch*), Switzerland's biggest department store, has top-notch brand-name merchandise and swarms of staffers. **Manor** (✉ *Bahnhofstr. 75, Kreis 1* ☎*044/2295699*) is dependable and affordable.

AN "A" FOR PACKAGING

It's hard to fight constant cravings for decadent chocolates when you're walking around Zürich, thanks to the many chocolate confiseries, especially the branches of Teuscher (Storcheng. 9, 044/2115153; Bahnhofstr. 46, 044/2111390; Jelmoli, Bahnhofstr. at Seidengasse, 044/2204387; Felix Café am Bellevue, Bellevueplatz 5y, 1 044/2518060). Not only do these serve up elaborate ice-cream sundaes and cakes, the shops blaze with boxes of pralines and champagne truffles all wrapped up in stunning fabrics, silk roses, and troll figurines. The beautiful boxes make fine keepsakes.

MARKETS

At **Bürkliplatz** (✉ *Lake end of Bahnhofstr., Kreis 1*) there's a flea market from 6 to 3:30 every Saturday from May to October. There's a curio market on the **Rosenhof** (✉ *Niederdorfstr. and Marktg., Kreis 1*) every Thursday from 10 to 9 and Saturday from 10 to 4 between April and Christmas. A **Christmas market** is held in the main train station and along Niederdorfstrasse starting in early December.

SPECIALTY ITEMS

BOOKS

The antiquarian bookshops in the upper streets of the Niederdorf area are rich with discoveries—and most have selections of books in English. **Biblion** (✉ *Kirchg. 40, Kreis 1* ☎*044/2613830*) specializes in antique books and bindings. The **EOS Buchantiquariat Benz** (✉ *Kirchg. 17 and 22, Kreis 1* ☎*044/2615750* ⊕*www.eosbooks.ch*) is a superb general bookshop spread over two storefronts. Both sell secondhand books as well as antiquarian tomes. The eclectic **medieval art & vie** (✉ *Spiegelg. 29, Kreis 1* ☎*044/2524720*) sells books, music, and replicas of medieval artifacts, including reproduction medieval shoes, jewelry, and water bottles.

COLLECTIBLES

In the center of town virtually every street has some kind of antiques or collectibles shop. Especially intriguing are "modern antiques" shops, which carry odds and ends from recent decades. **1000-Objekte** (✉ *Schoffelg. 3, Kreis 1* ☎*079/6605788*) has modern and antique glass and collectibles. **Eselstein** (✉ *Stadelhoferstr. 42, Kreis 1* ☎*044/2611056*) stocks items from the 1950s through the 1970s ranging from lamp shades to standing ashtrays, plus such finds as Russian samovars. **Hannibal** (⊠ *St. Jakobstr. 39, Kreis 4* ☎ *044/2426044*) is a delightful lumber room of postwar vases, chairs, pedal-operated trash bins, and rotary-dial telephones (remember them?).

MEN'S CLOTHES

Zürich's most elegant department store, **Grieder** (⊠ *Bahnhofstr. 30, Kreis 1* ☎ *044/2243636*), carries designs by Armani and Zegna, among others. **Trois Pommes** (⊠ *Weggeng. 1, Kreis 1* ☎ *044/2124710*) is the central boutique of a series of designer shops scattered through the Storchengasse area; the racks are heavily stacked with such high-profile international designers as Jil Sander, Versace, Donna Karan, and Dolce & Gabbana.

TOYS

AHA (⊠ *Spiegelg. 14, Kreis 1* ☎ *044/2510560*) sells hypnotic optical-illusion gifts in styles and sizes to suit all ages. **Pastorini Spielzeug** (⊠ *Weinpl. 3, Kreis 1* ☎ *044/2287070*) is a four-story mother lode of original and creative playthings, many hand-carved.

WOMEN'S CLOTHES

Beatrice Dreher Presents (⊠ *Gassen 14, Kreis 1* ☎ *044/2115548*) carries Chloë and Krizia. You can snag some of last season's fashions at deep discounts at Trois Pommes' bargain-basement **Check Out** (⊠ *Tödistr. 44, Kreis 1* ☎ *044/2027226*), where DKNY, Calvin Klein, and Dolce & Gabbana are jumbled on the racks. **En Soie** (⊠ *Strehlg. 26, Kreis 1* ☎ *044/2115902*) stocks gleaming, sometimes raw-textured silks, but although the fabrics are sophisticated, there's still an element of whimsy. At **Sonja Rieser** (⊠ *Froschaug. 2, Kreis 1* ☎ *044/2513847*) the selection of gorgeous handmade hats runs from elegant to wild. For the absolute latest, go to the main **Trois Pommes** (⊠ *Storcheng. 4, Kreis 1* ☎ *043/4972060*) for Balenciaga, Bluemarine, and Alaïa.

Eastern Switzerland & Liechtenstein

APPENZELL, SCHAFFHAUSEN, ST. GALLEN

Snowboarding in Heidiland, Ascent to Mt. Gonzen with snowshoes.

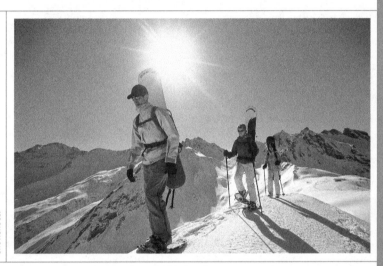

WORD OF MOUTH

"Once again, I found myself in Stein-am-Rhein-land heaven. When the town and castle come into view to the sound of the clacketty-clack of the train, it's a magical experience. I had wondered on my way there if I had made a mistake including it this time around—since I saw so many enchanting villages in the Alsace region—but when I turned a certain corner and started across that bridge over the Rhine, the experience was unreal. It's such a beautiful, beautiful place."   —Susan001

WELCOME TO EASTERN SWITZERLAND & LIECHTENSTEIN

TOP REASONS TO GO

★ **A bibliophile's paradise:** Pretend you live in the Rococo richness of the library at the Abbey of St. Gallen, with all the time in the world to read its 100,000 priceless books.

★ **The cows finally come home:** Take part in an Appenzell Alpfahrt festival, when cows are herded up into the nearby mountain slopes (in spring) or back down (in fall) by locals in their embroidered finery.

★ **Fast-forward to the 1400s:** Open a new window in Schaffhausen—the "City of Oriel Windows"— then discover the medieval magic of the preserved old town of Stein-am-Rhein.

★ **The Rhine maidens:** See Europe's third-largest river in its adolescent phase as it snakes its way to Germany. Take a lunch-boat ride, cycle along the river's grassy banks, or visit storybook castles.

★ **Lofty Liechtenstein:** Yes, it's fun to go to a tiny country for a day and get your passport stamped, but keep in mind it's mostly about high-finance banking here.

1 Schaffhausen and the Rhine. A trip from the Rhine Falls through Schaffhausen and upriver to Stein-am-Rhein transports you back to medieval and Renaissance times. The house facades, alive with colorful frescoes and oriel windows, attract tourists by the busload.

2 Bodensee to St. Gallen. Vast and windy, the Bodensee—the famous Lake Constance—offers a resort-town mellowness compared to the nearby city of St. Gallen, whose biggest draw is the manuscript-stuffed Abbey Library (as well as a decent 18th-century cathedral, a picturesque Old Town full of hearty restaurants, and its own symphony orchestra). Head south to Appenzell, whose idyllic rural appeal is literally milked to the fullest, with museums devoted to cheese making, cow herding, and the crafts of local dairy farmers.

3 Liechtenstein and the Walensee. If you don't brake quickly enough for tiny Liechtenstein, you may wind up in Austria. But you'll want to slow down for this fairy-tale realm lorded over by a princely castle (which may be viewed inside only by its princely family), a bevy of banks, and a post office famed for its unique stamps. Head back into Switzerland to see the spectacular Walensee lake.

GETTING ORIENTED

3

Quiet cousins to fast-paced, international Zürich, the eastern cantons often play the wallflower to more spectacular touristic regions, but are mistakenly overlooked. Lush and hilly, with orchards and gardens, its north dominated by the romantic Rhine, towered over by Mt. Säntis (8,200 feet), and dotted with lovely hidden lakes—as well as the enormous Bodensee (Lake Constance)—the region is as varied as it is beautiful.

Konstanz
liben Kreuzlingen
Bodensee
Roamanshorn
Frauenfeld
Amriswil
Rorschach
Gossau   St. Gallen   **2**
Wattwil   Appenzell   Rankweil
AUSTRIA
A L P S T E I N
Nesslau   Haag
C H U R F I R S T E N   **3** Buchs   **LIECHTENSTEIN**
Vaduz
Walensee   Sargans
ifels   *F L U M S E R   B E R G E*   Triesenberg
A3   A13   Malbun
Sargans
A1
A13

0 ——— 10 mi
0 ——— 10 km

Landquart

EASTERN SWITZERLAND & LIECHTENSTEIN PLANNER

How's the Weather?

The four seasons are clearly defined here: nicely balanced periods of sun and rain bring springtime blossoms and flowers with a vengeance, thanks to the many orchards and fields; summer temperatures zoom upward to between 70 and 90 degrees, depending whether it's a dry or wet one (although in recent years dry summers seem to be prevailing); the abundance of deciduous trees in this region means splashes of color in a crisp-aired, windy fall; and winter dumps lots of snow and brings temperatures hovering around -5 Celsius in town, down to -25 on some mountaintops.

Summers in eastern Switzerland provide the best weather and activities but also the greatest traffic, both on roads and in towns; spring and fall are good alternatives.

Although most places in this region are not too terribly crowded even in summer, Stein-am-Rhein is an exception.

It receives enough coach tours to virtually paralyze the village with pedestrians during high season; if you go, arrive earlier in the day or come on a weekday when crowds are a bit thinner.

Making the Most of Your Stay

This is the lazy part of Switzerland; a great place to enjoy the scenery while tooling down back roads or gazing out the train window at the greenery on the way to the next quiet town. Take along a stack of books to read on the hotel balcony or a picnic lunch for your stop in a meadow en route. In winter, pick a ski resort or a large town such as Schaffhausen or St. Gallen as your home base—unless you're looking for complete, peaceful seclusion, in other words, inescapable boredom. In summer, think of the many swimming opportunities offered by the Rhine and the Bodensee, pack at least one bathing suit, and take a leisurely lunch-boat ride. St. Gallen is the best place from which to take day trips to the region's highlights if you have a car.

Transportation Basics

Although eastern Switzerland is topographically the country's lowest region, it's still fairly rugged. It won't take long to see the major sights, but they are spread throughout the region, so leave time each day to be in transit. Train travel here is more complicated than in neighboring areas, requiring more intercity changes, so plan your itinerary accordingly. If you're planning to visit all the locations mentioned in this chapter as part of a circular tour, the easiest way to see the sights is with a car. The towns are all well connected by a network of roads—from expressways to narrow local routes meandering through the countryside—but because many regions are separated from one another by mountains or steep hills, public transportation is circuitous from one town to the other. Zürich is the public transportation hub for the four regions hereabouts: Schaffhausen/ Stein-am-Rhein; St. Gallen/Appenzell; the Toggenburg Valley; and Liechtenstein. Schaffhausen gets you most quickly to Stein-am-Rhein, the Rhine Falls, Arenenberg, Gottlieben, and Kreuzlingen/Konstanz; St. Gallen is also close to Arenenberg, Gottlieben, and Kreuzlingen/ Konstanz, as well as being central to Rorschach and the Appenzell region.

Hanging in the 'Hood

While the rest of the world hikes through the Berner Oberland in summer, many locals, especially from nearby Zürich, head for Mt. Säntis and its neighboring hills. The area offers something for all levels, whether you're panting to hike the 4½ hours all the way up to the top of the 1,500-foot peak, take an hour-long stroll around the cow pastures of the nearby hills, or drive directly to one of the many country restaurants for an outdoor pint, a meal, and a look at the sky-high views, it's all quickly reachable, some of it in less than an hour.

Finding a Place to Stay

During the summer high season, Stein-am-Rhein and Gottlieben are chock-full because there's no town around to catch the overflow—book early. St. Gallen has a large convention center; you should make your reservation in advance here, too. Prices also tend to escalate during conventions. Other destinations will usually still have a room or two on short notice. For romantic getaways, consider the castellated Drachenburg and Waaghaus in Gottlieben, a teeny-tiny village on the misty bank of the Rhine, or the secluded Park-Hotel Sonnenhof with a magnificent view in Liechtenstein. More and more hotels in this region are throwing away their Formica and commissioning hand-painted furniture to complement the beams they've so carefully exposed. The prices are somewhat lower on average here, with only slight variations from high to low season. Half board is rarely included.

WHAT IT COSTS IN SWISS FRANCS				
¢	$	$$	$$$	$$$$
RESTAURANTS				
under 15 SF	15 SF– 25 SF	25 SF– 40 SF	40 SF– 60 SF	over 60 SF
HOTELS				
under 100 SF	100 SF– 175 SF	175 SF– 250 SF	250 SF– 350 SF	over 350 SF

Restaurant prices are per person for a main course at dinner. Hotel prices are for two people in a standard double room in high season, including tax and service.

Go "Flea"-ing

Some of the least developed land is in Eastern Switzerland, which means plenty of old houses stuffed with plenty of old furnishings, art pieces, and gewgaws. This being Switzerland, commerce has responded: outdoor/indoor flea markets abound, as do secondhand thrift shops, called Bröckenhäuser (Brockenhaus in the singular)—every town has at least one. Antiques dealers regularly troll the area, but it's still possible to find a bargain here and there, especially in out-of-the-way villages. Let the hunt begin!

Fist Food

St. Gallen is almost as famous for its *Olma Bratwurst* as for the textiles it used to manufacture for shipment throughout the world. But while textiles are in decline, there's no chance the cream-color, grilled-to-perfection sausage will be disappearing from the region anytime soon. Locals get theirs from **Gemperli** (Schmidg. 34), who makes them from a recipe that dates back to 1438. You'll be offered mustard or even ketchup, but aficionados eat theirs plain. If sweets are your thing, try a *St. Galler Biber*—a gingerbread patty with almond paste filling—from **Konfiserie Scherrer** (Marktg. 28). One Biber can replace a whole meal; they are so rich you may find yourself living on lettuce and water for the next day.

GETTING AROUND

By Air

Unique Zürich Airport, just north of Zürich, is about 48 km (30 mi) south of Schaffhausen, about 75 km (46 mi) west of St. Gallen, and 130 km (81 mi) northwest of Liechtenstein.

Unique Zürich Airport (☎ *0900/300313*).

By Bus

The famous line of yellow Swiss Post postbuses are integrated into the national train and boat network, and provide much of the public transport in areas not served by trains, particularly to smaller towns.

Postbuses are also the prime means of transport for Liechtenstein, which has no rail service.

Bus schedules are usually posted outside town post offices, but you can also obtain information from any train station.

The smallest towns have one bus in the morning and one in the evening.

In larger towns, buses run several times a day. (☎ *0900/300300* ⊕ *www.sbb.ch*).

By Boat & Ferry

Swiss Federal Railways provides regular year-round service on the Bodensee through Schweizer Bodensee Schiffahrtsgesellschaft (Swiss Bodensee Cruiseline Co., ⊕ *www. sbsag.ch*), though fewer boats run in winter. The Schweizerisches Schiffahrtgesellschaft Untersee und Rhein ship company (⊕ *www.urh.ch*) offers a winning combination of a boat ride on the Rhine with romantic views of storybook castles, citadels, and monasteries. Boats run regularly up- and downstream, docking at Schaffhausen, Stein-am-Rhein, Gottlieben, Konstanz, and Kreuzlingen. Prices vary according to the distance traveled; a day pass costs 30 SF. A one-way trip from Schaffhausen to Kreuzlingen takes about 4½ hours. On both boat lines, you'll travel free if you have a Swiss Pass.

Schweizer Bodensee Schiffahrtsgesellschaft (☎ *071/ 4667888*). **Schweizerisches Schiffahrtgesellschaft Untersee und Rhein** (✉ *Freierpl. 8, Schaffhausen* ☎ *052/6340888*).

By Train

A connection by train from the Zürich Hauptbahnhof into the SBB Bahnhof Schaffhausen takes about 40 minutes; into SBB Bahnhof St. Gallen or Sargans, about an hour. Connections from the south (Graubünden) are more difficult, as both Austria and the Alps intervene.

Rail connections (☎ *0900 300 300* ⊕ *www.rail.ch*) are somewhat complicated in this area, especially if you want to visit more of Appenzell than its major towns. Schaffhausen and St. Gallen are the main hubs from which regional trains head into the countryside. The only railroads into the canton are the narrow-gauge line between St. Gallen and the town of Appenzell, and the Gossau Appenzell–Wasserauen line. To see more of the territory, you may return to St. Gallen on this same line by way of Herisau.

Although there is no regional rail pass available for eastern Switzerland, the general Swiss Pass rail pass (available from Switzerland Tourism and from travel agents outside Switzerland) includes St. Gallen and Schaffhausen city transit, as well as overall rail privileges.

By Car

The A1 expressway from Zürich heads for St. Gallen through Winterthur. To reach Schaffhausen from Zürich, take A1 to Winterthur, then head north on the cantonal highway E41/15. You also can leave Zürich by way of the A4 expressway past Unique Zürich Airport, crossing through Germany briefly and entering Schaffhausen through Neuhausen am Rheinfall.

From the south, the A13 expressway, shared with Austria, leads you from Chur along Liechtenstein to the east end of the Bodensee; from there, you take A1 into St. Gallen.

Liechtenstein is best reached by car; from Zürich, take the A1 expressway to Sargans, then change to the A13 heading north and take the Vaduz exit. From St. Gallen, follow the A1 northeast to the Bodensee, where it changes into the A13. Follow this south approximately 50 km (31 mi) to the Vaduz exit.

Driving in eastern Switzerland allows you to see the best of this region; Highway 13 goes along the south shores of the Untersee and Bodensee and continues up through the hills to Appenzell.

Neither St. Gallen nor Schaffhausen is a big enough city to warrant all-out panic, although you'll find it easiest to head directly for the center and abandon the car for the duration of your visit.

Try to get into a parking lot, as finding a spot on the street can be difficult. In Schaffhausen, there's underground |parking at the Stadttheater underneath Herrenacker. In St. Gallen, the Old Town is surrounded by underground parking lots. You'll find entrances on Burggraben, Oberergraben, and, most conveniently, on St. Georgenstrasse, right by the abbey.

Visitor Information

The tourist office for all of eastern Switzerland is based in St. Gallen.

There are small regional visitor information offices throughout eastern Switzerland.

Liechtenstein's office is in its capital.

Tourismusverband Ostschweiz (*Tourist Association of Eastern Switzerland* ⊠ *Bahnhofpl. 1a, St. Gallen* ☎ *071/2273737* ⊕ *www.ostschweiz-i.ch*).

Liechtenstein (⊠ *Städtle 37, Vaduz* ☎ *423/2396300* ⊕ *www. tourismus.li*).

By Foot Through Schaffhausen

The **Schaffhausen tourist office** (⊠ *Herrenacker 15,* ☎ *052/6324020* ⊕ *www.schaffhausen-tourismus.ch*) gives daily guided walking tours with English commentary of the Old Town, the monastery, and the Munot.

For a unique take on the city, try one of the nighttime guided walks, which focus on murders, pestilence, public hangings, and other dark events, available in English on request.

Updated by
Katrin Gygax

DESPITE ITS PROXIMITY TO ZÜRICH, this Germanic region, with Germany to the north and Austria to the east, maintains a personality apart—a personality that often plays the wallflower when upstaged by more spectacular touristy regions. Happily, the truth is that the region does not lack for a satisfying variety: its north dominated by the romantic Rhine, the region is lush with orchards and gardens, a generous share of mountains (including Mt. Säntis, at roughly 8,200 feet), and lovely hidden lakes, as well as the enormous Bodensee (Lake Constance). Because the east draws fewer crowds, those who do venture in find a pleasant surprise: this is Switzerland sans kitsch, sans the hard sell, where the people live out a natural, graceful combination of past and present. And although it's a prosperous region, with its famous textiles and fruit industry, its inns and restaurants cost noticeably less than those in adjoining areas.

The region covers a broad sociological spectrum, from the thriving city of St. Gallen, with its magnificent Baroque cathedral, to the plateau valley of Appenzell, where women were prohibited from voting in cantonal elections until the federal court intervened on their behalf in 1991 (federal law had granted women the national vote in 1971). On the last Sunday in April in Appenzell city you still can witness the *Landsgemeinde,* an open-air election on cantonal issues counted by a show of hands.

Architecture along the Rhine resembles that of Old Germany and Austria, frequent features being half-timbers and rippling red-tile roofs. In cities like Schaffhausen, masterpieces of medieval frescoes decorate town houses, many of which have ornate first-floor bay windows called oriels. In the country, farmhouses are often covered with fine, feathery wooden shingles as narrow as Popsicle sticks, which weathering has turned to chinchilla gray. Appenzell has its own famous architecture: tidy, narrow boxes painted cream, with repeated rows of windows and matching wood panels. The very countryside itself—conical green hills, fruit trees, belled cows, neat yellow cottages—resembles the naive art it inspires.

EXPLORING EASTERN SWITZERLAND

The cantons of Glarus, Schaffhausen, Thurgau, St. Gallen, and Appenzell harbor some of Switzerland's oldest traditions. Although the cities have plenty of energy, the countryside in these parts changes little over the years. In the northern part of the region are the old Rhine city of Schaffhausen, the dramatic Rheinfall, and the preserved medieval town of Stein-am-Rhein. The Bodensee occupies the northeastern corner of Switzerland, just below Germany. Farther south are the textile center of St. Gallen, the hilly Appenzell region, and the resort area of the Toggenburg Valley. The tiny principality of Liechtenstein lies just across the eastern border, within easy driving distance.

SCHAFFHAUSEN & THE RHINE

Known to many Swiss as Rheinfallstadt (Rhine Falls City), Schaff-hausen is the seat of the country's northernmost canton, which also shares its name. To gaze upon the grand mist-sprayed Rheinfall, argu-ably the most famous waterfall in Europe, is to look straight into the romantic past of Switzerland. Goethe and Wordsworth were just two of the world's best-known wordsmiths to immortalize the falls' power-ful grandeur.

SCHAFFHAUSEN

★ *48 km (29 mi) northeast of Zürich, 20 km (12 mi) west of Stein-am-Rhein.*

GETTING HERE

From/to Zurich, the fastest connection is the once-hourly S16 commuter train, which takes 58 minutes and costs 18.20 SF each way. There are two trains every hour to and from St. Gallen that connect through Win-terthur (travel time 86 mins, 28 SF each way). The S3 commuter does a scenic milk run up the Rhine to the Bodensee and St. Gallen every hour, stopping at almost every town along the way. Another favorite method of travel is by boat up the Rhine to the Bodensee. There are three to four (on Sunday) boats daily: the first leaves Schaffhausen at 9:10 AM, the last returns from Kreuzlingen at 2 PM or at 4 PM, going only as far as Stein-am-Rhein (30 SF for an all-day pass; the boats also offer lunch; Schweizerische Schifffahrtsgesellschaft Untersee und Rhein, 052/6340888, www.urh.ch). The Schweizerische Bodensee-Schifffahrts-gesellschaft (071/4667888, www.sbsag.ch) line also caters to guests traveling the Bodensee (Lake Constance). For departure times and prices for trains and buses for most destinations in this chapter, check with www.sbb.ch—the main Swiss public transportation Web site—or call 0900/300300 (1.19 SF per minute). Remember, if you have a Swiss Pass or another rail-discount card, it also applies to the buses.

Visitor Information (⊠ *Herrenacker 15* ☎ *052/6324020* ⊕ *www.schaffhausen-tourismus.ch*).

EXPLORING

A city of about 74,000, Schaffhausen was from the early Middle Ages on an important depot for river cargoes, which—because of the rap-ids and waterfall farther along—had to be unloaded there. The name *Schaffhausen* is probably derived from the skiff houses along the riv-erbank. The city has a small but beautiful Altstadt (Old Town), whose charm lies in its extraordinary preservation; examples of late Gothic, Baroque, and Rococo architecture line the streets. It doesn't feel like a museum, though; these buildings are very much in use, often as shops or restaurants, and lively crowds of shoppers and strollers throng the streets. Many streets (including Vorstadt, Fronwagplatz, Vordergasse, and Unterstadt) are pedestrian only.

Schaffhausen
and the Rhine

KEY
← Rail lines

SWITZERLAND

GERMANY

Bodensee

13

Roamanshorn

Amriswil

St. Gallen

Abwil

Gossau

Herisau

Kreuzlingen
& Konstanz

Arenenberg

Gottlieben

Weinfelden

THURGAU

Lipperswil

A1

Untersee

GERMANY

Wil

16

5 mi

5 km

A7

Frauenfeld

Aadorf

Stein-am-Rhein

A1

Schaffhausen

Neuhausen am
Rheinfall

Winterthur

Turbenthal

SCHAFFHAUSEN

Andelfingen

15

ZÜRICH

A1

Kloten

Bülach

GERMANY

A1

Zürich

SIGHTS TO SEE

3 Fronwagplatz. Lined with shops and cafés, this square is a favorite place for young people to stroll, especially in the evening. A large 16th-century fountain-statue of a prosperous burgher, the **Metzgerbrunnen,** watches over the marketplace. The **clock tower** once held the market scales; its astronomical clock (1564) records not only the time but also solar eclipses, seasons, and the course of the moon through the zodiac. Across the square, a reproduction of the 1535 **Mohrenbrunnen** (Moor's Fountain) represents Kaspar of the Three Kings. The original fountain is stored in the Museum zu Allerheiligen.

> **THE REDS ARE COMING!**
>
> Back in the 19th century, England's William Cox wrote, with characteristic British modesty, that the local cleanliness, behavior, and dress in Schaffhausen made him feel as if "I could think for a moment that I am in England." Others attribute the un-Swiss nature of the natives to the fact that they do not live surrounded by mountains, which are said to make most Alp dwellers introspective. Another reason may be the fine red wines produced by the region!

7 Gerberstube *(Tanners' Guildhall).* A pair of lions frames the doorway of the remarkable Baroque building. A two-handled tanner's knife used to stretch between the lions, but unfortunately the vibrations of nearby roadworks in the neighborhood caused it to collapse. A restaurant now occupies the building. ⊠*Bachstr. 8.*

4 Haus zum Ritter *(Knight's House).* The city's finest mansion dates from 1492. Its fresco facade was commissioned by the resident knight, Hans von Waldkirch. Tobias Stimmer covered all three stories with paintings on classical themes, which are now displayed in the Museum zu Allerheiligen; the reproduction of the original was made in the 1930s. ⊠*Vorderg. 65.*

NEED A BREAK? Snag an outdoor table at **Santa Lucia** (⊠*Schwertstr. 1* ☎*052/6252255*) for one of many spaghetti dishes offered, from the classic garlic and olive oil to smoked salmon with cream. Located smack-dab in the middle of the Old Town, it is perfect for people-watching.

8 Munot. Built between 1564 and 1585 in full circle form based on an idea by Albrecht Dürer, the massive stone ramparts served as a fortress allowing the defense of the city from all sides. From its top are splendid Schaffhausen and Rhine Valley views. ⊠*Munotstieg* 🎫*Free* ☉*May–Sept., daily 8–8; Oct.–Apr., daily 9–5.*

9 Münster zu Allerheiligen *(All Saints Cathedral).* This beautiful cathedral, along with its cloister and grounds, dominates the lower city. Founded in 1049, the original cathedral was dedicated in 1064, and the larger one that stands today was built in 1103. Its interior has been restored to Romanesque austerity with a modern aesthetic (hanging architect's lamps, Scandinavian-style pews). The **cloister,** begun in 1050, combines Romanesque and later Gothic elements. Memorial plates on the inside wall honor noblemen and civic leaders buried in the cloister's central garden. You'll also pass through the aromatic **herb garden;** it is re-created so effectively in the medieval style that you may feel you've stepped into a tapestry. ⊠*Klosterpl. 1* 🎫*Free* ⊙*Tues.–Fri. 8–5, weekends 8–8.*

THE DING-DONG TOLLS

Centerpiece of the main courtyard, the cathedral's enormous Schiller Bell was cast in 1486; it hung in the tower of the cathedral until 1895. Its inscription, VIVOS–VOCO/ MORTUOS–PLANGO/FULGURA–FRANGO ("I call the living, mourn the dead, stop the lightning"), allegedly inspired the German poet Friedrich von Schiller to write his "Lied von der Glocke" ("Song of the Bell").

🔟 **Museum zu Allerheiligen** *(All Saints Museum).* This museum on the cathedral grounds houses an extensive collection of ancient and medieval historical artifacts, as well as displays on Schaffhausen industry. The period rooms are definitely worth a look; they cover 15th- to 19th-century interiors. The best of these is the 15th-century refectory, which was rented out and all but forgotten until its rediscovery in 1924. Temporary exhibitions on various themes reach international caliber. Museum literature is available only in French or German. ⊠*Klosterpl. 1* 🕾*052/6330777* ⊕*www. allerheiligen.ch* 🎫*9 SF* ⊙*Tues.–Sun. 11–5.*

⑤ **Schmiedstube** *(Smiths' Guildhall).* With its spectacular Renaissance portico and oriel dating from 1653, this building is an embodiment of Schaffhausen's state of suspended animation. Framed over the door are the symbols of the tongs and hammer for the smiths, and that of a snake for doctors, who depended on the smiths for their tools and thus belonged to the guild. ⊠*Vorderg. 61.*

① **Schwabentorturm** *(Swabian Gate Tower).* Once a part of the city wall, the tower dates from 1370. Inside the arch on the keystone is a relief from 1933 that bears a wise caution for anyone crossing the street: LAPPI TUE D'AUGE UF ("Open your eyes, you idiot!"). The tower's counterpart, the **Obertorturm,** lies just off the Fronwagplatz.

② **Zum Goldenen Ochsen** *(At the Golden Ox).* This late-Gothic building had a Renaissance-style portico and oriel window added to it in 1609. Flanking the windows are three floors of exterior frescoes depicting historic and mythological figures, most from the Trojan War. ⊠*Vorstadt 17.*

⑥ **Zur Wasserquelle and Zur Zieglerburg** *(At the Spring and At the Brick Castle).* This Rococo duplex dates from 1738; since they are now private residences, you can see them only from the outside. Across the street are the **Tellenbrunnen,** a fountain-statue of Wilhelm Tell copied from the 1522 original, and, farther up Vordergasse, the **St. Johann-kirche** (St. John's Church), whose Gothic exterior dates from 1248. ⊠*Vorderg. 26/28.*

Schaffhausen

WHERE TO EAT

$$-$$$ ✕ **Beckenburg.** Well-heeled locals flock here to sample innovative twists
MEDITERRANEAN on Mediterranean staples, such as beef carpaccio with fresh ginger, Parmesan cheese, and olive oil. The tables are set far enough apart to give you lots of privacy, and the staff is attentive without being intrusive. Beechwood and metal tables and chairs complement the 300-year-old wood accents and the imposing Venetian chandelier that hangs over the room. The leafy outdoor graveled terrace is a nice place to decompress in summer. ⊠*Neustadt 1* ☎*052/6252820* ⊟*AE, DC, MC, V* ⊗*Closed Sun.*

$-$$ ✕ **Restaurant Falken.** This busy restaurant caters to crowds with a palate
SWISS for simple local fare—Rösti, breaded fish, and *Geschnetzeltes* (sliced veal in cream sauce). The *Tagesteller* (daily special) is an especially good deal at lunchtime. Though plain and cafeteria-like, it's an excellent choice for families; it even houses a small bowling alley. ⊠ *Vorstadt 5* ☎*052/6253221* ⊟*AE, DC, MC, V.*

$-$$ ✕ **Wirtschaft zum Frieden.** Dating back to 1789, this local favorite offers
CONTINENTAL three delightful settings: a small *Stübli* (Swiss pub) full of waxed and weathered wood, a graceful tile-stove dining room with antiques, and a private garden thick with wisteria and luxuriant trees. The Stübli serves up a wide variety of salads and soups, such as creamed curry soup with dates, while things get more elaborate in the upstairs dining room, with multicourse meals including lamb fillet, *Rösti,* and green beans tossed with bacon. ⊠*Herrenacker 11* ☎*052/6254767* ⊟*AE, DC, MC, V* ⊗*Closed Sun.–Mon.*

WHERE TO STAY

$$ ⌂ **Kronenhof.** This fine, quiet city hotel in the heart of Schaffhausen's Old Town has a traditional shutter- and flower-trimmed facade. Inside, however, all is modern, with tidy, well-constructed rooms cheered by birch furniture, cherry-stained paneling, and abstract prints. The newly refurbished "Antique Suite" is resplendent with stucco ceilings and hardwood floors. The American cafeteria look in the main restaurant seems at odds with the excellent, refined versions of local dishes, including fresh fish and homemade pasta. **Pros:** central location; cobblestone terrace café. **Cons:** the variation in style is a bit incoherent; service sometimes hurried. ⊠*Kirchhofpl. 7* ☎*052/6357575* ⊕*www.kronenhof.ch* ⟿*38 rooms, 2 suites* ⌂*In-room: no a/c, safe, refrigerator. In-hotel: restaurant, bar, public Internet, public Wi-Fi* ⊟*AE, DC, MC, V* ⊚|*BP.*

$-$$ ⌂ **Park-Villa.** Except for the no-nonsense elevator tacked onto the exterior, this Belle-Époque mansion has been transformed into a small hotel with little disruption to its grand but familial style. Many of the original furnishings—inlaid pieces, chandeliers, Persian rugs—remain. The upper floors are modern but retain their eccentric shapes; some have Rhine or fortress views. The fine old garden room is luxurious and a steal (the toilet is down the hall); all the other rooms have full baths. The hotel sits slightly uphill from the Old Town. **Pros:** you can pretend you live in an old mansion; tennis courts at this rate are rare. **Cons:** little refurbishment of late; somewhat musty. ⊠*Parkstr. 18* ☎*052/6356060*

⊕*www.parkvilla.ch* ⤳*21 rooms, 4 suites* ⟰*In-room: no a/c. In-hotel: restaurant, bar, tennis court, public Wi-Fi* ⊟*AE, DC, MC, V* ⎆|*BP.*

$$$–$$$$ ⊡**Rheinhotel Fischerzunft.** A Relais & Châteaux property, this option
★ has a modern sheen that's welcoming but, to some, may seem a bit out
of place in this medieval city on the Rhine. Of the 10 guest rooms—
some in fussy florals, others in sleek, jewel-tone solids—seven overlook
the river. Every guest, however, shares the lovely Rhine view at break-
fast. The restaurant's mixed nautical and Asian decor reflects the chef's
Franco-Chinese leanings: he trained in Hong Kong and has created a
brilliant, eclectic menu. **Pros:** an exquisite restaurant; rooms directly
on the river; excellent service. **Cons:** occasional mosquito attacks in
summer (remember that river); public salons that are so quiet you don't
dare speak. ✉*Rheinquai 8* ☎*052/6320505* ⊕*www.fischerzunft.ch*
⤳*6 rooms, 4 suites* ⟰*In-room: no a/c, safe, refrigerator, Ethernet.
In-hotel: restaurant* ⊟*AE, DC, MC, V* ⎆|*BP.*

SPORTS & THE OUTDOORS
Bicycles are a popular mode of transportation. They can be rented at
the **train station** (☎*051/2234217*) in Schaffhausen.

NEUHAUSEN AM RHEINFALL

Fodor'sChoice   *3 km (1¾ mi) south of Schaffhausen.*
★
GETTING HERE
The nicest way to get to the Rhine Falls is to walk (30 mins.) the Rhei-
nuferweg (Rhine Bank Trail) from Schaffhausen's Old Town: follow
the yellow hiking-trail signs. The S33 commuter train (0900/300300,
www.sbb.ch) leaves every half hour, takes five minutes and costs 3 SF
each way.

EXPLORING
Adjacent to Neuhausen, on the north bank of the Rhine, a series of
magnificent waterfalls powers the city's industry (arms, railroad cars,
aluminum).

The **Rheinfall** is 492 feet wide, drops some 82 feet in a series of three
dramatic leaps, and is split at the center by a bushy crag straight out of
a 19th-century landscape painting. The effect—mists, roaring water, jut-
ting rocks—is positively Wagnerian; Goethe saw in the falls the "ocean's
source," although today's jaded globetrotters have been known to find
them "cute." There's a footpath, the Rheinuferweg, that leads from
Schaffhausen's Old Town along the river to the falls (a 25- to 35-minute
walk). It is marked with the standard yellow hiking-trail signs.

From Neuhausen there's a good view toward **Schloss Laufen,** a 12th-
century castle that overlooks the Rheinfall.

STEIN-AM-RHEIN

FodorśChoice
★

20 km (13 mi) east of Schaffhausen.

GETTING HERE

The least complicated route from/to Schaffhausen is via the train (0900/300300, www.rail.ch) that departs every half hour (25 mins.); tickets cost 7.60 SF each way.

Visitor Information (⊠ *Oberstadt 3* ☎ *052/7422090* ⊕ *www.stein-am-rhein.ch*).

EXPLORING

Stein-am-Rhein, a nearly perfectly preserved medieval village and one of Switzerland's loveliest towns, lies at the point where the Rhine leaves the Bodensee. Crossing the bridge over the river, you see the village spread along the waterfront, its foundations and docks rising directly out of the water. Here restaurants, hotels, and shops occupy 16th- and 17th-century buildings, and the Rhine is calm and lazy—nothing like the sprawling industrial trade route it becomes farther downstream.

The **Rathausplatz** *(Town Hall Square)* and main street, Unterstadt, are flanked by tight rows of shingled, half-timber town houses, each rivaling the next for the ornateness of its oriels, the flamboyance of its frescoes. The elaborate decor usually illustrates the name of the house: Sonne (Sun), Ochsen (Ox), Weisser Adler (White Eagle), and so on. Most of the artwork dates from the 16th century. The **Rathaus** (Town Hall) itself was built between 1539 and 1542, with the half-timber upper floors added in 1745; look for its fantastical dragon waterspouts, typical of the region.

The Benedictine **Kloster St. Georgen** *(Monastery of St. George)*, a half-timber structure built in 1007, houses a cloister and a small museum devoted to examples of woodwork and local paintings. ⊠ *Edge of Old Town, just upstream from the last bridge over the Rhine before the Bodensee* ☎ *052/7412142* 🎫 *3 SF* ☉ *Museum: Apr.–Oct., Tues.–Sun. 10–5.*

Directly above the town, atop vineyards and woods, stands the 12th-century hilltop castle of **Hohenklingen,** which offers broad views of the Rhine Valley and the lake beyond, and houses an excellent restaurant. ☎ *052/7412137* 🎫 *Free* ☉ *Apr.–Oct., Tues.–Sun. 10–11; Nov.–Mar., Wed.–Sun. 10–11.*

WHERE TO EAT

$$-$$$
SWISS
★

✕ **Sonne.** Admire the 16th-century exterior frescoes before you go in—they're certainly worth a gape. Upstairs, you'll find a formal dining room (dark ceiling beams, damask fabrics, and Biedermeier furniture) where chef Philippe Combe's inventive, contemporary dishes based on seasonal ingredients—sliced prime rib of beef with garlic green beans and steamed new potatoes—command top prices. Downstairs in the bistro, he offers salads, regional sausages, and selections from the fine wine list, dished up in a spare, chic, gentrified pub: more beams, stone walls, stucco ceilings, and parquet floors. ⊠ *Rathauspl.* ☎ *052/7412128* ▭ *AE, DC, MC, V* ☉ *Closed Tues. and Wed.*

¢–$ ✕**Weinstube zum Roten Ochsen.** Yet another local establishment with a
SWISS   beautiful frescoed facade, this one glows with a deep-red wood-hued
interior that invites passersby into the warm little Weinstube. Inside,
dark antiques surround a *Kachelofen* (tile stove), and candles glow on
the tables. The menu mixes Swiss staples with Italian flavors—you'll
find veal saltimbocca alongside the traditional *Wurst-Käse-Salat*—
sliced *cervelat* sausages and cheese cubes with onions drizzled with
oil and vinegar dressing—it's tastier than it sounds. If you're tired of
meat, there's a good selection of crisp salads as well. ⊠*Rathauspl. 129*
☎*052/7412328* ▭*No credit cards.*

WHERE TO STAY

$$ 🏨**Adler.** With one of the most elaborately frescoed 15th-century facades
★   on the Rathausplatz, this hotel has a split personality: flamboyant on the
outside, no-nonsense inside. The decor is airy, slick, and immaculate,
with gray industrial carpet, white stucco, and blond wood through-
out. Double-glaze windows cut the noise from the square. A local
family runs the hotel, so family groups will fit right in. The cheerful
restaurant serves excellent regional cooking, along with some French
dishes. **Pros:** top-notch restaurant; excellent service. **Cons:** decor is in
serious need of attention, with noticeably absent frills. ⊠*Rathauspl.
15* ☎*052/7426161* ⊕*www.adlersteinamrhein.ch* ⇌*25 rooms* ⌂*In-
room: no a/c. In-hotel: restaurant, public Wi-Fi, no elevator* ▭*AE, DC,
MC, V* ☾*Closed Jan. and Feb.* ❏*BP.*

$$ 🏨**Rheinfels.** Even some of the bathrooms have ceiling beams in this
Fodor'sChoice   waterfront landmark, which was built between 1508 and 1517. The
★   public spaces have pine-plank floors and suits of armor on display, and
every room—modernized in beige and rose tones—has a Rhine view.
The hotel's suite has its own separate entrance, a one-car garage and a
boat jetty. The restaurant specializes in freshwater fish. The restaurant is
closed on Wednesday, except in July and August. **Pros:** the river is *right
there*; medieval atmosphere is a thrill; locals come from miles away for
the fish dishes. **Cons:** slightly musty room decor; proximity to a busy
thoroughfare. ⊠*Rhig. 8* ☎*052/7412144* ⊕*www.rheinfels.ch* ⇌*16
rooms, 1 suite* ⌂*In-room: no a/c, refrigerator. In-hotel: restaurant, no
elevator* ▭*MC, V* ☾*Closed Jan. and Feb.* ❏*BP.*

$ 🏨**Zur Rheingerbe.** Right on the busy waterfront promenade, this small
inn has wood-panel ceilings and big furniture reminiscent of Sears
(sculptured carpet, spindle beds). Some rooms overlook the Rhine, and
there's an apartment for long-term rentals on request. The excellent
first-floor restaurant (closed Wednesday) has a full-length bay window
along the riverfront. **Pros:** centrally located right on the town promenade; café for hours of people-watching; excellent rates, given location
and high-end restaurant. **Cons:** as is often the case in this region, rooms
are a bit sparse and lacking in style. ⊠*Schifflände 5* ☎*052/7412991*
⊕*www.rheingerbe.ch* ⇌*7 rooms* ⌂*In-hotel: restaurant, no elevator*
▭*AE, DC, MC, V.*

ARENENBERG

20 km (12 mi) east of Stein-am-Rhein, 40 km (25 mi) east of Schaffhausen.

East of Stein-am-Rhein the Rhine opens up into the Untersee, the lower branch of the Bodensee. In its center lies the German island of Reichenau. Charles the Fat, great-grandson of Charlemagne, was buried here. The villages on either side of the Untersee are dominated by castles.

Fodor'sChoice   On the Swiss side, behind the village
   ★   of Mannenbach (nearly opposite Reichenau), the **Arenenberg Napoleonmuseum** is housed in a magnificent castle given to the municipality

> MISSING LINKS
>
> Lovers of Napoleonic esoterica should want to visit two nearby châteaux with distant links to Bonaparte's glory. The Duchess of Dino, a companion of Hortense de Beauharnais (the de Beauharnais were the famous family the emperor married into) and mistress to the Duke of Talleyrand, went to live in Salenstein in 1817. Eugensberg Castle was built four years later by Eugène de Beauharnais, the son of Empress Joséphine. Ask for directions at the Arenenberg museum.

by Empress Eugénie of France in homage to her husband, Napoléon III, who grew up here with his mother, Hortense, sister-in-law of Napoléon I. Today the Schloss serves as a museum, and lovers of decorative arts will prize its ravishing period rooms dating from the Second Empire. Outside is a glorious park studded with ancestral statues. ⊠*Behind Mannenbach* ☎*071/6633260* ⊕*www.napoleonmuseum.tg.ch* ⊠*10 SF* ☉*Mid-Apr.–mid-Oct., Tues.–Sun. 10–5, Mon. 1–5; mid-Oct.–mid-Apr., Tues.–Sun. 10–5.*

GOTTLIEBEN

5 km (3 mi) east of Arenenberg, 45 km (28 mi) east of Schaffhausen.

The village of Gottlieben has a Dominican monastery-castle, where the Protestant reformers Jan Hus and Jerome of Prague were imprisoned in the 15th century by order of Emperor Sigismund and antipope John XXIII, who was himself confined in the same castle a few years later. Today, though the castle can be viewed only from the outside, Gottlieben offers a romantic half-timber waterfront promenade—and two fine old hotels—before you reach the urban complex of Kreuzlingen and Germany's Konstanz.

WHERE TO STAY

$$–$$$ ⚏ **Drachenburg und Waaghaus.** On the Rhine between the Bodensee and
Fodor'sChoice   the Zellersee, these two half-timbered apparitions of onion domes, shut-
   ★   ters, and gargoyles were first built in 1702 and retain their historic air despite modern expansion. The interiors live up to the exteriors' promise, though the Drachenburg is the most atmospheric. It has gleaming old staircases, four-poster beds, brocade, and crystal sconces scattered throughout. Rhine-view rooms are furnished like honeymoon suites. Its restaurants vary in ambience; the most sophisticated is the one in the original house. **Pros:** extremely quiet; tons of character; right on

the Rhine. **Cons:** in an isolated town; overtly theme-parkish. ✉*Am
Schlosspark* ☎*071/6667474* ⊕*www.drachenburg.ch* ↝*58 rooms, 2
suites* ⚿*In-room: no a/c, safe, refrigerator. In-hotel: 2 restaurants, bar,
public Wi-Fi, no elevator* ▤*AE, DC, MC, V* ⊘*Closed Dec. 24–Jan.
5* ◐*BP.*

BODENSEE TO ST. GALLEN

3

Along the shores of the Bodensee orchards stripe rolling hills that slowly
rise to meet the foothills of the Alps around St. Gallen. About 2,000
years ago this region lay on the northeastern border of the Roman
Empire, Arbon (Arbor Felix) being the first stop on the trade route for
goods coming into the empire from points east. Today the region is
mostly rural, with clusters of farmhouses dotting the grassy slopes. In
summer the lake teems with vacationers, but in other seasons it remains
a distinctly tranquil area.

BODENSEE

Known in English as Lake Constance, the Bodensee is about 65 km (40
mi) long and 15 km (9 mi) wide, making it second in size in Switzerland
only to Lac Léman (Lake Geneva). The strong German flavor of the
towns on its Swiss edge is seasoned with a resort-village mellowness;
palm trees fringe the waterfront. This isn't the Mediterranean, though;
as the lake is not protected by mountains, it is turbulent in stormy
weather and even on fine days is exposed to the wind. Nonetheless, it
draws European vacationers in summer for swimming, windsurfing, and
fishing. Many Swiss have built tidy homes along the lakefront.

SPORTS & THE OUTDOORS

HIKING As a summer resort destination, the area around the Bodensee is usually thronged with hikers. For timed hiking itineraries, topographical
maps, and suggestions on the areas best suited to your style of wandering, consult the Tourismusverband Ostschweiz (Tourist Association of
Eastern Switzerland; www.ostschweiz-i.ch).

SWIMMING People do swim in the Bodensee; there are several public beaches, usually more grass than sand. Most have changing rooms and concession
stands. **Arbon** (☎*071/4461333*) has a gravel beach—getting into the
water can be a little rough on tender feet. **Kreuzlingen** (☎*071/6881858*)
has some sand at the water's edge, though you'll be spreading your
towel on the grass. **Romanshorn** (☎*071/4631147*) is also mostly grass.

KREUZLINGEN & KONSTANZ

7 km (4 mi) east of Gottlieben, 46 km (28 mi) east of Schaffhausen.

The German city of Konstanz, with its Swiss-side twin of Kreuzlingen,
dominates the straits that open into the Bodensee. Though Kreuzlingen
itself offers little of interest to travelers, Konstanz has a lovely, concentrated Altstadt (Old Town) area. It's easily accessible from the Swiss

side, though your passport may be checked even if you pass on foot. Konstanz belonged to Switzerland until 1805; today the two border towns share the dominant German influence.

EN ROUTE
About halfway between Kreuzlingen and Rorschach (follow Highway 13 east along the Bodensee) you'll come to the small town of **Romanshorn.** An industrial town and an important ferry port for Friedrichshafen in Germany, this is also a surprisingly enjoyable resort with fine views of the Swiss and Austrian mountains.

Between Romanshorn and Rorschach on Highway 13, **Arbon** (known to the Romans as Arbor Felix) lies on a little promontory jutting out into the Bodensee, surrounded by lovely meadows and orchards. It was a Celtic town before the Romans came in 60 BC and built military fortifications. Evidence of the Romans can be found in an interesting collection of relics in the late-Gothic St. Martinskirche.

ST. GALLEN

14 km (9 mi) southwest of Rorschach, 94 km (59 mi) southeast of Schaffhausen.

GETTING HERE
There are two trains (0900/300300, www.sbb.ch) each hour from/to Zürich, clocking in at just over an hour each; the fare is 34 SF each way. Trains also arrive from and leave for Appenzell every half-hour, costing 13.80 SF each way.

Visitor Information Tourismusverband Ostschweiz (*Tourist Association of Eastern Switzerland* ⊠ *Bahnhofpl. 1a, St. Gallen* ☎ *071/2273737* 🖷 *071/2273767* ⊕ *www.ostschweiz-i.ch*).

EXPLORING
Switzerland's largest eastern city, bustling St. Gallen is dominated by students during the school year. The narrow streets of the Altstadt (Old Town) are flanked by a wonderful variety of boutiques and antiques shops. The city has been known for centuries as both an intellectual center and the source of some of the world's finest textiles. St. Gallus, an Irish missionary, came to the region in 612 to live in a hermit's cell in the Steinach Valley. In 719 an abbey was founded on the site where he died. Soon a major cultural focus in medieval Europe, the abbey built a library of awesome proportions.

Fodor'sChoice ★ The abbey was largely destroyed in the Reformation and was closed down in 1805, but its magnificent Rococo **Stiftsbibliothek** (*Abbey Library*), built between 1758 and 1767, still holds a collection of more than 100,000 books and manuscripts. The library hall itself is one of Switzerland's treasures. You enter behind the cathedral and change into the provided large, gray carpet slippers to protect the magnificently inlaid wood flooring. The hall is a gorgeous explosion of gilt, frescoes, and undulating balconies, but the most striking aspect by far is the burnished woodwork, all luminous walnut and cherry. Its contents, including incunabula and illuminated manuscripts that are more than 1,200 years old, constitute one of the world's oldest and finest scholarly collections. Also on display, incongruously, is an Egyptian mummy dating from 700 BC. ⊠*Klosterhof 6c* ☎*071/2273416* ⊕*www.stiftsbibliothek.ch* ⊠*10 SF* ⊘*Mon.–Sat. 10–5, Sun. 10–4. Closed mid-Nov.–early Dec.*

★ The **Kathedrale** *(Cathedral)* is an impressive sight. Begun in 1755 and completed in 1766, it is the antithesis of the library, though the nave and rotunda are the work of the same architect, Peter Thumb. The scale is outsize and the decor light, bright, and open, despite spectacular excesses of wedding-cake trim. ⊠*Klosterhof* ☎*071/2273381* ⊘*Daily 9–6, except during services.*

A-STITCHING WE WILL GO

St. Gallen's history as a textile capital dates from the Middle Ages, when convent workers wove linen toile of such exceptional quality that it was exported throughout Europe. The industry expanded into cotton and embroidery, before collapsing in 1918. Today St. Gallen dominates the small luxury market for fine handmade textiles, and magnificently historic finery is on view at the Textilmuseum (Textile Museum; Vadianstrasse. 2, 071/2221744, www.textilmuseum.ch, 12 SF, open daily 10–5).

NEED A BREAK? **Café Seeger** (⊠*Oberer Graben 2* ☎*071/2229790*) is a relaxing Viennese-style café and restaurant catering to stylish young patrons. The sidewalk seating area is a great place to watch St. Gallen go by.

The grounds of the abbey and the cathedral border the **Altstadt** (Old Town), which demonstrates a healthy symbiosis between scrupulously preserved Renaissance and Baroque architecture and a thriving modern shopping scene. The best examples of oriel windows, half-timbering, and frescoes can be seen along Gallusstrasse, Schmiedgasse, Marktgasse, and Spisergasse, all pedestrian streets.

For a good picnic spot, head to the **Mühleggbahn,** a self-service funicular that runs up the hillside to a lovely view of St. Gallen and the Bodensee. Once up top, take two immediate right turns to the wooden stairs leading to a paved path with park benches. ⊠*Off the abbey end of the Old Town* ☎*071/2439595* ⊠*2 SF* ⊘*Daily 5:40 AM–12:50 AM.*

WHERE TO EAT

$$$
SWISS
✕ **Am Gallusplatz.** Rubbing shoulders with the town cathedral, this award-winning St. Gallen landmark entices with a castlelated exterior, turreted and hued in pink. Inside, things get more stolid, with most of the action taking place in the main Rôtisserie room—a large chamber replete with cross-vaulted ceilings and heavy chandeliers. The menu is based on market-fresh ingredients and may include such favorites as *coq au vin* (chicken simmered in red wine) with fresh vegetables and potatoes but can also get nouvelle, as witness the veal Provençal. There's also an enormous wine list. ⊠*Gallusstr. 24* ☎*071/2233330* ⊕*www. gallusplatz.ch/* ☰*AE, MC, V* ⊘*Closed Mon.*

$$ ✕**Concerto.** The glassed-in terrace of the Tonhalle concert hall provides
MODERN SWISS a year-round garden setting and a beautiful view of its large park. The
all-day kitchen serves up inventive twists on local standards—trout with
spinach risotto and saffron sauce, for example—and has dishes for all
appetites and pocketbooks. The helpful waitstaff will also let you sit
with your coffee and book for a while during off-peak hours, making
it a good place to relax in between running from one place of inter-
est to another. The outside terrace is a quiet luxury in warm weather.
✉*Museumstr. 25* ☎*071/2420777* ▭*AE, MC, V.*

$$ ✕**David 38.** Is one of you in the mood for European and the other
ECLECTIC for Asian? On a quiet street outside the bustle of the Old Town (and
a favorite of local businesspeople), this hip, sleek eatery serves both
Asian-flavored dishes—beef teriyaki with bok choy—and the traditionally Mediterranean—the spaghetti in lemon sauce with jumbo shrimp is
a winner. The atmosphere is relaxed, and tables are spaced far enough
away from one another that it lends itself well to a bit of romance over
dinner. ✉*Davidstr. 38* ☎*071/2302838* ⊕*www.david38.ch* ▭*AE,
MC, V* ⊗*Closed Sun.*

$$$ ✕**Engelis.** *Engelis* are angels, and they make up the accents through-
MODERN SWISS out this small but well-appointed bistro with a soft white interior that
makes you think of Christmas, with stiff linens on the tables, candle-
sticks, and gold trim here and there. The kitchen staff adds a Mediter-
ranean flavor to traditional dishes, such as marinated octopus on a bed
of lentils or rack of lamb with white polenta and seasonal vegetables.
The Old Town location adds that little bit of Old Europe charm, as
does the outside seating in the cobblestone pedestrian street in warm
weather. The upstairs is no-smoking. ✉*Brühlg. 30* ☎*071/2233332*
⊕*www.engelis-restaurant.ch* ▭*AE, MC, V.*

$$ ✕**Netts Schützengarten.** In the corner of the local brewery, this award-
ECLECTIC winning restaurant polishes a 19th-century industrial look, with copper
pipes, exposed brick, and hardwood floors. Owner Köbi Nett's travels
have resulted in a far-reaching menu: sliced roast beef on dried tomatoes and arugula with roasted potatoes; Indonesian shrimp, chicken
and beef curry; Olma Bratwurst with onion sauce. The beer is tapped
directly from the vats next door. A spacious terrace doubles the size
of the restaurant in warm weather. ✉*St. Jakobstr. 35* ☎*071/2426677*
▭*AE, MC, V* ⊗*Closed Sun.*

$–$$$ ✕**Schlössli.** Tidy, bright, and modern despite its setting in a historic
SWISS building, this first-floor (second-floor to Americans) landmark has a less
★ woody atmosphere than peers like the Zum Goldenen Schäfli, but better
cooking from the award-winning chef. Look for inventive dishes such as
wafer-thin homemade ravioli with blue potato filling and white truffle
sauce, or local lamb shanks with chanterelle mushrooms, seasonal veg-
etables, and bread dumplings. The café draws casual family groups and
locals at lunch; businesspeople choose the slightly more formal dining
room that adjoins it. ✉*Am Spisertor, Zeughausg. 17* ☎*071/2221256*
▭*AE, DC, MC, V* ⊗*Closed weekends.*

$$ ✕**Zum Goldenen Schäfli.** Of the first-floor (second-floor to Americans)
SWISS restaurants that are St. Gallen's trademark, this is the most popular,
and its slanting floors groan under crowds of locals and tourists. The

low ceiling and walls are all aged wood, and it's easy to imagine coach-and-four passengers lifting a pewter stein in centuries gone by. The menu offers regional standards lightened up for modern tastes. Fillet of pork on a bed of noodles accompanied by crushed tomatoes and mushrooms in herb butter, for example, is a favorite. ⊠*Metzgerg. 5* ☎*071/2233737* 🖃*AE, DC, MC, V* ⊘*Closed Sun. No lunch Sat.*

WHERE TO STAY

$$$–$$$$ 🏨 **Einstein.** Tucked back into a slope at the edge of the Old Town, this
★ former embroidery factory is now an upscale business-class hotel, with sleek Hiltonesque interiors (polished cabinetry, subdued floral fabrics), a uniformed staff, and a five-star attitude. The generous breakfast buffet, laid out in the skylighted top-floor loft, is not included in the room price. The bar is dark, leathery, and American-business, appropriate to the clientele. An annex housing a business center, a gym, and two pools is due to be completed in 2009. **Pros:** St. Gallen's grand hotel; wonderful view from the top-floor restaurant and front rooms; great service. **Cons:** focus on business clients makes for a hectic pace. ⊠*Berneggstr. 2* ☎*071/2275555* ⊕*www.einstein.ch* 📶*62 rooms, 3 suites* ⚐*In-room: no a/c, refrigerator, Ethernet, Wi-Fi. In-hotel: restaurant, bar* 🖃*AE, DC, MC, V.*

$–$$ 🏨 **Vadian.** A narrow town house tucked behind half-timber landmarks in the Old Town, this is a discreet and tidy little place with an alcohol-free policy. Some of its tiny guest rooms have stucco walls, knotty-pine furniture, and grey carpeting; others are redone in clean lines and hardwood floors; all have modern tile baths and fluffy Swedish comforters. Rooms without bath are a better bargain. **Pros:** quality personal service, very central and yet still quiet. **Cons:** no-alcohol policy means partying in your room is frowned upon; no service after 10 PM. ⊠*Gallusstr. 36* ☎*071/2281878* ⊕*www.hotel-vadian.com* 📶*13 rooms, 6 with bath* ⚐*In-room: no a/c, no elevator* 🖃*AE, DC, MC, V* ⦿*BP.*

$$ 🏨 **Weissenstein.** With as quiet a location as you can get in the heart of the city, this hotel is all about relaxation. Comfy Swedish feather duvets cover large double beds; a rarity in a region where "double" usually means two singles pushed together. Bathrooms are small but up-to-date. In summer you can take your breakfast on the shady terrace. **Pros:** 21st-century styling, which is rare in this region; very quiet. **Cons:** about a 10-minute walk from the Old Town; dark and small breakfast room. ⊠*Davidstr. 22* ☎*071/2280628* ⊕*www.cityweissenstein.ch* 📶*20 rooms* ⚐*In-room: safe, refrigerator. In-hotel: restaurant, public Wi-Fi, no elevator* 🖃*AE, DC, MC, V* ⦿*BP.*

SPORTS & THE OUTDOORS

☺ **Säntispark.** Just outside St. Gallen lies this year-round, family-friendly sports and spa park. There is something to please (and exhaust) everyone—racquet sports, bowling, miniature golf, or billiards. Children can dive into the wave pool at the water park and enjoy the rides and playgrounds. For relaxing, the solarium, sauna, and massage center are available at an additional charge. Sports equipment can be rented. ⊠*From main train station in St. Gallen, 15 min by Bus 7 (Abtwil), or by car along Hwy. A1, exit Winkeln* ☎*071/3131515* ⊕*www.saentispark.ch*

⌨*18 SF for 1.5 hrs, each additional hr 1.50 SF* ☉ *Weekdays 9* AM*–10* PM, *weekends 8* AM*–10* PM.

SHOPPING

ANTIQUE PRINTS   An outstanding assortment of antique prints of Swiss landscapes and costumes is sold at a broad range of prices at **Stich-Galerie Osvald** (✉*Marktg. 26* ☎*071/2235016*). The pictures are cataloged alphabetically by canton for easy browsing.

TEXTILES & EMBROIDERY   Although the region's textile industry has now shrunk down to a few local specialists, it's still world-renowned for its quality. You'll find some fine examples at **Rocco Textil** (✉*Spiserg. 41* ☎*071/2222407*), which has a small but wonderful selection of embroidery, linens, and lace. The shop is an especially good source for custom work. **Akris** (✉*Felsenstr. 40* ☎*071/2277722*), the local couture house gaining international acclaim, sells its own line of luxury clothing, designed locally and manufactured in Switzerland.

APPENZELL

20 km (12 mi) south of St. Gallen, 98 km (60 mi) southeast of Schaffhausen.

GETTING HERE

Every half hour there is a direct train (0900/300300, www.sbb.ch) from/to St. Gallen that takes 48 minutes. If you want a change of scenery, an alternate route goes via Herisau. 10.40 SF each way for both routes.

Visitor Information Appenzellerland (✉*Hauptg. 4* ☎*071/7889641* ⊕*www.appenzell.ch*).

EXPLORING

Isolated from St. Gallen by a ridge of green hills, Appenzell is one of Switzerland's quieter regions. Fellow Swiss think of its people as hillbillies, citing their quirky sense of humor and old-fashioned costumes. The city of St. Gallen melts away into undulating hills spotted with doe-eyed cows, a steep-pastured, isolated verdure reminiscent of the Ozarks. Prim, symmetrical cottages inevitably show rows of windows facing the valley. Named Appenzell after the Latin *abbatis cella* (abbey cell), the region served as a sort of colony to the St. Gallen abbey, and its tradition of fine embroidery dates from those early days. The perfect chance to see this embroidery is during a local festival, such as the Alpfahrten, when cows are herded up or down the mountains. Women's hair is coiffed in tulle, and their dresses have intricate embroidery and lace, often with an edelweiss motif; men wear embroidered red vests and suspenders decorated with edelweiss or cow figures. These traditional costumes are taken very seriously; they can cost thousands of francs, but in this case, pride supersedes economy. A small highway (No. 3) leads into the hills through Teufen; the quaint Appenzell–Teufen–Gais rail line also serves the region.

The town of Appenzell blends some of the best and worst of the region, offering tourists a concentrated and somewhat self-conscious sampling of the culture. Its streets lined with bright-painted homes, bakeries full of *Birnebrot* (pear bread) and souvenir *Biber* (almond and honey cakes), and shops full of machine-made embroidery, Appenzell seems to watch the tourists warily and get on with its life while profiting from the attention. Its **Landsgemeindeplatz** in the town center is the site of the famous open-air elections (until 1991, for men only), which take place the last Sunday in April. Embroidery is big business here, but it's rare to find handmade examples of the local art; though women still do fine work at home, it's generally reserved for gifts or heirlooms. Instead, large factories have sprung up in Appenzell country, and famous fine-cotton handkerchiefs sold in specialty shops around the world are made by machine here at the Dörig, Alba, and Lehner plants.

> **WHAT'S IN A NAME?**
>
> True, the demanding embroidery technique for which the name Appenzell became famous can no longer be found in the town of its birth. Though this makes for a somewhat faux souvenir, the imports do a fine job of capturing the intricacies of Appenzell embroidery. In a sign-of-the-times switcheroo, **Margreiter** (Hauptg. 29, 071/7873313) carries a large stock of handkerchiefs turned out in the local factories. Very popular are ones embroidered with motifs of edelweiss. **Trachtenstobe** (Hauptg. 23, 071/7871606) offers high-quality lace, embroidery, and crafts.

The **Museum Appenzell** showcases handicrafts and local traditions, regional history, and an international embroidery collection—it's a good general overview of the area's history and culture. The building itself dates from 1560. An English-language guide is available. ⊠*Hauptg. 4* ☏*071/7889631* ⊕*www.museum.ai.ch* ☞*7 SF* ⊗*Apr.–Oct., daily 10–noon and 2–5; Nov.–Mar., Tues.–Sun. 2–5.*

WHERE TO EAT

$$ ✕**Hof.** One of Appenzell's most popular restaurants serves hearty
SWISS regional meats and cheese specialties, such as *Käseschnitte* (cheese toast)
★ and *Käsespätzli* (Spätzli with cheese), to locals and tourists who crowd elbow to elbow along shared tables and talk over the clatter from the bar. The rustic-wood decor, ladderback chairs, and the display of sports trophies add to the atmosphere. If you can still move after all that cheese, play skittles at the in-house lanes after dinner. ⊠*Engelg. 4,* ☏*071/7874030* ⊟*AE, DC, MC, V.*

$–$$ ✕**Traube.** The traditional interior here–wooden chairs with heart-shaped
SWISS backs, leaded-glass windows, hardwood floors–may get a little too cozy and smoky in cold weather, but in summer the place to sit is on the outside terrace or in the quiet garden hidden from the busy main street. The menu leans to meat and potatoes, with a few salads; fondue and Appenzeller *Chäshörnli* (cheese and macaroni) round out the mostly heavy offerings. The daily lunch special is usually around 20 SF. ⊠*Marktg. 7* ☏*071/7871407* ⊟*MC, V* ⊗*Closed Mon.*

WHERE TO STAY

$$ **★** ⊞ **Appenzell.** Although only built in 1983, this comfortable lodging has all the gabled Gemütlichkeit of its neighbors, with a view over the Landsgemeindeplatz and beyond to the mountains. Homey rooms, with polished wood, owe their airiness to the traditional rows of windows. The fine woodwork and antiques in the breakfast room are remnants of the previous house. The restaurant downstairs has the look of an upscale American pancake house, but the cooking is right on the regional target. **Pros:** central location; bakery on the ground floor with fresh breakfast items to choose from; helpful service. **Cons:** restaurant is filled to capacity in summer, which gets a bit loud. ⊠ *Landsgemeindepl.* ☎ *071/7881515* ⊕ *www.hotel-appenzell.ch* ↩ *16 rooms* ♿ *In-room: no a/c, Ethernet. In-hotel: restaurant, public Internet* ⊟ *AE, DC, MC, V* ⏍ *BP.*

$ ⊞ **Freudenberg.** This is a cookie-cutter modern chalet, but its setting on a velvety green hillside overlooking town is the most scenic and tranquil you'll find in the area. Built in 1969, it has guest rooms that are bright and airy, with Appenzeller murals and modern, white-tile bathrooms. Four rooms have balconies, and the broad, shaded café—festive in the evening with strings of yellow lights—shares the picture-pretty views. Ten minutes from the city center on foot, it is also easily accessible by car. **Pros:** child-friendly surroundings, including private playground; excellent value; good base camp for hikers. **Cons:** 10 minutes on foot on the way back are uphill; some bathrooms are small. ⊠ *Riedstr. 57* ☎ *071/7871240* ⊕ *www.hotel-freudenberg.ch* ↩ *7 rooms* ♿ *In-room: no a/c. In-hotel: restaurant, no elevator* ⊟ *AE* ⏍ *BP.*

$$$ ⊞ **Romantik Hotel Säntis.** This prestigious hotel has a crisp and formal ambience, though the earliest wing has been a hotel-restaurant since 1835. Old-style touches—inlaid wood, painted beams—mix comfortably with the jewel-tone rooms and gleaming walnut cabinetry; some rooms have four-poster or canopy beds. The restaurant serves regional specialties in either of two wood-lined dining rooms, one Biedermeier, the other a folksy Appenzeller style. Guests can borrow bikes for free. **Pros:** large and comfortable with all the amenities; a good choice for both loungers and the activity-happy. **Cons:** front view is onto the Landsgemeinde, which is a parking lot (albeit a small one). ⊠ *Landsgemeindepl.* ☎ *071/7881111* ⊕ *www.saentis-appenzell.ch* ↩ *31 rooms, 6 suites* ♿ *In-room: no a/c, safe, refrigerator. In-hotel: restaurant, bar, public Wi-Fi, no elevator* ⊟ *AE, DC, MC, V* ☉ *Closed early Jan.–early Feb.*

SHOPPING

CHEESES Picnickers can sample the different grades of Appenzeller cheese and its unsung mountain rivals at **Mösler** (⊠ *Hauptg. 13* ☎ *071/7871317*). **Sutter** (⊠ *Marktstr. 8* ☎ *071/7871333*) has a good selection of locally made cheeses.

LIQUEURS Butchers, bakers, and liquor shops up and down the streets offer souvenir bottles of Appenzeller Bitter (Alpenbitter), a very sweet aperitif made in town. A well-balanced eau-de-vie called Appenzeller Kräuter, made of blended herbs, is another specialty.

LIECHTENSTEIN & THE WALENSEE

When you cross the border from Switzerland into the principality of Liechtenstein, you will see license plates marked FL: this stands for Fürstentum Liechtenstein (Principality of Liechtenstein). You are leaving the world's oldest democracy and entering a monarchy that is the last remnant of the Holy Roman Empire—all 160 square km (59 square mi) of it. If you don't put the brakes on, you'll wind up quickly in Austria.

> ## THE PHILATOPHILE SMILE
>
> Liechtenstein is sometimes called the unofficial, per-capita world champion of stamp collecting. To buy some of its famous stamps, whether to send a postcard to a philatelist friend or to invest in limited-issue commemorative sheets, you must line up with the tour-bus crowds at the popular post office on the Städtle.

This postage-stamp principality was created at the end of the 17th century, when a wealthy Austrian prince, Johann Adam von Liechtenstein, bought out two bankrupt counts in the Rhine Valley and united their lands. In 1719 he obtained an imperial deed from Emperor Karl VI, creating the principality of Liechtenstein. The noble family poured generations of wealth into the new country, improving its standard of living, and in 1862 an heir, Prince Johann the Good, helped Liechtenstein introduce its first constitution as a "democratic monarchy" in which the people and the prince share power equally. Today the principality's 32,000 citizens enjoy one of the world's highest per-capita incomes—prosperous (though discreet) local industries range from making jam to molding false teeth—and pay virtually no taxes. Back in Switzerland, the Walensee and Flumserberg region is sparsely populated, with a long lake flanked on both sides by steep mountains with beginner to intermediate ski areas. In summer the action moves downhill, where swimmers enjoy the cool water at several beaches along the lake.

VADUZ (LIECHTENSTEIN)

31 km (18 mi) southeast of Appenzell, 159 km (98 mi) southeast of Schaffhausen.

GETTING HERE

There are no direct trains to Vaduz, Liechtenstein's capital city; you have to stop on the Swiss side of the Rhine and take a bus across the river. From/to St. Gallen via Buchs, by train (0900/300300, www.sbb.ch) and bus, the trip takes 79 minutes and costs 23.60 SF each way. If you're traveling from/to Zürich, take the two-hour fast train to Sargans, where a connecting bus takes you to Vaduz. Travel time: 150 minutes; cost: 36 SF each way.

Visitor Information Liechtenstein (✉ *Städtle 37, Vaduz* ☎ *423/2396300* 📠 *423/2396301* ⊕ *www.tourismus.li*).

EXPLORING

Arriving in downtown Vaduz (there are exits from the A13 expressway from both the north and the south), a visitor could make the mistake of thinking that Liechtenstein's only attraction is its miniature scale.

Liechtenstein's small **Postmuseum** demonstrates the principality's history as a maker of beautifully designed, limited-edition postage stamps. Have your passport stamped for 2 SF at the tourist office's hard-to-miss **Liechtenstein Center,** just a few steps down the street to the south, or at the information booth at the bus terminal in summer. ⊠*Städtle 37* ☎*423/2366105* ✆*Free* ☉*Daily 10–noon and 1:30–5.*

The **Kunstmuseum Liechtenstein** *(Liechtenstein Museum of Art)* offers ever-changing exhibitions, showing at anytime only a fraction of the country's extraordinary art collection, amassed by countless princes of Liechtenstein. Most of their treasures are now on view in the family's Palais Liechtenstein in Vienna—so spectacular a showcase it is worth a trip in itself to the city—but there are enough holdings to present exhibitions here, ranging from Roman mythological art to old masters. ⊠*Städtle 32* ☎*423/2350300* ⊕*www.kunstmuseum.li* ✆*12 SF* ☉*Tues., Wed., and Fri.–Sun., 10–5, Thurs. 10–8.*

The **Liechtensteinisches Landesmuseum** *(National Museum)*, in a former tavern and customhouse with a modern annex built into the cliff, covers the geology, history, and folklore of the principality. ⊠*Städtle 43* ☎*423/2396820* ⊕*www.landesmuseum.li* ✆*8 SF* ☉*Tues., Wed., and Fri.–Sun., 10–5, Thurs. 10–8.*

The **Ski Museum Vaduz** is a small shrine to the region's preferred pastime. Here you'll find numerous variations on the Alpine theme, including skis, sleds, ski fashion, and literature. ⊠*Fabrikweg 5* ☎*423/2321502* ⊕*www.skimuseum.li* ✆*6 SF* ☉*Weekdays 2–6, or by appointment.*

At the top of a well-marked hill road (you can climb the forest footpath behind the Engel restaurant) stands **Vaduz Castle.** Here His Serene Highness Hans-Adam II, reigning prince of Liechtenstein, duke of Troppau and Jaegerndorf, reigns in a gratifyingly romantic fortress-home with red and white medieval shutters, massive ramparts, and a broad perspective over the Rhine Valley. Originally built in the 12th century, the castle was burned down by troops of the Swiss Confederation in the Swabian Wars of 1499 and partly rebuilt during the following centuries, until a complete overhaul that started in 1905 gave it its present form. It is not open to the public, as Hans-Adam II enjoys his privacy. He is the son of the late beloved Franz Josef II, who died in November 1989 after more than a 50-year reign. Franz Josef's birthday, August 15, is still celebrated as the Liechtenstein national holiday. Hans-Adam II has been known to join the crowds below to watch the fireworks while wearing jeans; his two photogenic teenagers often make the party pages in Vienna, where the family museum is one of the city's finest cultural jewels.

WHERE TO EAT

$$$–$$$$
FRENCH
★

✕ **Real.** Here you'll find rich, old-style Austrian-French cuisine in all its buttery glory prepared by Martin Real, son of the unpretentious former chef, Felix Real (who still presides over the 20,000-bottle wine cellar). There's an abundance of game in season, richly sauced seafood, and soufflés. The ambience is old-school, and even the salads are prepared at your table. Downstairs, the more casual Stübli atmosphere is just right for *Geschnetzeltes mit Rösti* (veal in cream sauce with hash brown potatoes). ✉*Städtle 21,* ☎*423/2322222* ☐*AE, DC, MC, V.*

> **THE MOVEABLE FEAST**
>
> Ironically, prosperity has built the lower reaches of Liechtenstein into a modern community, full of big, new cream-color bungalows that hardly seem picturesque to tourists seeking traces of the Holy Roman Empire. In fact, most of the great art of the reigning family has been packed off to Vienna's newly renovated Palais Liechtenstein. Since they've now reopened this splendid 18th-century gallery to the public, no one can begrudge the fact that their family Schloss Vaduz is still private.

$
SWISS
★

✕ **Wirthschaft zum Löwen.** Though there's plenty of French, Swiss, and Austrian influence, Liechtenstein has a cuisine of its own, and this is the place to try it. In a wood-shingle landmark farmhouse on the Austrian border, the friendly Biedermann family serves tender homemade *Schwartenmagen* (the pressed-pork mold unfortunately known as headcheese in English), pungent *Sauerkäse* (sour cheese), and Käseknöpfli, plus lovely meats and the local crusty, chewy bread. Be sure to try the region's distinctive wines. When driving here on Route 16, keep an eye out for Schellenberg, posted to the left; if you zip past it, you'll end up in Austria. ✉*Schellenberg ✛10 km (6 mi) north of Vaduz off Rte. 16* ☎*423/3731162* ⊕*www.loewen. li* ☐*AE, MC, V* ⊗*Closed Wed. and Thurs.*

WHERE TO STAY

$$$$
★

🏨 **Park-Hotel Sonnenhof.** With a superb, nearly Himalayan view over the valley and mountains beyond, this hillside retreat offers understated but sumptuous luxury minutes from downtown Vaduz. Sit on your chaise lounge in the elegant garden and sip your dessert coffee as you study the adorable castle of the princes of Liechtenstein, perched on one of the adjacent hilltops. Directly ahead of you is the main building—a sort of hyper-chalet, but warmed up by awnings and cascading pink flowers. Inside, all is friendly luxe, with public salons full of antiques, rugs, woodwork, and familial touches. Upstairs, the clean, comfortable guest rooms are decorated in bright colors. The restaurant serves excellent, unstodgy French food and local fish. **Pros:** undeniably the most luxurious venue in this chapter, and a destination in and of itself; no worn edges here. **Cons:** restaurant is open to hotel guests only. ✉*Mareestr. 29* ☎*423/2390202* ⊕*www.sonnenhof.li* ⤶*17 rooms, 12 suites* ⌂*In-room: no a/c, safe, refrigerator. In-hotel: restaurant, pool, public Wi-Fi* ☐*AE, DC, MC, V* ⊗*Closed late Dec.–early Jan.* ⦿*BP.*

$$$

🏨 **Residence.** Rice-paper screens and down duvets mingle in a simple Japanese-European style. The smack-dab central location is a draw whether you're here on vacation or business, and both bath and conference rooms have state-of-the-art features. The restaurant serves market-fresh local fare and offers take-out if you're in the mood for a picnic. **Pros:** 21st-century design with all up-to-date conveniences; indulge your inner lazybones: everything is just three minutes away. **Cons:** a little sleek for the Holy Roman Empire experience; the reception desk is hidden away upstairs and badly marked. ⊠*Städtle 23* ☎*423/2392020* ⊕*www.residence.li* ↩*24 rooms, 5 suites* ⅋*In-room: no a/c (some), safe, refrigerator, Ethernet. In-hotel: restaurant, bar, public Wi-Fi* ▤*AE, DC, MC, V* ⦿*BP.*

SPORTS & THE OUTDOORS

BICYCLES &
MOTORCYCLES
In Triesen (4 km [2½ mi] south of Vaduz), bikes can be rented from **Bike Garage** (⊠*Landstr. 256* ☎*423/3900390*).

SHOPPING

POTTERY
Though shops on the main street of Vaduz carry samples of the local dark-glaze pottery, painted with folksy flowers and figures, the central source is 8 km (5 mi) north of Vaduz at **Schaedler Keramik** (⊠*Rte. 16, Nendeln* ☎*423/3731414*). Simpler household pottery is available for sale as well as the traditional and often ornate hand-painted pieces. Pottery making is demonstrated daily. The shop is open weekdays 8–5.

TRIESENBERG (LIECHTENSTEIN)

3 km (2 mi) southeast of Vaduz, 162 km (100 mi) southeast of Schaffhausen.

This cluster of pretty chalets clings to the mountainside, with panoramic views over the Rhine Valley. Triesenberg was settled in the 13th century by immigrants from the Valais in southwestern Switzerland.

The **Walser Heimatmuseum** *(Valais Heritage Museum)* traces the culture of these immigrants. Furnishings and tools from farmers and craftsmen are displayed, and an entertaining 20-minute slide show (in English) illustrates their Alpine roots. ⊠*Dorfenzentrum* ☎*423/2621926* ⊕*www. triesenberg.li* 💶*2 SF* ⏲*Mon.–Fri. 7:45–11:45, 1:30–5:45; Sat. 7:45–11, 1:30–5, Sun. by appointment only.*

MALBUN (LIECHTENSTEIN)

5 km (3 mi) southeast of Triesenberg, 167 km (103 mi) southeast of Schaffhausen.

In winter this 5,250-foot-high mountain resort near the Austrian border draws crowds of local families who come for the varied slopes, many of which are well suited to beginners. England's Prince Charles and Princess Anne learned to ski here while visiting the Liechtenstein royal family in Vaduz. In summer Malbun becomes a quiet, unpretentious resort with reasonable prices.

CLOSE UP

The Best Offense?

There is an article in Liechtenstein's constitution that states that every able-bodied man up to 60 years old must be prepared to defend his country at a moment's notice, but there hasn't been an official army since 1868. It wasn't always so: Liechtenstein was treaty-bound in the 18th century to contribute five men to the army of the Holy Roman Empire, as well as to cover the expenses of "half a cavalryman." This was increased to 80 men when Liechtenstein joined the German Confederation in 1814, but the expense of keeping an armed force was so steep that it was disbanded after the Austro-Prussian War came to a close. Since then, the only peacekeepers in the country have been the police force, which is augmented whenever necessary by a contingent of auxiliary service members. When all else fails, Switzerland has been known to offer its troops for civil service, such as helping to combat floods or mountain slides.

SKIING

Malbun is a sunny, natural bowl with low, easy slopes and a couple of difficult runs; you can ride a chairlift to the top of the Sareiserjoch and experience the novelty of skiing from the Austrian border back into Liechtenstein. Facilities are concentrated at the center, including hotels and cafés overlooking the slopes. The resort also has a **ski school** (☎ *423/2639770*). One-day lift tickets cost 48 SF; five-day passes cost 167 SF.

WHERE TO STAY

¢–$ ⊡ **Alpenhotel.** The Vögeli family's welcoming smiles and good food have made this remodeled chalet a Liechtenstein institution. The old rooms are small, with creaky pine trim; the higher-priced rooms are modern stucco. Winter or summer, there is a plethora of activities on offer in and around the hotel to make you sure you're getting your money's worth. **Pros:** breathtaking views of the mountains; exuberant staff; that soft down comforter. **Cons:** you're not at the end of the world, but you can see it from here. ⊠ *Malbun* ☎ *423/2631181* ⊕ *www.alpenhotel. li* ⊅ *22 rooms* ⊜ *In-room: refrigerator. In-hotel: restaurant, pool, no elevator* ⊟ *AE, DC, MC, V.*

SPORTS & THE OUTDOORS

Liechtenstein has a 162-km (100-mi) network of Alpine hiking trails, and another 243 km (150 mi) of valley hiking. Malbun and Steg are ideal starting points for mountain hikes. You can get trail maps at the tourist office or at magazine kiosks.

WALENSEE

38 km (23 mi) northwest of Malbun, 65 km (36 mi) southeast of Zürich, 127 km (78 mi) southeast of Schaffhausen.

Between Liechtenstein and Zürich, the spectacular, mirrorlike lake called the Walensee is a deep emerald gash that stretches 16 km (10 mi) through the mountains, reflecting the jagged Churfirsten peaks.

At the western end of the Walensee, **Weesen** is a quiet, shady resort noted for its mild climate and lovely lakeside walkway.

Six kilometers (4 mi) north of Weesen on a winding mountain road lies **Amden,** perched 3,116 feet above the Walensee in the relatively undiscovered region south of the Churfirsten Mountains.

SKIING
Despite its small size, **Amden** is a major winter sports center, offering modest skiing in a ruggedly beautiful setting. Easy and medium slopes with unspectacular drops and quick, short-lift runs provide good weekend getaways for crowds of local Swiss families. The highest trails start at 5,576 feet; there are two chairlifts, three T-bars, one children's lift, 25 km (16 mi) of downhill runs, and 8 km (5 mi) of cross-country trails. You can also take advantage of the **ski school** (☎055/6111115), a natural ice rink, and walking paths. One-day lift tickets cost 35 SF; six-day passes cost 165 SF.

SPORTS & THE OUTDOORS
For sports enthusiasts, **Amden** also has a public **open-air skating rink,** the heated indoor pool **Hallenbad Amden** (☎055/6111588), and an **outdoor tennis court** (☎055/6111292). There are also many **public beaches** that dot the southern shore of the Walensee.

STOP AND SMELL THE ROSES

Between the Walensee and Zürich, about 36 km (22 mi) northwest of Weesen, Rapperswil is a small town on the Zürcher See (Lake Zürich) with pleasant views, summertime waterfront strolls, and no fewer than three rose gardens, which is why it is known as the "Swiss City of Roses." If rainy, go instead to the forbiddingly Gothic 13th-century Schloss Rapperswil (055/2101862). Inside is a museum on Polish immigrants to Switzerland. It's open weekends from 1 to 5 in November, December, and March, and daily from 1 to 5 from April to October; admission is 5 SF.

Graubünden

AROSA, DAVOS, THE ENGADINE, ST. MORITZ

Davos

WORD OF MOUTH

"Oh, yes, absolutely see the Engadine!!! It's a really spectacular place that will give you dramatically different landscapes. The hiking and biking there are phenomenal! I rented a bike from the train station at St. Moritz and spent one day biking the Inn Valley and another biking the lakes (St. Moritz, Sils, Silvaplana). And, yes, you can get everywhere either by bike or Postbus or train."

—Svandav2000

WELCOME TO GRAUBÜNDEN

TOP REASONS TO GO

★ **Chic, chicer, chicest:** From Arosa to Zuoz, every skiing resort is a place to be "scene" by the elite of four continents. Sparkling St. Moritz, Davos, and Klosters are perfect for chilling out, but don't forget your Gucci sunglasses.

★ **Heidi's hideaway:** Shirley Temple immortalized the just-too-cute orphan but find out just how much her 1937 film differed from Joanna Spyri's beloved book with a visit to Maienfeld's Heidi Village.

★ **Beautiful sgraffiti:** The Lower Inn Valley is home to some picture-perfect villages, famous for their folkloric dwellings graced with sgraffiti wall decorations. For the best close-ups, head to Guarda—so beautiful it is under federal protection.

★ **Keeping body and soul together:** Palatial spa hotels and a landscape that inspired great painters and philosophers means Graubünden offers top-of-the-line rest and recuperation, "made in Switzerland."

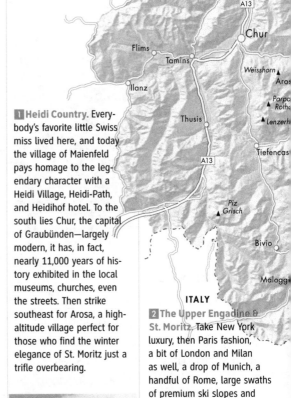

1 Heidi Country. Everybody's favorite little Swiss miss lived here, and today the village of Maienfeld pays homage to the legendary character with a Heidi Village, Heidi-Path, and Heidihof hotel. To the south lies Chur, the capital of Graubünden—largely modern, it has, in fact, nearly 11,000 years of history exhibited in the local museums, churches, even the streets. Then strike southeast for Arosa, a high-altitude village perfect for those who find the winter elegance of St. Moritz just a trifle overbearing.

2 The Upper Engadine & St. Moritz. Take New York luxury, then Paris fashion, a bit of London and Milan as well, a drop of Munich, a handful of Rome, large swaths of premium ski slopes and crystalline lakes, add the bubbling "champagne climate" of dry air and sun, mix well and pour onto a few acres in a gorgeous high-altitude valley. How can anything compare to St. Moritz?

LIECHTENSTEIN

Malbun

A3   A13

Sargans

Maienfeld

Bad Ragaz

Landquart

A13

Chur

Flims

Tamins

Weisshorn

Ilanz

Aros

Parpa
Roth

Thusis

Lenzerh

A13

Tiefencas

Piz
Grisch

Bivio

Malogg

ITALY

GETTING ORIENTED

Covering about 2,800 square miles, Graubünden is the largest canton in Switzerland, occupying more than one-sixth of the country. With high mountains nestling chic resorts like St. Moritz, Davos, and Klosters, the Grisons (to use the French name) offers as much attitude as altitude. Cross any of the passes south to the Engadine Valley for quaint sgraffito-covered villages and more fresh air than you've ever dreamed of.

3 **The Lower Engadine.**
Bustling Scuol has maintained its ancient feel despite modern amenities. Nature lovers will have all wishes fulfilled in the famed Swiss National park, while art lovers will adore flowerboxed Guarda and the magnificent fortress at Tarasp, which seems lifted from the pages of a medieval illuminated manuscript.

GRAUBÜNDEN PLANNER

How's the Weather?

Graubünden has essentially two climatic regions. In the lower Rhine Valley (Chur, Heidi-Land, etc), there are normally four distinct and equal seasons.

Up in the Engadine, there are four seasons as well, but their distribution is heavily skewed toward winter.

Snow can remain until May, and after a brief spring and summer you may experience flurries or frozen dew in August.

So even if traveling in summer, pack some warm clothing, like a sweater and a windbreaker.

The fall colors are well worth a trip—perhaps not as spectacular as New England, but very inspiring.

Finding a Place to Stay

Hoteliers in Graubünden invest fortunes in preserving Alpine coziness on both the outside and inside of their lodgings, which is not always the case in other parts of Switzerland. Wood is commonly used to soften interiors, and the source is often Arvenholz, the prized Swiss stone pine that grows here. Its wood is thick with knots and rich in natural color, which deepens over the years. Prices in this popular region are comparatively high. Even higher prices can be charged for the winter holiday period and in February; during the rest of winter you may find special lower-priced packages that include ski tickets. Summer rates are also generally lower. Many hotels close between seasons, from April to mid-June and from mid-October to mid-December, but the dates and months vary each year, so be sure to check. In a few winter resorts there are hotels that stay closed all summer; we have not included these in our listings.

Hotels publish tariffs in various ways; double-check to see whether you're paying per person or per room, as well as whether you have demipension (half board). If you plan to stay in one place for more than a day or two, half board can cut costs. You may also want to ask about GästeKarte (guest cards), small booklets given by hotels that provide various deals on local transit or attractions. These are distributed in some resort towns, including Klosters, Davos, and Flims/Laax. It is also worth noting that since March 2008 all hotels and restaurants in Canton Graubünden are no-smoking areas by law. The quality of the skiing and outdoor life, plus the allurements of the social life, means that many places are packed between Christmas and about January 15—so make reservations well in advance for this time.

If you are interested only in sports, you may wish to budget less for hotels by staying in more out-of-the-way villages and commute to such posheries as St. Moritz and Pontresina. After all, once you are in the Engadine, there are no great distances (Scuol to Sils Maria, for example, is about two hours by train and bus). Watch out if traveling between mid-October and November, or between Easter and beginning of June: Many hotels close for renovations and repairs.

Transportation Basics

Unless you intend to explore every nook and cranny of Graubünden or some of the more remote valleys, you will not really need a car. In fact, a car might cost more time and irritation than simply using public transportation. Virtually every village and major cable car, funicular or ski area is connected either by regular train service of the Rhätibahn (Rhaeteian Railway or RhB, for short) trains or Swiss post-buses. On occasion, hotels often have pick-up service (the Stern in Chur uses a beautiful 1930s Buick, a genuine "station" wagon). Note that if you intend to use public transportation (recommended) a fair amount, you should consider purchasing a Swiss Pass or one of the many other options. For example, an eight-day Swiss Pass (giving you unlimited transportation on trains, buses, and ships; 50% discounts on many funiculars or cable cars; plus entrance to museums and many other perks) costs 362 SF. Compare this to the basic cost for a car rental: about 680 SF for seven days—and you haven't tanked up yet or paid for parking.

Land of Plenty

Thanks to all those tourists, restaurants tend to stay open throughout the day for the hungry visitor. The way to be sure is to look for a sign that bears the word durchgehend, meaning without a stop. Some places, however, will serve only snacks—or close entirely—between around 2:30 and 5:30. If traveling in the low season (November or April), you may encounter quite a few closed doors. Finally, the rugged mountainscape is deceiving. Hikers and skiers will frequently encounter a cozy Bergbeizli, literally a mountain inn, where fine locally grown food is served up in a most congenial atmosphere.

WHAT IT COSTS IN SWISS FRANCS

¢	$	$$	$$$	$$$$
RESTAURANTS				
under 15 SF	15 SF–25 SF	25 SF–40 SF	40 SF–60 SF	over 60 SF
HOTELS				
under 100 SF	100 SF–175 SF	175 SF–250 SF	250 SF–350 SF	over 350 SF

Restaurant prices are per person for a main course at dinner. Hotel prices are for two people in a standard double room in high season, including tax and service.

Going Loco

Thanks to the Swiss Railways (SBB/CFF/FFS) and the affiliated *UNESCO World Heritage Status* narrow-gauge Rhätische Bahn (the Rhaeteian Railway, commonly referred to as the "Rhätibahn"), most destinations mentioned in the chapter are reachable by train; happily, Swiss postbuses stop in places where there is no train service.

Trains generally run from around 6 AM to 10:30 PM (schedules sometimes change between October and Easter).

With its signature picturesque red wagons, the Rhätibahn, or RhB network of trains that traverse Graubünden, is tailor-made for sightseeing thanks to its "panorama" cars (with big windows) that allow travelers to truly enjoy some of Switzerland's most spectacular scenery along 400 km (248 mi) of narrow-gauge tracks.

Special short trips for rail enthusiasts include excursions on three remaining steam locomotives and trips in open carriages over the Bernina Pass.

The legendary Glacier Express from St. Moritz to Zermatt and other trains traverse spectacular terrain, the bright-red cars crossing bridges built unbelievably high over gorges.

4

GETTING AROUND

By Bus

You can take the Swiss post-bus (postauto) system's *Palm Express* from Lugano in the Ticino to St. Moritz. The 3¾-hour trip passes through a corner of Italy and over the Maloja Pass. The bus runs twice daily from mid-June through mid-October; reservations are essential. Owners of a Swiss Pass will need to purchase the additional Alpine Ticket for 15 SF. Postautos are a good way to wind your way up Alpine switchbacks over the region's great passes—that is, if you're not inclined to motion sickness. You can also use them to make circle tours with some careful study of the schedule. Information is available at all post offices. The main ski resorts have "sport bus" shuttles, which connect the villages and mountain stations. The service is usually included in the price of your lift ticket or on presentation of a "guest card" (check to see if your hotel offers these discount booklets).

Palm Express (☎ *081/8376764 or 091/8078520* ⊕ *www.swisspost.com*). Note that the timetable and itinerary search is the same as Swiss Railways, so you will receive schedules for both bus and trains.

By Car

Graubünden is mountainous, with few major highways. Drivers can enter either by way of the San Bernardino Pass from the south or from the north on A13, the region's only expressway. Coming from Austria and Munich, the A27 leads into the Lower Engadine; roads over the Ofen and Bernina passes lead into the Engadine from the South Tyrol and Veltline areas of Italy respectively, and the approach to the Upper Engadine from Italy is over the Maloja Pass. The Oberalp and Lukmanier passes lead from Uri and Ticino respectively to the Surselva region to join A13.

The A13 expressway cuts a swift north–south route through Graubünden. A car is definitely necessary if you want to explore deeper into the countryside. Fine valley roads connect the rest of the area, though to move from one resort to another you may have to crawl over a mountain pass.

If you're traveling in winter, make sure to check the status of the passes beforehand. The San Bernardino old road and the Oberalp, Albula, and Flüela passes usually close, but the San Bernardino Tunnel and the Maloja, Bernina, Julier, and Ofen passes are usually open to traffic. Local road condition information is generally broadcast in German, French, and Italian, but you could also ask for the latest reports at the tourist offices. The Lukmanier is the only pass in the region that can stay open in winter.

Trains through the Vereina tunnel shuttle cars between Klosters and Sagliains (Susch–Lavin). The tunnel has made the Lower Engadine quickly accessible during the winter, when the Flüela pass is seldom open. Tickets are between 27 SF in summer and 40 SF in winter. Cars can also be taken by rail from Thusis to Samedan via the Albula tunnel; the service is limited and reservations are essential. The cost per car is 145 SF.

Car Transport/Rail Reservation (☎ *081/6511113*).

Visitor Information

Regional Tourist Office Graubünden Holidays (✉ *Alexanderstr. 24, Chur* ☎ *081/2542424* ⊕ *www.graubuenden.ch*).

By Train

Thanks to an extensive rail network, with trains running at a good frequency, a trip to Graubünden can be done without even a car—unless you insist on traveling up every tiny valley. A Swiss Pass gives you access to all trains and buses (supplemented at times by the Apline Pass). A FlexiPass can be used if you intend to use the trains only on certain days.

The Swiss Federal Railway trains that enter Graubünden travel only as far as Chur. From there the fine local Rhätische Bahn (RhB), awarded Unesco World Heritage status, takes over—from its brand-new train and bus station.

The *Bernina Express* runs from Chur to St. Moritz via the Albula route and on to Italy past the spectacular Bernina peaks, lakes, and glaciers. The *Engadine Star,* which began service in 2000, makes its way from Klosters to St. Moritz in a couple of hours. The glamorous *Glacier Express,* billed as "the slowest express in the world," connects St. Moritz with Zermatt via the Oberalp Pass, crossing 291 bridges during its 7½-hour journey. The train includes an antique burnished-wood dining car; you can book a table through Passaggio Rail.

Reservations for these trains are mandatory and can be made at almost any European rail station. As on the federal railways, a variety of reduced-price passes are available. For information on the local train network, contact Rhätische Bahn or the regional tourism office, Graubünden Holidays.

Passaggio Rail (✉ *CH-7000Chur* ☎ *081/2521425*).
Rhätische Bahn (☎ *081/2549100* ⊕ *www.rhb.ch*).
Swiss Federal Railway (*SBB/CFF/FFS* ☎ *0900/300300* ⊕ *www.sbb.ch*).

By Air

Engadine Airport is used mainly by private planes. At 5,600 feet, it's the highest airport in Europe. The closest international airports are Zürich (about 2 hours from Chur) and Lugano (about 2½ hours from St. Moritz).
Engadine Airport (✉ *Samedan, 5 km [3 mi] from St. Moritz* ☎ *081/8510851*).

Hikes & Walks

Arosa, Davos, and Lenzerheide-Valbella offer special hiking packages. You can walk from Davos to Arosa one day and from Arosa to Lenzerheide the next. No need to worry about booking a hotel or transporting your luggage, as it's all taken care of. Contact local tourist offices or the regional tourist office, Graubünden Holidays. Similar arrangements can be made in the Engadine; call Engadin Ferien (☎ *081/8300001* ⊕ *www.engadinferien.ch*) for information.

The Arosa tourist office offers guided tours and nature walks daily from June through October; you can visit a cheese maker, a regional museum, and a 15th-century chapel. The Davos and Klosters tourist offices arrange guided walks at least once a week from July to September. The Chur tourist office arranges guided tours from April to October every Wednesday at 2:30. To explore on your own, pick up a map from the tourist office and follow the green and red footprints on the pavement.

The Pontresina tourist office offers guided walking tours of its Old Town from mid-June to mid-October. It also offers guided botanical excursions, glacier treks, and hiking trips to the Swiss National Park, plus mushroom-picking outings in season (August and September). If you are staying in Pontresina, these trips are free; day visitors pay a small fee. Guides for all of the above tours speak English.

Updated
by Suzanne
Hégelé

ALTHOUGH THE NAMES OF ITS resorts—St. Moritz, Davos, Klosters, Arosa—register almost automatic recognition, the region wrapped around them remains surprisingly unsung, untouched by the fur-clad celebs who make stage sets out of its sports centers, aloof to the glamour trends—quirky, resilient, and decidedly apart. Nowhere in Switzerland will you find sharper contrasts than those between the bronze seven-day citizens who jet into St. Moritz and the stalwart native farmers who nurse archaic dialects and gather their crops by hand as their Roman-Etruscan forebearers did. Resort life in winter contrasts sharply with the everyday existence of the native mountain farmers.

As it straddles the continental divide, its rains pour off northward into the Rhine, eastward with the Inn to the Danube and Black Sea, and south to the River Po, the landscape here is thus riddled with bluff-lined valleys. The southern half basks in crystalline light and, except for the Italian-speaking Ticino, receives the most sunshine in the country. Its 150 valleys and 615 lakes are flanked by 937 peaks, among them Piz Buin (10,867 feet) in the north and Piz Bernina (13,307 feet), the canton's highest mountain, in the south. Like many Swiss cantons, Graubünden is culturally diverse. To the north it borders Austria and Liechtenstein, and in the east and south it abuts Italy. Swiss-German and Italian are widely spoken. The ancient Romansh language (literally, "Roman") is still predominant in the Lower Engadine and Surselva; it is estimated that 30% of Graubünden residents can speak it. The language dates back to the 1st century BC, when the area was conquered by the Romans and became a province called Rhaetia Prima. An alternative view on this point says the tongue predates the Romans and originated as long ago as 600 BC, when an Etruscan prince named Rhaetus invaded the region.

Anyone versed in a Latin language can follow Romansh's simpler signs (*abitaziun da vacanzas,* for example, is a vacation apartment), but Romansh is no easy matter to pick it up by ear. Nor do the Graubündners smooth the way: Rhaetian Romansh is fragmented into five dialects, which developed separately in formerly isolated valleys, so that depending on where you are, the word for *house* can be seen written on the facades of homes as *casa, chasa, chesa, tgaltgesa, or tgea.* Even the name *Graubünden* itself comes in a variety of forms: Grisons (French), Grigioni (Italian), and Grischun (Romansh). It originates from the "Gray Confederation," one of three leagues that joined together in 1471 to resist the feudal Habsburg rulers. After a period as a "free state," Graubünden became a Swiss canton in 1803. With these dialects and their derivatives cutting one valley culture neatly off from another, it's no wonder the back roads of the region seem as removed from the modern mainstream as the once-a-century world of Brigadoon.

EXPLORING GRAUBÜNDEN

A spine of 9,800-foot peaks fairly neatly bisects the region into two very different sections, which are connected by the Julier, Albula, and Flüela passes. In the north is the region's capital, Chur; to the west lies Surselva; and farther east are the famous ski resorts of Arosa, Klosters,

SKIING: SPORTY TO SNOBBISH

With Davos, site of the world's first ski lift, St. Moritz, arguably the world's ritziest resort, and a host of other hot spots within its confines, Graubünden has earned its reputation as an ultimate winter destination. You'll find downhill skiing and snowboarding for all skill levels, as well as miles of *Langlauf* (cross-country skiing) trails prepared for both the classic and skating techniques.

Sports shops can outfit you with the necessary equipment; in Davos and Flims-Laax you can even rent ski clothing. If you plan to spend a few days in one resort, check with local tourist offices for special packages. If you want to spend a day in a different resort within Graubünden, buy the lift ticket with your train ticket and the return fare will be nicely reduced. Remember that it was in Klosters that a fatal accident occurred in the entourage of England's Prince Charles, whose group was skiing off-piste—an unhappy reminder to always avoid unmarked zones.

and Davos. The southern part of the canton includes the Engadine, with its lakes, sophisticated resorts, and the National Park. The canton extends east to Austria and south toward Italy from the valleys of Bergell, Müstair, and Puschlav.

HEIDI COUNTRY

The Maienfeld region, with its hills and craggy peaks sloping down to sheltered vineyards, is the gateway from the north into Graubünden, but its claim to fame is that the legendary Heidi lived here. To the west in Surselva, the villages of Flims, Laax, and Falera together form the Alpine Arena, Graubünden's largest connected ski area. Arosa, to the east in the Schanfigg valley, is a quieter resort village that lies at the end of a spectacular, steep, winding road. The transportation hub of the region is Chur, the district capital.

CHUR

119 km (75 mi) southeast of Zürich, 77 km (48 mi) south of Appenzell.

GETTING HERE
The Swiss Federal Railway trains that enter Graubünden only travel as far as Chur. From here the local Rhätische Bahn (RhB) takes over. Frequent trains arrive in Chur from Zürich (37 SF, 1¼ hrs), Klosters (21 SF, 1 hr), Davos (27 SF, 1 hr), and Liechtenstein (19 SF, 1 hr). For departure times and prices for trains and buses for most destinations in this chapter, check with www.sbb.ch—the main Swiss public transportation Web site—or www.rhb.ch, or call 0900/300300 (1.19 SF per min). Remember, if you have a Swiss Pass or another rail-discount card, it also applies to the buses.

Visitor Information (✉ *Grabenstr. 5* ☎ *081/2521818* ⊕ *www.churtourismus.ch*).

Chur to Davos

AUSTRIA

SWITZERLAND

RHÄTIKON

SILVRETTA GRUPPE

GRIALETSCH GLACIER

SANKT GALLEN

GRAUBÜNDEN

PRÄTTIGAU VALLEY

SCHANFIGG

Piz Buin ▲

Saglains

Susch

Zernez

Brail

Weisshorn ▲

Schwarzhorn ▲

Piz Vadret ▲

Flüelapass ●

Klosters

Wolfgang

Golschnägrat

Jakobshorn ▲

28

Madrisahorn ▲

Saas

Weissfluhjoch ▲

Davos

Rinerhorn ▲

Alp Luzein

Küblis

Frauenkirch

Glaris

Schiers

Fideris

Arosa

Wiesen

Landquart

28

Weisshorn ▲

Parpaner Rothorn ▲

Lenzerhorn ▲

Alvaneu

Maienfeld

Parpan

A13

Valbella

Tiefencastel

Bad Ragaz

TO ZÜRICH

Pardiel

Lenzerheide

3

Chur

Reichenau

Albula River

Zillis

Thusis

A13

Via Mala

Tamins

Hinterrhein River

Rhein River

Flims

Laax

Ilanz

TO OBERALP PASSE AND LUKMANIER

6 mi

6 km

KEY

╟╌╌ Cable Carl Funicular

━━━ Rail lines

⛷ Ski Resorts

EXPLORING

A small city (and cantonal capital) of 35,000, with a modern downtown and a busy rail crossroads, Chur is actually the oldest continuously settled site north of the Alps. Recent discoveries of Stone Age tools place Chur's origins back to roughly 11,000 BC. The Romans founded Curia Raetorium on the rocky terrace south of the river; from here, they protected the Alpine routes that led to Lake Constance. By AD 284 the town served as the capital of a flourishing Roman colony, Rhaetia Prima. Its heyday was during the Middle Ages, when it was ruled by bishops and bishop-princes. Narrow streets, cobblestone alleys, hidden courtyards, and ancient shuttered buildings still abound. The southern *föhn* wind that blows up through the Rhine Valley accounts in great part for the wine grapes that grow along the steep slopes around the town.

4

The **Rathaus** *(Town Hall)* originated as two structures in 1464, which were connected in 1540. At ground level, under the arches, is the old marketplace. In the open hall on the second floor is a model of the Old Town, which can help you plan a tour of the city. The Grosser Ratsaal (Council Chamber) has a timber ceiling dating from 1493; the Bürgerratskammer (Citizens' Council Chamber) has wall panels from the Renaissance. Both chambers have old ceramic stoves, the one in the Ratsaal depicting the various deadly sins, the group of human behaviors Christian theology warns against. Embedded in the wall beside the door opening onto Reichsgasse is a rod of iron about a foot long—the standard measure of a foot or shoe before the metric system was introduced. Although both chambers are generally closed to the public, very small groups can contact the tourist office to arrange a visit. ✉ *Poststr.*

The **Kirche St. Martin** *(St. Martin's Church)* was built in 1491 after a fire destroyed the original dating from the 8th century. Since 1526 it has been Protestant. On your right as you enter are three stained-glass windows created in 1919 by Augusto Giacometti, the father of the Graubünden sculptor Alberto Giacometti. The steeple dates from 1917; with permission from the sacristan, you can climb to the top to see the bells. Of note, too, is the 1716 fountain beside the church, whose basin features the signs of the zodiac (with the exception of the figure on top, it is the original work). ✉ *Evangel. Kirchgemeinde, Kirchg. 12* ☎ *081/2522292* ⊙ *Weekdays 8:30–11:30 and 2–5.*

★ The **Rätisches Museum** provides a thorough, evocative overview of the canton's development. Displayed in a 1675 mansion, the collection includes not only furnishings and goods from that period, but also archaeological finds from the region, both Roman and prehistoric. There are also exhibitions of special interest on display most of the time. ✉ *Hofstr. 1* ☎ *081/2541640* ⊕ *www.raetischesmuseum.gr.ch* 💷 *6 SF* ⊙ *Tues.–Sun. 10–5.*

Opposite the Rätisches Museum, a stone archway under the **Hof-Torturm** *(Citadel Gate Tower)* leads into the court of the strong bishop-princes of Chur, once hosts to Holy Roman emperors passing through on their way to Italy or Germany—sometimes with whole armies in tow. The bishops were repaid for their hospitality by imperial donations to the

EATING WELL IN GRAUBÜNDEN

Graubünden, with its myriad dialects and potent blend of Latin and German blood, has a cuisine as novel and unexpected as its culture. The Graubünden idea of fast food is a *salsiz* (a kind of small, rectangular-shape salami of venison, liver, or beef) and a piece of bread. Besides regional specialties like the ubiquitous *Bündnerfleisch* (air-dried beef pressed into rectangular loaves and shaved into translucent slices), *Gerstensuppe* (barley soup), and *Nusstorte* (shortbread with a chewy walnut-and-caramel filling), you will find a broad range of international cooking, notably in the larger resorts. Italian influence is strong, and the Germanic *Spätzli* (tiny flour dumplings) coexist with gnocchi, risotto, and polenta.

You may feel you've stepped back into the Middle Ages when you sit down to *pizzoccheri neri* (buckwheat noodles with greens and potatoes, swimming in garlic butter and melted cheese) or to *maluns* (grated potatoes stirred in pools of butter until they form crisp balls). *Capuns* or *chrutcapuns* are bundles of Swiss chard smothered in butter and cheese and flavored with dried meat. These down-to-earth treats are making a comeback in either traditional or more modern interpretations. Year-round, but especially in fall, many menus feature wild game: the centuries-old hunting tradition is especially strong in this canton. Look for *Reh* or *Hirsch* (roe or red deer) and *Gems* (chamois), usually served with red cabbage, fruits, and chestnuts or in a *Pfeffer* (strongly flavored, peppery stew).

Most restaurants' wine lists include a selection of the red pinot noir and white Riesling Sylvaner from the Bündnerherrschaft region around Maienfeld, Jenins, and Malans as well as the hearty red Nebbiolo of the Veltlin. The latter is actually grown over the southern border in Valtellina, which was ceded to Italy in 1815, but some quantities have always been brought in bulk into the canton for bottling and can be considered, at least in spirit, to be Swiss. As an alternative to wine, try one of the regional mineral waters: Valser, Passugger, or Rhäzünzer.

Many restaurants in resort towns close from the end of April to mid-June and October to December; there are variations and exceptions, of course, so if you plan a visit in the off-season, check in advance.

people. The thick fortifications of the residence reflect the disputed powers of the bishops; by the 15th century irate inhabitants who repeatedly rebelled were rebuffed and punished with excommunication. By 1526 the Reformation had broken the domination of the Church, although the city remains a Catholic bishopric today. The Hofkellerei Stübli is now at the base of the tower. Head up to the second floor and you can have a drink in the paneled room, dating from 1522, once used for church meetings. ⊠*Hof 1.*

The **Kathedrale St. Maria Himmelfahrt** *(Cathedral of the Assumption)* was built between 1151 and 1272, drawing on stylistic influences from all across Europe. The structure on this site in prehistoric times was subsequently supplanted by a Roman castle, a bishop's house in the 5th century, and a Carolingian cathedral in the 8th century. The capitals of the columns are carved with fantastical beasts; at their bases are clustered less threatening animals, such as sheep and marmots. In the choir is a magnificent 15th-century altar of gilded wood featuring nearly 150 carved figures. This late-15th century work comes from the workshop of Jakob Russ in Ravensburg, Germany. ⊠*Hof* ☎*081/2522076* ☼*Daily 8–7.*

Obere Gasse, once the main street through Chur and a major route between Germany and Italy, is now lined with small shops and cafés. At the end stands the 16th-century Obertor (Upper Gate), guarding the bridge across the Plessur River. ⊠*Old Town, between the Obertor and Arcaspl.*

Collections at Graubünden's art museum, the **Bündner Kunstmuseum,** include works by well-known artists who lived or worked in the canton, including Angelika Kauffmann, Giovanni Segantini, Giovanni and Alberto Giacometti, and Ernst Kirchner. The building itself is a majestic neoclassical structure erected in 1875 as a private residence. ⊠*Postpl.* ☎*081/2572868* ⊕*buendner-kunstmuseum.ch* ☞*12 SF* ☼*Tue–Sun. 10–5.*

OFF THE
BEATEN
PATH

Via Mala. Heading south toward the San Bernardino pass on the A13, turn off at Thusis and follow the sign for the Via Mala (the "bad road"), which was used by the Romans and traders over centuries. It runs about 6 km (3½ mi) alongside the narrow Hinterrhein gorge. Shortly after the start of the gorge, you can climb down 321 steps (for a fee of 5 SF) to view the river, rock formations, a mid-18th-century bridge, and old road itself. Continue to **Zillis** to see the church's renowned 12th-century painted wood ceiling, whose 153 panels mostly depict stories from the Bible. It is one of the world's oldest original artistic works from the Romanesque era.

WHERE TO EAT & STAY

$–$$
ECLECTIC

✕**Calanda.** Young and old people meet here in this friendly, trendy place with a great big mural featuring the restaurant's specialty: chicken. Thanks to Herbert Max Wesner and his team, you can enjoy a simple charcoal-roasted, free-roaming bird on a bed of salad in mango sauce, salmon steak in banana leaf with vegetables and coconut sauce, or perhaps a crispy chicken breast covered with cherry tomatoes, coriander, and salsa. There is a changing specials menu daily, and Sunday brunch is also a popular affair at a reasonable 24 SF per person. ⊠*Postpl.* ☎*081/2530880* ⊕*www.calanda-chur.ch* ☼*Sun.–Wed. 9–11* PM, *Thurs.–Sat. 9–midnight* ⊟*V.*

$$

▥**Hotel ABC.** This *garni* (without a restaurant) business hotel is just yards from the train station. Happily, you can enjoy the convenience of a central location while safe in the knowledge that your slumber will not succumb to night tremors: there are no night trains running. The hotel occupies five floors of a corporate metal-and-glass box; the entry is hidden between shops. Amenities and guest rooms are state-of-the-art, and service is friendly and efficient. Regulars needing a straightforward stopover return for its cleanliness, comfort, and free breakfast buffet. A spa with fitness and relaxation rooms is due to be opened in late 2008. **Pros:** central location; free generous breakfast buffet; free Internet terminal. **Cons:** with no a/c, it can get stuffy during summer months; requires venturing out for food. ⊠*Bahnhofpl.,* ☎*081/2541313* ⊕*www.hotel abc.ch* ↩*40 rooms, 4 apartments* ⌂*In-room: no a/c, safe, refrigerator, Wi-Fi (fee). In-hotel: sauna, public Internet (free), public Wi-Fi (fee), parking (free)* ⊟*AE, DC, MC, V* ⑂*BP.*

$$–$$$

Fodor's Choice

★

▥ **Romantik Hotel Stern.** Like many of the good vintages on its wine list, this historic inn, built in 1677, just keeps getting better, especially under the loving care of Adrian Müller. The family-owned and -run hotel neighbors the town's main church, but don't worry about lost sleep; its bells are silent at night. Guest rooms are modern and wood-clad; you can relax on a rooftop terrace or by the fireplace in the lounge. Note that the elevator goes only to the third floor. The restaurant serves local wines and focuses boldly on regional dishes such as *capuns, maluns,* or the filling *Ratsherrenplatte,* which combines vegetables, Pizokel, and a beef fillet. **Pros:** an intimate ambience and welcoming host; finest restaurant in Chur, with both regional and gourmet seasonal dishes. **Cons:** church bells can be a little too close for comfort; some rooms are smaller than average due to dimensions of the old building. ⊠*Reichsg. 11* ☎*081/2585757* ⊕*www.stern-chur.ch* ↩*65 rooms* ⌂*In-room: no a/c, Ethernet, Wi-Fi (fee). In-hotel: restaurant, public Internet, public Wi-Fi (fee), parking (free), garage (fee), some pets allowed (fee)* ⊟*AE, DC, MC, V.*

NIGHTLIFE

The futuristic **Giger Bar** (⊠*Comercialstr. 23* ☎*081/2537506*) is a strange space created by Academy Award winner H.R. Giger, a Chur native who designed the sets for the famous film *Alien.*

MAIENFELD

17 km (11 mi) north of Chur.

GETTING HERE

Trains connect Chur and Maienfeld between 9 AM and 9 PM twice every hour (at 22 past and 5 minutes to the hour); between 6 AM and 9 AM trains leave three times per hour (the additional train is at 13 past). The journey takes no more than 15 minutes.

Visitor Information (⊠*Maienfeld* ☎*081/3301912 or 081/3025858* ⊕*www. buendnerherrschaft.ch*).

EXPLORING

Above this graceful little village full of fountains, vineyards, and old stucco houses, the Zürich author Johanna Spyri set *Heidi,* the much-loved children's story of an orphan growing up with her grandfather on an isolated Alpine farm. Taken away to accompany the invalid Clara in murky Frankfurt, she languishes until returning to her mountain home. Nursing her fatally ill son, Spyri spent time in Maienfeld and liked the mountains behind, but it's questionable whether actual people inspired her tale. Nonetheless, you can hike from Maienfeld along the **Heidi-Weg**

(Heidi Path), either on the short circular route or continuing across steep open meadows and through thick forest to what have now been designated Peter the Goatherd's Hut and the Alm-Uncle's Hut. Here you might meet today's version of that character, who enjoys a chat and can answer Heidi-related questions in English. Along the way you'll take in awe-inspiring Rhine Valley views from flowered meadows that would have suited Heidi beautifully.

> **SWEETEST STORY EVER TOLD**
>
> For the ultimate immersion in Heidi lore and folklore, check out *Heidi: Das Musical* (081/7202099, www.heidimusical.ch), performed on an impressive lakeside stage during July and August in nearby Walenstadt.

On both routes, you pass through **Heididorf** *(Heidi Village)*, in reality the hamlet of Oberrofels. Here you can find the house that was used as a model for the illustrations in the original *Heidi* books. It now houses Heidi-appropriate furnishings and life-size models of Heidi, Grandfather, and Peter. ☎081/3301912 ⊕*www.heidi-swiss.ch* ☜7 SF ⊙*Mid-Mar.–mid-Nov., daily 10–5.*

As an alternative to walking the route, you can take a two-hour tour in a **horse-drawn carriage** (☎*081/3301912*). The cost is 30 SF per person.

At the kitsch-happy **Heidihof Hotel** (☎*081/3004747*), an extended farmhouse, have a snack and take in the view or spend the night. For a more genuine "Heidi experience" you can sleep in straw at a nearby farm (inquire at the tourist office).

In Maienfeld, visit a few of the two dozen local wine merchants or enjoy a meal in the Knight's Hall of **Schloss Brandis,** a castle whose earliest portions date from the 10th century. ☎081/3022423 ⊕*www.schlossbrandis.ch* ⊙*Closed mid-July–mid-Aug.*

AROSA

★ *29 km (18 mi) southeast of Chur.*

GETTING HERE
The Rhätische Bahn (RhB) has departures to and from Arosa at least once an hour between 5:26 AM and 7:48 PM. The 9 AM train has open carriages in summer for an excellent sightseeing experience. Within town, you can ride the municipal buses for free if you have the Arosa Card.

Visitor Information (⊠*CH-7050* ☎*081/3787020* ⊕*www.arosa.ch*)

EXPLORING
Thanks to its high altitude, Arosa (5,900 feet) is a well-known winter and summer sports center, offering brisk hiking, paragliding, and other activities in summer and a long skiing or snowboarding season with a guarantee of snow. Its modest size, isolated location, quiet atmosphere, and natural beauty set it apart. There is little of the rush of Davos or the pretension of St. Moritz: this is a friendly, family-oriented spot staffed by upbeat, down-to-earth people. Even the well-heeled rarely dress for

dinner. On a winter walk you are more likely to be overtaken by sleds and horse-drawn carriages than by cars. "I spent weeks up there," wrote author Hermann Hesse in 1934, "and I found a level of vigor and youth I would never have thought possible." Arosa lies at the end of a beautiful, winding 29-km (19-mi) road with grades of more than 12% and more than 360 turns. Taking the train from Chur is a lot less nerve-wracking than driving.

The town has two sections: Inner-Arosa, where the Walsers ("immigrants" from the Valais) built their wooden chalets in the 14th century,

> ### WORD OF MOUTH
>
> "Arosa is a small skiing town, with limited activities for non-skiers (but if they are happy to sit with a book and take walks and admire the scenery…). Arosa is only 60 minutes by train from Chur, which has a lovely old town. You could also take the Bernina Express train, one of the best scenic excursion trains in Switzerland. I have only skied Arosa as a ski-over from Davos, but thought it was good."   —Cicerone

is at the end of the valley; Ausser-Arosa is near the train station and the Obersee (Upper Lake). Between the two is the impossible-to-miss casino, with its mosaic facade of screaming colors (it has now been converted into a theater/cinema). A convenient free bus shuttles through the town, and traffic is forbidden between midnight and 6 AM. After you deliver your luggage to your hotel, you probably won't be using your car again while in town.

Don't miss the light, water, and music show on the lake at 9:50 PM every Tuesday, Friday, and Sunday from mid-June to mid-October (except in the event of heavy rain or wind).

Drop into the Egghaus, one of the oldest and best-kept buildings from Arosa's past. It was first mentioned in a 1550 document and now houses the **Schanfigger Heimatmuseum.** Besides the tools of the mountain farmer's difficult trade, this little museum has put together a slide show on local history. The museum building itself, a mid-16th century wooden farmhouse, is a sight to behold. ⊠ *Poststr., Inner-Arosa* 🕾 *081/3771731* ⊕ *www.arosa-museum.ch* 🎫*3 SF* ⊙ *Late Dec.–early Apr., Tues. and Fri. 2:30–4:30; mid-June–mid-Oct., Mon., Wed., and Fri. 2:30–4:30.*

SKIING

Arosa's ski area is small compared with those of the Upper Engadine, Davos-Klosters, and the Alpine Arena (Flims-Laax). Closely screened in by mountains, the 5,900-foot-high resort has runs suitable for every level of skier. Its 15 lifts serve 70 km (43 mi) of trails. The slopes can be accessed directly from the valley at three points: the top of the village; behind the train station; and the Prätschli, a "feeder" lift to the main ski area. The black piste on the **Weisshorn** (8,700 feet) is challenging, but most of the runs there, as well as on **Hörnli** (8,200 feet), are easy to intermediate. You can get snow-sports instruction at the official **Swiss Ski School** (🕾*081/3771150*). Another option for ski lessons is the **ABC Snowsport School** (🕾*081/3565660*). For snowboarding lessons, try **Swiss Ski and Snowboard School** (🕾*081/3787500 or 081/3787505*).

Cross-country skiers or Nordic walkers will find instruction, guided tours, equipment, and information at the **Langlauf- und Schneeschuhzentrum Maran** (☎*081/3772215*), the Cross-country and Snow Shoe Center of Maran. All schools have English-speaking instructors. At press time a one-day lift ticket cost 56 SF; a six-day pass cost 259 SF (incremental increase each season likely). For cross-country skiing or snowshoeing, the Maran and Isla trails have 30 km (18 mi) of groomed trails. There are three official sled runs: Tschuggen, Prätschli, and Untersee. You can rent sleds at the train station or at **Stivetta Sport** (✉*Innere Poststr.* ☎*081/3772181* ⊕*www.aroserschlitten.ch*).

WHERE TO EAT

$–$$
SWISS

✕**Hotel-Restaurant Hold.** Set in a large chalet-style hotel, this busy family restaurant sits literally at the foot of the slopes. The menu is mostly traditional fare, including a range of *Spätzli* (little pasta dumplings) specialties—in curry sauce, or with Graubünden air-dried meat, for example—that will put an end to the greatest hunger pangs. Hardly the place for fashionistas, this is a top spot for kiddies: there are children's meals for under 10 SF, it's adjacent to the children's ski school, and it even has a small playroom. ✉*Poststr.* ☎*081/3771408* ⊟*AE, DC, MC, V* ⊘*Closed Easter–mid-June and mid-Oct.–early Dec.*

$$–$$$
FRENCH

✕**Le Bistro.** The decor fits the name, with tile floor, old French posters, dried flower bouquets hanging from the ceiling, and newspaper cuttings on the walls. The larger room is flooded with sunlight and bedecked in greenery with an immense view across the valley, yet come sundown the call from the cozier warmth of the front parlor room draws in those looking for romantic lighting and convivial chatter. The menu also leans toward French cuisine, with homemade pastry filled with oxtail and goose liver in a truffle sauce, or fried duck's liver and fig on apple chutney with fried quail's egg. For lighter fare, try the fish creations such as salmon lasagna. ✉*Hotel Cristallo, Poststr.* ☎*081/3786868* ⊟*AE, MC, V* ⊘*Closed mid-Apr.–late June and mid-Oct.–early Dec.*

WHERE TO STAY

$$–$$$

🏨**Alpensonne.** Family-owned and -run, this hotel is only about 200 yards from the ski lifts of Inner-Arosa. The public spaces are light and bright, if perhaps a little tired and worn. Faded brown curtains in the Café Stübli and carpets in the reception area could do with a change. That noted, those looking for a homey feel that is clean and comfy will not be disappointed. Guest rooms are in soft colors with lots of wood; some have showers only, and some of these are not yet tiled, so be sure to specify. Several family rooms are available, with multiple beds; the garden contains a kiddie playground. Note that rooms facing south have great views and are a good size. **Pros:** stunning views; close proximity to village and ski slopes. **Cons:** tired interiors; situated on main road through village; busy during the day, but night brings welcome reprieve as traffic is then forbidden. ✉*Poststr.* ☎*081/3771547* ⊕*www. hotelalpensonne.ch* ⟿*36 rooms, 5 apartments* ⌂*In-room: no a/c, safe, refrigerator, Ethernet (some & free). In-hotel: 2 restaurants, bar, sauna, bicycles, public Internet (free), public Wi-Fi (free), parking (free), garage (fee), some pets allowed (fee)* ⊟*AE, DC, MC, V* ⊘*Closed late Apr.– late June and mid-Oct.–early Dec.* ⦿|*BP or MAP.*

$$$$ ☷ **Arosa Kulm Hotel & Alpin Spa.** Originally a 19th-century wooden cha-
★ let, Kulm has expanded to become a full-fledged "alpine lifestyle" destination, and huge refurbishment has been carried out to ensure that
this landmark remains a cut above. The current modern structure is
sporty-luxury-hotel in style, with a large foyer warmed by a modern
fireplace and perked up by a bar. The Kulm's position on the farthest
edge of town, at the base of the slopes, is its biggest draw; from its wraparound windows you can take in acres of green hills or snowy slopes.
Guest rooms have soft prints and neutral tones; bathrooms are tile and
stone. In winter an Italian trattoria and a Thai restaurant join the main
Swiss-style restaurants. **Pros:** perfect location for views and skiing; sport
activities—putting green to bikes and sledges—for all ages; holistic spa
packages for a complete mind, body, and soul revamp. **Cons:** shopping
opportunities not as classy as this hotel merits; there is a smart-casual
dress code throughout, and black-tie is needed for HB restaurant gala
nights—come prepared. ⊠*Innere Poststr.* ☎*081/3788888* ⊕*www.
arosakulm.ch* ⇴*119 rooms, 15 suites* ♿*In-room: safe, refrigerator,
Ethernet (free), Wi-Fi (fee). In-hotel: 5 restaurants, 2 bars, 2 tennis
courts, pool, gym, spa, children's programs (ages 4–12), public Internet
(free), public Wi-Fi (fee), parking (free), garage (fee), some pets allowed
(fee)* ⊟*AE, DC, MC, V* ⊗*Closed late Sept.–early Dec. and mid-Apr.–
mid-June* ⊺⊙*BP and MAP.*

$–$$ ☷ **Sonnenhalde.** The sensor-touch heavy pine door that welcomes you
★ to this chalet-hotel garni is your first sign of the prevailing happy marriage of charm and modern comfort. Recent renovations seal this union
further. The welcoming family and small team of staff offer an energetic
and reliable service in a cozy space. The sizable light-drenched guest
rooms have wall-to-wall wood and rustic decor; thanks to moderniza-
tion, all now have en-suite showers. Some rooms easily accommodate
extra beds (for an additional fee). Tired aching muscles can be replen-
ished in the small but fortifying sauna, steam room, and relaxation area.
Pros: proximity to ski lifts and village. **Cons:** dining at the end of a long
day on the slopes requires venturing out. ⊠ *Arosa* ☎*081/3784444*
⊕*www.sonnenhalde-arosa.ch* ⇴*25 rooms* ♿*In-room: no a/c, safe,
refrigerator. In-hotel: spa, public Internet (fee), parking (free), garage
(fee), some pets allowed (free)* ⊟*AE, DC, MC, V* ⊗*Closed late Apr.–
late June and mid-Oct.–early Dec.* ⊺⊙*BP.*

$$$$ ☷ **Tschuggen Grand Hotel.** Grandiose by name, grandiose by nature—
Fodor's Choice well-heeled luxury seekers from all walks of life arrive in seventh heaven
★ as they step into the hushed, welcoming environs of this exclusive residence. There's something for everyone inside and out, yet the drive to
simply be and do nothing reaches new heights here. The lobby, lounge,
and bar are decked out with plush interiors—plump sofas allow for
some serious downtime in a congenial ambience. The famed Bergoase
spa, with striking modernistic pools, offers sensory serenity come rain,
snow, or shine. Throughout the 14-story hotel, floor-to-ceiling windows and ample balconies envelop guests in the natural beauty of the
surrounding mountains and wooded pine slopes. Inside, individually
designed guest rooms with leather bedheads, vibrant fabric accents,
and stucco ceilings are elegant; bathrooms are finished in local granite

and marble, while Molten Brown toiletries complete the experience. An extreme attention to detail seals this destination as one of the leading hotels of Switzerland. **Pros:** award-winning Bergoase spa; panoramic views; chic modern furnishings. **Cons:** unfetching stark glass-and-concrete exterior; perfection always comes at a cost. ⊠ *Arosa* ☎ *081/ 3789999* ⊕ *www.tschuggen.ch* ⌕ *98 rooms, 32 suites* ⟁ *In-Room: safe, refrigerator, Ethernet (free). In-hotel: 5 restaurants, bar, 2 pools, gym, spa, bicycles, children's programs (ages 3 up), public Wi-Fi (free), parking (free), garage (fee), some pets allowed (fee)* ⊟ *AE, DC, MC, V* ⊙ *Closed mid-April–mid-June* ⅼ◎ⅼ*BP, MAP.*

$$$ ⬚ **Waldhotel National.** Hallowed as the hotel where Thomas Mann wrote part of his famous *Magic Mountain*—back in the early 1900s this was a "cure-hotel" for ailing patients—this large, chalet-inspired retreat is set in its own wooded grounds above Arosa. Peace is everywhere, intoxicatingly enjoyed as you ski or sled your way home in winter. North-facing guest rooms look over the forest, and south-facing ones look over the village and the mountains. All are tastefully decorated and have touches of golden pine. The Kachelofa-Stübli serves local and French specialties. Hotel residents enjoy their meals in the airy and very popular Thomas Mann Restaurant (reservations essential); in winter season the Käse Hütte *(cheese hut)* restaurant is added. **Pros:** great location for the slopes; the peace, views, and Arosa itself; delicious food; family-friendly. **Cons:** wellness area a little cramped; some rooms could be updated. ⊠ *Arosa* ☎ *081/3785555* ⊕ *www.waldhotel. ch* ⌕ *79 rooms, 14 suites* ⟁ *In-room: no a/c, safe, refrigerator, Wi-Fi (fee). In-hotel: 2 restaurants, bar, pool, gym, spa, bicycles, children's programs (ages 3 up), public Internet (free), public Wi-Fi (fee), some pets allowed (fee)* ⊟ *AE, DC, MC, V* ⊙ *Closed mid-Apr.–mid-June and mid-Sept.–early Dec.* ⅼ◎ⅼ*MAP.*

NIGHTLIFE & THE ARTS

BARS   At the Hotel Eden, the **Kitchen Club** (⊠ *Jory-Jenny-Str.* ☎ *081/3787100*) is a disco inside a kitchen dating back to 1907. A young crowd dances among old pots and pans while the DJ perches above antique refrigerators. The après-ski crowd here is chic—you should change out of your ski bibs first. In the casino, **Nuts** (⊠ *Poststr.* ☎ *081/3773940*) plays the latest tunes for young people. For a more discolike experience, the **Gada Dancing** (☎ *081/3771766*) in the Hotel Carmenna plays tunes from the '70s and '80s in a refurbished stable.

MUSIC   From Christmas to mid-April and in summer, concerts are given at 5 PM on Tuesday on the hand-painted organ in Arosa's 500-year-old, wooden-roof **Bergkirchli** *(mountain chapel)*. A jazz festival takes place in July, and music courses are given from June through October; get the program from **Kulturkreis Arosa** (⊠ *Poststr.* ☎ *081/3538747*).

SPORTS & THE OUTDOORS

GOLF   Europe's highest tee (6,209 feet) is on the eighth hole of Arosa's 18-hole course at **Maran** (☎ *081/3774242*).

HIKING &   The **Arosa tourist office** (☎ *081/378–7020*) can arrange four-day walking
BIKING   or biking trips from Davos to Arosa.

SKATING &   Arosa has several skating rinks. At the indoor **Eissporthalle** (☎ *081/3771745*)
CURLING   you can watch ice hockey as well as take skating or curling lessons;
            there's an open-air rink alongside. Another option is the **InnerArosa rink**
            (☎ *081/3772930*), which is open from Christmas to mid-February.

PRÄTTIGAU & DAVOS

The name "Prättigau" means "meadow valley," and it's just that—
a lush landscape of alternating orchards, pastures, and pine-covered
mountains (though the main highway is a very busy route). The predominant language is German, introduced by "immigrants" from the
Valais in the 13th century, though most villages still have Romansh
names. Prättigau's most renowned ski resort is Klosters. Its equally
famous neighbor and ski-region partner, Davos, lies in the Landwasser
Valley, over the Wolfgang Pass. If you prefer an urban experience, head
to Davos; for a quieter village experience, look to Klosters.

KLOSTERS

49 km (29 mi) east of Chur.

GETTING HERE

The Rhätische Bahn (RhB), or a combination of Swiss railways and
the RhB, covers the distance in around one hour from Chur for 20 SF
one-way.

Visitor Information (✉ *Alte Bahnhofstr. 6* ☎ *081/4102020* ⊕ *www.klosters.ch*).

EXPLORING

At one time simply a group of hamlets, Klosters has become a small
but chic resort, made up mostly of weathered-wood and white-stucco
chalets. Author Peter Viertel and his wife, film luminary Deborah Kerr,
made this their home base for decades. The village has two districts:
Platz, which is older and busier, and Dorf, which lies on the main road
toward Landquart. Klosters is famed for its skiing—British royal family
members are faithful visitors—and makes the most of its access to the
slopes of the Parsenn, above Davos.

In Klosters Platz the church of **St. Jacob**, dating from 1492, is the only
remnant of the medieval monastery from which the village took its
name. Its windows were painted by Augusto Giacometti.

A brief visit to the folk museum **Nutli-Hüschi** shows the resort's evolution from its mountain roots. This pretty wood-and-stone farmhouse
with a stable was built in 1565. It shows how people lived and worked
in the Prättigau in centuries past through exhibits of kitchen utensils,
handcrafts, tools, and the spare regional furniture, including a child's
bed that could be expanded as the child grew. ✉ *Monbielerstr. at Tal-*
str. ☎ *081/4102020* ⬚ *3 SF* ☉ *Dec.–mid-Apr. and late June–mid-Oct.,*
Wed. and Fri. 3–5.

SKIING

Klosters is known for its vast range of downhill runs, which, together with those of Davos, total 320 km (200 mi). These are divided almost equally among easy, moderate, and difficult pistes. From the Gotschnagrat (7,494 feet), skiers can connect to the Parsenn slopes, and try, for example, the famous Weissflüh run down to the village of Küblis. The sunny Madrisa slopes above Klosters Dorf offer relatively easy skiing and snowboarding. For instruction or to go on a snowshoe trek, contact the **Swiss Ski & Snowboard School** (☎*081/4102828*), which has branches in both Platz and Dorf. The **Swiss Ski & Snowboard School Saas** (☎*081/4226660*), located near the train station in Klosters Platz, also offers the standard instruction plus special courses in carving, slalom skiing, and more; it has branches in both Platz and Dorf. There are 35 km (22 mi) of cross-country tracks, and you can get lessons at the **Nordic Ski School** (☎*081/4221040*). Lift tickets to the combined Davos/Klosters area cost 65 SF for one day and up to 282 SF for six days, depending on how many and in which areas you want to ski. Bar-code cards and KeyCards are used; you can activate them online (⊕*www.davosklosters.ch*). Train or bus transport back to Klosters from other villages within the ski area is included in the price of the regional ski ticket.

> ### UP, DOWN & AROUND
>
> With Davos and hyper-ritzy St. Moritz, Graubünden is one hot winter spot, noted for its downhill skiing and snowboarding, as well as miles of *Langlauf* (cross-country skiing) trails. You can participate in moonlight or torchlight skiing, usually followed by a get-together with fellow travelers. Sports shops can outfit you with equipment; in Davos and Flims-Laax you can even rent ski clothing. If you want to spend a day in a different resort within Graubünden, buy the lift ticket with your train ticket and the return fare will be just 1 SF.

WHERE TO EAT

$$–$$$
SWISS
Fodor's Choice
★

✕**Restaurant Gotschna** A homey rustic eatery slightly outside Klosters offers up traditional Swiss fodder for the whole family without the need for fuss or fanfare. Stone-clad floors and wall-to-ceiling *Arvenholz* (traditional pinewood interior of the region) decor ensconce you in the warmth and comfort of a true mountain abode. A straightforward menu of Bündner (the shorthand term for Graubünden) specialties is available. Rösti and fondue followed by homemade cakes or apple strudel while sitting among historic pictures and under ceiling lamps (romantically set low over each table) work wonders on the soul—it is all somehow reminiscent of a replenishing family gathering at the kitchen hearth. There is free parking and a garden to enjoy in the summer months. ✉*Serneuserstr., Serneus (5 km/ 3 mi north of Klosters)* ☎*081/4221428* ▭*AE, DC, MC, V* ☺*Closed Mon. and mid-Nov.–week after Easter and mid-Jun.–end-Oct.*

$–$$
SWISS

✕**Restaurant Höhwald.** This is a friendly, touristy restaurant up the hill from Klosters in Monbiel, with a large, open terrace that takes in valley and mountain views. The imposing timber-clad building stands proud in this majestic setting, and close by is a noted cross-country track.

As for the food, there is a wide selection of dishes to choose from, but be sure to try their Graubünden specialties, for example Capuns, Prättigauer *Knödlis (dumplings)*, and *Chäs-Gatschäder (a mixture of bread, milk, and cheese)*. Inside, decor runs to mounted animal trophies and old-world exposed beams; outside a breathtaking mountainscape enchants all eyes. ⊠ *Monbielerstr. 171, Klosters-Monbiel* ☎ *081/4223045* ⊟ *AE, DC, MC, V* ⊘ *Closed Tues. and mid-Apr.–May and mid-Oct.–mid-Dec.*

WHERE TO STAY

$$$–$$$$

Fodor's Choice
★

🛏 **Romantik Hotel Chesa Grischuna.** Located directly in the town center, this is one of Klosters' hotel landmarks, once patronized by the likes of Greta Garbo and Audrey Hepburn. Renovated from a farmhouse in 1938, the Grischuna has one of the most charming settings in Switzerland, beginning with its lobby graced by Swiss paintings, a regal pinewood Baroque ceiling, and folk antiques everywhere. As Klosters is a gathering place of international society, this place has plenty of public salons to accommodate the guests, and whether you bowl in the vaulted cellar, play cards, or dance to the piano music at happy hour you'll be surrounded by the coveted social mix of Klosters cognoscenti. Every guest room, including those in the nearby chalet annex, is full of old carved wood and antiques; some have balconies. The restaurant is legendary for its chic Gemütlichkeit, with carved-wood trim, romantic lighting, and a delicious mix of salads, snacks, and full-fledged meals at affordable prices. **Pros:** full of character and vibrant eclectic social scene; famed restaurant. **Cons:** rooms are small and can surprise those used to space; on busy through road in town center. ⊠ *Bahnhofstr. 12, Klosters-Platz* ☎ *081/4222222* ⊕ *www.chesagrischuna.ch* 🛏 *23 rooms, 19 with bath* ☾ *In-room: no a/c. In-hotel: restaurant, bar, public Wi-Fi (free), parking (free), garage (fee), some pets allowed (fee)* ⊟ *AE, DC, MC, V* ⊘ *Closed mid-Apr–end-June and end-Oct.–start-Dec.* ⦿ *BP.*

$$$

🛏 **Rustico.** Good things come in small packages here—guest rooms are on a petite scale but are very attractive, with parquet floors, country cottons, and white-tile showers. The lounge area has a fireplace and leads out to a summer terrace dominated by a Buddha. The restaurant (closed Wednesday in summer) is white-walled and brightened with regional artwork. It serves Euro-Asian dishes created in-house, such as fresh sushi and sashimi or lamb shanks Asian-style. After-dinner cigars are also on offer and can be enjoyed across the road in the new It's Bar. In winter many repair to the Walserhaus, a 266-year-old chalet that offers delicious traditional cheese and meat dishes. **Pros:** award-winning cuisine; enchanting personal hospitality. **Cons:** rooms are extremely small; there is no spa or sauna. ⊠ *Landstr. 194, Klosters-Platz* ☎ *081/4102288* ⊕ *www.rusticohotel.com* 🛏 *10 rooms, 2 suites* ☾ *In-room: no a/c, safe, refrigerator, Wi-Fi (fee). In-hotel: 2 restaurants, 2 bars, public Wi-Fi (fee), parking (free)* ⊟ *AE, DC, MC, V* ⊘ *Closed May–mid-June and 2 weeks in Nov.* ⦿ *BP.*

$–$$

Fodor's Choice
★

🛏 **Silvapina.** This delightful hotel in an old chalet-style building is family-run and family-welcoming. It is right by the station (trains don't run at night) and a few minutes' walk from the slopes. Guest rooms are done either all in wood or in white with touches of pine; south-facing rooms have balconies and are bright, clean, and airy. Apartments have small kitchens and fireplaces and are well kitted out for small families. Note that bathrooms have showers instead of tubs. The communal area and garden are homey and informal, with games for old and young. **Pros:** comfy and clean budget accommodation for families; 4-min walk to Madrisa cable car. **Cons:** next to train track, which can be distracting in the day; dated and tired dining area. ☒*Klosters-Dorf CH-7252* ☎*081/4221468* ⊕*www.silvapina.ch* ⇆*22 rooms, 5 apartments* ⚷*In-room: no a/c, kitchen (some), refrigerator (some), Wi-Fi (some). In-hotel: restaurant, bar, tennis court, sauna, public Internet terminal (free)* ☰*AE, MC, V* ☉*Third week Apr.–early June and Oct–early Dec.* ⍾*BP, MAP.*

$$$–$$$$ ⚏**Walserhof.** The most sophisticated establishment in Klosters, Walser-
★ hof was built in 1981 with the weathered boards from an old farm-house. Run by famed Swiss chef Armin Amrein and his discreet yet friendly wife Corina, the hotel and restaurant continue to draw refined, well-heeled patrons. Its restaurant and café are paneled with ancient carved wood; stone, stucco, and quarry tile are used elsewhere. From the intimate lounge with an open fire through such personal touches as the bed-turning in the evening make this venue a treasure. The superb Michelin star restaurant serves not only regional dishes but fresh, new creations such as cappuccino of curry and lemongrass with a spring roll and curry ice-cream, or veal cheek on a duck-liver parfait with celery-truffle puree. **Pros:** delicious food and outstanding wine list; relaxed personal service, yet intimate and discreet. **Cons:** location on main road heading out of village; some rooms have little space to move around in. ☒*Landstr. 141* ☎*081/4102929* ⊕*www.walserhof.ch* ⇆*11 rooms, 3 suites* ⚷*In-room: no a/c, safe, refrigerator, Ethernet, Wi-Fi (fee). In-hotel: restaurant, bar, sauna, public Wi-Fi (fee), parking (free), garage (fee), some pets allowed (fee)* ☰*AE, DC, MC, V* ☉*Closed Easter–late June and mid-Oct.–early Dec.* ⍾*BP.*

NIGHTLIFE

Revelers dance late into the night at the **Casa Antica** (☒*Landstr. 176* ☎*081/4221621*), in a 300-year-old converted barn. A popular after-dinner spot, **Chesa Bar** (☒*Bahnhofstr. 12* ☎*081/4222222*) has piano music and several intimate bar areas. In the Silvretta Parkhotel there's the **Kir Royal** (☒*Landstr. 190* ☎*081/4233435*) disco and a piano bar.

SPORTS & THE OUTDOORS

BIKING & The Klosters area has plenty of trails for exploring the countryside.
HIKING The 250 km (155 mi) of summer hiking routes are reduced to 30 km (19 mi) of prepared paths in winter. There are 120 km (74½ mi) of mountain-biking routes. To rent mountain bikes, try the **Hew Bike Shop** (☒*Klosters-Dorf* ☎*081/4223942*). Another source for mountain bikes is **Andrist Sport** (☒*Klosters-Platz* ☎*081/4102080*).

GOLF Not to be outdone by its neighbors, Klosters has also added a rela-tively tough 9-hole **Golf Klosters** (☎*081/4221133* ⊕*www.golf-klosters. ch* ☉*May–end Oct.*) with a unique feature: the caddy is included in the

greens fee. The seventh hole provides the additional handicap of a
jaw-dropping view of Klosters.

SKATING   Klosters's **Sportszentrum** (✉*Dog-*
gilochstr. 51, Klosters-Platz ☎*081/*
4102131) has rinks for skating,
hockey, curling, and ice bowling in
season. Skate rentals are available.

SLEDDING   Klosters is big on sledding. The
area has four sled runs: the 3.5-km
(2-mi) Rinerhorn run is also illuminated at night. A day card costs SF
47, while a sled can be rented for
SF 10 at the cable-car valley station
with a 50-franc deposit. Evening
runs on the lighted slope are 7–11

**THE FRESH AIR JUST
GOT FRESHER**

On March 1, 2008, Graubünden
became the third no-smoking
canton in Switzerland. Three-
quarters of the natives in this
canton voted for new laws to ban
smoking in public places; hotels,
restaurants, bars, and nightclubs
are allowed a designated smoking room should they wish it. This
trend is being followed by other
cantons throughout Switzerland,
as it is worldwide.

PM from January to March. They cost SF 20 for an evening. Schatzalp
to Davos Platz and Davos Dorf (⊕ *www.davos.ch/tobogganing-001-*
000203-en.htm). Day cards at Madrisa mountain cost SF 33. The run
here is 8.5 km long (5 mi) and ends in Saas, from which you can return
by bus to Klosters (buses leave every hour or so until 7:24 PM). Sled
rentals at the Madrisa cable-car station are SF 8. The fourth sled run
begins at the midway station of the Gotschna cable car. Day passes
cost SF 33; sled rentals at the station cost SF 10. Sleds are available for
rental at **Andrist Sport** (✉*Klosters-Platz* ☎*081/4102080*). **Sport Gotschna**
(✉*Klosters-Platz* ☎*081/4221197*) also rents sleds.

SWIMMING   The town's heated **outdoor swimming pool** (✉*Doggilochstr.* ☎*081/4221524*)
is open all summer. The indoor pool at the **Hotel Sport** (☎*081/4233030*)
has a wall of windows. The 14-meter indoor pool at the **Silvretta Parkhotel**
(☎*081/4233435*) is open to the public as well.

DAVOS

11 km (7 mi) southwest of Klosters.

GETTING HERE
To go to Chur or Zürich (51 SF one-way, 2½ hrs), change trains at
Landquart. For St. Moritz, take the train from Davos Platz and transfer
at Filisur. If heading to Scuol, train it from Davos Dorf and transfer
in Klosters. The Vereina tunnel provides year-round train service from
Klosters to Sagliains, near Susch–Lavin. Car-carrying trains leave from
just above Klosters—road signs indicate a train carrying cars and the
name Vereina—at 20 past and 10 to the hour between 7 AM and 10 PM.
The first passenger train is at 5:20 AM. Prices vary according to season.
A passenger car costs 27 SF in summer, 35 SF in winter, and 40 SF during the peak winter season from mid-December to mid-March during
daylight hours.

Visitor Information (✉*Promenade 67* ☎*081/4152121* ⊕*www.davos.ch*).

EXPLORING

At 5,116 feet, this highest "city" in Europe is good for cold-weather sports even in the soggiest of winters. It's famous for its ice sports and skiing, and almost more celebrated for hosting the annual World Economic Forum every January. The town and its lake lie in the Landwasser Valley, which runs parallel to the Upper Engadine, though they're separated by the vast Albula chain, reaching to more than 9,840 feet. On the opposite side of the valley stands the Strela chain, dominated by the Weissfluhgipfel.

Take note: this is a capital for action-oriented sports enthusiasts and not necessarily for anyone seeking a peaceful, rustic mountain retreat (especially at the end of December, when there's an invasion of ice-hockey fans for the international Spengler Cup). Davos is divided into the Platz and the Dorf (village), which together are one noisier-than-average urban strip, though Dorf is calmer. The town's first visitors came to take cures for lung diseases in the bracing mountain air. Now, except for a few token historic structures and brightly painted buildings, the town is modern and architecturally undistinguished, and the center of town can be filled with the exhaust of city traffic. But no matter how densely populated and fast-paced the town becomes, the slopes are still spectacular and the regulars return.

Davos was once famous as a retreat for people suffering from respiratory problems, such as tuberculosis. It was the inspiration for Thomas Mann's novel *The Magic Mountain*. The **Museum of Medicine**, which exhibits old-fashioned medical equipment, recalls the days when the streets were lined with spittoons. ⊠ *Platzstr. 1, Davos-Platz* ☎ *081/4135210* ☜ *3 SF* ☉ *Thurs. 5–7, and by appointment.*

Among the town's few architectural highlights, the late-Gothic **Kirche St. Johann** *(Church of St. John the Baptist)* stands out by virtue of its windows by Augusto Giacometti. Nearby is the 17th-century Rathaus (Town Hall). ⊠ *Rathausstutz 2.*

The **Kirchner Museum** boasts the world's largest collection of works by the German artist Ernst Ludwig Kirchner, whose off-kilter lines and unnerving compositions inspired the Expressionist movement. He traveled to Davos in 1917 for health reasons and stayed until his death in 1938. ⊠ *Promenade 82, Davos-Platz* ☎ *081/4106300* ⊕ *www.kirchner museum.ch* ☜ *10 SF* ☉ *Easter–mid-July and Oct.–Christmas, Tues.–Sun. 2–6; mid-July–Sept. and Christmas–Easter, Tues.–Sun. 10–6.*

The **Wintersportmuseum** has a collection of equipment from sleds to ski bindings. ⊠ *Promenade 43, Davos-Platz* ☎ *081/4132484* ⊕ *www.winter sportmuseum.ch* ☜ *5 SF* ☉ *Late June–mid-Oct., Tues. and Thurs. 4:30–6:30; Dec.–Apr., Tues., Thurs., and Sat. 4:30–6:30.*

SKIING

Davos can accommodate some 24,000 visitors on 325 km (202 mi) of runs. The steepish slopes of the **Parsenn-Gotschna** are accessed from town by the Parsenn funicular. For an alternative, try the **Rinerhorn,** a 15-minute ride by bus or train. Here the slopes lead to the hamlet of

Glaris, 7 km (4½ mi) from Davos. A must for the skilled skier is the descent from **Weissfluhgipfel** (9,330 feet) to **Küblis,** in the Prättigau. This magnificent, 13-km (8-mi) piste has a vertical drop of 6,560 feet and is classified as difficult at the top but moderate for most of its length. A real challenge for experts is the three-hour tour across the mountains to Arosa—which requires a guide and good weather conditions. An easy 2-km (1-mi) run is No. 11, the Meierhofer Tälli, which Davosers renamed the Hillary Clinton run, as it's her favorite here. **Jakobshorn,** a ski and snowboard area on the west-facing side, is reached by cable car and lift from Davos-Platz. The **Pischa** ski area, on the Flüela Pass road, is a free-ride paradise, and especially suitable for children and families—as is the **Bünda** slope in Davos-Dorf.

Lift tickets to the combined Davos–Klosters area cost 65 SF for one day, 282 SF for six days, and include transport between the ski areas. The **Snowsports School Davos** (⊠ *Promenade 157, Davos-Dorf* ☎ *081/4162454* ⊕ *www.ssd.ch*) gives skiing, cross-country, snowboard, and telemark lessons. If you need to get outfitted for skiing, including clothing, go to **PaarSenn** (⊠ *Promenade 159, Davos-Dorf* ☎ *081/4101013*). For the expert skier (freestyle, off-piste, and the like), the place to go is **Top Secret Snowboard and Freeski School and Shop** (⊠ *Brämabüelstr. 11, Davos-Platz* ☎ *081/4132040* ⊕ *www. topsecretdavos.ch*).

There are more than 75 km (47 mi) of prepared cross-country ski trails, for which there is no charge. The **Cross Country Ski School** (☎ *081/4162454* ⊕ *www.ssd.ch*) is in Davos-Dorf.

WHERE TO EAT

$–$$
SPANISH

✕ **Bar-Bistro Angelo.** If you have had enough Bündner specialties, try this restaurant, which doubles as a shop selling wines and spirits, pasta, and honey. The menu changes every few days depending on what produce is available. Simple chalkboard fare is the order of the day, yet vibrant artwork, live music from the piano, and a well-stocked bar create a cool, modern feel. Fresh- and saltwater fish are the specialty here, as are affordable prices. A fiery and fun Spanish evening serving up paella, with live Spanish music accompanying, for 28 SF per person is provided through February and March. Take-away is also possible. ⊠ *Promenade 119, Davos-Platz* ☎ *081/4137101* ⊟ *AE, DC, MC, V* ⊙ *Closed Sat.–Sun. 10:30–1:30* PM *in summer and closed Sun. at 4* PM *in winter.*

$$
SWISS AND
FRENCH
★

✕ **Bistro Gentiana.** A cozy bistro and number one in the region for fondues, this "café des artistes" dates back to the late 1880s, when it served as the town firehouse. Given an "art deco" overhaul, this is now a long-standing haunt for those seeking out snails, regional mushrooms, and age-old recipes for cheese and meat fondues. A convivial atmosphere with regional wines and cigars makes for a relaxed lunch or dinner. Cheese lovers should try the "Creation Gentiana" for two to four people. There is also a children's menu. Note there are two dinner services—if you don't want to be hurried out, reserve for the later 8:30 sitting. ⊠ *Promenade 53, CH-7270 Davos-Platz* ☎ *081/4135649* ⊟ *AE, DC, MC, V* ⊙ *Closed Weds. in summer.*

CLOSE UP

Inspiring Graubünden

Nietzsche's famous philosophical work *Thus Spoke Zarathustra* opens its second part with Zarathustra returning to the mountains "to seek the solitude of his cave." While the author's thinking may have been abstract, the cave and the mountains were probably quite real. For it was in Sils Maria, near St. Moritz, in the summer of 1883, that Nietzsche began writing this lengthy treatise on man and superman. His fundamental concept of recurrence came to him during a walk around nearby Silverplaner Lake.

For those seeking inspiration, Graubünden has always been a natural high. Countless artistic personalities have come to the canton for rest and relaxation and left with some great work of literature or art in their bags (or at least their heads, waiting to be created). Something in the clarity of the air and proximity to the sky seems to dispel all the cares and worries of the daily grind and set creative juices flowing.

For some, like Marcel Proust, it was the "bracing air, the aroma of hay and the sound of the brooks." For others, such as Hermann Hesse, the "powerful, severe beauty" of the mountains around Arosa provided the vim and vigor to edit his novel about religion and salvation, *Narcissus and Goldmund.* (He had been immobilized by a skiing accident, making it easier to devote himself to his work.) Nietzsche, for his part, felt he had arrived in the "Promised Land" on his first trip to the Engadine in 1879.

The gentle meadows and mysterious, aromatic forests of pine embraced by rugged snow-tipped mountains have all done their part to enthrall visitors. Goethe, Germany's greatest poet and

writer, traveled through the hair-raising Via Mala gorge on his way back from Italy and had to stop for a while to draw some sketches of the almost eerie sights. Decades later he recalled the trip: "The road over the Splügen mountains is indescribably beautiful, the Via Mala is the most frightening rocky pass in all of Switzerland."

Perhaps a similar thrill was felt by Robert Louis Stevenson when he came to vacation in Davos during the winter season of 1881–82. What the foggy and damp landscape of his native Scotland failed to do, Graubünden accomplished, enabling him to finish *Treasure Island.*

Davos also sparked the imagination of novelist Thomas Mann. In June 1912 he accompanied his wife, Katja, on a cure in the comfortable, Belle-Epoque rooms of the Schatzalp sanatorium. There he saw the first outlines of his novel *The Magic Mountain,* symbolizing Europe and its political and social choices: either to bask in illness and submit to death, or to choose life and social commitment.

Needless to say, his depiction of such an indolent society living in a morbid expectation of death—"flirting and taking their temperature"—did not please the people of Davos, whose community had made a name for itself as a serious spa for curing, or at least alleviating, tuberculosis.

The fame of *The Magic Mountain,* however, has long made up for any acrimony, and now healthy and positive-minded guests can stay at the Schatzalp, which has become a fine hotel.

WHERE TO STAY

$$–$$$ ⌂ **ArtHausHotel Quisisana.** This old symmetrical and sober building hued in a striking red seems to exude a mysterious pull. Inside, the walls are brightened by lively abstract paintings. The artist, Diego do Clavadetscher—who goes by the *nom d'artiste* Diegodo—is, in fact, the owner and manager (he also painted the facade). Here and there you'll find little minimalist touches—an ensemble of stones in an alcove, for example. Creative, freewheeling, relaxing, the hotel's guest rooms are fully functional, yet little works of art unto themselves. **Pros:** unique and quirky, with original art throughout; owner/artist welcomes guests with personal service. **Cons:** not a high-style hotel with requisite amenities; no sauna or aprés-ski facilities. ⊠ *Platzstr. 5, Davos-Platz* ☎ *081/4100510* ⊕ *www.arthaushotel.ch* ⊷ *19 rooms* ⌂ *In-room: no a/c, Wi-Fi (some & free). In-hotel: restaurant, bar, public Wi-Fi (free), parking (free), garage in winter (free)* ⊟ *AE, DC, MC, V* ⦿ *BP, MAP.*

$$–$$$ ⌂ **Bünda Davos.** This hotel, though not a very pretty building, is perfectly located right by the beginners' ski slope, the children's slope, and a ski school branch, as well as on the cross-country ski track. In addition, the Parsenn cable car is only a few minutes' walk. Guest rooms in the main building are small, some with showers instead of a tub, and two share a bathroom. Larger, more expensive rooms are in an annex, connected to the hotel by an underground passage. Moms and dads will note the good-sized garden with children's play area and large sun terrace. **Pros:** direct access to beginner and kids' skiing; great for families. **Cons:** slightly outside the center; not most characterful of places. ⊠ *Museumstr. 4, Davos-Dorf* ☎ *081/4171819* ⊕ *www.buenda davos.ch* ⊷ *41 rooms* ⌂ *In-room: no a/c, safe, refrigerator (some). In-hotel: restaurant, public Internet (free), Wi-Fi (free), parking (free), some pets allowed (fee)* ⊟ *MC, V* ⊙ *Closed mid-Apr.–May and mid-Oct.–Nov.* ⦿ *BP.*

$$$–$$$$
Fodor'sChoice
★   ⌂ **Schatzalp.** About 950 feet above town on a quiet, car-free slope, this spectacular hotel will transport you back to the grand spa days of Davos. It served once as a sanatorium and is described in Mann's *Magic Mountain*. The entire hotel is decorated in elegant Belle Epoque style, but many salons have now been given striking modern touches, such as exotic fabrics and contemporary furnishings. The vast hotel has grounds to match, and they include such fun-friendly features like a long hillside slide in summer and a sled run in winter. All south-facing guest rooms have balconies overlooking the looming mountain range, offering awe-inspiring vistas that are pure magic under snow; these views can also be savored from a table in the elegant Panorama restaurant. Spend summer afternoons enjoying the breeze on the long veranda or visiting the hotel's botanical garden, featuring high-altitude plants from five continents. Alternatively, join the weekly *Zauberberg Nacht*—a "Magic Mountain Night" open-air re-enactment evening harking back to the sanatorium days. The hotel is accessible only by its own funicular, the Schatzalp-Bahn, a 4-min ride from Davos-Platz near the Hotel Europe. **Pros:** Unique peaceful location; historic charm of building; boundless activities for all ages. **Cons:** those seeking fantastically appointed amenities in rooms may be disappointed. ⊠ *Schatzalp,*

Davos-Platz ☎*081/4155151* ⊕*www.schatzalp.ch* ⇨*92 rooms, Villa Guarda and Chalet.* &*In-room: no a/c, no TV (some), Wi-Fi (free). In-hotel: 2 restaurants, bar, pool, sauna, public Internet (free), Wi-Fi (free), parking (free), garage (fee), some pets allowed (fee)* ⊟*AE, DC, MC, V* ¶◎*|MAP* ☉*Closed Apr. and Nov.*

$$$$ ⊞**Steigenberger Belvéderè.** With its neoclassical stone fireplace, wedding-cake white plaster, and period details, this is a grand hotel in every sense of the word. The enormous white building with south-facing balconies is just above the main street. Guest rooms are decorated in woods ranging from rustic Arvenholz to classic mahogany. If it's cold outside, the murals of tropical birds and plants around the pool provide a comforting illusion. Special packages for sports, the great outdoors, and culture lovers are offered. There's a handy shuttle service to and from local environs. **Pros:** central location; outstanding concierge and personal service; half board is a nice way to ease up on the stiff prices. **Cons:** if you have to ask how much it costs…; reception area is chaotic at times. ⊠*Promenade 89, Davos-Platz* ☎*081/4156000* ⊕*www. davos.steigenberger.com* ⇨*97 rooms, 30 suites* &*In-room: no a/c, safe, refrigerator, Ethernet, Wi-Fi (fee). In-hotel: 3 restaurants, bar, pool, spa, public Internet (fee), public Wi-Fi (fee), parking (free), garage (fee), pets (fee)* ⊟*AE, DC, MC, V* ☉*Closed mid Apr.–mid-Jun. and mid-Oct.–mid-Nov.* ¶◎*|BP and MAP.*

NIGHTLIFE & THE ARTS

BARS In the Hotel Europe, the **Ex Bar** (⊠*Promenade 63, Davos-Platz* ☎*081/4154141*) is where hipsters gather to listen to DJ music.

CASINO The bright, glassed-in **Casino** (⊠*Hotel Europe, Promenade 63, Davos-Platz* ☎*081/4154141*) is one of the meeting places for *le tout Davos*, as it were. It opens at 2 PM daily and does not require formal dress.

DANCING The **Cabanna Club** (⊠*Promenade 63, Davos-Platz* ☎*081/4154141*) lures an energetic crowd with techno music—"scene-iors" usually head to the "Cava" (located under the Cabanna) to find more appropriate acoustic fare. The **Pöstli Club** (⊠*Promenade 42, Davos-Platz* ☎*081/4154500*) is a winter-only institution with a dance floor and music ranging from rock to folk and pop. In the Hotel Davoserhof, the **Rotliechtli Music Club** (⊠*Berglistutz 1, Davos-Platz* ☎*081/4149443*) attracts a young—or at least young at heart—crowd with somewhat traditional tastes in music.

MUSIC The annual Young Artists in Concert festival (⊕*www.davosfestival.ch*) is held from mid-July to early August. Young musicians from all over the world practice and perform in churches and in the Congress Center.

SPORTS & THE OUTDOORS

HIKING & Davos is threaded with more than 450 km (280 mi) of well-marked trails
BIKING perfect for hiking or biking in winter and summer. Mountain bikes can be rented at the train station or at **Ettinger Sport** (⊠*Talstr. 6, Davos-Platz* ☎*081/4135410* ⊠*Promenade 61, Davos-Platz* ☎*081/4106161*).

<table>
<tr><td>SAILING &
WINDSURFING</td><td>Sailing and windsurfing are popular on Davos Lake, where there's always a stiff breeze blowing. To rent boats or take a lesson with a sailing school, call **Segelschule Davosersee** (☎*0765663130* ⊕*www. davossail.ch*). **Hans-Martin Heierling** (☎*076/5663130*) offers lessons and rents boats as well.</td></tr>
<tr><td>SKATING</td><td>Davos has a long reputation as an important ice-sports center, with its enormous **Sports Center Davos** (✉*Talstr. 41* ☎*081/4153672*) and speed-skating rink, the biggest natural ice track in Europe. The Ice Stadium maintains one indoor and two outdoor rinks; rental skates are available.</td></tr>
</table>

THE LOWER ENGADINE

Like Dorothy landing in Oz, you may find your sudden arrival in this, the most picturesque and novel of Graübunden's many valleys, something of a shock. You'll hear people talk of *Schellenursli* (a legendary munchkin of a little boy with a bell), and there's even a sort of Scarecrow—on the *Hom Strom* holiday on the first day of March the children of Scuol make a figure out of hay to burn the winter away. Festivals and folklore abound, as do dense, fairy-tale forests and quaint village settings. "Allegra!" is the proper greeting on the street, reflecting the Romansh language and Latinate culture that have developed without obstruction here. The Roman roots of the region are also demonstrated in the houses—typically squat stucco bungalows with deep Etruscan-arch doors, thick Mediterranean walls, and sunken windows. Houses are large, with thick walls to keep the warmth in and the cold out. Windows are small, but the frames taper outward to let in as much light as possible. The outer walls are decorated using the *sgrafitto* technique—a signature of the Engadine (produced by whitewashing a layer of dark stucco, with symbols scraped in the paint—usually, the name of the original builder appears with a quote or a poem, and the extent and quality of the sgraffiti suggests the wealth and station of the owner). The Lower Engadine—more enclosed than its upper counterpart—shares the region's dry, crisp "champagne" climate.

GUARDA

★ *37 km (23 mi) east of Davos.*

The former main road through the Inn valley (Engadine) was higher up on the slopes than today's road. It passed through Guarda, one of a pleasant chain of small villages that includes Ardez and Ftan. Each has fine sgraffitied homes, but Guarda, where the architecture is government-protected, is particularly well suited for a leisurely exploration along its ancient cobbled streets. The dark-on-light etchings on the facades (contrasting sharply with the bright flowers on the windowsills) draw pedestrians from one photo op to the next. As its name implies, Guarda ("watch") sits high on a hillside looking out over the valley and the peaks to the south, which reach up to 9,840 feet.

CLOSE UP

The Bells of Chalandamarz

Old Man Winter is an especially tough customer in Graubünden, but the locals, going back to Roman days, have a one-day festival to spook him out of his snowshoes and send him packing. On March 1 the youngest schoolchildren (six- to eight-year-olds) gather in the village squares of the Engadine and many other towns and villages in other valleys to celebate Chalandamarz. The name derives from the Latin *calendae martius*, literally the March calendar. Dressed in traditional costumes, the girls with a riot of silk and paper flowers in their hair, the children march through the villages ringing bells of all sizes (known as *talocs*) and singing songs. In the old days they would stop at houses to collect food or other gifts that would be brought home to the families. Now cash is the preferred gift, used to fund the evening Chalandamarz dances.

The Chalandamarz procession in Guarda is special for two reasons. First, it takes place on the last day of February and only boys participate. Secondly, the town is the setting for the story "Schellenursli" ("A Bell for Ursli"), written by Selina Chönz with wonderful illustrations by Alois Carigiet. It tells of a young and poor goatherd named Ursli who, after many trials and tribulations, acquires the largest bell in town and is allowed to lead the procession. Within Switzerland, Schellenursli is as well known as Heidi. Graubünden has several Schellenursli trails. The one in St. Moritz, oddly, leads up to the "Heidihütte" where the 1970s TV series was shot.

WHERE TO STAY & EAT

$$–$$$
SWISS
★

Meisser. This picturesque, family-owned hotel, made up of three ancient farmhouses, has sgraffiti and flower boxes on the outside, antiques and honey-color pine inside. The former hay barn and woodshed are now a luxurious restaurant serving tasty dishes such as chamois with a walnut crust and elderberry sauce or *Lamm auf Alpenheu* (lamb simmered in aromatic local Alpine grasses); in summer an adjacent garden eatery opens. Guest rooms are simple and modern, though you can have a splendid carved-pine room if you pay a bit more. An adjacent, renovated 17th-century farmhouse has a half-dozen suites. **Pros:** unique ambience and style of the renovated farmhouses; special local cuisine. **Cons:** you are out in the sticks with nowhere to go except the big outdoors; local amenities such as an ATM are a 20-min drive. ⊠ *Guarda* 🕾 *081/8622132* ⊕ *www.hotel-meisser.ch* 🛏 *20 rooms, 5 suites* ⚴ *In-room: no a/c, safe, refrigerator (some), no TV (some). In-hotel: 3 restaurants, bar, Wi-Fi (free), parking (free), pets (fee)* ▭ *AE, MC, V* ⊗ *Closed Apr., May, and Nov.* ‖◎‖ *BP & MAP.*

SCUOL

13 km (8 mi) east of Guarda.

GETTING HERE

Journeying to Scuol by train is possible. A Chur-Scuol direct RegioExpress leaves at 20 past the hour (2 hrs, 76 SF). A Kloster-Scuol train leaves 28 minutes past the hour (43 mins, 43.20 SF). A St. Moritz-

Scuol train leaves two minutes past the hour with a change at Samedan (1 hr 17 mins, 25 SF).

Visitor Information (✉ *CH-7550* ☎ *081/8612222* ⊕ *www.scuol.ch*).

EXPLORING

The villages of Scuol and Tarasp-Vulpera effectively form one big resort. The area owes its popularity to the 20 mineral springs (traditionally used for liver cures), the beautiful surroundings (mountains and dense forests), and the proximity of the Parc Naziunal Svizzer. Previously popular only in summer, the villages now fill up in winter, thanks to skiing on the south-facing slopes of Motta Naluns.

A small town, Scuol has a petite but exemplary Old Town, with five fountains from which you can do a taste-test comparison of normal tap water against spring water.

★ For the inside-and-out spa experience, head for the **Bogn Engiadina Scuol,** one of Europe's most famous spas. It stands in the middle of town tucked against the mountainside—an elevator and a staircase in a silo-like modern construction lead down to the entrance (unless you prefer coming up from the center of the old village). The calming blue interior, fantastic aquatic murals, and shifting reflections from backlit pools start relaxing you before your toes even touch the water. Six pools, both indoor and outdoor, range in temperature from 60°F to 90°F. There are also saunas, solariums, steam rooms, and a massage area. A special Roman-Irish ritual treatment alternates between moist and dry heat, massage, and mineral baths. A therapy center offers mud baths, gymnastics, thalassotherapy, and electrotherapy (if you have a doctor's prescription). In addition to steeping in mineral water, you can drink it from four different sources near the entrance: wait for someone to serve you. Reservations must be made at least 24 hours ahead. ✉ *Town center* ☎ *081/8612000* 💲 *25 SF for bathing area with sauna for 2; 66 SF with Roman-Irish baths* ☉ *June–Apr., daily 9* AM*–10* PM.

NEED A BREAK? | For a delicious ice cream of organic milk, a good coffee, or a quick e-mail check, stop in at the **Glatscharia Balnot** (✉ *Stradun 402, Scuol (near the tourist office and bus station)* ☎ *081/8641643* ☉ *Daily 1–7*). The building is a riot of colorful, complex sgraffito ornamentation.

The other two villages lie on the opposite side of the river from Scuol. **Vulpera,** whose permanent residents number just five, has an 1876 Trinkhalle with its spring pumping out water rich in minerals said to be good for the digestive tract. From Vulpera you can take a 15-minute bus ride up to **Tarasp,** a cluster of houses, inns, and farms around a tiny lake. The Vulpera golf course straddles the road, so if you are traveling by car you may want to close your windows!

Fodor'sChoice | The village is dominated by the magnificently picturesque stronghold
★ | **Schloss Tarasp,** perched 500 feet above. Looking like illustrator Howard Pyle's model for the Castle Drachenhausen in his beloved children's classic *Otto of the Silver Hand,* Tarasp lords it over the valley with an impressive main tower, dating from the 11th century, when the castle

was built by the leading family of Tarasp. Tarasp became part of Austria in 1464; the imperial eagle still can be seen on the castle walls. In the early 1800s Napoléon gave Tarasp to the canton Graubünden, newly part of the Swiss federation. The castle went through several owners and subsequent neglect before passing into private hands in the early 20th century. You must join a tour to see the interiors, which range from the Romanesque chapel to the opulent "baronial" 19th-century reception rooms; the schedule varies quite a bit, so call ahead for tour times. Special midnight tours are conducted during the full moon. The bus from Vulpera departs roughly every hour. It's a 1½ hour walk from Scuol, following a well-marked path that goes over the Punt'Ota (high bridge). ☎081/8649368 ⊕www.schloss-tarasp.ch ☜10 SF ☉June–Oct., daily, times vary; Christmas–Easter, Tues. and Thurs., times vary.

SKIING & SNOWBOARDING

The region's ski area centers around 14 gondolas and lifts going up Scuol's **Motta Naluns**, at elevations between 4,100 and 9,184 feet. The 80 km (50 mi) of trails include the 12-km (7½-mi) Traumpiste (Dream Run), a good run of medium difficulty, with a few tough areas. There is a wide range of ski passes available for an equally wide range of prices on a sliding scale beginning at 50 SF for a day pass. Some passes even include use of the Bogn Engiadina Scuol spa. Tarasp has one short ski lift for beginners. Bus transport between Scuol/Sent and Scuol/Tarasp-Vulpera is free of charge if you have a ski pass.

Snowboarding is extremely popular on these broad, sunny slopes. Scuol's snowboard school, **The School** (☎081/8641723), is the oldest in Europe. You could also sign up with **Schweizer Schneesportschule Scuol** (☎081/8641723) for instruction in Alpine and cross-country skiing. There are 60 km (37 mi) of prepared cross-country tracks around Scuol. Rental equipment is available at sports shops in Scuol and next to the Motta Naluns cable-car station. As for children, they will find snowy excitement at the **Kinderland Nalunsin** (☎081/8612000) plus a daycare center for 7 SF per hour or 35 SF per day.

WHERE TO STAY

$$–$$$ ☐**Hotel Villa Post.** Landmarked by its distinctive turret, this former
★   post office provides simply and tastefully decorated guest rooms and a familial atmosphere ideal for those seeking a peaceful home away from home. Guests are welcomed with a drink in the hotel's own museum, which displays vintage tableware from the grand days of tourism in the early 20th century. And for a full blast of yesteryear, simply go to the sumptuously wood-paneled Arvenstube restaurant, an opulent pine setting for local specialties made from market-fresh ingredients. A nightcap in front of the fireplace on winter evenings rounds off a most restful experience. **Pros:** sense of history; fine dining; grand natural setting. **Cons:** anyone on the lookout for a buzzy social atmosphere should look elsewhere. ⊠Vulpera ☎081/8641112 ☐081/8649585 ⊕www. villa-post.ch ☞26 rooms ⚲In-room: no a/c, safe, refrigerator, Ethernet (free). In-hotel: restaurant, bar, parking. ⊟AE, MC, V ☉Closed May and Nov. ☺MAP.

The Little Red One

The Rhätibahn is not simply a means of transport but a journey that thousands love to experience every year. In July 2008 it won UNESCO World Heritage status, in recognition of its feats of engineering and the wondrous landscapes that it passes through. The monorail winds its way across glaciers, over viaducts and gorges, and past stupendous alpine scenery—along the way it discloses snapshots from a centuries-old way of life, all but forgotten in the bigger towns and cities.

The tracks of this wondrous travel experience thread a large section within Graubünden but also reach out to other cantons in Switzerland and can even transport you southward across the border to Italy. The network offers special services with named prestige trains—the top three are the Arosa Express, Bernina Express, and the Glacier Express. Each follows its own route and pre-booking is essential. Doing a little research to see which lines fit with your itinerary is well worth it. To ensure your chosen outpost is on one of the varied lines and to avoid disappointment it is best to check online or call ahead. For more details, call ☎081/288 4340 or visit www.rhb.ch.

$$

Fodor's Choice

★

🛏**Schlosshotel Chastè.** While many Swiss hoteliers are proud to claim a second generation of family ownership, this hidden treasure claims 500 years under the Pazeller family's care. Now a Relais & Châteaux treasure, it started as a farm, then supplied provisions to builders of Tarasp Castle, which looms above. The family has preserved the bulging, sgraffitied stucco exterior, and behind the magnificently carved Arvenholz wood door extraordinary effort has been made to match and modernize. Each room varies a bit: a canopy bed here, an antique trunk there. Rudolf Pazeller himself is the chef and offers a small but sophisticated menu; his fish dishes, such as the "Marriage of perch and char in white tomato sauce on southern vegetables and gnocchi," are outstanding. **Pros:** superb cuisine; enchanting rooms; untouched magical surroundings. **Cons:** the owner may be a little rude or grumpy; not always accommodating the needs of young children. ✉ *Tarasp* ☎ *081/8613060* ⊕ *www.schlosshotelchaste.ch* 🛏 *20 rooms* △ *In-room: no a/c, safe, Ethernet (fee). In-hotel: 2 restaurants, bar, parking, some pets allowed (fee)* ☐ *AE, DC, MC, V* ☉ *Closed Apr.–early June and mid-Oct.–mid-Dec.* ⦿ *BP.*

$$-$$$

🛏**Villa Engiadina.** This folly of towers and gables standing guard over Vulpera was built in 1902 and was transformed into a hotel in the late 1990s. Owing to the architecture, each room has a different shape and has been individually furnished. The rooms in the towers are especially attractive, offering a sprawling view of the valley. No. 107 has an antique bathroom, for example; No. 304 was once the house chapel. The restaurant offers (among other things) fresh vegetables from the hotel's own garden, while the homemade cakes have earned a reputation throughout the valley. Special offers for biking or golf weekends are available. **Pros:** the location; proximity of golf course. **Cons:** no elevator and lots of stairs, so may not be ideal for elderly people. ✉ *Vulpera* ☎*081/8612244* ⊕*www.villa-engiadina.ch* 📞*19 rooms, 4 suites* △*In-room: no a/c, safe, kitchen (some), refrigerator, Wi-Fi (fee, some). In-hotel: restaurant, bar, public Wi-Fi (fee), parking (free), some pets allowed (fee)* ☰*DC, MC, V* ⊗*Closed Apr. and Nov.* ⦿*BP, MAP..*

SPORTS & THE OUTDOORS

BIKING Rental bicycles are available at sports shops and the Motta Naluns cable-car station. For the adventurous, bikes can be taken on the cable car; once on the mountain, you can explore on your own or join a guided tour. Contact the tourist office for details.

ICE SPORTS Open-air ice rinks for hockey, curling, and skating are available in Scuol from early December to early March at **Sportanlage Trü** (☎*081/8612006*). **Eishalle Gurlaina** (☎*081/8640272*), in Scuol, has indoor skating facilities. There are three main sled runs, between 2½ and 7 km (1½ and 4½ mi) long. You can rent a sled at the Motta Naluns mountain station or from **Sport Conradin** (☎*081/8641410*). **Sport Heinrich** (☎☎*081/8641956*) rents sleds in Scuol.

ZERNEZ

27 km (17 mi) southwest of Scuol.

Visitor Information (✉*CH-7530* ☎*081/8561300* ⊕*www.zernez.ch*).

EXPLORING

This friendly little crossroads is the last town before the higher valley of the Inn and lies along the route over the Ofen Pass to the Val Müstair and Italy. Serious hikers sporting loden hats, knickers, and sturdy boots come to stock up on picnic goods and topographical maps before setting off for the Parc Naziunal Svizzer. In winter there are cross-country trails. The Alpine skiing areas of the Lower and Upper Engadine are accessible by public transport.

WHERE TO STAY

$ 🏠 **Chasa–Veglia Hotel Garni.** Located down a quiet side street, "the old house"—complete with converted barn—is a town treasure. The owner's wood-carving skills are on display at every turn, from the doors and chairs to ceilings and fretwork panels over the lighting fixtures. Rugs on parquet floors and a display of old farm and kitchen implements add to the atmosphere. One room is an exception, painted pink and decorated in an ultramodern style. Guest rooms are small; those without a bathtub have a shower, except for two rooms with only a toilet and sink. **Pros:** the charming hand-crafted interior. **Cons:** you will need to go elsewhere for dinner. ✉*Runatsch* ☎*081/2844868* ⊕*www.chasa-veglia.ch* 📞*11 rooms, 9 with bath* △*In-room: no a/c* ☰*No credit cards* ⊗*Closed May–mid-June and Nov.–late Dec.* ⦿*BP.*

PARC NAZIUNAL SVIZZER

Fodor'sChoice *Access roads from Zernez, Scuol, S-Chanf, and the Ofen Pass.*

★

The Swiss National Park is a magnificent federal preserve of virtually virgin wilderness. Established in 1914, it covers 173 square km (107 square mi), including the Macun lakes near Lavin. Minute compared with a U.S. or Canadian national park, it has none of the developments that typically hint of "accessibility" and "attraction": no campgrounds, no picnic sites, no residents, few rangers. This is genuine wilderness, every leaf protected from all but nature itself. Dead wood is left to rot and insects to multiply. Rangers see that rules are obeyed—no fires, dogs, bikes, skis, or tents are allowed, and picking plants is forbidden. Although the last bear was shot in the Lower Engadine in 1904, the park is home to large herds of ibex (the heraldic animal on the Graubünden flag), chamois, red and roe deer, and marmots. Don't forget binoculars; without them you might not see much fauna—the animals give a wide berth to the 80 km (50 mi) of marked paths. Remember these are wild animals and not likely to line up for Twinkies by the road. If big game fail to appear, you can just enjoy the scenery and watch out for a bearded vulture overhead. Before heading into the park, visit the brand new **Nationalpark-Haus** in Zernez, where you can watch a video in English, stock up on maps, and enjoy the natural-history exhibit, which includes a "marmot underground experience." Guided walks in English are available on Tuesday and Thursday; reserve one to two days in advance to join a group (10 SF for adults) or book a private guided walk.

Trails start out from parking lots off the park's only highway (visitors are encouraged to take buses back to their starting point)—a series of wild, rough, and often steep paths. Visitors are restricted to the trails except at designated resting places. The Il Fuorn–Stabelchod–Val dal Botsch trail marks botanical and natural phenomena with multilingual information boards and leads to a spectacular barren ridge at 7,672 feet; the round-trip journey takes about four hours. A three-hour route from picturesque S-chanf (pronounced sss-*chanff*) takes you into a deep glacial valley where ibex and chamois often gather; the return, by a riverside trail, passes a snack bar—just across the park border and thus permitted. ⊠*Nationalpark-Haus, Zernez* ⊹ *leaving the village toward Ofen Pass* ☎*081/8514141* ⊕*www.nationalpark.ch* ☜*7 SF* ☉*June–Oct., daily 8:30–6, Tues. 8:30 AM–10 PM.*

WHERE TO STAY

$–$$ ⊡**Hotel Parc Naziunal, Il Fuorn.** This century-old mountain inn in the Swiss National Park is on the highway and makes an ideal base for hikers. Choose from either old-style rooms without bath or pine-and-stucco rooms with bath. Multibed rooms are available for groups or individuals for 37 SF with breakfast and 19 SF without. The plain Swiss cooking is augmented by some game specialties. Near the hotel is one of the medieval iron-smelting ovens that gave Ofen Pass its name. **Pros:** only hotel in the national park; full of history; idyllic location for nature lovers, hikers, and bike enthusiasts. **Cons:** basic yet comfortable accommodation—do not expect plenty of amenities that are found in modern town or city hotel. ☒ *Il Fuorn, Zernez* ☎*081/8561226* ⊕*www.ilfuorn.ch* ⤺*37 rooms* ☁*In-room: no a/c, no TV. In-hotel: restaurant, parking (free)* ▤*AE, DC, MC, V* ☺*Closed late Oct.– mid-May* ⫪❍*BP, MAP.*

THE UPPER ENGADINE

Stretching from Brail to Maloja and with a gate to the Swiss National Park at S-chanf, this is one of the country's highest regions—the highest settlement is at 6,710 feet— and one of its most dazzling. From mountain peaks, such as Piz Corvatsch or Piz Nair, you can swoosh down world-class slopes or simply take in the dizzying view over the lakes and mountains. Besides summer and winter sports, both seasons are packed tight with cultural programs and events. Summer is also when the lowland farmers send their cows up to the high Alpine pastures so they can have a relaxing mountain holiday, too.

> **CREATURES GREAT & SMALL**
>
> This is no African big-game pre-serve. Sighting a group of ibex on a distant hill or great herds of male red deer, their antlers silhouetted above a snowy ridge, you may feel more privileged than when petting a dozen Yel-lowstone bison. If the big game makes no appearance, search your greedy soul and try to follow the park's advice: "Appreciate a but-terfly or an ant as much as a herd of chamois."

PONTRESINA

★ *38 km (24 mi) southwest of Zernez.*

GETTING HERE
Trains connecting with Pontresina by and large follow the same sched-ule as those to and from St. Moritz, with a change in Samedan. Pon-tresina to Chur trains leave at two minutes past the hour, a two-hour journey for 38 SF with the change at Samedan. The same trains go to Scuol, departing from Samedan. The Scuol–St. Moritz trains also take you to Pontresina, with a transfer at Samedan. Direct trains from Scuol to Pontresina are also possible.

Visitor Information (☒*Rondo Center* ☎*081/8388300* ⊕*www.pontresina.ch*).

EXPLORING
On a south-facing shelf along the Flaz Valley, Pontresina is an excep-tionally picturesque resort. It grew by converting its farmhouses to pen-sions and hotels for use by summer tourists. Today its climbing school is making a name for itself, and the village has become a popular hiking center. From here you can see clear across to the Roseg Valley, once filled with a glacier that has retreated to the base of Piz Roseg itself. The river Flaz winds through the valley from the Morteratsch glacier, which oozes down from Piz Bernina. Although the main street is built up with restaurants and shops, the resort still has a relaxed atmosphere. Every second Thursday in July and August there's a street market in

the lower part of the village, with locals selling fresh produce and handmade crafts. The altitude of Pontresina (6,000 feet) ensures wintry weather, and its access to skiing on the slopes of Diavolezza (9,751 feet) is convenient. In the off-seasons between Easter and mid-June and mid-October through Christmas, many hotels are closed.

The **Museum Alpin** gives some local history and documents the region's lifestyle over the centuries. It also exhibits the local flora, fauna, and mineral world; be sure to check out the room full of birds whose recorded songs can be heard at the push of a button. There's also an exhibit on mining in the Engadine. ⌧ *Via Maistra* ☎*081/8427273* ⊕*www.pontresina.ch/museumalpin* ⌧*5 SF* ☉*June–mid-Oct. and mid-Dec.–mid-Apr., Mon.–Sat. 4–6.*

> **THE NEIGHS HAVE IT**
>
> Horse-drawn carriages and sleighs in Pontresina can be booked through M. Kaiser (*081/8426274*); V. Rietberger (*081/8428353*) is another vendor offering sleigh and carriage rides. The Roseg Valley "horse omnibus" is run by L. Costa (*081/8426057*) as a scheduled service in summer and winter—this trip is very popular, so be sure to make a reservation.

SKIING
There's a small beginners' slope in the village at San Spiert. The compact ski areas of Diavolezza (9,768 feet) and, on the other side of the road, Lagalb (9,705 feet), on the Bernina pass, complement the much more extensive ones of St. Moritz. All three are about 20 minutes away by bus. Lift tickets cost 69 SF for one day, 348 SF for a six-day regional ticket. Rides on the Engadine bus service are included in the price of a regional ski ticket. Newcomers can learn the basics at the **Ski and Snowboard School** (☎*081/8388383*). Below the village, on the Engadine Marathon Trail, is the **Tolais Cross-Country Ski Center** (☎*081/8426844*).

WHERE TO EAT
$$–$$$ ✕**Steinbock.** Owned by the Walther family, proprietors of the neighSWISS   boring Hotel Walther, this 17th-century house has been modernized in keeping with Engadine style—lots of wood and warm colors. The Colani Stübli serves regional and seasonal specialties, such as polenta *cun gorgonzola*, a filling cornmeal dish. The game dishes served in autumn are exceptional, especially the *Gemspfeffer* (chamois ragout cooked in wine) with hazelnut Spätzli and red cabbage. For dessert you might try *Nusskrapfen* (puff pastry with a sticky nut filling). ⌧*Via Maistra* ☎*081/8393626* ▭*AE, DC, MC, V.*

$–$$ ✕**Café Puntschella.** Either way you look here, you can't go wrong: your SWISS   chair will face either the Roseg Valley or the spread of fresh-made pas★   tries. The menu can satisfy all kinds of cravings, from bowls of breakfast muesli to plates of *Rösti* (pan-fried potatoes). A nice salad buffet will take care of diners looking for lighter foods. Locals know to ask for the beignetlike *Quarkinis* with vanilla sauce—as well as a seat on the terrace. The staff are always welcoming with a friendly smile. ⌧*Via Mulin* ☎*081/8388030* ▭*V* ☉*Closed May and Nov..*

WHERE TO STAY

$$$$

Fodor'sChoice ★

Grand Hotel Kronenhof. A grand Versailles set amid mountain peaks, this breathtaking retreat was completed in 1898 and, happily, the exterior has changed little since. The lobby and dining rooms, with elaborate moldings, pink cherubs, and heavy chandeliers, are dazzling, especially the Rococo gold-and-gilt Grand restaurant, whose interior is fit for a king. Upstairs, the guest rooms are tastefully done with Biedermeier furniture. The lawn that sprawls out toward the Roseg Valley is a social center in summer and winter, with tennis courts doubling as an ice rink. While the Grand offers elegant international cuisine, the gorgeously wood-burnished Kronenstübli offers simpler regional fare: alpine macaroni with fried duck breast and liver, for example. **Pros:** beautiful grounds and location; activities and facilities galore; recent refurbishment is top-notch. **Cons:** this is a hard place to find fault with, so if you are happiest while grumbling or seeking out weak spots, you will be somewhat lost at sea here! ⊠*Pontresina* ☎*081/8303030* ⊕*www.kronenhof.com* 🛏*114 rooms* ₷*In-room: no a/c, safe, refrigerator, Ethernet, Wi-Fi (some, fee). In-hotel: 3 restaurants, bar, 2 tennis courts, 3 pools, gym, spa, children's programs (ages 3 up), public Internet (free), Wi-Fi (fee), parking (free), garage (fee), pets (fee)* ▤*AE, DC, MC, V* ☉*Closed mid-Apr.–mid-June and mid-Sept.–mid-Dec.* ❍*MAP.*

> **WORD OF MOUTH**
>
> "At Punt Muragl (081/8428232), off the highway between Samedan and Pontresina, you'll find the funicular for Muottas Muragl at 8,055 feet. Walk the Philosophers' Path, dotted with quotations from famous minds such as Socrates and Descartes. Head back down on the 4-km (2½-mi) sled run. The funicular fare is 27 SF. At the top (what photos!), visit the Berghotel Muottas Muragl (closed mid-Apr.– early Jun. and mid-Oct.–mid-Dec.) for a meal with a truly spectacular view." —MikeDall

$$

Hotel Station. Next to the entrance to the Roseg Valley, the cross-country skiing center, and the train station, the newly refurbished hotel offers dependable, low-key accommodations. Keeping things simple, tasteful, and clean, guest rooms are decked out in traditional wooden furniture with clean white walls and bold minimalist shower rooms. The bright and cheery restaurant offers simple fare at reasonable prices, nicely vibing with the rustic wood-wood-and-more-wood–chalet style of the Station. If you stay longer than a week, rates get cheaper. **Pros:** simple; easily accessible; affordable. **Cons:** proximity to train line. ⊠*Pontresina* ☎*081/8388000* ⊕*www.station-pontresina.ch* 🛏*21 rooms* ₷*In-room: no a/c, safe, Wi-Fi (free). In-hotel: restaurant, bar, sauna, public Wi-Fi (free), parking (free), covered parking (fee), some pets welcome (fee)* ▤*AE, DC, MC, V* ❍*BP.*

NIGHTLIFE & THE ARTS

BARS &
LOUNGES

Bar Pitschna Scena (⊠*Hotel Saratz* ☎*081/8394000*) has live music Thursday nights in summer and winter seasons. **Piano-Bar** (⊠*Sporthotel* ☎*081/8389400*) is a cozy, blond-wood bar. **The Pöstlikeller** (⊠*Hotel Post, Via Maistra* ☎*081/8389300*) features live music occasionally.

MUSIC The **Kurorchester Pontresina** plays chamber concerts daily between mid-June and mid-September at 11 AM in the Tais forest. Check with the tourist office for more information.

SPORTS & THE OUTDOORS

BICYCLING Touring and mountain bikes can be rented at the **Fähndrich Sport** (☎ *081/8427155*). **Flying Cycles** (☎ *081/8345750*) rents all kinds of bikes and can suggest scenic routes. To take on steep mountain descents like Lagalb–Poschiavo, contact **Engadin Ferien** (☎ *081/8300001*).

HIKING Pontresina and the top of the Alp Languard chairlift (open only in summer) are good starting points for hikers. The Diavolezza cable car, which runs in the summer, and the Rhaetian Railway also bring you to good hiking trails. For information on a variety of guided excursions and glacier hiking (34 SF), contact the tourist office. If you're staying overnight in Pontresina, some of the tours are free.

ICE SPORTS There's a large **natural ice-skating rink** at the **Sportpavilion Roseg** (✉ *Via Maistra* ☎ *081/8426346 or 081/8426349*). Rental skates and instruction are available. From December through March, 10 curling rinks with instructors are also available.

MOUNTAIN CLIMBING **Bergsteigerschule Pontresina** (✉ *Via Maistra* ☎ *081/8388333*), the biggest mountain climbing school in Switzerland, offers instruction in rock and ice climbing for people of all skill levels. The company also leads guided tours and ski tours in English.

ST. MORITZ

Fodor'sChoice ★ *5 km (3 mi) west of Pontresina, 85 km (53 mi) southeast of Chur.*

GETTING HERE

From Chur, trains leave all day (2 hrs, 38 SF) at four minutes to the hour until 8:56 at night. To Chur from St. Moritz, trains leave at four minutes past the hour, otherwise everything is the same. The trains going to St. Moritz also go to Pontresina, same timing and same price (2 hrs, 38 SF), although you must change at Samedan. St. Moritz-Scuol (1.21 hrs, 26 SF) follows the same schedule: at four minutes past the hour, with a change at Samedan. The trains from Scuol depart at 34 minutes past the hour.

Visitor Information (✉ *Via Maistra* ☎ *081/8373333* ⊕ *www.stmoritz.ch*).

EXPLORING

Who put the *ritz* in St. Moritz? The approach to this celebrated city may surprise newcomers who, having heard the almost magical name dropped in the same breath as Paris and Rome, expect either a supremely cosmopolitan Old World capital or a resort whose spectacular natural setting puts other resorts to shame. It is neither. What makes St. Moritz's reputation is the people who go there and who have been going there, generation by generation, since 1864, when hotelier Johannes Badrutt dared a group of English resorters—already summer regulars—to brave the Alpine winter as his guests. They loved it, delighted in the novelty of snowy mountain beauty—until then considered something to be avoided—and told their friends. By the turn of the century St. Moritz, Switzerland, and snow were all the rage.

Not that St. Moritz had been a stranger to tourism before that. Since 1500 BC, when Druidic Celts first passed through, people have made the pilgrimage here to take healing waters from its mineral springs. The Romans had a settlement here, and later a church was founded on the site, dedicated to Mauritius, an early Christian martyr. The first historical reference to the town dates from 1139, and in 1537 Paracelsus, the great Renaissance physician and alchemist, described the health-giving properties of the St. Moritz springs. More than 70% of latter-day pilgrims who visit St. Moritz come from abroad, still the cosmopolitan mix of socialites, blue bloods, and celebs that made the resort's name. St. Moritz catches social fire around the winter holidays—some New Year's Eve events have guest lists closed a year in advance—but the glitter fades by spring. Very ordinary people fill the streets come summer—the same hikers you might meet in any resort—and hotel prices plummet.

Then visitors see St. Moritz for what it really is: a busy, built-up old resort city sprawled across a hillside above an aquamarine lake, the St. Moritzer See, surrounded by forested hills and by graceful, though not the region's most dramatic, peaks. Piz Rosatsch, with its glacier, dominates the view, with Piz Languard (10,699 feet) on the east and Piz Güglia (7,492 feet) on the west. St. Moritz-Dorf is the most like a downtown, with busy traffic, yet due to recent investment by the locals, pedestrianization of the center and a new car park reached by the lake called Serletta has alleviated competitive parking. Escalators and a design gallery lead you to the shopping center. St. Moritz-Bad, the original spa-resort at the base of the lake, now bristles with brutish modern housing worthy of a Costa Moritza. At the top of the Dorf is St. Moritz's answer to Pisa—a leaning tower, all that's left of a 13th-century church. Other than that, don't expect a picturesque village that might appear on the lid of a chocolate box. St. Moritz has its fair share of unattractive buildings and, in winter, traffic snarls. But the latter have improved quite a bit since the creation of a pedestrian-only zone in the village. The town shows its best face from a distance, especially at dusk: from the *See* promenade—the popular walk around the lake—modern edges soften and the lake reflects the darkening mountains, warm hotel lights, and the grace that first made St. Moritz a star.

Even a hundred years of hype have not exaggerated its attractions as a winter sports center. The place that twice hosted the Olympic games (1928 and 1948)—and trademarked the shining sun as its logo—is still a sports marketing mecca, with excellent facilities for ice-skating, bobsledding, ski jumping, riding, and even winter golf, polo, and horse racing. But it does not have a corner on fine skiing: it shares a broad complex of trails and facilities with Sils, Silvaplana, Celerina, and Pontresina; only the slopes of Corviglia, Marguns, and Piz Nair are directly accessible from town.

The resort's events calendar is especially impressive. This is the place to see winter sports that were, or still are, found only here, such as polo and cricket played on snow, bob-sledding on natural ice, and horse racing on snow, which includes *skikjöring* (skiers pulled by rider-less horses). The frozen lake acts as the "white arena" for some events and provides the backdrop for oth-ers. A tent village complete with grandstands, palm trees, restau-rants, bars, and art exhibitions is installed on the lake from late Janu-ary through February. Watch for the annual winter Gourmet Festival in St. Moritz, when world-renowned chefs serve their specialties in local restaurants and hotels. The Grand Gourmet Finale is a gargantuan feast prepared by about 25 chefs and their assistants, usually presented on the frozen lake.

> ### GOOD FOR WHAT AILS YOU
>
> It is said that in the late 17th century the duke of Parma led a retinue of 25 followers over the mountain passes to taste St. Moritz's waters, and an 18th-century visitor from Germany described the coveted experience: "It puckers lips and tongue like the sharpest vinegar, goes to the head, and is like champagne in the nose."

Besides challenging sports, the town offers relaxation at the **St. Moritz Bad** *(spa complex)*. The local mineral springs have been known for more than 3,000 years; in 1535 the physician and alchemist Paracel-sus praised the water, which is the richest in iron and carbonic acid in Europe. Massages and most treatments are done in individual cabins with private baths. Peat baths and packs need a doctor's prescription, but you can take a mineral bath anytime; try one with natural aromas such as pine or rosemary (35 SF). ☎081/8333062 ⊙ *Weekdays 8–7, Sat. 8–noon.*

One of the few reminders that contemporary St. Moritz was once an Engadine village is the **Engadiner Museum,** a reproduction of the tradi-tional sgraffitoed home. In a building dating from 1906, the museum has displays of furniture, tools, and pottery in rooms decorated in styles from different periods. ⊠ *Via dal Bagn 39* ☎081/8334333 💶7 SF ⊙ *June–Oct., weekdays 9:30–noon, 2–5, Sun. 10–noon; Dec.–Apr., weekdays 10–noon, 2–5, Sun. 10–noon.*

The somewhat forbidding stone structure that houses the **Segan-tini Museum** showcases the work of Italian artist Giovanni Segantini (1858–99). His huge triptych *La Vita, La Natura, La Morte* hangs in the domed upper floor. Take a seat on the bench to absorb the meditations on life, nature, and death of this fine Impressionist artist. ⊠ *Via Som-plaz* ☎081/8334454 ⊕*www.segantini-museum.ch* 💶10 SF ⊙*Mid-May–mid-Oct. and early Dec.-early Apr., Tues.–Sun. 10–noon, 2–6.*

SKIING
Don't let the whirlwind of activities at St. Moritz make you forget that its raison d'être is skiing. You can reach the **Corviglia–Piz Nair, Suvretta,** and **Marguns** slopes, immediately above St. Moritz, from the Chantarella–Corviglia funicular in Dorf, the Signal cableway in Bad, the Suvretta chairlift, and the Marguns gondolas in Celerina. There are 80 km (50 mi) of difficult, intermediate, and easy runs and a half pipe for

snowboarders. The Upper Engadine ski region offers 350 km (217 mi) of prepared trails. The views from Corviglia, Piz Nair, and the Suvretta Paradise run are magnificent.

Descents behind Piz Nair (10,026 feet) eventually lead down to Marguns; they are often in shadow in early winter but have the best snow up to the end of the season. With the help of snowmaking equipment, conditions usually remain excellent until late April. The sunny Suvretta slopes are usually less crowded but do not benefit from snowmaking equipment. For instruction there are a number of choices, including the **Suvretta Snowsports School** (☎081/8366161). The **St. Moritz Ski School** (☎081/8300101), in town, is the oldest in Switzerland. You can join a group and go with an instructor on a free "snow safari" offered by any ski school, which begins in Sils and ends in Cellerina. Rental equipment is available at **Ski Service Corvatsch** (☎081/8387777) at the Corviglia valley and mountain stations. One-day tickets for St. Moritz are 69 SF; six-day regional passes cost 348 SF. Prices include transportation between ski stations on the Engadine) bus service. For reports on daily snow conditions, call the **hotline** (☎0844/844944); the English-language version comes last.

Cross-country skiing has its base in St. Moritz Bad, where the **Langlauf school** (⊠*Plazza Paracelsus 2* ☎081/8336233) offers lessons and excursions. You can try out the close-by Engadine Marathon track or the many side valleys. Near the school is a lighted circular trail of 3 km (2 mi) open from 5:30 PM to 9:00 PM.

WHERE TO EAT

$$$$ ✕ **Chesa Veglia.** When Stavros Niarchos, the Princess of Baroda, Eliza-
ITALIAN beth Taylor, and other legendary V.I.P.s used to visit St. Moritz, this
★ was their favored watering hole. So if you want to enter the snobbism sweepstakes, this is a great place to begin. A 17th-century *Bauern-hof* (farmhouse), it retains its raw beams and native carvings within a theme restaurant so self-consciously restored you may think you're in an American mall—an effect enhanced by the restaurant's fragmenta-tion into three theme rooms (an upscale grill, a Stübli, and a pizzeria). Despite the rustic-luxe setting, the main menu aspires to international cuisine; you can order *côte de boeuf à la moelle et aux truffes* (beef with marrow and truffles) and terrine *de lièvre* (hare pâté) at prices that are St. Moritz–high. There are good fruit tarts at teatime, when the atmo-sphere is at its most convincing. Later you'll find dinner and dancing with live entertainment and piano music in the grill. ⊠*Via Veglia 2* ☎081/8372800 ⚒*Reservations essential* ▤AE, DC, MC, V.

$–$$ ✕ **Engiadina.** With its plain linoleum and pine trim, this could pass for
SWISS a St. Moritz diner, though its raison d'être is fondue; champagne fon-due is the house specialty. Other favorites are *steak-frîtes* (steak with french fries) and, in winter, escargots. It's a popular oddity for this ritzy resort—more homespun than glitz and glamour. It is a low-key establishment for couples or a small group of friends. During summer months there are tables and chairs on the street, which enables a little people-watching. A nice plus: reasonable prices (for this area). ⊠*Plazza da Scuola 2* ☎081/8333265 ▤AE, DC, MC, V.

$$$$ ✕**Jöhri's Talvò.** Roland Jöhri's restaurant, in a 17th-century Engadine
FRENCH house, marries the best of Graubünden tradition with classic French
Fodor'sChoice elegance. Both the cooking and decor reflect this philosophy, from the
★ delicate linens softening weathered woodwork to the luxurious touches
that curb the heaviness of local dishes, like *capuns sursilvan* (a local
specialty from the Sursilvan area, capuns is spàtzli dough and curd
cheese with dried beef and ham wrapped in a swiss chard leaf and
cut into small pieces) with chanterelles. A popular fish menu could
include a house-style bouillabaisse or Arctic char from Sils Lake with
summer vegetables. Desserts are elaborate works of art. Be prepared
to spend as much on a meal as on a hotel room. ⊠*Champfèr ✚3 km
(2 mi) southwest of St. Moritz, about 330 feet from the postbus stop*
☎*081/8334455* ⚠*Reservations essential* ▤*AE, DC, MC, V* ✆*Closed
mid-Apr.–end-Jun. and end-Sep.–start-Dec.*

$–$$ ✕**Meierei.** On a winding, private forest road partway around the lake,
MODERN FRENCH this *Landgasthof* (country inn) is a rural mirage, an incongruity in the
★ city but spiritually allied to the mountains and lake. It started in the
17th century as a farm, was later a dairy restaurant, and then a hotel.
Today it's sought out for its restaurant, which serves light meals and
such modern combinations as fillet of venison with elderberry dumplings. Its sun terrace attracts day hikers, cross-country skiers, and
horseback riders. (If you're not a guest, you'll have to walk in, as only
guests may drive in.) The rustic themes of the dining areas are loosely
translated into guest-room decor. If you don't want a full meal, light
snacks are also on hand. ⊠*Via Dim Lej 5* ☎*081/8332060* ⊕*www.
hotel-meierei.ch* ▤*AE, DC, MC, V* ✆*Closed late Mar.–mid-June and
mid-Oct.–mid-Dec..*

$$–$$$ ✕**Veltlinerkeller.** Well priced for the area, this bright, genial restaurant
SWISS/AUS- has nothing swanky about it—lots of wood, ancient moldings in the
TRIAN/ITALIAN form of grapes, a few outsize game trophies, and a welcoming wood fire
where meat is roasted while you watch. The owner mans the grill, and
his touch with Italian-Romansh cooking is light and straightforward.
In addition to grilled meats and whole trout, there are good and varied
homemade pastas served family-style from crockery bowls. A tavern
by day, this becomes a specialty restaurant at dusk, when it draws
many of the resort's winter workers for a social drink or catch-up. The
nine double guest rooms upstairs are finished in slick quarry tile and
stucco, with cotton floral prints and all-tile baths. ⊠*Via dal Bagn 11*
☎*081/8221777* ▤*AE, DC, MC, V* ✆*Closed Oct.–May.*

WHERE TO STAY

$$$$ ✕🏠**Badrutt's Palace.** With its pseudo-Gothic stone and mismatched
★ sprawl of architectural excess, the Palace is Switzerland at its most
glitzy and glamorous. Back in the 1950s and 1960s, with master hotelier Cappy Badrutt at the helm, this spot was pure Hollywood and a
mecca for world high society during winter; today, although the celeb
count is lower, there are more than enough Rolls-Royces and Lear jets
discharging guests, and you'll find the Palace crammed with beautiful
people and wealthy wannabes. Nowhere in Switzerland will you find
more facilities—its own ski school, private cinema, and exclusive spa,
to name just a few. Seven restaurants entice, although the center ring

remains the beswagged and chandeliered Le Restaurant; the Grill Room enjoys a culinary reputation beyond the guest list. Guest rooms can be surprisingly discreet and rather like a lot of other hotel rooms at a third of the price—but it's not the drapes you're paying for here. **Pros:** every conceivable desire can be catered for; your chance to be treated like a king; excellent ski facilities. **Cons:** sky-high prices; lacking in distinctive atmosphere. ⊠ *Via Serlas* ☎ *081/8371000* ⊕ *www.badruttspalace.com* ✍ *159 rooms, 47 suites* ⚷ *In-room: no a/c, safe, refrigerator, Ethernet. In-hotel: 7 restaurants, bar, nightclub, 2 tennis courts, 2 pools, gym, spa, children's programs (ages 3–12), Wi-Fi (fee), parking (fee), some pets allowed (fee)* ⊟ *AE, DC, MC, V* ☉ *Closed end-Mar.–mid-Jun. and mid-Sept.–start-Dec.* ⧉ *BP, MAP.*

$ ⊞ **Bellaval.** Simple rooms at good value right at the train station are reason enough for guests staying here (especially those without a car), yet expectations are surpassed time and time again. Train lovers might consider the rooms facing the rails (the trains do not run at night); the other rooms face either the town, the lake, or both. The unpretentious restaurant, with a huge choice, draws many locals. The favorite sitting place, of course, is the section in the old Rhätibahn railcar, part of which turns into a popular bar at night, the RhBar. If you do not want to share communal showers, be sure to ask for a room with a private bathroom. **Pros:** next to train station; excellent food; easy on the wallet. **Cons:** no elevator, yet 3 flights of stairs. ⊠ *Via Grevas 55, St. Moritz-Dorf* ☎ *081/8333245* ⊕ *www.bellaval-stmoritz.ch* ✍ *23 rooms* ⚷ *In-room: no a/c, Wi-Fi (free). In-hotel: restaurant, bar, bicycles, public Internet, public Wi-Fi (free), parking (free), some pets allowed (fee)* ⊟ *AE, DC, MC, V* ⧉ *BP.*

$$–$$$ ⊞ **Corvatsch.** This family-run hotel in the middle of St. Moritz-Bad will make you feel right at home, even if the views from the windows are not the best in town. Friendly service and a drink by the crackling fire in the cozy "living room" are often all one needs at the end of a long day hiking or skiing. The large and airy restaurant can be highly recommended and has a great deal to choose from, including seasonal dishes featuring lots of venison and pastas. Guests needing a sauna can visit the neighboring Laudinella. This hotel offers cheaper deals for longer-staying guests. **Pros:** family hosts are very welcoming and helpful; the food is delicious and rated highly by locals. **Cons:** those looking for a "room with a view" should stay elsewhere; beds are not large. ⊠ *Via Tegiatscha 1, St. Moritz-Bad* ☎ *081/8375757* ⊕ *www.hotel-corvatsch. ch/* ✍ *27 rooms, 1 suite* ⚷ *In-room: no a/c, refrigerator, Ethernet (free). In-hotel: restaurant, bar, parking (free), garage (fee)* ⊟ *MC, V* ☉ *Closed Oct.–Dec. and end Apr.–June* ⧉ *BP.*

$$$$ ⊞ **Kulm.** This luxury hotel can claim its share of St. Moritz superlatives: it was the first hotel here (1856) *and* the first house to have electricity in all of Switzerland (1878). Modern comfort has come a long way since: for instance, the Panorama spa, with a saltwater grotto and top-notch fitness gym. Elsewhere, the hotel's discreetly done in slightly old-fashioned good taste—cream, gold, and scarlet. The facilities are top quality (9-hole golf course, putting green, ice skating and curling in winter), the breakfast room is pure Wedgwood,

and the à la carte restaurant—Rôtisserie de Chevaliers—is a romantic vaulted space, serving (predictably enough) old-style haute cuisine. In the Rôtisserie (open only in winter) and the main dining room, jacket and tie are a must, but more casual dining options are also available. Half board is normal, but B&B possible outside winter season. **Pros:** excellent location and views; golf course on site. **Cons:** exterior is not the most attractive; spiffy dress codes. ⊠ *Via Maistra* ☎ *081/8368000* ⊕ *www.kulmhotel-stmoritz.ch* ⤺ *173 rooms, 41 suites* ⚖ *In-room: no a/c, safe, refrigerator, Ethernet (free). In-hotel: 5 restaurants, 2 bars, 2 tennis courts, pool, gym, spa, bicycles, children's programs (ages 3 up), public Internet (fee), public Wi-Fi (fee), parking (fee), some pets allowed (fee)* ⊟ *AE, DC, MC, V* ☉ *Closed mid-Apr.–late Jun. and mid-Sep.–start Dec.* ⓄⒷ *BP and MAP.*

$$–$$$
★
Languard. Set in the town center, this delightful little hotel garni stands between the Eden and the Kulm, sharing their lovely mountain views. Details like sgraffiti, carved ceilings, and fine darkened pine in some rooms preserve the best from its earlier days. The big corner guest rooms deserve their higher price; back rooms are small, but all have tile baths. Front rooms have mountain and lake views. In the small sitting area, check out the collection of skiing trophies won by the owner's father, who used to run St. Moritz's ski school. **Pros:** affordable place with five-star views; central location. **Cons:** too small to have a spa or sauna facility. ⊠ *Via Veglia 14 (off Via Maistra)* ☎ *081/8333137* ⊕ *www.languard-stmoritz.ch* ⤺ *21 rooms, 1 suite.* ⚖ *In-room: no a/c, safe, refrigerator (some), Wi-Fi (fee). In-hotel: public Wi-Fi (fee), parking (free), some pets allowed (fee)* ⊟ *AE, DC, MC, V* ☉ *Closed late Apr.–early June and mid-Oct.–early Dec.* ⓄⒷ *BP.*

$$$–$$$$
Schweizerhof. This big-city hotel in the center of town was built in 1896 and is still grand. Public areas are heavy with carved wood and moldings, and the Victorian splendor is almost oppressive. A lighter touch is the painted ceiling of the guests' dining room, with its glittering birch forest. Guest rooms leave romantic fantasy behind—they're slick postmodern with burled-wood cabinets and contemporary color schemes. The informal Acla restaurant serves up solid meals such as chateaubriand and Wiener schnitzel. An outdoor restaurant opens in summer, and the hotel has its own mountain hut on the Suvretta slope. The rooftop wellness center offers saunas, steam baths, massages, and superb views over the lake. **Pros:** central location; views over lake from top floor. **Cons:** front-of-house staff occasionally surprises with poor service and incompetence; guest rooms are finished with soft interiors more suited to a motel; faded grandeur. ⊠ *Via dal Bagn* ☎ *081/8370707* ⊕ *www.schweizerhofstmoritz.ch* ⤺ *73 rooms, 10 junior suites* ⚖ *In-room: no a/c, safe, Wi-Fi (fee). In-hotel: 3 restaurants, bar, spa, children's programs (ages 3 up), public Internet, public Wi-Fi (fee), parking (free), garage (fee), some pets allowed (fee)* ⊟ *AE, DC, MC, V* ⓄⒷ *BP & MAP.*

$$$$
★
Suvretta House. The hotel has many assets: a unique location outside the village with stupendous views of Piz Corvatsch and the Silvaplana Lake, a private ski school, and access to the Corvilgia slopes just outside the front door. In the health complex you can soak in an outdoor hot

tub (even in winter) or dream under the sauna's night sky reproduced with tiny lights; elsewhere you can enjoy the driving range and 6-hole golf course. Jacket and tie are requested after 7 PM in the lobby and main dining room, but a casual downstairs area reserved for guests has English-style lounges, an informal restaurant, and even a children's restaurant. **Pros:** beautiful location and views; private ski school. **Cons:** anybody disliking dress codes should stay elsewhere; very soft beds. ✉ *Via Chasellas 1, St. Moritz-Suvretta* ☎*081/8363636* ⊕*www.suvretta house.ch* ☛*154 rooms, 21 junior suites, 9 suites.* ♨*In-room: no a/c, safe, refrigerator, Wi-Fi (fee). In-hotel: 5 restaurants, 2 bars, 2 tennis courts, pool, gym, spa, bicycles, children's programs (ages 3 up), public Internet (fee), public Wi-Fi (fee), parking (free), garage (fee), some pets allowed (fee)* ▭*AE, DC, MC, V* ☾*Closed start-Apr.–end Jun. and start Sep.–mid-Dec.* ⓘ*MAP.*

$$$–$$$$
Fodor$Choice
★

🏨**Waldhaus am See.** This is another world, a good hotel perched on a peninsula overlooking the lake and mountains with a merely peripheral view of St. Moritz's urban turmoil (well filtered through double glass) across the highway. With a big, sunny balcony, dining rooms with views, and a clientele ranging from family clans to senior citizens, it's a vacation lodge geared to leisurely stays. The reasonably priced restaurant stocks more than 1,500 wines, and owner-entrepreneur Claudio Bernasconi has introduced Switzerland's most extensive whiskey bar (which holds the record for the *Guinness Book of World Records*' largest selection of whiskies). Guest rooms are plain, with pine trim and some dated plumbing, though many modern baths have been added in recent years. **Pros:** peaceful; location with stunning views; whiskey bar; good toothpick design! **Cons:** dated in places; if you have a room in the building behind the main hotel the view will be limited. ✉ *Via Dim Lej 6* ☎*081/8366000* ⊕*www.waldhaus-am-see.ch* ☛*50 rooms, 2 apartments* ♨*In-room: no a/c, safe, refrigerator, Ethernet (fee). In-hotel: 2 restaurants, bar, gym, bicycles, public Internet, public Wi-Fi (free), some pets allowed (fee)* ▭*AE, DC, MC, V* ⓘ*BP & MAP.*

NIGHTLIFE & THE ARTS

To find out what's happening, check the English-language section in the weekly *Engadine Information* brochure, available at the tourist office, hotels, and shops.

BARS &
LOUNGES

The après-ski clique favors the Steffani Hotel's **Cava** (✉ *Via Traunter Plazzas* ☎*081/8369696*). Choose from the world's largest selection of whiskies at the **Devil's Place** (✉ *Via Dim Lej* ☎*081/8366000*). This bar in the Waldhaus am See is mentioned in the *Guinness Book of World Records*. For elegant but informal surroundings, try the **Grischuna** (✉*Schulhauspl.* ☎*081/8370404*). Hotel Hauser's open-air **Bar Roo** (✉ *Via Traunter Plazzas* ☎*081/8375050*) attracts those who've spent the day on the slopes.

CASINOS

The **Casino St. Moritz** (✉ *Via Mezdi 29* ☎*081/8375454*) is located in the Kempinski Grand Hôtel des Bains in St. Moritz-Bad and offers roulette, poker, black jack, and slot machines with a "fantasy jackpot." It's open Sunday through Thursday until 3 AM, Friday and Saturday until 4 AM. It closes in May and November.

DANCING **Anton's Bar** (⊠ *Via Chasellas 1* ☎*081/8363636*), a winter-season spot at the Suvretta House, is jacket-and-tie formal. **Diamond** (⊠ *Via Maistra 33* ☎*081/8349767*), as a club, lounge, and restaurant, is a place with wide appeal to the young and chic. In Badrutt's Palace, the **King's Club** (⊠ *Via Serlas* ☎*081/8371100*), has a Moorish decor. Open only in winter, it has a steep cover charge on weekends. For more formal dancing to live music, try the winter-only **Sunny Bar** (⊠ *Via Maistra* ☎*081/8368000*). This old-style dance hall is in the Kulm. In the basement of the Steffani Hotel is **Vivai** (⊠ *Via Traunter Plazzas* ☎*081/8336939*), which opens for both the winter and summer seasons.

> **NO STANDING HERE**
>
> On the world's one and only Cresta Run, riders on skeletons (a metal toboggan) rush headfirst down a winding ice channel from St. Moritz to Celerina, accelerating to about 90 mph. You can watch the runs every morning from the path or the roof of the Junction Hut. If you'd like to try the run, contact the St. Moritz Tobogganing Club (*081/8333117*). It's a private club, but they do allow temporary memberships (for 600 SF) that will give you five runs. The Cresta is open from late December to the last day of February. Note that the run is not open to women.

MUSIC The musical highlight in St. Moritz is the **Snow & Symphony Music Festival** (☎*081/8344646*), which takes place over 14 days in early spring. Prize-winning classical and jazz musicians, chamber orchestras, and a symphony orchestra give roughly 20 concerts. The performances are held in hotels and on mountaintops. The **Engadine Festival** (☎*081/8520588.*) takes place from mid-July to late August, with smaller-scale performances throughout the Upper Engadine. The **St. Moritz Chamber Orchestra** gives free daily concerts in summer at 10:30 AM in the spa center's hall or park. Contact the tourist office for more information.

SPORTS & THE OUTDOORS

BOBSLEDDING In 1890 and 1891 the first bobsled races were held on the road between St. Moritz and Celerina. The present-day run, built each year from natural ice, follows roughly the same course; it's the only one of its kind in the world. You can watch the **Olympia Bob Run** (☎*081/8300200*) races for around 5 SF. Or you can tear along the run yourself by riding behind an experienced pilot. The ride costs 210 SF; book well in advance. The run is open from late December through early March.

GOLF Samedan's 18-hole **Engadine Golf Course** (☎*081/8510466*), the oldest on the continent, is about 10 minutes by car from St. Moritz. It's open from late May to early October. The **St. Moritz Golf Club** (☎*081/8368236*) has a 9-hole course in the Kulm Park.

HIKING There are dozens of hiking and walking routes around St. Moritz, all well signposted. Maps are available at the tourist office. Most cable cars, funiculars, and some chairlifts run in summer, providing access to higher trails, including the magnificent Via Engiadina path along the mountainside at roughly 6,560 feet to the beginning of the valley.

The full walk takes about six hours, but you can descend to valley level earlier if you are tuckered out.

ICE-SKATING & CURLING The lakeside outdoor **Ludains Skating Rink** (✉*St. Moritz-Bad* ☎*081/8335030*) is open from mid-July to late April. Skate rentals are available. The skating and curling rinks at the **Kulm** (☎*081/8368000*) hotel are open to the public in winter; rental skates and curling lessons are available.

Ticino

BELLINZONA, LOCARNO, LUGANO

Lago di Dentro Cadlimo Piz Tanelin

WORD OF MOUTH

"If you are regretting missing Italy, consider the Ticino, Switzerland's Italian region. I call it Italy Lite; all the wonders of Italy (food, wine, enthusiastic people, language) and none of the inconveniences."
                                                                                    —Catbert

"Locarno was nice. We enjoyed walking around the old town and along the lake. It was so different from the rest of the country— I still don't know how it became part of Switzerland."
                                                                                    —Margo

WELCOME TO TICINO

TOP REASONS TO GO

★ **Luscious Lugano:** Nowhere in the Ticino do Italian chic and Swiss quality mingle so perfectly. But there is more going on here than people-watching and ice-cream tasting: Churches, museums, and the restored Old Town also demand attention.

★ **Land o' Lakes:** Gaze at the verdant mountains, cozy villages, and palm-fronted shores from the vantage point of the elegant old ferry boats that ply the waters of the Lago Maggiore and Lago di Lugano.

★ **Castle-topped Bellinzona:** Old cobblestone streets, shady arcades, and the three fortresses that once upon a time held the line between Italy and the wild Swiss take the visitor back to a time when this region belonged to Milan.

★ **Get a view:** Monte Bré (near Lugano) can be climbed on foot or by funicular, which is faster and far less tiring. Either way, the view from the top is one that will literally take your breath away.

1 Sopraceneri. Capital of the Ticino, Bellinzona has always been a famous crossroads thanks to three passes—the St. Gotthard, the Lukmanier, and the San Bernardino—from the north. The town's great castles—Castelgrande, Montebello, and Sasso Corbaro—prove that Bellinzona was always in the firing line. To the west along Lago Maggiore lies Locarno, Switzerland's sunniest town, with its bevy of Baroque and Renaissance churches (including the cliff-top Santuario della Madonna del Sasso). Just beyond are the lakeside promenades of Ascona, so beloved by painters, and the Brissago Islands, Switzerland's most beautiful botanical garden.

2 Sottoceneri. South of Monte Ceneri, the Ticino changes. While the countryside shelters many Italianate villages clustered around ancient bell towers, the bustling city of Lugano draws all eyes. There are really two Luganos. Sophisticated, modern Lugano is Switzerland's fourth most-important financial center; Lugano of the old-world charm is another, its arcades and twisting streets so reminiscent of a small Italian town. Fashionable boulevards and art-filled museums compete with the fabled waterside promenade, Il Lungolago, and lose out to its stupendous vistas of the blue lake and bluer peaks. On Lago di Lugano's southern shores lie a gaggle of gorgeous villages: Gandria, Campione, and Morcote.

GETTING ORIENTED

Even in Switzerland, this Italian-cultured canton is something of a step-daughter to the other cantons. It does have everything to make it Swiss: high mountains, gorgeous lakes with clean waters, and excellent service. And yet the air has that unmistakable redolence of the Mediterranean. A little inaccessible—wedged into Italy, it hides "behind" a virtual curtain of snow-capped peaks—the Ticino is a happy harbor for Switzerland's Italian-speaking minority.

5

| 0 | | | 7.5 mi |
| 0 | | | 7.5 km |

TICINO PLANNER

Finding a Place to Stay

The hotel industry of this Mediterranean region of Switzerland capitalizes on its natural assets, with lakeside views of Lago Maggiore and Lago di Lugano, and swimming pools and terraces that pay homage to the omnipresent sun.

As Ticino is at its best in spring and fall, and packed with sun-seekers in summer, many hotels close down for the winter. Tourist offices often publish lists of those remaining open, so if you're planning to come in low season—and even in January the lake resorts can be balmy—check carefully.

Keep in mind that most hotels are not air-conditioned, in spite of hot spells in July and August. Vacation resorts don't depend on the demipension (half-board) system like many of their mountain counterparts, but arrangements can be made.

And remember, there are several festivals in all towns in summer, notably Locarno and Lugano—expect full hotels.

Otherwise, the Ticino is moderately well visited throughout most of the year, except in late fall and after the Christmas/New Year period.

How's the Weather?

No one complains about the weather in the Ticino. Palm trees, magnolia, century plants, and full-bodied wines suggest why so many "northerners" come to the canton for their vacation: the weather is milder than elsewhere in Switzerland in winter, while stark summer temperatures are moderated by the lakes and the mountains.

There can be some surprises, though, since you are in the Alps. Sudden storms and drops in temperature are a possibility. So make sure you have a few warm clothes along and something waterproof.

If you intend to trek up the valleys or up to the summit of a mountain, you will definitely need something warm along besides robust hiking boots and sunglasses. Winters are cold up in the mountains, but around the lakes several degrees warmer than elsewhere in Switzerland.

Lush and Mediterranean, the Ticino is gorgeous in springtime; the season starts as early as mid-March here, making the region a popular late-winter escape.

In summertime, lakeside activity surges, and the weather can at times be hot. Warm summer nights are incredibly romantic, particularly on the Lago di Lugano.

Crowds fill the promenades at Lugano and Locarno throughout the summer, but neither waterfront becomes unpleasantly jammed—although the road from Bellinzona to Locarno and Lugano is usually packed.

Great Grotto Grits

The best place to sample Ticino's down-to-earth delicacies is in a "grotto," one of the scores of traditional country restaurants scattered across the region. Some are set deep in the mountains and forests, others can be reached only by boat and have little more than a few picnic tables and a string of festive lights. Some serve only cold meats, but a few offer one or two hot dishes. To experience an authentic grotto, avoid the ones with "ristorante" in their names; the categories of eating establishments are carefully regulated, so these will always be pricier—and not the real thing.

Making the Most of Your Stay

The important parts of the Ticino are all fairly close to one another, but depending on the amount of time you have, you might want to choose one or two home-base locations. Locarno or Ascona will allow you easy and quick access to the Verzasca and Maggia Valleys and to all the sites and sights along Lago Maggiore. Lugano gives you fast access to the Lago di Lugano and the gems of Gandria, Morcote, and Campione. From Bellinzona, you will have good access to everything. And there's lots to do if you want to. If not, you can enjoy long meditative walks in the mountains or along the lakes. Shopping in Lugano, touring the lakes by ferry, or hopping a funicular up a mountain, followed by a simple meal in a "grotto," will give you classic Ticinese moments. On the other hand, more active types will have lots of sports options available, from skiing and snowboarding in winter to swimming, climbing, or golf during the warm months. If in need of a big city, remember that Milan is 1–1½ hours away by train from Lugano.

WHAT IT COSTS IN SWISS FRANCS				
¢	$	$$	$$$	$$$$
RESTAURANTS				
under 15 SF	15 SF– 25 SF	25 SF– 40 SF	40 SF– 60 SF	over 60 SF
HOTELS				
under 100 SF	100 SF–175 SF	175 SF–250 SF	250 SF–350 SF	over 350 SF

Restaurant prices are per person for a main course at dinner. Hotel prices are for two people in a standard double room in high season, including tax and service.

Transportation Basics

As with most of Switzerland, bus lines and railroad tracks crisscross the area.

Good thing, as parking in towns is difficult, making a car more a liability than a pleasure.

Add to that the fact that the Ticinese are not completely considerate drivers, which causes much additional chaos on the roads, especially during rush hours.

Happily, Lugano, Locarno, and Bellinzona are very well connected by train, and all the main sights within the towns can be seen on foot.

There is regular bus service to Ascona from Locarno, or up the Verzasca and Maggia valleys.

Lugano to Morcote, and so on, can be easily done by bus as well.

Two alternatives, of course, are the boats for sights along the Lake Lugano's shore, or alternatively renting bicycles (do one way by bike and return either by bus or by ferry).

5

GETTING AROUND

By Air

The nearest international airport is in Italy. Malpensa, near Milan, is one of the biggest hubs in southern Europe.

Swiss International Air Lines, known as Swiss, Switzerland's domestic carrier, has direct connections to Lugano's airport, Aeroporto Lugano-Agno, from Zürich's Unique Airport, Cointrin in Geneva, and other European destinations.

To get to Lugano from Aeroporto Lugano-Agno, take one of the frequent shuttle buses or a taxi.

Starbus (☎ *091/9948878*) connects Milan's Malpensa and Linate airports with Lugano.

Aeroporto Lugano-Agno (✉ *7 km [4½ mi] west of Lugano, Agno* ☎ *091/6051226*).

Linate (✉ *10 km [6 mi] east of Milan* ☎ *0039/274852200*).

Malpensa (✉ *50 km [31 mi] northwest of Milan* ☎ *0039/0274852200*).

Regional Tourist Office

Ticino Turismo (✉ *Palazzo Civico, Bellinzona* ☎ *091/8252131* 🖷 *091/8254120* ⊕ *www.ticino.ch*).

By Boat & Ferry

Lago di Lugano and Lago Maggiore are plied by graceful steamers that carry passengers from one waterfront resort to another, offering excellent views of the mountains. Steamer travel on Lago di Lugano is included in the Swiss Pass; tickets can be purchased near the docks before departure. On Lago di Lugano, the Navigazione Lago di Lugano (Navigation Company of Lake Lugano) offers excursions around the bay to Gandria and toward the Villa Favorita. Boats owned by Navigazione Lago Maggiore-Bacino Svizzero (Swiss Navigation Company of Lake Maggiore) cruise Lago Maggiore. Discounts are given for Swiss and Swiss Boat passes.

Navigazione Lago di Lugano (✉ *Casella Postale 56, Lugano* ☎ *091/9715223* ⊕ *www.lakelugano.ch*). **Navigazione Lago Maggiore-Bacino Svizzero** (✉ *Lungolago Motta, Locarno* ☎ *0800/5510801* ⊕ *www.navlaghi.it*).

Tour Options

The *Wilhelm Tell Express* carries you by paddle steamer and rail from Luzern over the St. Gotthard Pass and into Locarno and Lugano with a guide and running commentary in English. Inquire at any rail station for details. The *Bernina Express*, Europe's highest Alp-crossing railway, takes you from Chur to St. Moritz in the *Glacier Express;* then you cross the Alps over the Bernina Pass into Italy (in summer it's even possible in an open-air train car) and continue into Lugano by postbus.

By Car

There are two major gateways into the Ticino: the St. Gotthard Pass, in the northwest, and the San Bernardino Pass, to the northeast. From the St. Gotthard Pass, the swift A2 expressway leads down the Valle Leventina to Bellinzona, where it joins with A13, which cuts south from the San Bernardino. A2 directs the mingled traffic flow southward past Lugano to Chiasso and the Italian border, where the expressway heads directly to Como and Milan. As an alternative, there's the St. Gotthard Tunnel—17 km (11 mi) of dense air and darkness speeding you through the Alps rather than over them. If traffic is light, it can cut an hour off your travel time, but if the passes are closed and it's holiday migration time, tunnel traffic can be nasty.

A car is a real asset here if you intend to see the mountain valleys—and a hindrance in the congested lakeside resorts. Lugano is particularly difficult to drive through, and the parking garages are usually packed. Traffic between Bellinzona and Locarno can move at a crawl during high season. There are a handful of main roads between towns, but secondary roads peter out. Wherever you are in the Ticino, the Italian (read: fast and risky) driving style dominates.

By Train

The St. Gotthard route connects south from Zürich, cuts through the pass tunnel, and heads into Bellinzona and Lugano. Side connections lead into Locarno from Brig, crossing the Simplon Pass and cutting through Italy. Swiss Pass travelers do not have to pay Italian rail fares to cross from Brig to Locarno via Domodossola. Trains connect out of Zürich's airport and take about three hours to Lugano, Locarno, and Ascona; from Geneva, catch the Milan express, changing at Domodossola, Locarno, and Bellinzona. Trains do not go directly into Ascona but stop at Locarno: you must connect by taxi or local bus. For train information from Lugano, call the Swiss Federal Railway, here called the Ferrovie Federali Svizzere (FFS).

Secondary rail connections here are minimal and can make all but the most mainstream rail sightseeing a complicated venture; most excursions will require some postbus connections. Nevertheless, there is a regional discount pass called the Holiday Pass FART. The pass is valid for the Lugano and Locarno areas and gives you unlimited free travel for three or seven consecutive days on bus and train and a 30–50 percent discount on others.

Ferrovie Federali Svizzere (FFS) (☎ 0900/300300, 1.19 SF per min).

By Bus

The Palm Express scenic post-bus route carries visitors from St. Moritz to Lugano via the Maloja Pass and Italy.

Reservations are strongly recommended.

It takes about four hours and can be arranged at any train station or tourist office.

You can also contact Railtour Suisse.

There's a convenient postbus sightseeing system here that you can use to get around the region, even into the backcountry.

La Posta (post and telegraph office) publishes illustrated booklets with suggested itineraries and prices.

You can get these through the Autopostale Ticino-Moesano or through local tourist and post offices.

Postbus excursion prices are reduced with the Locarno or Lugano Holiday Passes.

Even better, they are free with the Swiss Pass.

Autopostale Ticino-Moesano (✉ Via S. Balestra, Lugano ☎ 091/8078520 ⊕ www.post.ch).

Railtour Suisse (☎ 031/3780000).

Updated by
Alexis Munier

VISITORS A BIT WEAK ON their geography might hear the names Lugano, Ascona, Locarno, and Bellinzona and assume—quite naturally—that they're in Italy. Color photographs of the region might not even set them straight: nearly every publicity shot shows palm trees and mimosas, azure waters, and indigo skies. Surely this is the Italian Mediterranean or the coast of the Adriatic. But behind the waving date palms are telltale signs: fresh paint, manicured gardens, punctual trains. There's no mistake about it: it's a little bit of Italy, but the canton Ticino is decidedly Swiss.

For the German Swiss, it's a little bit of paradise. They can cross over the St. Gotthard or San Bernardino passes and emerge into balmy sunshine, fill up on gnocchi and polenta in shaded *grotti* (rustic outdoor restaurants), drink merlot from ceramic bowls, gaze at the waters of Lago Maggiore (Lake Maggiore)—and still know their lodging will be strictly controlled by the Swiss Hotel Association. Plus, they never even have to change currency. The combination is irresistible, and so in spring, summer, and fall they pour over the Alps to revel in low-risk Latin delights.

And the Ticinese welcome them like rich, distant cousins, to be served and coddled and—perhaps just a bit—tolerated. For the Italian-speaking natives of the Ticino—a lonely 8% of the Swiss population—are a minority in their own land, dominated politically by the German-speaking Swiss, from whom they are set apart by language as well as culture. Their blood and politics are as Mediterranean as their climate: in a battle over obligatory seat belts, the Ticinese consistently voted to reject the federal intrusion. They were voted down by their Germanic neighbors—a 70% majority—and when they protested, it was brought to vote again, and again they were defeated. Nowadays the Ticinese defy the federal law—and the local policemen, Ticinese themselves, of course, turn a blind and supportive eye.

Their Italian leanings make perfect sense: an enormous mountain chain blocks them from the north, pushing them inexorably toward their lingual roots. Most of the territory of the Ticino belonged to the pre-Italian city-states of Milan and Como until 1512, when the Swiss Confederation took it over by force. It remained a Swiss conquest—oppressed under the then-tyrannical rule of Uri, Schwyz, and Unterwalden, the very cantons now revered for forming the honorable Confederation of Switzerland—until 1798, when from the confusion of Napoléon's campaigns it emerged a free canton, and in 1803 it joined the confederation for good.

It remains a canton apart nonetheless, graceful, open, laissez-faire. Here you'll instantly notice differences in manner and body language among Ticinese engaged in conversation; you'll also notice fewer English-speaking Swiss. The climate, too, is different: there's an extraordinary amount of sunshine here, more than in central Switzerland and even more than in sunny Italy, immediately across the border. Mountain-sports meccas aside, this is the most glamorous of Swiss regions: the waterfront promenades of Lugano, Locarno, and Ascona, lined with pollards, rhododendrons, and bobbing yachts, blend a rich social mix of jet-set resorters. A drive of a few miles brings the canton's impoverished past into view: foothill and mountain villages still scattered with low-roof stone cabins, although nowadays those cabins often prove to have been gentrified into chic vacation homes.

Although they're prosperous, with Lugano standing third in banking, after Zürich and Geneva, the Ticinese hold on to their past, a mountain-people culture that draws them to hike, hunt, and celebrate with great pots of risotto stirred over open outdoor fires. It's that contrast—contemporary glamour combined with an earthy past—that grants travelers a visit that's as balanced and satisfying as a good merlot.

EXPLORING TICINO

The canton is geographically divided into two regions by the small mountain range (1,817 feet) called Monte Ceneri, which rises up south of the valley below Bellinzona. Extending northeast and northwest of Monte Ceneri in the windswept Sopraceneri region are several mountainous valleys, including Valle di Blenio, Valle Maggia, Valle Verzasca, and Valle Leventina. Included in this region north of or, literally, above Monte Ceneri are Locarno and Ascona, which share a peninsula bulging into Lago Maggiore. The more developed southern region, Sottoceneri ("below Ceneri"), is home to business and resort towns, notably Lugano.

SOPRACENERI

The mountainous valleys of Valle di Blenio, Valle Maggia, Valle Verzasca, and Valle Leventina reach, like the fingers of a hand, south from the Alps into the basin of Lago Maggiore and Monte Ceneri, in the Sopraceneri. At the tips are the sun-kissed resorts of Locarno and Ascona, both on the northern edge of Lago Maggiore. Here the true spirit of the canton is still evident in the numerous small valley communities, each of which was politically autonomous at fewer than 100 inhabitants. The Sopraceneri reveals a slightly slower-paced, homier side of the Ticino, leaving the flashier offerings to Lugano in the south.

BELLINZONA

Fodor'sChoice *141 km (88 mi) south of Luzern, 150 km (93 mi) south of St. Moritz.*
★
GETTING HERE
Transportation gateway to the Ticino, Bellinzona is not only on the Zürich–Milan route but has frequent trains running nearly every half-hour to and from Locarno (25 mins, 8 SF) and Lugano (30 mins, 12 SF). Note that the Swiss Federal Railway is here called the Ferrovie Federali Svizzere (FFS). Buses to smaller villages leave from the bus depot at the train station. For schedules for destinations in this chapter, check either the Swiss Railway's Web site, www.sbb.ch, or call 0900/300300

(1.19 SF per min). Remember, if you have a Swiss Pass or another rail-discounting card, it also applies to the buses.

Visitor Information (✉ *Palazzo Civico* ☎ *091/8252131*).

EXPLORING

All roads lead to Bellinzona, the fortified valley city that guards the important European crossroads of the St. Gotthard and San Bernardino routes. The capital of the Ticino, its importance through the ages is evident in the three massive fortified castles that rise over its ancient center. As the only example of late medieval military architecture preserved along the Alpine range, the castles and fortifications have been named a World Heritage Site by UNESCO. They were built by the Sforza and Visconti families, the dukes of Milan who ruled northern Italy and its environs for centuries. In the 15th century many of the surrounding valleys began falling into the hands of the expanding Swiss confederation. Bellinzona, however, remained Italian until Milan itself—as well as Bellinzona—was occupied by the French in 1503. Bellinzona decided to cast its lot with the Swiss Confederation. Ironically, the names of the castles built in part to keep the Swiss at bay were then changed to Schwyz, Uri, and Unterwalden—the three core cantons of the Swiss Confederation. Eventually the names were changed again, and the for-

EATING WELL IN THE TICINO

Of all the Swiss regions, the Ticino can be the most pleasurable in which to eat, as the stylish and simple cuisine of Italy has been adopted virtually intact. Because the Ticinese were once a poor mountain people, their everyday cooking shares the earthy delights of another once-poor mountain people, the Piedmontese, whose steaming polenta and rib-sticking gnocchi break bread with game and meaty porcini mushrooms. *Manzo brasato* (savory braised beef with vegetables), *busecca* (vegetable soup with tripe), and osso buco are standards, as are any number of variations on risotto. Game offerings usually include *coniglio* (rabbit), *lepre* (hare), and *capretto* (roast kid). Wherever you eat, *il piatto del giorno* (the daily special) can help you economize.

As in the rest of Switzerland, local cold meats come in a broad variety, from myriad salamis to prosciutto *crudo*, the pearly pink cured raw ham made famous in Parma. Any food product made locally is called *nostrano*, and the prosciutto crudo nostrano is worth asking for, as you won't find a match for its forthright, gamey flavor back home. Eat it with bread and sweet butter to balance the salt. Most cooks import Italian cheeses—Parmigiano-Reggiano, sharp pecorino—though there are good, hard, white mountain varieties (Piora, Gesero) in most shops. Tiny *formaggini*—little molds of ultra-fresh goat cheese—taste best with coarsely ground black pepper and olive oil. Or try the *zincarlin,* a fresh cheese mixed with parsley, garlic, and pepper.

The local wine is merlot; a warm, generous wine counted as one of the top Swiss reds. The wine is often poured into an individual *boccalino,* a traditional ceramic pitcher, or a small ceramic bowl, to be drunk from like a cup. Instead of beer to quench locals' thirsts, a mix of *gazosa* (lemon-lime soda) and *vino nostrano* (the house red wine) is de rigueur. If you want a real Italian-style espresso, one-finger deep and frothing with golden foam, ask for *un liscio.* Otherwise they'll serve it with cream, Swiss style, and might even charge you extra. If you want a shot of grappa (grape brandy) thrown in, ask for it *corretto*—literally, "correct." Or finish off your meal with a shot of *Nocino,* a traditional walnut liqueur also known as *Ratafiá* (from *rata fiat,* meaning "it's done"). Walnuts picked before San Giovanni's day (June 25) are soaked in grappa and mixed with a secret combination of herbs and spices. Most Nocino is produced privately from closely guarded recipes—no two taste alike.

tresses are known today as Castelgrande, Castello di Montebello, and Castello di Sasso Corbaro.

The three castles have been exceptionally well restored, and each merits a visit (a walk along the ramparts at night is particularly appealing), but the city itself should not be overlooked: it's a classic Lombard town, with graceful architecture, red cobblestones, and an easy, authentically Italian ambience. It's relatively free of tourists and thus reveals the Ticino way of life, complete with a lively produce market on Saturday featuring boar salami, wild mushrooms, and local cheeses.

The **centro storico** *(Old Town)*, with its heavy-column arcades, wrought-iron balconies, and shuttered facades, exhibits the direct influence of medieval Lombardy. The small area is distinguished by red cobblestones.

The **Palazzo Civico,** located in the Old Town on the Piazza Nosetto, is a splendid Renaissance structure that was rebuilt in the 1920s. Its courtyard is framed by two stacked rows of delicate vaulted arcades decorated with sgraffiti depicting Bellinzona in the 19th century. The top floor consists of an airy loggia.

The **Castelgrande** was first mentioned in a document from the 6th century. The current structure, however, dates from the 1200s. The massive exterior is dominated by two heavy, unmatched towers and the remaining portion of a crenellated wall that once stretched all the way to the river. Modern renovations have added an elaborate complex of restaurants and museums, including historical and archaeological exhibitions. The 14th-century ceiling murals, created to embellish the wooden ceiling of a local villa (now demolished), offer a peek at privately commissioned decorative art. A dramatic audiovisual history of Bellinzona and the Ticino Valley is shown in one room. ⊠ *Monte San Michele* ☎ *091/8258145* 💷 *5 SF, 10 SF combination ticket for Castelgrande, Castello di Montebello, and Castello di Sasso Corbaro* ⊙ *Daily 10–6.*

> **WORD OF MOUTH**
>
> "The three castles in Bellinzona are most interesting. They do live opera in the summer at the largest (and lowest); the view from the smallest (and highest) castle is wonderful and you can do a pleasant hike down from the top back into town (take a taxi to the top)."   —BTilke
>
> "In Bellinzona, we had a great lunch on the square and walked to the three castles. They don't have furnished rooms (as at Gruyères or Chillon)—still, the views are great. I remember seeing a post bus stop at one castle, so it's probably easy to get from one to the other."   —LLindaC

The sober, late-Renaissance facade of the **Chiesa Collegiata di San Pietro e San Stefano** *(Collegiate Church of St. Peter and St. Stephen)*, begun in the 16th century, stands across from the Castelgrande. Its Baroque interior is richly decorated with frescoes and stucco work by a host of Ticino artists. Of particular note is the late-18th century Crucifixion attributed to Simone Peterzano that serves as a central altar painting. ⊠ *Piazza Collegiata* ☎ *091/8252131.*

The most striking of Bellinzona's three castles is the **Castello di Montebello.** Its core, the oldest section located behind two drawbridges, dates from the 13th century; the palace and courtyard are from the 15th century, with spectacular walkways around the top of the encircling walls. The center structure houses an attractive, modern Museo Civico (Municipal Museum) and the Museo Archeologico (Archaeology Museum), with exhibits on local history and architecture, including an impressive collection of Gothic and Renaissance stone capitals. ⊠ *Salita ai Castelli* ☎ *091/8251342* ⊕ *www.castellodimontebello.com*

CLOSE UP

Ticino's Fossil Trove

Rooted firmly on the southern shores of Lago di Lugano, the 3,595-foot Monte San Giorgio has been an irresistible draw for paleontologists since the mid-19th century. Scientific excavations in its five successive strata have regularly churned out extremely well-preserved fossils, allowing scientists to study the evolution of various groups of marine creatures of the geological era known as the Middle Triassic (245–230 million years ago). Thousands of the reptiles, fish, and invertebrates found here—some of them unique specimens—have made their way into museums of paleontology in Zürich, Lugano, and Milan.

No wonder, then, that UNESCO added the entire region—an area measuring 2,098 acres and extending across the communities of Meride, Riva San Vitale, and Brusino Arsizio—to the list of World Heritage Natural Sites in July 2003. This designation for Monte San Giorgio is Switzerland's second such honor, coming two years after that for the glaciers spanning the Jungfrau, Aletsch, and Bietschhorn summits.

✉️ *5 SF, 10 SF combination ticket for Castelgrande, Castello di Montebello, and Castello di Sasso Corbaro* 🕙 *Easter–Nov., daily 10–6.*

The **Castello di Sasso Corbaro** is a massive and forbidding fieldstone construction; the almost complete absence of curvature is typical of the Sforza style. It was designed by a Florentine military engineer and built in 1479 for the duke of Milan, who insisted the work be completed in six months, as indeed it was. Temporary art exhibitions are held in the Belvedere and in the Emma Paglia Room. Ambitious walkers can reach the castle in about 45 minutes by treading uphill from the Castello di Montebello along a switchback road through woods; if you're driving, follow the signs to Artore. ☎️ *091/8255906* ✉️ *5 SF, 10 SF combination ticket for Castelgrande, Castello di Montebello, and Castello di Sasso Corbaro* 🕙 *Easter–Nov., daily 10–6.*

Chiesa San Biagio *(Church of St. Biagio)*, one of Bellinzona's two Italianate churches, is a spare medieval treasure guarded on the exterior by an outsize fresco of a soldierly Christ. The 12th-century late-Romanesque structure suggests a transition into Gothic style. Alternating natural red brick and gray stone complement fragments of exquisitely colored 14th-century frescoes. ✉️ *Via San Biagio 13, Bellinzona-Ravecchia* ☎️ *091/8252131.*

Chiesa Santa Maria delle Grazie *(Church of St. Mary of Grace)* was first mentioned in the 15th century, when it was part of a Franciscan monastery, which has now been turned into a retirement home. The church's most remarkable feature is the huge fresco on a wall segmenting the main nave painted by an unknown Lombard artist some time around 1500. It depicts the Crucifixion in the center, surrounded by 15 vignettes from the life of Christ. The church fell victim to a fire in 1996, but was completely restored and reopened in 2006. ✉️ *Via Convento, Bellinzona-Ravecchia* ☎️ *091/8252131.*

The city's art gallery, **Museo Villa dei Cedri,** sporadically dips into its coffers—made up of a donated private collection—to mount worthwhile exhibits. Behind the garden and grounds, the city maintains a tiny vineyard used to produce its very own merlot, available for sale inside. ⊠*Piazza San Biagio 9* ☎*091/8218520* ⊕*www.villacedri.ch* ⊠*8 SF* ☉*Tues.–Fri. 2–6, weekends 11–6.*

WHERE TO EAT

$$$-$$$$ ✕**Castelgrande DeLuxe.** Now that the oldest of the city's castles has been

MODERN ITALIAN   renovated, its chic, modern restaurant merits a visit. Don't expect a

★   quick cafeteria lunch served to shorts-clad tourists: this is a serious experience, with a daringly cool, post-Memphis decor and sophisticated efforts from the Italian chef, such as goose liver with blueberries or pigeon and pearl onions in sweet-and-sour sauce. The wine list flaunts more than 70 Ticino merlots. Just downstairs, there's a lighter atmosphere at the more casual Grotto restaurant. Its stunning summer terrace is a great spot to soak up views and sunshine. ⊠*Monte San Michele* ☎*091/8262353* ⊕*www.castelgrande.ch* ⊟*AE, DC, MC, V* ☉*Closed Mon.*

$$$ ✕**Malakoff.** In this small family restaurant just up the hill from the town

ITALIAN   center, chef Rita Fuso prepares traditional and innovative Italian fare

★   from impeccable high-quality ingredients. The pasta is homemade, and the vegetables and meats often come from local farms; some of the herbs come from the Fusos' own garden. Try seasonal variations on standard regional fare, such as the exquisite lemon and ricotta-filled ravioli in a butter-sage sauce. The best bet (and a great value at around 30 SF) is the daily two-course special, such as homemade rabbit terrine with salad followed by loin of lamb in morel sauce. ⊠*Carrale Bacilieri 10* ☎*091/8254940* ⊟*MC, V* ☉*Closed Sun.*

$$-$$$ ✕**Osteria Sasso Corbaro.** From the heights of the ancient Castello di Sasso

MEDITERRANEAN   Corbaro, this atmospheric restaurant serves meals inside a beautifully restored hall. In the summer you can dine al fresco at sturdy granite tables in the shady, walled-in courtyard. The cooking is Mediterranean with French touches including fresh seafood—a top choice is the pan-fried foie gras with carmelized apples. Good local wines round out the experience. Take the 45-minute walk up from the rail station for a stunning view to help burn off those extra calories before you indulge in desserts like creamy panna cotta and homemade tiramisu layered with ice cream. ⊠*Castello Sasso Corbaro* ☎*091/8255532* ⊟*AE, DC, MC, V* ☉*Closed Mon. and Nov.–Feb.*

WHERE TO STAY

$$ 🏠**Grotto Paudese.** Immaculate, friendly, and family-run, this grotto-cum-bed-and-breakfast perches high above the town in the tiny hamlet of Paudo. Its rooms, a mere handful, are tastefully simple if a bit small; the owners squeeze in the occasional antique chest of drawers. There's an unsurpassed view of the twinkling valley and the Alps beyond. The adjoining grotto is warmly traditional, turning out a robust daily meal (homemade pasta, polenta, and the like). The inn is roughly a 15-minute drive up from Bellinzona. Going east into the Val Morobbia, follow signs for Pianezzo and then for Paudo. **Pros:** a rare

traditional experience; hilltop location benefits from much-appreciated cool breezes. **Cons:** the windy road should be avoided by those who suffer from motion sickness; two of the four rooms share a hall shower. ⊠ *Paudo* ☎ *091/8571468* ⊐ *4 rooms* ⟨⟩ *In-room: no a/c, no phone, no TV, no shower (some). In-hotel: restaurant, bar* ⊟ *V* ⊘ *Closed Mon. and Tues. and mid-Dec.–Feb.* ⊚ *BP.*

$$ \text{\$\$} $$

$$ \text{\$\$} $$ ⊞ **Locanda Brack.** The shady terrace, discriminating wine list, and excellent homemade pastas using mostly organic ingredients are what attract visitors and locals alike to this osteria (closed Monday–Wednesday) perched on the hillside of Gudo, right between Bellinzona and Locarno. But Marco and Gesa Brack also run a very fine bed-and-breakfast in the converted farmhouse. Each room has either a balcony with a spectacular view of the Ticino valley, or a peaceful terrace nestled into the hillside. Furnishings are simple and tasteful. **Pros:** nearly 90% of the culinary ingredients used are organic; owners are passionate to share their unique philosophy of life and homemade wine. **Cons:** remote location between Locarno and Bellinzona; besides the hotel osteria, limited dining choices. ⊠ *Via delle Vigne* ☎ *091/8591254* ⊐ *7 rooms* ⟨⟩ *In-room: no a/c, dial-up, Internet. In-hotel: restaurant, bar, pool* ⊟ *MC, V* ⊘ *Closed Dec.–Feb.* ⊚ *BP.*

LOCARNO

25 km (16 mi) west of Bellinzona, 45 km (28 mi) northwest of Lugano.

GETTING HERE

From Bellinzona, trains are a 20–30 minute ride for 8 SF. Trains from Bern are frequent. The trip lasts about 4 hours; trains pass through Luzern and the Gotthard or the newly opened Lötschberg base tunnel and the Centovalli and cost 75–85 SF. From Geneva, the fastest and most scenic route passes through Domodossola and the Centovalli on a trip that takes around 4½ hours. The Centovalli is all twists and turns, so if you suffer from motion sickness, you may wish to avoid these routes.

Visitor Information (⊠ *Via Largo Zorzi 1* ☎ *091/7910091*).

EXPLORING

Superbly placed on the sheltered curve of the northernmost tip of Lago Maggiore and surrounded on all sides by mountains, Locarno is Switzerland's sunniest town. Subtropical species of flora flourish here, with date palms and fig trees, bougainvillea and rhododendron, and even aloe vera burgeoning on the waterfront. Its two-legged fauna are no less colorful: every spring, summer, and fall the arcaded streets and cafés teem with exotic characters in fur coats and T-shirts, lamé, and leather. Don't forget your sunglasses—you don't show your face in Locarno without a stylish set of shades, especially during August, when the town makes worldwide news with its film festival, showcasing the latest cinema on an outdoor screen in the Piazza Grande; it also hosts international artists in concert.

5

Modern Locarno is actually made up of three communities so tiny and close together that you often don't notice you've moved from one to another: Locarno, Muralto, and Minusio. The town's raison d'être is its waterfront, which has a graceful promenade curving around the east flank of the bay, and a beach and public pool complex along the west. Its clear lake is often as still as glass, reflecting the Ticinese Alps across to the south. Locarno's Lombard-style arcades and historic landmarks continually draw visitors inland as well. There are a few pedestrians-only streets in the heart of the Old Town.

★ The **Piazza Grande** is the heart of the Old Town and its social center: from under the crowded arcades shoppers spill onto the square to lounge in cafés and watch each other drink, smoke, and pose.

Chiesa Nuova (*New Church* ⊠ *Via Cittadella*) is an exuberantly decorated Baroque church (1630) with a disproportionately large statue of St. Christopher on the facade.

Down the street from the New Church, the **Casa dei Canonici** (*House of the Canons* ⊠ *Via Cittadella*) dates from the same period. Note the lovely interior courtyard; it's now a private house.

The harmonious, almost delicate **Chiesa di San Francesco** (*Church of St. Francis* ⊠ *Via S. Francesco*) and its convent stand cheek-by-jowl with the painfully bulky, modern building that houses the city's Department of Education, Culture, and Sports. The history of the parish goes back to the early 13th century, when it was allegedly founded by Saint Anthony of Padua. The current church was begun in 1538, however, on the remains of earlier constructions. The most remarkable aspect of the interior, perhaps, is the series of frescoes, some of which are unfortunately in very poor shape. Note the fine marble carvings and paintings on the side altars. Concerts are performed every spring and fall in the church sanctuary; contact the tourist office for more information.

The 17th-century **Chiesa di Sant'Antonio** (*Church of St. Anthony* ⊠ *Piazza Sant'Antonio*) stands on a small plaza in the midst of narrow streets lined with splendid old houses in both medieval and Baroque styles.

Immediately to the left of the Church of St. Anthony stands the **Casa Rusca**, an 18th-century residence that now serves as the city art gallery. Its permanent collections include the work of Jean Arp, and temporary exhibits highlight both Swiss and international artists. ⊠ *Piazza Sant'Antonio* ☎ *091/7563185* 🗺 *7 SF* ☉ *Tues.–Sun. 10–5.*

Built in 1300 as a stronghold of the dukes of Milan, Castello Visconteo was soon virtually destroyed by the invading Swiss Confederates. Today it contains a **Museo Civico e Archeologico** *(Municipal and Archaeological Museum)*, with Roman relics—including a major glass collection—and Romanesque sculpture. ⊠ *Piazza Castello 2* ☎ *091/7563461* 🗺 *7 SF* ☉ *Apr.–Oct., Tues.–Sun. 10–noon, 2–5.*

★ Offering a god's view of Locarno and the lake, the **Santuario della Madonna del Sasso** *(Sanctuary of the Madonna of the Rock)* breathtakingly crowns the hilltop hamlet of Orselina—pilgrims make the steep hike up to it, but most opt for the short funicular that starts from close to the train station (round-trip costs 6.60 SF). Open to regular visitors by appointment only, the sprawling church complex stands where, in 1480, Brother Bartolomeo da Ivrea had a vision of the Virgin Mary; the sanctuary was completed seven years later and was gradually enlarged to include a monastery, a Way of the Cross, and a church. Within the sanctuary you'll find several side chapels featuring statues depicting scenes from the New Testament, such as the Last Supper. Several halls are incongruously filled with modern votive candleholders. The church, which was given a neo-Renaissance facade in the late 19th century, is a lavishly decorated affair. Among its artistic treasures are Bramantino's 1520 *The Flight into Egypt* and Ascona-born Antonio Ciseri's *Christ Carried to the Sepulcher*, a dramatic, Caravaggesque procession scene painted in 1870. Admission rates depend on the number of visitors. There is talk of renovation in the next few years, so be sure to call ahead. ⊠ *Via Santuario 2, Orselina* 2 ☎*091/7436265* ✆*By appointment only.*

> **WORD OF MOUTH**
>
> "A great way to tie in with the Bernina Express rail route is to take the Palm Express Swiss postal bus, one of the finest of the fabled Swiss postbus rides and so named because it links Lugano and the Swiss Riviera to St. Moritz. From Lugano it heads out along the shores of idyllic Lake Lugano (passing ancient Gandria) and then enters Italy, going overland to Lake Como and stopping for a break at cute Menaggio, one of Lake Como's marquee resorts. Hugging the lake, it traverses a wide valley to Chiavenna and then re-enters Switzerland to end in St. Moritz." —PalQ

OFF THE BEATEN PATH

Cimetta. A winter-sports center with views of Monte Rosa, the Swiss Alps, and the Italian Apennines, Cimetta (5,482 feet) can be reached only by chairlift; first you must catch a hypermodern cable car designed by the Ticinese star architect Mario Botta from the district of Orselina (accessible using the funicular near the train station) to Cardada, then a chair lift to the resort. But don't be put off; the ride is part of the fun: as the lake falls away below, you'll sail over meadows and wooded hills. Cimetta is also a hiker's paradise. The round-trip costs 33 SF. ☎*091/7353030* ☉*Apr.–Oct., daily 8–8; late Dec.–Mar., Mon.–Thurs. 9–6, Fri.–Sun. 8–8.*

WHERE TO EAT

$$$

ITALIAN

Fodor's Choice

★

✕**Osteria del Centenario.** Across from the waterfront east of the town center, this new restaurant serves innovative Franco-Italian cuisine that's unashamedly nouvelle and absolutely top quality, from its moderately priced business lunch to the all-out 81 SF, five-course, *menu de dégustation* (sampling menu). Specialties include prawns with olives and lavender on a bed of wilted spinach. You can have an aperitif on the lakefront terrace before sitting down to a meal in a chic environment with modern art lining the walls, warm terracotta tiles, and dark-wood furnishings. ⊠ *Viale Verbano 17, Locarno-Muralto* ☎*091/7438222* ⊕*www.osteria centenario.ch* ▤*AE, MC, V* ☉*Closed Sun. and Mon.*

$$
ITALIAN
✕ **Casa del Popolo.** The politics lean left at this popular restaurant, whose sprawling terrace spills out onto "Corporation Square" (Piazza Corporazione), but the Italian favorites are done just right for all. Try the amazingly delicate *piccata alla Milanese* (veal cutlets pounded thin, coated in egg, and sautéed), the spicy *penne all'arrabbiata* (pasta with red pepper and tomato sauce), or any of the 20 varieties of pizza. Red-checkered tablecloths and occasional appearances by the local politico round it all out. A great deal, but note that the crowds may come more for the ambience than the cuisine itself. ✉ *Piazza Corporazione* ☎*091/7511208* ▭*No credit cards.*

> **THE MIGHT OF THE GARTER**
>
> Along the wisteria-lined waterfront there are cafés where visitors mingle with the locals engaged in the time-honored mid-morning Italian habit of putting the world right. Back in 1925, four visitors had something else in mind, when Briand, Stresseman, Mussolini, and Chamberlain signed the Locarno Pact here. It might have been called something different, as the story goes that the meeting was to be held elsewhere but the French minister's mistress insisted on Locarno. If so, one admires her taste.

WHERE TO STAY

$$–$$$
▥ **Cittadella.** Perched near Lago Maggiore, this Old Town option has guest rooms that are pleasing, some up under the rafters, all with classic stone-tile floors in cream and red. They may verge on the simple, but they're good value. Even better, the popular trattoria downstairs offers inexpensive regional food—pizzas, pastas, simply prepared fish—with fancier fish dishes on tap in the more formal restaurant upstairs. Preparations are light, flavors subtle with oils and herbs, deliciously evident in the buttery monkfish medallions with cracked pink pepper. **Pros:** surprisingly peaceful location in the heart of the old town; tasty local seafood virtually at your feet. **Cons:** top-floor rooms can get stuffy in the summer; reserve online—sometimes difficult to get through to the staff by phone. ✉ *Via Cittadella 18* ☎*091/7515885* ⊕*www.www.cittadella.ch* ✑*10 rooms* ♿*In-room: no a/c, no phone. In-hotel: 2 restaurants, no elevator* ▭*AE, DC, MC, V* ⊙*BP* ☉*Closed Sun.–Mon. in June–July; Mon. in Aug.–May.*

$$
▥ **Dell' Angelo.** What better place to start your day or experience the goings-on in Locarno than at the tip of Piazza Grande. The Dell' Angelo was based on a 1674 structure but rebuilt in 1976, with ground-floor arches and solid, iron-trimmed balconies. Inside are wrought-iron grilles, fluffy bedspreads, and darkly stained furniture, but you can admire the chintz and damask under the faded remains of frescoed vaulting in the upstairs breakfast room. The restaurant on the ground floor features wood-oven pizzas and other delights. **Pros:** the only hotel in the Old Town center; fourth-floor terrace has dreamy lake views—ask to have your breakfast served here if the sun is out. **Cons:** somewhat staid interiors; lobby has a decidedly worn feel; not all staff speak flawless English. ✉ *Piazza Grande* ☎*091/7518175* ⊕*www.hotel-dell-angelo.ch* ✑*55 rooms* ♿*In-room: safe. In-hotel: restaurant, parking (fee)* ▭*AE, MC, V* ⊙*BP.*

$$ 🛏**Hotel Navegna.** It may not look like much from the outside, but this is
Fodor'sChoice a true diamond in the rough, right on the lake farther up the shore from
★   the promenade. The rooms are simply furnished in bright florals, and
there's a fireplace in the living room for damp days. But it's the inventive Ticinese cooking that earns raves for proprietor Enrico Ravelli,
who supplies the kitchen with fresh poultry, eggs, vegetables, and herbs
from his own farm in the hills. **Pros:** the phenomenally delicate homemade pastas shouldn't be missed; gregarious owner is an attraction in
himself. **Cons:** to reach the hotel's isolated location on foot, count on
a 30-minute walk from the train station (by car, it's easiest to reach the
hotel via the Minusio exit from the A13 highway). ⊠ *Via alla Riva 2,
Locarno-Minusio* 🕾*091/7432222* ⊕*www.navegna.ch* ⇥*20 rooms*
⚲*In-room: no a/c. In-hotel: restaurant, bicycles* ▱*MC, V* ⊗*Closed
late Dec.–Easter* 🍴*BP.*

NIGHTLIFE & THE ARTS

BARS   The **Bar Lungolago** (⊠ *Via Bramantino 1, Locarno* 🕾*091/7515246*)
draws a young and style-conscious crowd. **La Regina** (⊠ *Via Naviglio
Vecchio 4* 🕾*091/7514111*) is a popular spot to sip cocktails on their
glass-covered terrace. A fun experience on a hot summer night is the
little **Katjaboat** (⊠ *Viale Verbano 25, Locarno* 🕾*079/6863990* ⊗*Nov.–
Feb.*), a bar docked opposite the Hotel Rosa-Seegarten; it occasionally
sets off into the lake broadcasting jazzy sounds and crooners.

CASINO   The **Casinò di Locarno** (⊠ *Via Largo Zorzi 1, Piazza Grande*
🕾*091/7511535*) has 150 slot machines and other various gambling
options. It's open every day from noon to 3 AM, and until 4 AM on Friday and Saturday nights.

FILM   The **Locarno International Film Festival** (⊠ *Via B. Luini 3a* 🕾*091/7562121*
⊕*www.pardo.ch*), gaining ground on the prestige front because of
the caliber of the films it premieres, takes place every August in the
Piazza Grande.

MUSIC   One of the latest events to be held on the Piazza Grande is **Moon and
Stars** (⊠*Piazza Grande* 🕾*0900/800800 in Switzerland only* ⊕*www.
moonandstarslocarno.ch*), a series of evening concerts by international
pop stars held during the second week of July.

THEATER   The **Teatro di Locarno** (⊠*Palazzo Kursaal, Via Largo Zorzi 1*
🕾*091/7561093*) hosts international theatrical companies from September through May. For tickets, contact the Locarno tourist office.

VALLE MAGGIA

*4 km (2 mi) northwest of Locarno, 30 km (19 mi) northwest of
Lugano.*

GETTING HERE

Getting into Ticino's valleys usually requires buses, which have infrequent departures from the Locarno train station. The trip up Valle
Maggia, for example, costs 29 SF and lasts nearly 1½ hours to Cevio.
The Ferrovie Autolinee Regionali Ticinesi runs a train into Valle Maggia

up to Ponte Brolla (departures are more frequent in the earlier morning and later afternoon, where you must take a bus. Valle Maggia is 4 km (2 mi) northwest of Locarno, 30 km (19 mi) northwest of Lugano.

EXPLORING

A drive through this rugged agricultural valley that stretches northwest from Locarno will give you a sense of the tough living conditions endured for centuries by Ticinese farmers, whose descendants today quarry granite. The valley is cut so far into the earth in part that sunlight in winter never seems to reach bottom—a stark contrast to sunny Locarno, only a short distance south. Until the 1920s many

> **FAITH, HOPE & CLARITY**
>
> Beyond Bignasco, to the east, lies the Val Lavizzara. At Peccia the road splits again, with Val Sambuco to the east. Nearly at the end of this valley, in tiny Mogno, stands a beautiful modern chapel built in 1994 by world-renowned Ticinese architect Mario Botta (who has designed headline-making structures, including the San Francisco Museum of Modern Art). Constructed in simple lines, the minimalist chapel is built of granite ashlars in two colors, creating remarkable patterns.

Valle Maggia natives emigrated to the United States; some returned, bringing with them several English phrases that still pepper the local dialect. As you pass through Gordevio, Maggia, Someo, and Cevio—the latter, the valley's main village—you feel as if you're in a time capsule. There's little commercialization, and the mostly 17th-century houses call to mind a movie set. Bignasco, just beyond Cevio, is the last village before the valley splits in two as you continue north.

ASCONA

3 km (1¾ mi) west of Locarno.

GETTING HERE

From Locarno, pick up the bus (2.80 SF, tickets are available at machines) on the lake end of the Piazza Grande. It leaves every 15 minutes. You can also take the ferry over for a more romantic, 30-minute ride (16 SF round-trip). No trains head to Ascona. The tourist office is the one based in Locarno.

EXPLORING

Although it's only a few minutes from Locarno, tiny Ascona has a life of its own. Little more than a fishing village until the end of the 19th century, the town was adopted by a high-minded group of Northerners who arrived to develop a utopian, vegetarian artists' colony on **Monte Verità,** the hillside park behind the waterfront center. Influenced by Eastern and Western religions as well as the new realms of psychology, its ideals attracted thousands of sojourners, including dancer Isadora Duncan and psychologist C. G. Jung. You can visit the group of Monte Verità buildings, including the unusual flat-roof, wooden Casa Anatta, and view papers and relics of the group's works. ☎091/7910327 🖃6 SF ☉Apr., May, and Sept., Tues.–Sun. 2:30–6:30; July and Aug., Tues.–Sun. 3–7.

Monte Verità's influence spread and its reputation grew throughout the world. Today the still-small village of 5,000 attracts artists, art restorers, and traditional bookbinders to its ancient, narrow streets.

★ On the waterfront, however, it's a sun-and-fun scene, with the pedestrians-only **Piazza Motta** crowded with sidewalk cafés and the promenade on the water's edge swarming with boats.

Behind Piazza Motta, a charming labyrinth of lanes leads uphill past art galleries (not all showing gallery-quality work) to **Via Borgo,** lined with contemporary shops and galleries.

OFF THE BEATEN PATH

Isole di Brissago. Alpine drama and subtropical colors are wed in Brissago, yet another flowery lakefront resort at the lowest elevation in Switzerland, which is an easy excursion by car or bus from Ascona. The main attraction, however, lies offshore: federally preserved as botanical gardens, the Brissago Islands are set like jewels in the lake and teem with more than 1,000 species of subtropical plants. Plaques identify the flora in Italian, German, and French; an English guide to the plants is for sale at the gate (8 SF). Have lunch or drinks at the restaurant, in a beautifully restored 1929 villa that now doubles as a seminar center. Boats bound for the islands depart regularly from Brissago, Porto Ronco, Ascona, and Locarno. You must leave with the last boat back to the mainland—usually around 6 PM—so check the schedule carefully when planning your excursion. Purchase your ticket at the entrance to the gardens or when you book your boat trip; Swiss Boat Pass discounts apply. ☎091/7516140 for boat, 091/7914361 for tour ⛴Boat: 16 SF round-trip from Ascona, 26 SF round-trip from Locarno; gardens: 8 SF ☉Daily 9–6 ☉Mid-Oct.–Mid-Mar.

WHERE TO EAT

$$
FUSION
✕**Seven.** Locals and tourists alike flock to Seven for more than just its sleek, minimalist interior. On a Friday or Saturday night, this is *the* place to see and be seen in the greater Locarno area. The restaurant/bar/lounge operates on a "seven" theme: the menu consists of seven sets of seven dishes, including feisty Asian, classic Italian, and so-called "garden" fare. Though you may be drawn to more glamorous choices like the pike-perch with broccoli, vanilla, and almonds, the risotto is outstanding. Creamy, soft, but with a hint of chewiness to the rice; it's one of the few restaurants to get it truly right. ✉*Via Moscia CH-6612* ☎*091/7807777* ☲*AE, DC, MC, V.*

$$
ITALIAN
✕**Hostaria San Pietro.** If you're looking for a bite in the Old Town, take out your map and try your best to find this charming restaurant. Tucked away in a maze of tiny streets, this little gem offers creative Italian-influenced pasta and fish dishes. Sample its fresh local catch (often a fish fillet in lemon basil sauce), plump ravioli stuffed with vegetables and toasted almonds, or any of the grilled specialties. The most romantic tables are in the intimate garden, slipped between the walls of neighboring houses. ✉*Passagio S. Pietro 6* ☎*091/7913976* ☲*AE, DC, MC, V* ☉*Closed Mon. and Jan.*

$$ ✗**Grotto du Rii.** On your way to or from Italy, this beautiful stone grotto-
ITALIAN   house with lush flowers pouring out of its window boxes is straight
Fodor'sChoice   out of a fairy tale. The rooms inside cast their spell as they are cozily
★   crammed with all manner of folkloric charm—carriage-wheel lamps,
mounted animals, fireplace inglenooks. Enjoy the rosemary-infused
wine on the terrace, followed by *brasato* (beef shoulder) with polenta
and the daring *dolce sorpresa* (surprise dessert). On Tuesday night the
four-course meal accompanied by Ticinese musicians is a good deal. The
restaurant is a short walk from the Centovalli train station. Intragna,
whose church tower is the tallest in the Ticino, is a good spot from
which to begin a hike into the hills. ⊠ *Via Cantonale, Intragna (9
km/5 mi northwest of Ascona)* ☎*091/7961861* ⊕*www.grottodurii.ch*
☉*Closed Wed. in Sept.–June.*

$$ ✗**Osteria Nostrana.** The tables of this bustling restaurant spread into the
ITALIAN   piazza overlooking the lake. Inside, rough wooden ceilings, marble-top
tables, chandeliers, and a hodgepodge of photos and posters add to its
charm. Look for the spaghetti Enzo (with porcini mushrooms, bacon,
and cream) along with daily and seasonal specials. If you haven't met
your weekly pizza quota, try their simple Margherita—a crispy classic that never goes out of style. The wine list, with more than 100
Italian and Swiss vintages, deserves consideration. ⊠*Piazza Motta*
☎*091/7915158* ▭*AE, DC, MC, V.*

WHERE TO STAY

$$$–$$$$ ▦**Castello Seeschloss.** Dating from 1250, this Romantik property is a
★   romantic enough hotel as is—not even taking into account its garden
setting and position across from the waterfront. Its interior is rich with
frescoes, beams, and heavy masonry, recently lightened with a contem-
porary touch. Each room is different: a wrought-iron bed in the back
tower, a blue wooden canopy bed in Room 203, or the lavish front
tower room with a loft. There is a private courtyard for summer-night
dining, along with an isolated pool. **Pros:** lakeside rooms have original
16th- to 18th-century frescoes; deluxe tower rooms start not much
higher than standard doubles. **Cons:** not all rooms have a/c—be sure
to request one; tower rooms can be reached only by spiral staircase.
⊠*Piazza Motta* ☎*091/7910161* ⊕*www.castello-seeschloss.ch* ⟲*45
rooms* ⚿*In-room: no a/c (some), safe, refrigerator. In-hotel: 3 restau-
rants, bar, pool* ▭*AE, DC, MC, V* ☉*Closed Jan. and Feb.* ▦|*BP.*

$$$$ ▦**Giardino.** The Great Gatsby would feel in his element in this Relais
Fodor'sChoice   & Châteaux property that's as glamorous as a Mediterranean villa
★   yet fabulously modern. The luxury borders on decadence: the sheets
are pure linen, ground-floor rooms have small, private gardens, and
there's a landscaped pool. The restaurants are excellent: try Aphrodite,
with modern Italian and vegetarian cuisine and rates among the best
in Switzerland. Restaurant Ecco surprises with so-called "molecular"
cuisine, which attempts to find new ways of cooking based on busting
preconceived rules with scientific experientation. It may sound bizarre,
but the results are often delicious. **Pros:** Sundays often feature ballet
recitals or jazz or opera performances; spectacular lush garden setting.
Cons: overflowing with German and Swiss-German tourists; some say
that regular guests seem to get preferential treatment. ⊠*Via Segnale*

10 ☎*091/7858888* ⊕*www.giardino.com* ⇔*54 rooms, 18 suites, 5 apartments* ⬠*In-room: safe, refrigerator, Wi-fi, plasma TV. In-hotel: 2 restaurants, bars, pool, gym, salon, spa, bicycles, babysitting* ⊟*AE, DC, MC, V* ⊘*Closed mid-Nov.–Apr.* ⦿*MAP.*

$$$ ⛳ **Tamaro.** The shuttered windows of this 18th-century patrician house look out on the waterfront; inside, you can lounge in sitting rooms richly furnished with antiques, books, and even a grand piano. The rooms range from lavish corner doubles with lake views and reproduction antiques to tiny quarters overlooking the courtyard that are an excellent value. **Pros:** personable staff who aren't afraid to show a good sense of humor; there's a private sun terrace high over the street with fine lake views. **Cons:** not all rooms have a/c—be sure to request one; rooms have no Internet access, but free Wi-fi is available in the lobby. ⬚*Piazza G. Motta 35* ☎*091/7854848* ⊕*www.hotel-tamaro. ch* ⇔*51 rooms* ⬠*In-room: no a/c (some), safe, refrigerator. In-hotel: 3 restaurants, pool, bicycles, parking (fee)* ⊟*AE, DC, MC, V* ⊘*Closed mid-Nov.–Feb.* ⦿*BP.*

NIGHTLIFE & THE ARTS

The ideals that brought Isadora Duncan here still bring culture to Ascona: every year it hosts a series of world-class jazz and classical music concerts. The lakefront piazza serves as an open-air stage for almost daily summer entertainment, with mime, theater, and live pop bands. Locarno's August film festival is only a cab ride away across the peninsula.

BARS & DANCING — At Hotel Eden Roc, **Eden Bar** (⬚*Via Albarelle 16* ☎*091/7857171* ⊕*www.edenroc.ch*) is the place to sip bellinis (peach liqueur with champagne) and listen to live music.

MUSIC — **JazzAscona New Orleans & Classics** (☎*091/7910091* ⊕*www.jazzascona.com*) seeks out performers a cut above standard Dixieland and swing groups, and brings an amazing international selection of them to its open-air bandstands in June and July. The **Settimane Musicali** (☎*091/7910091* ⊕*www.settimane-musicali.ch*) bring in orchestras, chamber groups, and top-ranking soloists to Ascona and Locarno. Events run from late August to mid-October.

SOTTOCENERI

Although Monte Ceneri is no Everest, it marks the borderline between the Sopraceneri with its vastly different southern cousin "below" the Ceneri. The Sottoceneri is the Ticino with attitude, where culture and natural beauty join forces with business and commerce. The resort town of Lugano is an international glamour magnet, but even there the incredible scenery and traditional warmth haven't been completely upstaged.

SWITZERLAND

0   5 mi

0   5 km

ITALY

Lugano
see detail
map

Gandria

di Lugano

ITALY

Agno

Paradiso

Campione

Ponte Tresa

Monte
San Salvatore

Argegno

Melide

Monte
Generoso

Ghirla

Morcote

S233

Riva
San Vitale

A2

Chiasso

Sottoceneri

KEY

⊢•⊣ *Cable Car/ Funicular*
⊢—⊣ *Rail lines*

LUGANO

45 km (28 mi) southeast of Ascona, 39 km (24 mi) southeast of Locarno.

GETTING HERE

From Bellinzona, trains take about 30 minutes and cost 11.60 SF (unless you purchase a cheaper Zürich–Lugano direct ticket); trains leave several times per hour. Trains from Locarno run at least once an hour (with a change usually in Bellinzona or Giubiasco); the trip lasts nearly one hour and costs 16.20 SF. Lugano is 1–1 ½ hours away from Milan, with very frequent connections, 12.80 SF. Trains coming from Geneva pass either through Bern/Luzern, or Zürich for 5- to 6-hour journeys. Postal buses spider out from Lugano to hamlets and main towns from the depot on Via Serafino Balestra.

Visitor Information Lugano (✉ *Piazza della Riforma* ☎ *091/9133232*).

EXPLORING

Strung around a sparkling bay like Venetian glass beads, with dark, conical mountains rising primordially out of its waters and icy peaks framing the scene, Lugano earns its nickname as the Rio of the Old World. Of the three world-class waterfront resorts, Lugano tops Ascona and Locarno for architectural style, sophistication, and natural beauty.

Too bad it recently lost its main museum—the fabulous old master painting collection of Baron Hans-Heinrich Thyssen-Bornemisza has been packed off to Madrid and is no longer in state at Lugano's Villa Favorita. This isn't to say that it has avoided the pitfalls of a successful modern resort: there's thick traffic right up to the waterfront, much of it in manic Italian style, and it has more than its share of concrete waterfront high-rise hotels with balconies skewed to produce "a room with a view" regardless of aesthetic cost. Yet the sacred *passeggiata*—the afternoon stroll to see and be seen that winds down every Italian day—asserts the city's true personality as a graceful, sophisticated resort. It's not Swiss, not Italian…just Lugano. Note: Many phone numbers in Lugano have—an inexplicable oddity—a Locarno prefix.

MAIN ATTRACTIONS

5 **Chiesa di Santa Maria degli Angioli** *(Church of St. Mary of the Angels).*
★ The simple facade doesn't prepare you for the riches within. Begun in the late 15th century, the church contains a magnificent fresco of the *Passion and Crucifixion,* as well as *The Last Supper* and *Madonna with the Infant Jesus,* all by Bernardino Luini (1475–1532). ⊠*Piazza Luini, Old Town.*

6 **Giardino Belvedere** *(Belvedere Gardens).* This lakefront sculpture garden frames a dozen modern works with palms, camellias, oleanders, and magnolias. At the far west end there's a public swimming area. ⊠*On lake side of Quai Riva Antonio Caccia near Piazza Luini, Old Town* 🎫*Free* ⊙*Daily 24 hrs.*

8 **Il Lungolago** *(lake promenade).* This 2-km (1-mi) waterfront path lined
★ with pollarded lime trees, funereal cypresses, and graceful palm trees stretches from the Lido all the way to the Paradiso neighborhood. Il Lungolago is the place to see and be seen—while taking in the views, of course. At night luminous fountains turn the lake near the Parco Civico into a special attraction.

7 **Museo d'Arte Moderna** *(Museum of Modern Art).* Consistently outstanding temporary exhibitions are the hallmark of this museum. Recent exhibits have included works by George Baselitz, Jeanne Claude and Christo, Egon Schiele, and Chagall. Brochures are available in English. The museum has only one or two exhibitions a year, which last several months, so check out the museum's Web site to find out this year's schedule. ⊠*Villa Malpensata, Riva Antonio Caccia 5, Lungolago* 🕿*058/8667201* ⊕*www.museodartemoderna-lugano.ch* 🎫*12–25 SF.*

9 **Museo Cantonale d'Arte** *(Cantonal Art Museum).* A group of three palaces dating from the 15th to the 19th centuries was adapted for this museum. Its exhibits include paintings, sculpture, and photography, including some important avant-garde works. The permanent collection holds works by Klee, Turner, Degas, Renoir, and Hodler, as well as contemporary Ticinese artists. Descriptive material is available in English. ⊠*Via Canova 10, Old Town* 🕿*091/9104780* ⊕*www. museo-cantonale-arte.ch* 🎫*Permanent collection 7 SF, plus 10 SF for temporary exhibits* ⊙*Daily 10–5.*

Lugano

TO TRAIN STATION

V. Massagno
Gerso
V. San Gottardo
V. Zoppi
V. Gatti
V. Cantonale
V. Monte · Ceneri
V. Ginevra
V. Berna
V. Dufour
V. Ciseri
V. d'Alberti
Viale Stefano Franscini
V. Giuseppe
V. Maderno
Corso · Elvezia
V. Antonio · Fusoni
Curti
V. Lambertenghi
Piazzale P. Pelli
V. Speranza
V. al Chios
Via Pietro Capelli
Viale
Cassarate
V. Serafino Balestra
V. del Tigl
V. Campo Mar
V. Alberto Giacometti
V. Emilio
Bossi
V. Fr. Somaini
V. Luigi Canonica
V. Lavizzari
Villa Favorita Castagnola Parks
Corso Pestalozzi
V. G.B. Pioda
V.C. Frasca
Quartiere Maghetti
Corso Elvezia
Pza. Castello
Viale Carlo Cattaneo
Via Foce
V. P. Peri
V. Pretorio
V. Nizzola
V. d. Calducci
V. Stauffacher
Pza. dell' Indipendenza
S.M. Chiattone
Pza. Dante
V. M. Luini
Posta
V. Canova
Pza. Cioccaro
G. Vegezzi
Albizzi
Pza. della Riforma
V. Cattedrale
V. Pessina
V. dei Solari
Pza. Maraini
Riva Giocondo Albertolli
Pza. R. Rezzonico
Imbarcadero Centrale
V. San Lorenzo
V. T. Tasso
V. Giuseppe
Motta
V. Nassa
Riva V. Vela
Pza. Luini
Riva Antonio Caccia

Lago di Lugano

- ① ② ③ ④ ⑤ ⑥ ⑦ ⑧ ⑨ ⑩ ⑪ ⑫ ⑬

KEY

- ✦✦✦ Funicular
- 🛈 Tourist Information

0   1/4 mile
0   400 meters

Cattedrale di San Lorenzo **3**

Chiesa di Santa Maria degli Angioli **5**

Giardino Belvedere **6**

Lido **13**

Il Lungolago **8**

Museo d'Arte Moderna **7**

Museo Cantonale d'Arte **9**

Museo Cantonale di Storia Naturale **12**

Museo Civico di Belle Arti **11**

Palazzo Civico **2**

Parco Civico **10**

Parco del Tassino **4**

Piazza della Riforma **1**

A GOOD WALK

Begin at the **Piazza della Riforma**, which is dominated by the **Palazzo Civico**, or town hall. Look up to the gable above the clock to see the city's coat of arms. (The building also houses the tourist office, whose entrance is on the lake side.)

On the western side of the square the Piazza della Riforma bleeds into the **Piazza Rezzonico,** which contains a large fountain by Otto Maraini dating from 1895.

Heading out of the Piazza della Riforma on the north side, onto the Via Luvini, you come to the **Piazza Dante,** which is dominated by a large department store and a bank. From here, if you pop over one street east to the busy Via Pretorio, you can get a look at Lugano's oldest building, the Pretorio (1425), at No. 7. Back at Piazza Dante, turn left down Via Pessina, which leads you into the **Piazza Cioccaro,** on your right. Here the funicular from the train station terminates and the typical *centro storico* (Old Town) begins, its narrow streets lined with chic clothing shops and small markets offering pungent local cheeses and porcini mushrooms.

From the Piazza Cioccaro walk up the shop-lined staircase street of Via Cattedrale. The street curves left, ending at the **Cattedrale di San Lorenzo**. Take a moment to enjoy the view from the church square.

Head back and then south along the waterfront promenade known as **Il Lungolago**, and at the Imbarcadero Centrale (Central Wharf) take the underpass to cross the road, coming back up at the Piazza della Riforma.

Leave the piazza at the northeast side through a portico onto the Via

Canova. After crossing over the Via della Posta/Via Albrizzi, you come to the **Museo Cantonale d'Arte**, on your right.

Continue straight ahead to the 17th-century church of San Rocco, with its neo-Baroque facade. Turn left onto Via Carducci before you reach the church and you'll find a small orange-tile pedestrian entranceway into the **Quartiere Maghetti**—a town within a town. It's a tangle of streets full of porticoes, little squares, shops, and offices, a modern take on old forms, created in the early 1980s by the architects Camazind, Brocchi, and Sennhauser.

Exit the Quartiere Maghetti onto Via Canova (you'll be behind the church now) and continue east, crossing Via Stauffacher. On your left is the open **Piazza dell'Independenza.** Cross over the wide Corso Elvezia to enter the **Parco Civico.** Inside the grounds, in addition to the nearly 15 acres of greenery, you'll find the **Museo Civico di Belle Arti** and **Museo Cantonale di Storia Naturale.**

From here you can opt to spend the afternoon at the **Lido**, the city's public beach and pool, just east of the park across the River Cassarate.

Or you can head back to town along the waterfront promenade, and take in the stunning mountain views: straight ahead, the rocky top of Monte Generoso (5,579 feet), and flanking the bay at right and left, respectively, Monte San Salvatore and Monte Brè.

Remember it is best to start your tour through the city in the morning, before it gets too hot. Note that the museums are closed on Monday.

⓫ Museo Civico di Belle Arti *(Municipal Art Museum).* The restored Villa Ciani, with its lofty vaulted ceilings and tile floors, displays hundreds of works by Swiss and European artists from the 15th to the 20th centuries. Especially noteworthy is the extensive collection of paintings by Futurist artist Umberto Boccioni, Cesare Tallone, and Impressionists Monet, Rousseau, and Matisse. English-language brochures are available. ⊠ *Villa Ciani, Parco Civico* ☎*058/8667214* 🎟*12 SF* ☉*Tues.–Sun. 10–noon, 2–6.*

ALSO WORTH SEEING

❸ Cattedrale di San Lorenzo *(Cathedral of St. Lawrence).* Behind this church's early Renaissance facade is a Baroque interior with recently restored frescoes and a baptismal font dating from 1430. The church has pre-medieval origins: it became a collegiate church in 1078. Eight centuries later it became a cathedral. ⊠ *Via Cattedrale, Old Town.*

> ### SYLVAN GLADES
>
> For an idyllic daytime excursion, take a short tram trip out of Lugano's city center to the fabled Castagnola parks, which surround the Villa Favorita (the famous Thyssen-Bornemisza estate now closed to the public). The Parco degli Ulivi (Olive Park) spreads over the lower slopes of Monte Brè and offers a romantic landscape of silvery olive trees mixed with wild rosemary; you enter it from the Sentiero di Gandria (Gandria Footpath). Parco San Michele (St. Michael Park), also on Monte Brè, has a public chapel and a broad terrace that overlooks the city, the lake, and the Alps.

⓭ Lido. The city's public beach has two swimming pools and two restaurants. To reach it, you'll have to cross the Cassarate River. Heading east from the Parco Civico, cross Viale Castagnola and then turn toward the lake. The main swimming-area entrance is just ahead on the right. Everyone from families to scenesters comes here to cool off. ⊠ *Via Cassarate 6* ☎*058/8666880* 🎟*Beach 9 SF* ☉*May and Sept., daily 9–7; June–Aug., daily 9–7:30.*

⓬ Museo Cantonale di Storia Naturale *(Cantonal Museum of Natural History).* A museum since 1854, it contains exhibits on fossils, animals, and plants (there's a large section on local crystals that is especially interesting for people intending long hikes in the mountains), mostly those typical of the region. The museum is located in a high school. Note, too, that all labels are in Italian. ⊠ *Viale Cattaneo 4, Parco Civico* ☎*091/8154761* ⊕*www.ti.ch/mcsn* 🎟*Free* ☉*Tues.–Sat. 9–noon, 2–5.*

❷ Palazzo Civico *(Town Hall).* This Neoclassical Lombard structure dates from 1844. Inside there's a large inner yard surrounded by a four-sided arcade, with a wide vestibule on the piazza side. It houses the town council and tourist office. ⊠*Piazza della Riforma, Old Town.*

❿ Parco Civico *(City Park).* A green oasis in the city center, the park has cacti, exotic shrubs, and more than 1,000 varieties of roses, as well as an aviary, a tiny deer zoo, and a fine view of the bay from its peninsula. ⊠*South of Viale Carlo Cattaneo, east of Piazza Castello.*

❹ **Parco del Tassino** *(Tassino Park).* On a plateau just behind and south of the train station, this park offers lovely bay views from its rose gardens. A small deer park and playground make it very child-friendly. ⊠ *Take Bus 2 east to San Domenico stop in Castagnola, or use funicular from Old Town to train station* 🆓 *Free.*

❶ **Piazza della Riforma** *(Reformation Square).* In the early 19th century, several buildings were removed in order to enlarge the square—providing ★ more room for the present-day café tables. Commonly referred to simply as "la Piazza," it's the social and cultural heart of the city and the site of markets and open-air music performances. ⊠ *Just north of the Imbarcadero Centrale, Old Town.*

WHERE TO EAT

$$$–$$$$
ITALIAN
Fodor'sChoice
★
✕ **Al Portone.** Silver and lace dress up the stucco and stone here, but the ambience is strictly casual. Here father and son chefs Roberto and Silvio Galizzi pursue *nuova cucina* (contemporary Italian cuisine) with ambition and flair. Tall, dark, and quirkily handsome, Silvio has become something of a local celebrity; in addition to hosting his own cooking show, his recently published cookbook, *Cucina Bello,* is making waves. You might choose duck liver with mango chutney and pears, lobster in squid-ink sauce, or lamb with eggplant and zucchini stew (depending on the season). Or you could *lascia fare a Roberto e Silvio* (leave it to Roberto and Silvio)—as they call their menu de dégustation. ⊠ *Viale Cassarate 3, Lugano-Cassarate* ☎*091/9235511* 🖃*AE, DC, MC, V* 🕾*Closed Sun.–Mon., and mid-July–mid-Aug.*

$$
ITALIAN
✕ **Da Raffaele.** Having a meal in this family-run Italian restaurant feels like being let in on a neighborhood secret. Start with a pasta, like the marvelous homemade orecchiette (ear-shape pasta) or *mezzelune* (half moons) stuffed with ricotta and spinach, then try something from the grill, like *gamberoni alla griglia* (grilled shrimp). The staff doesn't speak English, but their warmth needs no translation. The restaurant is just outside the city center in a residential neighborhood, but is easily reached by car or bus (take Bus 8 or 9 from the train station to the last stop, Viganello). ⊠*Contrada dei Patrizi 8/Via Pazzalino, Lugano-Viganello* ☎*091/9716614* 🖃*AE, MC, V* 🕾*Closed Sun., last wk of July, first 2 wks of Aug. No lunch Sat.*

$
ITALIAN
✕**Grotto Figini.** Absolutely authentic, this grotto pulls in a rowdy local crowd for a boccalino of good merlot and a satisfying, rib-sticking meal of polenta and grilled meats. Don't expect English or other tourists, and don't take personally the stares you'll receive when you first walk in. The grotto is set apart in a short stretch of woods on a hill in Gentilino, above Lugano-Paradiso. After your meal you can stroll down the shady road to see old *grotti* hidden in the overgrown hillside. ⊠ *Via ai Grotti, Gentilino* ☎*091/9946497* 🖃*V* 🕾*Closed Mon. and mid-Dec.–Feb.*

$–$$
ITALIAN
★
✕**La Tinera.** Tucked down an alley off Via Pessina, this cozy basement taverna squeezes loyal locals and tourists onto hard wooden chairs and benches for authentic regional specialties, hearty meats, and pastas. Ticinese wines are served in traditional ceramic bowls—try a strong red to cut through the thick polenta taragna (the best buckwheat and polenta mix: once you try it you'll never eat the bland yellow version

CLOSE UP

Viewtiful!

The serious view hound may want to reach the top of one of the three peaks that define the landscape around Lugano. Monte Brè (*091/9713171 www.montebre.ch, Funicular 20 SF round-trip open daily, times vary greatly depending on the month, closed Jan.–Feb.*) has a funicular that departs every 30 minutes from the east end of Lugano in Cassarate. At the top are several well-marked hiking trails, as well as an "art trail" in the summit village of Brè, a path studded with pieces of sculpture. Monte San Salvatore (*091/9852828 www.montesansalvatore.ch Times vary greatly depending on the month*) can be reached via the funicular in

Paradiso every 30 minutes, 26 SF round-trip, closed mid-November–mid-March. At the top are a huge relief model of the entire Sottoceneri region and marked "nature itinerary" paths, which have signs pointing out flower and tree specimens. For yet more spectacular views take a boat from Lugano across to Capolago, where you can take the 40-minute cogwheel train up Monte Generoso (*091/6305111 www.montegeneroso. ch Train 39 SF round-trip Closed early Nov.–early Dec and early Jan.–mid-March*), which runs daily, with times varying depending on the month; the top has a restaurant and lots of marked hiking trails.

again) with Luganighe, cumin-flavored local sausages. End your meal with strong expresso matched with light, melt-in-your-mouth tiramisu. ⊠ *Via dei Gorini 2, Old Town* ☎091/9235219 ▤*AE, DC, MC, V* ⊗*Closed Sun. and Aug.*

$$$

SEAFOOD

✕**Locanda del Boschetto.** At the end of a cul-de-sac in a residential neighborhood (not far from the Lugano South exit on the autostrada), the grill is the first thing you see in this grotto-style ristorante, a specialist in pure and simple seafood *alla griglia* (grilled). Homemade pasta is another specialty, and when the two are combined, as in the house favorite *linguini allo scoglio,* you'll leave your plate cleaner than a whistle. The decor is a study in linen and rustic wood, and the service is helpful and down-to-earth. Reserve in advance to guarantee a table. ⊠ *Via Boschetto 8, Paradiso* ☎091/9942493 ▤*AE, DC, MC, V* ⊗*Closed Mon., last two weeks of Aug., and first 2 wks of Nov.*

$$–$$$

ITALIAN

✕**Orologio.** Snowy white tablecloths and chairs stand out against shiny, dark hardwood floors in this open, minimalist restaurant. The attentive staff is quick to bring you modern Italian dishes such as thinly sliced octopus with olive oil, jumbo shrimp with saffron and fresh garlic, or lamb cutlets with caramelized spring onions and almond potatoes—but they retreat to let you linger over coffee. Favored by locals, it's one of the few greats in town with few or no tourists in sight. ⊠ *Via Nizzola 2, Old Town* ☎091/9232338 ▤*AE, DC, MC, V* ⊗*Closed Sat. and Sun. July and Aug. and 2 wks in early Aug.*

$$$$

CONTEMPORARY

ITALIAN

★

✕**Santabbondio.** Ancient stone and terra-cotta blend with pristine pastels in this upgraded grotto, where subtle, imaginative, new Italian cuisine *du marché* (based on fresh produce) is served in intimate little dining rooms and on a shady terrace. Watch for perch with mango and sage or beef fillet with figs in balsamic vinegar to confirm the local opinion:

chef Martin Dalsass is one of the canton's best. There's a good selection of open wines to wash everything down with. You'll need a car or cab to get here, but it's worth the trip. ⊠ *Via Fomelino 10, Lugano-Sorengo* ☎ *091/9932388* ▤ *AE, DC, MC, V* ⊙ *Closed Sun.–Mon. and Jan.–Feb.*

WHERE TO STAY

$$$–$$$$ ▦ **Du Lac.** This comfortable, bright hotel offers more lakefront luxury than many of the glossier hotels farther down the same beach. Owned by the same family since it was founded in 1920, this lodging has been regularly renovated. Huge, impressive needlework tapestry art reproductions, handmade by the owner's father, cover the walls of the generously sized lobby and restaurant. The rooms are all spacious and face the lake; those on the sixth floor are the quietest. **Pros:** there's a private swimming area on the lake; eager-to-please staff round out a friendly, personalized atmosphere. **Cons:** lobby furnishings are behind-the-times; not all rooms have a/c, but they do have fans. ⊠ *Riva Paradiso 3, Lugano-Paradiso* ☎ *091/9864747* ⊕ *www.dulac.ch* ⬂ *52 rooms, 1 suite* ⚿ *In-room: no a/c (some), safe, refrigerator, Wi-Fi. In-hotel: restaurant, bar, pool, gym, beachfront* ▤ *AE, DC, MC, V* ⊙ *Closed Jan.–Feb.* ⑩ *BP.*

$$–$$$ ▦ **International au Lac.** Next to the Church of St. Mary of the Angels, this UNESCO-honored historic hotel is across from the lake. The interiors are floridly decorated, with gilded paintings, antiques, and heavy, sumptuous furniture. Family-run for over a hundred years, it's also the only hotel in the Old Town with a large garden and pool. City location is perfect for exploring, but can get a bit noisy—light sleepers should request the quieter side rooms. **Pros:** you'll forget you're downtown when lounging at the pool or in the back garden; hotel features seasonal, live classical music. **Cons:** some rooms feel as if they haven't been renovated since the hotel's 1908 opening; not the place to stay if you need up-to-date amenities and luxury toiletries. ⊠ *Via Nassa 68, Old Town* ☎ *091/9227541* ⊕ *www.hotel-international.ch* ⬂ *80 rooms* ⚿ *In-room: no a/c (some), safe. In-hotel: restaurant, bar, pool, parking (fee)* ▤ *AE, DC, MC, V* ⊙ *Closed Nov.–Easter* ⑩ *BP.*

$–$$ ▦ **Pestalozzi.** This older hotel right in the middle of town and a few steps

ITALIAN away from the lake offers excellent value. The newly restored rooms are simple, clean, and functionally furnished. The restaurant offers a new menu for each day featuring mostly Ticinese dishes, including several vegetarian selections. One peculiarity: traditionally, no alcohol is served, so for an exploration of local wines, you will have to find another place. **Pros:** a favorite among thrifty travelers; just a stone's throw from the Old Town. **Cons:** if your room has no a/c, pray that the mercury doesn't rise; not all rooms have TVs, so you'll have to go out for that lakeside gelato instead of spending Saturday watching last season's episodes of *Desperate Housewives* dubbed in Italian. ⊠ *Piazza Indipendenza* ☎ *091/9214646* ⊕ *www.pestalozzi-lugano.ch* ⬂ *55 rooms* ⚿ *In-room: no a/c (some), no TV (some), shared shower (some), Wi-fi. In-hotel: restaurant* ▤ *AE, MC, V.*

$ ▦ **San Carlo.** Ideally located on the main shopping street, this friendly hotel is one of the best deals in town. It's near the funicular and a block from the waterfront, but manages to remain peacefully quiet after sundown. The rooms are exceptionally tiny, but clever carpentry makes the most out of small spaces, creating niches for a mirror, a television, or a hideaway bed. The breakfast room is small, so breakfast in bed is encouraged. **Pros:** each room is uniquely crafted; terrific prices. **Cons:** some rooms are adjoining, so be sure to lock your doors; walls tend to be thin. ⊠ *Via Nassa 28, Old Town* ☎ *091/9227107* ↳ *20 rooms* ⊕ *www.sancarlohotel.ch* ↳ *In-room: no a/c (some), shared bathroom (some). In-hotel: no-smoking rooms (some), public Internet* ☰ *AE, DC, MC, V* ⦿ *BP.*

$$$$ ▦ **Splendide Royale.** One of the last palace-style hotels in Ticino, this
Fodor's Choice   landmark villa was first converted into a hotel in 1887 and, gorgeously,
★   much of the Victorian luster of its public spaces—with their marble, pillars, terrazzo, chandeliers, and antiques—has been respectfully preserved. The famous clientele, including Sophia Loren, Lauren Bacall, Gloria Swanson, Igor Stravinsky, and Tina Turner have all signed the lobby's Livre d'Or. More modern types can opt for the 1983 wing, where discreetly modern rooms are decorated in beech, beige, and gold. The balconies and terraces open onto lake or garden views—for the Cinerama version of Lake Lugano, head to the elegant La Veranda restaurant. **Pros:** the historic suites here are showstoppers, replete with 19th-century frescoes and Venetian chandeliers; even the smallest rooms here feature heated bathroom floors. **Cons:** the 1983 wing feels more *Miami Vice* than *Pride and Prejudice*; some ancient common areas and corridors could use a freshening-up. ⊠ *Riva A. Caccia 7* ☎ *091/9857711* ⊕ *www.splendide.ch* ↳ *88 rooms, 8 suites* ↳ *In-room: safe, Wi-Fi, refrigerator. In-hotel: restaurant, bar, pool, sauna, gym* ☰ *AE, DC, MC, V* ⦿ *BP.*

$$$–$$$$ ▦ **Ticino.** Set on a time-stained square and around the corner from pic-
★   turesquely porticoed Via Nassa, this 500-year-old former monastery is fully protected as a historical monument. Shuttered windows look out from every room onto a glassed-in garden, while vaulted halls are lined with art and antiques. Guest rooms are unpretentious yet elegant, with pleasing details such as embroidered towels and special orthopedic mattresses. The formal restaurant is full of dark-wood wainscoting and leather banquettes, and blends Ticinese, Mediterranean, and French cuisine. **Pros:** hotel is just steps from the funicular to the train station; excellent food—the restaurant is famous for its fresh seafood and rack of lamb with herbs. **Cons:** rooms can be quite small and stuffy in the summer; dinner service can be slow—prepare to take your time and enjoy every course. ⊠ *Piazza Cioccaro 1, Old Town* ☎ *091/9227772* ⊕ *www.romantikhotels.com/lugano* ↳ *18 rooms, 2 suites* ↳ *In-room: no a/c (some), safe, refrigerator. In-hotel: restaurant, bar* ☰ *AE, DC, MC, V* ⊙ *Closed Jan. No lunch weekends* ⦿ *BP.*

$$$$ ▦ **Villa Principe Leopoldo & Residence.** Spectacularly perched on the Col-
★   lina d'Oro hillside high over Lake Lugano, this mansion offers a nonpareil location and old-world service. Although the villa was built in 1868 on behalf of Prince Leopold of Hohenzollern, most of the public rooms and guest rooms are staidly modern and snoozily traditional—gracefully lush but with little patina or fireworks. You may not care

once you take a glance at the stunningly arranged pool-and-terrace complex encircled by a double staircase (a slightly Baroque touch right out of Bel Air). Fabulous creations from chef Dario Ranza, such as pink grapefruit risotto with shrimp or sea bass baked in a salt crust, make dining here a notable experience. **Pros:** beautiful views of Lake Lugano and the surrounding mountains; set in a landscaped park, the hotel is worlds away from the noise and traffic of the city below. **Cons:** staff as well as guests can be pretentious–watch their faces as you drive up in a compact rental alongside the red Ferraris and Rolls Royces. ⊠ *Via Montalbano 5, Collina d'Oro* 🕾*091/9858855* ⊕*www. leopoldohotel.com* ⟿*50 rooms, 24 suites* ♿*In-room: safe, refrigerator. In-hotel: 2 restaurants, 2 bars, 2 tennis courts, 2 pools, gym* ▤*AE, DC, MC, V* ❢❙*BP.*

> ### HESSE'S HAVEN
>
> In the tower of the Casa Camuzzi, a fabulous jumble of old houses on a hilltop in Montagnola, the Herman Hesse Museum (091/9933770, www.hesse-montagnola.ch, 7.50 SF, open Mar.–Oct., Tues.–Sun. 10–6:30; Nov.–Feb., weekends 10–5:30) is tiny but impressive. The Nobel Prize–winning author lived here the last 43 years of his life, writing *Siddhartha* and *Steppenwolf.* His rooms have been meticulously preserved; you can see his papers, books, desk, glasses, even his straw hat. Take the postbus marked Agra-Montagnola from Lugano's train station.

$$ **Park-Hotel Nizza.** Tucked into the dense tropical foliage of the lower slopes of Monte San Salvatore, this former villa mixes old and modern comforts. Most rooms are small, but all are quiet and comfortable; panoramic views of the lake below don't cost extra. The hotel has its own farm and vineyards on the hill behind—the source of the organic produce used by the kitchen. The restaurant makes its own wine, with some very original labels designed by the owner. Summer meals are served in the garden; there's a special farmer's breakfast on Tuesday and a cocktail party on Friday evening. ⊠ *Via Guidino 14, Lugano-Paradiso* 🕾*091/9941771* ⊕*www.villanizza.com* ⟿*28 rooms* ♿*In-room: no a/c, safe, refrigerator. In-hotel: restaurant, bar, pool, public Internet* ▤*AE, MC, V* ☾*Closed late Oct.–3 wks before Easter* ❢❙*BP.*

NIGHTLIFE & THE ARTS

BARS Just off the Piazza delle Riforma, **Bottegone del Vino** (⊠ *Via Magatti 3, Old Town* 🕾*091/9227689*) has a great selection of wine accompanied by good local cheeses and tapas. It's closed on Sunday. **Hotel Eden** (⊠*Riva Paradiso 1, Old Town* 🕾*091/9859200*) has a popular piano bar. For a refined, if uncrowded, place to enjoy a cocktail, head to the palatial **Splendide Royale** (⊠*Riva A. Caccia 7, Lungolago* 🕾*091/9857711*).

CASINO In addition to slot machines and gaming tables, the three-floor **Casinò Lugano** (⊠ *Via Stauffacher 1, Old Town* 🕾*091/9737111*) has a bar and restaurant.

DANCING **Discoclub Underground** (⊠ *Via Soave 7 Old Town* 🕾*079/4588903*) has a multitude of cocktails and limitless people-watching opportunities. On

Friday and Saturday nights **Morandi** (☒ *Via Trevano 56, Molino Nuovo* ☎*091/9712291*) is the number-one club catering to the over-30 crowd and a great place to dance to songs from the '70s and '80s. The lively **Living Room** (☒ *Via Trevano 89a, Molino Nuovo* ☎*091/9233281* ⊕*www.livingroom.ch*) has a dance floor and lounge, and hosts some of the better European electro and rock up-and-comers.

MUSIC The free **Blues to Bop Festival** livens up the Piazza della Riforma at the end of August. In July **Estival Jazz** brings jazz and world music to the Piazza della Riforma. From April to June, the city hosts its **Lugano Festival,** which draws world-class orchestras and conductors.

SHOPPING

Cute novelty shops and antiques stores line the staircase street of **Via Cattedrale.** All the top designers can be found in the shops lining the pedestrian-only **Via Nassa.** If it's Italian and international designer clothing bargains you're after, explore the factory outlet store called **Fox Town** (☒ *Via Angelo Maspoli, Mendrisio* ☎*091/6405020*). It's open daily from 11 to 5.

> **EMPTY YOUR POCKETS**
>
> Somehow, there's a fascination about smuggling, even if you've never brought so much as a single cigarette over your allowance through the green Nothing-to-Declare channel. The subject is brought to life at the Museo Doganale (*091/9239843 Free admission; open Mid–March.–Oct., daily 1:30–5:30*), set across Lago di Lugano from Gandria, surrounded by Italy. Known as the "Smuggler's Museum," it bristles with ingenious containers, weapons, and contraband exhibits, which explore the romantic history of clandestine trade between Italy and Switzerland. You can catch a boat from the jetty in Gandria.

GANDRIA

Fodor'sChoice *7 km (4 mi) southeast of Lugano.*
★

Although today its narrow waterfront streets are crowded with tourists, the tiny historic village of Gandria merits a visit, either by boat or by car. Gandria clings vertiginously to the steep hillside; a labyrinth of stairways and passageways lined with flower-filled balconies hangs directly over open water. Souvenir and crafts shops now fill its backstreet nooks, but the ambience of an ancient fishing village remains.

CAMPIONE

18 km (11 mi) south of Gandria, 12 km (7 mi) south of Lugano.

In the heart of Swiss Italy lies Campione. Here, in this southernmost of regions, the police cars have Swiss license plates but the police officers inside are Italian; the inhabitants pay their taxes to Italy but do it in Swiss francs. Its narrow streets are saturated with history, and the surrounding landscape is a series of stunning views of Lago di Lugano and Monte San Salvatore.

In the 8th century the lord of Campione gave the tiny scrap of land, less than a square kilometer (½ square mi) in area, to the monastery of St. Ambrosius of Milan. Despite all the wars that passed it by, Campione remained Italian until the end of the 18th century, when it was incorporated into the Cisalpine Republic. When Italy unified in 1861, Campione became part of the new Kingdom of Italy—and remained so. There are no frontiers between Campione and Switzerland, and it benefits from the comforts of Swiss currency, customs laws, and postal and telephone services. Despite its miniature scale, it has exercised disproportionate influence on the art world: in the Middle Ages a school of stonemasons, sculptors, and architects from Campione and the surrounding region worked on the cathedrals of Milan, Verona, Cremona, Trento, and Modena—even the Hagia Sophia in Istanbul.

NIGHTLIFE & THE ARTS

Today Campione is a magnet for gamblers, thanks to its **Casino** (⊠*Piazza Milano 1* ☎*091/6401111*), now housed in a brand-new building designed by star architect Mario Botta, which looks like some huge brown UFO that has landed on the little town. When you're not playing the tables you can have dinner in the restaurant or enjoy a show. Men are required to wear a jacket, but they don't have to wear a tie in summer.

EN ROUTE
If you wish to see all of Switzerland's monuments in a few hours, then stop in the town of **Melide** 8 km (5 mi) south of Lugano. The **Swissminiatur** (☎*091/6401060* ⊕*www.swissminiatur.ch* ☎*15 SF* ☉*Mid-Mar.–mid-Nov., daily 9–6*) has all the sights and sites you could wish for at a 1:25 scale installed on a 3.5-acre plot. These include such diverse monuments as Heidi's Village, Château de Chillon, Basel's Münster, and the Madonna del Sasso in Locarno. Every year sees the replacement of an old monument with a new one. And nearly 3.5 km (2 mi) of miniature train tracks have been laid out and are busily used by passenger and freight stock.

MORCOTE

Fodor's Choice ★ *11 km (7 mi) northwest of Campione, 10 km (6 mi) south of Lugano. A half-hour bus ride connects you to Lugano.*

At the southernmost tip of the glorious Ceresio Peninsula is the atmospheric village of Morcote, its clay-color houses and arcades looking directly over the waterfront.

A steep and picturesque climb leads up to the **Chiesa di Madonna del Sasso** *(Church of the Madonna of the Rock)* , with its well-preserved 16th-century frescoes; its elevated setting affords wonderful views.

★ The **Parco Scherrer** is a remarkable garden created over a period of decades by the Swiss businessman Arthur Scherrer (1881–1956). This folly rising from the lakeside brings together architectural samples from around the world—an Egyptian sun temple, a Siamese teahouse, and an Indian palace, for example—within the setting of a carefully land-

CLOSE UP

A Century of Wine

Roughly 6,000 tons of wine grapes—about 7 percent of Switzerland's total production—are grown each year in the rolling hills of the Ticino. Leading the way is the popular merlot grape, introduced in 1905. It wasn't a success solely because it grows well in this region. An epidemic of phylloxera was destroying the country's vineyards, and the merlot grape proved to be the most resistant.

Merlot now accounts for 80% of the region's wine production. Thanks to technological advances, the Ticino also produces white and blush varieties. A sampling of merlot in the region's grotti, restaurants, and vineyards will reveal a wide range of wines, including some very fine vintages with top-quality barrel maturation. If you want to learn more about the wines of the region, you might wish to follow *le strade del vino* (the wine roads), which map out 69 restaurants, 43 wine producers, and five *enotecas* of note. For information, contact **Ticinowine** (☎ *091/6901353* ⊕ *www.ticinowine.ch*).

scaped garden. ⊕*www.lugano-tourism.ch* ☜*7 SF* ⊗*Mid-Mar.–Nov., daily 10–5; July and Aug., daily 10–6.*

WHERE TO STAY

$$–$$$
★ ⊞ **Carina Carlton.** Somehow, this family-run hotel has managed to fit a host of pretty and spacious rooms, a restaurant, a generous terrace, and an outdoor pool into the narrow strip between the mountain and the lake. It's a wonderful place to enjoy the peace of the lake—and a mere 20 minutes from Lugano. The restaurant awaits for lunch or dinner with a wide range of Swiss, Ticinese, and Italian dishes. **Pros:** filled with repeat guests, many of them Swiss or Italian; comprehensive restaurant menu is definitely worth a try. **Cons:** no a/c, but thankfully there's a fan in every room; noisy cars driven in the usual aggressive fashion can be heard along the shore road. ⊠*Riva da Sant' Antoni* ☎*091/9961131* ⊕*www.carina-morcote.ch* ⤢*22 rooms* ᗢ*In-room: no a/c, safe, refrigerator. In-hotel: restaurant, pool, public Internet* ⊟*AE, DC, MC, V* ⑂|*BP* ⊗*Closed mid-Oct–mid-Mar.*

$$–$$$
Fodor'sChoice
★ ⊞ **Dellago.** Combining a soothing atmosphere, personal service, and unpretentious savoir faire, this stylish refuge right on the lake spoils its guests. At dinnertime the casual lakeside terrace lures many locals, devotees of chef Andreas Lauer, who whips up astounding entrées such as tender mahi-mahi fillet glazed with ginger, sesame, and chili, served on a bed of coconut-lemongrass risotto, and sumptuous desserts like chocolate ravioli laced with blood-orange sauce and rum-raisin ice cream. Individually decorated rooms are equipped with a range of treats: ask for surround-sound stereo, a private rooftop hot tub, a DVD player, or a plasma TV. **Pros:** breakfast is replete with homemade jams, fine teas, and a selection of unusual breads; there's a hotel paddle boat for excursions on the lake. **Cons:** rooms facing the busy street are noisy; no a/c, but fans in every room. ⊠*Lago di Lugano, Melide* ☎*091/6497041* ⊕*www. hotel-dellago.ch* ⤢*16 rooms 4 suites* ᗢ*In-room: no a/c (some). In-hotel: restaurant, bar* ⊟*AE, DC, MC, V* ⑂|*BP.*

Luzern & Central Switzerland

BÜRGENSTOCK, RÜTLI MEADOW, WEGGIS, WILLIAM TELL COUNTRY

Benedictine monastery in Einsiedeln, Canton Schwyz

6

WORD OF MOUTH

"I'm a scenery lover myself. And, IMHO, scenery is what Switzerland excels at. Unfortunately, Switzerland can also excel at rainy weather. What's nice about Luzern is there are plenty of different museums to see if the weather is bad." —greuzi

"Visiting the legendary Rütli Meadow—the 'birthplace' of Switzerland—in the heart of Wilhelm Tell Country was an ascension-into-heaven moment." —Cheyne2

WELCOME TO LUZERN & CENTRAL SWITZERLAND

TOP REASONS TO GO

★ **Luzern:** The must-see spot on the tour, it offers not only the things you've heard of—the Chapel Bridge, the Lion Monument—but other treasures like the Rosengart Picassos and that perfect table for two under the chestnut trees on the lakeside promenade.

★ **Mountain majesty:** Thanks to cable cars and cog railways, hill thrills—and some of the most staggering panoramas—can be yours atop Mts. Pilatus, Titlis, and Rigi.

★ **William Tell country:** As with all good legends, the story of the famous archer who shot an apple from his son's head with a crossbow may have little basis in fact, but don't tell that to the crowds who visit his home turf in and around Altdorf.

★ **A paddleboat steamer ride:** Smart white steamers—some of them beautifully kept and picturesque old paddle-steamers—ply Lake Luzern and offer a voyage back into time.

1 Luzern. The little big city, Luzern offers a full cultural palette: wander through the medieval solidity of the Old Town; shop your way through the many boutiques; take a boat cruise to a yodeling beat; and listen to Cecilia Bartoli sing in Jean Nouvel's architectural wonder, the Kultur- und Kongresszentrum.

2 Luzern Environs. Towering over Luzern, Mt. Pilatus is dramatic and impressive, with a restaurant teetering on its razor-sharp ridge at the top. Take the "golden round-trip," which includes a bus from Luzern, a cable car trip to the top, a cogwheel train back down the other side, and a boat ride back to Luzern. Head south to Engelberg—noted for its outdoor sports—where you can take the gondola up to the top of Mt. Titlis, gasping at the view, the loftiest in central Switzerland.

3 William Tell Country. Hallowed by myths, the Urnersee is the southern—and by far most romantic—leg of Lake Luzern. Dramatic mountains run steeply into the lake as sharp peaks stab into the clouds, a landscape that has inspired many a master, from Rossini to Wagner, Schiller to Twain (bring along your sketchbook or journal). Weggis and Vitznau are the "Riviera" towns, sheltered by coves and address to the rich. Farther south, pay your respects to the historic Rütli Meadow; the picturesque Tell Chapel, just across the lake; and Altdorf, where Wilhelm Tell first became a legend.

GETTING ORIENTED

To enter Luzern is to approach the very heart of historic Switzerland, for the sharply indented shoreline of the Vierwaldstättersee (Lake Luzern) was the cradle of the Swiss Confederation, forged here in the 13th century on the Rütli Meadow as the world's first democracy. Most-visited Luzern, with its Old Town, sits on one end of the lake; the quieter but equally historic Altdorf, "home" of Wilhelm Tell, on the other. In between is probably the most beautiful stretch of lakeshore in Switzerland.

LUZERN & CENTRAL SWITZERLAND PLANNER

Visitor Information

The principal tourist bureau for the whole of central Switzerland, including the lake region, is Zentralschweiz Tourismus (Central Switzerland Tourism; www.lakeluzern.ch).

The main tourist office for the hub city of Luzern is in the Bahnhof, off Track 3.

There are also local tourist offices (see town listings) and an accommodations service in many of the region's towns, often near the train station.

Happily, the Luzern tourist office offers English-language walking tours of the city.

Their usual schedule is daily from May to October and Wednesday and Saturday from November to April.

Their tours take about two hours and cost 18 SF.

In addition, Schiffahrtsgesellschaft des Vierwaldstättersees (⊠ Werftestr. 5, Luzern ☎ 041/3676767) offers history and Alpine theme cruises with English commentary daily from May to October.

Luzern (⊠ Bahnhof: Zentralstr. 5, ☎ 041/2271717 ⊕ www. luzern.com).

Small Town, Big Style

In a town of fewer than 60,000 inhabitants, where a local philanthropist can afford to buy prime real estate to put her private art collection on display, where the lakeside is teeming with villas, and the concert hall attracts international greatness in the form of Cecilia Bartoli and Renée Fleming, the Ugly Tourist can stick out like a sore thumb in Luzern.

Although residents appreciate the value of comfortable clothes, this is definitely not the place to let it all hang out: huge droopy T-shirts, ill-fitting Bermuda shorts, and baseball caps will get you looks of distain, seated only in McDonald's, and denied entrance to most churches and museums. Of course we don't mean you in particular, it's those other guys...

Take the Slow Boat to...

One of the joys of traveling in this region is touring Lake Luzern on one of its time-stained 19th-century paddleboat steamers. These are a slow but extremely scenic and therefore worthwhile mode of transportation; you'll find locals on day trips traveling along with you. Remember that this is a very unrushed part of the country, where people tend to enjoy the slow moments and avoid the hectic ones; impatience may get you ignored, so chill and enjoy.

The Vierwaldstättersee (to use the German name for Lake Luzern) has a very good network of steamers—only two are historic paddlesteamers, however—which connect virtually every community on the lakeside. The larger boats have full restaurant facilities and even the smaller ones offer refreshments. As elsewhere in Switzerland, they link, where practical, with both the train and postbus services. The round-trip/excursion tickets offer best value for the money.

Services are frequent in the peak season with, for example, hourly departures from the lovely boat dock in Luzern, but in the off-peak season services are limited, so check on availability when you arrive. Swiss Passes allow deep discounts.

Finding a Place to Stay

All budgets are covered in central Switzerland, from backpacker-type multibed rooms to luxurious suites with 1,000-thread-count silk sheets. In the mountains, high season means the winter ski season, in the valleys summer is more expensive. As the terrain and climate vary radically between balmy lakefronts and icy heights, check carefully for high and low seasons before booking ahead. Resorts such as Weggis and Vitznau cut back service considerably in winter, just when Engelberg comes alive. Book early for ever-popular Luzern. Prices drop by as much as 25% in winter, approximately November through March. Rates are often calculated on a per-person basis, so it's wise to confirm rates, particularly if you're traveling as anything other than a couple.

Seven Days of Madness

Although Carnival (called Fasnacht in German) is celebrated throughout the country, the party aspect is taken most seriously in Luzern. On the first Thursday seven weeks before Easter each year, seven days of madness follow, alive with parades, confetti, dancing, singing, and, of course, the odd bit of drinking. The parades begin with an orderly parade of Guggä—elaborately costumed brass and drums bands that can turn any pop tune into a festive event—that soon (d)evolves into a writhing, rowdy old-town festival that goes more or less nonstop throughout the week. Guests are encouraged, if not downright expected, to join in. Most locals take the week off—there's no getting any work done anyway. To paraphrase Chuckles the Clown: a little song, a little dance, a little confetti down your pants.

How's the Weather?

The geographic heart of Switzerland enjoys four distinct seasons, temperate in the valleys and more extreme in the mountains. Spring, summer, and fall are perfect for warm-weather outdoor activities.

Fall becomes crisp around October and winter brings snow to the highlands.

Keep in mind that snow can stay as late as May and come as early as August over 6,500 feet.

Avoid walking in creek beds: a hidden rainstorm high in the mountains can turn a trickling brook into a rushing torrent in a matter of seconds and has swept away many a hiker or canyoner.

If you're going up and down mountains, dress like an onion: the warmth of the valley, needless to say, can be quickly replaced by a cold breeze 5,000 feet higher.

6

WHAT IT COSTS IN SWISS FRANCS

¢	$	$$	$$$	$$$$
RESTAURANTS				
under 15 SF	15 SF–25 SF	25 SF–40 SF	40 SF–60 SF	over 60 SF
HOTELS				
under 100 SF	100 SF–175 SF	175 SF–250 SF	250 SF–350 SF	over 350 SF

Restaurant prices are per person for a main course at dinner. Hotel prices are for two people in a standard double room in high season, including tax and service.

GETTING AROUND

Transportation Basics

When visiting this area, you must change modes of transit frequently to see it all.

Part of the region's interest is the variety of boats, trains, and other less common modes of transportation you'll take to reach the sights.

On any given day, you may walk through the lovely Old Town of Luzern, ascend Mt. Pilatus by cable car and descend by cogwheel train, take a lake steamer, or drive to the Rütli Meadow.

Many of the towns in this region are scattered around the unusually shaped Vierwaldstättersee, so sometimes a ferry will be faster than a freeway.

In other instances, you'll find a train often makes more sense than a car.

The Swiss Federal Railways (SBB, 0900/300300, www.sbb.ch) manages trains, boats, and buses.

Direct rail connections from Geneva, Zürich, and Basel run through Luzern, from which there is public transportation to every part of the region.

By Boat & Ferry

It would be a shame to see this historic region only from the shore; some of its most impressive landscapes are framed along the waterfront, as seen from the decks of one of the cruise ships that ply the lake.

Rides on these are included in a Swiss Pass or a Swiss Boat Pass.

Individual tickets can be purchased at Luzern's departure docks; the fee is based on the length of your ride.

You can arrange any combination of transportation, such as a leisurely cruise from Luzern to Flüelen at the lake's southernmost point, lasting about 3½ hours and costing 45 SF for second class, 69 SF for first class.

A return train trip, via the Arth-Goldau railroad line, takes little more than an hour.

The discount Tell Pass gives you free boat rides.

Information Schiffahrtsgesellschaft des Vierwaldstättersees (⊠ *Quay in front of train station* ☎ *041/3676767* ⊕ *www.lakeluzern.ch*).

Swiss Federal Railways (☎ *0900/300300* ⊕ *www.rail.ch*) also covers boat information.

By Bus

The postbus network carries travelers faithfully, if slowly, to the farthest corners of the region. It also climbs the St. Gotthard and the Furka passes (remember, these are closed in winter).

For schedules and prices, call Swiss Federal Railways. If you're staying in Luzern, purchase the LucerneCard, offering unlimited rides for three days for 33 SF.

The Tell Pass (regional train pass; for more information, see By Train on next page) includes free postbus travel.

Information Swiss Federal Railways (☎ *0900/300300* ⊕ *www.rail.ch*).

By Train

Luzern functions as a rail crossroads, with express trains connecting hourly from Zürich, a 49-minute trip, and every two hours from Geneva, a 3½- to 4-hour trip changing at Bern. Trains enter from the south via the St. Gotthard Pass from the Ticino and via the Furka Pass from the Valais. For rail information, call the Bahnhof.

Swiss National Railways is enhanced here by a few private lines (to Engelberg, Pilatus, the Rigi Kulm) that make it possible to get to most sights.

If you don't have a Swiss Pass, there's a central Switzerland regional discount pass, called the Tell Pass, on sale from April to October. The 15-day pass grants you five days of unlimited free travel on main routes, 10 days at half fare.

The seven-day pass gives you two days free, five at half fare. (Besides the national lines, most private rail lines will also accept the pass.)

The ticket can be bought at rail or boat ticket offices, on cruise boats, from travel agencies, or from tourist offices.

The 15-day pass costs 210 SF second class, 244 SF first class; the seven-day pass costs 158 SF second class, 180 SF first class.

Plan your itinerary carefully to take full advantage of all discount rates; before you buy a regional pass, add up your excursions à la carte. Remember that many routes always charge half price.

All boat trips and the private excursions to Rigi and Pilatus are free to holders of regional passes—but getting to the starting point may cost you half the ususal price. If you plan to cover a lot of ground, however, you may save considerably.

Choose your free days in advance: you must confirm them *all* with the first inspector who checks your pass.

Information Bahnhof (⊠ *Bahnhofpl.* ☎ *0900/300300* ⊕ *www.sbb.ch*).

By Air

The nearest airport to Luzern is Unique Zürich Airport, which is approximately 54 km (33 mi) northeast of Luzern.
Airport Information Unique Zürich Airport
(☎ *0900/300313*).

By Car

It's easy to reach Luzern from Zürich by road, approaching from national expressway A3 south, connecting to A4 via the secondary E41 in the direction of Zug, and continuing on A4, which turns into the A14, to the city.

A convenient all-expressway connection between the two cities is due to open in 2010.

From Basel in the northwest, it's a clean sweep by the A2 to Luzern.

Approaching from the south, take the A2 to Altdorf, where a tunnel sweeps you through to the shores of the lake.

If you're heading for resorts on the north shore, leave the expressway at Flüelen and follow the scenic secondary route.

Although Mt. Rigi and Mt. Pilatus aren't accessible by car, nearly everything else in this region is.

The descent from Andermatt past the Devil's Bridge, which once carried medieval pilgrims from the St. Gotthard Pass and drew thrill seekers during the 19th century, now exemplifies awe-inspiring Swiss mountain engineering: from Göschenen, at 3,627 feet, to the waterfront, it's a four-lane expressway.

6

Updated by
Katrin Gygax

WITH THE MIST RISING OFF the waves and the mountains looming above the clouds, it's easy to understand how Wagner could have composed his *Siegfried Idyll* in his mansion beside the lake. This is inspiring terrain, romantic and evocative. When the waters roil up, you can hear the whistling chromatics and cymbal clashes of Gioacchino Rossini's thunderstorm from his 1829 opera, *Guillaume Tell*. It was on Lake Luzern, after all, that Wilhelm Tell—the beloved, if legendary, Swiss national hero—supposedly leaped from the tyrant Gessler's boat to freedom. And it was in a meadow nearby that three furtive rebels and their cohorts swore an oath by firelight and planted the seed of the Swiss Confederation.

The Rütli Meadow on the western shore of Lake Luzern is the very spot where the confederates of Uri, Schwyz, and Unterwalden are said to have met on the night of November 7, 1307, to renew the 1291 Oath of Eternal Alliance—Switzerland's equivalent of the U.S. Declaration of Independence. With this oath, the world's oldest still-extant democracy was born, as the proud charter territories swore their commitment to self-rule in the face of the Habsburgs' Holy Roman Empire. Every August 1, the Swiss national holiday, citizens gather in the meadow in remembrance of the oath, and the sky glows with the light of hundreds of mountaintop bonfires.

Wilhelm Tell played an important role in that early rebellion, and his story, especially as told by German poet and playwright Friedrich von Schiller in his play *Wilhelm Tell* (1805), continues to stir those with a weakness for civil resistance. Here, around the villages of Altdorf, Bürgen, and the stunningly picturesque lakeside Tell Chapel, thousands come to honor the memory of the rebellious archer and, well, tell tales.

Yet for all its potential for drama, central Switzerland and the area surrounding Lake Luzern are tame enough turf: neat little towns, accessible mountains, smooth roads, resorts virtually glamour-free—and modest, graceful Luzern (Lucerne) astride the River Reuss much as it has been since the Middle Ages.

An eminently civilized region, Zentralschweiz (Central Switzerland) lacks the rustic unruliness of the Valais, the spectacular extremes of the Berner Oberland, and the eccentricity of Graubünden. It's also without the sophistication and snob appeal of the cosmopolitan mix of Geneva, Basel, and Zürich. Instead, villages here range neatly around their medieval centers; houses are tidy, pastel, picture-book cottages, deep-roofed and symmetrical, each rank of windows underscored with flowers. Luzern, the capital, hosts arts festivals and great shopping but little native industry. Serene and steady as the Reuss that laps at the piers of its ancient wooden bridges, it's an approachable city in an accessible region.

Central Switzerland's popularity with tourists has spawned an infrastructure of hotels, restaurants, museums, excursions, and transportation that makes it one of the easiest places in Switzerland to visit, either by car or by rail—and one of the most rewarding. As Wagner exclaimed, "I do not know of a more beautiful spot in this world!"

EXPLORING LUZERN & CENTRAL SWITZERLAND

Called variously the Vierwaldstättersee, the Urnersee, or the Luzerner-see—it depends on which end you are standing—Lake Luzern and its environs take in not only the four cantons that abut the lake—Luzern, Uri, Schwyz, and Unterwalden—but the canton of Zug as well. Unter-walden itself is divided politically into two half-cantons: Obwalden (upper) and Nidwalden (lower). It was the canton of Schwyz that gave Switzerland its name.

The narrow, twisting lake flows from Flüelen, where the Reuss opens into the Urnersee, its southernmost leg. This is the wildest end of the lake, where much of the Tell story was set. The north end of the lake is flanked by the region's highest points, Mt. Pilatus (6,953 feet) and Mt. Rigi (5,894 feet). Luzern lies in a deep bay at the lake's northwest extreme and at the point where the rivers Reuss and Emme part ways. Zug stands apart, on the northern shore of its own Lake Zug, which is divided from Lake Luzern by the mass of Mt. Rigi.

LUZERN

57 km (36 mi) southwest of Zürich.

GETTING HERE

Luzern's centrally located main station brings hourly trains in from Basel (31 SF one-way), Bern (35 SF one-way), and Zurich (23 SF one way). Geneva trains arrive through Bern or Olten (72 SF one-way). Directly outside the station's entrance is the quay where lake boats that form part of the public transit system can take you to a variety of towns along the Vierwaldstättersee, including Weggis, Vitznau, Flüelen (with a bus connection to Altdorf), and Brunnen. For departure times and prices for trains and buses for most destinations in this chapter, check www.sbb.ch—the main Swiss public transportation Web site—or call 0900/300300 (1.19 SF per min). Remember, if you have a Swiss Pass or another rail-discounting card, it also applies to the buses. Central Switzerland has its own discount Tell Pass; for info, *see Essentials at end of this chapter or* log on to www.lakeluzern.com.

Visitor Information (✉*Bahnhof [Train Station]: Zentralstr. 5* ☎*041/2271717* ⊕*www.luzern.com*).

EXPLORING

Luzern city is a convenient home base for excursions all over central Switzerland. The countryside here is tame, and the vast Vierwaldstät-tersee offers a prime opportunity for a lake steamer cruise. Where the River Reuss flows out of Lake Luzern, Luzern's Old Town straddles the narrowed waters. There are a couple of discount passes available for museums and sights in the city. One is the LucerneCard that costs19 SF for 24 hours and grants unlimited travel on all public transportation in Luzern, a 50% discount at select museums, and further price reduc-tions. If you're staying in a hotel, you may also want to pick up a special visitor's card; once stamped by the hotel, it entitles you to discounts at

Luzern (Lucerne)

TO TRAIN STATION

Friedentalstrasse

Friedentalstr.

Kantonsspital

Reussport Tunnel

Spitalstrasse

Friedbergstrasse

Brambergstrasse

Wettsteinpark

St.-Karli-Strasse

Luegetenstr. Geissmattstr.

Mühlemattstr.

Diebold Schilling-Str.

Old Town Wall

Reuss

Sentimattstrasse

Dammstrasse

Baselstrasse

Geissmatt-brücke

15

Museggstrasse

St.-Karli-Quai

Löwengraben

Weimarkt

Kramg.

Kornmarkt

Kanonenstrasse

Château Gütsch

Baselstrasse

Reuss

5

4

Mühlenplatz

6

7

Pfistergasse

Reuss-brücke

Rathaus-Steg

3

Gibraltarstrasse

Schützenstr.

Bruchstr.

Hirschengraben

Münzgasse

Burgerstrasse

9

Gütschwald

Sonnenberg Tunnel

Klosterstrasse

Pilatusstr.

8

Hirschengraben

Winkelriedstr.

Zürichstrasse

Fluhmattstrasse

Bergstrasse

Denkmalstr.

Landschaustrasse

Abendweg

Dreilindenstr.

Hitzlisbergstr.

Dreilindenstr.

14

13

Kapuzinerweg

Weystrasse

12

Löwen-
platz

Löwenstr.

Adligenswilerstr.

TO VERKEHRSHAUS →

Museggstrasse

11

Zinggentorstr.

Haldenstrasse

St.-Leodegar-Str.

Hertensteinstr.

Haldenstrasse

**Kursaal
(Casino)**

Carl Spittelerquai

Nationalquai

Schweizerhofquai

Schwanen-
Platz

Luzernersee

Furrengasse

Rathausquai

Seebrücke

10

Kapell-
brücke

Bahnhofstrasse

Bahnhof-
platz

Europa-
platz

1

theaterstr.

Pilatusstrasse

2

Frankenstrasse

Zentralstrasse

Bahnhof

Inseliquai

KEY	
••••	*Funicular*
┼┼┼┼	*Rail lines*
═══	*Tramway*

0   200 yards

0   200 meters

most museums and other tourist-oriented businesses. Both passes are available at the tourist office.

OLD TOWN & BEYOND

MAIN ATTRACTIONS

❸ **Altes Rathaus** *(Old Town Hall).* In 1606 the Luzern town council held its first meeting in this late-Renaissance-style building, built between 1602 and 1606. It still meets here today. ✉ *Rathausquai, facing the north end of Rathaus-Steg.*

⓬ **Bourbaki-Panorama.** The panorama was the IMAX theater of the 19th
★ century; its sweeping, wraparound paintings brought to life scenes of epic proportions. The Bourbaki is one of only 30 remaining in the world. Painted by Édouard Castres between 1876 and 1878 (he was aided by many uncredited artists, including Ferdinand Hodler), it depicts the French Army of the East retreating into Switzerland at Verrières, a famous episode in the Franco-Prussian War. As you walk around the circle, the imagery seems to pop into three dimensions; in fact, with the help of a few strategically placed models, it does. There's a recorded commentary in English. Its conical wooden structure is surrounded by a modern glass cube filled with shops, movie theaters, and a restaurant. ✉ *Löwenpl. 11* ☏ *041/4123030* ⊕ *www.bourbakipanorama.ch* 🎫 *8 SF* ⊘ *Nov.–Mar., Mon. 1–5, Tues.–Sun. 10—5; Apr.–Oct., Mon. 1–6, Tues.–Sun. 9–6.*

❼ **Historisches Museum** *(History Museum).* Housed in the late-Gothic armory dating from 1567, this stylish institution exhibits numerous city icons, including the original Gothic fountain that stood in the Weinmarkt. Reconstructed rooms depict rural and urban life. ✉ *Pfisterg. 24* ☏ *041/2285424* ⊕ *www.hmluzern.ch* 🎫 *10 SF* ⊘ *Tues.–Sun. and holidays 10–5.*

❾ **Jesuitenkirche** *(Jesuit Church).* Constructed in 1666–77, this Baroque
Fodor'sChoice church with a symmetrical entrance is flanked by two onion-dome towers,
★ added in 1893. Inside, its vast interior, restored to its original splendor, is a dramatic explosion of gilt, marble, and epic frescoes. Nearby is the Renaissance **Regierungsgebäude** (Government Building), seat of the cantonal government. ✉ *Bahnhofstr., just west of Rathaus-Steg* ☏ *041/2100756* ⊕ *www.jesuitenkirche-luzern.ch* ⊘ *Daily 6 AM–6:30 PM.*

❿ **Kapellbrücke** *(Chapel Bridge).* The oldest wooden bridge in Europe
Fodor'sChoice snakes diagonally across the Reuss. When it was constructed in the early
★ 14th century, the bridge served as a rampart in case of attacks from the lake. Its shingle roof and grand stone water tower are to Luzern what the Matterhorn is to Zermatt, but considerably more vulnerable, as a 1993 fire proved. Almost 80% of this fragile monument was destroyed, including many of the 17th-century paintings inside. However, a walk through this dark, creaky landmark will take you past polychrome copies of 110 gable panels, painted by Heinrich Wägmann in the 17th century and depicting Luzern and Swiss history, stories of St. Leodegar

A GOOD WALK

Start at the **Kultur- und Kongresszentrum,** near the train station, which gives you a beautiful view of all the places you'll see in Luzern. Walk down Pilatusstrasse to see the city's latest addition to its cultural offerings, the **Sammlung Rosengart.**

Cut north to Bahnhofstrasse, taking a left to the modern bridge, the Rathaus-Steg, and head north to the **Altes Rathaus,** across the bridge. This late-Renaissance building is on Rathausquai, the city's main avenue.

Turn left and climb the stairs past the ornately frescoed Zunfthaus zur Pfistern, a guildhall dating from the late 15th and early 16th centuries, to the Kornmarkt, where the grinding din of the grain market was once heard. Cut left to the **Weinmarkt,** a fountain square.

Leave the square from its west end, turn right on Kramgasse, and head west across the Mühlenplatz to the **Spreuerbrücke,** an unlikely exhibition space for dark paintings of the medieval plague epidemic.

Crossing the bridge to the left bank, you'll find a pair of museums, the **Natur-Museum** and the **Historisches Museum.**

From the end of the Spreuerbrücke, cut back upriver along Pfistergasse, veer left on Bahnhofstrasse, and turn right into Münzgasse to the **Franziskanerkirche.**

Return to Bahnhofstrasse and head to the **Jesuitenkirche.** Continuing east past the Rathaus-Steg Bridge, you'll see the **Kapellbrücke,** the oldest bridge of its kind in Europe.

After crossing the Kapellbrücke, break away from Old Town through thick pedestrian and bus traffic at Schwanenplatz to Schweizerhofquai.

Double back and take the first right, St. Leodegarstrasse, to the **Hofkirche.**

Go back down the church steps, doubling back on St. Leodegarstrasse, turn right, and continue on to Löwenstrasse.

Turn right and walk up to Löwenplatz and the **Bourbaki-Panorama,** which dominates the square with its mix of Victorian and modern architecture.

Beyond the plaza, up Denkmalstrasse, is the **Löwendenkmal,** called by Mark Twain "the most mournful and moving piece of stone in the world."

Immediately adjoining the small park that shades the lion lies the **Gletschergarten.**

Return down Denkmalstrasse and, at Löwenplatz, turn right on Museggstrasse, which cuts through an original city gate and runs parallel to the watchtowers and crenellated walls of Luzern, constructed around 1400. The fifth tower is the **Zytturm.**

TIMING
The Old Town is easy to navigate and ideal for walking. You can take in the sights on this route in about three hours; to this add another hour each to see the Natur-Museum and Historisches Museum, and time to linger at the Kapellbrücke and the Löwendenkmal. Note that both the Natur-Museum and the Historisches Museum are closed Monday.

and St. Mauritius, Luzern's patron saints, and coats of arms of local patrician families. ⊠*Between See-brücke and Rathaus-Steg, connecting Rathausquai and Bahnhofstr.*

❶ **Kultur- und Kongresszentrum** *(Culture*
★ *and Convention Center).* Architect Jean Nouvel's stunning glass-and-steel building manages to both stand out from and fuse with its ancient milieu.

GETTING AROUND

Parking is limited, and Luzern's Old Town is pedestrian-only; it is best to park your car and walk. All destinations in this region mentioned here are small, reachable by train or boat, and can easily be traveled on foot once you get there.

The lakeside center's roof is an oversized, cantilevered, flat plane; shallow water channels thread inside, and immense glass plates mirror the surrounding views. The main draw is the concert hall, which opened in 1998. Although the lobbies are rich in blue, red, and stained wood, the hall itself is refreshingly pale, with acoustics so perfect you can hear the proverbial pin drop. Among the annual music events is the renowned International Music Festival. A museum focuses on rotating exhibits of new international artists. ⊠*Europapl. 1* ☎*041/2267070* ⊕*www.kkl-luzern.ch.*

❷ **Sammlung Rosengart** *(Rosengart Collection).* A father-and-daughter team amassed this amazing group of works by major late-19th- and 20th-century artists. Now housed in a former bank building, the collection, opened to the public in 2002, reveals their intensely personal approach; the Rosengarts acquired according to their own tastes instead of investment potential. Here you can see Miró's *Dancer,* Léger's *Contraste de formes,* and works by Cézanne, Monet, Matisse, Klee, and Chagall. There's an especially rich selection of Picassos; the artist painted the daughter, Angela Rosengart, five times. ⊠*Pilatusstr. 10* ☎*041/2201660* ⊕*www.rosengart.ch* 🖼*18 SF* ☉*Apr.–Oct., daily 10–6; Nov.–Mar., daily 11–5.*

❹ **Weinmarkt** *(Wine Market).* What is now the loveliest of Luzern's several fountain squares drew visitors from all across Europe in the 15th to 17th centuries with its passion plays. Its Gothic central fountain depicts St. Mauritius (patron saint of warriors), and its surrounding buildings are flamboyantly frescoed in 16th-century style. ⊠*Square just west of Kornmarkt, north of Metzgerrainli.*

ALSO WORTH SEEING

❽ **Franziskanerkirche** *(Franciscan Church).* Since its construction in the 13th century, this church has been persistently remodeled. It still retains its 17th-century choir stalls and carved wooden pulpit. The barefoot Franciscans once held a prominent social and cultural position in Luzern, which took a firm stance against the Reformation and today remains approximately 70% Roman Catholic. ⊠*Franziskanerpl., just off Münzg.*

⓮ **Gletschergarten** *(Glacier Garden).* This 19th-century tourist attraction was excavated between 1872 and 1875 and has been dramatically pocked and polished by Ice Age glaciers. A private museum on the site displays impressive relief maps of Switzerland. ⊠*Denkmalstr. 4* ☎*041/4104340* ⊕*www.gletschergarten.ch* 🖾*12 SF* ⊙*Apr.–Oct., daily 9–6; Nov.–Mar., daily 10–5.*

⓫ **Hofkirche.** This sanctuary of St. Leodegar was first part of a monastery founded in 750. Its Gothic structure was mostly destroyed by fire in 1633 and rebuilt in late-Renaissance style, so only the towers of its predecessor were preserved. The carved pulpit and choir stalls date from the 17th century, and the 80-rank organ (1650) is one of Switzerland's finest. Outside, Italianate loggias shelter a cemetery for patrician families of Old Luzern. ⊠*St. Leodegarstr. 6* ☎*041/4182020* ⊙*Call for hrs.*

OFF THE BEATEN PATH **Verkehrshaus.** Easily reached by steamer, car, or Bus 8 or 6, the Swiss Transport Museum is almost a world's fair in itself, with a complex of buildings and exhibitions both indoors and out, including live demonstrations, dioramas, and a "Swissorama" (360-degree screen) film about Switzerland. Every mode of transit is discussed, from stagecoaches and bicycles to jumbo jets and space capsules. The museum also houses the country's first IMAX theater. If you're driving, head east on Haldenstrasse at the waterfront and make a right on Lidostrasse. Signs point the way. ⊠*Lidostr. 5* ☎*041/3704444* ⊕*www.verkehrshaus.ch* 🖾*24 SF* ⊙*Apr.–Oct., daily 10–6; Nov.–Mar., daily 10–5.*

⓭ **Löwendenkmal** *(Lion Monument).* The Swiss guards who died defending ★ Louis XVI of France at the Tuileries in Paris in 1792 are commemorated here. Designed by Danish sculptor Berthel Thorwaldsen and carved out of a sheer sandstone face by Lucas Ahorn of Konstanz, this 19th-century wonder is a simple, stirring image of a dying lion. The Latin inscription translates "To the bravery and fidelity of the Swiss." ⊠*Denkmalstr.*

❻ **Natur-Museum** *(Natural History Museum).* Unusually modern display ↻ techniques bring nature lessons to life here. The museum focuses on local natural history, with panoramas of early Luzern settlers and live animals for children to meet. ⊠*Kasernenpl. 6* ☎*041/2285411* ⊕*www. naturmuseum.ch* 🖾*6 SF* ⊙*Tues.–Sun. 10–5.*

❺ **Spreuerbrücke** *(Chaff Bridge).* This narrow covered bridge dates from 1408. The weathered wood structure's interior gables hold a series of eerie, well-preserved 17th-century paintings by Kaspar Meglinger of the *Dance of Death.* Medieval in style and inspiration, they chronicle the plague that devastated all of Europe in the 14th century. ⊠*Between Geissmattbrücke and Reussbrücke, connecting Zeughaus Reuss-Steg and Mühlenpl.*

⓯ **Zytturm** *(Time Tower).* The clock in this fifth watchtower was made in Basel in 1385 and still keeps time. ⊠*North of and parallel to Museggstr.*

WHERE TO EAT

$$ ✕**Bodu.** A touch of Paris in the heart of Luzern, this comes replete with
FRENCH   advertising posters from the '20s and '30s, simple wooden tables, and a
green-and-yellow checkered floor. The darker, barlike entrance leads to
the bright main room with a terrace overlooking the river. Sumptuous
dishes like duck breast with apples in calvados sauce with noodles and
vegetables, or ravioli stuffed with spinach and ricotta in a mushroom
and cheese cream sauce, are based on fresh market ingredients. Be pre-
pared to pay 3 SF for tap water if you don't order anything else to drink.
✉*Kornmarkt 5* ☎*041/4100177* ⊟*AE, DC, MC, V.*

$$ ✕**Galliker.** Step past the ancient facade and into a room roaring with
SWISS   local action. Brisk waitresses serve up the dishes *Mutti* (Mom) used to
★   make: fresh *Kutteln* (tripe) in rich white wine sauce with cumin seeds;
real *Kalbs-kopf* (chopped fresh veal head) served with heaps of green
onions and warm vinaigrette; and authentic Luzerner *Kügelipaschtetli.*
Occasional experiments in a modern mode—such as steak with wasabi sauce—prove that Peter Galliker's kitchen is no museum. Desserts
may include raspberries with peppermint ice cream. ✉*Schützenstr. 1*
☎*041/2401002* ⊟*AE, DC, MC, V* ⊘*Closed Sun., Mon., and mid-
July–mid-Aug.*

$$$–$$$$ ✕**Old Swiss House.** This popular establishment has been feeding travelers
SWISS   since 1931. Originally built as a farmhouse in 1858, it pleases crowds
★   with its beautifully contrived collection of 17th-century antiques, leaded
glass, and an old-world style now pleasantly burnished by more than 77
years of service. The standing menu includes specialties from around the
country: cubed fillet of beef in a green-pepper mustard sauce with fresh
buttered noodles, lake fish with spinach and lemon ricotta ravioli, and
chocolate mousse. In warm weather, enjoy your meal in the outdoor
seating area, which spills out into the pedestrian zone. ✉*Löwenpl. 4*
☎*041/4106171* ⊟*AE, DC, MC, V* ⊘*Closed Mon. and Feb.*

$$ ✕**Pfistern.** One of the architectural focal points of the Old Town water-
SWISS   front, this floridly decorated guild house—the guild's origins can be
traced back to 1341—provides an authentic medieval setting in which
to sample reasonably priced local fare. Lake fish with steamed new
potatoes or *pastetli* (meat pies with puff pastry) are worthy local
options. Inside, it's woody and publike, if slightly down-at-the-heels,
but in summer the small first-floor balcony or the airy cobblestone riverside arcade provides one of the best seats in town. ✉*Kornmarkt 4*
☎*041/4103650* ⊟*AE, DC, MC, V.*

$$ ✕**Rebstock/Hofstube.** Formerly a 16th-century tavern, this spot is now a
FRENCH   meeting place for Luzern's art and media set. The lively brasserie hums
with locals lunching by the bar, and the more formal old-style restau-
rant glows with wood and brass under a low-beamed parquetry ceiling.
Fresh market ingredients are combined for modern, international fare,
including chicken simmered in white wine, rabbit stewed with rosemary,
and classic garlic snails, as well as East Asian and vegetarian specialties.
There is ample outside seating when it's warm, including a small garden.
✉*St. Leodegarpl. 3* ☎*041/4103581* ⊟*AE, DC, MC, V.*

EATING WELL IN CENTRAL SWITZERLAND

Rooted in the German territory of Switzerland and the surrounding farmlands, central Switzerland's cuisine is down-home and hearty. In the mountains there are Alpine cheese specialties (*Aelpler Magrone*—pasta, butter, cheese, and fried onions); in the region's orchard country there are such cherry specialties as *Zuger Kirschtorte*, a rich white cake soaked with cherry schnapps. Pears from the local orchards are dried, then spiced and poached in sweetened red *Dole* (wine).

Luzern takes pride in its *Kügelipaschtetli*, puff-pastry nests filled with tiny veal meatballs, chicken, or sweetbreads; mushrooms; cream sauce; and occasionally raisins. But here the real *cuisine du marché*, based on fresh market ingredients, focuses on lake fish.

Lake Luzern produces an abundance of *Egli* (perch), *Hecht* (pike), *Forellen* (trout), and *Felchen* (whitefish); Lake Zuger produces its own exclusive *Röteln*, a red-bellied relative of the trout.

Restaurants—especially along waterfronts—trade heavily in these freshwater fish, whether they come from the region or not. Ask, and you may get an honest answer: the sources vary, but the style of preparation remains local. In Luzern, whole fish is traditionally sautéed with tomatoes, mushrooms, and capers.

WHERE TO STAY

$$$–$$$$ ★ **Des Balances.** Built in the 19th century on the site of two ancient guildhalls, this waterfront property is full of style. State-of-the-art tile baths, up-to-date pastel furnishings, and one of the best sites in the heart of the Old Town make this the slickest in its price class. Rotes Gatter ($$–$$$$), the hotel's chic restaurant, has a combination as desirable as it is rare: a soigné interior, shimmering river views, and a sophisticated menu. The restaurant has a more casual, less expensive bistro area as well. **Pros:** all rooms have great views; the river terrace is exceptional. **Cons:** top-floor rooms tend to be rudimentary. ⊠ *Weinmarkt* 🕾 *041/4182828* ⊕ *www.balances.ch* 🛏 *50 rooms, 7 suites* ⌂ *Inroom: no a/c, safe, refrigerator, Ethernet. In-hotel: restaurant, public Wi-Fi* ⊟ *AE, DC, MC, V* ⍩ *BP.*

$$$ **Hofgarten.** This gracious 12th-century house close to the Hofkirche and the Löwendenkmal has been artfully modernized with an eclectic mix of colors and themes. One room contains a 5-foot-tall antique stove (still operable), and another resembles the interior of a clipper ship. Some white-tiled bathrooms have cool steel sinks. The Hofgarten has one of Luzern's best vegetarian restaurants, with dishes that could satisfy even a meat lover. **Pros:** leafy garden terrace in summer; very quiet. **Cons:** doesn't get much sun. ⊠ *Stadthofstr. 14* 🕾 *041/4108888* ⊕ *www.hofgarten.ch* 🛏 *19 rooms* ⌂ *In-room: no a/c. In-hotel: restaurant, parking (fee)* ⊟ *AE, DC, MC, V* ⍩ *BP.*

$$$–$$$$ **The Hotel.** Noted French architect Jean Nouvel, who also designed Luzern's Kultur- und Kongresszentrum, focuses on ultrahip design; parquet floors are this lodging's only remaining old-world touch. Metal

blocks act as cupboards, and mirrors, puffy chairs, and dark walls add to the look. But the highlight of each room is the enlarged movie still that covers the ceiling. Fellini, Wenders, and von Trier are represented, among others, and yes, the photograph is positioned so that you see it best while lying on your bed. An Asian/French fusion restaurant attracts locals as well as hotel guests. **Pros:** heaven for style junkies; hip restaurant. **Cons:** the odd staff member suffers from hype-head. ⊠*Sempacherstr. 14* ☎*041/2268686* ⊕*www.the-hotel.ch* ⬅*10 rooms, 15 suites* ⌂*In-room: refrigerator, Ethernet. In-hotel: restaurant, bar, public Wi-Fi* ⊟*AE, DC, MC, V.*

$$$ **Krone.** Spotless and modern, this hotel softens its edges with pastel linens and walls; look in the recessed niche of one of the interior walls for a stone shrine retained from the original structure. The rooms facing the Weinmarkt have high ceilings and tall windows that let in lots of light. Guest rooms to the back have no direct sun but are still bright and a little larger. The ground-floor cafeteria-style restaurant has a no-alcohol policy. **Pros:** very friendly and helpful staff; good central location. **Cons:** restaurant has a no-alcohol policy. ⊠*Weinmarkt 12* ☎*041/4194400* ⊕*www.krone-luzern.ch* ⬅*25 rooms* ⌂*In-room: no a/c, refrigerator. In-hotel: restaurant* ⊟*AE, DC, MC, V* ❙⊚❙*BP.*

$–$$ **Löwengraben.** For something completely different, spend a night in jail—which this hotel was until as recently as 1998. Bright paint, comfortably simple beds, modular bathroom facilities, and the odd antique furnishing take the blues out of the jailhouse and replace it with funky charm. Although the rooms are small—think cell-sized—the fun atmosphere that radiates from the bars (one is called Alcatraz) and restaurants downstairs adds to the draw. There's even a suite in the old warden's office, with a large barred window. **Pros:** very innovative venue; cheerful service. **Cons:** not for claustrophobics or for stays cursed by endless rainy days. ⊠*Löwengraben 18* ☎*041/4107830* ⊕*www. jailhotel.ch* ⬅*51 rooms, 4 suites* ⌂*In-room: no a/c, no TV. In-hotel: 2 restaurants, 2 bars* ⊟*AE, MC, V* ❙⊚❙*BP.*

$$$–$$$$ **Montana.** This 1910 palace glows with beeswaxed beauty, its luxurious original woodwork, parquet, and terrazzo are all in superb condition. The public rooms flank the ground floor's south side, and on a clear day offer a magnificent view of the lake and the mountains. The guest rooms are made up in art deco style, with bold patterns and funky furniture. Those in back overlook a hillside, while the front doubles (slightly costlier) have balconies overlooking the city and lake. The building is perched on a slope above town, accessible by funicular from the lakeshore Haldenstrasse or by car. **Pros:** good jazz concerts in a you-are-there venue; large terrace hovers over the lake. **Cons:** away from the city center; difficult to find. ⊠*Adligenswilerstr. 22* ☎*041/4190000* ⊕*www.hotel-montana.ch* ⬅*52 rooms, 10 suites* ⌂*In-room: no a/c, safe, refrigerator. In-hotel: restaurant, bar, public Wi-Fi, parking (no fee)* ⊟*AE, DC, MC, V* ❙⊚❙*BP.*

$$$$ **National Hotel.** This monumental landmark, founded in 1870, was once home base to Cesar Ritz, the man who invented the world's first modern luxury hotel. It is no surprise, then, that the inner sanctums of this lodging trumpet a florid splendor, down to the last cupola,

crown molding, and Corinthian column. The hotel's mansarded facade stretches the length of two city blocks, dominating the lakeside promenade. The French provincial guest rooms have brass beds; the domed bar is decked with mahogany and aglitter with crystal. **Pros:** splendid marble-columned breakfast hall; promenade restaurant under chestnut trees. **Cons:** the adjoining Casino makes for the occasional overly boisterous guests. ⊠*Haldenstr. 4* ☏*041/4190909* ⊕*www.national-luzern. ch* ⟋*78 rooms, 10 suites* ⟐*In-room: no a/c, safe, refrigerator, Ethernet. In-hotel: 4 restaurants, bar, pool, gym, public Wi-Fi, parking (fee)* ▭*AE, DC, MC, V.*

$$$$ ⚀ **Palace Hotel.** This waterfront hotel drinks in the broadest possible
★ lake views. Built in 1906, it has been brilliantly refurbished so that its classical look has a touch of postmodernism. Rooms are large enough for a game of badminton, and picture windows afford sweeping views of Mt. Pilatus. The hotel's elegance also seeps into its restaurant, Jasper ($$-$$$$). The contemporary cuisine—think veal with celery mousse and truffle sauce—is faultlessly prepared and formally presented. The bar has a clubby look—leather chairs, brass fixtures, and a long oak bar. **Pros:** lakefront setting, right off the promenade; grand interiors. **Cons:** backs onto a main throroughfare. ⊠*Haldenstr. 10* ☏*041/4161616* ⊕*www.palace-luzern.com* ⟋*178 rooms, 45 suites* ⟐*In-room: no a/c, safe, refrigerator, dial-up, Ethernet. In-hotel: 2 restaurants, bar, gym, public Wi-Fi, parking (fee)* ▭*AE, DC, MC, V.*

$-$$ ⚀ **Schlüssel.** This crisp, no-nonsense lodging on the Franziskanerplatz attracts young bargain hunters. It's a pleasant combination of tidy modern touches (quarry tile, white paint) and antiquity: you can admire the fine old beams in the lobby or in the low, cross-vaulted "crypt"-esque restaurant. Locals come here for Swiss specialties like cheese fondue or Fleischvögel–pounded beef steaks wrapped around stuffing in a sausage shape. Two of the rooms overlooking the square's Franciscan church have small balconies. **Pros:** staff makes that extra effort. **Cons:** be prepared for insistent morning church bells. ⊠*Franziskanerpl. 12* ☏*041/2101061* ⊕*www.luzern-schluessel.ch* ⟋*10 rooms* ⟐*In-room: no a/c. In-hotel: restaurant, public Wi-Fi* ▭*MC, V.*

$$$$ ⚀ **Schweizerhof.** Built in the 1840s and since 1861 owned by the same family that expanded it in the 1860s, this imposing structure has hosted Napoléon III, Leo Tolstoy, and Mark Twain—and Richard Wagner lived here while his lakefront home at Tribschen was being completed. The guest rooms all have sweeping views of the lake and mountains. Their period style has a modern twist: gilt mirrors, richly colored carpets, and marble-and-tile bathrooms cover the luxury bases, and Internet access and voice mail keep you connected. **Pros:** top-of-the-line comfort combined with state-of-the-art technology. **Cons:** a nearby supermarket looms a little close in the back. ⊠*Schweizerhofquai 3* ☏*041/4100410* ⊕*www.schweizerhof-luzern.ch* ⟋*86 rooms, 1 suite* ⟐*In-room: safe, refrigerator, Ethernet. In-hotel: 2 restaurants, bar, gym, public Wi-Fi, parking (fee)* ▭*AE, DC, MC, V.*

¢-$ ⚀ **Tourist.** Despite its collegiate atmosphere, this cheery, dormlike spot
★ is anything but a backpackers' flophouse. It has a terrific setting on the Reuss around the corner from the Old Town. Its spare, modern

architecture is brightened with fresh, trendy colors and framed prints, and rooms that don't have a river view face the quiet backyard instead. The coed four-bed dorms (sex-segregated in high season) draw sociable travelers with their rock-bottom prices. There are also seven private-bath doubles. **Pros:** shared baths are well maintained; the staff is young and helpful. **Cons:** no parking (but public parking is across the river). ⊠*St. Karli Quai 12* ☎*041/4102474* ⊕*www.touristhotel.ch* 🛏*11 rooms, 1 suite* ♿*In-room: no a/c, no phone. In-hotel: bar, laundry facilities, public Internet* 🚏*AE, DC, MC, V.*

$$$–$$$$ 🏨**Wilden Mann.** The city's best-known hotel creates a gracious and
★ authentic experience of old Luzern, with stone, beams, brass, and burnished wood everywhere. Even the street is atmospheric—across the way is a 16th-century pharmacy. The hotel's reputation extends to its restaurants: the Burgerstube is cozy with its dark beams and family crests, whereas vaulting and candlelight make the Liedertafel more formal. Both menus strike a fine balance between local cooking and French cuisine, with main dishes such as pike-perch with chanterelle mushroom ravioli and desserts like port wine cherries. **Pros:** friendly service; medieval architecture straight out of Middle Earth. **Cons:** some ceilings are a bit low. ⊠*Bahnhofstr. 30* ☎*041/2101666* ⊕*www.wilden-mann.ch* 🛏*42 rooms, 8 suites* ♿*In-room: no a/c, refrigerator. In-hotel: 2 restaurants, public Wi-Fi* 🚏*AE, DC, MC, V* 🍽*BP.*

$$ 🏨**Zum Weissen Kreuz.** This completely modernized historic hotel in the bustling heart of the Old Town has a tongue-in-cheek combination of sleek modern lines with gilded frames and fat cherubs. The rooms are small but well-designed, with hardwood floors and retro '60s furnishings. The entire hotel, including the popular pizzeria with its wood-burning pizza oven, is no-smoking. There's a webcam showing Luzern on the roof—you can check the weather ahead of time. **Pros:** rare no-smoking treat in hard-smoker territory; young, enthusiastic staff. **Cons:** some room views are limited. ⊠*Furrerg. 19* ☎*041/4188220* ⊕*www. hotel-wkreuz.ch* 🛏*21 rooms, 1 suite* ♿*In-room: no a/c, refrigerator. In-hotel: restaurant, public Internet, public Wi-Fi* 🚏*AE, DC, MC, V.*

NIGHTLIFE & THE ARTS

For information on goings-on around town, go to the tourist office for a copy of the German/English *Luzern City Guide,* published quarterly by the city. Get it stamped by your hotel for discounts on museums, public transit, and special events.

NIGHTLIFE

BARS &   In the Hotel Montana, **Louis Bar** (⊠*Adligenwilerstr. 22* ☎*041/4190000*)
LOUNGES   offers live jazz in the style of Louis Armstrong. While you're there, sip one of the 80 Scotch whiskies behind the bar. The beautiful **Meridiani** (⊠*Klosterstr. 12* ☎*041/2404344*) bar pours everything from coffee to cognac. Students and young professionals mix and mingle at **Oops** (⊠*Zentralstr. 10* ☎*041/2102255*). If you need a jolt, choose from 60 different kinds of coffee.

Opus (✉ *Bahnhofstr. 16* ☎ *041/2264141*) specializes in fine wines, many served by the glass. **Roadhouse** (✉ *Pilatusstr. 1* ☎ *041/2202727*) is a British pub with live rock and roll acts.

CASINO The most sophisticated nightlife in Luzern is found in the **Grand Casino Luzern** (✉ *Haldenstr. 6* ☎ *041/4185656* ⊕ *www.grandcasinoluzern.ch*), an early-20th-century building on the lake's northern shore near the grand hotels. You can play *boule* (a type of roulette) in the Gambling Room; dance in the Club; watch the cabaret in the Casineum; or have a meal in Olivio, a Mediterranean restaurant with views of the mountains and the lake.

THE ARTS

FILM Movie theaters, concentrated on the south bank along Pilatusstrasse and Bahnhofstrasse, usually screen films in their original language. You can also catch a show in the Bourbaki-Panorama development.

FOLKLORE The *Night Boat* (☎ *041/3194978*) sails from the Landungsbrücke—a dock right on the Bahnhofplatz-Europlatz—every evening from May through September. This pleasant lake cruise has meals, drinks, and a folklore show. Performances at the **Stadtkeller** (✉ *Sternenpl. 3* ☎ *041/4104733*) come with yodelers, dirndled dancers, and more.

MUSIC Luzern, the cultural hub of central Switzerland, hosts the annual **Lucerne Festival** (✉ *Hirschmattstr. 13* ☎ *041/2264480*) from mid-August to mid-September in the Kultur- und Kongresszentrum. Outstanding performers come from all over the world; past guests have included mezzo-soprano Cecilia Bartoli and pianist András Schiff. Performing at the Kultur- und Kongresszentrum, the **Luzerner Symphonieorchester** (✉ *Europapl.* ☎ *041/2103060* ⊕ *www.lucernefestival.ch*), the local orchestra in residence, has a season that runs from October through June.

THEATER The **Luzerner Theater** (✉ *Theaterstr. 2* ☎ *041/2281414* ⊕ *www.luzerner-theater.ch*), directly on the waterfront on the Bahnhof side of town, is home to Luzern's principal theater group, which stages plays in German and operas in their original language.

SPORTS & THE OUTDOORS

BICYCLING

The standard Swiss practice of renting bicycles from the **train station** (✉ *Bahnhofpl.* ☎ *051/2273261*) comes in handy here, as the lake-level terrain offers smooth riding.

BOATING

Pedal-, motor-, and sailboats are available in Luzern through **Marina Charter** (✉ *Alpenquai 13* ☎ *041/3607944*). **SNG Luzern** (✉ *Alpenquai 11* ☎ *041/3680808*), open weekdays only, offers fair-weather boat rentals from April to October and year-round hour-long boat tours for 15 SF. **Werft Herzog AG** (✉ *Nationalquai* ☎ *041/4104333*) specializes in motorboats for up to 10 passengers.

SWIMMING
At the **Lido** (⊠*Lidostr.* ☎*041/3703806*), past the casino and near the Verkehrshaus, you can swim in Lake Luzern from May to September, daily from 9 to 8.

SHOPPING

The best shopping in the region is concentrated in Luzern, which, although it no longer produces embroidery or lace, still offers a wide variety of Swiss handicrafts as well as the luxury goods appropriate to its high profile. The pedestrian zone along Hertensteinstrasse is packed with boutiques and department stores. In summer most shops stay open until 9 PM; on Sunday morning they open after 11 AM. On Thursday night year-round, shops stay open until 9.

DEPARTMENT STORES
The main department store in town is **Globus** (⊠*Pilatusstr. 4* ☎*041/2270707*); it's a good place to hunt for souvenirs. **Migros** (⊠*Hertensteinstr. 9* ☎*041/4170740*) specializes in groceries and inexpensive items.

EMBROIDERY
The main producer of Swiss embroidery is **Sturzenegger** (⊠*Buobenmatt 2* ☎*041/4101958*) of St. Gallen, which sells its own machine-made lace and embroidered goods as well as Hanro and Calida underwear. The store also stocks a conservative line of women's dresses and blouses.

HANDICRAFTS & GIFTS
Aux Arts du Feu (⊠*Schweizerhofquai 2* ☎*041/4101401*) offers high-end china and crystal. **Bookbinders Design** (⊠*Hertensteinstr. 3* ☎*041/4109506*), an upscale stationer, stocks precision writing instruments and brightly colored, handmade, recycled-paper products. **Schmid-Linder** (⊠*Denkmalstr. 9* ☎*041/4104346*) carries an extensive line of Swiss embroidery and linen, as well as cuckoo clocks, cowbells, and a large stock of wood carvings from Brienz, in the Berner Oberland.

MARKETS
From May to October, a **Flohmärt,** or flea market, takes place every Saturday from 8 to 4 at Untere Burgerstrasse, not far from the Franziskanerkirche. For locally made crafts, there's a **Handwerksmarkt** on the Weinmarkt. It takes place on the first Saturday of every month from April through December.

WATCHES
Competition is fierce, and the two enormous patriarchs of the watch business advertise heavily and offer inexpensive souvenirs to lure shoppers into their luxurious showrooms. **Bucherer** (⊠*Schwanenpl. 5* ☎*041/3697700*) represents Piaget and Rolex. **Gübelin** (⊠*Schweizerhofquai 1* ☎*041/4105142*) is the exclusive source for Audemars Piguet, Patek Philippe, and its own house brand.

WOMEN'S CLOTHING

The czarina of women's fashion in Luzern is Christina De Boer, who runs a group of designer boutiques. **Christina De Boer** (⊠ *Werchlaubeg. 14* ☎*041/4106239*) is an exclusive boutique with cashmere fashions and high-end labels such as Jil Sander and Rena Lange. **Rive Gauche** (⊠*Pilatusstr. 14* ☎*041/2108916*) has a wide variety of mid-range labels such as Gabriele Seba.

LUZERN ENVIRONS

Since Luzern doesn't have the sprawling suburbs associated with most cities, bucolic landscapes are just a short day trip away. Craggy mountaintops, lush hills dotted with grazing cows, and peaceful lakeside villages—along with one of the most famous mountains in Switzerland—are easily reached by boat, train, or car.

MT. PILATUS

Fodor'sChoice ★ *10 km (6 mi) southwest of Luzern.*

6

GETTING HERE

If you don't have time for the four-hour hike, there are two ways to get to the top of Mt. Pilatus (www.pilatus.ch): from Luzern by bus to Krienz and from there to the summit by cable car (76 SF round-trip) and back, or by returning down the other side by cogwheel train to Alpnachstad and getting on the boat back to Luzern (83 SF round-trip).

EXPLORING

Unlike Queen Victoria, who rode to the summit of this 6,953-foot mountain by mule in 1868, you can travel there and back by cable car for a hefty 74 SF from Luzern. Take a bus from the train station in Luzern to the suburb of Kriens, where you catch a tiny, four-seat cable car that flies silently up to Fräkmüntegg (4,600 feet); then change to the 40-seat cable car that sails through open air up the rock cliff to the summit station (5,560 feet). From here a 10-minute walk takes you to the **Esel,** at the center of Pilatus's multiple peaks, where views unfold over the Alps and the sprawling, crooked Lake Luzern.

At the top, a grand 19th-century "mountaineer's" hotel is the centerpiece of the surprisingly stroller-friendly mountain peak. Glorious views are everywhere, as you'll discover walking along the blissfully flat main trail; this leads in and out of the mountain, and comes replete with striking cavern windows that offer drop-dead vistas. The main view takes in Luzern, which looks

> **BEHIND THE NAME**
>
> Mt. Pilatus was named either from the Latin *pileatus* (wearing a cap), to refer to its frequent cloud covering, or, more colorfully, for the ghost of Pontius Pilate, who supposedly haunts the summit. (His body, it was said, was brought here by the devil.) For centuries it was forbidden to climb the mountain and enrage the ghost, who was said to unleash deadly storms.

Luzern Environs

10
Littau
Malters
Kriens
LUZERN
Mittaggüpfi
Mt. Pilatus
Hergiswil
Alpnachstad
GROSSCHLIERENTAL
A8
Kerns
Sarnen
0   5 mi
0   5 km

Verkehrshaus
Luzern see detail map
Meggen
Weggis
Stansstad
Stans
Ennetmoos
Stanserhorn
Aa

A14
A2

Küssnacht
Rigi Kulm
Rigi-Kaltbad
Luzernersee
Bürgenstock
Ennetbürgen
Beckenried
NIDWALDEN
Klewenalp
ENGELBERGERTAL
Schwalmis
Srisen
Grafenort
Wissigstock

Zuger
Arth
Goldau
8
Rigi Scheidegg
Lauerzer See
Vitznau
Gersau
Brunnen
Schwyz
Vierwaldstättersee
Seelisberg
The Tellskapelle
Rütli Meadow
A2
Urnersee
Axen
Flüelen
Altdorf
URI
Bürglen
A2

Alpinacher See

KEY
•─• Cable Car/ Funicular
├─┤ Rail lines
🚢 Ferry
⛷ Ski Resorts

Gräfimattstand
Melchtal
Nünalphorn
Engelberg

SWITZERLAND

like a tiny Lionel train-set toy village from way up here. The hotel, once graced by Victoria, is now just a restaurant, but consider reserving a spot here for lunch: the surrounds still reverberate to a 19th-century vibe and the food is spiced up by the views just outside the elegant sash windows.

A super variation for the return trip to Luzern from Mt. Pilatus involves riding one of the steepest cogwheel trains in the country—often down gradients inclined nearly 48%—through four tunnels that pierce sheer rock, to Alpnachstad. From there, take the train or the ferry, which leaves from the jetty across from the train station, back to Luzern, all for 83 SF. To go on to Engelberg, get off the Luzern-bound train at Hergiswil, where you can cross the track and climb aboard the small, private Stans-Engelberg train that heads up the Engelbergertal (Engelberg Valley).

STANS

10 km (6 mi) southeast of Mt. Pilatus, 10 km (6 mi) south of Luzern.

Visitor Information (⊠ *Bahnhofpl. 4* ☎ *041/6108833* ⊕ *www.stans.ch*).

In the heart of lush valley terrain and mossy meadows, Stans is an old village whose appealing Old Town center is dotted with the deep-roof houses typical of central Switzerland. This was the home of the beloved Heinrich Pestalozzi, the father of modern education. When the French army invaded the village in 1798, slaughtering nearly 2,000 citizens, it was Pestalozzi who gathered the orphaned children into a school, where he applied his progressive theories in the budding science of psychology to the practice of education. Instead of rote memorization and harsh discipline, Pestalozzi's teaching methods emphasized concrete examples (using plant specimens to teach botany, for example) and moral as well as intellectual development—quite a liberal education. He also championed the idea of fostering a child's individuality.

The bell tower of the **Pfarrkirche St. Peter und St. Paul** *(Church of Sts. Peter and Paul)* is in Italian Romanesque style with increasing numbers of arched windows as it rises. The incongruous steeple was added in the 16th century. ⊠ *Knirig. 1.*

On the town square stands a 19th-century **monument to Arnold von Winkelried,** a native of Stans who martyred himself to lead the Swiss Confederates to victory over the Austrians at the battle of Sempach in 1386. The Austrians, armed with long spears, formed a Roman square so that the Swiss, wielding axes and halberds, couldn't get in close enough to do any damage. Shouting, "Forward, confederates, I will open a path!" von Winkelried threw himself on the spears, clasping as many of them as he could to his breast—creating an opening for his comrades. ⊠ *Knirig., facing the Pfarrkirche St. Peter und St. Paul.*

EN ROUTE

A two-part journey on a nostalgic 1893 funicular and an ultramodern cable car takes you to the **Stanserhorn** (6,200 feet), from whose peak you can see the Titlis, the highest point in central Switzerland. You can also see the Jungfrau. ⊠ *Stans* ☎ *041/6188040* 🎫 *52 SF round-trip* ⊗ *Apr.–Nov., daily 8:30–4:30.*

OFF THE BEATEN PATH

Mount Titlis. Set 19 km (12 mi) south of Stans, this is perhaps the most spectacular of the many rocky peaks that surround the Obermatt's long, wide bowl. Thanks to a sophisticated transportation system that benefits skiers, hikers, climbers, and sightseers alike, it's possible to ride a small cable car up to the tiny mountain lake (and famous ski area) called Trübsee (5,904 feet). From there, change and ascend to Stand to catch the famous Rotair cable car, which rotates to give 360-degree panoramas on its way up to the summit station on the Titlis. At the top is a multilevel structure that seems to conjure up Disney's Space Mountain: four rock-embedded, fortress-thick floors lead to shops, an ice grotto (serving drinks from a solid-ice bar), and a restaurant whose views take in the JuraMountains, the Graubünden and Bernese Alps, and what from this perspective looks like a puny Pilatus. Warning: at this altitude most people are affected by mountain sickness; this usually

CLOSE UP

Watch Your Step!

Dozens of people are injured or even killed while hiking in the Alps, many of them travelers who misjudge the steep inclines and unsteady ground. Although all the trails are regularly maintained and most high-level walkways have railings, there are hazards every hiker should keep in mind. For example, slippery conditions in the loose gravel or on patches of grass after it rains or snows can often lead to a fall.

The best way to ward off injury is to bring a good pair of hiking boots and a walking stick, and to maintain a slow and careful pace. Pay attention to weather conditions: summer storms can develop suddenly. These days locals take along a cell phone just in case; reception is good in almost every corner of the country.

takes the form of a mild headache, so it might be best to take aspirin before heading up to this snowy wonderland. Mt. Titlis is found looming over the village of Engleberg (3,280 feet), located at the top of the village of Obermatt. Engleberg is a popular resort for skiers from nearby Zürich, but its slopes are limited in comparison with those of St. Moritz, Wengen, and Zermatt. From Luzern the resort is easily reached on an hourly train that also stops in Stans. Engelberg clusters at the foot of its Benedictine **Kloster** *(monastery),* founded in 1120; inside there's one of the largest organs in the country. Until the French invaded in 1798, massacring thousands, this monastery ruled the valley. The monastery grounds are open to the public daily and include a cheese shop, a small vegetable garden, and a florist. ⊠*Engelberg* ☎*041/6395050* ⊕*www. titlis.ch* ✆*82 SF round-trip.*

WILLIAM TELL COUNTRY

Perhaps it was only destiny that Switzerland was born right here. Take one look at the spectacular mix of snowy peaks, sapphire lakes, and picturesque meadows surrounding the Urnersee—the southern leg of Lake Luzern—and you'll realize this very beauty may have inspired the pact signed in 1291 between the clans of Schwyz, Unterwalden, and Uri. This Oath of Eternal Alliance announced the creation of a new realm—the world's first democracy. Believe it or not, this is not the only iconic historical event in this region. Although now considered by some to be mere myth, this is also the hallowed ground where Wilhelm Tell (to use the German spelling) was born and played out the legend that has thrilled millions to this day. Every year, thousands of Swiss make a pilgrimage here, taking a lake steamer from Luzern all the way down to the Urnersee (or driving the same route along the northern lakefront highway to Brunnen) to find their way to the Rütli Meadow—the birthplace of Switzerland—and to then trace the story of Tell in neighboring lakeside villages. If you want to "go high" and get a bird's-eye view of the area, opt for the excursion up to the top of majestic Rigi Kulm, the summit of Mt. Rigi, by train or cable car.

If you choose to take a lake cruise, depart at any convenient time (schedules are available at the ticket and tourist offices) from the main docks by the train station; the boat will be marked for Flüelen. First-class seats are on top; each level has a restaurant-café. The exterior seats are only slightly sheltered; if you want to sit inside, you may feel obligated to order a drink. Take advantage of the boat's many stops—you can get on and off at will.

BÜRGENSTOCK

20 km (13 mi) southeast of Luzern.

GETTING HERE
Trains depart from Luzern 10 times a day (45 minutes); you then transfer to a cog railway for a five-minute ride up to Bürgenstock. Lake steamers, departing from Luzern, shorten the trip to 30 minutes.

EXPLORING
The rich have always headed to Lake Luzern, thanks, in good part, to the famous Bürgenstock hotel resort. This haute-monde hideaway,

perched atop its own Alp, lured many celebs to these parts—Audrey Hepburn, Sophia Loren, Sean Connery, and Shirley MacLaine once colonized the chalets around here. Now partly under renovation, the hotel takes a back seat to the area's wonderful hiking. Most Flüelen-bound boats go to the base of the Bürgenstock, where visitors can take a funicular to the isolated resort at the top of a ridge. Though the plateau isn't terribly high—only 1,500 feet—it rises dramatically above the water and offers striking views over the region. Bürgenstock also can be approached by car, up a steep, sometimes dangerous road, from Stansstad, on the road between Luzern and Stansand—but watch out: it was designed with so many switchbacks to prevent playboys speeding their Ferraris.

WHERE TO STAY

$$$–$$$$

Fodor's Choice

★

Bürgenstock Hotels & Resort. Where only an eagle's nest should be, a quartet of hotels—dating from 1873, 1904, 1991, and 2007—take luxury to new heights, literally. Perched 1,600 feet over Lake Luzern, this complex was masterminded by the famous Frey family. Unfortunately, a large chunk is undergoing massive renovation, and now news comes that this will be ongoing until 2011. Hopefully, they will not touch the fin de siècle splendor: 19th-century frescoes, Art Nouveau wickerwork chairs, stained-glass windows, and the 14th-century late-Gothic chapel. And few can complain about the latest and greatest in facilities—they blasted out hillsides to accommodate pools and a stunning golf course. Long host to kings, queens, and celebs like Walt Disney and Charlie Chaplin, the hotel still welcomes V.I.P.s (who often arrive on the heli-pad). Guest rooms range from small to spacious; all are understated, but many will be getting a new face-lift in the years ahead. The full-service health club, with such spa services as aromatherapy and massage, is a great place to get pampered. Bring along your hiking boots, as the hotel has a restaurant perched on top of the nearby Hammetschwand Peak, along with one down by the lake. The food is nouvelle and slimming but, of course, you'll need chubby wallets. **Pros:** for both hikers and loafers; beautiful restaurant down by the lake—and an elevator there and back. **Cons:** high rollers only. ⊠ *Bürgenstock* ☏ *041/6129010* ⊕ *www.buergenstock-hotels.ch* ⬧ *200 rooms, 75 suites* ⬧ *In-room: no a/c, safe, refrigerator, Ethernet. In-hotel: 5 restaurants, bars, 9-hole golf course, 2 tennis courts, 3 pools, gym, spa, bicycles, public Wi-Fi* ⊟ *AE, DC, MC, V* ⎮�⎮BP.

WEGGIS

★ *25 km (15 mi) northeast and across the lake from Bürgenstock, 20 km (12 mi) northeast of Luzern.*

GETTING HERE

Boats come from Luzern and Flüelen every 1 to 1½ hours during daylight hours. A bus between the two towns goes every hour, a boat every 1 to 1½ hours during daylight hours (7.20 SF one-way). Weggis has a cable car up to the top of the Rigi (www.rigi.ch), while Vitznau has a cog-wheel train (each ca. once per hour, 37 SF one-way).

Visitor Information (⊠ *Seestr. 5* ☏ *041/3901155* ⊕ *www.weggis.ch*).

EXPLORING

With a pretty waterfront park and promenade, Weggis is a summer resort town known for its mild, almost subtropical climate—little wonder that it is a magnet for Switzerland's retired set. It's far from the highway and accessible only by the secondary road, so you get a pleasant sense of isolation. The famed **Mt. Rigi** (1,798 meters [5,900 feet]) is just a cable-car ride away from Weggis: follow signs for the Rigibahn, a station high above the resort (a 15-minute walk). From here you can ride a large cable car to **Rigi-Kaltbad,** a small resort on a spectacular plateau; walk across to the electric rack-and-pinion railway station and ride the steep tracks of the Vitznau–Rigi line to the summit of the mountain. Take an elevator to the **Rigi-Kulm** hotel to enjoy the views indoors or walk to the crest (45 minutes) to see as far as the Black Forest in one direction and Mt. Säntis in the other. Or consider climbing to the top, staying in the hotel, and getting up early to see the sun rise over the Alps—a view that astounded both Victor Hugo and Mark Twain. With Lake Luzern on one side and Lake Zug on the other, Mt. Rigi can seem like an island.

You have the option of returning to Luzern from Weggis by taking a different railway down, from Rigi to Arth-Goldau; the two lines were built by competing companies in the 1870s in a race to reach the top and capture the lion's share of the tourist business. The line rising out of the lakefront resort of Vitznau won, but the Arth-Goldau line gets plenty of business, as its base terminal lies on the mainstream St. Gotthard route. The round-trip fare from Vitznau or Arth-Goldau to Rigi-Kulm is 62 SF.

SKIING

Mt. Rigi, at 5,900 feet, has two funicular railways, three cable cars, seven lifts, 30 km (19 mi) of downhill runs, 14 km (9 mi) of cross-country trails, 14 km (9 mi) of ski-hiking trails, and curling.

WHERE TO EAT & STAY

$$–$$$
CONTEMPORARY

✕**Renggli's.** This very popular restaurant is ideally located on the waterfront, with its own private dock and a terrace overlooking the lake. The focus is on local lake fish specialties and seafood, accompanied by market-fresh side dishes. If you're a meat eater, the schnitzel or tournedos are also excellent. ✉*Seestr. 21* ☎*041/3900170* ▭*AE, DC, MC, V* ☉*Closed Wed. in July and Aug.*

$$$–$$$$
★

🏠**Beau-Rivage.** Built in 1908 but much modernized, this attractive business-class resort concentrates its comforts on a small but luxurious waterfront site, with a large restaurant above the manicured lawn, a small swimming pool with mountain views, and comfortable lounge chairs at the lake's edge. Its guest rooms glow with rosy wood, brass, and pastel fabrics. It's at the center of town, near the boat landing. **Pros:** a great place to just be; impeccable service. **Cons:** backs onto the main road. ✉*Gotthardstr. 6* ☎*041/3927900* ⊕*www.beaurivage-weggis.ch* ⮐*40 rooms* ᴧ*In-room: no a/c, safe, refrigerator. In-hotel: restaurant, bar, pool, public Wi-Fi* ▭*AE, DC, MC, V* ☉*Closed Nov.–Mar.* ⏹|*BP.*

6

$$$–$$$$
★

Post Hotel Weggis. Very hip in a town that leans more towards hip-replacement, this completely refurbished 1960's concrete block has been been redesigned to an inch of its life, with excellent results. If Weggis is Florida, this hotel is South Beach; its "playrooms," each with

> **BICYCLING & TENNIS**
>
> The tourist office (☎ *041/3901155*) at Weggis rents bicycles and has information about public tennis courts.

a balcony and view of the lake, are festooned in leopard- or tiger-print wallpapers and carpeting, with neon highlights—an apple-green vase, say, or a hot red coffee table. The toys inside include flatscreen TVs, a cutting-edge sound system with an iPod docking station, Blu-ray players, and a PlayStation 3. Across the street, the hotel bar is directly on the lake. **Pros:** fabulous baths; top service. **Cons:** the nightlife is hotel-confined. ✉ *Seestr. 8* ☎ *041/3922525* ⊕ *www.poho.ch* ☎ *45 rooms* △ *In-room: no a/c, safe, refrigerator, Ethernet. In-hotel: restaurant, bar, pool, gym, spa, public Wi-Fi* ☐ *AE, DC, MC, V* ۞ *Closed Nov.–Mar.* ⟨◎⟩*BP.*

$$
Rigi-Kulm. This high-altitude hotel is perfect for mountain-lovers; built in 1950 using elements of the former 19th century hotel (parquet floors, mirrors, sandstone staircases) and recently upgraded, the rooms mix clean-lined interior design with antique furnishings. Southern rooms have great views. (But: if it rains, the views disappear.) A short walk from the summit, at 5,900 feet, it's accessible by cable car from Weggis or by cogwheel from Vitznau or Arth-Goldau. Or you can climb up from Weggis, allowing either three hours or, as Mark Twain required, three days, depending on your penchant for resting. **Pros:** a sunny perch above the clouds of November–February. **Cons:** once you're here, you're here. ✉ *Rigi Kulm* ☎ *041/8550303* ⊕ *www. rigikulm.ch* ☎ *40 rooms* △ *In-room: no a/c, no TV. In-hotel: restaurant* ☐ *AE, DC, MC, V* ⟨◎⟩*BP.*

VITZNAU

4 km (2½ mi) southeast of Weggis, 26 km (16 mi) east of Luzern.

Visitor Information (✉ *Seestr.* ☎ *041/3980035* ⊕ *www.vitznau.ch*).

For a quintessentially scenic, quiet spot, stop over in Vitznau, a tiny waterfront resort that competes with Weggis in balmy weather. Small as this village may be, it looms large on the tourist radar. Not only is Vitznau address to the magnificently palatial Park Hotel (opened 1902), it is home to Switzerland's first-ever cog railway (opened May 21, 1871); the Mülefluh fortress (the first artillery fortress in the country); the shipyards where Lake Luzern's fabled paddleboat steamers were initially built; and today it's the best place to see the world's largest Swiss flag, proudly displayed on a face of Mt. Rigi overlooking Vitznau.

WHERE TO STAY

$$$$
★

Park Hotel. Set in a fairy-tale lakefront palace, this isolated but lavish retreat dominates the tiny lakefront village of Vitznau. Constructed in 1902 and enlarged in 1985, it's a vaulted and beamed Edwardian dream in impeccable modern form. Even the corridors are grand, with massive oak doors and Persian runners over quarry tile. Guest rooms are decorated in timeless pastels, and lakefront rooms command dreamy Alpine views. The back rooms overlook the slopes of the Rigi, dotted with grazing cows. With the hotel's restaurants—one a chandeliered extravaganza—and all the activities available, you could easily find yourself not wanting to budge. **Pros:** one-stop vacationing; luxuriously relaxing. **Cons:** off the beaten track. ⊠*Kantonstr.* ☎*041/3996060* ⊕*www. parkhotel-vitznau.ch* ⇆*71 rooms, 32 suites* ⌂*In-room: no a/c, safe, refrigerator. In-hotel: 2 restaurants, bar, 2 tennis courts, pool, gym, beachfront, bicycles, public Internet, public Wi-Fi* ⊟*AE, DC, MC, V* ⊗*Closed Nov.–mid-Apr.* ⊙|*BP.*

$–$$ ☷**Rigi.** Less than a third of the price of the grandiose Park Hotel, this solid lodging has modernized interiors and a welcoming atmosphere in its public areas. A dozen rooms have balconies with lake views; four have small kitchenettes. The hotel is one block from the boat landing and close to the Rigibahn. Both the restaurant and the Stübli serve good, simple fish dishes, and there's a pleasant garden terrace. **Pros:** centrally located; pleasant service; calm atmosphere. **Cons:** some traffic noise in daytime; could use a slight facelift. ⊠*Seestr.* ☎*041/3972121* ⊕*www. rigi-vitznau.ch* ⇆*36 rooms* ⌂*In-room: no a/c, refrigerator (some), kitchen (some). In-hotel: 2 restaurants* ⊟*AE, DC, MC, V* ⊙|*BP.*

¢   ☷**Schiff.** Just across the street from the luxurious Park Hotel and shar-
★   ing much the same view, this old roadhouse, perched on the slope of the hill, offers down-to-earth, cheap rooms with shared bathrooms in '50s summer cottage–style rooms. The vine-trellised terrace restaurant, wide open to the water and mountain skyline, serves inexpensive lakefish dishes, traditional ice-cream desserts, and a very decent pint. **Pros:** decidedly friendly; the Park's grounds are open to visitors. **Cons:** bath and toilet are down the hall. ⊠*Kantonstr.* ☎*041/3971357* ⇆*4 rooms without bath* ⌂*In-room: no a/c, no phone, no TV. In-hotel: restaurant, no elevator* ⊟*AE, DC, MC, V* ⊗*Closed Oct. and Nov.* ⊙|*BP.*

SPORTS & THE OUTDOORS

SWIMMING Because of a quirk of climate, Vitznau's bay is naturally warmer than Luzern's Lido, making this a great place to swim.

EN
ROUTE From Vitznau a boat tour will take you across Lake Luzern to **Beckenried,** from which a cable car leads up to Klewenalp (5,250 feet), a small resort overlooking the lake. The area is excellent for hiking, with breathtakingly panoramic views of the lake and mountains on clear days. If you're driving, you could also follow the north shore to Gersau, a tiny lake resort that was an independent republic—the world's smallest—from 1332 to 1798. From Gersau the boat snakes around the sharp peninsula of the Seelisberg; the 1980 completion of a 9¼-km (6-mi) tunnel through the peninsula, south of the lake, opened the way for even swifter north–south travel between Luzern and points north and the St. Gotthard route and points south.

RÜTLI MEADOW

Fodor'sChoice   *14 km (8 mi) southeast of Vitznau, 15 km (10 mi) northwest of Altdorf*
★   *on Urnersee, 35 km (22 mi) southeast of Luzern.*

GETTING HERE

The lake steamers from Luzern make frequent stops here.

EXPLORING

At the south end of Lake Luzern, past the gorgeously scenic Seelisberg Peninsula, the narrow, majestic Urnersee accesses some of the most historic—or, at least, romantic—landmarks in the region. The **Schillerstein**, on the right as you cruise past the peninsula, is a spectacular natural rock obelisk extending nearly 85 feet up out of the lake, onto which has been carved a gigantic dedication: TO THE AUTHOR OF WILHELM TELL, FRIEDRICH VON SCHILLER. 1859. About 10 minutes beyond the rock, the lake steamer pulls up at the quaint, 19th-century landing dock for perhaps the most historically significant site in central Switzerland: the Rütli Meadow, where the confederates of Schwyz, Unterwalden, and Uri are said to have met in 1307 to renew the 1291 Oath of Eternal Alliance.

You head up the hillside for a five-minute walk to emerge on a grassy plateau where you'll find a rock and flagpole to honor the sacred spot. Nearby is a medieval rock bench nestled by towering trees—the perfect spot to think about another monumental event that took place here centuries later: amid threats of a 1940 German invasion, General Guisan, Swiss army commander in chief, summoned hundreds of officers to the meadow to reaffirm their commitment to the Swiss Confederation in a secret, stirring ceremony. Afterward, head back down the hill to study the small video presentation (perhaps also take a photo of a costumed historical interpreter) and be sure to stop in the time-burnished, 19th-century chalet snack shop, with its lovely stained-glass salons and picturesque wood verandas.

ALTDORF

20 km (12 mi) south of Rütli Meadow, 35 km (22 mi) southeast of Luzern.

GETTING HERE

On the main train and car route linking the area south of the Alps with the north, Altdorf was a main stop on the journey when it took weeks, not hours, to get from Zürich to Milan. As a consequence, there are hourly train connections from Zürich, Luzern, or Lugano (stop in Flüelen and take the bus into Altdorf's center, the Telldenkmal stop). The lake steamers from Luzern take about 2½ to 3½ hours to Flüelen, depending on the number of stops along the way. Train and boat tickets to Altdorf will include the five-minute bus trip from Flüelen to Altdorf's Telldenkmal stop.

Visitor Information (⊠ *Schützeng. 11* ☎ *041/8720450).*

Was Wilhelm Tell Norwegian?

According to an 18th-century story by Gilg Tschudi, Wilhelm Tell performed his heroic deeds in 1307. But that puts him several centuries behind two 11th-century Norwegians named Eindridi and Hemingr. To force Eindridi to accept Christianity, King Olaf is said to have ordered him to shoot a "writing plate" from his son's head. Eindridi's wife persuaded the king to drop the matter. Hemingr was not so lucky. After the hunter won several athletic challenges, an irate King Harald ordered him to shoot not a mere apple, but a hazelnut from his son's head. Hemingr made the shot and, like Tell, took his revenge on the ruler.

A century later, a tippler named Toko bragged about his skill with a bow. The Dane was forced by a king to shoot an apple off his son's head. As Tell would later do, Toko kept an arrow destined for the king should he fail. Toko was then forced to ski down a cliff into the North Sea, a feat he miraculously survived.

A 17th-century English ballad tells of Adam Bell, Clim of the Clough, and William of Cloudesley—outlaws who live off the king's deer, Robin Hood style. In the ballad, William of Cloudesley is the man with the bow:

"An apple upon his [son's] head he set,
And then his bowe he bent;
Syxe score paces they were outmet,
And therefore Cloudesley went…"

Toko's story was in a book that includes the tale of Amleth, a Danish prince, which Shakespeare used for his play *Hamlet*. If Shakespeare had chosen Toko's story, who knows what form Tell's legend might have taken?

EXPLORING

Schiller's play *Wilhelm Tell* sums up the tale for the Swiss, who perform his play religiously in venues all over the country—including the town of Altdorf, just up the road from the Rütli Meadow. Leave the steamer at Flüelen, the farthest point of the boat ride around the lake, and connect by postbus to Altdorf, the capital of the canton Uri and, by popular if not scholarly consensus, the setting for Tell's famous apple-shooting scene.

Though there are no valid records of Wilhelm Tell's existence, and versions of the legend conflict with historical fact, no one denies the reality of his times, when central Switzerland—then a feudal dependent of Austria but by its own independent will not yet absorbed into the Holy Roman Empire—suffered brutal pressures and indignities under its local rulers. The mythical Gessler was one of those rulers, and his legendary edict—that the proud Swiss should bow before his hat suspended from a pole in the village square at Altdorf—symbolizes much crueler oppressions of the time. Schiller's Tell was a consummate hero: brisk, decisive, a highly skilled helmsman as well as marksman, and not one for diplomatic negotiations. He refused to kneel and provoked his famous punishment: to shoot an apple off his young son's head before a crowd of fellow townsmen. If he refused, both would be killed. Tell quietly tucked an arrow in his shirt bosom, loaded another into his crossbow, and shot the apple clean through. When Gessler asked what the second arrow was for, Tell replied that if the first arrow had struck his child, the second arrow would have been for Gessler and would not have missed.

For this impolitic remark, Tell was sentenced to prison. While deporting him across Lake Luzern, the Austrians (including the ruthless Gessler) were caught in a violent storm (remember your Rossini) and turned to Tell, the only man on board who knew the waters, to take the helm. Unmanacled, he steered the boat to a rocky ridge, leapt free, and pushed the boat back into the storm. Later he lay in wait in the woods near Küssnacht and shot Gessler in the heart. This act of justified violence inspired the people to overthrow their oppressors and swear the Oath of Eternal Alliance around a roaring bonfire, laying the groundwork for the Swiss Confederation.

There's an often-reproduced **Tell monument** in the village center, showing a proud father with crossbow on one shoulder, the other hand grasping his son's hand; it was sculpted by Richard Kissling in 1895.

SPORTS & THE OUTDOORS

BIKING   You can rent bikes at the **train station** (☎*051/2214532*) in Flüelen. Mountain bikes and motorbikes can be rented and serviced in Altdorf through **Zweirad Affentranger** (✉*Gotthardstr. 53* ☎*041/8701315*).

BÜRGLEN

3 km (1¾ mi) southeast of Altdorf, 40 km (25 mi) southeast of Luzern.

Wilhelm Tell was supposedly from the tiny, turreted town of Bürglen, just up the road from Altdorf.

The **Tell-Museum** devoted to him displays documents and art related to the legend. ✉*Postpl.* ☎*041/8704155* ⊕*www.tellmuseum.ch* 🖼*5 SF* ☾*July–Aug., daily 10–5 and Sept.–Oct., daily 10–11:30, 1:30–5.*

THE TELLSKAPELLE

Fodor'sChoice   *14 km (9 mi) north of Altdorf, 41 km (26 mi) southeast of Luzern.*
★
GETTING HERE
The lake steamer from Luzern stops here as well as at the Rütli Meadow (directly across the lake), so these two sights are a good combination. Boats leave Luzern between about 11:30 AM and 5:30 PM, four times a day from spring through fall, twice a day in winter at around 11 AM and 3 PM. You can also take a taxi from Brunnen (about SF 50 each way), but set a time for your driver to pick you up again: there is no stand at the Tellskapelle. The steamer also stops in Brunnen.

EXPLORING
Have your Nikons ready for this magnificently picturesque lakeside chapel set at the foot of the Axen mountain. A shrine to Wilhelm Tell, it is adjacent to the **Tellsplatte**, which was the rocky ledge onto which

Tell, the rebellious archer, leaped to escape from Gessler's boat, pushing the boat back into the stormy waves as he jumped. Built in 1500, it was restored in high Victorian fashion in 1881. It contains four frescoes of the Tell legend (painted at the time of restoration), showing the taking of the oath on the Rütli Meadow, Tell shooting the apple on his son's head, Tell's escape, and Gessler's death. This is but one of the many scenic highlights that line the shore of the Urnersee, some of which are incorporated into "The Swiss Way" (Der Weg der Schweiz; www.weg-der-schweiz.ch/). Since Switzerland's septicentennial, central Switzerland has marked and developed this historic foot trail, which covers 35 km (21½ mi) of lakefront lore in 26 sections, each honoring one of Switzerland's cantons. You'll trace the mythical steps of Wilhelm Tell and the genuine steps of medieval forerunners, climb through steep forests and isolated villages, and visit the holiday resort of Brunnen. Complete information and maps can be requested through Zentralschweiz Tourismus (Central Switzerland Tourism). This trail weaves in and out of the famous Axenstrasse, a road carved in the 19th century out of the living rock (in certain stretches), offering spectacular vistas and lakeside perches.

SCHWYZ

20 km (12 mi) south of Rütli Meadow, 35 km (22 mi) southeast of Luzern.

Visitor Information (⊠ *Obersteisteg 14* ☎ *041/8555950* ⊕ *www.schwyz-tourismus.ch*).

This historic town is the capital of the canton Schwyz, root of the name Switzerland and source of the nation's flag. Switzerland's most precious archives are stored here as well. Traces of an independent settlement at Schwyz have been found from as far back as the Bronze Age (2500 BC–800 BC), but it was its inhabitants' aid in the 1291 Oath of Allegiance that put Schwyz on the map.

You can see the beautifully scripted and sealed original document as well as battle flags and paintings of the period in Schwyz's **Bundesbriefmuseum** *(Federal Charter Museum)*. ⊠ *Bahnhofstr. 20* ☎ *041/8192064* ⊕ *www. bundesbriefmuseum.ch* 🖃 *4 SF* ⊗ *May–Oct., Tues.–Fri. 9–11:30, 1:30–5, weekends 9–5; Nov.–Apr., Tues.–Fri. 9–11:30, 1:30–5, weekends 1:30–5.*

Fodor's Choice ★ Schwyz has several notable Baroque churches and a large number of fine old patrician homes dating from the 17th and 18th centuries, not least of which is the **Ital-Redinghaus** with its magnificent interior, antique stoves, and fine stained glass. A visit to this grand house includes a peek inside the neighboring **Bethlehemhaus,** the oldest wooden house in Switzerland, dating from 1287. There is no parking on the grounds; park on the nearby town square and walk 50 yards to the entrance off Reichsstrasse. ⊠ *Rickenbachstr. 24* ☎ *041/8114505* ⊕ *www.irh.ch* 🖃 *5 SF* ⊗ *May–Oct., Tues.–Fri. 2–5, weekends 10–noon and 2–5.*

Curiously, many of Schwyz's splendid houses owe their origin to the battlefield. The men of Schwyz had a reputation as fine soldiers and were in demand in other countries as mercenaries during the 16th and 17th centuries. They built many of the houses you can see today with their military pay.

Schwyz's most famous landmark is the **Rathaus** *(Town Hall)*; its richly frescoed exterior (1891) depicts the Battle of Morgarten, where the Austrian army was defeated by the Swiss. The building is still used as the Town Hall. ⊠*Hauptpl. 1.*

Basel

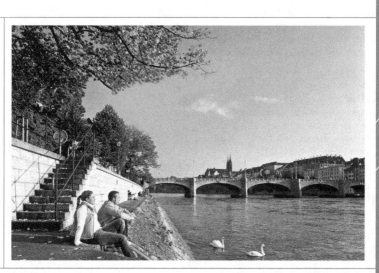

Couple on the Rhine shore of Lesser Basel with a view of the Mittlere Bruecke and the Cathedral.

WORD OF MOUTH

"Basel is a fascinating city and I am sure you'll love it—I did. Cross the river on one of the funny little ferries: it's a nice, inexpensive treat."
—Ingo-11

"For sure look up the Tinguely Museum—lots of sculptures that whirl, groan, giggle, and mutter. At this museum, you can make them move; in most other places you can only look at them. There are also amusing and colorful works by his long-time amour, Nikki de Sainte-Phalle."
—Colonna

WELCOME TO BASEL

TOP REASONS TO GO

★ **Three corners:** Not many cities offer a more cosmopolitan mix. Here Switzerland merges with Germany and France, and Basel is home to some 150 nationalities.

★ **Art attack:** This city of the arts has galleries full of old master paintings and some pictures so contemporary the paint is still drying—more than 30 museums cater to every taste.

★ **Fasnacht:** Each spring during its three-day Lenten celebration the city streets are filled with spectacularly costumed revelers, bands, and pipers.

★ **Münster madness:** Not only is this cathedral an amazing piece of architecture, it also offers fabulous views of the city and the river Rhine.

★ **Noble dust:** A short boat ride from Basel, the Colonia Augusta Raurica is the oldest Roman settlement on the Rhine, complete with a restored 1st-century BC theater.

1 A bridge too far. Having the first bridge across the Rhine, built in 1225, brought wealth to Basel. Its position now where the Mittlere Rheinbrücke stands offers fine views of the city. The three kings on the facade of Hotel Les Trois Rois were a traditional decoration for a thoroughfare of magnitude. Overlooking the waters, the beloved Làllekönig gargoyle is also worth a glance.

GETTING ORIENTED

Shouldering the Swiss Jura Mountains, the German Black Forest, and the French Vosges, Basel is Switzerland's third-largest city and the central conurbation for the northwest of the country. Bordering both banks of the Rhine, Basel is 730 feet above sea level—the lowest altitude of any Swiss city north of the Alps. From here the river turns 90 degrees north and widens into a majestic waterway.

2 Kunstmuseum. The Museum of Fine Arts and its younger sister, the Museum of Contemporary Art, are fine establishments in which to meet up with old masters and modern upstarts.

3 Medieval district. The Altstadt (Old Town) borders the marketplace, which lies in front of the majestic red Town Hall, and is host to a thriving consumables market. Winding alleyways lead off to a maze of shopping possibilities.

7

BASEL PLANNER

How's the Weather?

Basel is located in the Rhine Valley, which affords it an agreeably mild climate.

Warm Mediterranean air also wafts this way from the Rhône Valley.

On average the sun is supposed to shine for 1,680 hours; the average temperature in January, the coldest month, is 1 Celsius (34 F), in July, the warmest, 19 Celsius (66 F).

Fog is rare, unlike in other Swiss regions, and the average rainfall is the lowest north of the Rhône.

Tour Options

Basel Tourismus organizes two-hour walking tours of the city, which start from the tourist information office in the Stadt Casino and cater to German, French, and English speakers.

Tours take place from May to mid-October, Monday through Saturday at 2:30.

From mid-October to April the walking tours are held every Saturday at 2:30. The cost is 15 SF.

Transportation Basics

Basel is a transportation hub, with French, German, and Swiss train stations. Be sure to get off at the Swiss station Schweizerische Bundesbahnen (SBB) on Centralbahnstrasse; many a weary traveler has walked an hour from the German side of town. Klein-Basel (Small Basel), east of the Rhine in German territory, is an industrial center (with some new sights); the more affluent Grossbasel (Greater Basel) on the western side contains most of the sights and the Altstadt (Old Town). To reach the Altstadt from the SBB, head north (left) on Heuwaage-Viadukt, turn right on Steinenvorstadt and continue until you reach the central square, Barfüsserplatz. To reach outlying areas, take the tram. Indeed, the best way to see Basel is on foot or by tram, as the landmarks, museums, and even the zoo radiate from the old town center on the Rhine, and the network of rails covers the territory thoroughly. Taxis are costly, less efficient, and less available than the ubiquitous tram.

Feeling Festive

From three days of Carnival craziness during Fasnacht at the beginning of the year to the bejeweled Christmas market that mark the end of it, Basel hosts events all year round. Fasnacht is spectacularly celebrated with fifes, drums, and fabulous oversize masks. You'll spot the stock characters year-round: Ueli the clown; the Vogl Gryff (griffin); and the Lällekönig, who sticks out a mechanical tongue. There are also daily happenings, such as the Marktplatz market, weekly ones like the Barfüssermarkt on Barfüsserplatz every Thursday, and many more. Plus seasonal events such as super-glam Art Basel every June, one of the world's leading contemporary art shows. Basel even has its own marathon, run every September since 2005, and also hosts the Davidoff Swiss Indoors each October, the world's third-largest indoor tennis tournament. Look for the Basel Tattoo in July, featuring top-class professional bands with a total of more than 1,000 participants from Switzerland and abroad. Plus, there is the Herbstmesse (Autumn Fair) in October–November with its fun fairs and wine convention.

Making the Most of Your Time

If you are in town for just a day, your best bet is to take a stroll through Basel's Old Town, making sure to see the Münster and the sweeping views from the terrace overlooking the Rhine.

Art enthusiasts could decide to circle from here directly to the Kunstmuseum, and shoppers may want to head down one of the winding alleyways into the Freie Strasse or the Marktplatz.

A leisurely late-afternoon walk across the Mittlere Rheinbrücke and upstream along the sunny Kleinbasel riverside promenade (Oberer Rheinweg) is a good way to see the town in its best light.

If you are sticking around for longer, then take in some of the city's smaller museums, perhaps in the picturesque St. Alban quarter. From here take a ferryboat across the river and head east to the Museum Tinguely.

Or organize your day around a trip to Riehen; the Fondation Beyeler's stunningly well-rounded (and beautifully presented) collection of 20th-century art can be reached in a mere 20 minutes by tram.

In summer you could opt to take a boat trip to the Roman ruins of Augusta Raurica, east of Basel.

Or take a driving tour of, or catch a local train to, some of the small villages scattered south of the city, such as Balsthal, Holderbank, Oberer Hauenstein, Langenbruck, and Liestal to experience the more rural delights of the area.

Cool off in very hot weather like the locals by taking a dip in the Rhine; swimmers can often be seen from the Mittlere Rheinbrücke, and there are a number of popular bathing spots along the banks.

Visitor Information

The main tourist information desk in Basel is in the Stadt Casino at Barfüsserplatz, and is open weekdays 8:30–6:30, Saturday 9–5, Sunday and holidays 10–4; there is also a branch located in the SBB Bahnhof train station on Centralbahnstrasse.

Basel Tourismus (*Basel Tourism* ✉ *Stadt Casino, Steinenberg 14, Grossbasel* ☎ *061/ 2686868* ⊕ *www.basel.com*).

Penny Pinchers

Hotel guests in Basel receive a complimentary Basel Mobility Ticket, which allows free use of all public transportation within the city during their stay. Many museums offer free entry between 4 PM and 5 PM on selected weekdays as well as on the first Sunday of each month.

Most Baslers eat their main meal at lunchtime, so look out for the "Tagesmenu" (Daily Menu) at restaurants, as this will offer a reasonably priced couple of courses.

Most students find refuge from expensive restaurants at the self-service joints situated in the larger Migros and Coop supermarkets. On Markplatz, a big daily market sells fruit, veggies, bread, cheese sandwiches, and even egg rolls.

GETTING AROUND

By Air

Basel uses EuroAirport (just across the border in France), which is shared with Mulhouse in France and Freiburg in Germany. Direct flights link Basel to most major European cities, including Zürich. The nearest intercontinental airport is Unique.

Regular bus service runs between EuroAirport and the SBB train station in the center of Basel. The trip takes about 15 minutes and costs 3.80 SF per person.

One-way taxi fare from the airport to the Basel center is approximately 50 SF; it takes about 15 minutes in light traffic and up to 30 minutes at rush hours (around 7:30 AM to 8:30 AM, noon to 2 PM, and 5 PM to 7 PM). There are normally cabs at the taxi stand, but if you need to call one from the airport, make sure you leave the building on the Swiss side.

EuroAirport (☎ 061/3252511 ⊕ www.euroairport.com).

Unique Zürich Airport (Flughafen Zürich AG) (☎ 0900/ 300313 ⊕ www.unique.ch).

33er Taxi (☎ 061/3333333).

Mini Cab (☎ 061/7777777).

Taxi-Zentrale (☎ 061/2222222).

By Car

The German autobahn A5 enters Basel from the north and leads directly to the Rhine and the center of the city. From France the autoroute A35 (E9) peters out at the frontier, and secondary urban roads lead to the center. The A2 autobahn leads off to the rest of Switzerland. Since most of the city's sights are within walking distance of downtown, it's advisable to park your car for the duration of your visit. Head straight for an all-day garage, such as the Parkhaus Elisabethen, on Heuwaage near the SBB train station. Expect to pay around 25 SF per day.

By Train

There are two main rail stations in Basel. The Schweizerische Bundesbahnen (locally known as the SBB Bahnhof) in Grossbasel connects to destinations in Switzerland, France, and with the Intercity to Germany. The Deutsche Bundesbahn (known as the Badischer Bahnhof) in Kleinbasel runs services to Germany.

Deutsche Bundesbahn (⊠ Schwarzwalderstr. and Riehenstr., Kleinbasel ☎ 061/6901215). **Schweizerische Bundesbahnen** (⊠ Centralbahnstr., Grossbasel ☎ 0900/300300).

By Tram

Most Basel trams run every six to eight minutes all day, and every 15 minutes in the late evening. Tickets must be bought at the automatic machines at every stop. Stops are marked with green-and-white signs; generally the trams run from 5:30 or 6 in the morning until midnight. *Mehrfahrtenkarten* (multijourney cards) allow you 12 trips for the price of 10 and can be purchased from the ticket office at Barfüsserplatz. *Tageskarten* (day cards), from the ticket machines at the tram stops, allow unlimited travel all day within the central zone for 8 SF. Guests at hotels in Basel receive a complimentary Basel Mobility Ticket for free use of all public transportation for the duration of their stay. Holders of the Swiss Pass travel free on all Basel public transport systems.

Updated by
Sharon-Anne
Wilcox

ALTHOUGH IT LACKS THE GILT and glitter of Zürich and the Latin grace of Geneva, in many ways Basel (Bâle in French) is more sophisticated than either. Situated at the frontier between two of Europe's most assertive personalities—France and Germany—and tapped directly into the artery of the Rhein (Rhine), the city has grown remarkably urbane, cosmopolitan, and worldly-wise, yet is delightfully eccentric as well. Its imagination has been fed by centuries of intellectual input: Basel has been host to Switzerland's oldest university (1460) and patron to some of the country's—and the world's—finest minds. As a northern center of humanist thought and art, it nurtured the painters Konrad Witz and Hans Holbein the Younger, as well as the great Dutch scholar Erasmus. And it was Basel's visionary lord mayor Johann Rudolf Wettstein who, at the end of the Thirty Years' War, negotiated Switzerland's groundbreaking—and lasting—neutrality.

Each day more than 30,000 French and German commuters cross into Basel. Banking activity here is surpassed only by that of Zürich and Geneva, and every month representatives of the world's leading central banks meet at the Bank for International Settlements in the city center. Enormous international pharmaceutical firms—among them Novartis and Roche—crowd the riverbanks. Yet Basel's population remains modest, hovering around 188,000; its urban center lies gracefully along the Rhine, with no building so tall as to block another building's view of the cathedral's twin spires. Two blocks from the heart of the thriving shopping district you can walk along medieval residential streets cloaked in perfect, otherworldly silence to Münsterhügel (cathedral mount), where the Romanesque-Gothic cathedral offers superb views over the Old Town and the Rhine all the way to the surrounding mountains.

The high number of museums per capita is a reflection of Basel's priorities: the city has more than 30, including the world-class Kunstmuseum, the Museum Tinguely, and the Fondation Beyeler. As high culture breeds good taste, Basel has some of the most varied, even quirky, shopping in Switzerland, all within walking distance. But you can still get a beer and a bratwurst here: natives almost exclusively speak German or their own local version of *Schwyzerdütsch,* called *Baseldütsch.* On the Marktplatz, hungry shoppers stand in front of a mobile kitchen, holding bare *Wienerli* (hot dogs) and dipping the pink tips into thick golden mustard. They also indulge in *Kaffe und Kuchen*—the late-afternoon coffee break the neighboring Germans live for—but locals have their own version: instead of a large slice of creamed cake, they select tiny sweet gems—two or three to a saucer, but petite nonetheless—and may opt for a delicate Chinese tea instead of a Kaffee.

The Celts were the first to settle here, around 500 BC, on the site of the cathedral mount. During the 1st century BC the Romans established a town at Augst, then called Colonia Augusta Raurica; the ruins and the theater, 10 km (6 mi) outside town, can be visited today. By the 3rd century the Romans had taken the present cathedral site in Basel proper, naming the town Basilia (royal stronghold). Germanic invaders banished them around 450, and it wasn't until the Holy Roman emperor Henry II took Basel under his wing in the 11th century that stability returned. His image and that of his wife, Kunegunde, adorn the cathedral and the Rathaus (Town Hall). Henry built the original cathedral—on the site of a church destroyed in 916 by a raiding band of Hungarian horsemen—and established Basel as one of the centers of his court. In 1006 the bishop of Basel was made ruler of the town, and throughout the Middle Ages these prince-bishops gained and exerted enormous temporal and spiritual powers. Though prince-bishops are no more, Basel still uses one of their symbols in its coat of arms—a striking black staff.

Yet Basel is first and foremost a Renaissance city in the broadest sense of the word: a city of intellectual and artistic rebirth. In 1431 the Council of Basel, an ecumenical conference whose chief objective was church reform, was convened here, bringing in—over a period of 17 years—the great sacred and secular princes of the age. One of them, who later became Pope Pius II, granted permission for the founding of the university and established Basel as the cultural capital it remains today.

Art and academia over the ages haven't made Basel a stuffy place, however. The Baslers' Lenten celebration of Fasnacht (related to Mardi Gras, or Carnival) turns the usual workings of the city on its ear. The streets are filled with grotesquely costumed revelers bearing huge home-made lanterns scrawled with comments and caricatures relating to local current events. Although the festivities last only three days, you'll see masks displayed and sold everywhere all year long, and you'll hear strains of fife-and-drum marches wafting from the guildhalls' upper windows in rehearsal for the celebration. Like confetti lodged between the cobblestones, there always seems to be a hint of Fasnacht, age-old and unpredictable, even in Basel's most sedate and cultivated corners.

EXPLORING BASEL

The Rhine divides the city into two distinct sections: on the south-western bank lies Grossbasel (Greater Basel), the commercial, cultural, and academic center. Directly upriver from Grossbasel wind the quiet medieval streets of St. Alban, where you can stroll along the Rhine, peek into antiques shops, then dine in a cozy bistro. The opposite bank, to the northeast, is Kleinbasel (Little Basel), a Swiss enclave on the "German" side of the Rhine that is the industrial quarter of the city. Here is the convention center, chain stores galore, and hotels with terraces that afford glorious views of the Münster (cathedral).

Numbers in the text correspond to numbers in the margin and on the Basel map.

OLD TOWN

If you stand in the middle of the Marktplatz, or even just watch river traffic from the Mittlere Rheinbrücke, it's easy to envision the Basel of centuries ago. On a bend of the Rhine, Basel's Old Town is full of majestic Gothic spires and side streets that are largely unchanged since the 1600s. Still, woven through the delicately preserved architecture of the Old Town are impressive state-of-the-art museums and miles of shop-lined pedestrian zones.

TOP ATTRACTIONS

9 **Basler Papiermühle/Schweizer Papiermuseum und Museum für Schrift und Druck** *(Basel Paper Mill/Swiss Museum for Paper, Writing and Printing).* Though its name sounds esoteric, this museum, in a beautifully restored medieval waterfront mill with a still functioning waterwheel, is surprisingly accessible. Demonstrations of papermaking, typesetting, and bookbinding reveal much about the ancient craft. You can participate in a papermaking process, beginning with the pulpy raw material simmering in the "visitors' vat." Kids can try out quills and ink or spell out their names in pieces of type for printing. Most descriptions have an English translation, but some special exhibits are described in German text only. ⊠ *St. Alban-Tal 35, St. Alban* ☎ *061/2259090* ⊕ *www. papiermuseum.ch* 🎟 *12 SF* ⊘ *Tues.–Sun. 2–5.*

Fasnacht-Brunnen *(Carnival Fountain).* Created by the Swiss artist Jean Tinguely, known for his work in mechanized media, this witty, animated construction was commissioned by the city in 1977. Its whimsically styled metal figures busily churn, lash, and spray with unending energy. It is especially impressive in winter when the jets of water freeze, creating unique airborne sculptures. ⊠ *Theaterpl., Grossbasel.*

26 **Fondation Beyeler** *(Beyeler Foundation).* For decades, the most prestigious art collectors and world-famous billionaires would make a pilgrimage to Basel to worship at the feet of one of modern art's greatest gallery owners, Ernst Beyeler. Magnificent Monets, legendary Toulouse-Lautrecs, and the finest Giacometti sculptures were the Swiss "souvenirs" these power-players came home with—that is, if Herr Beyeler approved of you. At the end of his phenomenal career, he wound up deeding his own incomparable collection to the public, and in the Basel suburb of Riehen commissioned noted architect Renzo Piano to build a public museum to house it. Today, the holdings of Ernst and Hildy Beyeler present an astonishingly well-rounded collection of 20th-century and contemporary art, and Piano's simple, introverted lines direct attention to the 200 paintings and objects. Rightly so, as the collection's catalog reads like a who's who of modern artists—Cézanne, Matisse, Lichtenstein, and Rauschenberg.

In this limpid setting of natural light and openness, Giacometti's wiry sculptures stretch toward the ceiling and Monet's water lilies seem to spill from the canvas into an outdoor reflecting pool. Indigenous carved figures from New Guinea and Nigeria stare into faces on canvases by Klee and Dubuffet. A stellar selection of Picassos is juxtaposed with views of blue skies and neighboring fields. The harmony of the collection notwithstanding, personal preference is a perceivable theme. The tram trip from Schifflände takes about 20 minutes. Public tours in English are often offered on Sunday, or private tours can be arranged. ⊠ *Baselstr. 101, Riehen* ☎ *061/6459700* ⊕ *www.beyeler.com* 🎟 *23 SF* ⊘ *Thurs.–Tues. 10–6, Wed. 10–8.*

Fodor'sChoice
★

7

A GOOD WALK

Six bridges link the two halves of the city; the most picturesque is the **Mittlere Rheinbrücke**. On the corner at Schifflände, you can see a facsimile of the infamous **Lällekönig**, a 17th-century gargoyle mechanized to stick out his tongue and roll his eyes at his rivals across the river. Walking across the bridge, you'll see Basel's peculiar, gondola-like ferryboats (you can ride one for 1.60 SF). Back across the Mittlere Rheinbrücke in Grossbasel, turn left up a steep alley called the **Rheinsprung**, banked with 15th- and 16th-century houses. Turn right at Archivgässlein, and you'll come to the **Martinskirche**, the city's oldest parish church, dating from 1288.

Continue along Martinsgasse to the elegant neighboring courtyards of the **Blaues und Weisses Haus**, meeting place of kings. Just beyond, turn left and head past the basilisk fountain into Augustinergasse. At No. 2 is the **Naturhistorisches Museum**, and just beyond the **Museum der Kulturen Basel**, which house great natural history and prehistory collections. Augustinergasse leads into the Münsterplatz, dominated by the striking red-sandstone 12th-century **Münster**, burial place of Erasmus. Walk around to the cathedral's river side to the Pfalz terrace for wide views of the river, the Old Town, and the Black Forest.

From the Münsterplatz, head down Rittergasse and go past its elegant villas and courtyards to the first busy cross street. Ahead of you is St. Alban-Vorstadt, which leads to the **St. Alban-Tor**, one of the original 13th-century city gates. St. Alban-Tal leads from St. Alban-Vorstadt down to St. Alban-Rheinweg on the Rhine to the **Museum für Gegenwartskunst** (Museum of Contemporary Art). Take St. Alban-Rheinweg along the riverside, ascend the Wettstein Bridge stairways, and head left onto St. Alban-Graben to find the **Kunstmuseum,** home of one of Europe's oldest public collections. Continue down St. Alban-Graben to the intersection of Steinenberg. A few blocks straight ahead into Elisabethenstrasse will take you to the **Haus zum Kirschgarten,** a showcase of 18th- and 19th-century decorative arts. To circle back into the Old Town, however, veer right on Steinenberg, which goes by the **Kunsthalle.** Just beyond the art gallery, the whimsical Tinguely-Brunnen, or **Fasnacht-Brunnen,** puts on a show on the Theaterplatz.

Continue on Steinenberg until it opens out onto the bustling Barfüsserplatz and the **Puppenhaus Museum** and the **Historisches Museum**. Behind the tram concourse on Barfüsserplatz, follow the pedestrian zone to Leonhardsberg, which leads left up the stairs to the late-Gothic **Leonhardskirche.** Continue along the church walk into Heuberg street, the spine of one of the loveliest sections of old Basel. A network of small streets here is lined with graceful old houses from many periods: Gothic, Renaissance, Baroque, Biedermeier. On Spalenvorstadt perches the **Holbeinbrunnen,** styled from a drawing by Hans Holbein. The Spalenvorstadt stretches to the 14th-century **Spalentor** gate. Nearby Petersplatz is home to the 13th-century **Peterskirche**, behind which pose an exemplary row of houses, some of them only a single window wide.

⑫ Haus zum Kirschgarten *(Kirschgarten House)*. This 18th-century home was built as a palace for a young silk-ribbon manufacturer. Nowadays it contains the 18th- and 19th-century collections of the city's Historical Museum, displayed as furnishings in period rooms. The timepieces, porcelain, and faience are especially outstanding. ✉*Elisabethenstr. 27–29, Grossbasel* ☎*061/2058600* ⊕*www. hmb.ch* 🎫*7 SF (1st Sun. of month free; Tues.–Sat. 4–5 free)* 🕑*Tues.–Fri., Sun. 10–5, Sat. 1–5.*

⑯ Historisches Museum *(History Museum)*.
★ Housed within the **Barfüsserkirche** (Church of the Shoeless Friars), which was founded by the barefoot Franciscans in 1250 and rebuilt during the mid-14th century, the museum has an extensive collection of tapestries, wooden sculptures, coins, armor, and other vestiges of Basel's past. An underground gallery displays fully reconstructed **medieval and Renaissance guild rooms,** complete with stained glass, ceramic stoves, and richly carved wood. Downstairs, in the back of the church, the **Münster Treasury** contains priceless reliquaries in gold. Despite its status as one of the finest examples of Franciscan architecture north of the Alps, the church was deconsecrated in the 19th century and turned into a warehouse until it was rescued in 1894 and converted to its present-day use as a museum. Most descriptions are in German only. ✉*Barfüsserpl., Grossbasel* ☎*061/2058600* ⊕*www.hmb.ch* 🎫*7 SF (1st Sun. of month free; Mon., Tues.–Sun. 4–5 free)* 🕑*Tues.–Sun. 10–5.*

⑬ Kunsthalle *(Basel Art Gallery)*. A must-do for lovers of contemporary
★ art, managed through Basel's community of artists, the Basler Kunstverein, this museum has hosted landmark, precedent-setting exhibits of contemporary art since 1872. In addition to showing the work of several modern masters from an early stage of their careers (Klee and Picasso), the gallery was the first in Europe to display works by American Abstract Expressionists. It is renowned as one of the world's most active institutions dedicated to the presentation of modern art. The building was renovated in 2004 and features an on-site theater that hosts video installations, performances, and local and foreign films. ✉*Steinenberg 7, Grossbasel* ☎*061/2069900* ⊕*www.kunsthallebasel. ch* 🎫*10 SF includes admission to Architektur museum* 🕑*Tues., Wed., Fri. 11–6, Thurs. 11–8:30, weekends 11–5.*

YOU GOTTA HAVE ART

With a renowned collector's hand-picked paintings (the Fondation Beyeler), an homage to unique mechanized art (the Museum Tinguely), and one of the world's oldest public art collections (the Kunstmuseum), Basel easily earns a high rank in the art world, especially each June when it hosts one of the world's most glamorous modern art fairs, Art Basel (www.artbasel.com). The Basel-Card is a must, offering unlimited admission to participating museums for one, two, or three days. It can be purchased for 20 SF, 27 SF, or 35 SF (for one, two, or three days) at Basel Tourismus and at most hotels.

7

26

25

TO DEUTSCHE
BUNDESBAHN
(BADISCHER BAHNHOF)

Riehenstrasse

Wettsteinallee

Wettsteinallee

Wettsteinallee

Wettsteinplatz

Grenzacherstrasse

Theodorsgraben-
Anlage

Solitude
Park

Schaffhauser-Rheinweg

Rhein

St. Alban-Rheinweg

10   **9**

St. Alban-
Tal

St. Alban-Vorstadt

Weidengasse

8

Zürcherstrasse

Gellertstrasse

St. Alban-Anlage

Lange Gasse

Hardstrasse

Schule

Engelgasse

St. Jakobs-Str.

Münchensteinerstrasse

Kant.
Handelsschule

St. Alban-Ring

Sissacherstr

St. Alban

A2

St. Jakobs-Str.

**Güterbahnhof
Wolf**

7

CLOSE UP

Fasnacht

Dating from the Middle Ages, Fasnacht, Switzerland's best-known festival, draws people from all over the world. Beginning at 4 AM on the Monday following Ash Wednesday, all lights are turned off and the city is illuminated by the lanterns of the *Cliques* (carnival associations). The event features a blast of fifes and drums, boisterous *Guggemusik* (played by enthusiastic, rather than talented, marching bands), and a covering of confetti. The streets are absolutely packed with zillions of onlookers who have fortified themselves against the cold morning with a bowl of the traditional *Mehlsuppe* (flour soup). A colorful masked procession traverses the Old Town until dawn, and continues for the next two days. Nearby Liestal stages its own spectacular ceremony, during which burning stacks of wood are paraded through the town and finally heaped together. While other Fasnacht celebrations in Switzerland are usually held on or around February 27 and 28, Basel holds its festival a week later—check with the tourist board Web site for all the spectacular details.

⓫ Kunstmuseum *(Museum of Fine Arts).* In a city known for its museums, the Kunstmuseum is Basel's heirloom jewel. It was built between 1932 and 1936 to house one of the oldest public art collections in Europe, owned by the city since 1661; the imposing facade gives way to an inner courtyard studded with statues. Inside is the world's largest assemblage of paintings by members of the Holbein family, an exceptional group of works by Konrad Witz, and, in fact, such a thorough gathering of the works of their contemporaries that the development of painting in the Upper Rhine is strikingly documented. Other Swiss artists are well represented: from Basel's own Arnold Böcklin to Klimt-like Ferdinand Hodler. The museum's other forte is its international 20th-century collection, from Georges Braque to Jasper Johns. ⊠ *St. Alban-Graben 16, Grossbasel* ☏ *061/2066262* ⊕ *www.kunstmuseumbasel.ch* 🎫 *12 SF, includes admission to Museum für Gegenwartskunst* ☉ *Tues., Thurs.– Sun. 10–5, Wed. 10–7.*

Fodor'sChoice ★

❷ Lällekönig. When a famous gate tower on the Grossbasel side was destroyed, lost along with it was the notorious Lällekönig, a 15th-century gargoyle of a king whose mechanized clockwork caused the apparatus to stick out his tongue and roll his eyes at the "lesser" citizens across the river. Kleinbasel residents seek symbolic revenge even today, though. Every year during the Vogel Gryff festival, a birdlike figure dances to the midpoint of the bridge, gives the Lällekönig a flash of his backside, and takes the party back to Kleinbasel. You can see a working facsimile of the Lällekönig on the corner of what is now a chain restaurant at Schifflände while the original still ticks and taunts away in the nether regions of the Historical Museum. ⊠ *Schifflände, Grossbasel.*

★

㉑ Marktplatz *(Marketplace).* Flowers, fruits, and vegetables are sold most mornings from open stands in this central square, Basel's historic and modern heart. In fall and winter passersby purchase bags of hot roasted chestnuts, the savory scent of which wafts through the square. ⊠ *Tram crossroads at foot of Rathaus, south of Marktg.* ⊘ *Market: Mon.–Sat. 6 AM–1:30 PM.*

❶ **Mittlere Rheinbrücke** (*Middle Rhine Bridge*). Basel's most historic bridge
★ is a good metaphor for the city's successful mix of custom and commerce. It is used as a catwalk for many of Basel's centuries-old celebrations, while beneath its span processions of barges continually glide through its low-slung arches. First built around 1225, the bridge made possible the development of an autonomous Kleinbasel and the consequent rivalry that grew between the two half towns. A stone bridge replaced the wooden one at the turn of the 20th century. ⊠ *Schifflände, Grossbasel.*

❼ **Münster** (*Cathedral*). Basel's cathedral evolved into its current form
★ through a combination of the shifts of nature and the changing whims of architects. The site started as a 9th-century Carolingian church, then became a cathedral, which was consecrated by Henry II in 1019. Additions, alterations, and reconstructions in late Romanesque–early Gothic style continued through the 12th and 13th centuries. When Basel's devastating earthquake destroyed much of the building in 1356, subsequent reconstruction, which lasted about a century, adhered to the newly dominant Gothic style. The facade of the north transept, the **Gallusporte** (St. Gall's Door), is a surviving remnant of the original Romanesque structure. It's one of the oldest carved portals in German-speaking Europe—and one of the loveliest. Slender, fine-tooled columns and rich high-relief and freestanding sculptures frame the door. Each of the evangelists is represented by his symbol: an angel for Matthew, an ox for Luke, a lion for Mark, and a bulbous-chested eagle for John. Above, around the window, a wheel of fortune flings little men off to their fates.

Inside on the left, following a series of tombs of medieval noblemen whose effigies recline with their feet resting on their loyal dogs, stands the strikingly simple **tomb of Erasmus.** Below the choir, you can see the delicately rendered death portraits on the double **tomb of Queen Anna of Habsburg** and her young son, Charles, from around 1285. The vaulted **crypt** was part of the original structure and still bears fragments of murals from 1202. The Münster will be undergoing restoration on different parts of the building for at least another five years.

The Münsterplatz square itself is one of the most satisfying architectural ensembles in Europe, its fine town houses set well back from the cathedral, the center filled with pollarded trees. ⊠ *Münsterpl., Grossbasel* ⊕ *www.baslermuenster.ch* ⊘ *Easter–mid-Oct., weekdays 10–5, Sat. 10–4, Sun. 11:30–5; mid-Oct.–Easter, Mon.–Sat. 11–4, noon 11:30–4.*

NEED A BREAK? It's hard to beat the plaza tables of **Zum Isaak** (⊠ *Münsterpl. 16, Grossbasel* ☎ *061/2614712* ⊕ *www.zum-isaak.ch*) for scenic value; it has a direct view of the cathedral's towers. It's open for lunch, dinner, or just a piece of Madame Iselin's *Schoggikuchen* (chocolate cake) and coffee.

㉕ Museum Tinguely. Stay alert and be ready to get involved—the fascinating
🕐 mechanized artworks of 20th-century master Jean Tinguely invite close
★ inspection and interaction. As you circle the installations, some a story
high, you may wonder: how do they work? what do they mean? and
where did he find this stuff? Born in Fribourg, Tinguely is best known
for his whimsical *métamécaniques* (mechanical sculptures), which transform machinery, appliances, and items straight from the junk heap
into ironic and often macabre statements. For instance, *Le Ballet des
Pauvres,* from 1961, suspends a hinged leg with a moth-eaten sock, a
horse tail and fox pelt, a cafeteria tray, and a blood-soaked nightgown,
all of which dangle and dance on command. The wing projecting over
the Rhine has a splendid river view of Basel. Many of the museum's
"sculptures" are activated at preset times, typically every 5–15 minutes, and it pays to wait and see them in action. Schedules are listed on
each work's nameplate, and information sheets are available in English.
✉*Paul Sacher-Anlager 1, Kleinbasel* ☎*061/6819320* ⊕*www.tinguely.
ch* 💷*15 SF* ⊙*Tues.–Sun. 11–7.*

㉒ Rathaus *(Town Hall).* This bright red late-Gothic edifice, built to honor
★ the city's entry into the Swiss Confederation in 1501, towers over the
Marktplatz. Only the middle portion actually dates from the 16th century; pseudo-Gothic work was added in 1900. A massive clock with
figures of the Madonna, the emperor Henry II, and his wife, Kunegunde,
adorns the center of the facade; all around it is a series of colorful
frescoes, painted in 1608. Step into the courtyard, where the frescoes
continue. ✉*Marktpl., Grossbasel.*

NEED A
BREAK? Choose a few jewel-like pastries and order leaf-brewed tea in the carved-
wood environs of the clubby upstairs tearoom of the **Confiserie Schiesser**
(✉*Marktpl. 19, Grossbasel* ☎*061/2616077* ⊕*www.confiserie-schiesser.
ch*), steeping since 1870 in its prime location opposite the Town Hall.

Rheinsprung. A row of 15th- and 16th-century houses line this steep
little alley in Grossbasel. Number 11 housed Basel's university when it
was founded in 1460. ✉*Grossbasel* ✛*parallel to and south of Rhine,
between Eiseng. and Stapfelbg.*

ALSO WORTH SEEING

❹ Blaues und Weisses Haus *(Blue House and White House).* Built between
1762 and 1768 for two of the city's most successful silk merchants,
these were the residences of the brothers Lukas and Jakob Sarasin. In
1777 the emperor Joseph II of Austria was a guest in the Blue House,
and the roster of subsequent visitors' names—including Czar Alexander
of Russia, Emperor Francis of Austria, and King Friedrich Wilhelm III
of Prussia, who met for dinner here in 1814—brings this historic site's
guest book over the top. The restored houses look more cream and
grey these days, and house the city's justice department, but are clearly
labeled for curious passers-by. ✉*Martinsg., Grossbasel.*

㉓ Fischmarkt *(Fish Market).* Fishmongers once kept their catches market-
fresh here on this square, whose fountain basin served as a sort of
communal cooler. The fountain itself dates from 1390 and holds figures

of the Virgin Mary, St. Peter, and John the Baptist. ⊠*Northwest of Marktpl., Grossbasel.*

⑰ Leonhardskirche *(St. Leonard's Church).* Like virtually all of Basel's churches, this one was destroyed in the 1356 earthquake before being rebuilt in the Gothic style, although its original Romanesque crypt remains. Its High Gothic wooden pulpit is distinctive. Free organ concerts are often held on Friday evenings. ⊠*Leonardskirchpl., Grossbasel* ⊙*Daily 9–5.*

㉔ Les Trois Rois Hotel *(Three Kings Hotel).* The statues on the facade depict the biblical three wise men and are thought to date from 1754. The young general Napoléon Bonaparte stayed here in 1797 (an opulently decorated suite is still named after him), followed by other stellar guests, including Princess Victoria, Charles Dickens, and Picasso. In 1887 the great Hungarian-born Jewish writer Theodor Herzl stayed here during the first Zionist Congress, which laid the groundwork for the founding of the state of Israel. ⊠*Blumenrain 8, Grossbasel.*

❸ Martinskirche *(St. Martin's Church).* The excellent acoustics make this church popular for concerts, although it's rarely used for services. The lower portions of the tower date from 1287, making it the oldest parish church in town; the upper part was rebuilt after the earthquake of 1356. The fountain outside, with the statue of a warrior in battle dress, dates from the 16th century. ⊠*Martinsg., Grossbasel.*

❻ Museum der Kulturen Basel *(Basel Museum of Cultures).* Although undergoing a radical renovation over the next two years, the museum will still host short-term (each running up to eight months) exhibitions during this time. These could be based on a theme that runs through all societies, which, of course, allows the museum to show many of its permanent exhibits in this context, or the exhibition may concentrate on one culture. Still worth a look. ⊠*Münsterpl. 20, Grossbasel* ☎*061/2665600* ⊕*www.mkb.ch* ᠅*16 SF (1st Sun. of month free)* ⊙*Tues.–Sun. 10–5.*

❿ Museum für Gegenwartskunst *(Museum of Contemporary Art).* Bringing Basel's art collections up to the present, this museum focuses on works from the 1960s forward. The fittingly modern building looks as though it has shouldered its way in between the street's half-timber houses. The exhibitions change frequently, so pick up a brochure from a tourist office to see which artists' works will be on view at the time you visit. The language of the exhibition materials typically corresponds to the nationality of the artists. ⊠*St. Alban-Rheinweg 60, Grossbasel* ☎*061/2066262* ⊕*www.kunstmuseumbasel.ch/* ᠅*12 SF, Tues.–Sat. 4–5 free, includes admission to Kunstmuseum* ⊙*Tues.–Sun. 11–5.*

❺ Naturhistorisches Museum *(Natural History Museum).* All aspects of the natural sciences—from the history of the earth to indigenous minerals, from extinct to living mammals, from mammoths to insects—are featured here. A tour is like an expedition into the remotest corners of the planet, where natural objects, large and small, wait to be discovered, inspected, and contemplated. Most descriptive materials are in German only. ⊠*Augustinerg. 2, Grossba-sel* ☎*061/2665500* ⊕*www.nmb.bs.ch* 🔳*7 SF (1st Sun. of month free, Tues.–Sat. 4–5 free)* ⊙*Tues.–Sun. 10–5.*

(19) **Peterskirche** *(St. Peter's Church).* Evidence of Basel's late-Gothic heyday, the 13th-century St. Peter's Church sits across from **Petersplatz,** a lovely park next to the **Universität** (University). In the rose window–lighted chapel are some interesting 14th-century frescoes. Call for information about services. ⊠*Across Peters-Graben from Peterspl., Grossbasel* ☎*061/2618724.*

WORD OF MOUTH

"The best atmosphere in Basel is definitely during Art Basel, the annual cutting-edge art exposition which usually takes place mid-June. A lot of trendy people and stars like Brad Pitt around (but no hotel rooms!). During those ten days, you think you're in a different town. If ever possible, I never miss that event." —Ursula152

(20) **Pharmazie-Historisches Museum** *(Museum of Pharmaceutical History).* Although pharmaceuticals as the topic of an entire museum may seem like too much of a necessary thing, this collection showcases Basel's roots in the industry that dominates the banks of the Rhine today. There are original and re-created pharmacy counters and all kinds of beakers and flacons, and old remedies. To balance out the scientific quota, there is also a look at the history of alchemy. The museum is housed in Zum Vorderen Sessel, a home once frequented by Paracelsus. You can request an English-language information sheet. ⊠*Totengässlein 3, Grossbasel* ☎*061/2649111* ⊕*www.pharmaziemuseum.ch* 🔳*5 SF* ⊙*Tues.–Fri. 10–6, Sat. 10–5.*

(15) **Puppenhaus Museum** *(Dollhouse Museum).* Bordering on the Barfüsser-platz, this museum has several floors filled with 18th-, 19th-, and 20th-century toys (including a cast of 2,500 Teddy bears) and dollhouses on a 1:12 scale, all artistically displayed. ⊠*Steinenvorstadt 1, Grossbasel* ☎*061/2259595* ⊕*www.puppenhausmuseum.ch* 🔳*7 SF* ⊙*Daily 10–6.*

(8) **St. Alban-Tor** *(St. Alban's Gate).* This original medieval city gate is set amid a lovely garden near remnants of the town's ramparts. Parts of the gate date from the 13th century. ⊠*St. Alban-Berg, St. Alban.*

(18) **Spalentor** *(Spalen Gate).* Like the St. Alban-Tor, the Spalentor served as one of Basel's medieval city gates. More imposing than graceful, the 14th-century structure has a toothy wooden portcullis; note Basel's coat of arms atop the gate. ⊠*Spalenvorstadt, Grossbasel.*

Statue of Helvetia. What would the woman pictured on most Swiss coins do if freed from the confines of currency? With spear and shield set aside (and with a packed suitcase in hand), this humanistic interpretation shows her seemingly contemplating the possibilities from a perch not far from the border of her homeland and the wide world beyond. ⊠*Kleinbasel, northeastern bank of Rhine, on the edge of Mittlere Rheinbrücke, Kleinbasel.*

⑭ **Zoologischer Garten** (*Zoological Garden*). Referred to by Baslers as *Zolli*, ☺ this zoo is famed for its armored rhinoceroses, gorillas, hippopotamuses, and fabulous Vivarium filled with fish and reptiles. Animal enclosures are scattered around and almost hidden by its garden environment. Very child-friendly, the zoo has a handy and enormous restaurant. ✉*Binningerstr. 40, Grossbasel* ☎*061/2953535* ⊕*www.zoobasel.ch* 🖾*16 SF* ⊘*Jan., and Feb., Nov., and Dec., daily 8–5:30; Mar., and Apr., Sept., and Oct., daily 8–6; May–Aug., daily 8–6:30.*

OFF THE BEATEN PATH

Langenbruck & Environs. In the German-speaking countryside south of Basel, known as the Baselbiet, you'll find a handful of stately little villages with sturdy old guest houses and a range of historic sites—from medieval to Roman—to explore. Take the winding forest road (A12) west of the freeway between Liestal and Oensingen, watching for Balsthal, Holderbank, Oberer Hauenstein, and Langenbruck; the industrial stretch just south of Liestal is less attractive. By train these towns take a matter of minutes to reach. Trains leave regularly from the SBB Bahnhof. **Landgasthof Bären** (☎*062/3901414* ⊕*www.baeren-langenbruck.ch*) in Langenbruck offers superb regional cooking, inexpensive Tagesmenus (daily specials), and locally brewed beer.

Vitra Design Museum. Ten kilometers (6 mi) across the border in the German town of Weil am Rhein, the main building of this museum is a startling white geometric jumble designed by famed American architect Frank O. Gehry as part of an avant-garde building complex associated with the Vitra furniture manufacturer. The Gehry section generally hosts traveling architectural exhibits. The permanent collection, including the soaring Wall of Chairs (just what it sounds like), is displayed in the nearby Vitra Fire Station, accessible only on the guided tour. To get here by car, take A5/E35 north from Basel toward Karlsruhe; turn right just after German customs onto Route 532, parallel to the parking lot, and turn left after exiting at Weil am Rhein. The museum is 1½ km (about 1 mi) ahead on the right. Or from the Deutscher Bundesbahn in Basel (also known as the Badischer Bahnhof), take Bus 55 toward Kandern to the Vitra stop (takes about 20 minutes from Claraplatz). Bring your passport and call ahead to arrange for an English-speaking tour guide. ✉*Charles-Eames-Str. 1, Weil am Rhein, Germany* ☎*49/76217023200* ⊕*www.design-museum.de* 🖾*€7.50. Guided architectural tour, Tues.–Sun. 12–2 PM, €9* ⊘*Tues.–Sun. 11–6.*

COLONIA AUGUSTA RAURICA (AUGST)

Founded in 44–43 BC, Augst is the oldest Roman settlement on the Rhine, and today has been largely reconstructed as a noted museum of ancient Roman antiquities (one suspects the Swiss might have done the same with Rome's Colosseum if they had gotten their hands on it). The site is reachable by car from Basel in 15 minutes or in summer via a leisurely boat trip up the river. From the SBB Bahnhof take train S1 to Kaiseraugst, or bus 70 from Basel-Aeschenvorstadt to Augst; thereafter it takes approximately 10 minutes from both these stops to walk to the Roman Museum. To view the restoration areas scattered around the almost suburban neighborhood, be prepared for a fair bit of walking.

SIGHTS TO SEE

★ **Augusta Raurica.** The remains of this 2,000-year-old Roman settlement have been extensively rebuilt, with substantial portions of the ancient town walls and gates, streets, water pipes, and heating systems all in evidence. The 1st-century BC theater, described as the best-preserved ancient complex north of the Alps, has been gloriously restored in the last few years.

Römermuseum *(Roman Museum)*. Roman daily life is vividly depicted in this rebuilt ocher-hue home. Everything, from the thermal baths to the ancient board games in the sitting rooms has been completely re-created. The museum also exhibits a trove of Roman-era coins and silver unearthed in 1962. The objects, dating mostly from the 4th century, are believed to have been buried by the Romans in 350 to protect them from the ravages of the Alemanni, the German tribes who drove the Romans out of Switzerland. Trilingual (English/French/German) brochures are available. ⊠ *Giebenacherstr. 17, Augst* ☎ *061/8162222* ⊕ *www.augustaraurica.ch* ☜ *7 SF* ⊙ *Mar.–Oct., Mon. 1–5, Tues.–Sun. 10–5; Nov.–Feb., daily 10–noon, 1:30–5.*

> **PHOTO-OP**
>
> Set in the heart of the prettiest area of Old Basel, the fanciful Holbeinbrunnen fountain found its inspiration in several other artworks. Created by an unknown 16th-century stonemason, it depicts a group of dancing farmers, copied from a drawing by Hans Holbein; above stands a bagpiper, copied from a Dürer engraving. The fountain itself is a replica, the original having been moved to the Historical Museum, and can be found on Spalenvorstadt, 2 blocks up the tram tracks toward Spalentor.

WHERE TO EAT

WHAT IT COSTS IN SWISS FRANCS				
	¢	$	$$	$$$	$$$$
AT DINNER	under 15 SF	15 SF–25 SF	25 SF–40 SF	40 SF–60 SF	over 60 SF

Prices are per person for a main course at dinner.

THE SCENE

Classic but boundary-pushing, bank-breaking but exquisite gourmet cuisine has long been one of Basel's fortes, along with medium-priced but fine restaurants, with new trends popping up and disappearing in the blink of an eye. Snuggled between three countries, Basel has inherited the culinary interests of each, and excels with offering its own specialties and those of its neighbors…and beyond.

Eating out here, as anywhere in Switzerland, can be a costly delight, and top-of-the-range restaurants are plentiful. Stucki Bruderholz, a landmark establishment, has been renovated and remains the "in" place for gourmets, especially with its new trendy lady chef. Zum Goldenen Sternen and Teufelhof never go out of fashion with their mouthwatering and boundary-challenging modern French-flavored cuisine. At the other end of the scale, you will never have to go far for a German-style sausage, Italian pasta, or mouth-watering confectionary as small local restaurants and cafés can be found in practically every street you walk down. Other than the top-drawer places, Basel is, in fact, full of comfortable haunts lined with carved wood and thick with the mingled odors of cooking meat and cigar smoke. The city's down-to-earth fare owes its roots to the Germanic hordes who arrived here to rout the ancient Romans, bringing with them homely-fare like schnitzel, and *Spätzli* (tiny flour dumplings), all to be washed down with beer.

As for dining specialties, the proximity of the Rhine means that most Basel restaurants serve a variety of freshwater fish. If the city could claim a regional specialty, it would be salmon. (These days much of it is shipped in from elsewhere, but the Rhine variety is making a come-back.) The meaty fish is best served *nach Basler Art* (Basel-style), mean-ing in a white-wine marinade with fried onions on top. Try it with a bottle of the fruity local Riesling-Sylvaner.

Asian fusion restaurants are newly popular, but these tend to come and go as do theme restaurants like the new Das Neue Rialto, which sells food and the designer furniture you sit on to eat it. This is a great con-cept in a city renowned for its art-filled atmosphere and, after all, this is Switzerland, where anything you sit on or see that takes your fancy you should be able to order to go, no?

For a satisfying and pocket-friendly lunch, supermarket canteens and many of the small local restaurants offer lunch specials (*Tagesmenu*). These are often a dish of the day accompanied by a starter or salad and maybe even a dessert and are the best way to eat well on a budget.

More and more restaurants are becoming smoke-free, while others have no-smoking sections. These no-smoking sections, however, often seem to have been randomly selected and the smell of smoke still pervades within (children's eating and play sections in supermarket restaurants often seem to be placed next to the smokers section for some bizarre reason).

$$$
MODERN FRENCH
Fodor's Choice
★
✕ **Bel Étage/Weinstube** Monica and Dominique Thommy transformed a grand old Heuberg mansion into a cultural center boasting two res-taurants, a trendy bar, and even medieval ruins in the basement. They have now handed over their mission of mixing art and gastonomy to the younger hands of Nathalie Reinhardt and Raphael Wyniger. Actu-ally set within the complex of the Hotel Teufelhof, the formal Bel Étage showcases Michael Baader's masterly culinary inventions, including duck breast and pie with truffle juice and turnip cabbage and silsnap-per fish fillet with passion-fruit vinaigrette, saffron spaghettini, and bok choy. Sip wines by the glass, then buy the bottles you'd like to take home in the house wine shop. The casual, high-tech *Weinstube* serves ever-changing seasonal dishes. ⊠ *Leonhardsgraben 49, Gross-basel* ☎ *061/2611010* ⊕ *www.teufelhof.com* ⊟ *AE, DC, MC, V* ⊗ *Bel Étage closed Sun. and Mon. No lunch Sat.*

$–$$ ✕ **Brauerei Fischerstube.** If you're serious about sampling the local color,
SWISS   stop in here for a cold one. The Fischerstube, Basel's smallest brewery,
★   produces its own lagers and ales in the deep, frothing copper tanks you
see at the end of the room. If you like their Ueli Bier, named for a Fasnacht clown, you can buy a keg to take home. The look is beer-friendly,
with freshly renovated plain walls and sanded wooden tables, offering
a range from simple fare like oven-fresh pretzels to heartier local dishes
of steak or grilled *Würstli* (sausages). In summer the roof beer garden
out back is very popular. ✉ *Rheing. 45, Kleinbasel* ☎ *061/6929200*
⊕ *www.uelibier.ch* ⌖ *Reservations essential* ▭ *AE, DC, MC, V.*

$ ✕ **Café Pfalz.** This bookish little self-service café boasts a great position
CAFÉ   down a narrow street on the square by the cathedral, where so many
of Basel's seasonal events take place. This is a popular but small venue
offering lunchtime veggie plates, sausages, and quiche in a trim beech-
wood-and-black contemporary setting. The impressive salad bar usually
holds 30 different varieties. There is also at least one hot daily special.
To quench your thirst, try a freshly squeezed delight from the juice
bar or one of 15 different types of tea. ✉ *Münsterberg 11, Grossbasel*
☎ *061/2726511* ⊕ *www.salat-laden.ch* ▭ *No credit cards* ⊙ *Closed
weekends. No dinner.*

$$$ ✕ **Chez Donati.** Now under the wing of Les Trois Rois hotel, this much-
ITALIAN   loved establishment has been serving up a selection of Italian stan-
dards for 50 years, and is famous for its antipasti. Other specialties
include osso buco with saffron risotto and scampi with their special
house sauce. The traditional, gilt-framed Venetian paintings are supple-
mented with modern art (the Art Basel crowd has long convened here,
including once-regulars Andy Warhol and Jean Tinguely). Dine while
enjoying the view of the Rhine from your white-draped table. ✉ *St.
Johanns-Vorstadt 48, Grossbasel* ☎ *061/3220919* ⊕ *www.lestroisrois.
com* ▭ *AE, DC, MC, V* ⊙ *Closed Sun.–Mon., also July–Aug.*

$$ ✕ **Das Neue Rialto.** If you find you're sitting pretty in this new trendset-
MODERN FRENCH   ting restaurant, you can always bring your chair home with you. Chef
★   Andrea Berger allows you to enjoy her culinary creations in a 20th
century–inspired designer space where all the furniture is for sale. Set
on the second floor of the Rialto swimming pool complex near the Zoo,
this hot spot offers plenty of seasonal dishes—lamb fillets served with
tomato-potatoes and the sole with steamed arugula and rice balls are
two top options. The restaurant is smoke-free inside. ✉ *Birsigstr. 45
CH-4054* ☎ *061/2053145* ⊕ *www.dasneuerialto.ch* ⌖ *Reservations
essential* ▭ *AE, DC, MC, V* ⊙ *Closed Sun. No dinner Mon.–Tues.
No lunch Sat.*

$$ ✕ **Löwenzorn.** This is a classic, comfortable gathering place serving typ-
SWISS   ical Swiss food. The menu features everything from traditional and
filling *Kalbsläberli und Röschti* (veal liver with grated potato) to the
more sophisticated roasted pike-perch with capers, olives, and dried
tomatoes served with rice. Regulars come for a beer, a full plate, and
some laughs with the friendly staff. With stained-glass lamps, ceramic
stoves, and woodwork, it's a nice mix of bistro and beer hall, and a
popular place to hang out during Fasnacht ✉ *Gemsberg 2–4, Grossba-
sel* ☎ *061/2614213* ⊕ *www.loewenzorn.ch* ▭ *AE, DC, MC, V.*

$ ✕ **Restaurant/Café Papiermühle.** With the splashing of the paper mill's
SWISS   waterwheel in the background, this is a restful spot for lunch or an
★ afternoon snack (it's only open until 6 PM except on Friday). The hand-
scrawled chalkboard usually includes two set meals, brunch favorites
(quiches and *Birchermüsli,* the original, creamy, fruity version of muesli),
salads, soups, and pasta dishes. After 2 PM hot food is no longer served,
but sandwiches and other snacks are still available and hand signals will
be all you need to point out one of the delicious homemade cakes on
display. Every Friday night from 7 PM until midnight there is an Italian
antipasti buffet. Sunday mornings find this one of Basel's most popular brunch locations. ⊠ *St. Alban-Tal 37, St. Alban* ☏ *061/2724848*
⊕ *www.papiermuseum.ch* ▭ *No credit cards* ⊘ *Closed Mon.*

$$$ ✕ **St. Alban-Eck.** This bistro, a five-minute walk behind the Kunstmu-
FRENCH   seum, is a well-known landmark in the Old Town. In a half-timber
historic home, it's a real *petit coin sympa* (friendly little place), with
plank wainscoting in natural wood, framed historic prints, and net
curtains. The cuisine gracefully mixes Swiss and French favorites. Try
one of their market-fresh grilled sole with green asparagus and a saffron
sauce or some local beef fillet with fresh chanterelle mushrooms, both
complemented by seasonal vegetables. ⊠ *St. Alban-Vorstadt 60, St.
Alban* ☏ *061/2710320* ⊕ *www.st-alban-eck.ch* ⚏ *Reservations essen-
tial* ▭ *AE, DC, MC, V* ⊘ *Closed Sun., July–Aug. No lunch Sat.*

$$$ ✕ **Schlüsselzunft.** This extremely popular historic guildhall has been
FRENCH   spruced up, and its elegant little restaurant reopened in winter 2007.
★ The main eatery, with its famous traditional ceramic stove, draws a
crowd with its special business set lunch, but dinner also features well-
bred seasonal cuisine such as sautéed Swiss pike fillet on ratatouille
with basil butter and saffron noodles—another winner is the grilled veal
cutlets with a reduced port sauce, noodles, and fresh vegetables. Also on
the premises is an inexpensive courtyard brasserie-café called the Schlüs-
selhöfli, with a menu that changes daily. ⊠ *Freie Str. 25, Grossbasel*
☏ *061/2612046* ⊕ *www.schluesselzunft.ch* ⚏ *Reservations essential*
▭ *AE, DC. MC, V* ⊘ *Closed Sun., June, July, and August.*

$$$–$$$$ ✕ **Stucki Bruderholz.** Freshly renovated and featuring one of Switzerland's
FRENCH   most promising new chefs, Tanja Grandits—Gault Millau's Cook of
★ the Year 2006—this legendary restaurant continues to hit new heights.
Grandits is renowned for her abilities to conjure creations that have
been described as "filigree art " by taking regional products and add-
ing a touch of the exotic. "I simply know what goes with what" is how
she explains her eclectic dishes. Exciting seasonal choices include St.
Pierre fillet with fennel sauerkraut and a herb and honey vierge sauce,
and the beef fillet with nutmeg-flavored pesto, candied crisp summer
vegetables, and a potato-hazelnut foam. The service at this restaurant
in the residential neighborhood of Bruderholz is formal. Take tram
No. 15 from Marktplatz, direction Bruderholz, to Radio Studio Basel.
⊠ *Bruderholzallee 42, Bruderholz* ☏ *061/3618222* ⊕ *www.stucki-
bruderholz.ch* ⚏ *Reservations essential* ▭ *AE, DC, MC, V* ⊘ *Closed
Sun. and Mon.*

$$$
FRENCH
Fodor'sChoice
★
✕**Zum Goldenen Sternen.** Dating from 1506, this *Gasthof* claims to be the oldest restaurant in Switzerland, even though the building was moved to its current Rhine-side site. Impeccable restoration retains the antique beams, stenciled ceilings, and unvarnished planks, without seeming bogus (in summer you can also opt for *al fresco* eating on the river terrace out front or in the garden out back). Though it could easily play a secondary role, the food does its best to live up to the setting: tenderloin of pork "Basel-style" with bacon, prune sauce, browned potatoes and market vegetables; Lake Neuenburg char with a verjus sauce, stewed artichokes, olives, and sautéed potatoes with rosemary. There's also a seven-course tasting menu that changes monthly. ⊠*St. Alban-Rheinweg 70, St. Alban* ☎*061/2721666* ⊕*www.sternen-basel. ch* ⌕*Reservations essential* ⊟*AE, DC, MC, V.*

$$
SWISS
✕**Zur Harmonie.** It's well worth deciding to take the time to walk up to this *Jugendstil* (Art Nouveau) charmer, with its parquet floors and etched mirrors, for an informal lunch in a friendly and relaxed atmosphere. Choose from a selection of delicious French and Swiss favorites, such as veal *cordon bleu,* bread-crumbed schnitzel stuffed with cheese and ham and served with French fries and vegetables, or the mussels "Harmonie-style," featuring red peppers, or perhaps even a plate of snails, cooked in the style of the Burgundy region. ⊠*Petersgraben 71, Grossbasel* ☎*061/2610718* ⊕*www.harmonie-basel.ch* ⌕*Reservations essential* ⊟*AE, DC, MC, V* ☉*Snacks only Sat.–Sun.* 5 PM–6 PM.

WHERE TO STAY

WHAT IT COSTS IN SWISS FRANCS				
	¢	$	$$	$$$	$$$$
FOR TWO PEOPLE	under 100 SF	100 SF–175 SF	175 SF–250 SF	250 SF–350 SF	over 350 SF

Prices are for two people in a standard double room, including tax and service.

THE SCENE

Grand as a palace? Way-cool as a converted prison? An art lover's paradise? Or cozy and a little run down just like Grannie's? The hotel scene in Basel is definitely varied. But with its industry, its banking, and its busy convention center offering a different trade fair most months, this is a city that prides itself on being especially business-friendly. Many hotels therefore place their priorities with their business clientele (a never-ending supply), and invariably humble tourists take second place.

But don't write off the city's business-oriented hotels as a place to stay—these often drop their prices bigtime over the weekend and offer superb amenities. In many hotels the lobbies are minimalist chic, with signs to the meeting rooms and business facilities more prominent than any paintings on the wall. At the top of the pile, hotel-wise, has to be Les Trois Rois, which feels like a palace and is frequented by visiting heads of state and the glitterati. Originality also abounds, ranging from the converted cloister-cum-prison that is now Au Violon, through the artist's canvas of a hotel, Teufelhof, to the relaxed, intellectual dorm-like feel of Rochat. Many hotels offer a river view and a calm, relaxed, designer interior. Cheaper hotels range from the all-orange extravaganza of Easyhotel to the homely feel of Hecht am Rhein, where smoking is still not a crime.

All in all, the hotel scene in Basel is not known for its ever-changing establishments but instead for its stability. The hotel you stayed in 10 years ago is probably still there, and will welcome you again with open arms into its recently exquisitely renovated interior. When there's a trade fair in town, prices shoot through the roof, and every bed for miles can be filled, so book well ahead. This is also true at Fasnacht, during Art Basel, and many of the other city happenings, when prices can rise as much as 40%. Breakfast tends to be included only in the more budget-oriented hotels, while the expensive ones, like Les Trois Rois, stick it on top of their bill. All Basel hotels equip their guests with free travel passes (Basel Mobility Ticket) for use in the city during their stay.

$$$–$$$$ **Basel.** This all-modern hotel plays an important part in its Old Town neighborhood as in the evening its bars and restaurants fill up with an interesting mix of businessmen, locals calming down after work, and tourists. The wood-panel guest rooms are accented with contemporary leather furniture and chrome; polished marble adds luster to the baths. **Pros:** great central location just off the market square is great for catching trams, and it's close to the river too; friendly and accommodating staff. **Cons:** during the week the hotel clientele is almost exclusively business executives. ⊠*Am Spalenberg, Münzg. 12, Grossbasel* ☎*061/2646800* ⊕*www.hotel-basel.ch* ☞*69 rooms, 3 suites* ♻*In-room: safe, refrigerator, Wi-Fi. In-hotel: 2 restaurants, room service, bar, public Internet, public Wi-Fi, parking (fee), some pets allowed* ☲*AE, DC, MC, V* ⓧ*EP.*

$$–$$$ **Best Western Merian am Rhein.** Overlooking the Rhine, this hotel has a modern, airy look accented with touches of gray wood, russet leather, and Le Corbusier chairs. The hotel is most famed for its Café Spitz, whose name has been allowed as a city meeting place since the early 13th century. Now a chic restaurant, this tranquil eatery features overlarge Art Nouveau lampshades and is painted in a wine red, accentuated by warm checks to match the newly renovated reception. In summer, opt for the lovely restaurant terrace with views of the cathedral. **Pros:** ask for a cheaper but plainer business room to save money. **Cons:** you pay more for a Rhine view. ⊠*Rheing. 2, Kleinbasel* ☎*061/6851111* ⊕*www.hotelmerianbasel.ch* ☞*63 rooms* ♻*In-room: no a/c, safe, refrigerator, Ethernet. In-hotel: restaurant, room service, public Internet, public Wi-Fi, parking (fee), some pets allowed, no elevator* ☲*AE, DC, MC, V* ⓧ*CP.*

$–$$ **Central.** This establishment is under the same management as the
★ Euler, where, in fact, you head to pick up your room key (it is connected to its parent hotel by a corridor). Guest rooms can be on the small side,

but are tasteful and cheerful; dashes of vivid color can include tangerine bedspreads. **Pros:** you can use the excellent facilities of the Euler at a reduced price. **Cons:** elevator doesn't reach all levels; feels spartan compared to Euler. ✉*Kücheng. 7, Grossbasel* ☎*061/2758000* ⊕*www. hoteleuler.ch* ⤴*22 rooms* ⚒*In-room: no a/c, Wi-Fi. In-hotel: parking (fee), some pets allowed* ☐*AE, DC, MC, V* ☉*EP.*

¢–$ ☒ **EasyHotel.** Located in Kleinbasel, the first EasyHotel in Switzerland opened in 2005. Guest rooms are compact, minimalist, and contemporarily decorated with orange detail; some come without windows (these have air-conditioning and are bargains). Downstairs are vending machines, but the restaurant next door is open from 9 AM to midnight. Note: rooms can only be booked via the Web site. **Pros:** for a central location, simple uncluttered rooms, and the ease of booking immediately day or night on the Internet, this hotel chain is hard to beat. **Cons:** no lobby; TVs are extra. ✉*Riehenring 109, Kleinbasel* ☎*0900/327927 (1.50 SF min)* ⊕*www.easyhotel.com* ⤴*24 rooms* ⚒*In-room: no a/c (some), no phone, Ethernet (fee),Wi-Fi (fee). In-hotel: no-smoking rooms* ☐*AE, MC, V* ☉*EP.*

$$$ ☒ **Euler.** An archetypal old-world hotel, this 140-year-old landmark has
★   been tastefully renovated throughout to bring out the best in its original features. The bar is split between the new reception lounge, where a pianist plays each evening, and the greatly reduced-in-size restaurant. Up in the guest rooms, duvets billow over bed frames in some of the cushier rooms and suites; standard rooms are on the small side, and are furnished with reproduction antique furnishings. **Pros:** within easy walking distance of train stations and the middle of town. **Cons:** glazed windows cut out noise from bustling tram hub outside, so need to be kept closed. ✉*Centralbahnpl. 14, Grossbasel* ☎*061/2758000* ⊕*www. hoteleuler.ch* ⤴*60 rooms, 6 suites* ⚒*In-room: safe, refrigerator, Ethernet, Wi-Fi. In-hotel: restaurant, room service, bar, public Internet, parking (fee), some pets allowed* ☐*AE, DC, MC, V* ☉*EP.*

$$$$ ☒ **Grandhotel Les Trois Rois.** Voltaire, Napoléon, Kaiser Wilhelm II, and
Fodor's Choice now you? Basel's leading rendezvous for the rich and famous ever since
★   three 11th-century kings (Conrad II, Henry III, and Rudolf III) once convened here, the Drei Könige—to use its German name—has long been an integral part of Basel history. Once a small inn on the banks of the Rhine, then a coach stop, it was given a regal makeover in 1835. Today, the furnishings have regained their 19th-century grandeur, with ravishing colors of cream, gilt, and powder blue; ornate woodwork, paintings and tapestries nudge the opulence factor ever higher. The lobby is a symphony of beiges, walnuts, and Secession-style armchairs; the bar, a resplendent statement in rouge-reds and sunny oranges. There is a feast here for the stomach as well as the eyes: the formal Cheval Blanc restaurant, which has been awarded a Michelin star under new chef Peter Knogl, serves up French *cuisine classique* on the broad, awning-shaded Rhine terrace (well heated into fall); the Brasserie proffers a stunning glass wall overlooking the river; while Chez Donati pays its respects to Piedmontese Italian food and hot modern art. All in all, while expanded, restored (by the Counts des Boisrouvray), and a virtual tourist attraction (those three statues of kings on the facade), this hotel

remains surprisingly intimate and understated in the best Swiss way. Note: Riverside rooms get higher rates, but you can be sure the Rolling Stones and opera star Montserrat Caballé splurged on them. **Pros:** regal prices are reflected in regal service. **Cons:** breakfast is extra and very pricey; ambience of the rooms is somewhat spoiled by the large flat-screen TVs. ⊠*Blumenrain 8, Grossbasel* ☎*061/2605050* ⊕*www.lestroisrois.com* ➔*83 rooms, 18 suites* ⊘*In-room: safe, refrigerator, Wi-Fi. In-hotel: 3 restaurants, bar, gym, public Internet, public Wi-Fi, parking (fee), some pets allowed* ⊟*AE, DC, MC, V* ⊠*EP.*

WORD OF MOUTH

"I enjoyed Hotel au Violon, which is very central. Stayed in a Category B room overlooking the square but quiet at night. Charmingly creaky wood floors, nice celery/off-white color scheme, and the fanciest shower stall I've ever seen."   —Travelnut

$ 🚻**Hecht am Rhein.** Situated between two more expensive hotels, this
★ budget lodging offers faded comfort and a friendly staff. The guest rooms here seem bigger than in the neighboring establishments, and are simply furnished with aged leather chairs, wood-backed beds, and an astonishing selection of art prints. Each floor has a seating area and clean, bright, and inviting showers and toilet facilities. There is also a welcoming breakfast room. The popular terrace restaurant serves pizza in summer. **Pros:** the price is right for an unassuming place to stay with a great riverside location; no extra charge for a river view. **Cons:** one refrigerator on each floor; smoking allowed throughout. ⊠*Rheing. 8, Kleinbasel* ☎*061/6901515* ⊕*www.hotelbasel.ch* ➔*30 rooms* ⊘*In-room: no a/c, no TV. In-hotel: restaurant, some pets allowed, no elevator* ⊟*AE, DC, MC, V* ⊠*BP.*

$ 🚻**Hotel Brasserie Au Violon.** The former residents here—priests and pris-
★ oners—never had it so good. Housed in a 12th-century building that served as a cloister and then a prison, the hotel now captivates its clientele with subdued elegance, a peaceful location, and a terrific restaurant. There are some reminders of the building's austere past—guest rooms overlooking the courtyard still conform to cell-block arrangements, with uniformly tight square footage. Guest rooms facing the town offer more space. The brasserie, with its mirrored bar, art deco fixtures, and iron-leg tables, serves French classics. **Pros:** when restaurant is open, take the convenient lift from Barfüsserplatz up the hill. **Cons:** safes only available at reception. ⊠*Im Lohnhof 4, Grossbasel* ☎*061/2698711* ⊕*www. au-violon.com* ➔*20 rooms* ⊘*In-room: no a/c, no TV (some). In-hotel: restaurant, some pets allowed, no-smoking rooms* ⊟*AE, MC, V* ⊠*EP* ⊘*Closed between Christmas and New Year's.*

$$–$$$ 🚻**Krafft.** Smack on the waterfront, this spot offers a can't-get-better
Fodor'sChoice location for people-watching. Set in an elegant mansion, the Kraft has
★ been renovated throughout with an airy and elegant feel; the wooden flooring has been restored, and guest rooms are simply furnished with Swiss designer furniture. The traditional dining room and ever-popular waterfront terrace offer spectacular views of the Old Town, while the cosy downstairs Petit Krafft is welcoming on colder days. Across the street the new addition, Dépendence, offers 12 new rooms and

the Consum wine/snack bar. **Pros:** refreshment station on each floor; no-smoking restaurants, but smoking room provided. **Cons:** only one refrigerator on each floor; the bars and restaurants are very popular and can be loud. ⊠*Rheing. 12, Kleinbasel* ☎*061/6909130* ⊕*www. krafthotel.ch* ⊋*45 rooms* ⚥*In-room: no a/c, safe, Wi-Fi. In-hotel: 2 restaurants, bar, public Internet, public Wi-Fi, some pets allowed* ⊟*AE, DC, MC, V* ⦿*CP.*

$–$$ ⛲ **Rochat.** If you like the feel of educated peace, then the location of this modest but roomy property is a great asset; it's across from the university and makes you feel well removed from the shopping masses. The main building, a brownstone dating from 1898, has a dorm-like feel, while the whitewashed annex with its twisting hallways comes across as a scaled-down inn. **Pros:** good breakfast buffet; service polite and to the point. **Cons:** try not to get lost in the rabbit warren of corridors; there are stairs in between the elevators, so not easily accessible for wheelchair users. ⊠*Petersgraben 23, Grossbasel* ☎*061/2618140* ⊕*www.hotelrochat.ch* ⊋*50 rooms* ⚥*In-room: no a/c (some), safe, refrigerator. In-hotel: restaurant, public Internet, public Wi-Fi, some pets allowed, parking (fee)* ⊟*AE, DC, MC, V* ⦿*BP.*

$$$ ⛲ **Teufelhof.** Two hotels in one: the Art Hotel has nine rooms that are
★ works of art in their own right, as each is regularly redecorated by a different Swiss artist; the simple rooms of the adjoining Gallery Hotel function collectively as a canvas for one particular artist to show off work or for an artistic theme (at present the rooms all feature work from disabled artists). An in-house theater puts on shows in German from mid-September to early May. In-room TVs are available upon request. **Pros:** great location—only three tram stops away from the main station. **Cons:** noisy in summer with windows open, as there is no air-conditioning. ⊠*Leonhardsgraben 49, Grossbasel* ☎*061/2611010* ⊕*www.teufelhof.com* ⊋*29 rooms, 4 suites* ⚥*In-room: no a/c, safe, no TV, Wi-Fi. In-hotel: 2 restaurants, room service, bar, public Internet, public Wi-Fi, some pets allowed, no elevator in Gallery Hotel* ⊟*AE, DC, MC, V* ⦿*BP.*

NIGHTLIFE & THE ARTS

For a complete listing of events, pick up a copy of *Basel Live,* a booklet published every two weeks (written partially in English). Also note *Events Highlights,* a flyer printed every six months in English. Both are available at the tourist office and usually at hotel desks. If you'd like to play it by ear, the Steinenvorstadt is crowded with cinemas, bars, and young people, and on the Kleinbasel side there are late-night bars along the Oberer Rheinweg.

NIGHTLIFE

BARS & LOUNGES

The extremely popular **Bar des Arts** (⊠*Barfüsserpl. 6, Grossbasel* ☎*061/2735737*), a bistro/pub/lounge, pulls in an interesting mix of patrons. It began as an arty experiment, but the crimson interior of **Bar**

Rouge (⊠ *Level 31 Messeturm, Am Messepl., Kleinbasel* ☎*061/3613031*) has caught on. The bar is on the top floor of the trade-fair tower. Opposite the Zoo, **Acqua** (⊠ *Binningerstr. 13, Grossbasel* ☎*061/2716300*), with its "waterfall" artworks in the hallway, has remained trendy since it opened over three years ago.

Campari Bar (⊠ *Steinenberg 7, Grossbasel* ☎*061/2728383*), behind the Kunsthalle and Tinguely Fountain, pulls in an artsy crowd with its pop-art interior and tree-canopied terrace. With its back-to-the-1970s feel and central position just off the Barfüsserplatz., **Baragraph 4** (⊠ *Kohlenberg 10, Grossbasel* ☎*061/2618864*) pulls a mixed crowd for its beer and cocktails; generous with their peanuts. **Sperber** (⊠ *Münzg. 12, Grossbasel* ☎*061/2646800*) has the feel of an English pub, with live music some evenings.

DANCING & NIGHTCLUBS

A wood-trimmed and mirrored club near the zoo that offers garage, electro, funk, and jazz, **The Annex** (⊠ *Binningerstr. 14, Grossbasel* ☎*061/2830070*) is open Fridays and Saturdays. **Atlantis** (⊠ *Klosterberg 13, Grossbasel* ☎*061/2289696*) offers live music, club nights, and a restaurant with a summer roof terrace. You have to be 25-plus to enjoy the three floors of music at **Disco-Bar Club 59** (⊠ *Steinenvorstadt 33, Grossbasel* ☎*061/2815950*) where the DJ rages through disco to rock and reggae.

THE ARTS

Advance bookings for many live performances can be made inside Bider & Tanner at **au Concert** (⊠ *Aeschenvorstadt 2, Grossbasel* ☎*061/2722229*). You can also purchase tickets at **Ticketcorner** (⊠ *On the 5th floor inside Manor department store, Greifeng. 22, Kleinbasel* ☎*061/6854699*).

FILM

Movies in Basel are usually shown in the original language with subtitles. Most theaters are along Steinenvorstadt in the Old Town, and the titles and times are prominently posted. In summer there are open-air cinemas in various locations, such as on the Münsterplatz.

MUSIC

The **Musik-Akademie der Stadt Basel** (⊠ *Leonhardsstr. 6, Grossbasel* ☎*061/2645757*) is an important music academy drawing top-drawer international performers. The **Stadt Casino** (⊠ *Steinenberg 14, Grossbasel* ☎*061/2737373*) hosts the Basel Symphony Orchestra, the Basel Chamber Orchestra, and a wide range of visiting performers.

THEATER

The **Musical Theater** (⊠ *Feldbergstr. 151, Kleinbasel* ☎*061/6998899*) is the venue for touring companies. **Theater Basel** (⊠ *Theaterstr. 7, Grossbasel* ☎*061/2951133*) hosts opera, operetta, and dance performances, as well as drama (usually in German); it is closed from the end of June to mid-August.

SHOPPING

The major downtown shopping district stretches along **Freie Strasse** and **Gerbergasse,** where you can find many one-of-a-kind boutiques. More reasonably priced shops along **Steinenvorstadt** cater to a younger crowd.

DEPARTMENT STORES

Coop City (✉ *Gerberg. 4, Grossbasel* ☎ *061/2699250*) carries a wide selection of clothing and household goods, as well as groceries in the basement. **Globus** (✉ *Marktpl. 2, Grossbasel* ☎ *061/2684545*) is an upscale department store with gourmet edibles and sleek clothes. Whether you're in need of socks, toothpaste, or chocolate on the cheap, head to **Manor** (✉ *Greifeng. 22, Grossbasel* ☎ *061/6854699*). In the main train station, the supermarket **Migros** (✉ *Centralbahnpl., Grossbasel* ☎ *058/5758412*) stays open until 10 PM seven days a week.

SPECIALTY STORES

ANTIQUE BOOKS

Among many fine competitors, **Erasmushaus** (✉ *Bäumleing. 18, Grossbasel* ☎ *061/2289933*) has one of the city's largest collections of fine antique manuscripts, books, and autographs; mostly in German but including some multilingual art publications. If they cannot help you in the search for a particular tome, they will be happy to supply the names of the other specialist shops in the Basel area.

CALLIGRAPHY

Abraxas (✉ *Rheinsprung 6, Grossbasel* ☎ *061/2616070*) is a great source for fine writing instruments and paraphernalia, from thick paper and delicate fountain pens to luxurious sealing waxes and reproductions of antique silver seals. **Scriptorium am Rheinsprung** (✉ *Rheinsprung 2, Grossbasel* ☎ *061/2613900*) mixes its own ink and undertakes commissions on demand.

CRAFTS & GIFTS

Though primarily specializing in home furnishings, **Atelier Baumgartner** (✉ *Spalenberg 8, Grossbasel* ☎ *061/2610843*) also stocks Swiss and European handicrafts, including music boxes and nutcrackers from the Erzgebirge region of Germany. **Heimatwerk** (✉ *Schneiderg. 2, Grossbasel* ☎ *061/2619178*) sells a selection of exquisite Swiss crafts. **Zem Baselstab** (✉ *Schnabelg. 8, Grossbasel* ☎ *061/2611016*) has Fasnacht figurines and other Swiss and Basel paraphernalia.

ENGLISH-LANGUAGE MEDIA

Bider & Tanner (✉ *Aeschenvorstadt 2, Grossbasel* ☎ *061/2069999*). **Thalia Bücher** (✉ *Freie Str. 32, Grossbasel* ☎ *061/2642626*).

FOOD SPECIALTIES

Bachmann & Co (✉ *Gerberg. 51, Grossbasel* ☎ *061/2613583* ✉ *Blumenrain 1, Grossbasel* ☎ *061/2609999* ✉ *Centralbahnpl. 7, Grossbasel* ☎ *061/2712627*) carries a Basel specialty called *Leckerli,* a chewy cookie made of almonds, honey, dried fruit, and kirsch. **Glausi's** (⊠*Spalenberg 12, Grossbasel* ☎*061/2618008*) has a fine selection of Swiss cheeses and even ages its own. The famous **Läckerli-Huus** (⊠*Gerberg. 57, Grossbasel* ☎*061/2642323*) sells a variety of sweets, including wonderful *Leckerli*. A large selection of gift canisters and a shipping service make getting gifts home a cinch. **Schiesser** (⊠*Marktpl. 19, Grossbasel* ☎*061/2616077*), a convivial tearoom that opened in 1870, sells

> **THAT TIME OF YEAR ALL YEAR**
>
> Highly specialized handiwork comes from **Johann Wanner** (Spalenberg 14, Grossbasel, 061/2614826), which sells Christmas goods year-round, including handblown, hand-painted, and hand-molded ornaments, tin Victorian miniatures, Tartan ribbons, Advent cards and calendars, and Christmas cards.

carefully crafted (and costly) confections in its downstairs shop.

LINENS

Caraco (⊠*Gerberg. 77, Falknerstr. entrance, Grossbasel* ☎*061/2613577*) sells handmade Swiss lace and embroidered goods. **Schlossberg Boutique** (⊠*Gerberg. 26, Grossbasel* ☎*061/2610900*) offers all manner of household linens for the bedroom, dining room, and kitchen. **Sturzenegger** (⊠*Theaterstr. 4, Grossbasel* ☎*061/2616867*) specializes in household items, including table decorations edged with St. Gallen lace, but these often sell out immediately.

LINGERIE

Beldona (⊠*Freie Str. 103, Grossbasel* ☎*061/2731170*) stocks classy Swiss lingerie. **Fogal** (⊠*Freie Str. 4, Grossbasel* ☎*061/2611220*) sells Swiss hosiery; look out for its tray of clearance goods. **Sturzenegger** (⊠*Theaterstr. 4, Grossbasel* ☎*061/2616867*) carries an extensive line of undergarments with labels such as Hanro.

MEN'S CLOTHES

Classic Herrenmode (⊠*Fischmarkt 5, Grossbasel* ☎*061/2610755*) carries formal and casual shirts, cashmere pullovers, and underwear. Serving gentlemen for more than 100 years, **Fein-kaller & Co.** (⊠*Gerberg. 48, Grossbasel* ☎*061/2611233*) has an impeccable selection of designer wear from Armani to Brioni and Isaia.

SHOES

Müki (⊠*Münsterberg 14, Grossbasel* ☎*061/2712436*) focuses on functional yet stylish European-made kids' shoes, plus designer minis from Dolce & Gabbana and Moschino. **Rive Gauche** (⊠*Schneiderg. 1, Grossbasel* ☎*061/2611080*) carries high-end designer shoes. This is the place to satisfy that Prada, Miu Miu, or Marc Jacobs craving.

TOYS

Bercher & Sternlicht (⊠*Spalenberg 45, Grossbasel* ☎*061/2612550*) has miniature trains and accessories. **Spielegge** (⊠*Rümelinspl. 7, Grossbasel* ☎*061/2614488*) places an emphasis on wood, with chisel-carved puppets and whimsical watercolor puzzles of fairy-tale scenes. **Spiel-huus** (⊠*Eiseng. 8, Grossbasel* ☎*061/2649898*) is a good source for board games and reasonably priced children's toys, as well as fanciful Fasnacht costumes.

WOMEN'S CLOTHES

Le Mouton à Cinq Pattes (⊠ *Eiseng. 6, Grossbasel* ☎ *061/2620007*) sounds the siren call of a bargain; you'll find mostly cut-rate French and Italian styles. **Trois Pommes** (⊠ *Freie Str. 74, Grossbasel* ☎ *061/2729255*) dominates the high end of fashion, with Jil Sander, Prada, Gucci, and Dolce & Gabbana.

Fribourg & Neuchâtel

The summit of the Moleson in canton of Fribourg

WORD OF MOUTH

"There's just something about the entire character of the place that makes it what I would call 'real hometown Swiss'—its so non-touristy, so serene, and so much like what Switzerland probably is like without all the visitors."   —Wayne4

"Medieval Gruyères is one of Europe's finest walled towns, with very intact walls girdling a lovely old town with a castle of your dreams. Head to nearby Broc for a Willy Wonka experience: the Nestlé Chocolate factory."   —PalenQ

WELCOME TO FRIBOURG & NEUCHÂTEL

TOP REASONS TO GO

★ **Stir the melting pot:** Fondue—officially known as fondue fribourgeoise—was invented here partly to honor the region's famous, fabulous Gruyère cheese.

★ **Switzerland's largest lake:** Lac Neuchâtel is a great place for a boat trip, to try out wakeboarding, or to savor the fine fish served on its shores.

★ **You say Schloss:** And I say Château. In either language, this area has some of Switzerland's most impressive castles, from Grandson to Gruyères.

★ **Home-grown talent:** Whether it's the clockwork extravaganzas of Tinguely or the disturbing alienlike creations of Giger, these two sculptors are true eye-knockers.

★ **Gorgeous Gruyères:** Step into a postcard in this perfect specimen of a medieval stronghold, its single main street cozy within the ramparts.

1 Fribourg. One of Switzerland's best-kept secrets, Fribourg's medieval Old Town features steep, cobbled streets and bridges in all styles from wooden to suspension. Get enlightened with the cathedral's noted Art Nouveau stained glass.

2 Gruyères. Be sure to visit a modern and traditional demonstration dairy, both making famous regional cheeses like Vacherin Fribourgeois and Gruyère, then tour this car-free village, picture-box perfect with its castle and geranium-clad houses.

3 Murten. This bilingual lakeside resort with its boat-lined waterfront seems far too peaceful to have been home to a fierce battle—but back in 1476 the Swiss Confederates trounced the Burgundians here.

4 Neuchâtel. Flanked by vineyards and facing Lac Neuchâtel, this French-accented city celebrates the grape each fall with a weekend of parades and feasting. Enjoy its architecture—Romanesque to Rococo—and discover the Bronze Age lifestyle of stilt-house people at Laténium or the birthplace of precision timekeeping in "Watch Valley."

GETTING ORIENTED

This area is roughly organized like a hand. At the wrist are the Alpine foothills of Fribourg; these curve gently down to the palm of flatter Neuchâtel, with the long ellipse of Lac Neuchâtel. Beyond lie the Jura's rugged fingers, which form valleys in the Jura Mountains and finally come to rest on the plateaus.

8

FRIBOURG & NEUCHÂTEL PLANNER

The Good Table

Both Fribourg and Neuchâtel have a plethora of top-quality, French-influenced, *gastronomique* (ultragourmet) restaurants. They offer far cheaper lunch menus (three or more courses) or at least an *assiette du jour* (daily special) for less than 20 SF. No one here lays down strict dress codes. Ever sensible, the Swiss expect common sense from their customers: the fancier the restaurant, the fancier the attire, but you won't be thrown out for not wearing a tie. Restaurants open about 6 in the evening, though diners tend to arrive closer to 7:30, and kitchens wind down between 9:30 and 10. Lunch is usually served from 11:30 to 2, but you can often get simple fare even after that. For a quick, cheap meal that still has local flavor, try a crêperie. The closer you are to France, the more of these you'll find.

How's the Weather?

Spring and fall are beautiful times to visit anywhere in this region. During the summer temperatures reach an average of 18–20° C (65–68°F), which is comfortable, but crowds tend to pick up, especially in Gruyères. During a heatwave it's not unusual for temperatures to soar to 30° C (86°F). In winter the average temperature is 0–3° C (32–38°F). In the pre-Alps region there can be long periods of snowfall. January is great for winter sports. You can't be sure of snow in December, and in February some canton or other (not to mention the Germans, English, Dutch, and Italians) will invariably have school vacations, so slopes get pretty crowded. When the snow lasts, March is also ideal for skiing.

Feeling Festive

When the Alpine grass thins out in the fall, the cows of Haute Gruyères are led down to the village with huge bells around their necks and flowers and pine branches attached to their horns. Not to be outdone by their beasts, the cowherds wear their Sunday best: a dark blue jacket with embroidered edelweiss motifs and puffy short sleeves that optically double the width of the wearer's shoulders. To avoid two weeks of continual congestion on the roads, the foothill villages of Charmey (last Saturday in September) and Albeuve (first Saturday in October) have the herds descend together, making a folk festival of it—La Désalpe. Decorated cows, heifers, sheep, goats, and even pigs are paraded through the streets from 9 AM until about 3 PM. The partying goes on all day, with flag throwing, marching bands, alpenhorn playing, and stalls selling Bénichon (Kilbi in Swiss German) specialties. This harvest feast fetes not only the return of the cattle from the high pastures to the plains but also the season's final yield: chimney-smoked ham, served hot with moutarde de Bénichon (sweet mustard); mutton stew with plump raisins and potato puree; and tart poires-à-Botzi (pears poached in liquor and lightly caramelized). Don't worry if you miss La Désalpe itself, the restaurants across the region serve versions of Bénichon all fall.

Making the Most of Your Time

Though the major sights themselves don't require too much time to visit, they are scattered throughout the region, so it takes a while to get to them. You can easily explore much of this area by train or bus, while renting a car allows you to combine locations more efficiently.

If you have only one or two days, try to take in one or more of the cities. Neuchâtel and Fribourg have very different characters, and a day can easily be spent walking around the city centers, visiting a few of their museums, and sampling their restaurants.

If you cut out the museums, then each of these could be combined with a trip to one of the smaller towns we mention nearby. Check the distances in the chapter, and if traveling by public transport, ask the local tourist office in advance about what is possible.

More time allows you to tour the area and take in its subtle differences. If you start at Fribourg, cut south to the castle at Gruyères, and from there circle northwest through the ancient town of Murten on your way to Neuchâtel.

From Neuchâtel head south along the Route du Vignoble (Vineyard Road) to the château town of Grandson and onto Yverdon-les-Bains. Or spend some time pursuing the many sporting opportunities that the different seasons and towns have on offer.

Alternatively, summer is the perfect time to take a long trip on the Lake of Neuchâtel or to enjoy a hike.

Throughout the year you'll encounter lighter tourist traffic here than in any other region. Summer is a lovely time, when forest glades become ripe with the smells of the woods, but crowds tend to pick up, especially in Gruyères. Spring and fall are beautiful times to visit anywhere in this region. January is great for winter sports.

WHAT IT COSTS IN SWISS FRANCS

¢	$	$$	$$$	$$$$
RESTAURANTS				
under 15 SF	15 SF–25 SF	25 SF–40 SF	40 SF–60 SF	over 60 SF
HOTELS				
under 100 SF	100 SF–175 SF	175 SF–250 SF	250 SF–350 SF	over 350 SF

Restaurant prices are per person for a main course at dinner. Hotel prices are for two people in a standard double room in high season, including tax and service.

Finding a Place to Stay

As they become more tourist-oriented, Fribourg and Neuchâtel are developing a better hotel infrastructure. Fribourg is the best-equipped, though there's still only a handful of choices in the Old Town. In Neuchâtel most lodgings are along the lake. Don't expect air-conditioning either; assume hotels don't have it unless it's specified. Many hotels offer more than one meal plan, so even if BP (breakfast plan) is specified in a review, ask about other plans.

Around the Whirl

Bicycling is popular here, and itineraries are varied. You can struggle up Alpine passes, bounce over mountain-bike trails, or coast along the flat-lands around the lakes. Route maps can be picked up in most tourist offices or train stations. Swiss Federal Railways (CFF/SBB) offers reasonably priced rentals at most train stations. Bikes must be reserved at least one day in advance, three in summer. In addition, tourist offices in Fribourg run a unique program called Bike Broye. They've charted 20 different biking itineraries (a vineyard or abbey tour, for example), each of which comes with an overnight package. Reserve at least three weeks in advance; for July, two months in advance.

GETTING AROUND

By Air

Frequent flights from the United States and the United Kingdom arrive on Swiss and other international carriers, either at Geneva's Cointrin or Unique Zürich airports.

Fribourg lies between Geneva's Cointrin Airport (138 km [86 mi] to the southwest) and Unique Zürich Airport (180 km [112 mi] to the northeast). Train connections to both are good.

The Bern-Belp Airport is a small international airport 34 km (21 mi) northeast of Fribourg, near Bern.

Airport Information **Bern-Belp Airport** (☎ *031/9602111*). **Cointrin Airport** (☎ *022/ 7177111, 0900/571500 for arrivals and departures*). **Unique Zürich Airport** (☎ *0900/ 300313*).

By Bus & Tram

Postbus connections, except in the principal urban areas, can be few and far between.

Consequently, you should plan excursions carefully using the bus schedules available at the train station, or phone the local tourist office for advice.

By Boat & Ferry

There are frequent boat trips on the lakes of Neuchâtel and Murten (Morat) in summer and usually a host of themed evening trips. Contact La Navigation Lacs de Neuchâtel et Morat for more information.

Boat & Ferry Information **Navigation Lacs de Neuchâtel et Morat** (☎ *032/7299600* ⊕ *www.navig.ch*).

By Car

An important and scenic trans-Swiss artery, the A12 expressway cuts from Bern to Lausanne, passing directly above Fribourg.

A parallel route to the northwest extends the A1 between Zürich and Bern, connecting Bern to Murten, Payerne, and Lausanne.

There is an expressway, the A5, between Neuchâtel and Yverdon, but as this runs through a lot of tunnels, if you have the time take the national road for a scenic view of the lake shore.

The charms of this varied region can be experienced easily by car, and there are scenic secondary highways throughout.

Keep in mind that some towns, like Gruyères, are car-free or have pedestrians-only centers; in these cases, parking lots are easy to find.

By Train

The main train route connecting Basel, Zürich, and Geneva passes through the Fribourg station between Bern and Lausanne. Neuchâtel has hourly connections to main Swiss cities.

Regional train services to smaller destinations leave from the larger towns of Fribourg and Neuchâtel, though buses may be a more direct route. Ask the local tourist office for information.

Information (☎ *0900/300300 [1.19 SF per min]*).

Updated
by Suzanne
Hégelé

SHOULDERED BY THE MORE PROMINENT cantons of Bern and Vaud, the cantons of Fribourg and Neuchâtel are easily overlooked by hurried visitors. If they do stop, it is usually for a quick dip into Fribourg and Gruyères. That leaves the rest of this largely untouched area to the Swiss, who enjoy its relatively unspoiled nature and relaxed approach to life.

Although the strict cantonal borders are a messy reflection of historic power struggles, the regional boundaries are unmistakable, even to an outsider. Fribourg starts in the pre-Alpine foothills above Charmey and rolls down across green hills, tidy farms, and ancient towns until it reaches the silty shores of the Murten, Neuchâtel, and Biel lakes. The region of Neuchâtel begins in these silt-rich fields (which grow everything from lettuce to tobacco), sweeps across Lac Neuchâtel to its château- and vineyard-lined western shore, and rises up to the Jura Mountains.

The Röstigraben (or Hash-Brown Trench, so called because Swiss Germans eat lots of *Rösti*) is the tongue-in-cheek name for the linguistic border where French meets German. It runs through Fribourg and butts up against the northern borders of Neuchâtel. In some towns you can walk into a *boulangerie* (bread bakery) selling dark *Vollkornbrot* (whole-grain bread) or find a family named Neuenschwand that hasn't spoken German for generations.

Nature's delights take pride of place here. But no matter what aspect of history interests you, you should find something to please you here: from prehistoric menhirs and the lifestyle of stilt-house people at Laténium, near Neuchâtel, to imagining the Battle of Murten from the city's ramparts. Perhaps you'd prefer Grandson's castle, with Charles the Bold's ridiculously bejeweled hat and life-size, fully armored replicas of jousting knights. If you love Gothic churches and religious art, you can have your fill, especially in Fribourg and Neuchâtel. There's stained glass at Romont, and the sheer romantic thrill of medieval towns like storybook Gruyères.

FRIBOURG

With its landscape of green hills against the craggy peaks of the pre-Alps, Fribourg is one of Switzerland's most rural cantons. Its famous Fribourgeois cows—the Holsteins (black and white, the colors of the cantonal coat of arms)—provide the canton with its main income, although light industry is replacing the cows. Fondue was invented here, as was Gruyère cheese and Switzerland's famous *crème-double* (double cream).

FRIBOURG

★ *34 km (21 mi) southwest of Bern, 74 km (46 mi) northeast of Lausanne.*

GETTING HERE

Direct trains from Fribourg to major Swiss cities: Geneva, two per hour (1 hr 25 mins, 41 SF); Lausanne, two per hour (45–50 mins, 23 SF); Bern, two per hour (22–35 mins, 12.80 SF); Basel via Bern, no direct link (1 hr 30 mins, 48 SF); Zurich, two per hour, with every other train running direct (1 hr 24 mins, 53 SF). Buses leave from behind Fribourg's train station for villages in the surrounding canton. For departure times and prices for trains and buses for most destinations in this chapter, check with www.sbb.ch—the main Swiss public transportation Web site—or call 0900/300300 (1.19 SF per min). If your knowledge of French or German is good, then Fribourg and Neuchâtel offer Web sites with information on regional services: www.tpf.ch and www.trn.ch. Remember, if you have a Swiss Pass or another rail-discount card, it also applies to the buses. Fribourg is 34 km (21 mi) southwest of Bern.

Visitor Information (✉ *1 av. de la Gare* ☏ *026/3501111* ⊕ *www.fribourg tourism.ch*).

EXPLORING

Between the rich pasturelands of the Swiss plateau and the Alpine foothills, the Sarine River (called the Saane by German speakers) twists in an S-curve, its sandstone cliffs joined by webs of arching bridges. In one of the curves of the river is the medieval city of Fribourg. The city grew in overlapping layers; it's an astonishing place of hills and cobblestones, ramparts and Gothic fountains, ancient passageways and worn wooden stairs, red-orange rooftops and sudden views. Only on foot can you discover its secret charm as one of the finer ensembles of medieval architecture in Europe.

Fribourg is a stronghold of Catholicism; it remained staunchly Catholic even during the Reformation. The evidence is everywhere, from the numerous chapels and religious orders to the brown-robed novitiates walking the sidewalks. Fribourg University, founded in 1889, remains the only Catholic university in Switzerland. It is also the only bilingual institution of its kind and reflects the region's peculiar linguistic agility. Two-thirds of the people of Canton Fribourg are native French speakers, one-third are native German speakers, and many switch easily between the two. In the Basse-Ville neighborhood, old-timers still speak a unique mixture of the two languages called Boltz. The city is officially bilingual, although French predominates.

At its very core, and a good place to start a walk, is the **Basse-Ville** *(Lower City)*, tucked into a crook of the river. Here you'll find the 11th- through 16th-century homes of the original village as well as a lively café and cellar-theater scene.

The oldest bridge in this city of bridges is the **Pont de Berne** *(Bern Bridge)*, to the north of the Basse-Ville. Once the only access to the territory of Bern, it's made entirely of wood.

As the town expanded from the Basse-Ville, it crossed the river over the Pont du Milieu (Middle Bridge) to a narrow bank, the Planche-Inférieure, with its picturesque terraced houses. As the town prospered, it spread to the more stately 16th- and 17th-century **Planche-Supérieure**, a large, sloping, open triangular *place* (square) that was once the busy livestock market. It is now lined with several upscale restaurants and cafés. From here you can walk up to the **Chapelle de Lorette** (Loreto Chapel), once a favored pilgrimage site, for the best view of Fribourg.

When the Pont St-Jean was built in the 17th century, making the northern bank of the river readily accessible, the merchant houses and walled cloisters of the **Neuve-Ville** *(New Town)* popped up.

From the steep, partially cobbled Rue Grand-Fontaine (best avoided at night unless you like red-light districts), you can spy narrow passageways and hidden courtyards, or you can take the funicular up and walk down the Rue des Alpes to the **Hôtel de Ville**, or Rathaus (Town Hall). This is the seat of the cantonal parliament, built on the foundations of the château of Berthold IV of Zähringen, who founded the town of Fribourg in 1157. The symmetrical stairways were added in the 17th century, as were the clockworks in the 16th-century clock tower.

From the Place de Tilleul, the shop-lined Rue de Lausanne and Rue des Alpes climb upward, their tightly spaced 18th-century buildings hiding terraced gardens of surprising size. The 19th- and 20th-century section of the city begins at the top of Rue de Lausanne; nearby are the main buildings of the university. The 21st century has arrived in the form of the Fribourg Center shopping mall, close to the station.

★ A block away from the Hôtel de Ville, the Gothic **Cathédrale St-Nicolas** *(St. Nicholas Cathedral)* rears up from the surrounding gray 18th-century buildings. Its massive tower was completed in the 15th century, two centuries after construction of the cathedral was begun in 1283. Above the main portal, a beautifully restored tympanum of the Last Judgment shows the blessed being gently herded left toward Peter, who holds the key to the heavenly gates; those not so fortunate head right, led by pig-face demons, into the jaws and cauldrons of hell. Inside, you can see the famous 18th-century organ as well as the rare, restored 1657 organ. The exceptional stained-glass windows, installed between 1873 and 1983, are executed in a number of styles, including Pre-Raphaelite and Art Nouveau. In the **Chapelle du St-Sépulcre** (Chapel of the Holy Sepulchre) a group of 13 figures dating from 1433 portrays the entombment of Christ. If you can handle the 365 steps, climb up the tower for a panoramic view. (During services, you won't be allowed in.) ⊠ *Rue St-Nicolas* 🎫 *Free, tower 3.50 SF* ☉ *To tourists: Mon.–Fri. 9–6, Sat. 10–4, Sun. 2–5; tower Mar.–Nov., Mon–Fri. 10–noon and 2–5, Sat. 10–4, Sun. 2–5.*

From the cathedral, slip through the rue des Épouses to the Grand-rue, lined with 18th-century patrician

> **GO FOR THE VIEWS!**
>
> Climb the 365 steps of the tower of Cathédrale St-Nicolas for a stunning panoramic view.

homes. At the end of this street is the **Pont de Zaehringen** *(Zähringen Bridge)*, with views over the Pont de Berne, the Pont de Gottéron, and the wooden remains of the ancient towers that once guarded the entrance to the city. You're now in the area where Duke Berthold IV first established his residence and founded the city in 1157.

NEED A BREAK?

The terrace of **Le Café du Belvédère** (⊠ *36 Grand-rue* ☎ *026/3234407*) has a fabulous view up the river to the Planche-Supérieure. Inside it's a *café littéraire* by day and a lively bar and meeting spot at night. An eclectic mix of '70s plastic furniture and a huge, rounded plastic bar contrast wonderfully with the wood-beamed, old-cottagey feel of the building. The friendly staff serves a selection of teas, coffees, and homemade syrups as well as alcohol, and you can get Asian delights from the excellent Thai restaurant upstairs.

The 13th-century **Église des Cordeliers** *(Church of the Franciscan Friars)*, north of the cathedral, is attached to a Franciscan friary. The lightness of its white walls and the rose-, gray-, and alabaster-color ceiling contrast with the Gothic darkness of the cathedral. A 16th-century polyptych by the anonymous Nelkenmeister, or Maîtres à l'Oeillet (who signed their works only with red and white carnations), hangs over the high altar. A carved wood triptych, believed to be Alsatian, and a 15th-century retable of the temptation of St. Anthony by the Fribourg artist Hans Fries adorn the side walls. At the entrance to the cloister leading to the friary is a 13th-century five-panel fresco depicting the birth of the Virgin Mary. ⊠ *6 rue de Morat* ☎ *026/3471160* ☑ *Free* ☉ *Mon.–Sat. 9–6, Sun. noon–6.*

Near the Église des Cordeliers, the **Musée d'Art et d'Histoire de Fribourg** *(Fribourg Museum of Art and History)* is housed in the Renaissance Ratzé Mansion and, incongruously, an old slaughterhouse connected by an underground passage. The mansion displays 12th- to 19th-century art and history, including several works by Hans Fries. The 19th-century slaughterhouse, a stark stone structure modernized with steel-and-glass blocks, provides the setting for a provocative mix of sacred sculptures and the kinetic, scrap-iron whimsies of native son Jean Tinguely (1925–91). The attic gallery displays 19th- and 20th-century paintings from Swiss artists as well as from Delacroix, Courbet, and others. Take a breather in the quiet sculpture garden overlooking the river. Limited descriptive material in English is available upon request, and guided tours in English can be booked in advance. ⊠ *12 rue de Morat* ☎ *026/3055140* ⊕ *www.fr.ch/mahf* ☑ *6–8 SF* ☉ *Tues., Wed., and Fri.–Sun. 11–6, Thurs. 11–8.*

Once the city's tram terminal, the **Espace Jean Tinguely–Niki de Saint Phalle** now houses a selection of whirring, tapping, spinning metal sculptures by Jean Tinguely and a wall full of the voluptuous, colorful work of his wife, Niki de Saint Phalle. Her works are titled in English while his need no explanation. Kids (16 and under free) are often fascinated by Tinguely's work. Something is happening somewhere all the time: skis are walking, a potted plant is turning, a toy rabbit is being hit on

8

the head. ⊠2 *rue de Morat* ☎026/3055140 ⌑4–6 SF ⊘ *Wed. and Fri.–Sun. 11–6, Thurs. 11–8.*

The **Musée Suisse de la Machine à Coudre** *(Swiss Sewing Machine Museum)* displays an example of almost every sewing machine ever built (more than 250). There's also a collection of contraptions created to ease the life of handworkers and housewives before the age of electricity, including useful household firsts such as vacuum cleaners and washing machines. A side room is packed with curiosities from bygone days, such as chestnut-hulling boots. Owner Edouard Wassmer will charm you with anecdotes and history. ⊠58 *Grand-rue* ☎026/4752433 ⊕*www.museewassmer.com* ⌑7 SF ⊘ *By appointment only.*

WHERE TO EAT

$$

MODERN FRENCH

✕**Auberge de Zaehringen.** The oldest private house in Fribourg, now a brasserie, has been owned by only three families during its 700 years. The warmly lighted restaurant offers gracious service in a no-smoking environment, with traditional dishes on its menu such as beef fillet in a green pepper sauce. There are more exotic choices, too, like grilled salmon with mango and eggplant. Book a few days ahead for this popular spot, although in off hours they are ready to welcome guests out for a simple break of coffee and cake. ⊠13 *rue de Zaehringen* ☎026/3224236 ⌑*Reservations essential* ⊕*www.auberge-de-zaehringen.ch* ⊟AE, DE, MC, V ⊘*Closed Sun.*

$$–$$$

CONTINENTAL

✕**Auberge de la Cigogne.** In the Basse-Ville a friendly husband-and-wife team have created a flower-filled cozy restaurant (seating 35 to 40) from a former blacksmith shop. Opposite the wooden bridge, the building dates from 1771, and its fresco is the last one in Rococo-style in Fribourg. The menu is daring and changes five times a year, featuring dishes like caramelized veal with ginger and lemon served with spiced basmati rice; or turbot grilled on the bone with homemade orange butter and puréed potatoes flavored with virgin olive oil. For vegetarians there is a polenta cake, which once cut into oozes buffalo mozzarella; or ask for the seasonal house dish. ⊠24 *rue d'Or* ☎026/3226834 ⊕*www.la-cigogne.ch* ⊟AE, DC, MC, V ⊘*Closed Sun. and Mon.*

$$–$$$

MODERN FRENCH/MOD-ERN SWISS

Fodor's Choice

★

✕**Des Trois Tours.** If you have a penchant for innovative, excellent food that is superbly presented, try this award-winning restaurant gastronomique just outside town. You can eat in the sunny, plant-filled bistro; in the more discreet ocher-and-blue dining room; or on the shady terrace in summer. Fast beforehand, because a *menu du marché* (market menu) costs 110 SF to 135 SF, and you'll want to relish it all. Perhaps you'll eat your way from the lasagna of crepes and wild mushrooms to the mosaic of fruits and sorbets via a mouthwatering series of mains and a groaning cheese trolley, but then again, perhaps not. To reach this spot, take the bus from Fribourg train station to Bourguillon; it leaves every hour from track No. 13 until early evening (10- to 15-mins journey, 2.70 SF). There is also a night bus. Taxis take around the same amount of time and cost 20–30 SF ⊠15 *rte. de Bourguillon, Bourguillon* ☎026/3223069 ⌑*Reservations essential* ⊟AE, DC, MC, V ⊘*Closed Sun. and Mon., plus late July–early Aug., late Dec.–early Jan.*

EATING WELL IN FRIBOURG & NEUCHÂTEL

The cuisines of these two regions all use robust, seasonal food: perch from the lakes, game and mushrooms from the forested highlands, and, of course, the dairy products of Fribourg and Gruyères. In the lake towns, menus are thick with *perche* (perch), *sandre* (a large cousin of the perch), *bondelle* (a pearly-fleshed trout found exclusively in Lac Neuchâtel), or *silure* (catfish). Mushrooms are another strong suit, from the delicate *Schwämli* (*chanterelles* in French) to the robust *Steinpilz* (*bolets* in French), fat, fleshy mushrooms with a meaty texture and taste. These are particularly wonderful when sautéed and served with slices of dark bread or with local rabbit or venison, along with a glass of Neuchâtel pinot noir.

Many regions of Switzerland are known for fondue, but Fribourg is the source of *fondue fribourgeoise*, the combination of the canton's two greatest cheeses—Gruyère and Vacherin Fribourgeois—into a creamy *moitié-moitié* (half-and-half) blend. The Vacherin can be melted alone for an even creamier fondue, and potatoes can be dipped instead of bread.

Those familiar cows dotting the green landscape of the Fribourg countryside yield more than cheese, however. An additional debt of gratitude is owed them for producing crème-double, a Gruyères specialty that rivals Devonshire cream.

A rich, extra-thick, high-fat cream that—without whipping—almost supports a standing spoon, it is served in tiny carved-wood *baquets* (vats), to be spooned over a bowl of berries and meringues.

8

$$ ✕ **L'Epée.** It's a good idea to make reservations at this popular brasserie
FRENCH in the Basse-Ville. The food is delicious (often with unique spices and garnishes added) and reasonably priced, the staff is friendly, and the view up to the cathedral and the Neuve-Ville is a real draw—from inside or the terrace, by day or night. Options include ricotta-filled ravioli in an onion and mushroom sauce, an oh-so-tender rack of lamb with basil, and meringues with *vin cuit* (cooked wine) and Gruyère cream. ⊠ *39 Planche-Supérieure* ☎ *026/3223407* ⊟ *DC, MC, V* ⊘ *Closed Sun. and late July–late Aug. No dinner Mon.*

¢ ✕ **Xpresso Café.** On the fourth floor of the Fribourg Center, this café–
FRENCH crêperie does waffles and crepes—both savory and sweet. You can also choose from a wide selection of teas and coffees. Set in a shopping center, this outpost of a popular Swiss chain offers a perfect time-out from heavy-duty retail therapy. ⊠ *12 av. de la Gare* ☎ *026/3417808* ⊟ *No credit cards.* ⊘ *Closed Sun. No dinner.*

WHERE TO STAY

$–$$ ▨ **Auberge aux 4 Vents.** Guests book as early as four months ahead
Fodor'sChoice for this quirky, high-style country inn noted for its fabulous gardens
★ and themed rooms. Of the guest rooms, "Babylone" is exceedingly picturesque with its red-and-white tiled interior and raised bed, while "Bleue" flaunts a cast-iron bath on rails—you can trolley out into the open air for a bath under the stars. "Anges" has a stunning red velvet-draped bed, while "Grandfey" is a turn-off—too close to the northern

autoroute exit. Downstairs, the restaurant is nightclub-glamorous, a perfect setting for meeting the exceedingly photogenic couple that run this fun spot. The hotel can be reached by bus from Fribourg (Bus No.1 direction Portes de Fribourg/St. Leonard; get off at Poya [fare 2.70 SF], and then it's a charming 10-minute walk up the Rue de Grandfey). Be sure to check out the Web site for a preview taste of the creative eccentricities of the owners. Many say "fantastique," but formal traditionalists may feel out of place here. **Pros:** individuality and unique quirky character of venue; personal style of the owners. **Cons:** not convenient to central Fribourg. ⊠ *124 rue de Grandfey* ☎ *026/3473600* ⊕ *www. aux4vents.ch* 🛏 *8 rooms* ♻ *In-room: no a/c, no TV (some), Wi-Fi (fee). In-hotel: restaurant, bar, pool, public Wi-Fi (fee), parking (free), some pets allowed (fee), no elevator* ⊟ *MC, V* ☾ *Closed first 3 wks of Jan. and every Wed.* ⑩ *BP.*

$$ 📺 **Best Western Hôtel de la Rose.** In a typical 17th-century sandstone house, this hotel is within walking distance of museums, churches, the cathedral, and the Old Town. The hotel is friendly and familial, all rooms have been recently renovated and offer tea- and coffeemaking facilities. Ask for a quiet room away from the main street. This option is favored for business meetings and, as such, has all modern facilities but in an historic setting. Comfort is ensured, and old-world charm has not been lost in renovations. The restaurant Chez Dino offers Italian and international fare with a fairly good wine list to boot. **Pros:** excellent central location; high-quality service; friendly disposition of staff. **Cons:** on Fribourg's noisy main street—ask for a back room if you are a light sleeper; no air-conditioning, a nuisance in summer months. ⊠ *1 rue Morat* ☎ *026/3510101* ⊕ *www.hoteldelarose.ch* 🛏 *40 rooms* ♻ *In-room: no a/c, safe, refrigerator, Wi-Fi (free). In-hotel: restaurant, bar, public Wi-Fi (free), public Internet (fee), parking (fee), some pets allowed (fee)* ⊟ *AE, DC, MC, V* ⑩ *BP.*

¢ 📺 **Ibis.** Near the northern *autoroute* (expressway) exit and a mere six-minute drive from Fribourg city, this modern budget hotel appeals to those traveling by car. At the edge of town, it's close to the casino and the convention center (Le Forum). Guest rooms are simple, appointed in turquoise and ocher; triple-glazed windows keep out most of the noise from the main road. Some rooms have pull-out beds so children under 12 can stay for free. Two rooms are accessible and fully equipped for people in wheelchairs. The hotel has air-conditioning. **Pros:** bargain-basement, straightforward establishment—you get what you pay for; easy to find; surprisingly spacious rooms. **Cons:** no evening meals available; not the best location if you travel car-free, as it is not central; if you loathe motel-style accommodation, give Ibis a wide berth. ⊠ *21 rte. du Lac Granges-Paccot (3.5 km/2 mi north of Fribourg)* ☎ *026/4697900* ⊕ *www.accorhotels.com* 🛏 *82 rooms* ♻ *In-room: Wi-Fi (fee), In-hotel: bar, public Wi-Fi (fee), parking (no fee), some pets allowed (fee)* ⊟ *AE, DC, MC, V* ⑩ *EP.*

$$–$$$ 📺 **Romantik Hotel Restaurant Au Sauvage.** The Sauvage began in the 1600s
★ as a cloister, became an inn during the cattle-market days in the 18th and 19th centuries, and is now a sophisticated auberge with a striking blend of minimalism and medieval details. In the guest rooms, thick,

whitewashed stone walls hide TVs, while sleek bathrooms include elegant vanities. The small dining room (closed Sunday and Monday, and all of July), under the original vaulted ceiling, serves French-influenced seasonal cuisine, such as beef in a pesto-and-cheese crust and fish served with exotic fruit and green curry. **Pros:** enchantingly steeped in medieval history; central location. **Cons:** staff does not always speak English willingly (if at all). ⊠ *12 Planche-Supérieure* ☎*026/3473060* ⊕*www. hotel-sauvage.ch* ⇆*17 rooms* ⌂*In-room: no a/c, safe, refrigerator, Wi-Fi (free). In-hotel: restaurant, bar, public Wi-Fi (free), parking (free), some pets allowed (fee)* ⊟*AE, MC, V* ⍟*BP.*

NIGHTLIFE

BARS To get a feel for Fribourg's nightlife, try one of the cellar bars scattered throughout the Old Town, such as **La Cave de la Rose** (⊠*1 rue de Morat* ☎*026/3510101*), which stays open into the wee hours of the morning. **Elvis et Moi** (⊠*13 rue de Morat* ☎*026/3220755*) offers live music and DJs in a kitschy, Elvis-inspired interior. It's open Tuesday to Saturday from 5. An 18th-century inn, seemingly in the middle of nowhere, has been turned into **Planet Edelweiss** (⊠*Mariahilf 1* ✛*Düdingen* ☎*026/4920505*), a lively *restaurant de nuit* and disco. Its diverse crowd (ranging from bankers to farmers) doesn't get going until after 10, and the bar stays open until 2 AM Sunday–Thursday, 4 AM Friday and Saturday. The 12-minute taxi ride from town runs about 25 SF.

CASINO Near the northern autoroute exit, the **Casino de Fribourg** (⊠*11 rte. du Lac, Granges-Paccot* ☎*026/4677000*) opened in 2003. In addition to roulette, blackjack, poker, and 100 poker machines, the casino has a restaurant and offers regular shows. A five-minute taxi ride from town costs around 12 SF.

EN ROUTE ⌚ On the way from Fribourg or Charmey to Gruyères, chocoholics should consider stopping at the tantalizing **Nestlé Chocolaterie** *(chocolate factory)*, in the otherwise unassuming town of Broc. Founded by Alexandre Cailler in 1889 and bought by Nestlé in 1929, it offers a 40-minute tour and video, followed by a chocolate tasting. Look for chocolate-brown signs marking the way. ⊠*Broc* ☎*026/9215151* ▱*Free* ⊙*May–Oct., Mon.–Sun. 9:30–4.*

GRUYÈRES

Fodor'sChoice *35 km (21 mi) south of Fribourg.*
★

GETTING HERE

To connect with Gruyères via public transport, buses from Fribourg are your best bet. Take a bus to Bulle and change to another bus that heads directly to Gruyères (a trip of 1 hr 15 mins, six to seven connections per day). Alternatively, take the bus to Bulle, then change to a train and get off at the town of Gruyères in front of the cheese dairy La Maison du Gruyère. Walk up to the town (approx. 10 minutes). This option takes 1 hour, and there are hourly connections. If training from Lausanne or

8

Cheese: Fribourg's Calling Card

A traveler cruising Switzerland's emerald hills and villages far from industrial turf can't help but notice the damp, fresh, earthy ephemera of the dairy that hangs in the air—a mild, musky tang that scents the cream, thickens the chocolate, and alchemizes the cheese.

And nowhere else will you smell this as strongly as in the region of Fribourg—this is the region that gave birth to the most famous cheese that goes into fondue, Gruyère, and it sits shoulder-to-shoulder with two other areas that gave us great cheeses: Emmentaler (near Bern) and Tête de Moine from the Jura Mountains.

Today, as always, Swiss cheese is most delightfully experienced in that most satisfying of all Swiss dishes, fondue, which first became fashionable in America during the 1950s ski craze. Those who have not acquired the habit feel uncomfortably replete after only a few mouthfuls.

Halfway through the repast a halt is called, presumably to draw breath, and the pause is mellowed by a small glass of Kirsch—the perfect digestif (guests are warned never to drink water or beer after fondue but only white wine, Kirsch, tea, or coffee). Whether you favor fondue, raclette, or *salées au fromage* (cheese cakes), cheese is the star in this region.

The word fondue comes from the French *fondre* ("to melt"). With its pungent crushed garlic and sting of kirsch stirred through the creamy molten mass, its flavors are relatively complex. Different regions press the subtlety further by blending local cheeses: Proportions of aged Gruyère and milder Emmental vary,

and in Fribourg, it's also made with a creamy Vacherin.

No matter which province you try it in, it is comforting to know that the convivial system of sharing fondue around a table dates back to the ancient peasant tradition of circling around a common pot for the family meal. For that matter, cheese is available around the clock.

A good Swiss breakfast won't be served without a fan of brown-skinned slices of Gruyère, Emmentaler (the one with the holes that gave "Swiss cheese" its name), or Appenzeller.

Cubed cheese may show up in your lunch salad of *Käsesalt*. And after a French-style meal, there's always the cheese course.

One of the most unique options is the Tête de Moine from the Jura, which is shaved off in spiraling ruffles with a crank.

The great commercial cheese factories of Gruyères and Emmental are vast factories, but head into the hills of Fribourg and you'll still see old copper pots sizzling over wood fires.

Each family of cheesemakers stirs its own daily milk, gathers up the thick curd in broad cheesecloth, squeezes out excess whey with a wooden press, and molds the cheese into a round wheel.

Each cheese is then stamped with the family brand and delivered to a modern cooperative *affineur* who carefully supervises its aging until the farmer reclaims the finished product, to sell or keep as he likes.

Zürich, transfer to a local train at Palézieux—this rail journey takes about five hours.

Visitor Information (⊠ *Village Center* ☎ *026/9211030* ⊕ *www.gruyeres.ch*).

EXPLORING

Rising above the plain on a rocky crag and set against a backdrop of Alpine foothills, the castle village of Gruyères seduces from afar. This perfect specimen of a medieval stronghold comes complete with a cobbled main street, stone fountains, and well-preserved houses whose occupants try to outdo each other with picturesque facades and gera-nium displays in summer. The town was once the capital of the Alpine estates of the Burgundian counts of Gruyères, and its traditional crest bears a stylized crane (*grue*). Gruyères is car-free, so you'll have to park in one of three lots outside town and walk up from the Maison du Gruyère.

★ Between 1080 and 1554, 19 counts held political power over this region, and they built and expanded the **château.** Little is known about them except for the last, Michel. A lover of luxury and a big spender, he expanded the estates and then fled his creditors in 1555. In 1849 a wealthy Geneva family bought the castle and encouraged painter friends to decorate a room now known as Corot's Room, as it features four of his landscapes. Also worth seeing is the Knights' Room with its impressive 19th-century fresco cycle depicting local legends, and the aptly named Fantastic Art Room for contemporary work. A new 18-minute multimedia show called *Gruyères* is now shown daily in the old caretaker's lodge and is worth making time for, bringing to life the history of the castle in animated form (available in eight languages). ☎ *026/9212102* ⊕ *www.chateau-gruyeres.ch* 🎟 *9.50 SF* ⊙ *Apr.–Oct., daily 9–6; Nov.–Mar., daily 10–4:30.*

Most people will get enough of an idea about the enormously tal-ented but equally tormented H. R. Giger just by sitting in the Giger Bar, opposite the **Giger Museum.** Here you can admire ceiling buttresses that look like elongated backbones with ribs, and his ingenious trademark chairs: yet more spines and ribs, with pelvises for headrests. Giger won an Academy Award for his set design for the horror film *Alien;* he's not likely to win any prizes for his cheerful, healthy outlook on life (or women). That said, a few of his sculpture/furniture pieces are very good. Just avoid looking at the walls if you want to enjoy lunch afterward. ⊠ *Château St. Germain* ☎ *026/9212200* ⊕ *www.hrgigermuseum.com* 🎟 *12 SF* ⊙ *Apr.–Oct., daily 10–6; Nov.–Mar., Tues.–Fri. 1–5, weekends 10–6, closed Mon.*

Before going up to town, you can visit the very touristy **Maison du Gruyère,** a demonstration *fromagerie* (cheese dairy) where the famous cheese is produced with fully modernized equipment. Demonstrations are given three to four times a day, depending on the season. ⊠ *Pringy-Gruyères* ☎ *026/9218400* ⊕ *www.lamaisondugruyere.ch* 🎟 *7 SF* ⊙ *June–Sept., daily 9–7; Oct.–May, daily 9–6.*

WHERE TO EAT

$–$$ ✕ **Auberge de la Halle.** Set amid Gru-
SWISS yères's most historic buildings, the
exterior of this venue is an imposing medieval structure, adorned in
flowing flower boxes. Inside, the
unfussy interior of this medieval
hostelry, with its massive raftered
ceiling, wood-panelled walls, and
smooth stone floor, feels like a 16th-
century burgher's home. Choose the
front rooms for people-watching or
the back terrace for admiring the
town ramparts while you savor tra-
ditional Gruyères dishes, such as fondue with potatoes. They have a
signature dish called Soupe de Chalet, which is worth a try. ⊠ *24 rue
de Bourg* ☎ *026/9212178* ⊕ *www.chalet-gruyeres.ch* ⊟ *AE, MC, V*
☿ *Closed Tues.–Wed. Oct.–Apr.*

> **LOCAL SPECIALTIES**
>
> Gruyères is known for its blue-
> and-white or dark-red-and-white
> pottery decorated with the *grue*,
> as well as for creamy, nutty
> cheeses (Vacherin and Gruyère,
> spelled without the town's s),
> and the 48% butterfat crème-
> double, which is served with a
> bowl of berries or crumbly,
> sweet meringues.

WHERE TO STAY

$–$$ 🏨 **Hostellerie des Chevaliers.** Standing outside the main gates of Gruyères,
★ this traditional, family-friendly hotel has the same views overlooking
the valley and the castle as in-town lodgings, without the noise. Guest-
room decor mixes regional antiques, handsome woodwork, and ceramic
stoves with contrasting color schemes. Though the hotel no longer has a
restaurant, breakfast is served in the dining room, and additional meal
plans are offered using the restaurant of the Hostellerie St-Georges. A
small detail to note is the art exhibit between the hotel and the adjacent
conference-center underpass. **Pros:** quieter location than other options
yet still very central; friendly, personal service. **Cons:** no restaurant
in-house; rooms and beds are outdated, even taking into account the
antique style. ⊠ *Gruyères* ☎ *026/9211933* ⊕ *www.gruyeres-hotels.
ch* ⇄ *34 rooms* ⌂ *In-room: no a/c, safe, refrigerator. In-hotel: parking
(free), some pets allowed (fee)* ⊟ *AE, DC, MC, V* ☿ *Closed Jan. and
Feb.* ⋈ *BP.*

$$ 🏨 **Hostellerie St-Georges.** With delicious views out the windows, this
hotel is a treat. Tastier still is the excellent restaurant, anchored by a
massive fireplace. At lunch you have the option of taking in the vistas
from the large, light-filled winter garden. As for the guest rooms, the
four larger double rooms are spacious and cheerful, and have traditional
wood decor and white, edelweiss-embroidered bed linen, plus a slew of
breathtaking mountain and Sarine valley views. Ten smaller rooms are
also available. Bathrooms are sizable and clean, if a little old-fashioned.
Pros: fine food and atmospheric dining is second to none; stunning
views. **Cons:** flies can be a problem during summer months; small and
noisy rooms are at front of house, so ask for larger back rooms with
views. ⊠ *Main street* ☎ *026/9218300* ⊕ *www.st-georges-gruyeres.ch*
⇄ *14 rooms* ⌂ *In-room: no a/c, safe, refrigerator, Wi-Fi (free). In-hotel:
restaurant, public Wi-Fi (free), parking nearby (free), some pets allowed
(fee)* ⊟ *AE, DC, MC, V* ☿ *Closed Nov.–Mar.* ⋈ *BP.*

CLOSE UP

La Désalpe

When the Alpine grass thins out in the fall, the cows of Haute Gruyères are led down to the village stables—in style, with huge bells around their necks and flowers and pine branches attached to their horns. Not to be outdone by their beasts, the cowherds wear their Sunday best: a dark blue jacket with embroidered edelweiss motifs and puffy short sleeves that optically double the width of the wearer's shoulders. With their black-trimmed straw caps, fancy pipes, and bushy beards, the men are the real stars of the day. The women, in red-checked aprons and flat straw hats, stay in the background.

To avoid two weeks of continual congestion on the roads, the foothill villages of Charmey (last Saturday in September) and Albeuve (first Saturday in October) have the herds descend together, making a folk festival of it. Decorated cows, heifers, sheep, goats, and even pigs are paraded through the streets from 9 AM until about 3 PM. The partying goes on all day, with flag throwing, marching bands, alpenhorn playing, and stalls selling Bénichon specialties. (Originally a benediction of the church, Bénichon has become a harvest celebration.)

Watch for the *poyas* adorning the front walls of Gruyères farmhouses. These are naive-style paintings of cows filing up to the high pastures in spring. They advertise which breed the farmer owns and symbolize hope for a productive summer. (Before the 1820s, cheese was only made up on the Alps, where the cows had the lushest grass; so farmers had four months a year to make their living.)

8

$$-$$$ ★ **Hôtel De Ville.** Set on the cobbled stone village square, this welcoming countryside hotel has large, airy guest rooms; tastefully renovated, they mix bright Tuscan colors with traditional pine furniture. Back rooms overlook the valley, front rooms the village. The honeymoon suite, with a pretty, cotton-trimmed four-poster bed, is available for a romantic getaway (including four-course meal and champagne for two). The restaurant serves steaming fondue, raclette, local trout from Gruyères, and other Swiss dishes. Special low rates in the quiet season are attractive. **Pros:** authentic, traditional country hotel in enchanting medieval setting; private terrace encircled by castle walls for private dining. **Cons:** rich fondue smell may be too pungent for the faint-hearted. There is no elevator. ⊠ *Main street* ☎*026/9212424* 🛏*8 rooms* ⚎*In-room: no a/c, Wi-Fi (fee). In-hotel: restaurant, public Wi-Fi (fee), parking nearby (free)* ⊟*AE, DC, MC, V* ⦿*BP.*

$$ **La Fleur de Lys.** From its vaulted, stenciled reception area to its pine-and-beam restaurant, this is a welcoming little hotel set in a pink-hued historic building. The plain, spacious guest rooms contain '50s-style wooden furniture, and a large rear terrace and garden have a wonderful view of the mountains and town castle. They serve traditional Swiss and continental fare in the restaurant—top options include the fillet of rabbit with basil and the sautéed lamb casserole with saffron—changing the menus to follow the local seasonal specialties. Breakfast is an extra 15 SF per person. **Pros:** idyllic central location with beautiful views; intimate, friendly service. **Cons:** high-tech modern amenities are not

a part of this rustic abode; should you be looking for a buzzing social scene look elsewhere. ✉*14 rue du Bourg* ☎*026/9218282* ⊕*www. hotelfleurdelys.ch* 🛏*10 rooms* 🛆*In-room: no a/c, Wi-Fi (free). In-hotel: restaurant, public Wi-Fi (free), parking nearby (free), some pets allowed (fee)* ▭*AE, DC, MC, V* ⊙*Closed Feb.* ⊚*EP.*

OFF THE
BEATEN
PATH

Fromagerie d'Alpage. For a more authentic, historical perspective on cheese making than the Maison du Gruyère provides, visit the Magnin family's cheese-making operation on the edge of Moléson village. Watch the true Vacherin Fribourgeois cheese or the local Lutin de Moléson being made in a cauldron over an open fire in the low-roofed chalet, just as it has been made since the 17th century. There is also a 15-minute video, subtitled in English, describing the process of cheese making. A small restaurant serves traditional local dishes. ✉*12 pl. de l'Aigle, Moléson-sur-Gruyères* ☎*026/9211044* ⊕*www.fromagerie-alpage.ch* 💳*3 SF* ⊙*May–Oct., daily 9–7; demonstrations May at 10; June–Aug. at 10 and 2:30; Sept. at 10. Reservations advised.*

SKIING

At 3,609 feet, **Moléson,** Gruyère's "house mountain," offers skiing up to 6,568 feet and wraparound views of the pre-Alps and on to Lac Léman (Lake Geneva). The area has three cable cars, four lifts, 20 km (12 mi) of downhill ski runs, and 8 km (5 mi) of cross-country trails.

BULLE

5 km (3 mi) northwest of Gruyères, 31 km (19 mi) southwest of Fribourg.

GETTING HERE

Trains from Fribourg to Bulle, one per hour, change in Romont (45 mins, 16.80 SF). There is direct bus service from Fribourg station, one per hour (32 mins, 14.20 SF).

EXPLORING

With 16,000 inhabitants, the town of Bulle has many attractions worthy of a larger destination: a castle (not open to the public), three-storied patrician houses lining the cobblestone main street, and a scenic backdrop so perfect you might think it has been painted.

You can learn about Gruyères traditions at the **Musée Gruérien,** which contains displays of folk costumes, handicrafts, and farm tools—it even has a full reproduction of a flagstone farmhouse kitchen and dining room. ✉*25 rue de la Condémine* ☎*026/9127260* ⊕*www.musee-gru-erien.ch* 💳*8 SF* ⊙*Tues.–Sat. 10–noon, 2–5, Sun. 2–5.*

ROMONT

15 km (9 mi) northwest of Bulle, 49 km (30 mi) southwest of Fribourg.

GETTING HERE

Trains from Fribourg to Romont, two direct per hour (30 mins, 9.20 SF).

EXPLORING

The best way to approach this 13th-century town of two broad streets is to leave the highway and drive up to its castle terrace. The fortress's 13th-century ramparts surround the town, forming a belvedere from which you can see the Alps—from Mont Blanc to the Berner Oberland. You'll also find a 12th-century Cistercian convent, the 17th-century Capuchin monastery, and the lovely 13th-century Collégiale, one of the purest examples of a Gothic church in Switzerland, with period (and modern) windows, sculptures, choir stalls, a screen, and an altarpiece.

Inside the castle, the **Vitromusée** *(Stained-Glass Museum)* shimmers with crisscrossing shafts of colored light from its glass panels, both ancient and contemporary. A slide presentation traces the development of the craft, and a workshop area demonstrates current techniques. The museum now includes a donated collection of reverse painting on glass. ⊠*Château* ☎*026/6521095* ⊕*www.vitromusee.ch* 🎫*10 SF* ☉*Mar.– Nov., Tues.–Sun. 10–1, 2–6; Nov.–Mar., Thurs.–Sun. 10–1, 2–5.*

PAYERNE

8

15 km (9 mi) north of Romont, 18 km (11 mi) west of Fribourg.

GETTING HERE

Trains from Fribourg to Payerne, one direct per hour (30 mins, 7.80 SF); from Neuchátel to Payerne, two per hour, change at Murten or Yverdon (47–52 mins, 17–21 SF).

Visitor Information (⊠*10 pl. du Marché* ☎*026/6606161* ⊕*www.payerne.ch*).

EXPLORING

The meandering streets in this market town are filled with pastel-painted 18th-century buildings, now shops and restaurants. Above them stands a magnificent 11th-century *église abbatiale (abbey church)*, one of the finest examples of Romanesque art in Switzerland. You can visit its restored austere abbey, including a grand barrel-vaulted sanctuary and primitive capital carvings on the pillars. The church often hosts painting exhibitions and organ concerts. *026/6626704* 🎫*3 SF if no exhibition* ☉*Summer: Tues.–Sun. 10–noon, 2–6; winter: Tues.–Sun. 10–noon, 2–5.*

ESTAVAYER-LE-LAC

7 km (4 mi) northwest of Payerne, 51 km (32 mi) southwest of Neuchâtel.

GETTING HERE

Trains from Fribourg to Estavayer-le-Lac, one direct per hour (35 mins, 11.40 SF); from Neuchâtel to Estavayer-le-Lac, one per hour, change at Yverdon (41 mins, 18.20 SF).

Visitor Information (⌂*11 rue de L'Hôtel de Ville* ☎*026/6631237* ⊕*www. estavayer-le-lac.ch*).

EXPLORING

Modest Estavayer-le-Lac, on the shore of Lac Neuchâtel, can still be navigated using a map drawn in 1599. It has retained much of its medieval architecture, from the arcades of the town center to the gracious, multitowered medieval **Château de Chenaux,** which now houses city government offices.

For something completely different, visit the quirky **Musée de Grenouilles** *(Frog Museum).* Here are displays of 108 embalmed frogs posed like people in scenes of daily life from the 19th century. Other exhibits include an authentic 17th-century kitchen, various military and household artifacts dredged from Lac Neuchâtel, and more than 200 Swiss railroad lanterns. ⌂*13 rue des Musées* ☎*026/6632448* ⊕*www. museedesgrenouilles.ch* ⌦*5 SF* ⊗*Mar.–June, Sept., and Oct., Tues.– Sun. 10–noon, 2–5; July and Aug., daily 10–noon, 2–5; Nov.–Feb., weekends 2–5.*

WHERE TO STAY

$ 🏨 **Hotel du Lac.** Although this blocky, semi-modern hotel is short on old-world charm, it's the only lodging in town with a lakeside location. The harbor and grassy park are completely relaxing; in spring you can watch the swans nesting from the terrace. Guest rooms are unpretentious and in need of renovation (they seem to have got stuck somewhere in the 1970s). Despite this, rooms are clean and comfortable, and some have balconies. Families are welcome, and interconnecting rooms are available. **Pros:** only lakeside hotel in town; unpretentious and affordable. **Cons:** dated decor; not strong on character and individual charm. ⌂*6 rte du Débarcadère* ☎*026/6635220* ⊕*www.hotel-restaurant-du-lac.ch* ⌦*36 rooms* ⌂*In-room: no a/c, safe, Wi-Fi (fee). In-hotel: restaurant, public Wi-Fi (free), parking (fee), some pets allowed (free)* ▤*AE, DC, MC, V* ⌾*BP.*

MURTEN

★   *19 km (12 mi) northeast of Estavayer-le-Lac, 17 km (11 mi) north of Fribourg.*

GETTING HERE

Trains from Fribourg to Murten, one per hour (25 mins, 10.40 SF); from Neuchâtel to Murten, one direct per hour (24 mins, 11.40 SF).

Visitor Information Murten (✉ *Franz-Kirchg. 6* ☎ *026/6705112* ⊕ *www. murtentourismus.ch*).

EXPLORING

The ancient town of Murten, known in French as Morat, is a popular resort on the Murtensee/Lac de Morat (Lake Murten). The bilingual town has a boat-lined waterfront, Windsurfer rentals, a lakeside public pool complex, grassy picnic areas, and a promenade as well as a superbly preserved medieval center. Leave your car in the parking area in front of the 13th-century gates and stroll the fountain-studded cobblestone streets. Climb up the worn wooden steps to the town ramparts for a view of the lake over a chaos of red roofs and stone chimneys.

The town's most memorable moment came on June 22, 1476, when the Swiss Confederates—already a fearsomely efficient military machine—attacked with surprising ferocity and won a significant victory over the Burgundians, who were threatening Fribourg under the leadership of Duke Charles the Bold. Begun as a siege 12 days earlier, the battle cost the Swiss 410 men, the Burgundians 12,000. The defeat at Murten prevented the establishment of a large Lothringian kingdom and left Switzerland's autonomy unchallenged for decades. Legend has it that a Swiss runner, carrying a linden branch, ran from Murten to Fribourg to carry the news of victory. He expired by the town hall, and a linden tree grew from the branch he carried. Today, to commemorate his dramatic sacrifice, some 15,000 runners participate annually on the first Sunday in October in a 17-km (11-mi) race up the steep hill from Murten to Fribourg. As for the linden tree, it flourished in Fribourg for some 500 years until 1983, when it was ingloriously felled by a drunk driver. It has been replaced with a steel sculpture.

The **Musée de Morat** *(Murten Museum)* is in the town's old mill, complete with two water-powered mill wheels. On view are prehistoric finds from the lake area, military items, and trophies from the Burgundian Wars. ✉ *4 Ryf* ☎ *026/6703100* ⊕ *www.museummurten.ch* 🎫 *6 SF* ⊙ *Apr.–Nov., Tues.–Sat. 2–5, Sun. 10–5.*

WHERE TO EAT

$$–$$$ ✕ **Ringmauer.** Whether in the simpler brasserie or the dining section, this
FRENCH rustic restaurant in the city wall offers good value for money. Try the *confit de canard* (duck leg in a garlic and parsley sauce) or the regional pan-fried perch fillets. There is a daily menu that changes. You can enjoy the terrace in summer and take your predinner drinks by the fire in winter. There are also 28 guestrooms to take advantage of, which are decorated with paintings by Swiss artists. ✉ *Deutsche Kirchg. 2* ☎ *026/6701101* ▤ *MC, V* ⊙ *Closed Sun. and Mon.*

WHERE TO STAY

$$–$$$ ▥ **Hotel Murtenhof & Krone.** An ensemble of patrician houses dating back
Fodor'sChoice to 1428 nestled in the heart of Murten's Old Town conjures memo-
★ ries of centuries gone by. Yet step inside, and the modern sits well alongside the revered history of this establishment, thanks to the sensibilities of the Joachim family, which has been running the show since 1978. Guest rooms are individually designed and vary greatly. Suites

8

are more substantial and proffer luxury amenities; try out the Royal Senior suite if 16th-century Baroque drawing rooms are your thing! The tavern and veranda are pleasant venues for the generous morning spread, and a changing á la carte menu for fine dining in the restaurant keeps guests sated. **Pros:** individuality and heritage of establishment very much cherished; location for lake views and in the heart of the peaceful Old Town; kindly and quirky staff. **Cons:** some say the walls are a tad too thin! ⊠*Rathausg. 1–3* ☎*026/6729030* ⊕*www. murtenhof.ch* 🛏*57 rooms, 5 suites* ♿*In-room: no a/c, safe, refrigerator, Ethernet (free), Wi-Fi (free). In-Hotel: restaurant, bar, public Internet (free), Wi-Fi (free), parking (free), garage (fee), some pets allowed (fee)* ☰*AE, DC, MC, V* ⫯❂⫯*BP.*

$–$$ 🏨 **Hotel Schiff am See.** The Schiff nabbed an ideal setting; its sheltered terrace gives onto a shady park and the waterfront promenade. Inside, you'll find an eclectic collection of heavy wood furniture and antiques, sometimes overwhelmed by the floral wallpapers that can make some guest rooms feel cluttered. The gourmet restaurant, Lord Nelson ($$–$$$), has lake views and wraps around the garden. Specialties include local fish and inventive combination meat dishes such as beef tournedos and giant shrimp. The Schiff is a "velo-hotel"; bicycles are welcome, and the staff can help you rent one in town. **Pros:** peaceful waterside location; ferry docks in front of hotel making a daytrip to nearby Neuchâtel tempting. **Cons:** heavy and dated floral guestrooms; no elevator. ⊠*Direkt am See* ☎*026/6723666* ⊕*www.hotel-schiff.ch* 🛏*15 rooms* ♿*In-room: no a/c, safe, refrigerator. In-hotel: restaurant, bar, some pets allowed (fee)* ☰*AE, DC, MC, V* ⫯❂⫯*BP.*

$$$$ 🏨 **Le Vieux Manoir au Lac.** Truly worthy of Relais & Châteaux status, a
★   manicured park spreads around this stately, turreted mansion just 1 km (½ mi) south of Murten on Lac de Morat. Most of the guest rooms have lake views and have been individually "themed" by various artists and designers. The names alone—Flying Carpet, Iron Heart—conjure magical spaces. The lakeside location provides a range of water sports and outdoor activities on the doorstep, and the three restaurants ($$$–$$$$) offer seasonal sampling menus with a Mediterranean, French-continental, and local bent. Options might include chateaubriand with spring onions and béarnaise sauce or a pan-fried Norwegian lobster served with a fennel and cardamom puree. **Pros:** pretty lakeside location within walking distance of medieval Murten; romantic candlelit dinner for two on the pier—book a few days ahead. **Cons:** frequent functions can disturb the prevailing tranquility; restaurants are somewhat pricey. ⊠*18 rue de Lausanne, Murten-Meyriez* ☎*026/6786161* ⊕*www.vieuxmanoir.ch* 🛏*34 rooms* ♿*In-room: safe, refrigerator, Wi-Fi (fee). In-hotel: 3 restaurants, bar, spa, beach, watersports, bicycles, public Wi-Fi (fee), parking (no fee), some pets allowed (fee)* ☰*AE, DC, MC, V* ⫯❂⫯*BP.*

LAC NEUCHÂTEL

The region of Neuchâtel belonged to Prussia from 1707 to 1857, with a brief interruption caused by Napoléon and a period of dual loyalty to Prussia and the Swiss Confederation between 1815 and 1857. Yet its French heritage remains untouched by Germanic language, diet, or culture. Some boast that the inhabitants speak "the best French in Switzerland," which is partly why so many summer language courses are taught here.

NEUCHÂTEL

★ *28 km (17 mi) northwest of Murten, 48 km (30 mi) northwest of Fribourg.*

GETTING HERE

Direct trains from Neuchâtel to major Swiss cities: Geneva, one per hour (1 hour 10 mins, 37 SF); Lausanne, one per hour (41 mins, 24 SF); Bern, two per hour (40–50 mins, 17.60 SF); Basel, one per hour (1½ hrs, 34 SF); Zürich, one per hour (1 hr 35 mins, 49 SF). Trains from Fribourg to Neuchâtel, one direct per hour (53 mins, 19 SF). Take Bus No. 7 to Place Pury to get Littoral Neuchâtel buses (www.tnneuchatel. ch; 1.85 to 3 SF) to countryside villages.

Visitor Information (✉ *Hôtel des Postes* ☎ *032/8896890* 🖷 *032/8896291* 🌐 *www.neuchateltourisme.ch*).

EXPLORING

At the foot of the Jura Mountains, flanked by vineyards, and facing southeast, the city of Neuchâtel enjoys panoramic views of Lac Neuchâtel and the range of the middle Alps, including the majestic mass of Mont Blanc and the Bernese Oberland. Lac Neuchâtel, at 38 km (24 mi) long and 8 km (5 mi) wide, is the largest lake located entirely within Switzerland. (The much larger lakes of Geneva and Constance are shared with France and Germany, respectively.) A prosperous city, Neuchâtel has a reputation for precision work, beginning with watchmaking in the early 18th century. In fact, the whole Neuchatel region is referred to by locals as "Watch Valley, the Land of Precision." The city itself lies on the Watchmaking Route—a 200 km (125 mi) journey with 27 stops running from Geneva to Basel. There are traditional workshops, museums, and countless other insights into the ingenuity of this craftmanship and time itself.

Broad avenues in the lower part of town bordering the lake are lined with neo-Romanesque yellow-sandstone buildings, which inspired author Alexandre Dumas to call Neuchâtel "a city with the appearance of an immense *joujou* [toy] dressed in butter." The cathedral and the 12th-century castle, which today houses the cantonal government, sit gracefully above the city's bustling old marketplace. You can stroll (or cycle or rollerblade) along the lakeside promenade as far as Hauterive, the next village to the north. Neuchâtel's biggest annual festival is the winemakers' three-day celebration of the grape harvest, the *fête des vendanges*. It's celebrated the last weekend of September with parades and fanfare throughout the city.

The extent of French influence in Neuchâtel is revealed in its monuments and architecture, most notably the **Église Collégiale** *(Collegiate Church)*. The handsome Romanesque and Burgundian Gothic structure dates from the 12th century, with a colorful tile roof. The church contains a strikingly realistic and well-preserved grouping of life-size painted figures called *le cénotaphe*, or monument, to the counts of Neuchâtel. Dating from the 14th and 15th centuries, this is considered one of Europe's finest examples of medieval art. Anyone not wanting to climb steep streets can reach the church from the Promenade Noire off the Place des Halles by an inconspicuous elevator—*ascenseur publique.* ⊠*12 rue de la Collégiale* ☎*032/8896000* ☎*Free* ☉*Weekdays 8–noon, 1:30–5.*

The **Tour des Prisons** *(Prison Tower),* which adjoins the Collegiate Church, has panoramic views from its turret. On your way up, stop in one of the original wooden prison cells. ⊠*Rue Jehanne-de-Hochberg* ☎*No phone* ☎*1 SF* ☉*Apr.–Sept., daily 8–6.*

The architecture of the **Old Town** presents a full range of French styles. Along Rue des Moulins are two perfect specimens of the Louis XIII period, and—at its opposite end—a fine Louis XIV house anchors the Place des Halles (market square), also notable for its turreted 16th-century **Maison des Halles.** The **Hôtel de Ville** *(Town Hall* ⊠*Rue de l'Hôtel de Ville)* opened in 1790 east of the Old Town. It was designed by Pierre-Adrien Paris, Louis XVI's architect. There are also several fine patrician houses, such as the magnificent **Hôtel DuPeyrou** (⊠*1 av. DuPeyrou),* home of the friend, protector, and publisher of Jean-Jacques Rousseau, who studied botany in the nearby Val-de-Travers. Most of the Old Town is a pedestrians-only zone, though public buses do run through it. You can stroll as far as Marin-Epagnier (east side) and Vaumarcus (west side).

Behind the Hôtel Du Peyrou, the new **Galeries de l'Histoire** *(History Gallery)* houses models of Neuchâtel from the year 1000 to 2000. ⊠*7 av. DuPeyrou* ☎*032/7177920* ⊕*www.mahn.ch* ☎*Free* ☉*Wed.–Sun. 1–5.*

★   Thanks to a remarkably unprovincial curator, the **Musée d'Art et d'Histoire** *(Museum of Art and History)* displays a striking collection of paintings gathered under broad themes—nature, civilization—and mounted in a radical, evocative way. Fifteenth-century allegories, early Impressionism, and contemporary abstractions pack the walls from floor to ceiling: interacting, conflicting, and demanding comparison. You may climb a platform (itself plastered with paintings) to view the higher works. This aggressive series of displays is framed by the architectural decorations of Neuchâtel resident Clement Heaton, whose murals and stained glass make the building itself a work of art.

This novel museum also has the honor of hosting three of this watch-making capital's most exceptional guests: the **automates Jaquet-Droz,** three astounding little androids, created between 1768 and 1774, which once toured the courts of Europe like young mechanical Mozarts. Pierre Jaquet-Droz and his son Henri-Louis created them, and they are moving manifestations of the stellar degree to which watchmaking had evolved by the 18th century. Le Dessinateur (the Draughtsman) is an automated dandy in satin knee pants who draws graphite images of a dog, the god Eros in a chariot pulled by a butterfly, and a profile of Louis XV.

La Musicienne (the Musician) is a young woman playing the organ. She moves and breathes subtly with the music and actually strikes the keys that produce the organ notes. L'Écrivain (the Writer) dips a real feather in real ink and writes 40 different letters. Like a primitive computer, he can be programmed

ON THE CALENDAR

Neuchâtel's biggest annual festival is the winemakers' three-day celebration of the grape harvest, the *fête des vendanges*, held the last weekend of September.

to write any message simply by the change of a steel disk. The automatons come alive only on the first Sunday of the month, at 2, 3, or 4 (or by appointment), but the audiovisual show re-creates the thrill. ✉*1 esplanade Léopold-Robert* ☎*032/7177920* ⊕*www.mahn.ch* 🎫*8 SF, free Wed.* ⊗*Tues.–Sun. 11–6.*

Named after the Swiss writer and artist Friedrich Dürrenmatt, the **Centre Dürrenmatt,** perched high above Neuchâtel, houses an exhibition area devoted to modern literature and visual arts. Architect Mario Botta designed a curving, skylit underground space connected to Dürrenmatt's former home (now a private library and offices). Many of Dürrenmatt's paintings are disturbing, reflecting a bleak worldview that tends to be softened by the humor, albeit acerbic, in his writing. Letters and excerpts of his books are also on display, and each artwork is accompanied by a quote. ✉*74 chemin du Pertuis-du-Sault* ☎*032/202060* ⊕*www.cdn.ch* 🎫*8 SF* ⊗*Wed.–Sun. 11–5.*

� ★ The **Laténium,** an interactive archaeological museum, displays artifacts discovered in and around the lake and explains (in French and German) how they were recovered. The lifestyles of the *la Tène* Celts and Bronze Age lake dwellers are skillfully depicted. A sculpted menhir from Bevaix, a village southwest of Neuchâtel, resembles a man. Inside the museum you can see the remains of a 60-foot-long Gallo-Roman barge; outside in the park, its reconstruction is moored near a full-scale wooden Bronze Age house on stilts. There is a pamphlet in English, and guided tours in English can be booked in advance. ✉*Espace Paul VougaHauterive* ☎*032/8896917* ⊕*www.latenium.ch* 🎫*9 SF* ⊗*Tues.–Sun. 10–5.*

OFF THE BEATEN PATH

Col de la Vue des Alpes. From Neuchâtel, take the road to La Chaux-des-Fonds for 15 km (9½ mi) to the pass Col de la Vue des Alpes where the parking area on this high ridge affords, on a clear day, spectacular views of the Alps, including the Eiger, Mönch, Jungfrau, and Mont Blanc.

WHERE TO EAT

¢–$ FRENCH ★ ✕ **Bach & Buck.** Simply furnished and seating 70, this crêperie-cum-tea room opposite the Jardin Anglais is an ideal spot to grab a cheap but tasty meal. Its location close to the university ensures a young crowd, many of whom head here to enjoy a choice from more than 120 types of crepes: sweet and savory, meat or vegetarian with gluten-free, and wheat and buckwheat varieties cater for many diets. A selection of more than 30 teas can also be enjoyed while playing one of the video games or perusing one of the comic books they have on offer. Make a quick visit to the neighboring shop, Art' The, to pick up a bag of home-made tea and associated utensils for a charming memento to take home. ⊠29 av. du 1er-Mars 🕾032/7256353 ⊕www.artthe.ch ▤No credit cards ⊗Closed Sun. in July and Aug.

$$–$$$
MODERN
FRENCH,
MODERN SWISS

✕**Café Au Boccalino.** Just north of Neuchâtel, this restaurant gastronomique has a tiny winter-garden brasserie and a main dining room discreetly decorated in pale gray and muted blue. Despite its proximity to the lake, there's neither terrace nor view, and charming owner-chef Claude Frôté wants it that way. Customers should come for his innovative regional food (an evening menu will cost between 110 SF and 180 SF) and, above all, his wine. He keeps 25,000 bottles in stock, and connoisseurs can reserve a predinner *apéro* in the cellar (for up to 12 people). Try traditional tripe, pork tongue, foie gras of duck with passion fruit, or veal poached with vanilla and mint. ⊠11 av. Bachelin, St-Blaise 🕾032/7533680 ⚖Reservations essential ▤AE, DC, MC, V ⊗Closed Sun. and Mon.; mid-July–mid-Aug.; and late Dec.–early Jan.

$$–$$$
SWISS

✕**Du Banneret.** Chef Angelo de Marco often emerges to greet diners in the brasserie portion of this popular restaurant, housed in a late-Renaissance building at the foot of the Rue du Château. Dishes are mostly regional fare, such as homemade pasta with fresh wild mushrooms and lake trout. In the upstairs dining room the food takes a strong Italian twist. In good weather it is fun to enjoy the street-side tables that are at the base of the steep alleys and next to a fountain. ⊠1 rue Fleury 🕾032/7252861 ▤DC, MC, V ⊗Closed Sun. and Mon.

$$–$$$
FRENCH

✕**Le Cardinal Brasserie.** Stop and have a perfect café crème (coffee with cream) or a light meal along with the Neuchâteloise at one of the most authentic cafés in the Old Town. This place models itself on a traditional Parisian brasserie, and the striking Art Nouveau interior certainly helps: the molded ceiling, etched windows, and blue-and-green decorative tile all date from 1905. Fish is the specialty, and large platters of *fruits de mer* (shellfish) in season are a delicious treat. A "menu of the day" special usually costs 18 Swiss francs. ⊠9 rue du Seyon 🕾032/7251286 ⊕www.lecardinal-brasserie.ch ▤AE, DC, MC, V.

WHERE TO STAY

$$$$
★

🔲 **Beau-Rivage Hotel.** This thoroughly elegant, restored 19th-century hotel sits gracefully on the lakeshore; on a clear day there's a splendid view of the Alps. The warmly lit interior, with high ceilings and wild-cherry wood, exudes calm. Two-thirds of the spacious rooms have lake views, and the generous bathrooms are decked out in white marble. The sophisticated dining room, done in pale green, offers a fine selection of wines, after-dinner cigars, and brandies. The veranda-bar is comfortingly low key and open for snacks and drinks throughout the day and into the evening. The spa, gym, and air-conditioning complete the deluxe hotel experience. Breakfast is an additional 28 Swiss francs per person. **Pros:** high standard of service and facilities not easy to find in this region; outstanding views; lakeside location. **Cons:** perhaps a tad too corporate and lacking in character for some; fourth-floor rooms are darker and smaller than the rest. ⊠1 esplanade du Mont Blanc 🕾032/7231515 ⊕www. beau-rivage-hotel.ch ⇌65 rooms ⚙In-room: safe, refrigerator, Ethernet (fee), Wi-Fi (fee). In-hotel: restaurant, concierge, bar, gym, spa, public

Internet (fee), public Wi-Fi (fee), parking (free), covered parking (fee), some pets allowed (fee) ⊟AE, DC, MC, V.

$-$$ ⊞ **Café-Hôtel de L'Aubier.** In the pedestrian zone at the foot of Neuchâ-
★ tel's cantonal château, this delightful hotel offers light, modern, spacious guest rooms whose warm color schemes are inspired by the spice
they are named after. Cheaper rooms have their own sink but share a
bathroom. The central location sometimes makes it noisy on weekends. The café (closed Monday breakfast and Sunday) and terrace offer
inexpensive but good organic fare: breakfasts, salads, and desserts (try
the chocolate tart), with a selection of teas and coffees. **Pros:** central
location in pedestrian zone; bright, light, and modern atmosphere.
Cons: can tend toward noisiness on weekends due to central location; no
breakfast on Mondays. ⊠*1 rue du Château* ☎*032/7101858* ⊕*www.
aubier.ch* ⏂*9 rooms, 3 with bath* ⏃*In-room: no a/c, no TV (some).
In-hotel: restaurant, some pets allowed (fee)* ⊟*MC, V* ⏃*EP.*

$ ⊞ **Hotel Du Marché.** Opening directly onto the Place des Halles, this is a
delightful place for a hearty plat du jour or a carafe of local wine. Inside,
pass through the lively bar-café to the steamy, old-wood brasserie for
a bowl of tripe in Neuchâtel wine or salt pork with lentils. Upstairs,
a pretty little dining room (closed Sunday) serves more sophisticated
fare. Plain, functional guest rooms with tidy tile bathrooms down the
hall are good value. Double-glazed windows keep out the noise. **Pros:**
in the heart of the city; good choice of food. **Cons:** no en-suite bathrooms; no parking, but it should be easy to find nearby. ⊠*4 pl. des
Halles* ☎*032/7232330* ⊕*www.hoteldumarche.com* ⏂*10 rooms* ⏃*In-
room: no a/c, Ethernet (free). In-hotel: 2 restaurants, bar.* ⊟*AE, DC,
MC, V* ⏃*BP.*

$$-$$$ ⊞ **La Maison du Prussien.** In the gorge of Vauseyon, 10 minutes from
Neuchâtel, this restored 18th-century brewery nestles alongside a roaring woodland stream. Polished beams, yellow-sandstone highlights,
and lush views are undeniably atmospheric. Every guest room is different, but all have authentic beams and whitewashed walls, while three
have fireplaces. The glass-roofed winter-garden restaurant ($$$-$$$$;
closed Sunday) offers innovative seasonal cuisine, or you can enjoy a
simpler lunch on the terrace overlooking the stream. Take the tunnels
under Neuchâtel toward La Chaux-de-Fonds, exit toward Pontarlier-
Vauseyon, and watch for the hotel's signs. **Pros:** traditional old-world
charm and authentic restoration; quiet location. **Cons:** those looking
for sports or pampering will be missing the point of this place—peaceful
historic location and venue are the basis for unwinding here. ⊠*Au
Gor du Vauseyon, 11 rue des Tunnels* ☎*032/7305454* ⊕*www.hotel-
prussien.ch* ⏂*6 rooms, 4 suites* ⏃*In-room: no a/c, safe, refrigerator,
Wi-Fi (free). In-hotel: restaurant, bar, public Wi-Fi (free), parking (free),
some pets allowed (fee)* ⊟*AE, DC, MC, V* ⏃*Closed mid-July–mid-
Aug. and late Dec.–early Jan.*

SPORTS & THE OUTDOORS

SWIMMING There are **public beaches** at many villages and resorts on the lake. A
municipal complex (⊠*Nid du Crô, 30 rte. des Falaises* ☎*032/7226222*)
has outdoor and indoor pools.

NIGHTLIFE

Neuchâtel has an ever-changing selection of restaurants de nuit and *bars musicaux,* establishments that pulse with disco music until the wee hours of the morning and sometimes serve food—along the lines of steak *frites* (steak and fries)—to keep you going. **Café Trio** (⊠*3 rue des Moulins* ☎*032/7242224*) is open until 2 on Friday and Saturday. Swinging into the night on Fridays and Saturdays (from 10:30 PM to 4 AM), at **Casino de la Rotonde** (⊠*14 faubourg du Lac, CH-2000 Neuchâtel* ☎*032/7244848* ⊕*www.la-rotonde.ch*) are the **Discothèque Golden Eyes** and **Latino Labodega,** both offering music.

EN ROUTE

To the west of Neuchâtel lie some of Switzerland's best vineyards, their grapes producing chiefly white and rosé wines that are light and slightly sparkling. The wines are bottled before the second fermentation, so they have a rather high carbonic acid content. **Château Boudry** offers wine tasting by appointment and houses the **Musée Cantonale de la Vigne et du Vin** (Cantonal Museum of Vines and Wines). ⊠*Château Boudry, Boudry* ☎*032/8421098* ⊕*www.chateaudeboudry.ch* 🗲*Museum 5 SF* ⊙*Museum Wed.–Sun. 2–6 or by prior arrangement.*

GRANDSON

29 km (18 mi) southwest of Neuchâtel.

This lakeside village in Canton Vaud has a long history. It is said that in 1066 a member of the Grandson family accompanied William of Normandy (better known as the Conqueror) to England, where he founded the English barony of Grandson. Otto I of Grandson took part in the Crusades.

When the Burgundian Wars broke out in the late 15th century, the ★ **Château de Grandson** *(Grandson Castle),* built in the 11th century and much rebuilt during the 13th and 15th centuries, was in the hands of Charles the Bold of Burgundy. In 1475 the Swiss won it by siege, but early the next year their garrison was surprised by Charles, and 418 of their men were captured and hanged from the apple trees in the castle orchard. A few days later the Swiss returned to Grandson and, after crushing the Burgundians, retaliated by stringing their prisoners from the same apple trees. After being used for three centuries as a residence by the Bernese bailiffs, the castle was bought in 1875 by the de Blonay family, who restored it to its current impressive state, with high, massive walls and five cone turrets. Inside, you can see reproductions of Charles the Bold's Burgundian war tent and two jousting knights astride their horses—in full armor. There are also *oubliettes* (dungeon pits for prisoners held *in perpetua*), torture chambers, and a model of the Battle of Grandson, complete with 20-minute slide show (in English if you get in quickly enough to push the right button). Cassette-guided tours of the town are available from a desk at the Tourist Office (Maison des Terroirs). The dungeons now house an extensive vintage car museum, with motorbikes and even a penny farthing bicycle. ☎*024/4452926* ⊕*www.grandson.ch* 🗲*12 SF* ⊙*Apr.–Oct., daily 8:30–6; Nov.–Mar., daily 8:30–5.*

YVERDON-LES-BAINS

6 km (2½ mi) southwest of Grandson, 38 km (24 mi) southwest of Neuchâtel.

GETTING HERE

Trains from Fribourg to Yverdon-les-Bains, one direct per hour (54 mins, 16.80 SF); from Neuchâtel to Yverdon-les-Bains, two direct per hour (18 mins, 13.40 SF).

Visitor Information (✉ *2 av. de la Gare* ☎ *024/4236101* ⊕ *www.yverdon-les-bains.ch/tourisme*).

EXPLORING

This pastel-color lakefront town at the southernmost tip of Lac Neuchâtel has been appreciated for its thermal waters and sandy, willow-lined shoreline since the Romans first invaded and set up thermal baths here. In the 18th century its fame spread across Europe. Today the **Thermal Center** is completely up to date, with indoor and outdoor pools, whirlpools, and massage jets. Swim caps are mandatory, and children under 3 are not permitted. ✉ *22 av. des Bains* ☎*024/4230232* 🔲*19 SF* ⊘*Mon.–Sat. 8 AM–10 PM, Sun. 8–8.*

In the center of the Old Town sits the turreted, mid-13th-century **Château de Yverdon-les-Bains.** Most of the castle is now a museum, with exhibits on locally found prehistoric and Roman artifacts, Egyptian art, natural history, and of course, local history. A special room is dedicated to the famous Swiss educator Johann Heinrich Pestalozzi (1746–1827), who spent 20 years here. His influential ideas on education led to school reforms at home and in Germany and England. ☎*024/4259310* 🔲*8 SF* ⊘*Jun.–Sep., Tues.–Sun. 11–5; Oct.–May, Tues.–Sun. 2–5.*

In front of Yverdon's **Hôtel de Ville** *(Town Hall)* —an 18th-century building notable for its French-inspired neoclassical facade—stands a bronze monument of Pestalozzi, grouped with two children. The charming, bustling town center is closed to traffic. Along the waterfront you'll find parks, promenades, a shady campground, and a 2-km (1¼-mi) stretch of little beaches.

EXCURSION INTO THE JURA

Straddling the French frontier from Geneva to Basel is a range of low-riding mountains (few peaks exceed 4,920 feet), which fall steeply down to the mysterious River Doubs, Lac des Brenets, and Doubs Falls to the north and to Lac Neuchâtel and Lac de Bienne to the south. The secret of this region, known as the Jura, is the sunny plateau atop the mountains, with lush pastures and gentle woods just made for excellent hiking, biking, horseback riding, and cross-country-skiing opportunities. In addition to the Jura mountain range is Jura, the youngest Swiss canton: in 2004 it celebrated the 25th anniversary of its independence.

LA CHAUX-DE-FONDS

22 km (14 mi) north of Neuchâtel.

Actually part of Canton Neuchâtel, La Chaux-de-Fonds (called "Tschaux" by locals) sits high on the Jura plateau. In the early 18th century watch making was introduced as a cottage industry to create income for an area otherwise completely dependent on farming. Over the years the town became the watch-making capital of Switzerland. Destroyed by fire at the end of the 18th century, the city was rebuilt on a grid plan around the central, broad, tree-lined avenue Léopold-Robert. It is a city of incongruities: pastel-painted town houses and stone villas, working-class cafés and cultural institutions.

Famed architect Charles-Édouard Jeanneret, otherwise known as Le Corbusier, was born here. His birthplace can be seen, although not toured, along with the École d'Art, where he taught, and several villas he worked on between 1906 and 1917. The tourist office has a brochure outlining a walk that passes by his array of designed buildings. Only two are open to the public, the most noted of which is the **Villa Turque,** set north of the main avenue. It has a glowing terracotta-brick facade, rounded wings, and curved edges. A 20-minute video about Le Corbusier is available in English. ⊠*147 rue du Doubs* ☎*032/9123123* ⊕*www.fribourgtourisme.ch* ⊠*Free* ⊗*1st and 3rd Sat. of month 10–4.*

La Maison Blanche is a newly renovated residence that Le Corbusier had built for his parents in 1912. Set against an attractive backdrop of trees in landscaped gardens, this impressive white villa takes about one hour to savor. ⊠*12 ch. de Pouillerel CH-2300* ☎*032/9109030* ⊕*www.maisonblanche.ch* ⊠*10 SF* ⊗*Fri., Sat., and Sun. 10–5 and 1st Sat. of each month for public guided visit at 11.*

The **Musée des Beaux-Arts** *(Museum of Fine Arts),* a striking neoclassical structure, was designed by Le Corbusier's teacher, L'Éplattenier. It contains works by noted Swiss artists, such as Léopold Robert, as well as three of Le Corbusier's works: a furniture set, an oil painting *(Femme au Peignoir),* and a tapestry *(Les Musiciennes).* Perhaps the most famous artist in the collection is, rightly, Swiss: Ferdinand Hodler (1853–1918), who was born in Bern but spent most of his career in Geneva. His most beautiful works are his Swiss landscapes, touched as they are with accents of Symbolism and Art Nouveau. The museum also usually has a temporary exhibit. ⊠*33 rue des Musées* ☎*032/9130444* ⊠*8 SF, Sun. 10–noon free* ⊗*Tues.–Sun. 10–5.*

★ The **Musée International d'Horlogerie** *(International Timepiece Museum)* displays a fascinating collection of clocks and watches that traces the development of timekeeping and the expansion of watch making as an art form. You can see audiovisual presentations on the history and science of the craft, observe current repairs on pieces from the collection in an open work area, and browse the gift shop, which sells replicas as well as the latest timepieces by stellar local watch-making firms (Corum, Girad-Perregaux, Ebel, and so on). Some explanatory material is in English, and group tours in English can be arranged. ✉*29 rue des Musées* ☎*032/9676861* ⏛*www.mih.ch* 🎫*12 SF* ⏰*Tues.–Sun. 10–5.*

WHERE TO EAT & STAY

$–$$ ✕**Auberge de Mont-Cornu.** Just southeast of town, this converted farm-
SWISS   house has an idyllic setting. Friendly staff serve everything from simple sandwiches to traditional regional dishes; the fondue with cream is renowned. The desserts are beautifully presented and hard to refuse. The salons are wood-paneled and chock-full of authentic extras; a grandfather clock, a gramophone with record, and a huge glazed-tile oven. In summer, sit outside in the flower-filled garden and take in the view of wooded hills and the sound of distant cowbells. ✉*116 Mont-Cornu* ☎*032/9687600* ⏛*Reservations essential* 🍴*AE, MC, V* ⏰*Closed Mon. and Tues. and Dec.–Feb.*

$$$ 🏨**Grand Hôtel les Endroits.** Set in a tranquil green suburb above town, this modern, family-run hotel offers just about everything. Guest rooms are spacious and light, with discrete pastels and warm wood set off by touches of black. Many have balconies or open onto a grassy area. Eat local seasonal produce cooked by the owner Jean-Pierre Vogt and his brother Fritz in the no-smoking restaurant ($$–$$$), in the brasserie (¢–$), or on the large terrace. There is a workout room, sauna, and Jacuzzi for relaxing. **Pros:** welcoming hosts; tasty food; front desk staff speak good English, which is not always the case in this region. **Cons:** exterior of building is starkly modern and could belie the warm hospitality that lies within; interiors are reminiscent of 1980s. ✉*94 bd. des Endroits* ☎*032/9250250* ⏛*www.hotel-les-endroits.ch* 🛏*42 rooms, 4 suites* ⏛*In-room: no a/c, safe, refrigerator, Wi-Fi (fee). In-hotel: 2 restaurants, bar, gym, sauna, bicycles, children's' playroom, public Wi-Fi (fee), parking (free), some pets allowed (fee)* 🍴*AE, DC, MC, V* 🍽*BP.*

SAIGNELÉGIER

26 km (16 mi) northeast of La Chaux-de-Fonds.

A small, fairly modern town, Saignelégier is known mostly for its lush surroundings, horseback riding, and cross-country skiing. The Marché-Concours National de Chevaux (National Horse Fair), held since 1897, takes place on the second Sunday in August and draws crowds from throughout Switzerland and France, as does the Fête des Montgolfières (Hot-Air Balloon Festival) the second weekend of October.

WHERE TO EAT & STAY

$$$–$$$$ ✕**Hôtel-Restaurant Georges Wenger.** One of Switzerland's top gourmet
SWISS   restaurants is just 6 km (4 mi) from Saignelégier. Chef Georges Wenger
Fodor'sChoice   creates elegant, savory dishes with both a regional and seasonal bent
★   and has a flair for unusual combinations, such as langoustines with a subtle, gingery almond-milk and rhubarb sauce. An excellent selection of cheeses and a fine wine cellar round out the experience. If you feel you can't tear yourself away, you can spend the night; upstairs are a handful of luxurious, individually decorated rooms. There is also an online boutique selling Georges Wenger products, enabling you to recall

8

and savor his flavors back home. It should not come as a surprise that Wenger has two Michelin stars and Relais & Châteaux standing—in other words, make your reservations well in advance. ✉ *2 rue de la Gare, Le Noirmont* 🕾 *032/9576633* ✍ *Reservations essential* ⊕ *www. georges-wenger.ch* ⊟ *AE, DC, MC, V* ⊘ *Closed late July–early Aug., late Dec.–late Jan., and Mon. and Tues.*

Bern

Flower market on the Federal Square, Bern

9

WORD OF MOUTH

"I guess I'm in the minority, but I like Bern. I admit to being a museum junkie, and we enjoyed the Alpine Museum, the Paul Klee Museum, Albert Einstein's apartment, and the Swiss Parliament. There's a compact, attractive historical center with charming theme fountains throughout."

—Jean

"The only thing I didn't like about Bern—the shops' prices."

—FainaAgain

WELCOME TO BERN

TOP REASONS TO GO

★ **Lived-in history:** UNESCO only made Bern a World Heritage Site in 1983, but the city's cobblestone arcades and clock towers have been beautifully preserved since the 1400s.

★ **Feats of Klee:** The spectacular Zentrum named for Paul Klee—the whimsical painter artist who hopscotched across art—is a tour de force of vibrant creativity.

★ **Undercover shopping:** Bern's got it all—from couture fashion to artisan chocolatiers—and, thanks to those famous arcaded streets, you can even enjoy window shopping in rainy weather.

★ **The Zibelemärit:** Think of an object—a train car, an alarm clock, a teddy bear—and you will likely see it rendered in onion at November's city-wide celebration of the humble veg.

★ **Those sunbathing Swiss:** Warm summer days lure swimmers to the Marzili's sweeping lawns and swift, icy stretch of river below the Federal parliament building.

1 Old Town. Watch the clock turn back to 1191, when the Zytglogge marked Bern's outer edges and the city sloped gently down to the river by the Untertorbrücke. Today the historic Rathaus, Münster, painted fountains, and 18th-century guildhalls rub shoulders with arcades and cellars full of restaurants and quirky boutiques.

2 City Center. The swath of land between the Zytglogge and the Hauptbahnhof is Bern's most commercially vibrant, a dense warren of narrow streets and pedestrian passageways studded with shops, hidden alleys, grand architecture, and the Swiss Federal Government complex.

GETTING ORIENTED

Few capital cities are as charming and compact as Bern, Switzerland's political nerve center. Alluring medieval streets, frolicsome fountains, and palpable history coexist so easily with outdoor markets and traditional cheese-and-potatoes that it's easy to forget this is actually a fully wired, surprisingly young 21st-century urban center.

enbergstr.

Aare
Langmauerweg
Postgasshalde
Rathauspl.
amgasse   Gerechtigkeitsg.   Junkerngasse
ünstergasse   Gerberngasse
           Münster   OLD TOWN
Münsterpl. Münster
arstrasse   Platform
           Schifflaube

Nydegg Stalden
Untertorbrücke
Nydeggbrücke
Aarg aue rstalden
Alter

Grosser Muristalden
Kleiner Muristalden

Zentrum Paul Klee

Kollerweg   Muristrasse
        Gryphenhübeliweg
Marienstrasse
Thunstrasse   Dufourstr. Jungfraustr.
eum für
amunikation
        Hallwylstr.

0   300 yards
0   300 meters

9

3 Museum District. The Kirchenfeld neighborhood is a masterpiece of late 19th-century urban planning, where a top array of Bern's museums are grouped together in a tight, easy-to-visit cluster on the south bank of the river Aare.

BERN PLANNER

Transportation Basics

The most efficient, flexible, cheap, and enjoyable way to navigate Bern's cobblestones is on foot.

Cars that attempt to enter the downtown area are steered right back out again, and parking is scarce unless you opt for a (modern, well-lit) municipal parking garage; taxis suffer the same fate, and fares reflect the torturous routing.

Public transport, which means buses and trams, is both plentiful and easy to use.

Bern is easy to navigate: count on 10 minutes to walk at a steady clip from the Hauptbahnhof to the Bärengraben; about five to take the bus.

From the station, the main shopping street, Spitalgasse, leads straight through Bärenplatz; this square and the adjacent Bundesplatz mark the center of town.

Most sights are on or near Spitalgasse, which becomes Marktgasse, Kramgasse, and Gerechtigkeitsgasse.

Trams and buses are handy for getting outside the Altstadt.

Bern's Best Photo-Ops

As Albert Einstein discovered to his delight in 1902, the weather has been bested in Bern. "Both sides of the road are completely lined by old arcades so that one can stroll from one end of the city to the other in the worst downpour without getting noticeably wet," he wrote to his fiancé in 1902. Sturdy 15th-century pillars support the low vaulted roofs of these picturesque *Lauben* (arcades), which extend to the edge of the sidewalk along miles of Altstadt streets. Steeply angled cellar doors at street level lead down to additional underground eateries and businesses, while brilliantly colored and carved *Brunnen* (fountains), historically the city's water sources and congregation points, punctuate the main thoroughfares. Ten of the most prominent fountains are the work of Hans Gieng, who created them between 1542 and 1549.

Tour Options

Bern Tourismus (☎031/3281212 ⊕www.berninfo.com) guides lead 90-minute English-language walking tours of the Altstadt at 11 AM daily between April and October, on Saturday the rest of the year. Upon request they also organize group tours conducted by bus or down the Aare in rafts. Reserve at the tourist center in the Hauptbahnhof; the walking tour costs 18 SF.

Visitor Information

Bern Tourismus, based in the Hauptbahnhof, distributes free brochures and maps, organizes tours, publishes Bern Guide, administers www.berninfo.com, and operates a 3-D multimedia history presentation called *Bern Show* at its satellite information center next to the Bärengraben. Bern-Cards, on sale at either counter, grant free access to the permanent collections of most Bernese museums.

Bern Tourismus (⊠ *Tourist Center at railway station, City Center*, ☎031/3281212 ⊕www.berninfo.ch).

To Market, To Market

Bern has been a market town since the Middle Ages, and seasonal outdoor markets are still an integral part of daily life. The most elaborate is the Zibelemärit (Onion Market), a Fasnacht-tinged remnant of a 15th-century Autumn Market that lasted two weeks; 19th-century farmers' wives, notably from Fribourg, developed the habit of coming to Bern on the first day of the market to sell their excess produce, in particular onions, and today half of the 700 stalls that line the City Center on the fourth Monday in November display a vast assortment of items made with onions—everything from wreaths to alarm clocks to soup. The Weihnachtsmarkt (Christmas Market) fills the air throughout December with the scent of evergreens and holiday excitement; window boxes burst into bloom following the one-day Geranienmarkt (Geranium Market) in mid-May.

The Bernese also descend on daily, weekly, and monthly markets, their wicker baskets and wheeled carts in tow. The often organic fruits and vegetables that await them form swaths of color on wooden tables with computerized pan scales. It's courteous to ask for assistance rather than serve yourself, but hesitate and they will move on to weigh a handful of apricots or a wedge of cheese for the next customer. Butchers and fishmongers display locally raised meat and fish in mobile cooling trailers; fresh herbs may be had in season; and a tangle of shoppers and carts spills out from coffee bars lining the squares. Note that the socializing happens largely along the perimeter—market shopping demands your full attention.

Making the Most of Your Time

The Bernese do not scurry around their city, and neither should you—its considerable charms are best discovered at a slow, steady pace with a plan to get from A to B but no fixed idea how. It is technically possible to see the major sights in a day, but you'd miss seeing the sun set over medieval rooftops, you wouldn't be able to linger in restaurants, and this is a city that comes out at night. Do pace yourself as you wander the streets, do visit the museums at a steady clip, and do get a running start on the narrow curved steps up the Münster steeple. Indulge any urges to explore Marzili or Matte, to pursue your curiosity at the markets, to take a sudden chocolate break, to feed the bears, or to admire the fountains—although it is indeed strange to find the latter sitting in the middle of main-street traffic.

How's the Weather?

Architecture can be a big tip-off: covered stone arcades, dark underground cellars, small windows, and thick stone walls were all medieval coping tactics in the face of bad weather.

Bern can be cold and wet and miserable in winter, its indoor spaces warmed with fires and packed with people.

But it is mild and sunny from spring through autumn, when every restaurant that can sets up camp in the street, windows are thrown open, and people take to the river by the Marzili with unrestrained glee.

Summer is warm, and July through mid-August is vacation season.

Note that many restaurants close up shop for vacation for a few weeks during the summer season.

9

GETTING AROUND

By Air

Germany's national airline, Lufthansa, operates flights from **Bern-Belp Airport** (✉ *Belp* ☎ *031/9602111* ⊕ *www.flug-hafenbern.ch*) to Munich; the regional carrier Darwin flies direct to London City and Lugano. The Bern-Belp ticketing office handles local queries for both companies.

Bern's small airport, located 9 km (6 mi) south of the city in Belp, has daily connections to Munich and London City. Shuttle bus service between the Hauptbahnhof and the airport is coordinated with arriving and departing flights; the fare each way is 15 SF and the ride takes 20 minutes. A taxi from the airport to the Hauptbahnhof costs about 50 SF.

By Taxi

Bernese taxis are clean and plentiful, but circuitous downtown traffic routing renders them cumbersome and expensive; a ride from the Hauptbahnhof to the Bärengraben costs about 20 SF.

Call or find an official taxi stand; they won't respond if hailed. The two top companies are Bären Taxi (☎031/3711111) and Nova Taxi (☎031/3313313).

By Car

Bern sits squarely on the map of Swiss expressways. The A1 connects the city with Basel and Zürich to the north, with Lac Léman and Geneva to the south, and via Lausanne with the Valais. The A6 to the Berner Oberland runs just east of the city. Downtown pedestrian zones make parking in city garages a virtual necessity; electric signs on major incoming roads post current numbers of empty spaces.

By Bus & Tram Within Bern

Service by Bernmobil (⊕ *www.bernmobil.ch*) is extensive, with fares costing between 1.90 SF and 3.20 SF. Buy tickets from the dispensers placed at every stop by finding the name of the stop closest to your destination on the map, then selecting the fare listed for it. The machines give change. All public transportation is free for holders of a BernCard, which costs 20 SF for 24 hours, 31 SF for 48 hours, or 38 SF for 72 hours and may be purchased from the Hauptbahnhof and Bärengraben tourist centers, any museum, or any hotel. Swiss Pass holders travel free.

By Train

Bern is a train-based city, and the only European capital to have three high-speed connections: the ICE from Berlin takes 8½ hours, the TGV from Paris takes 4½ hours, and the Pendolino from Milan (known in Switzerland as the Cisalpino) takes 3½ hours. There are daily departures for Rome and, between June and August, Barcelona; Bern's Hauptbahnhof (✉ *Bahnhofpl.* ☎ *0900/300300* ⊕ *www. sbb.ch*) is also a major hub for trains within Switzerland. Intercity trains, which make the fewest stops, leave every 30 minutes: count an hour to reach Zürich or Basel, less than two for Geneva, four hours to Lugano. A tight network of local and regional trains keeps Bern connected to surrounding communities. Touch-screen consoles (in English) by the main arrival and departures board sell tickets for any destination in Switzerland.

Updated by
Katrin Gygax

ALTHOUGH BERN IS THE FEDERAL CAPITAL, you won't find much cosmopolitan nonsense here: the *cuisine du marché,* based on the freshest ingredients available in the local market, features fatback and sauerkraut, the annual fair fêtes the humble onion; and the president of the Swiss Confederation has been known to take the tram to work. Warm, friendly, down-to-earth, the Bernese are notoriously slow-spoken; ask a question, and then pull up a chair while they formulate a judicious response. Their mascot is a common bear; they keep some as pets in the center of town. Walking down broad medieval streets past squares crowded with farmers' markets, past cafés full of shirt-sleeved politicos, you might forget that Bern is the geographic and political hub of a sophisticated, modern, and prosperous nation.

In fact, at first glance, you might take the city (Berne in French) for a thriving country town rather than a major European capital. Arriving in the city center, either by car or by train, most visitors see only its Old Town and miss altogether the modern sprawl of banking and industry that surrounds it. Although Bern is full of patrician houses and palatial hotels, there is no official presidential residence: the seven members of the coalition government, each of whom serves a year as president, have to find their own places to live when in Bern.

Bern wasn't always so self-effacing.

It earned its pivotal position through a history of power and influence that dates from the 12th century, when Berchtold V, Duke of Zähringen, expanded his fortress at the tip of a sharp meander in the River Aare. He chose the site for its impregnable location and its proximity to the great kingdom of Burgundy, which spread across France and much of present-day French-speaking Switzerland. Then he named his new city for the first animal he killed in the local woods (an unlucky but immortal brown bear).

By the 14th century Bern had grown into a strong urban republic. When the last Zähringens died, the people of Bern defeated their would-be replacements and, in 1353, chose to become the eighth canton to join the rapidly growing Swiss Confederation. It was an unlikely union: aristocratic, urban Bern allied with the strongly democratic farming communities of central Switzerland. But it gave the Bernese security against the Habsburg Holy Roman Empire and cleared the way for westward expansion.

Setbacks did occur—the wooden city was gutted by fire in 1405—but by the late 15th century three decisive victories over the Duke of Burgundy had made Bern the most powerful city-state north of the Alps, with a territorial reach that soon extended southwest to Geneva and municipal coffers full of gold, silver, and precious textiles. The Reformation reached Bern in 1528; by the mid-16th century the city had assumed the leading role in Switzerland and Swiss affairs.

Bern stayed on top. The 17th and 18th centuries saw a boom in development fueled not so much by commerce as by the export of troops and military know-how—the ruling aristocracy saw its raison d'être

9

in politics, foreign policy, the acquisition of additional territory, and the forging of alliances. The landed gentry, meanwhile, grew fat on the fruits of the city's rich agricultural lands. Napoléon seized those lands briefly from 1798 until his defeat in 1815, and the 1814 Congress of Vienna forced Bern to part with its western and eastern territories, forming the Cantons of Vaud and Aargau, but by the 1830s the Bernese were back in charge. When the Swiss Confederation took its contemporary, federal form in 1848, Bern was a natural choice for its capital.

Yet today it's not the massive Bundeshaus (Federation Building) that dominates the city, but instead its perfectly preserved arcades, fountains, and thick, sturdy towers—all remnants of its heyday as a medieval power. Bern owes its architectural unity to a major fire that swept through town in 1405, destroying most of the houses, then mainly of wood. It was rebuilt in sandstone, and its arcades stretch on for some 6 kilometers (4 mi). They're the reason UNESCO granted Bern World Landmark status, with the pyramids and the Taj Mahal.

EXPLORING BERN

From the time it was built on a high, narrow peninsula above the rushing Aare, Bern's streets have followed the river's flow. The original town began by what is now the Nydegg bridge—it controlled the ferry crossing there—and spread westward, uphill to the *Zeitglockenturm* (known locally as the *Zytglogge*), a clock tower constructed in 1191 to mark Bern's first significant western gate. Further expansion in 1256 stretched the city to where the Käfigturm now stands; one last medieval growth spurt, hot on the heels of a resounding victory over the Burgundians in 1339, moved the city walls west yet again to the present-day train station, the *Hauptbahnhof*.

The bustling, commercial city center radiates out from that train station. To get to the *Altstadt* (Old Town), follow the trams across Bärenplatz and through the Käfigturm. Marzili and Matte, former working-class and still flood-prone neighborhoods, lie together along the riverbed of the Aare. All of these areas are easily explored on foot, but in Marzili and Matte you may want to take your cue from the locals: walk down, ride up. The cluster of museums in Kirchenfeld, on the south side of the river, is a short (spectacular) walk or tram ride away.

Numbers in the text correspond to numbers in the margin and on the Bern map.

OLD TOWN & CITY CENTER

Fire destroyed the original, predominantly wooden structures that comprised the Altstadt, the historical heart of the city that perches above the Aare. The Bernese rebuilt using local sandstone, and today's arcaded, cobblestone streets radiate medieval appeal. Eclectic upscale boutiques inhabit some of the oldest buildings, downhill from the Zytglogge; Marktgasse and Spitalgasse favor chain and department stores.

MAIN ATTRACTIONS

⑧ **Bärengraben** *(Bear Pits).* Bern almost certainly gets its name from the
local contraction of the German *Bären*, due to Berchtold V's supposed
★ first kill in the area, and the image of a bear is never far away, from the
official coat of arms to chocolate morsels. The city has kept live bears
since 1513, when victorious Bernese soldiers brought one back from
the Battle of Novara and installed it in a hut on what is now Bärenplatz; the current neo-Gothic castle structure and wooded location date
from 1857. Keeper-approved treats are sold between the two pits on
the river side; plaques and pamphlets in English describe the bears and
their lifestyle. ✉*Grosser Muristalden 6, Bärengraben* ☎*031/3281212*
💰*Free* ⊙*Daily 9:30–5.*

⑫ **Bundeshaus** *(Houses of Parliament).* Conceived as a national monument and the beating heart of the Swiss Confederation (the seven-mem-
ber Federal Government, the 46-member Council of States, and the
200-member National Council all meet here), this massive, majestic
domed complex built between 1852 and 1902 takes its symbolism seriously. Twenty-six fountains out front represent the Swiss Cantons; solemn statues inside depict the swearing of the oath on which the Union
is founded; and two huge murals, one in each Chamber, represent the
Vierwaldstättersee (Lake Lucerne) and a Landsgemeinde (outdoor cantonal assembly) scene, respectively the place where Swiss democracy
was founded and the means by which it flourished. ✉*Bundespl. 3, City
Center* ☎*031/3228522* ⊕*www.parlament.ch* 💰*Free* ⊙*Guided tours
only: Mon.–Sat. at 9, 10, 11, 2, 3, and 4; available in English.*

⑥ **Einsteinhaus** *(Einstein's House).* The sofa comes from Princeton, but the
★ rest of this genteel apartment has been lovingly re-created to evoke the
world of 1905, the miracle year in which then-tenant Albert Einstein,
a badly paid, newly married young clerk in Bern's Patent Office, developed and published his *Special Theory of Relativity.* All signage is in
English. ✉*Kramg. 49, Altstadt* ☎*031/3120091* ⊕*www.einstein-bern.
ch* 💰*6 SF* ⊙*Oct.–third week of Dec., Feb.–Mar.,Tues.–Fri. 10–5, Sat.
10–4; Apr.–Sept., daily 10–5.*

② **Heiliggeistkirche** *(Church of the Holy Ghost).* Built in the shadow of the
huge Christoffelturm on the site of a disused monastery hospital, this
Baroque church, laid out like a Huguenot temple, turned out to be a sur-
vivor as town walls, houses, gates, and fountains crashed down around
it to create today's busy transport hub. Serenity does still reign within,
where natural light floods the green sandstone supporting a magnificent vaulted stucco ceiling. ✉*Spitalg. 44, City Center* ☎*031/3003340*
⊕*www.ohk.ch* 💰*Free* ⊙*Tues.–Fri. 11–6:30.*

⑬ **Kunstmuseum** *(Museum of Fine Arts).* The permanent collection, one of the
★ largest and most diverse in Switzerland, begins with the Italian Trecento
(notably Duccio and Fra Angelico) then follows Swiss art from Niklaus
Manuel in the 15th century through Albert Anker and Ferdinand Hodler
in the 19th and on to Giovanni Giacometti and Cuno Amiet in the 20th.
The Impressionists are covered from Manet through Monet, the Nabis
by Bonnard. Picasso bridges the gap between Toulouse-Lautrec and

A GOOD WALK

Bern's downtown is not large, but it can be steep and there's a lot to absorb. Shops in the arcades often represent worlds to be discovered, you will never be far from a café, and the operative word throughout the city is "slow"—the Bernese way of life is to make time and enjoy it.

Begin in the main hall of the Hauptbahnhof, facing the arrivals and departures board, then turn 180 degrees and head through the main bank of escalators into the Christoffel-unterführung (Christoffel underpass). The polished granite tiles in the floor will lead you to the remnants of the city's third gate, the **Christoffelturm**, and a 15th-century bridge. Ride the escalator up to the Loeb department store.

To your left, on the far side of Spitalgasse, is the **Heiliggeistkirche**, named for a medieval monastic order and consecrated in 1729. Duck inside for a peek at its colorful Baroque ceiling, then follow the trams left past the cheerful Pfeiferbrunnen (Bagpiper Fountain) to the first intersection, Bärenplatz.

Keep following the trams (carefully) through the **Käfigturm**, a 17th-century prison tower built on the site of the city's 13th-century main gate, and continue down the street (now called Marktgasse) to admire the Anna Seilerbrunnen (Anna Seiler Fountain), an allegory on moderation named for the woman who founded Bern's main hospital in 1354.

The Schützenbrunnen (Musketeer Fountain), originally positioned to face the home of a 16th-century rifle society, is a little farther along, past the stately Kaiserhaus (a department store until 1972), on your right.

At the next intersection, the end of Marktgasse, follow the trams to the left to the Kindlifresserbrunnen, atop which an ogre (most likely a Fasnacht character) sits munching on several small children.

The imposing 18th-century **Kornhaus**, behind the fountain, is home to two restaurants and the 21st-century Kornhausforum (Media and Design Center).

Walk through the former market hall between the restaurants and head down Zeughausgasse to the front of the Französische Kirche (French Church). Nip inside for a look at the elegant 13th-century rood screen and wall paintings that range from intricate ivy to the Last Judgment, then loop around the other side of the church along Nägeligasse back to the Kornhausplatz. On your left is the neo-Baroque Stadttheater, Bern's Opera House.

Cross the street before the bridge and examine the dramatic 1849 equestrian monument to Rudolf von Erlach, the Bernese victor over the Burgundians in the 1339 Battle of Laupen, then head inland again to the intersection where the trams turn.

On your left, dominating the town center, is the mighty **Zytglogge**, Bern's original western gate and communal horological reference point since 1530.

Walk through the tower past the standard measurements on the left wall and turn around to view the actual clock face. If the minute hand is approaching the hour, you'll be treated to a show.

From the Zytglogge continue down Kramgasse, Bern's medieval main street. The painted figures and insignia above some houses indicate their connections to specific guilds; others date from the city's 18th-century height of prosperity. Note the grand Zähringerbrunnen (Zähringer Fountain) and the Simsonbrunnen (depicting Samson).

At No. 49, the **Einsteinhaus** is where a young man named Albert struggled to make his name in physics.

Take nearby Kramgasse (called Gerechtigkeitsgasse from this point on) and continue down the hill.

The Gerechtigkeitsbrunnen (Justice Fountain), considered the jewel of Bern's fountains, presents the emperor, the pope, the sultan, and the mayor of Bern.

As you pass the Hotel zum Goldenen Adler, the 18th-century successor to the city's oldest guesthouse, veer left where the main street becomes Nydeggasse and aim downhill into Nydeggstalden.

The **Nydeggkirche**, set back from the road on your right, occupies the site of Duke Berchtold's original fortress and thus represents the oldest part of the city.

From the church courtyard, head for the far end of the church and take the covered Burgtreppe stairs down to Mattenenge, turning left then right when you get to the bottom.

Both routes will leave you facing Bern's oldest river crossing, the Untertorbrücke, or Lower Gate Bridge, with the Läuferbrunnen (Messenger Fountain) and its bear-human duo sheltering under a tree to your left.

Cross the swift, blue-green Aare and head left past the Landhaus to the paved footpath marked ROSENGARTEN and zigzag to the right on Lerberstrasse.

When you reach Aargauerstalden you will be rewarded with a fetching view of the Altstadt (Old Town).

From here, head back down the hill to the traffic circle and cut directly across it to watch the city's mascots flirt with onlookers in the **Bärengraben**.

Walk straight through the carefully tended **Rosengarten** to see the best view of all—the city's bridges, rooftops, and, on clear days, the Gurten, Bern's local hill.

Meander through the flowerbeds and take the cobblestone footpath below the restaurant back down to Alter Aargauerstalden, the traffic circle, and the Bärengraben.

Cross back to the Altstadt by way of the Nydeggbrücke and veer left into Junkerngasse, a street named for its 17th-century upper-crust inhabitants.

At the top of Junkerngasse sits the pride of the city: the magnificent, Gothic **Münster**.

Turn left before the cathedral, however, and walk out onto the Münsterplattform (a medieval graveyard turned Reformation-era art dump turned pleasure garden) for a look at the grand front facades of the houses you just passed.

9

Bern

Universität
Hauptbahnhof

KEY

▭ Tram line
▭ Bus lines

ALTENBERG

Alter Aargauerstalden
Aargauerstalden

MATTE

DALMAZI

MARZILI

Läuferbrunnen
Gerechtigkeitsbrunnen
Vennerbrunnen
Simsonbrunnen
Zähringerbrunnen
Mosesbrunnen
Kindlifresserbrunnen
Franz. Kirche
Schützenbrunnen
Anna Seilerbrunnen
Pfeiferbrunnen
Ryffibrunnen
Mühlenplatz
Schwelle
Marzilibahn Funicular
Helvetiaplatz
Zeitglockenturm

Kornhausbrücke
Untertorbrücke
Nydeggbrücke
Kirchenfeldbrücke
Dalmazibrücke

TO GURTEN →

0   300 yards
0   300 meters

Bärengraben **8**
Bernisches Historisches
Museum **17**
Bundeshaus **12**
Christoffelturm **1**
Einsteinhaus **6**

Erlacherhof **10**
Heiliggeistkirche **2**
Käfigturm **3**
Kornhaus **4**
Kunsthalle Bern **15**
Kunstmuseum **13**

Münster **11**
Museum für
Kommunikation **19**
Naturhistorisches
Museum **18**
Nydeggkirche **7**
Rosengarten **9**

Schweizerisches
Alpines Museum **16**
Zentrum Paul Klee ... **14**
Zytglogge/
Zeitglockenturm **5**

Braque; Kirchner, Kandinsky, and Klee represent German expressionism through Blue Rider to Bauhaus. Mondrian and Meret Oppenheim round out the 20th century; temporary exhibits often take it from there. ⊠ *Hodlerstr. 8–12, City Center* ☎ *031/3280944* ⊕ *www.kunst museumbern.ch* ☎ *8 SF* ⊘ *Tues. 10–9, Wed.–Sun. 10–5.*

MARKET DAYS
The main fruit, vegetable, and flower market fills Bärenplatz with fresh produce, herbs, and flowers on Tuesday and Saturday (daily, during shopping hours between May and October).

⓫ **Münster** *(Cathedral).* Master Builder Matthäus Ensinger already had
Fodor'sChoice Strasbourg's cathedral under his belt when he drew up plans for what
★ became the largest and most artistically important church in Switzerland. The city broke ground in 1421 on the site of a smaller church that was dismantled once the cathedral's choir could accommodate Sunday worshippers, and work continued, with minor interruptions, for about 180 years. The finishing touch, the tip of the open, octagonal, 328-foot **steeple,** was added almost 200 years after that, in 1893. Today Switzerland's highest church tower houses two towerkeepers (in an apartment below the spire) and presents wraparound views of Bern and the surrounding mountains.

The Reformers dismantled much of the Catholic Münster's interior decoration and paintings (dumping them in the Münsterplattform, next door), but the exterior 15th-century representation of the Last Judgment above the **main portal** was deemed worthy and spared. The archangel Michael stands between ivory-skinned angels with gilt hair (heaven) on the left and green demons with gaping red maws (hell) on the right; painted images of the Annunciation and the Fall of Man flank the carved figures as you pass through the doors. Elaborately carved pews and choir stalls, within, are crowned by 15th-century **stained glass** windows that show an easy mix of local heraldry and Christian iconography. The organ, above the main entrance, is often used for concerts. ⊠ *Münsterpl. 1, Altstadt* ☎ *031/3120462* ⊕ *www.bernermuenster.ch* ☎ *Steeple 5 SF* ⊘ *Easter–Oct., Tues.–Sat. 10–5, Sun. 11:30–5; Nov.–Easter, Tues.–Fri. 10–noon, 2–4, Sat. 10–noon, 2–5, Sun. 11:30–2 (tower closes 30 min before church).*

❼ **Nydeggkirche** *(Nydegg Church).* A plaque on the outside wall of the church indicates where vestiges of Duke Berchtold's 12th-century Nydegg Castle (destroyed about 1270) still poke through the landscape; the church itself was begun in 1341, and its wooden pulpit dates from 1566. ⊠ *Nydegghof 2, Altstadt* ☎ *031/3525829* ⊕ *www.nydegg.ch* ⊘ *Apr.–Oct., daily 9–5; Nov.–Mar., daily 9–noon, 2–5.*

❾ **Rosengarten** *(Rose Garden).* The lower Altstadt's hilltop cemetery was
☾ converted to a public park in 1913. Today its lawns, arbors, playground,
★ and formal gardens draw leisurely couples and families with young children. The gardens are planted with azaleas, irises, rhododendron, and rose varieties such as Ingrid Bergman (deep velvet red), Maria Callas

9

(bright magenta), Christopher Columbus (peach), Cleopatra (red tips, orange interior), and Lady Di (small, pink). ⊠*Alter Aargauerstalden/ Laubeggstr.* ☎*031/3281212* 🎫*Free.*

NEED A BREAK? **Open from early March to late November, the Restaurant Rosengarten** (⊠*Alter Aargauerstalden 31b* ☎*031/3313206* ⊕*www.rosengarten.be*) serves dishes such as salmon tartare with crème fraîche and wasabi, Tandoori chicken kebabs, veal saltimbocca, and Brie sandwiches against a backdrop of panoramic Altstadt views.

⓮ **Zentrum Paul Klee** *(Paul Klee Center).* Engaged creativity are the watchwords in this undulating, light-filled complex inspired by the life and art of Paul Klee and designed by Renzo Piano. The permanent collection is the world's largest of works by Klee (about 200 are on display at any given time); temporary exhibits focus on his artistic environment and legacy. The Ensemble Paul Klee performs regular, varied, and colorful short concerts in the auditorium; guest artists from the worlds of theater and dance present productions, readings, and workshops (in German) with a pictorial slant. The Kindermuseum Creaviva, a sunny, paint-spattered area visible from the Restaurant Schöngrün on the north end of the interior Museum Street, is open to children over four and anyone else who would like to make art. A sculpture garden, free Internet terminals, and multilingual (audio) tours of the permanent collection round out the possibilities—come early and plan to spend the day. All signage is in English. To get to the Zentrum, head out from the city's central Hauptbahnhof. Head up the main escalators to the tram and bus stops on Bubenbergplatz and ride the No. 12 bus for 10 minutes to the end of the line. ⊠*Monument im Fruchtland 3, Schöngrün* ☎*031/3590101* ⊕*www.zpk.org* 🎫*16 SF (collection only)* ☉*Collection, Tues.–Sun. 10–5; Museum Street, Tues.–Sun. 9–5:30.*

❺ **Zytglogge/Zeitglockenturm** *(Clock Tower).* Though its exterior dates from 1771, the internal walls of Bern's first western gate reach back to the 12th century and represent the city's core. The calendar clock on the Kramgasse side began keeping Bern's official time in 1530; the gilded rooster to the left of the mechanical figures crows four minutes before every hour to begin the sequence of marching bears, fools, and gilded knights who strike the bells. The astronomical clock to the rooster's right keeps track of the day, the month, the zodiac, and the moon. Tours of the horological masterpiece behind it all are conducted in English. ⊠*Kramg. at Hotelg., Altstadt* ☎*031/3281212* ⊕*www.zeitglockenturm.ch* 🎫*Tour 10 SF* ☉*Tours May–Oct., daily 2:30; Nov.–Apr., by request.*

ALSO WORTH SEEING

❶ **Christoffelturm** *(Christoffel Tower).* Timelines (in English), 14th-century maps, 19th-century photographs, and St. Christopher's huge limewood head give context to the thick stone foundations of Bern's third city gate. The tower was built between 1344 and 1366 and destroyed in 1865 after a tight vote in favor of the train station. Its ruins have been

Bern's Artistic Son

It's ironic that expressionist painter Paul Klee (1879–1940), one of Switzerland's most prolific and talented artists, wasn't a Swiss citizen during his life. Though he was born near Bern and spent most of his life in the country, his nationality was determined by the lineage of his father, who was German.

Born into a family of musicians, Klee played with chalk as a toddler and filled his schoolbooks with caricatures and images copied from magazines. At age 19 he left Bern to study drawing in Munich, but he couldn't support himself with his art and returned to his parents in 1902. Four years later he had saved enough from his work as a violinist with the Bern Music Society to marry pianist Lily Stumpf and move to Munich, where they lived until 1926.

A trip to Tunisia in 1914 clarified Klee's artistic calling. "Color has taken possession of me," he wrote, upon encountering desert light. "I am a painter." His signature became color—rendered in oil, watercolor, ink, or all three—and almost childlike paintings with a highly developed sense of poetry, music, and dreams. Recognition followed in the 1920s, with exhibitions in Paris and New York and a teaching postion at the Bauhaus from 1921. In 1933 the Nazis labeled him a degenerate, his academic position in Düsseldorf was terminated, and he and Lily emigrated to Switzerland. The apartment they took the following year in Bern's Elfenau district became his studio for the rest of his life.

In 1935 Klee began to show symptoms of severe fatigue and what was misdiagnosed as the measles turned out to be (determined after his death) scleroderma. He continued to paint, however, and produced more than 1,000 works the year before his death in the Ticino, where he had gone to convalesce. His ashes are buried in Bern's Schosshalde cemetery, next to today's Zentrum Paul Klee.

incorporated into the underground shopping mall of the train station. ⊠ *Christoffel-unterführung, City Center.*

⑩ Erlacherhof *(Erlach House).* Mayor Hieronymus von Erlach did not live to see the elegant mansion he commissioned in 1746, but it remains the only private edifice in Bern with a formal courtyard and a garden terrace (visible from the Münsterplattform). Commandeered by the French in 1798, it was purchased by the city in 1832 and served as the Swiss Federal Parliament building from 1848 to 1858. It now houses government offices. ⊠ *Junkerng. 47, Altstadt* ☎ *031/2216201.*

❸ Käfigturm *(Prison Tower).* The current tower, completed in 1643, served as the city's prison until 1897. Reconfigured as the Confederation's Political Forum in 1999, it now hosts political events and exhibitions. ⊠ *Marktg. 67, City Center* ☎ *031/3227007* ⊕ *www.kaefigturm.admin.ch* 🎫 *Free* ☉ *Weekdays 8–6, Sat. 10–4 during exhibitions.*

❹ Kornhaus *(Granary).* Wine stocked the cellar and grain filled the top three floors of this granary for 100 years during Bern's Golden Age. Then the 1814 Vienna Congress separated the city from its territories and this monumental Baroque storage depot lost its function overnight.

The cellar was renovated in 1893 and painted four years later; today it houses a restaurant, where waiters scurry past images of Bernese women in traditional costume, Renaissance musicians, and a who's who of folkloric characters. The **Kornhausforum** (Media and Design Center) organizes contemporary design, architecture, video, photography, and applied art exhibits upstairs. ⊠*Kornhauspl. 18, Altstadt* ☎*031/3129110* ⊕*www.kornhausforum.ch* ✆*9–12 SF, varies by exhibit* ⊘*Tues.–Fri. 10–7, weekends 10–5.*

WORD OF MOUTH

"Zentrum Paul Klee [is] fabulous. Amazing architecture (Renzo Piano); even if you don't like Klee, the building—inside and out—and the grounds are worth it. Exhibition is great and we were entranced by the children's area with plenty of hands-on…and workshops. Of course, everyone checks email at the free Internet set-ups in the museum."

—escargot

NEED A BREAK?
Outdoor tables, a sunny central location, light meals, homemade pastries, 10 kinds of coffee, and open doors from 8 AM 'til midnight give the **Kornhaus Café** (⊠*Kornhauspl. 18, Altstadt* ☎*031/3277270*) a constant, marketlike buzz.

MUSEUM DISTRICT

Kirchenfeld is a quiet, leafy neighborhood due south of the Altstadt, with radial streets and unexpected vistas. It was constructed in 1881 according to a district plan and quickly filled with embassies, consulates, and the bulk of Bern's museums.

A GOOD WALK

Begin at Casinoplatz and dip downhill onto the Kirchenfeldbrücke. Far below on your left is the Matteschwelle, a weir almost as old as the city that steers river water around and through the Matte district (most of the time—in August 2005 the entire neighborhood flooded up to the first floor). On your right is a panoramic view of the Bundeshaus and the less precarious Marzili area.

Keep left as you come off the bridge and duck inside the **Kunsthalle Bern** to check the pulse of contemporary art, then cross the street and aim to the left of the building labeled Schulwarte; a little farther along its facade on the right is the entrance to the **Schweizerisches Alpines Museum**. Return to the corner with a new appreciation for the art of mapping mountains and cross Helvetiaplatz to the castlelike **Bernisches Historisches Museum**. The self-consciously epic statue in the middle of the square commemorates the advent of telegraphic communication in Europe. Exit the museum when you've exhausted Bernese history and follow its walls in either direction, to the left down Bernastrasse for the low-key **Naturhistorisches Museum** or to the right down Helvetiastrasse for the interactive **Museum für Kommunikation**. From Helvetiaplatz cross the Kirchenfeldbrücke back to the Altstadt.

WHAT TO SEE

⑰ **Bernisches Historisches Museum** *(Bern History Museum).* Indonesian shadow puppets, Japanese swords, Polynesian masks, Indian figurines, and Celtic jewelry fill the ground floor, and the Islamic collection is exquisite, but head to the basement for the real focus: Bern and its place in Swiss history. Armor and arms, lavish church treasure (including sculptures from the Münster), magnificent silver, tapestries "acquired" in 1476–77 when the Bernese pushed Charles the Bold back into France, and several of Hans Gieng's original fountain statues lead the charge. The top floor is devoted to Einstein; major signage is in English. ⊠*Helvetiapl. 5, Kirchenfeld* 🕾*031/3507711* ⊕*www.bhm.ch* 🗐*18 SF* ⊙*Tues.–Sun. 10–5.*

> **DID YOU KNOW?**
>
> Albert Einstein wrote and published his *Special Theory of Relativity* in Bern, in 1905.

OFF THE BEATEN PATH

Gurten. Bern's very own hill presents a delightful alternative to the city on clear afternoons. The view moves from the Jura Mountains in the west to the Alps in the east by way of Bern itself; multiple lawns, terraces, and restaurants allow for picnics, cafeteria service, or formal dining as you gaze. The bright red funicular to the top takes three minutes; head left to the east for a diagram labeling more than 200 distant peaks or right for a 360-degree view from the top of the Gurtenturm. You can also walk up from Wabern. ⊠*Wabern* ⊹*tram No. 9, stop Gurtenbahn* 🕾*031/9703333* ⊕*www.gurtenpark.ch* 🗐*Funicular 10 SF round-trip, 6 SF one-way* ⊙*Funicular Mon.–Sat. 7 AM–11:40 PM, Sun. 7 AM–10 PM.*

⑮ **Kunsthalle Bern** *(Bern Art Gallery).* A completely different animal from the Kunstmuseum across town, this groundbreaking contemporary art venue built in 1918 by and for artists (among them Kirchner, Klee, and Giacometti père) seeks to confront, provoke, and engage viewers with the artistic phenomena of today. This translates each year to between six and seven exhibits of work by living artists; they become part of a history that includes Wassily Kandinsky, Henry Moore, Jasper Johns, Sol LeWitt, Bruce Nauman, Christo, and Grandma Moses. ⊠*Helvetiapl. 1, Kirchenfeld* 🕾*031/3500040* ⊕*www.kunsthalle-bern.ch* 🗐*8 SF* ⊙*Tues. 10–7, Wed.–Sun. 10–5.*

⑲ **Museum für Kommunikation** *(Museum of Communication).* This resolutely ♺ interactive museum keeps its focus on the act of communication rather ★ than the means. Exhibits examine body language across cultures, the views of Switzerland's minority populations, the history of the Swiss postal service, and the evolution of telecommunication through to the Internet. The world's largest collection of postage stamps is also here. All signage is in English. ⊠*Helvetiastr. 16, Kirchenfeld* 🕾*031/3575555* ⊕*www.mfk.ch* 🗐*12 SF* ⊙*Tues.–Sun. 10–5.*

⑱ **Naturhistorisches Museum** *(Museum of Natural History).* The biggest ♺ draw here is the stuffed body of Barry, a St. Bernard who saved more than 40 people in the Alps between 1800 and 1812, but start with the Alpine minerals, diamonds, and fossils in the basement, working up to

9

wild animals in the city. Birds' nests, skeletons large and small, interactive temporary exhibits, and more than 200 wildlife dioramas round out the highlights. Basic signage is in English. ✉ *Bernastr. 15, Kirchenfeld* ☎ *031/3507111* ⊕ *www.nmbe.ch* 💰 *8 SF* ⊘ *Mon. 2–5, Tues., Thurs., and Fri. 9–5, Wed. 9–6, weekends 10–5.*

⓰ Schweizerisches Alpines Museum *(Swiss Alpine Museum)*. A slideshow
★ overview of Switzerland's relationship with its mountains acts as an introduction to this detailed museum. Exhibits include massive topographical models and relief maps; audiovisual consoles covering topics such as the Roman introduction of viticulture, power generation, and global warming; Alpine farming implements, toys, and skis; frank descriptions of mountain life; ceremonial masks; and Hodler's seven-part mural of the Matterhorn's conquest. You'll leave with a hearty appreciation for Swiss tenacity. All signage is in English. ✉ *Helvetiapl. 4, Kirchenfeld* ☎ *031/3500440* ⊕ *www.alpinesmuseum.ch* 💰 *10 SF* ⊘ *Mon. 2–5:30, Tues.–Sun. 10–5:30.*

WHERE TO EAT

THE SCENE

Traditional dining in Bern is a pretty grounded affair, characterized by Italian home cooking and German-style meat and potatoes. Two particular local favorites are the *Bernerplatte*—great slabs of salt pork, beef tongue, smoked bacon, pork ribs, and mild pork sausage cooked down in broth then heaped on top of juniper-scented sauerkraut, green beans, and boiled potatoes—and *Berner Rösti,* shredded potatoes pan-fried with onions, butter, and chunks of bacon. Other—healthier—options include creative vegetarian cuisine, refined gastronomic delicacies, fresh fish—often caught in the nearby Aare river—and ethnic foods. Most menus change with the seasons, featuring asparagus in spring, berries in summer, and wild game in fall; food presentation can be sophisticated; and service is almost universally friendly.

Many of Bern's established restaurants are dark, often underground, and accessible through a kind of cellar storm door that looks much like the one Dorothy just missed getting to when the tornado hit her Kansas farm. But once you're down there, you'll find the atmosphere cozy and warm, with a hint of the medieval—especially in the simpler, beer-hall type venues. Another option is sitting at one of the few tables that are usually outside each restaurant, but under the famous Bernese arches, so you're sheltered from summer showers on a hot July evening, say, or a biting spring breeze. As soon as the weather permits, indoor restaurants are abandoned—but still open—as diners flock outdoors.

Be sure to make reservations, especially if you want to eat outside in warm weather. Popular garden restaurants that attract both tourists and locals will be packed at lunch, so you might try arriving a little before noon—but don't try the other extreme and come late, as most kitchens switch to the snack menu after 2—if they're still open.

WHAT IT COSTS IN SWISS FRANCS				
¢	$	$$	$$$	$$$$
AT DINNER	under 15 SF	15 SF–25 SF	25 SF–40 SF	40 SF–60 SF	over 60 SF

Prices are per person for a main course at dinner.

$–$$
SWISS
✕**Altes Tramdepot.** The cavernous, stripped-down barn space, voluminous outdoor seating with leafy views of the Altstadt, and hints of Munich in the menu all underline the fact that your Bernerplatte with homemade Spätzli, cordon bleu, Weisswurst, or warm pretzel filled with ham would be incomplete without a house beer. There are two vegetarian dishes if you're not here for the meat. Dark, light, and "normal" varieties are brewed in copper vats behind the bar and specialty beers appear at Easter, in October, or during the full moon. The kitchen stays open from 11 AM to midnight every day of the year. ⊠*Grosser Muristalden 6, Bärengraben* ☎*031/3681415* ⊟*AE, DC, MC, V.*

$$–$$$
SWISS
Fodor'sChoice
★
✕**Della Casa.** Probably the ultimate place to sample a Bernerplatte, luscious veal liver with Rösti, superlative game (in season), or hearty ox-tail stew with fried macaroni, this institution beloved of Swiss politicians is affectionately nicknamed "Delli" and has been operating nearly as long as the Federal parliament building, down the street. The yellowed "Säli" on the ground floor and the wood-paneled restaurant upstairs share the same big, generous kitchen; the veteran waitresses shepherd you through the menu; and there's no need to rush—your second portion awaits on a warming table nearby. ⊠*Schauplatzg. 16, City Center* ☎*031/3112142* ⊟*AE, DC, MC, V* ⊘*Closed Sun. year-round; Apr.–Sept., no dinner Sat.*

$–$$
ECLECTIC
✕**Gartenrestaurant Marzilibrücke.** Red-and-yellow pillows punctuate the white benches and wood tables inside this bohemian spot on the Marzili side of the river; the shaded gravel garden out front and the gourmet pizza zone around back more than double the restaurant's size in summer. The staff may seem casual, but the menu's sweep of Indian curries, lentils, and naan; local fish; Thai curry; pasta; schnitzel; and Caesar or Greek salad is presented with timely flair. Italian and Spanish wines dominate; Sunday brunch is served from 10 to 2. ⊠*Gasstr. 8, Marzili* ☎*031/3112780* ⊟*AE, DC, MC, V* ⊘*No lunch Sat.*

$$–$$$
SWISS
✕**Harmonie.** Plain wooden chairs, blue tablecloths, warm orange trim, and the telltale whiff of cheese all indicate, correctly, that this family-run establishment within sight of the Zytglogge does Swiss cuisine well. Whether classic (Gruyère), *moitié-moitié* (half Gruyère, half Vacherin), or gussied up with truffles and champagne, fondue will arrive trailing copious amounts of bread and, ideally, a *pot* of Vaudois white. *Käseschnitte* (open-face sandwiches with melted cheese), *Chäshörnli* (macaroni and cheese), traditional pork sausage, veal, beef, rack of lamb, and sides of crispy brown Rösti or *Spätzli* (dumplings) complete the picture of a nation well fed. ⊠*Hotelg. 3, Altstadt* ☎*031/3131141* ⊟*AE, DC, MC, V* ⊘*Closed weekends.*

$$$–$$$$
FRENCH
✕**Jack's Brasserie.** Time moves a little slower here amid the civilized elegance of lazy cigarette smoke and china teapots. Picture windows face the train station; gilt ceiling details, grapevine motifs, and leopard-

9

print banquettes warm up the wood paneling; and the day's papers hang from lampposts at discreet intervals between tables. The menu changes every week, but the classic French theme is constant—expect tartares and minestrone in summer, cassoulet or veal liver in winter, and chateaubriand year-round. There's an excellent selection of Swiss wines and expensive but top-flight French reds. ⊠ *Bahnhofpl. 11, City Center* ☎ *031/3268080* ☐ *AE, DC, MC, V.*

$$–$$$
MEDITERRANEAN

✕ **Kornhauskeller.** Entering the Kornhauskeller is like entering a cathedral, except that the stunning vaulted ceilings and frescoes are underground and the lounge-bar in the gallery stocks 92 whiskeys, 30 rums, 15 bourbons, and a selection of Cuban cigars. The building has focused on food throughout its long life, first as a wine cellar/granary, then as a beer hall, now as a classy, popular restaurant where crostini, carpaccio, lemon risotto, and gnocchi with artichoke occupy the same menu as calves' liver, veal schnitzel, and a regal Bernerplatte. ⊠ *Kornhauspl. 18, Altstadt* ☎ *031/3277272* ☐ *AE, DC, MC, V* ☯ *No lunch Sun.*

$$–$$$
ITALIAN
★

✕ **Lorenzini.** If Bern were Italian, every place might look like this one. Cushioned brown benches and black wooden chairs surround white-clad tables with silver bread bowls. Eclectic photos, prints, and paintings adorn the walls, and marble statues stand tucked in alcoves. The staff exudes the barest hint of attitude, and Tuscany and Piedmont jostle for space on the wine list. The kitchen presents mouthwatering homemade pastas and desserts, with a signature dish of escalope of veal with ham, sage, and saffron risotto. The open-air atrium, crammed with tables and summer diners, is decorated with olive trees, grape vines, and pink geraniums. And, there are two bars. ⊠ *Theaterpl. 5/Hotelg. 8, Altstadt* ☎ *031/3117850* ☐ *AE, DC, MC, V* ☯ *Closed Sun.*

$
ECLECTIC

✕ **Markthalle.** The name says it all: the global food court you see today—in which Japanese, Turkish, Indian, and tapas eateries rub shoulders with a gelato stand and a white-linen formal restaurant that offers tasting menus with tidbits from around the globe—was once a market hall full of produce and independent vendors. The wine shop does tastings; the tea-and-herbs emporium brews cups from China, India, Japan, South Africa, and Sri Lanka; and stand-up bars keep things animated late into the evening. ⊠ *Bubenbergpl. 9, City Center* ⊕ *www.markthalle-bern.ch* ☐ *AE, MC, V.*

$$$$
MEDITERRANEAN

✕ **Meridiano.** The curved gold ceiling, white baby grand, brown suede bench nooks, and sweeping view of the Altstadt complete with operatic Alpine backdrop make this chic, contemporary space a wonderful spot for romance. And the complex, vibrant and award-winning Mediterranean menu includes such dishes as fried duck liver on a bed of candied melons, or sautéed filet of veal with wild garlic pesto and fresh chanterelle mushrooms. Chef Fredi Boss oversees the kitchen; ask for a seat on the terrace in summer—the view is spectacular. ⊠ *Hotel Allegro, Kornhausstr. 3, Kornhausbrücke* ☎ *031/3395500* ☐ *AE, DC, MC, V* ☯ *Closed Sun. and Mon. No lunch Sat.*

$$–$$$
MEDITERRANEAN

✕ **Schwellenmätteli.** A chest-high glass barrier stands between you and white water at the tip of this sun-soaked, airy restaurant-lounge and bar. Built like a ship's prow past the edge of the Matteschwelle weir, this unique establishment maintains a hip, beachlike atmosphere with its chaises longues, teak bar stools, and cushioned wicker chairs. The dining area, inside or beneath a retractable roof, serves Mediterranean-inspired dishes like lemongrass-cream soup, rhubarb-strawberry chutney with baked Vacherin, red snapper with lemon risotto and grilled vegetables, and *cabillaud* (cod) saltimbocca with saffron potatoes. ☒ *Dalmaziquai 11, Schwellenmätteli* ☎ *031/3505001* 🖃 *AE, MC, V.*

> ### CASANOVA WAS HERE
>
> The history of Zum Zähringer dates back to the time when Badgasse (Bath Street) was Bern's red-light district and the inn on the corner was a favorite with Giacomo Casanova.

¢ ✕**Tibits.** Everything on the menu can be ordered to go, and its integration into the train station building makes this airy space a favorite with travelers. But linger in the wicker chairs or spread books across the long tables; the children's corner has toys, storybooks, a blackboard, and high chairs. The food is 100% vegetarian and sold by weight from a buffet that can yield three courses; homemade sandwiches and soups such as pumpkin, lentil, or green pea with peppermint fill in the gaps. To drink: fresh fruit and vegetable juices, organic wine, flavored coffee, herbal tea, and cocktails such as Rooibos Vodka. ☒ *Bahnhofpl. 10, City Center* ☎ *031/3129111* 🖃 *No credit cards.*

VEGETARIAN
Fodor's Choice
★

\$\$–\$\$\$ ✕**Verdi.** Music is a leitmotif along walls studded with opera posters, paintings, programs, scores, photos, and clippings; there are also low ceilings, wooden beams, gilt mirrors, velvet drapes, stone walls, and a balcony overlooking a huge working fireplace. The real star, however, is the menu, which sees truffles, cream, and polenta transition to tomatoes, basil, fennel, and lemon soup with salmon ravioli as the weather warms up. Rack of lamb with a caponata of eggplants, onions, capers, olives, and tomatoes is a year-round favorite. The wine cellar, visible through glass doors off the dining room, ranges all over Italy. ☒ *Gerechtigkeitsg. 5, Altstadt* ☎ *031/3126368* 🖃 *AE, DC, MC, V.*

ITALIAN
★

\$\$–\$\$\$ ✕**Zimmermania.** A deceptively simple local favorite and one of the most typically French bistros in Bern, this cultural transplant tucked away on a backstreet near the Rathaus has been serving classics like *entrecôte café de Paris* with French fries, *escargots* in herb garlic butter, and calf's head since 1848. In a city that celebrates the onion, this is a good place to try onion soup. Lunch specials are under 20 SF; wines come from Switzerland, Italy, and France. ☒ *Brunng. 19, Altstadt* ☎ *031/3111542* 🖃 *MC, V* ☺ *Closed Sun. and Mon.*

FRENCH
★

\$\$–\$\$\$ ✕**Zum Zähringer.** This is a four-parter, with a formal, elegant salon called "Dine and Wine," a less formal bistro with a somewhat smaller offering on the menu, a covered terrace overlooking the river Aare, and a garden area that hosts barbecues in summer. All share the same kitchen, which serves up dishes such as pork cutlets with root vegetables and French fries; *Sauerbraten* (beef marinated in red wine) with mashed potatoes; and baked filets of pike-perch with capers, tomato cubes, and new potatoes. ☒ *Badg. 1, Matte* ☎ *031/312 0888* 🖃 *MC, V* ☺ *Closed Sun. No lunch Sat. and Mon.*

CONTEMPORARY
Fodor's Choice
★

9

WHERE TO STAY

THE SCENE

Bern has plenty of quality hotels, many of them splendorous with 19th-century characteristics: lobbies with 20-foot-tall ceilings ornately tinged with stucco moldings; balconies with curlicue Belle Epoque iron railings; domed corner turrets; and miles of marble floors. A step or two below, price-wise, are some older venues that still tend toward the generic. But today's owners and managers are waking up to the fact that flowered prints and dusty blue carpeting are just a little too 1980s, even if they're very clean. These new entrepreneurs are ripping up old flooring to expose and polish up the often centuries-old parquet underneath; they're whitewashing the walls; installing state-of-the-art entertainment systems; upgrading the bathrooms (or just plain adding them); and fixing up the rooms with simple, modular furniture that keeps the prices at a level the average tourist can afford.

Given Bern's geographical characteristics, almost all the hotels listed in this chapter are located within the same medieval central-city core—which can easily be crossed on foot in 10 minutes at most. Most of the streets are pedestrian, or "traffic-calmed" to the extent that most drivers don't venture into the Old Town at all. What this all adds up to: leave your car in a parking lot for the duration of your stay, as you'll have plenty of opportunity to wander the streets on foot.

What's true of practically every hotel staff member in Bern is that they are professional, helpful, cheerful, accommodating, and—this is Switzerland after all—most of them speak at least three languages comfortably, and one of those is sure to be English. If you can, be sure to book in advance—music festivals, trade conventions, markets, sports events, and parliamentary sessions (March, June, September, and December) can fill rooms fast. Rates drop on weekends, when there is less demand.

WHAT IT COSTS IN SWISS FRANCS				
	¢	$	$$	$$$	$$$$
FOR TWO PEOPLE	under 100 SF	100 SF–175 SF	175 SF–250 SF	250 SF–350 SF	over 350 SF

Prices are for two people in a standard double room, including tax and service.

$$ 🖼 **Ador.** Functional, yet nonetheless nicely appointed and located just west of the Hauptbahnhof near tram stops and a movie theater, this boxy hotel is a good deal if you're price-conscious but still want something stylish. The stone lobby sparkles, and vending machines on each level replace in-room refrigerators; rooms have modular furniture, dark parquet floors, and white-tile baths; they are also designed for wheelchair use. **Pros:** well-designed modern interiors; close to everything. **Cons:** uninspiring exterior located on a block heavy with early '70s concrete. ⊠ *Laupenstr. 15, City West* ☎ *031/3880111* ⊕ *www.hotelador.ch* 🛏 *52 rooms* 🚪 *In-room: no a/c, safe, Ethernet. In-hotel: restaurant, public Internet, public Wi-Fi, parking (fee)* 🖃 *AE, DC, MC, V* 🍽 *BP.*

$$$ 🔲**Allegro.** In a town renowned for its antiquity, the Allegro stands out as thoroughly modern. Styles range from the interior Atrium rooms, with one-way glass windows, flat-screen TVs, and backlit smoked-glass headboards to penthouse suites with private balconies, pan-

> **OH, BELLE EPOQUE!**
>
> Original works of art by Steinlen, Hodler and Klimt grace the walls of the Belle Epoque hotel.

oramic city views, rounded leather furniture, and Jacuzzis. Unusual for Switzerland: there is an ice machine on every floor. The modern Chinese restaurant Yù has a wall of falling water. **Pros:** heated tiled floors in bathrooms; upper south-facing rooms with Alpine views. **Cons:** somewhat stiff staff. ✉*Kornhausstr. 3, Kornhausbrücke* ☎*031/3395500* ⊕*www.allegro-hotel.ch* ⟳*167 rooms, 4 suites* ♿*In-room: safe, refrigerators, dial-up. In-hotel: 3 restaurants, bar, gym, public Wi-Fi, bicycles, airport shuttle, parking (fee)* ⊟*AE, DC, MC, V.*

$$$ 🔲**Belle Epoque.** Pay close attention to the walls in this boutique gem,
★ they're furnished entirely with Belle Epoque originals: Steinlen graces the bathrooms and breakfast area, Hodler and Klimt spice up suites named for them, and the bar has photos of Toulouse-Lautrec standing next to the Moulin Rouge poster behind you. Windows are triple-glazed for silence, bathrooms have vanities, closets disguised as traveling trunks hide televisions, and period consoles pick up BBC World Service radio. Each of the three suites has a DVD player, Dolby Surround Sound, and original LPs. **Pros:** well-stocked breakfast buffet; on a charming & quiet cobblestone street. **Cons:** live jazz on Sunday draws boisterous crowds. ✉*Gerechtigkeitsg. 18, Altstadt* ☎*031/3114336* ⊕*www.belle-epoque. ch* ⟳*14 rooms, 3 suites* ♿*In-room: no a/c, safe, refrigerator, dial-up. In-hotel: restaurant, bar, public Wi-Fi* ⊟*AE, DC, MC, V.*

$$$$ 🔲**Bellevue Palace.** A pretension-free mix of Belle Epoque elegance
Fodor'sChoice and contemporary ease defines this impeccable hotel built in 1913 to
★ accommodate government visitors. Intricate moldings, golden beige brocade, crystal chandeliers, and Art Nouveau stained glass lure political events and weddings here. Guest rooms are outfitted with warm yellows, reds, and blues; granite bathrooms with heated floors; and occasional flat-screen TVs. The fifth floor has sleek modern lines, glass showers, and sloped ceilings. The elegant Bellevue Grill uses seasonal ingredients to create artful dishes and menus. **Pros:** two extremely loungeable lobbies for decompressing; fabulous Alpine views from south-facing rooms and outdoor dining terrace; elegant design. **Cons:** Wi-Fi is fee-based. ✉*Kocherg. 3–5, Altstadt* ☎*031/3204545* ⊕*www. bellevue-palace.ch* ⟳*117 rooms, 13 suites* ♿*In-room: safe, refrigerator, Internet. In-hotel: restaurant, bar, public Wi-Fi, parking (fee)* ⊟*AE, DC, MC, V* ⦿*BP.*

$$–$$$ 🔲**Bern.** With an imposing facade that looks like a 19th-century bank, this energetic property, on a busy street behind the Kornhaus, contrasts totally with the clean, modern lines inside. Guest rooms have colorful block carpeting, curved light fixtures, chairs shaped like punctuation marks, and the occasional architectural flourish such as rounded windows or sloping eaves. Most of the clientele are businesspeople

9

but the hotel is equally suited to children. **Pros:** kids stay free; expert service. **Cons:** restaurants are a bit stale, style-wise. ⊠ *Zeughausg. 9, City Center* ☎ *031/3292222* 🖷 *031/3292299* ⊕ *www.hotelbern. ch* 🖙 *100 rooms* ♿ *In-room: no a/c, safe, refrigerator, Ethernet. In-hotel: 3 restaurants (1 seasonal May–September), public Wi-Fi* ⊟ *AE, DC, MC, V* ⊠ *BP.*

$$$ ⬚ **Best Western Bären/Bristol.** The joint occupants of a full city block, halfway between the Hauptbahnhof and the Bundeshaus, these business-class Siamese twins are favorites with parliament officials and bankers—and perfectly placed at the heart of Bern's commercial district. Clean, modern, and functional, the guest rooms are outfitted with sleek curved wood, round glass tables, starched white duvets. A large proportion are no-smoking—a rarity in this country. **Pros:** good value; very central; practical desks. **Cons:** a bit of a clunker compared to the elegant hotels in the area. ⊠ *Bären: Schauplatzg. 4, City Center* ☎ *031/3113367, 800/780–7234 in U.S.* 🖙 *57 rooms* ⊕ *www.baerenbern.ch* ⊠ *Bristol: Schauplatzg. 10, City Center* ☎ *031/3110101, 800/780–7234 in U.S.* 🖷 *031/3119479* ⊕ *www.bristolbern.ch* 🖙 *92 rooms* ♿ *In-room: safe, refrigerator, dial-up. In-hotel: bar, spa, bicycles, public Wi-Fi* ⊟ *AE, DC, MC, V* ⊠ *BP.*

$ ⬚ **Goldener Schlüssel.** This 500-year-old (and oldest in Bern) property is within earshot of the Zytglogge bells; its solidly popular restaurant serves a mix of rib-sticking favorites like bratwurst with Rösti, and a few Indian dishes like Gujarati thali. The service is friendly and enthusiastic. The recently renovated rooms are small but nicely conceived, with dark parquet floors, modular furniture, white pillows, and duvet covers, and flatscreen TVs; all have showers. The top floors offer medieval-rooftop views. **Pros:** good bang for the buck; quiet location. **Cons:** small rooms. ⊠ *Rathausg. 72, Altstadt* ☎ *031/3110216* ⊕ *www.goldener-schluessel. ch* 🖙 *34 rooms* ♿ *In-room: no a/c, safe. In-hotel: restaurant, public Internet, public Wi-Fi* ⊟ *MC, V* ⊠ *BP.*

$$$ ⬚ **Innere Enge.** Exposed beams, Art Nouveau accents, pristine Alpine views, and jazz memorabilia from greats like Lionel Hampton, John Lewis, Hazy Osterwald, and Clark Terry punctuate the spacious, sunny rooms in this half-timbered inn that dates to the early 1700s. The park-like setting, five minutes by bus from the Hauptbahnhof, provides a tranquil alternative to city streets; Marians Jazzroom warms things up in the basement during the school year. Napoléon's beloved Josephine once had lunch in the Park Pavilion. **Pros:** lush private park; large outdoor terrace. **Cons:** quite a way from the center. ⊠ *Engestr. 54, Innere Enge* ☎ *031/3096111* ⊕ *www.zghotels.ch* 🖙 *11 rooms, 15 suites* ♿ *In-room: refrigerators, no a/c (some), safe, dial-up. In-hotel: restaurant, public Wi-Fi, parking (no fee)* ⊟ *AE, DC, MC, V* ⊠ *BP.*

$$ ⬚ **Kreuz.** There may not be a frill in sight, and there must have been a Spartan on the design committee, but all that is counterbalanced by up-to-date modern furnishings in well-outfitted guest rooms, personable service, and a housekeeping team that works hard upholding the stereotype of the Swiss as a fussy people with a penchant for cleanliness. **Pros:** excellent location; free Internet; very good staff. **Cons:** although modern, the gym is very small; front rooms may catch noise from the street. ⊠*Zeughausg. 39/41, Altstadt* ☎*031/3299595* ⊕*www. hotelkreuz-bern.ch* ↘*90 rooms* ♻*In-room: no a/c, refrigerator. In-hotel: restaurant, gym, public Internet* ☐*AE, DC, MC, V* ♥❘*BP.*

$ ⬚**Landhaus.** The river views are idyllic and the wood floors creak authenticity in this airy young hostel with a Foosball table by the reception, live jazz in the laid-back restaurant, communal kitchen space, and a grocery store. Rooms range from dorm-style cubicles (for 33 SF) with sold-separately linens and breakfast to all-inclusive doubles with shower. Every guest room has modern stainless steel bed frames and a sink. The bistro restaurant offers take-out service if you'd rather eat in your room or in the surrounding greenery. **Pros:** ideal location: central yet green; helpful service; good place to meet other travelers. **Cons:** more youth hostel than hotel. ⊠*Altenbergstr. 4–6, Altenberg* ☎*031/3314166* ⊕*www.landhausbern.ch* ↘*6 rooms, 2 with bath, 2 dormitories* ♻*In-room: no a/c. In-hotel: restaurant, bar, kitchen, public Wi-Fi, no elevator* ☐*AE, DC, MC, V* ♥❘*BP.*

¢–$ ⬚**Marthahaus.** Bright, sunny rooms—some with a balcony—have light wood, white walls, sinks, and up to five beds; the reception is open round the clock; breakfast—served in an airy, cheerful bistro-style room—can be served from 4:30 AM; and the staff will do your laundry at this quiet, comfortable turn-of-the-century pension north of Bern's Altstadt. Mixed-sex dormitory space costs 45 SF. There's an intimate common room with a TV. **Pros:** staff is very accommodating; cooking facilities, bicycles, and an Internet terminal are free. **Cons:** a brisk walk from the center. ⊠*Wyttenbachstr. 22a, Lorraine* ☎*031/3324135* ⊕*www.marthahaus.ch* ↘*40 rooms, 4 with shower, 6 dormitories* ♻*In-room: no a/c, kitchen, Wi-Fi. In-hotel: bicycles, public Internet, public Wi-Fi, parking (fee)* ☐*MC, V* ♥❘*BP.*

$ ⬚**Nydeck.** Mirrors work magic in this small, tidy corner hotel near the Nydeggbrücke; light-wood parquet floors, sage-green headboards and upholstery, white-striped duvet covers, pink geraniums, and medieval city views complete the job. Compact white-tile bathrooms have glass showers, hair dryers, and vanities; double-glazed windows keep street noise at bay. The Junkere bar, downstairs, spills into a delightful sidewalk terrace in summer. **Pros:** cheerful environment; perfect medieval neighborhood setting. **Cons:** the bed seems bigger than the room in some instances. ⊠*Gerechtigkeitsg. 1, Altstadt* ☎*031/3118686* ⊕*www.hotelnydeck.ch* ↘*12 rooms* ♻*In-room: no a/c. In-hotel: bar, public Wi-Fi, no elevator* ☐*AE, DC, MC, V* ♥❘*BP.*

$$$ ⬚**Savoy.** Halogen-lighted hallways lead to pleasant rooms with rose carpets, yellow walls, sleek wood, and white bedcovers in this neatly tailored hotel across the street from the Stauffacher bookstore. The Hauptbahnhof and Bern's markets are just a block away. Most of the doubles have two sinks, the fourth floor has rooftop views, suites have extra seating areas, and any room facing the *Hof* (inner courtyard) will be absolutely quiet. **Pros:** rooms have soundproofed windows; very friendly staff. **Cons:** interiors could use a bit of an overhaul. ⊠*Neueng. 26, City Center* ☎*031/3114405* ⊕*www.zghotels.ch* ↘*50 rooms, 6 suites* ♻*In-room: no a/c (some), safe, dial-up. In-hotel: restaurant, public Wi-Fi* ☐*AE, DC, MC, V* ♥❘*BP.*

NIGHTLIFE & THE ARTS

Twice a year, Bern Tourismus publishes and widely disseminates *Bern Guide*, a free, pocket-size, bilingual (German/English), and comprehensive guide to what's on in the city (exhibits, nightlife, festivals, shopping, excursions, and useful telephone numbers). The Web site *www. berninfo.com* fills in any remaining gaps.

NIGHTLIFE

The Bernese like to party, and nightlife options accordingly run the gamut from plush velvet seating and Belle Epoque refinement to jazz lounges, casual sidewalk bars, and plugged-in clubs where DJs spin the latest. Bärenplatz and Kornhausplatz bubble over with revelers on summer evenings; many restaurants transition into bars as the night wears on.

BARS

Adriano's (⊠ *Theaterpl. 2, Altstadt* ☎ *031/3188831* ⊕ *www.adrianos. ch*) is a friendly, glassed-in coffee bar that serves fresh croissants from 7 AM (10 AM on Sunday), sandwiches throughout the day, and wine or beer to a sidewalk crowd come nightfall. Exquisite Belle Epoque paintings and outdoor jazz grace the **Bar Toulouse-Lautrec** (⊠ *Hotel Belle Epoque*). Well-heeled travelers come to see and be seen at the indoor-outdoor **Bellevue Bar** (⊠ *Hotel Bellevue Palace*). The wood-paneled Weinstube dates from 1635, and the owners are traditionally single blonde women at the **Klötzlikeller** (⊠ *Gerechtigkeitsg. 62, Altstadt* ☎ *031/3117456* ⊕ *www. kloetzlikeller.ch*), Bern's last true wine cellar beneath the arcades. The Riviera vibe at the outdoor **Terrasse** and indoor **Color-Lounge** (⊠ *Dalmaziquai 11, Schwellenmätteli* ☎ *031/3505001* ⊕ *www.schwellenmaetteli. ch*), both part of the Schwellenmätteli restaurant complex, lure thirty-something hipsters down to the river.

CASINO

All 261 slot machines and 11 gaming tables at the Kursaal's **Grand Casino Bern** (⊠ *Kornhausstr. 3, Kornhausbrücke* ☎ *031/3395555* ⊕ *www.grand casino-bern.ch*) function until 4 AM from Thursday through Saturday.

DANCING

Smart young professionals stop after work for a mellow glass of wine and stay until 4 AM for weekend dance parties at **Du Théâtre** (⊠ *Hotelg. 10/Theaterpl. 7, Altstadt* ☎ *031/3185067* ⊕ *www.lorenzini.ch*). **Shakira** (⊠ *National Hotel, Hirschengraben 24, City Center* ☎ *031/3811988* ⊕ *www.shakira.ch*) specializes in Latin music, salsa dancing, and tropical drinks. The Prodigy, Moby, and The Roots all played the sophisticated, musically multitalented **Wasserwerk Club** (⊠ *Wasserwerkg. 5, Matte* ☎ *No phone* ⊕ *www.wasserwerkclub.ch*) early in their careers.

THE ARTS

Bern's three-pronged arts scene covers opera and symphonic classics, seasonal festivals, and cubbyhole theaters buried underground.

FILM

If a film was made in English, Bernese cinemas generally show it in English. Local newspapers list screening times (look for "E" to confirm the language) and most theaters advertise current programs on big boards underneath the Käfigturm and in the Christoffelunterführung. The open-air **OrangeCinema** (⊠ *Grosse Schanze* ☎ *0800/078078* ⊕ *www.orangecinema.ch*) sets up camp in front of the university each July and shows recent mainstream favorites through August.

MUSIC & THE PERFORMING ARTS

The **Berner Symphonie-Orchester** (☎ *031/3282424* ⊕ *www.bernorchester. ch*) performs orchestral work and chamber music, primarily in the **Kultur-Casino** (⊠ *Herreng. 25, Altstadt*). The **Stadttheater** (⊠ *Kornhauspl. 20, Altstadt* ☎ *031/3295111* ⊕ *www.stadttheaterbern.ch*) presents seven full-scale operas, 10 dramas (in German), and three contemporary dance pieces each year. **Bern Billett** (⊠ *Nägelig. 1a, Altstadt* ☎ *031/3295252* ⊕ *www.bernbillett.ch*) handles ticket sales for the Kultur-Casino and the Stadttheater.

Altstadt streets empty briefly in mid-July as A-list rockers like James Blunt, Billy Idol, and David Gray draw crowds to the four-day open-air **Gurten Festival** (⊕ *www.gurtenfestival.ch*). **Marians Jazzroom** (⊠ *Engestr. 54, Innere Enge* ☎ *031/3096111* ⊕ *www.mariansjazzroom.ch*) hosts top international jazz, blues, and gospel artists between September and May; the **International Jazz Festival** (⊕ *www.jazzfestivalbern.ch*) amplifies that program for two months starting in March.

Marionettes, stick puppets, hand puppets, shadow puppets, and masks come to life on stage at the **Berner Puppen Theater** (⊠ *Gerechtigkeitsg. 31, Altstadt* ☎ *031/3119585* ⊕ *www.berner-puppentheater.ch*). The **Theater am Käfigturm** (⊠ *Spitalg. 4, City Center* ☎ *031/3116100* ⊕ *www. theater-am-kaefigturm.ch*), three levels below Spitalgasse, presents pantomime, modern dance, avant-garde plays, satires, burlesques (in Swiss German), and the occasional piece aimed at children.

SPORTS & THE OUTDOORS

BICYCLING

There are about 300 km (185 mi) of marked trails in and around Bern. Leave ID and a 20 SF deposit with **Bern Rollt** (⊠ *Bahnhofpl. and Zeughausg., City Center and Altstadt* ☎ *079/2772857* ⊕ *www.bernrollt. ch*) between May and October and you can ride for free from 7:30 AM to 9:30 PM.

SWIMMING

Swimmers have headed into the cold, swift Aare just before its U-turn around the Altstadt since Bern was founded. These days a hot Sunday may see scantily clad (or, in certain sections, naked) crowds of more

6

than 10,000 sprawled on beach towels on the grass, swimming laps in the pools, or bobbing happily in the river (a system of handrails projected over the water prevents bathers from traveling too far downstream). Known universally as **The Marzili** (⊠ *Marzilistr. 29, Marzili* ☎ *031/3110046* ⊕ *www.aaremarzili.ch*), this sunny stretch of riverbank below the Bundeshaus presents a unique, and entirely free, take on the city.

Heated mineral-rich indoor baths, open-air saltwater pools, underwater massage jets, bubble beds, whirlpools, a mushroom fountain, eucalyptus steam baths, and a sauna park are highlights at the sprawling **Solbad Schönbühl** (⊠ *Mattenweg 30, Schönbühl* ☎ *031/8593434* ⊕ *www.solbad. ch*), open year-round to the north of Bern. Bathing suits and towels can be rented on-site; admission to the baths is 28 SF.

SHOPPING

Bern's official store hours are 9 to 6:30 weekdays and 8 to 4 on Saturday. Thursday hours are extended to 9; stores in the Hauptbahnhof may open on Sunday. Smaller stores, particularly in the Altstadt, may stay shuttered Monday morning, close for lunch, close before 9 on Thursday, and/or open as late as 10.

DEPARTMENT STORES

Quality, stylish, often vibrantly colorful home accessories and cooking gear fill the upper stories at **Globus** (⊠ *Spitalg. 17–21, City Center* ☎ *031/3134040*). On the lower levels, luscious hats and scarves, cosmetics, and designer labels give way to foodstuffs—from specialty oils through cheese—in the upscale supermarket downstairs. **Loeb** (⊠ *Spitalg. 47–51, City Center* ☎ *031/3207111*) sells model trucks, Legos, and children's clothing on the top floor, descending through craft supplies, luggage, housewares, and mid-range clothing brands to assorted stationery, hosiery, and Swiss-themed souvenirs on the ground floor.

MARKETS

Some say the best time to browse the annual **Zibelemärit** *(Onion Market)* is just after it opens at 4 AM on the fourth Monday in November, when stalls are candlelighted; you may be treated to a predawn dusting of snow, and confetti battles do not yet rage. Throughout December, hot mulled wine adds spice to the arts and crafts, evergreen, and seasonal produce stalls lining Münsterplatz and Waisenhausplatz during the **Weihnachtsmarkt** *(Christmas Market)*, which keeps regular shop hours. Tuesday and Saturday are Bern's formal year-round market days, with most of the action concentrated in the morning along Bundesplatz, Bärenplatz, Waisenhausplatz, Schauplatzgasse, Gurtengasse, and Bundesgasse in the center of town. The main **fruit, vegetable, and flower market** fills Bundesplatz and Bärenplatz with fresh produce, herbs, and flowers (daily, during shopping hours on Bärenplatz between May and

October). The nearby Münstergasse hosts a **meat and cheese market.** The **trader's market** on Waisenhausplatz adds late-night hours on Thursday between May and October and forms an awning-covered warren of handmade soaps, antique copper pots, silver jewelry, handmade hammocks, tie-dyed scarves, and incongruous objects like panama hats. Arts and crafts stalls create a **craft fair** on the Münsterplattform every first Saturday of the month between March and December. The **flea market,** held on Matte's Mühleplatz the third Saturday of the month from May to October, has the look and feel of an antiques-laden tag sale.

SHOPPING STREETS

No street or side alley in downtown Bern is without interest to shoppers, and you never know what fabulous discovery may await at the end of an intriguing passageway or the bottom of cellar stairs. **Spitalgasse** and **Marktgasse** form the city center's main shopping drag; parallel streets such as **Neuengasse, Aarbergergasse,** and **Amthausgasse** can also be very rewarding. The Altstadt, from **Brunngasse** to **Junkerngasse** by way of **Kramgasse** and **Gerechtigkeitsgasse,** is lined and honeycombed with fine specialty boutiques.

SPECIALTY STORES

BOOKS

It is easy to get lost in the sprawling trilingual **Stauffacher** (⊠*Neueng. 25–37, City Center* ☎*031/3136363*) emporium of books, maps, and multimedia, but there are far worse fates. The substantial English Bookshop occupies the third floor of the west wing; regular readings (some in English) are held in the Café Littéraire. At **Thalia** (⊠*Spitalg. 47–51, City Center* ☎*031/3202020*), a German-language chain lodged in the basement of the Loeb department store, globes, dictionaries, multi-lingual travel guides, English-language fiction and biographies, a play area for kids, and a sizable selection of books about Switzerland are highlights.

CHOCOLATE

Chocolate-covered plums and truffles made with Bailey's, kirsch, or coconut white chocolate lead the charge at **Abegglen** (⊠*Spitalg. 36, City Center* ☎*031/3112111*). **Beeler** (⊠*Spitalg. 29, City Center* ☎*031/3112808*) shapes chocolate to look like members of the Federal Council. **Eichenberger** (⊠*Bahnhofpl. 5, City Center* ☎*031/3113325*) concocts its strong, dark house mix of cacao by hand on the first floor. The self-styled prince of Bernese chocolatiers, **Tschirren** (⊠*Kramg. 73, Altstadt* ☎*031/3111717*), has been making its divine assortment of artfully rough-hewn truffles since 1919.

GIFTS & SOUVENIRS

The warrenlike **Boutique Nelli** (⊠*Gerechtigkeitsg. 3, Altstadt* ☎*031/3111040*) has a whimsical selection of glassware by local artists, candles in rainbow colors, soap shaped like fruit, and imaginative kitchen gadgets. Victorinox, Wenger, and Swiss Military knives

9

dominate the window at **Hei-matwerk** (⊠*Kramg. 61, Altstadt* ☎*031/3113000*), a high-quality emporium of Swiss-made music boxes, toys, handicrafts, textiles, and ceramics. Colorful handmade wooden figures and candelabras, delicate shaved-wood trees, and lacy wooden cutouts pull focus at **Holz Art** (⊠*Münsterg. 36, Altstadt* ☎*031/3126666*). Most of the fine,

SUNDAY TEA

Many chocolatiers' shops have tearoom areas at the back and are, therefore, allowed to open on Sunday. If you go, be sure to try the Bernese specialty *Lebkuchen,* a dense, flat spice cake made with hazelnuts, honey, and almonds.

often Swiss-themed, embroidery and linens at **Langenthal** (⊠*Marktg. 15, City Center* ☎*031/3118786*) were made in Switzerland.

HOME ACCESSORIES
Cachet (⊠*Amthausg. 22, City Center* ☎*031/3118466*) stocks culturally resonant items such as iron Japanese teapots, colored grass baskets, camel rugs, Turkish lamps, multicolored bottles, whimsical mobiles, and soulful carved-wood furniture from India, Indonesia, and Pakistan. Clean, livable, often joyously colorful and affordable designs channel faraway locales at **Interio** (⊠*Spitalg. 4, City Center* ☎*058/5762400*), where you could outfit a house but might settle for satiny cotton sheets, gossamer curtains in bright colors, hammered steel Moroccan bowls, floating candles, silk pillows, or Indian cotton placemats.

TOYS
The big, old red cash register works; colorful mini-kites twirl out front; child-sized umbrellas have animal handles; and the plush toys range from snow owls to llamas at **Bilboquet** (⊠*Münsterg. 37, Altstadt* ☎*031/3113671*). **Chlätterbär** (⊠*Amthausg. 3, City Center* ☎*031/3111196*) sells fully stocked wooden kitchens, xylophones, beaded jewelry, drum sets, hand puppets, and wooden dollhouse furniture. The owner of the **Puppenklinik** (⊠*Gerechtigkeitsg. 36, Altstadt* ☎*031/3120771*) has a passion for restoration; the result is a huge collection of vintage dolls, toys, teddy bears, and puppets from around the world. There are very few hard edges at **U-Tiger** (⊠*Gerechtigkeitsg. 79, Altstadt* ☎*031/3279091*), where cloud sofas, green dragon bean bags, quilted soccer fields, and fuzzy sheep hot water bottles headline the creative selection of room furnishings for children.

Berner Oberland

GSTAAD, INTERLAKEN, JUNGFRAUJOCH, LAUTERBRUNNEN, MÜRREN, WENGEN

Mürren

WORD OF MOUTH

"Now I know what those 'Beware: Switzerland is Addictive' posters mean!"

—KalpanaKar

"I didn't know I HAD any knee problems until the Kleine Scheidegg trail. I literally walked down backwards, with my husband calling out course corrections. Great scenery though—even backwards."

—dmcwriter

WELCOME TO BERNER OBERLAND

TOP REASONS TO GO

★ **Top of the world:** At 11,400 feet, the Jungfraujoch peak isn't the highest place on the planet, but you could probably see it from here.

★ **Twin peaks:** The upwardly mobile head to the adjacent, mountaintop villages of Wengen and Mürren to find the Switzerland of cheese, chalet, and chic cliché.

★ **Shangri-la found:** The Lauterbrunnen Valley is Yosemite blown up to the nth dimension, complete with 76 cascading waterfalls (among Europe's highest).

★ **Gstaad, dahling:** Money attracts money, and there's certainly lots of it here. Mere mortals can indulge in exquisite meals, skiing, and overnight stays in paradise.

★ **Old Switzerland, in a nutshell:** Ballenberg is a delightfully reconstructed Swiss village—à la America's Williamsburg—with traditional crafts on show.

1 Jungfrau Region. A transportation hub, bustling Interlaken has upward of 130 hotels and makes the perfect base camp (with a lively nightlife for city mice). A short ride away are the magnificent summits of summits—the Eiger, Mönch, and Jungfrau (with the highest train station in the world). Nestling below are the villages of Grindelwald, Lauterbrunnen, Wengen, and Mürren, all chalets and geraniums. In winter they have the ambience that every North American "alpine village" resort aims for—and misses.

Brienzersee. In the Oberland a wide variety in altitude creates a great diversity of scenery, so you can bathe comfortably in Lake Brienz after skiing on the Jungfrau slopes in July. Waterfront Brienz is home to famed wood-carvers and the storybook museum village of Ballenberg. Nearby, the plot thickens in Meiringen—Sherlock Holmes saw his last here at Reichenbach Falls.

Thunersee. This idyllic lake is named for Thun, a resort town of medieval dignity. Between bouts of waterskiing and wakeboarding, castle-hop to your heart's content: the shoreline villages of Spiez, Hilterfingen, and Oberhofen all have fairy-tale-worthy extravaganzas.

Simmental & Gstaad. From Spiez, the highway leads southwest into the Simmental Valley, where forest gorges hide Gstaad, so chic and modish a winter resort Elizabeth Taylor still owns a chalet here.

GETTING ORIENTED

Blessed with nine valleys, the lovely lakes of Thun and Brienz, jet-set Gstaad, and the ageless grandeur of the Jungfrau, this compact region contains a universe of sights. No wonder Switzerland's tourist industry began here in the early 1800s, with English gentry flocking to gape at this aristocrat of Alpine scenery.

10

BERNER OBERLAND PLANNER

When to Go

The Oberland has four distinct seasons, each more beautiful than the last. Valley springs and summers are perfect for outdoor activities, from hiking and biking to swimming. Falls becomes crisp around October and winter brings snow. Keep in mind that snow can stay as late as May and come as early as August over 6,500 feet.

Winter versus summer? Everyone loves the magic of snow, but an ermine mantle can easily lend a sameness to all those mountains—something you avoid if you enjoy an Alpine summer. Warm weather, however, brings a global-warmed haze, which can ruin your photos of spectacular valleys, so be sure to pack your camera's UV filter.

If crowds aren't your thing, try the early spring/late fall off-season. Cultural offerings are limited to traditional arts and crafts, although Gstaad hosts the Yehudi Menuhin Music Festival every July/August.

Sports enthusiasts will be in their element: hiking, biking, waterskiing, sailing, parasailing and gliding, bungee-jumping, skiing, snowboarding, and sledding are just a few activities available.

No Wait, Not Those Kinds of Udders...

Cows, cheese, skiing and—Hooters? Of all the gin joints in all the world—a Hooters in Interlaken? It seems that a couple of lusty Swiss guys went golfing in Florida, stopped in at a local joint for a quick bite and a drink, and came home extremely enthusiastic about a new restaurant concept.

After five years going, business at Höheweg 57 (033/8226512) is brisk, with locals, tourists, families, and surprised North Americans flocking to the establishment. As a relatively new venture, the establishment is less cynical than in the States (not much silicone to be found here) and has more of an innocent novelty feel about it (picketing feminists having better things to do). Bottoms up!

Tour Options

Auto AG Interlaken offers guided coach tours and escorted excursions within the Berner Oberland. There are bus tours to Mürren and the Schilthorn (including trips on the cable car), to Grindelwald and Trümmelbach Falls, to Kandersteg and the Blausee, and to Ballenberg.

Guests are picked up at either the Interlaken West or East train station or at the Metropole or Interlaken hotel. Some tours are available with English commentary. The tourist office is the best source of information.

If you're traveling without either a Swiss Pass or a Regional Pass, remember that guided tours to the Jungfraujoch or to the Schilthorn, arranged through the railway and cable companies themselves, cost less than independent round-trip tickets.

For a nostalgic tour of the streets of greater Interlaken by horse-drawn carriage, line up by the Interlaken West train station.

Contact Oberland Tours Grindelwald (☎033/8281717 *for reservations*). **Horse-drawn carriage** (✉*Charles Wyss Kutschenbetrieb* ☎033/8222403).

Finding a Place to Stay

This is the most-visited region in Switzerland. Translation: book as early as possible.

High season here means winter, with summer making up a second-place high season.

Decide on which experience you want: the townie feel of a place like Interlaken, which has many bars, night clubs, restaurants, and movie theaters; the much quieter Grindelwald, with fewer venues; or the clifftop-secluded Mürren or Wengen, where you'll be getting most of your evening's entertainment from the hotel—usually including meals.

Accommodations in the area range from Gstaad's hyper-luxe Palace hotel to Balmer's youth hostel, where you can sleep in a boisterous group tent pitched on the premises in summer.

Main Regional Tourist Offices

Berner Oberland Tourismus dispenses tourist information for the entire region. It's not oriented toward walk-ins, so write or call ahead. The Interlaken Tourist Office, at the foot of the Hotel Metropole, provides information on Interlaken and the Jungfrau region. Arrange your excursions here.

Berner Oberland Tourismus (⊠*Jungfraustr. 38, Interlaken* ☎*033/8283737* 🖷*033/8283734* ⊕*www.berner oberland.ch*). **Interlaken Tourist Office** (⊠*Höheweg 37,* ☎*033/8265300* 🖷*033/8265375* ⊕*www.interlaken.ch*). **Meiringen-Hasliberg** (⊠*Bahnhofstr. 22, Meiringen* ☎*033/ 9725050* 🖷*033/9725055* ⊕*www.alpenregion.ch*).

WHAT IT COSTS IN SWISS FRANCS

¢	$	$$	$$$	$$$$
RESTAURANTS				
under 15 SF	15 SF–25 SF	25 SF–40 SF	40 SF–60 SF	over 60 SF
HOTELS				
under 100 SF	100 SF–175 SF	175 SF–250 SF	250 SF–350 SF	over 350 SF

Restaurant prices are per person for a main course at dinner. Hotel prices are for two people in a standard double room in high season, including tax and service.

Grime Every Mountain?

Brrr! What global warming? On Christmas Day, you might not notice any greenhouse effects when standing atop the Jungfrau but, unfortunately, acid rain, deforestation, erosion, and overdevelopment have all begun to corrode the biggest air-conditioning machine in the world, those erstwhile pristine Swiss Alps.

In fact, a bit of Switzerland crumbled away on July 13, 2006, with the headline-making rockfall from the Eiger's notorious north face due to the melting of the rock permafrost (which, also, incidentally, is the "glue" that keeps all those cable-car girders in place—hopefully). Little wonder the Bernese Oberlanders (who love to track storms from valley to valley) remain weather-obsessed. When nature cooperates, however, the Oberland has four distinct seasons, each more beautiful than the next. But keep in mind that snow can stay as late as May and come as early as August over 6,500 feet.

Winter versus summer? Everyone loves the magic of snow but an ermine mantle can easily lend a sameness to all those mountains—something you avoid if you enjoy an Alpine summer. Warm weather, however, brings a global-warmed haze, so be sure to pack your camera's UV filter.

10

GETTING AROUND

Transportation Basics

Happily and spectacularly, cars aren't a necessity here, as Mürren, Wengen, and Gstaad are car-free, and rail connections are excellent. The region is threaded with narrow-gauge or cog-wheel tracks and aerial cableways and plenty of chairlifts will have you singing "Ain't No Mountain High Enough" in no time. If you're planning a circular tour of the region, a car will navigate the valleys a little faster, though. Direct rail connections from Geneva, Zürich, and Basel run through Bern, from which there is public transportation to every part of the region. Thun is the hub for Gstaad and Spiez; Interlaken takes you on to Brienz, Lauterbrunnen, and Grindelwald; and hypermagical Lauterbrunnen takes you up to Wengen and Mürren.

By Boat & Ferry

Round-trip boat cruises around Lake Thun and Lake Brienz provide an ever-changing view of the craggy foothills and peaks. The round-trip from Interlaken to Thun takes about four hours; the trip to Spiez takes about two hours and includes stopovers for visits to the castles of Oberhofen, Spiez, and Thun. A round-trip from Interlaken to Brienz takes around 2½ hours, to Iseltwald about 1¼ hours. These boats are public transportation as well as pleasure cruisers; just disembark whenever you feel like it and check timetables when you want to catch another.

Tickets are flexible and coordinate neatly with land transit: you can cruise across to Thun and then take a train home for variety. Buy tickets and catch boats for Lake Thun at Interlaken West station. For Lake Brienz, go to Interlaken East. The official boat company for both lakes is Schiffsbetrieb BLS Thuner- und Brienzersee.

Boat & Ferry Information Schiffsbetrieb BLS Thuner- und Brienzersee (☎ 033/3345211).

By Bus

Postbuses (called postautos or postcars) travel into much of the area not served by trains, including most smaller mountain towns. **Swiss Rail** (☎ 0900/300300 ⊕ www.sbb. ch) is the leading company, and even offers private motorcoach tours to many points of interest. **Gray Line Switzerland** (☎ 044/3831705) has a wide range of routes.

By Air

Belp Airport in Bern brings you within an hour via train of Interlaken, the hub of the Berner Oberland. Near Basel, EuroAirport (across the border in France) is 2¼ hours by train. The Unique Zürich Airport is 2½ hours away. Geneva's Cointrin is less than three hours away.

Airport Information Belp (☎ 031/9602111). **Cointrin** (☎ 022/7177111). **EuroAirport** (☎ 061/3252511). **Unique Zürich Airport** (☎ 0900/300313).

By Train

Trains from Bern to Interlaken run once an hour between 6 AM and 11 PM, some requiring a change at Spiez. From Zürich, a direct line leads through Bern to Interlaken and takes about three hours, departing hourly; a more scenic trip over the Golden Pass route via Luzern takes about two hours.

From Basel trains run twice an hour via Olten (approximately a three-hour trip). Trains run hourly from Geneva (a 2½-hour ride). Trains stop at the Interlaken West station first. Next stop is Interlaken East.

West is the more central, but check with your hotel if you've booked in advance: some of the town's fine hotels are clustered nearer the East station, and all Brienzersee boat excursions leave from the docks nearby. For train information in Interlaken, ask at Interlaken West.

The Berner Oberland is riddled with federal and private railways, funiculars, cogwheel trains, and cable lifts designed with the sole purpose of getting you closer to its spectacular views.

A Swiss Pass lets you travel free on federal trains and lake steamers, and gives reductions on many private excursions.

If you're concentrating only on the Berner Oberland, consider a seven-day Regional Pass, which offers 450 km (279 mi) of free rail, bus, and boat travel for any three days of your visit, with reduced fare for the remaining four days, as well as discounts on some of the most spectacular (and pricey) private excursions into the heights. The price is 164 SF (first class) and 114 SF (second class).

A five-day pass allows you two days of free travel for 136 SF (first class) and 94 SF (second class), with reduced fare for the remaining three days. These regional passes also grant a 50% discount for travel to Luzern, Zermatt, and Brig.

With a Family Card (20 SF), children who are under 16 and accompanied by at least one parent travel free.

Discount passes pay for themselves only if you're a high-energy traveler; before you buy, compare the price à la carte for the itinerary you have in mind.

Train Information Swiss Rail (☎0900/300300 ⊕www. sbb.ch). For special discounts and passes in Berner Oberland: **Golden Pass Rail Centre** (☎0900/245245 ⊕www.mob.ch).

By Car

Swift and scenic roads link both Bern and Zürich to Interlaken. From Bern, the autoroute A6 leads to Spiez, then A8 continues as the highway to Interlaken. From Zürich, the planned autoroute link with Luzern is incomplete; travel by Highway E41 south, then pick up the autoroutes A4 and A14 in the direction of Luzern. South of Luzern, pick up the A4 again in the direction of Interlaken.

From Geneva the autoroute leads through Lausanne and Fribourg to Bern, where you catch A6 south, toward Thun. A long, winding, scenic alternative: continue on the autoroute from Lausanne to Montreux, then to Aigle; then, head northeast up the mountain on A11 from Aigle through Château-d'Oex to Gstaad and the Simmental.

Driving in the Berner Oberland allows you the freedom to find your own views and to park at the very edges of civilization before taking off on foot or by train. If you are confining yourself to the lakefronts, valleys, and lower resorts, a car is an asset.

But several lovely resorts are beyond the reach of traffic, and train, funicular, and cable-car excursions take you to places ordinary tires can't tread; sooner or later, you'll leave the car behind and resort to public transportation. Remember that Wengen, Mürren, and Gstaad are all car-free.

10

Updated
by Suzanne
Hégelé

THERE ARE TIMES WHEN THE reality of Switzerland puts postcard ide-
alization to shame, surpassing tinted-indigo skies and advertising-image
peaks with its own astonishing vividness. Those times happen most
often in the Berner Oberland, for this rugged region concentrates some
of the best features of rural Switzerland: awesome mountain panoramas, massive glaciers, crystalline lakes, gorges and waterfalls, chic ski
resorts, dense pine forests, and charming gingerbread chalets.

After contemplating the Staubbach Falls in 1779, the great German
writer Johann Wolfgang von Goethe was moved to write one of his most
celebrated poems, "Gesang der Geister über den Wassern" ("Song of the
Spirits over the Waters"). After Rousseau spread word of the region's
natural phenomena among Paris society, the Romantics began to beat
a path to the area, Lord Byron in the lead—it is said he conceived his
Manfred here in barren, windswept Wengernalp. Shelley followed, then
William Thackeray, John Ruskin, the composer Johannes Brahms, and,
from America, Mark Twain; British master landscape painter J. M. W.
Turner recorded the views; and Queen Victoria herself came, beginning
a flood of tourism that permanently changed the Berner Oberland's—
and Switzerland's—profile.

Before the onslaught of visitors inspired many locals to switch from
farming to innkeeping, agriculture was the prime industry—this is still
true today, evidenced by the frequent sight of brown-and-white cows
dotting the hillsides, as though conveniently placed for photo-ops. The
houses of the Berner Oberland are classics: the definitive Swiss chalet,
whose broad, eaved roofs cover fancifully scalloped and carved gables.
Facades are painted with the family dedication on wood, which has
weathered to dark sienna. From early spring through autumn, window
boxes spill torrents of well-tended geraniums and petunias, and adjacent woodpiles are stacked with mosaiclike precision in readiness for
dropping temperatures.

The region is arranged tidily enough for even a brief visit. Its main
resort city, Interlaken, lies in green lowlands between the gleaming
twin pools of the Brienzersee and the Thunersee, which are linked by
the River Aare. Behind them to the south loom craggy, forested foothills, and behind those foothills stand some of Europe's noblest peaks,
most notably the snowy crowns of the Eiger (13,022 feet), the Mönch
(13,445 feet), and the fiercely beautiful Jungfrau (13,638 feet). Because
nature has laid the region out so conveniently, it has become the most
popular in Switzerland for tourism, with its excursion and transportation systems carrying enormous numbers of visitors to its myriad
viewpoints, overlooks, and wonders. The railroad to the Jungfraujoch
transports masses of tour groups to its high-altitude attractions, and on
a peak-season day its crowded station can look like the Sistine Chapel in
August or the Chicago Board of Trade. But the tourist industry handles
the onslaught with ease, offering such an efficient network of boats,
trains, and funiculars, such a variety of activities and attractions, and
such a wide range of accommodations, from posh city hotels to rustic
mountain lodges, that every visitor can find the most suitable way to
take in the marvels of the Bernese Alps.

The Jungfrau
Region

KEY
•—•—• Cable Car/ Funicular
⊢—⊢—⊣ Rail lines
🎿 Ski Resorts

EXPLORING BERNER OBERLAND

The central, urban-Victorian resort of Interlaken makes a good base
for excursions for visitors who want to experience the entire Jungfrau
region, which includes the craggy, bluff-lined Lauterbrunnen Valley and
the opposing resorts that perch high above it: Mürren and Wengen.
Busy Grindelwald, famous for its variety of sporting possibilities, and
isolated Kandersteg, ideal for hiking and cross-country skiing, are both
easily accessible from Interlaken. Each lies at the dead end of a gorge
road that climbs into the heights. Spreading east and west of Interlaken
are the Brienzersee and Thunersee, both broad, crystalline lakes, surrounded by forests, castles, and waterfront resorts, including Brienz,
Thun, and Spiez. From Spiez you can head southwest through the forest
gorge of the Simmental to the Saanenland and glamorous Gstaad. Connections by rail or car keep most highlights within easy reach.

THE JUNGFRAU REGION

The thriving resort town of Interlaken lies between two spectacularly
sited lakes, the Brienzersee (Lake Brienz) and the Thunersee (Lake
Thun), and is the gateway to two magnificent mountain valleys, one

leading up to the popular sports resort of Grindelwald, the other into Lauterbrunnen and the famous car-free resorts of Wengen and Mürren. Looming over both valleys, the Jungfrau and its partner peaks—the Eiger and Mönch—can be admired from various high-altitude overviews.

INTERLAKEN

58 km (36 mi) southeast of Bern.

GETTING HERE

Interlaken has two train stations (www.sbb.ch), the centrally located Interlaken West, where trains arrive from Bern, Thun, and Spiez, and Interlaken Ost (East), which connects you to Brienz and the Jungfrau region. The direct train that comes from Bern every half hour stops at both stations and costs 26 SF each way. Buses to towns nearby leave from the train stations, both of which have taxis to help you schlep your luggage to your hotel; there are also carriage rides for the romantically inclined. For departure times and prices for trains and buses for most destinations in this chapter, check with www.sbb.ch—the main Swiss public transportation Web site—or call 0900/300300 (1.19 SF per min). Remember, if you have a Swiss Pass or another rail-discount card, it also applies to the buses.

Visitor Information (✉ *Höheweg 37* ☎ *033/8265300* 🖨 *033/8265375* ⊕ *www.interlaken.ch*).

EXPLORING

Often touted as a town without character, Interlaken has patiently borne the brunt of being called "the best place in Switzerland to get away *from*"—but this, it turns out, is tribute to the town's nearby location to many of the wonders of the Bernese Alps. As a gateway to the entire Berner Oberland, this bustling Victorian resort town is the obvious home base for travelers planning to visit both the region's two lakes and the mountains towering behind them. And have no fear—there's more than enough character and *Gemütlichkeit* to go around.

The name *Interlaken* has a Latin source: *interlacus* (between lakes). At 1,870 feet, Interlaken dominates the Bödeli, the branch of lowland between the lakes that Interlaken shares with the adjoining towns of Unterseen, Wilderswil, Bönigen, and Matten. The town's two train stations, Interlaken East and Interlaken West, are good orientation points; most sights are just a few minutes' walk from one of the stations. There are unlimited excursion options, and it is a pleasant, if urban, place to stay put as well, as its setting is spectacular and its ambience genteel.

The **Höheweg** is the city's main promenade, its tree- and flower-lined walkways cutting through the edge of the broad green parklands of the Höhematte. This 35-acre park once provided pasture ground for herds of the Augustinian monastery that dominated medieval Interlaken. Cows still graze in fenced-off areas.

★ Mark Twain once sojourned at the **Victoria-Jungfrau Grand Hotel & Spa** on the Höheweg, designed to take in the view of the snowy Jungfrau that towers above the town. Topped by a magnificent Victorian-style cupola and spire, and lushly appointed with glittering salons, only one room, the mammoth 19th-century Brasserie restaurant, has survived the hotel's numerous renovations. The hotel originated as two humbler inns, the Jungfrau (1864) and the Chalet Victoria (1865), named in honor of the English queen who journeyed here in the 19th century and put the Oberland on the tourist map; these were merged and expanded in 1895, and the facade redesigned and landmark tower added in 1899. Repair here at least once to enjoy drinks in one of the hotel's many bars and dine on its grassy terrace—this is Interlaken as luxe as it gets. ⊠*Höheweg 41* ☎*033/8282828* ⊕*www.victoria-jungfrau.ch.*

Between the Höheweg and the River Aare you'll find the beautifully landscaped grounds, complete with a floral clock, surrounding the **Kursaal.** Built in 1859 in a dramatic combination of Oberland-chalet and Victorian styles, the Kursaal (meaning a public room at a resort) was renovated in 1968 and has become once again a social focal point for the city. Plays and concerts are presented here, mostly during the high season, and folklore evenings are held in the adjoining Spycher (storehouse).

The **Schlosskirche** *(Castle Church)* was once the chapel for the Augustinian monastery. All that remains of the monastery, founded in 1133, and the convent that shared its grounds, are a 14th-century chancel and a wing of the cloister. The rest of the convent was incorporated into a private castle in 1745. ⊠*At end of Höhematte, south of Hotel du Nord.*

On the north side of the River Aare is the tiny town of **Unterseen,** with its picturesque Old Town and Marktplatz (Marketplace). Founded in 1279 on land rented from the Augustinians, Unterseen retains some of the region's oldest buildings, including the 17th-century **Stadthaus** (city hall) and the 14th-century **church,** its steeple dating from 1471. The **Schloss Unterseen** (Unterseen Castle), built in 1656 for the reigning Bernese nobleman, stands at the opposite end of the square from these structures, near a medieval arched gateway. You can get here via a 10-minute bus ride from Interlaken's center, or even by walking; it's near the Interlaken West train station.

Fronting on the Unterseen Marktplatz is the **Touristik-Museum der Jungfrau Region,** which traces the history of tourism in the area over the last 200 years. Exhibits include models of early transportation and primitive mountain climbing and skiing equipment. ⊠*Obere Gasse 26* ☎*033/8266464* ⊠*5 SF* ☉*May–mid-Oct., Tues.–Sun. 2–5.*

Fodor's Choice Lovers of Old Swiss style should consider trekking out some 8 km ★ (5 miles) from Interlaken to take in **St. Beatus-Höhlen.** Whether or not you're into natural caverns remains to be seen, but no one could resist St. Beatus's extraordinary entry hillside pavilion: a Hansel-and-Gretelesque extravaganza of 19th-century Alpine Gemütlichkeit, replete with dollhouse-issue waterfall. Beauty is not just skin deep, however, for the deep St. Beatus caves are marvels, too. Their legend goes back to the 6th century, when the missionary St. Beatus arrived on the Thunersee to find the local population terrorized by a dragon who lived in the lake and surrounding grottoes. Exorcised by Beatus, the fleeing dragon fell to his death on the rocks plunging down to the lake. The caves then became the hermit's home; today you can see the stalagmites, stalactites, and pools inside. There's even a replica of Ponzo, the dragon, for children to explore, and a Ponzo-decorated steamship plies the Thunersee. You can reach the caves by taking Bus 21 from the Interlaken West train station or by crossing by boat from Interlaken West station to Sundlaunen, then a quarter-hour hike to the caves. ⊠ *Opposite Interlaken on east coast near Sundlaunen* ☎ *033/8411643* ⊕ *www.beatushoehlen.ch* ☜ *18 SF* ⊘ *Mid-Mar.–mid-Oct., daily 10:30–5.*

★ Adorned with a spectacular, turreted, Gothic, chalet-style restaurant, **Harder Kulm** (4,297 feet) can be bested thanks to an eight-minute funicular ride; from there, hike uphill to catch views south over the city, the lakes, and the whole panorama of snowy peaks. The restaurant offers sumptuous meals on a sunny terrace, with views of the surrounding mountains. The funicular runs every 20 to 30 minutes. ⊠ *Funicular station north of River Aare near Interlaken East, across Beaurivagebrücke* ☎ *033/8287339* ☜ *Funicular round-trip: 25 SF* ⊘ *Funicular: May–end of Oct., Mon.–Sat. 9–6, Sun. 8–6.*

An old-fashioned, red funicular railway leads to the top of the 2,194-foot **Heimwehfluh** mountain, where you will get views over both lakes and an elevated peek at the Jungfrau, the Eiger, and the Mönch. A restaurant and playground have been built at the top, complete with a 985-foot-long bobsled run, and there's a show of model trains every 30 minutes. The funicular station is a five-minute walk from the Interlaken West station down the Rugenparkstrasse, with departures every 15 minutes. If you hike to the top, the train show costs just 8 SF. ☎ *033/8223453* ⊕ *www.heimwehfluh.ch* ☜ *20 SF, includes model train show* ⊘ *Late Apr.–Oct., daily 9:30–5.*

For the most splendid overview in the region, make the ambitious trip to the 6,445-foot peak of the **Schynige Platte** for a picnic, or wander down any of numerous footpaths, or visit its Alpine Botanical Garden, where more than 520 varieties of mountain flowers grow. A cogwheel train dating from 1893 takes you on the round-trip journey, though you may opt to walk either up or (more comfortably) down. Make sure to specify when you buy your ticket. Trains run from approximately 7:45 AM to 6 PM. To get here, take the six-minute ride on Bernese Oberland Railway from Interlaken East to Wilderswil. ⊠ *Wilderswil* ☎ *033/8287233* ☜ *One-way 37.40 SF; round-trip 62.80 SF* ⊘ *Late May or early June–late Oct., daily, depending on snow conditions.*

WHERE TO EAT

$$–$$$ ✕ **Alpenblick.** Just 2 km (1 mi) south of Interlaken, this carved wood-
SWISS   and-shingle 17th-century landmark attracts both locals and travelers
★   with its two restaurants. The Dorf Stube serves old-style Swiss cuisine (try the Felchenfilet from Brienz lake nearby or an Alpenblick Rösti). Or opt for the Gourmet Stübli, a showcase for chef Richard Stöckli's

renowned international fare, such as octopus carpaccio with tuna, avocado, and wasabi, or chicken curry with pine nuts, raisins, and honeyed herbs. The established wine cellar offers Swiss and international wines; should you have a few too many glasses there is always the option of staying over, as this is also a hotel. There is a variety of rooms available in two chalets. ⊠*Oberstr. 8, Wilderswil/Interlaken* ☏*033/8283550* ⟁*Reservations essential.* ⊕*www.hotel-alpenblick.ch* ⊟*AE, DC, MC, V* ⊗*Closed Mon.–Tues.* .

$$–$$$ ✕**Im Gade.** This welcoming hybrid of carved-wood coziness and sleek
SWISS formality fills up with appreciative locals who recognize fresh, fine
★ cooking and alert service. Details count here: even that dab of smoky sauerkraut in your crisp mixed salad is made on the premises. Choose seasonal specialties such as salmon with lime mousse and ratatouille, or pork fillet with truffles. A new owner has taken over but has succeeded in maintaining the high standards, especially with the fishy favorites. ⊠*Hotel du Nord, Höheweg 70* ☏*033/8275050* ⊟*AE, DC, MC, V* ⊗*Closed mid-Nov.–mid-Dec.*

$$–$$$ ✕**Krebs.** This establishment has been in Interlaken—and the Krebs fam-
ECLECTIC ily—since 1875. A classic old-world resort spot—recently reopened in May 2008 after a complete renovation—it offers a well-balanced mix of tradition and modern comfort, with starched collar–style service. Along with the decor, the traditional Swiss cuisine and homey daily plates have been transformed and updated, and now upscale French and Asian creations are also offered—tenderloin of pork with Banyuls sauce and pan-fried shiitake and yellow Chinese noodles could be a good dish to start. A sunny, front-porch serving area overlooks the street, but head for the more formal dining room, glassed-in yet still opening onto the main promenade ⊠*Bahnhofstr. 4* ☏*033/8227161* ⊟*AE, DC, MC, V* ⊗*Closed Nov.–Apr.*

$–$$ ✕**Restaurant Laterne.** You'll find this unpretentious local favorite with a
SWISS sports-bar ambience a bit off the tourist track, east of the center near
★ the A8 ring road (a 10-minute walk from Interlaken East). The rustic tile-and-wood setting is a perfect backdrop for the hearty meat dinners and Swiss specialties: seven kinds of Rösti served in iron skillets and eight kinds of cheese fondue. To top it all off, the prices are reasonable. ⊠*Obere Bönigstr. 18* ☏*033/8221141* ⊟*AE, DC, MC, V.*

$$–$$$ ✕**Schuh.** With a luxurious shady terrace spilling into the Höhematte in
SWISS summer and mellow piano sounds enhancing the old-fashioned elegance inside, this sweet shop and café-restaurant serves everything from tea to rich, hot Swiss meals. No matter that recipes are used that date all the way back to 1818—most of the ingredients and dishes are freshly made in-house on a daily basis. Leave room for the chocolate specialties and pastries, like the glossy strawberry tarts, which you'll also find in the adjoining shop. ⊠*Höheweg 56* ☏*033/8229441* ⊟*AE, DC, MC, V.*

$–$$ ✕**Stellambiente.** For something nicely out of the ordinary, try this res-
MODERN SWISS taurant in the Stella Swiss Quality Hotel. This small family-run gem
★ defies its outdated '60s exterior and residential neighborhood setting. Inside—along with marvelous, friendly service—you'll be able to enjoy modern, flavorful cuisine: order the "surprise" menu and you'll be treated to six inventive courses served on beautiful, individually selected

10

pieces of china. Also on tap are several vegetarian options with locally grown ingredients and an extraordinary variety of salads. In summer, the attractive terrace, complete with fountain, turns dining into a garden idyll. ⊠ *Waldeggstr. 10* ☎*033/8228871* ⊟*AE, DC, MC, V.*

WHERE TO STAY

$ ⭐ ☷ **Alphorn.** Comfortably old-fashioned, this lovely family-run Victorian bed-and-breakfast sits on a quiet side street between Interlaken West and the Heimwehfluh. Some rooms have tapestry wallpaper, waxed parquet floors, and original plaster moldings; florals and other patterns abound. Service is warm and welcoming. The bar/breakfast room is bright and light with an alphorn adorning the wall. Do not expect high class, but do expect affordability, and savor the age-old Swiss guarantee of clean comfort. **Pros:** free Internet in lobby; peaceful location; ideal for budget seekers. **Cons:** some rooms are tiny; the single beds pushed together to make a double with two separate covers can surprise those not used to this Swiss tradition. ⊠*Rothornstrasse 29a* ☎*033/8223051* ⊕*www.hotel-alphorn.ch* ☞*10 rooms* ☖*In-room: no a/c, safe. In-hotel: bar, public Internet (free), Wi-Fi (free), parking (free), some pets allowed, no-smoking rooms.* ⊟*AE, MC, V* ⦿*BP.*

⭐ ☷ **Balmer's.** This popular youth hostel gives families and young travelers bare-bones rooms at rock-bottom prices. Kitchen access, washers and dryers, videos, two fireplaces, a convenience store, self-service suppers, and a bar/nightclub add to the lively, collegiate-party atmosphere. The English-speaking staff can help find the cheapest deals for all outdoor activities, train tickets, or packages. Guest rooms, some with sinks, are available with one to five beds. You can also go for an even cheaper bed in the group tents (for 6 people) pitched at the edge of town, roughly from June through September. The tent site boasts a pool and parking lot. The guest house is for smaller groups or families. Checkout is at 10 AM; there are lockers and storage for luggage. **Pros:** cheap, sociable accommodation; free bus pass for guests throughout Interlaken; storage facilities available. **Cons:** could be considered noisy for young families during summer months as it is a hot spot for backpackers and has a nightclub on site. ⊠*Hauptstr. 23–25* ☎*033/8221961* ⊕*www.balmers. com* ☞*50 rooms, tent village* ☖*In-room: no a/c. In-hotel: restaurant, bar, nightclub, pool, bicycles, laundry facilities, public Internet (fee), Wi-Fi (fee), parking, some pets allowed, no-smoking rooms.* ⊟*AE, MC, V* ⦿*CP.*

$$ ☷ **City Hotel Oberland.** With its city-crossroads position this downtown hotel occupies both sides of the street and keeps expanding. Its storybook exterior bristling with mansard windows and stucco trim, the main hotel offers guest rooms with old-world dimensions and a heavy-on-the browns decor; the newer wing across the pedestrian alley (in a building pierced by a life-size statue of a cow) has '80s modern rooms, with warm wood tones and funkily designed bathrooms. Personality challenged these may be, but they are comfortable, a plus in this crowded city. The hotel restaurant is extremely popular—it offers the usual Swiss suspects but most dishes go beyond yum to yum-yum. **Pros:** central location for shops and nightlife; a decent breakfast to set you up for sightseeing could save you lunch expenses. **Cons:** noisy

neighborhood; limited parking for number of guests the hotel caters for. ⊠*Postg. 1* ☎*033/8278787* ⊕*www.city-oberland.ch* ⇗*191 rooms* ⚘*In-room: no a/c (some), safe, Wi-Fi (fee). In-hotel: 2 restaurants, room service, 2 bars, laundry service, public Internet (fee), Wi-Fi (fee), parking (free and fee), some pets allowed (fee), no-smoking rooms.* ⊟*AE, DC, MC, V* ⦿*BP.*

$$-$$$ ⊡**Hotel Interlaken.** When they say this is the oldest hotel in town, they don't fool around: it's been hosting overnight guests since 1323—first as a hospital, then as a cloister, and by the early 15th century as a tavern-hotel. Felix Mendelssohn and Lord Byron may have once slept here, but today the comfortable guest rooms are quite up to date, with sleek furnishings and pastel accents. A multicultural air is added by the elaborate Japanese garden and the Italian, Swiss, and excellent Cantonese menus on offer. It's a short walk to the Interlaken East train station, making excursions a snap. **Pros:** location in historic part of Interlaken and close to train station; friendly, helpful service. **Cons:** no air-conditioning; no leisure/wellness facilities. ⊠*Höheweg 74* ☎*033/8266868* ⊕*www. interlakenhotel.ch* ⇗*60 rooms* ⚘*In-room: no a/c, safe, refrigerator, Ethernet (fee), Wi-Fi (fee). In-hotel: restaurant, room service on request, bar, laundry service, public Internet (fee), Wi-Fi (fee), free parking, some pets allowed, no-smoking rooms.* ⊟*AE, DC, MC, V* ⦿*BP.*

$$-$$$ ⊡**Hotel Royal–St. Georges.** If you are a fan of Victoriana, this impeccably restored 100-year-old grand hotel is a dream come true, with original moldings, built-in furnishings, and fantastical Art Nouveau bath fixtures. In the lobby you pass beautifully carved columns on your way to the staircase that sweeps you upstairs. All guest rooms are spacious and clean, some more modern than others, with the more traditional better suited to the Belle Epoque vibe. The wellness facilities offer a great retreat after a long day of sightseeing. **Pros:** architecturally enjoyable for lovers of Art Nouveau; there is a wealth of nearby excursions suggested by hotel staff. **Cons:** updated modern rooms are out of the '80s and feel somewhat out of place here. ⊠*Höheweg 139* ☎*033/8227575* ⊕*www.royal-stgeorges.ch* ⇗*93 rooms, 3 suites* ⚘*In-room: no a/c, safe, refrigerator, Wi-Fi (fee). In-hotel: restaurant, bar, spa, laundry service, public Internet (fee), Wi-Fi (fee), parking (free), some pets allowed (free), no-smoking rooms.* ⊟*AE, DC, MC, V* ⊗*Closed Nov.–Jan.* ⦿*BP, MAP in summer.*

$$$-$$$$
★
⊡**Lindner Grand Hotel Beau Rivage.** This Interlaken old-timer is steeped in luxury. Set well back from the road and surrounded by gardens, it maintains an unruffled calm. Rich in brocades, muted tones, and patterned carpets, the rooms have views of either the mountains or the quiet Aare. Delicate market-fresh cuisine is served in the highly regarded, hearth-warmed restaurant. Try the crab soup with lemon tortellini followed by the chicken in pepper glaze on the enchanting summer terrace. The location, close to the Interlaken East train station, is perfect. **Pros:** fabulous views; extremely friendly staff; culinary highlights. **Cons:** some rooms on the small side; needs renovating to maintain five-star status; rooms at the back are very close to train tracks. ⊠*Höheweg 211* ☎*033/8267007* ⊕*www.lindnerhotels.ch* ⇗*89 rooms, 12 suites* ⚘*In-room: no a/c, safe, refrigerator, Ethernet (fee), Wi-Fi (fee). In-hotel: 3 restaurants, room*

10

*service, bar, pool, gym, bicycles (free), laundry service, Internet (fee),
Wi-Fi (fee), parking (free), some pets allowed, no-smoking rooms.*
☐*AE, DC, MC, V* ¶⃝*BP* ☺*Open all year round.*

$–$$ ⌨ **Splendid.** Location is key here: you can't get more central to shopping
and nightlife. It's a modest, family-run Victorian dwelling with some
woodsy rooms and the occasional spindle bed enlivening the decor.
Historic tales of the building's past fascinate: the dining room was once
used as an operating theater when the hotel had to be used as a military
hospital in World War II, while the on-site Buddy's Pub was first built
in England and moved here as the first public pub in Switzerland. The
back guest rooms overlook a quiet street; the corner bays are prettiest.
The proprietor is a hunter, so game in season is fresh and local. **Pros:**
warm welcome from the family hosts; central location. **Cons:** can get
noisy at night, as you're in the center of the action. ✉*Höheweg 33*
☎*033/8227612* ⊕*www.splendid.ch* ⌕*35 rooms* ♿*In-room: no a/c,
safe. In-hotel: restaurant, bar, public Wi-Fi (free), parking (free), some
pets allowed, no-smoking rooms.* ☐*AE, MC, V* ☺*Closed Nov.–mid-
Dec.* ¶⃝*BP, MAP (in summer).*

$$$$ ⌨ **Victoria-Jungfrau Grand Hotel & Spa.** Grand says it all. Mark Twain
Fodor's Choice may have slept in this 1865 landmark, but its restoration has taken it
★ firmly into the 21st century, with glitzy postmodern touches such as the
burled-wood entryway. The vast Belle Epoque atrium lobby spirals off
into innumerable bars, tea salons, and the concierge desks, where the
front desk staff may seem frenzied by the awesome demands of 400
occupied beds. There are plenty of facilities, including indoor master
golf, and a knockout spa. Guest rooms are gorgeous, from fresh gingham fabrics and waxed wood floors to marble columns. Nearly all take
in the obligatory view over the central Interlaken meadow and on to
the Cinerama-wide range of Alps, with the snowy peak of the Jungfrau
crowning the far distance. A casual restaurant, La Pastateca, joins the
flashy formal dining room, La Terrasse, but don't forget to check out
the Brasserie, a mammoth, leaded-glass-and-carved-wood Victorian
concoction almost as delicious as its meals. **Pros:** location with view
across to Jungfrau and two lakes; wonderful spa. **Cons:** this is such a
gargantuan place you can feel like a mouse among many; some say it is
overpriced. ✉*Höheweg 41* ☎*033/8282828* ⊕*www.victoria-jungfrau.
ch* ⌕*212 rooms, 95 suites* ♿*In-room: no a/c (some), safe, refrigerator,
Ethernet, Wi-Fi (fee). In-hotel: 3 restaurants, 2 bars, 2 tennis courts,
pool, gym, spa, bicycles, children's programs (4–10 yrs), public Internet
(fee), public Wi-Fi (fee), parking (free), some pets allowed (fee)* ☐*AE,
DC, MC, V* ¶⃝*BP, MAP.*

NIGHTLIFE & THE ARTS

BARS   At the Happy Inn Lodge you'll always find a lively, mixed crowd at
Brasserie 17 (✉*Rosenstr. 17* ☎*033/8223225*). **Buddy's Pub** (✉*Höheweg
33* ☎*033/8227612*), at Hotel Splendid, is a popular spot where locals
and visitors actually mingle. Feeling homesick? Believe it or not, there's
actually a **Hooters** (✉*Höhenweg. 57* ☎*033/8226512*) here, offering
tongue-in-cheek American ambience—somewhat surprisingly, you'll
find families here soaking up the vibe.

CASINO
The **Casino Kursaal** (☎ *033/8276210*) has American and French roulette, as well as 124 slot machines; it's open Sunday–Thursday, noon–2 AM, Fri.–Saturday, noon–3 AM. Las Vegas it's not, but a congenial atmosphere prevails.

DANCING
In the Hotel Metropole, the dance club **Black & White** (✉ *Höheweg 37* ☎ *033/8236633*) attracts an upscale crowd. **High-Life** (✉ *Rugenparkstr. 2* ☎ *033/8221550*), near Interlaken West, brings back easygoing oldies. **Johnny's Club** (✉ *Höheweg 92* ☎ *033/8260160*), in the Carlton Europe Hotel, has been the definitive after-hours club for years. Don't get here too early, as the place comes alive at midnight. **The Metro Bar** (✉ *Hauptstr. 23–25* ☎ *033/8221961*), in the Balmers youth hostel, attracts painfully young people.

> ## STEPPIN' OUT
>
> For groups of 10 or more, dinner folklore shows—yodeling and all—are presented at the Kursaal in the Folklore-Spycher (Off Höheweg, 033/8276100). Call ahead; if another group has booked, individuals can join the party. With dinner only; shows start at 7. At the breathtaking, sky-high restaurant at Harder Kulm (033/8223444), reached by funicular, on Friday only from June through September you can hear typical Ländler (traditional dance) music—and not only the tourists participate. Go ahead, try a few steps yourself.

THEATER
FodorsChoice
★
For a real introduction to the local experience, don't miss the **Tellfreilichtspiele**, an outdoor pageant presented in Interlaken every summer by a cast of Swiss amateurs. Wrapped in a rented blanket—which you'll need, since evenings can be chilly, even from June to September—and seated in a 2,200-seat sheltered amphitheater that opens onto illuminated woods and a permanent "medieval" village set, you'll see 250 players in splendid costumes acting out the epic tale of Swiss hero Wilhelm Tell. The text is Schiller's famous play, performed in German with the guttural singsong of a Schwyzerdütsch accent—but don't worry; with galloping horses, flower-decked cows, bonfires, parades, and, of course, the famous apple-shooting climax, the operatic story tells itself. Tickets range from 26 SF to 48 SF and are available through the **Tellbüro** (✉ *Bahnhofstr. 5A* ☎ *033/8223722* ⊕ *www.tellspiele.ch*). Travel agents and hotel concierges can also secure tickets.

SPORTS & THE OUTDOORS

MOUNTAIN CLIMBING
Contact **Alpin Center Interlaken** (✉ *Wilderswil* ☎ *033/8235523* ⊕ *www.alpincenter.ch*) to join tours led by accredited mountain guides.

SAILING
Lake Thun offers the area's best sailing. From April through October, Interlaken's **Von Allmen Sailing School** (☎ *033/8225693*) offers courses and boat rental.

10

LAUTERBRUNNEN

Fodor'sChoice
★

10 km (6 mi) south of Interlaken.

GETTING HERE

The Bernese Oberland Railway (BOB) runs hourly trains from Interlaken Ost station to the village of Lauterbrunnen; the trip takes about half an hour and stops in such hamlets as Wilderswil and Zweilütschinen.

Visitor Information Wengen-Mürren-Lauterbrunnen (✉ *Across from train station on Bahnhofplatz* ☎ *033/8568568* ⊕ *www.wengen-muerren.ch*).

EXPLORING

Acclaimed by Lord Tennyson as "the stateliest bit of landstrip," the Lauterbrunnen valley is often ranked as one of the five most beautiful places in Switzerland (we give it the number-one spot). A Swiss Shangri-la, it encloses a nearly perfect set piece of earth, sky, and water. The mountains here seem to part like the Red Sea as two awesome, bluff-lined rock faces line the vast valley, where grassy meadows often lie in shadow as 1,508-foot rocky shoulders rise on either side. What really sets this mountainous masterpiece apart are the more than 70 waterfalls (Lauterbrunnen means "only springs") that line the length of the 2-mi-long valley. Some plummet from sky-high crags, others cascade out of cliff-face crevasses, while many are hidden within the rocks themselves; the largest, the Staubbach Falls, were once immortalized by Goethe, Wordsworth, and Lord Byron, who described them as "the tail of a white horse blowing in the breeze." For scenery supreme, Lauterbrunnen clearly can't be topped.

The relentlessly picturesque panorama opens up as you get off the train. This tidy town of weathered chalets also serves as a starting point for the region's two most famous excursions: to the Schilthorn and to the Jungfraujoch. Super-efficient parking and a rail terminal allow long- and short-term parking for visitors heading for Wengen, Mürren, the Jungfraujoch, or the Schilthorn. Consider choosing this valley as a home base for day trips by train, funicular, or cable, thereby saving considerably on hotel rates. But don't ignore its own wealth of hiking options through some of the most awe-inspiring scenery in Europe. Several famous trails line the valley, including the **Panorama Spazierweg**, which connects Lauterbrunnen with Wengen: get a map of it (and lots of brochures) from Lauterbrunnen's tourist office, which is located on the main street.

Magnificent waterfalls adorn the length of the Lauterbrunnen Valley, the most famous being the 984-foot **Staubbachfälle** *(Staubbach Falls)*, which are illuminated at night and visible from town. These falls draw you like a magnet through the village of Lauterbrunnen itself, past a bevy of roadside cafés and the town center (marked by a church and a small Museum of the Lauterbrunnen Valley), and they are found just opposite a centuries-old, flower-bedecked graveyard. At the other side of the valley are the Mürrenbachfälle, which at 250 meters (820 feet) are among the tallest in Europe (the tourist office has a brochure outlining a hike to the top 10 waterfalls). Five minutes by car and 40

CLOSE UP

Hero of 1,001 Travel Posters

Shadowed by the Eiger, Mönch, and the Jungfrau peaks, the vista of the Lauterbrunnen Valley has been captured in innumerable books and postcards. If you wanted to bag this panoramic photo, you used to head to mountaintop Wengen, but it is now so overbuilt you can't get That View. Instead, head for the Panorama Spazierweg trail: take the underpass at Lauterbrunnen's train station to exit on the left side of the village and find the Stocki Road and take the left turn up the hillside. The entire hike to Wengen takes 1½ hours, but the most picturesque part is reached in 15 minutes. Here, in a section lined with cow gates and little barns, case out the right meadow to get the best vantage spot. Another 15 minutes on the trail deposits you at a tiny hut with benches and a cross. Get some more great shots from here, then return to the valley floor. Sir Edmund Hillarys can continue up to Wengen—an hour-long, very steep hike.

minutes on foot beyond the Staubbachfälle are the spectacular **Trümmel-bachfälle** *(Trümmelbach Falls)*, a series of 10 glacier waterfalls hidden deep inside rock walls at the base of the Jungfrau, which you can access by a tunnel lift. Approach the departure point via a pretty, creek-side walkway and brace yourself for some steep stair climbing. Be sure to bring along a light jacket—the spray can be more than refreshing in the cool Alpine air. ⊠ *Follow signs from town* ☎ *033/8553232* ⊕ *www. truemmelbach.ch* 🎫 *11 SF* ☉ *Apr.–early Nov., daily 9–5; July and Aug., daily 8:30–6.*

WHERE TO STAY

$–$$ ★ 🛏 **Hotel Silberhorn.** Though across from the train station and next to the cable car to Mürren, this family-owned hotel, set in a lovely garden, is surprisingly quiet and a wonderful option. Knotty *Arvenholz* (pine) panels the spic-and-span guest rooms. On clear days you may want to chill out in one of the wicker chairs on the sunny porch. The dependable restaurant ($$–$$$) offers satisfying meals of Rösti and meat fondues in a swanky woodlined salon. The more casual Gaststube overlooks a truly soigné fireplace room, replete with cathedral ceiling, exposed timbers, and lots of happy guests. **Pros:** excellent cuisine; peaceful and comfortable with amazing views. **Cons:** not many of the standard services a modern hotel offers: laundry, room service, elevator...should these be vital, look elsewhere. ⊠ *Lauterbrunnen* ☎ *033/8562210* ⊕ *www. silberhorn.com* 🛌 *30 rooms* � *In-room: no a/c. In-hotel: 2 restaurants, bar, public Internet (free), Wi-Fi (free), parking (free), no-smoking rooms.* ▤ *AE, DC, MC, V* ⏹ *BP, MAP.*

10

¢ Fodor'sChoice ★ 🛏 **Matratzenlager Stocki.** Set on one of the most enviable patches of real estate in the Bernese Alps—it occupies what might be called a front-and-center orchestra seat to the Lauterbrunnen Valley spectacular—this adorable hostel welcomes you with a Hansel-and-Gretel chalet exterior just steps from the Panorama Spazierweg trail. The million-euro views, however, are enjoyed by penny pinchers—this is a full-fledged hostel, replete with communal baths and beds (the dorms are lined with 10 double-decker beds all pushed together: get ready to sleep a few inches away from total strangers). Lending an eminently civilized touch to it all is Greti Graf-Feuz, the manager who speaks perfect English and has the bearing of a grande dame. Reservations are made by calling or through the tourist office. One word—fabulous. **Pros:** great value for money; some windows feature some of the most sought-out views in Bernese Oberland. **Cons:** unless the peace, views, and socializing with other guests are top priority, you could feel that entertainment

> **THE SKY'S NO LIMIT!**
>
> If you have the stomach for it, hop on a breathtaking helicopter tour of the amazing mountain ranges from Air Glaciers (at the Heliport, south of town off the main road, 033/8560560); the truly intrepid like riding the many valley thermals here and go paragliding—inquire at the tourist office about Gleitschirmfliegen.

and facilities are definitely lacking—no TV, games, or bar. ⊠*Stocki Str.* ☎*033/8551754* ⬚*30 beds* &*In-room: no a/c, no phone, no TV. In-hotel: kitchen area available, laundry facilities, some pets allowed (free), no-smoking rooms.* ⊟*No credit cards* ☉*Closed early Nov.–first snowfall* ⎮◯⎮*BP.*

¢–$ **Staubbach.** Located just across from the famous Staubbach Falls and directly on Lauterbrunnen's main street—handily lined with cafés—is this excellent option. Young owners have turned this local landmark into a stylish hotel, with modern guest rooms that shimmer with teak and pinewoods. Although the emphasis is on keeping the prices low, there's no skimping on personal warmth and charm. Needless to say, the views of the falls are astounding and, consequently, most people ask for a south-facing room. The fact that this side also faces the main road (which has its share of roaring buses) means you should also consider the three other directions of the compass. Families will be pleased to note the children's play area. **Pros:** views across to Staubbach falls; budget destination with charm and style. **Cons:** no restaurant; in-room facilities are limited (no TV or telephone). ⊠*Hauptstr.* ☎*033/8555454* ⊕*www.staubbach.ch* ⬚*31 rooms* &*In-room: no a/c, no phone, no TV, Wi-Fi (some for fee). In-hotel: public Internet (fee), Wi-Fi (fee), parking (free), some pets allowed (fee)* ⊟*MC, V* ☉*Closed Nov.–mid-Dec.* ⎮◯⎮*BP.*

MÜRREN

Fodor's Choice   *7 km (4 mi) southwest of Lauterbrunnen, 16 km (10 mi) south of Inter-*
★   *laken, plus a 5-min cable car ride from Stechelberg.*

GETTING HERE

With no roads for cars, access here is only via the cable car from Lauterbrunnen (connecting with the Grütschalp Berg Bahn) or the cable cars up to the Schilthorn departing from Stechelberg village.

Visitor Information Wengen-Mürren-Lauterbrunnen (⊠ *Sportzentrum* ☎*033/8568568* ⊕*www.wengen-muerren.ch*).

Moo

It's difficult to grow more than grass on the steep slopes of the Alps, so much of the area has traditionally been used to graze sheep, goats, and, of course, cattle, who supply fresh milk to the cheese and chocolate industries that makes up such an important part of the country's agricultural economy. The Brown Swiss cow, said to be the oldest breed in the world, has been a reliable producer of dairy products for centuries. Browns are highly prized in the region, as they adapt to all kinds of weather, have strong feet and legs, and produce more milk (which also happens to be higher in protein than that from other cows). Their robust nature has made them increasingly popular throughout the world, resulting in a current global population of about 7 million.

The seasonal movement of livestock from lowland pastures to Alpine meadows is a tradition that goes back to ancient times. In spring, herders in regional costume spruce up their animals with flowers and embroidered bell collars and move them up to the grazing areas in a ceremony known as the *Alpaufzug* (Alpine ascent). In fall they come down the same way in the *Alpabfahrt* (Alpine descent). All cows are fitted with bells to help make them easier to find if they wander away from the rest of the herd, and the collective clang can echo through an entire valley. If you're driving along during one of the ceremonies, be prepared to pull over for a half hour or more while the cows lumber on past, taking up the entire road.

EXPLORING

Like Wengen, this Noah's Ark village is perched on a mountaintop shelf so high up—5,413 feet, to be precise—that you may feel like James Stewart starring in *Vertigo* (or Cary Grant swinging atop Mt. Rushmore in *North by Northwest*). The Hollywood reference is apropos, as these two villages have always lured the rich and famous. Birthplace of downhill and slalom skiing (in the 1920s), Mürren offers extraordinarily peaceful mountain nights and an unrivaled panorama of the Jungfrau, Mönch, and Eiger, all set so close you feel you can almost reach out and touch them. Skiers may want to settle here for daredevil year-round skiing at the top (the annual Inferno Race in January is the longest downhill in the world); hikers can combine bluff-top trails with staggering views. This is a car-free resort, so no parking lots spoil the scenery. You'll have to get upwardly mobile in other ways. Mürren is usually accessed from the center of Lauterbrunnen village by an aerial cable car and Bergbahn cogwheel rail (round-trip 25 SF) from Grütschalp, but these can be shut for maintenance (global warming's permafrost melt has increased closings); alternatively, take the bus to Stechelberg—located at the far end of the valley—where two even more dizzying cable cars (round-trip 21 SF) have you reaching for the sky in no time. Upon arrival, Mürren splays out along a long mountain ridge road lined with hotels, restaurants, shops, a few historic chalets, and a large **Sportzentrum** sports center. The village is not overly picturesque, but having your

10

Kaffee und Kuchen on a nearly levitating restaurant terrace will give you that top-of-the-world feeling.

Mürren boasts some of the longest downhill runs because it is at the foot of the **Schilthorn** (9,742 feet) mountain, famed for its role in the James Bond thriller *On Her Majesty's Secret Service*. The peak of this icy Goliath is accessed by a four-stage cable-lift ride past bare-rock cliffs and stunning slopes. At each level you step off the cable car, walk across the station, and wait briefly for the next cable car. At the top is the much-photographed revolving restaurant **Piz Gloria,** where you can see clips of the film thriller in the Touristorama—if you can tear yourself away from the restaurant panorama, which slowly rolls past your window (sit here for 50 min-

> **LA–LI–O–HO–LA**
>
> As a winter sports center, Lauterbrunnen has a vast array of outdoor activities, from cross-country skiing and Nordic walking to ice climbing and snowshoe trekking. Come summer, more cultural fare is on offer, especially the Folkloreabend evenings, which feature Trychler ("cowbell shakers"), the local brass band, costumed dance groups, yodellers, and flag throwers, who gather to perform at the old school house near the Staubbach waterfall. They are held on many Friday eves (but not all), June–August, at 8:30 PM. Also check out the village's annual Nordic Festival every September.

utes and you'll go full circle). The cable-car station is in the town of Stechelberg, near the spectacular Mürrenbachfälle (Mürrenbach Falls). ⊠*Stechelberg* ☎*033/8260007* ⊕*www.schilthorn.ch* ✉*Round-trip cable car Stechelberg–Schilthorn 96 SF; 72 SF 7:25–8:55 or after 3:25 in May and mid-Oct.–mid-Nov.* ☉*Departures daily yr-round, twice hourly 6:25 AM–4:25 PM; last departure from the top 6:03 PM in summer, 5:03 PM in winter.*

A more affordable way to Mürren is the **aerial cable car** built in 2006, whose station sits across the street from Lauterbrunnen's train station. You then connect to the cogwheel rail from Grütschalp, which runs along the cliff and affords some magnificent views. The whole trip takes about 30 minutes and drops you at the Mürren rail station, at the opposite end of town from the cable-car stop. There are departures every 15 to 20 minutes. As you ascend, point your binoculars at the gleaming dome on the Jungfraujoch across the valley: you can almost hear the winds howling off the Aletsch Glacier. ⊠*Lauterbrunnen* ☎*0900/300300* ⊕*www.sbb.ch* ✉*25 SF.*

SKIING

Mürren provides access to the **Schilthorn,** where you'll find a 15-km (9-mi) run that drops all the way through Mürren to Lauterbrunnen. At 5,413 feet, the resort has one funicular railway, two cable cars, seven lifts, and 65 km (40 mi) of downhill runs. A one-day pass covering the Schilthorn region costs 56 SF; a seven-day pass costs 265 SF.

For lessons, contact Mürren's **Swiss Ski & Snowboard School** (☎*033/8551247*) at Chalet Finel, directly behind the Hotel Jungfrau.

CLOSE UP

Licensed to Thrill

Atop Mount Schilthorn perches an amazing sight: the flying-saucer-like lair of Ernst Blofeld, the bald-headed villain from *On Her Majesty's Secret Service* (and the model for Austin Powers' arch-nemesis, Dr. Evil). Or at least that is what it was in the 1969 Bond movie. As eye-popping as granite-featured George Lazenby and the over-the-top plot (Blofeld means to use beautiful women as carriers for a lethal ecovirus), the Piz Gloria was ultimately blown up in the film, but the "hideout" was so memorable that

it kept its stage name and became Europe's first revolving restaurant, still famous for its James Bond breakfast (no martinis, however), which allows you to watch the sun come up over the peaks. According to Joanna Lumley, one of the Bond Girls in the film: "Ringed by range after range of mountains, the view was unparalleled, perfect; too perfect—it looked like a painted backcloth. A props man was given the task of enticing birds to fly around to show it was real."

WHERE TO STAY

$ ★ 🏨**Alpenruh.** Clad in time-burnished pine, fitted out with cute gables and some great gingerbread wood trim, the Alpenruh is as picturesque a hotel as you can get in Mürren. Its perch is spectacular, nearly cantilevered over the vast valley and with reach-out-and-touch vistas of the great Jungfrau and Eiger. No place in Mürren has such a fetching and gorgeous dining terrace. Because the prices here are on the gentle side, the guest rooms verge on plain. The owners also run the Mürren cable car up to the Schilthorn, and you can trade in the hotel's buffet for breakfast atop the revolving Piz Gloria. During key weeks, room rates are upped to include board. **Pros:** picturesque house with jaw-dropping views straight out of a postcard; simple, tasteful interiors at low prices. **Cons:** nearby cable-car girders may mar the view from some rooms; only three bathrooms have bathtubs—if you like a long hot soak après-ski be sure to book one of them. ⊠ *Mürren* ☎*033/8568800* ⊕*www.alpenruh-muerren.ch* ➯*26 rooms* ⚒*In-room: no a/c, safe, refrigerator. In-hotel: 2 restaurants, bar, spa, public Internet, some pets allowed (fee)* ⊟*DC, MC, V* ⦿❙*BP, MAP.*

$$ ★ 🏨**Hotel Bellevue.** Distinguished by its lovely yellow-brick-and-shutter facade, this older landmark, with welcoming owners, presents itself as a traditional ski lodge with full modern comforts. Each room has a tiny balcony, and the decor is fresh pine and gingham. The main dining room is suave in Swedish woods, while the casual Jägerstübli is set around a big fireplace and—those with delicate constitutions beware—hunting trophies. Free entry to the nearby Mürren sports center (tops for swimming and the ice rink) is a big plus, especially for families. **Pros:** a welcome "home away from home" abode; small and perfectly fitted to suit the scene outside. **Cons:** there is one room without a balcony—be sure to avoid this. ⊠ *Mürren* ☎*033/8551401* ⊕*www.muerren.ch/bellevue* ➯*20 rooms* ⚒*In-room: no a/c, Wi-Fi (fee). In-hotel: 2 restaurants, bar, sauna, bicycles to rent, children's play area, public Internet (free), public Wi-Fi (free), some pets allowed (10 SF)* ⊟*MC, V* ☉*Closed*

10

Easter–early Jun. and end of Oct.–
mid-Dec. ⟨◯⟩*BP, MAP.*

$$$–$$$$ ⊡ **Hotel Eiger.** With a front-row
Fodor'sChoice   perch directly across from the Eiger,
★   Mönch, and Jungfrau, this is the
most stylish hotel in Mürren. With
one five-story wing dating back to
the 1920s and an even larger, snaz-
zier wing from the early 1990s,

> **IT'S ALL DOWNHILL FROM HERE**
>
> For a handy Web site about winter sports in the region, log on to www.jungfrauwinter.ch.

most rooms flaunt balconies with "peak" views. In addition, the hotel
has room to spare for a spa replete with an indoor pool with staggering
views of the ermine-mantled mountains. Inside, all is *Gemütlichkeit*-
elegant: the adorable bar has a big fireplace hood, while regular guest
rooms come with elegant pine wainscoting and suites can go all out
with exposed timber beams and gorgeous fabrics. If you want to enjoy
the high life—in more ways than one—head here. **Pros:** fantastic views;
plush and cozy environment; adjacent to the Bergbahn clifftop station.
Cons: the windows do not open for safety reasons, so claustropho-
bics beware; the location is all about peace and tranquillity. ⊠ *Mürren*
☎ *033/8565454* ⊕ *www.hoteleiger.com* ✆ *49 rooms* △ *In-room: no
a/c, safe, refrigerator (some), Wi-Fi (fee). In-hotel: 2 restaurants, room
service, bar, pool, spa, public Internet (free), public Wi-Fi (fee), some
pets allowed (fee)* ⊟ *AE, D, MC, V* ⟨◯⟩*BP, MAP.*

JUNGFRAUJOCH

Fodor'sChoice   *Half-day cog railway excursion out of Interlaken, Lauterbrunnen, or*
★   *Grindelwald.*

GETTING HERE
The long slog uphill starts at Interlaken Ost; change in Lauterbrunnen
and also in Kleine Scheidegg (don't worry about missing your stop—
everyone else is going there, too). A round-trip costs 177.80 SF. Con-
tacts: 033/8287233, www.jungfraubahn.ch.

EXPLORING
The granddaddy of all high-altitude excursions, the famous journey to
the Jungfraujoch, site of the highest railroad station in Europe, is one
of the most popular adventures in Switzerland. From the station at
Lauterbrunnen you take the green cogwheel Wengernalp Railway nearly
straight up the wooded mountainside, and watch as the valley and the
village shrink below. From the hilltop resort of **Wengen** the train climbs
up steep grassy slopes past the timberline to **Kleine Scheidegg,** a tiny,
isolated resort settlement surrounded by vertiginous scenery. Here you
change to the **Jungfraubahn,** another train, which tunnels straight into
the rock of the Eiger, stopping briefly for views out enormous picture
windows blasted through its stony face.

The **Jungfraujoch terminus** stands at an elevation of 11,400 feet; you
may feel a bit light-headed from the altitude. Follow signs to the Top
of Europe restaurant, a gleaming white glass-and-steel pavilion. The
expanse of rock and ice you see from here is simply blinding.

If you're not sated with the staggering views from the Jungfraujoch terminus, you can reach yet another height by riding a high-tech 90-second elevator up 364 feet to the **Sphinx Terrace**: to the south crawls the vast Aletsch Glacier, to the northeast stand the Mönch and the Eiger, and to the southwest—almost close enough to touch—towers the tip of the Jungfrau herself. Note: even in low season you may have to wait in line for the elevator.

More than views are offered to the hordes that mount the Jungfraujoch daily. From June to the middle of September you can sign up for a beginner's ski lesson or a dogsled ride, or tour the chill blue depths of the **Ice Palace**, a novelty reminiscent of a wax museum, full of incongruous and slightly soggy ice sculptures. Admission to the attraction is included in the price of the excursion.

> **FATAL ATTRACTION**
>
> Landmarked by its famous "White Spider" (the conjunction of snowy crevasses), the Eiger's notorious north face was first climbed in summer in 1938, but it was not until 1961 that the first group of climbers successfully conquered the almost vertical rock face. It took them six days to reach the top. As you look up from the comfort of the Jungfrau Railway train, the surprise is not that more than 45 people should have lost their lives on the north face, but that anyone should have succeeded. Legend has it that townspeople make bets to see who will make it and who will not.

A few things to keep in mind for the Jungfraujoch trip: take sunglasses, warm clothes, and sturdy shoes; even the interior halls can be cold and slippery at the top. Some sensitive individuals may experience fatigue or headaches while at the top from the high altitude, which usually disappears on the train ride down. Return trains, especially toward the end of the day, can be standing room only. To save money, take a guided tour with English commentary (called Jungfrau Tour, as opposed to *Jungfrau individuel*), which costs less. Tours leave once a day from Interlaken West, with stops at Interlaken East, Wilderswil, Lauterbrunnen, and Wengen before climbing to Kleine Scheidegg; the return trip is via Grindelwald. You can get to Lauterbrunnen or Grindelwald on your own steam, but you'll have to return the way you came and miss the full round-trip tour. ☎ 033/8287233 ✉ *Round-trip Interlaken East–Lauterbrunnen–Wengen–Jungfraujoch (back via Grindelwald) 177.80 SF* ⊙ *May–Oct., daily 6 AM (first train up)–5:50 PM (last train down); Nov.–Apr., daily 6 AM (first train up)–4:40 PM (last train down). The schedule is weather-dependent in winter: call ahead.*

10

WENGEN

Fodor'sChoice
★

10 km (6 mi) north of Mürren.

GETTING HERE

Famously, cars cannot drive to Wengen and the only transport is provided by the little Wengernalp Mountain Railway, or Wengernalpbahn. This departs and arrives from the lower valley floor town of

Lauterbrunnen and chugs up the mountainside to Wengen every quarter-hour, with departures as early as 6 AM and as late as 11:30 PM (depending on the season; www.jungfraubahn.ch).

Visitor Information Wengen-Mürren-Lauterbrunnen (⊠ *Village Center* ☎ *033/8568568* ⊕ *www.wengen-muerren.ch*).

EXPLORING

Lord Byron, Consuelo Vanderbilt (when Duchess of Marlborough), and other social "climbers" put Wengen on the map, spreading the word about its incomparable eagle's-nest perch on a plateau over the Lauterbrunnen Valley. Few places offered such magnificent panoramas, such elegant hotels, and because of its setting, its *Alpenglöh* was said to be the glowiest in Switzerland. Alas, success breeds its own problems. Today you can barely drink in the famous view 4,068 feet over the valley, as hundreds of chalets now elbow each other to get out of the way. Innerwengen, the town center, is crowded with large buildings and shops with plate-glass windows. But once up on your hotel balcony—the higher the better, of course—you may experience the wonder of yore.

The "upwardly" mobile still head here because the town is home to some of the Oberland's most challenging skiing (which connects with the trail network at Grindelwald), chicest hotels, and pinkest sunsets. You can aim for centrally located upscale hotels, near shopping and nightlife options, or head downhill to pleasant, more isolated lodgings, all artfully skewed toward the view. Half board is just short of obligatory, as only a few restaurants are not attached to a hotel. It's a car-free town; most hotels have porters that meet the trains.

In summer Wengen is a wonderful place to hike. You can also be inspired—and thrilled—by taking the famous **Männlichen Cable Car** (⊕ *www.maennlichen.ch*), the world's longest cable car route. From Wengen it soars up to the top of the Männlichen ridge, a nearly five-minute ride. In Männlichen, hike up to the viewing station for a spectacular view of the Grindelwald and Lauterbrunnen valleys framed by the Eiger and Jungfrau peaks. The center of town is the Berggasthasu Männlichen (Mountain Guest House), home to several restaurants and a bevy of guest accommodations. The cable car descends down to another great town, Grindelwald. Many, however, opt to bi-ped their way down to **Kleine Scheidegg** (a tiny hamlet that serves as a hub for the mountain trains)—a steep and nearly two-hour descent that is one of the most beloved and scenic hikes in the world.

But Wengen is not just about legs, it's about heads: get out onto those forest trails and you may understand why Byron was inspired to compose *Manfred* when he hiked to nearby Wengernalp in 1816, kick-starting the 19th-century Romantic movement in the process.

SKIING

Just over the ridge from Grindelwald, **Wengen** (4,265 feet–11,316 feet) nestles on a sheltered plateau high above the Lauterbrunnen Valley; from there a complex lift system connects to Grindelwald, Kleine Scheidegg,

Postcards from the Ledge

Here are some musings from **Gruezi**'s trip report posted on Fodor's popular Talk Forums (www.fodors.com): all in all, charming, and with a you-are-*more*-than-there vibe:

"I absolutely love great hiking and gorgeous mountain views, but I don't do well hanging thousands of feet above ground in a little metal box connected to a wire 'clothesline,' or walking around the edge of a lovely but very high mountain. So I have to plan carefully to assure my mountain adventures are more joyful than frightful.

But I wanted to visit the Berner Oberland because it is such a Fodor's favorite and I was intrigued by the villages of Grindelwald, Wengen, and Mürren. After much research, I opted on Wengen and the Hotel Alpenrose (my room was the size of a nun's cell but lovely, with a stunning view toward the Lauterbrunnen Valley). And, on the last night, my husband joined me for a special date in this romantic village.

The proprietor of Mary's Restaurant—a pretty 25-minute walk in the Staubbachbankli direction, from just below Wengen's train station—helped me choose a hike to Biglenalp. Up, up, up I went, with a lot of pine trees in my face, but after an hour I reached a plateau with gorgeous in-your-face views of Jungfrau and Eiger and Mönch.

The next day, my acrophobic self scoped out the "skytrain"—the famous cable car, Europe's longest—up to the Männlichen ridge. The most favored hike in this area is from Männlichen to Kleine Scheidegg. From the ground the skytrain looked a bit scary, but I was determined to take the hike and the only other way to get there was a two-hour hike. Posted travel time by skytrain was five minutes. Heck, I can do anything for five minutes I bravely told myself!

After an early breakfast at 7 AM, I headed for the skytrain. Soon I was sitting on board—in a cold sweat. No one else was there! OMG, is there no attendant? Am I riding in this alone? Have I lost my mind? I am not this brave! At a few seconds before 8, the attendant and three other passengers hopped on, the door closed, and we started up.

I began my personal five-minute timer, found a focal point on the floor, and did my yogic breathing. This worked really well—for about three minutes! Then I tried positive self-talk. Checked my watch a few thousand times. Five minutes had passed and we hadn't landed yet! Now I'm panicking. The next two minutes felt like two hours. I started counting down from 100. At about 47 we docked but the doors did not open. When they finally did, about a bazillion feet above sea level, I walked very quickly across an open grid floor to wonderful, blessed terra firma.

I turned around and looked at the view and almost fainted. Literally. Sit down. Deep breaths. It was a simply amazing vista. Absolutely gorgeous views everywhere, and I was proud of myself for sure. Then I set off on perhaps the most beautiful and glorious walk I've ever taken. Think Ireland greenery with the Alps, big beautiful Swiss cows and goats with tinkling bells, and throw in some gorgeous views to the Eiger, Jungfrau, and over the Grindelwald valley. Sheer heaven."

10

and Männlichen. Wengen has six funicular railways, one cable car, 31 lifts, and 250 km (155 mi) of downhill runs. The Lauberhorn run is tough; it's used for the World Cup Ski Races in January. One-day lift tickets for Kleine Scheidegg–Männlichen cost 59 SF. A two-day pass costs 110 SF. Lift passes for the Jungfrau–Top-Ski-Region are available only for two or more days. A two-day ticket costs 126 SF; a three-day ticket, 173 SF; and a seven-day, 334 SF. For a handy Web site about skiing here, log on to: ⊕ *www.jungfrauwinter.ch*.

WHERE TO STAY

$–$$ ▦ **Bären.** This family-run chalet-style lodging just below the center of town is straightforward and bright, with good views and low rates. Guest rooms are done in blues, yellows, and pale wood, accented by watercolors painted by the owner's mother. Front rooms have balconies, so be sure to ask for a view when booking. The nearby playground with a trampoline is a winner for young children. They also offer a chalet called '*Kleiner Bär*' with two rooms for families. Half board is quite a deal, as the dinners are outstanding, and they save trekking around the village after a long day on the slopes. **Pros:** family hosts are ace; food is top-notch; free Internet and wireless connection a bonus. **Cons:** this is a fairly modest, straightforward establishment, so don't look for any luxury in-room amenities. ⊠ *Wengen* ☎ *033/8551419* ⊕ *www.baeren-wengen.ch* ⊅ *14 rooms, 2-bed chalet* ⅄ *In-room: no a/c, Wi-Fi (free). In-hotel: restaurant, bar, public Internet (free), public Wi-Fi (free), some pets allowed (fee).* ▭ *MC, V* ⊗ *Closed mid-Oct.–mid-Dec. and for 2 wks after Easter* �ʘ *BP, MAP.*

$$$$ ▦ **Beausite Park Hotel.** Grandly situated on the hill above Wengen (more than a bit of a hike from the town center, but that may be a virtue), this hotel offers the kind of views that made Wengen world-famous—a Cinerama vista of mountain majesty with the buildings of the town nearly hidden by trees. Happily, the southern-exposure guest rooms come with balconies to drink in the beauty. Pampering is offered elsewhere: sink into a couch in the lounge, relax with a massage, or enjoy a dip in the bio-pond or indoor pool to cool off. The restaurant is done in dull baby blue, and the bar is very stylish. Rooms are spacious and mostly modern—some have elegant brass beds and a more traditional, rustic style. **Pros:** peaceful park location; families situated perfectly for skiing in winter; family-run. **Cons:** 10-min walk uphill from cable car (good idea to pay for ski gear to be kept by slopes); back rooms can be dark due to trees. ⊠ *Wengen* ☎ *033/8565161* ⊕ *www.parkwengen. ch* ⊅ *40 rooms* ⅄ *In-room: no a/c, safe, refrigerator, bar, Ethernet (fee). In-hotel: restaurant, bar, 2 pools, spa, public Internet, some pets allowed (fee)* ▭ *DC, MC, V* �ʘ *BP, MAP.*

$$$–$$$$ ▦ **Hotel Alpenrose.** Wengen's first lodging, this welcoming inn—downhill ★ and away from the center—has been run by the same family for more than a century. The decor is homey, with knotty pine, painted wood, rugs, and skirted lamp shades throughout. Guest rooms with south-facing balconies are slightly more expensive and well worth it—the sweeping views of the valley are sublime. The bar/salon is spacious and comfy, with an open fire, candles, fresh flowers, and overhead beams ensuring the inn's warmth envelops guests at every turn. There

is an emphasis on good half-board meals, the restaurant being for hotel guests only. **Pros:** traditional family-run business; relaxing salon for tired skiers or hikers. **Cons:** not in central Wengen; no wellness or spa facilities. ⊠ *Wengen* ☎*033/8553216* ⊕*www.alpenrose.ch* ⊠*50 rooms* ⚐*In-room: no a/c, refrigerator. In-hotel: restaurant, bar, public Internet (free), public Wi-Fi (free)* ⊟*AE, MC, V* ⊗*Closed Easter–mid-May and early Oct.–Christmas* ⫮*BP, MAP.*

$–$$ ⊞**Hotel Hirschen.** Many of Wengen's hotels have been buffed to a high gloss, but there are a few that still provide delightful rustic accommodations. So if you really just want to indulge in the peaceful and great outdoors hereabouts, your dream of a *Heidi* hideaway can be realized here at this small chalet-style hotel. The couple that runs this inn provides satisfying home-cooked dinners for guests and gives useful tips about walks and skiing. The hotel is directly on the ski slopes, adjacent to hiking paths, and only five minutes from the trains. Note that the restaurant closes during the summer, giving way to bed and breakfast only. **Pros:** small, intimate family atmosphere; directly on hiking paths and ski piste. **Cons:** those not attuned to walking everywhere will not be content here—there is a steep path from the station to the hotel; rustic and simple rooms can rub some people the wrong way. ⊠ *Wengen* ☎*033/8551544* ⊕*www.wengen.com* ⊠*7 rooms* ⚐*In-room: no a/c, no phone, Wi-Fi (fee). In-hotel: restaurant, bar, laundry service, Wi-Fi (fee), some pets allowed (fee), no-smoking rooms* ⊟*V, MC* ⊗*Closed Apr.–June and Sept.–Dec.* ⫮*BP, MAP.*

$–$$
Fodor'sChoice ⊞**Schweizerheim.** It's worth the hike to this family-run pension nestled well below the beaten path for the flawless full-valley views, ★ the pristine gardens, and the terrace picnic tables balancing precariously over the Lauterbrunnen Valley. The rooms are a dated mix of wood paneling, Formica, linoleum, and carpet, but the experience is welcoming and fun—and the owner is a Swiss hand-organ celebrity. The restaurant serves guests only, and half board is possible and very pleasing. The staff is multilingual. **Pros:** hot water and power showers galore; staff are fluent in English. **Cons:** no Web site to check out or make bookings in advance; a disdain for hiking will veto this hotel as a choice for you. ⊠ *Wengen* ☎*033/8551112* ⊠*24 rooms, 2 apartments* ⚐*In-room: no a/c. In-hotel: restaurant, bar, some pets welcome (free)* ⊟*MC, V* ⫮*BP.*

$$$$
Fodor'sChoice ⊞**Regina.** It's all about atmosphere in this genteel Victorian hotel. ★ With its frou-frou trim, Art Nouveau colors, and mountainside setting, this is the most gracious hotel in Wengen. Thanks to the Meyer family, a genuinely familial mood is palpable, which you sense immediately upon entering the plush and handsome lobby. Most large guest rooms have balconies and are finished with a very elegant touch; rooms under the eaves have loft beds. Paintings and rustic antiques (such as a huge wooden sled) are scattered throughout. The half board for an extra 45 SF per person, is a treat; the conservatory-like dining room shares the chef with the hotel's popular restaurant, Chez Meyer's ($$$–$$$$), adorned with vintage family photos and serving a creative seasonal menu. **Pros:** luxurious, modern interiors; fine award-winning cuisine; welcoming hosts. **Cons:** some rooms are tired and outdated.

10

✉ *Wengen* ☎*033/8565858* ⊕*www.hotelregina.ch* ➟*80 rooms* ♨*In-room: no a/c, Wi-Fi (fee). In-hotel: 3 restaurants, bar, gym, spa, public Wi-Fi (fee), some pets allowed (fee)* ☰*AE, DC, MC, V* ☺*Closed Nov.* ☺|*BP, MAP.*

SPORTS & THE OUTDOORS

ICE SKATING Wengen has a **Natureisbahn** *(outdoor ice rink)* in winter and a partially sheltered indoor rink. For hours of operation, contact the **tourist office** (☎*033/8551414*).

GRINDELWALD

Fodor's Choice *19 km (12 mi) southeast of Interlaken.*
★

GETTING HERE
Bernese Oberland Railway (www.jungfraubahn.ch) trains frequently run the 35-minute route between Grindelwald and the Interlaken Ost station.

Visitor Information (✉ *Village Center* ☎*033/8541230* ⊕*www.grindelwald.ch*).

EXPLORING
Grindelwald (3,445 feet) may be surrounded by the peaks of the Wetterhorn, Schreckhorn, Mönch, and Jungfrau, but it is best known as the "Eiger village"—it faces front and center the terrifying north face of the peak that has claimed so many mountain climbers' lives. In the summer of 2006 the Eiger almost claimed Grindelwald itself as its newest victim: headlines around the world described the large chunk of rock face that broke off (due to global warming) and plummeted down the mountainside, covering Grindelwald in dust for several days. Not counting its sheer Alpine beauty, the town remains among the most popular in the Berner Oberland for the simple reason that it is the most accessible of the region's mountaintop resorts. Strung along a mountain roadway with two convenient train stations, it makes an excellent base for skiing, shopping, and dining—if you don't mind a little traffic. Once you get off the main road, there are gorgeous alpine hikes in all directions.

★ From Grindelwald you can drive, take a postbus, or hike up to the **Oberergletscher,** a craggy, steel-blue glacier—act fast though, it has already melted by 30% since 1963, and forecasts have it shrinking another 20% by 2030. You can approach its base along wooded trails, where there's an instrument to measure the glacier's daily movement.

★ For an equally fascinating experience, travel down into the valley to Grund, below Grindelwald, and visit the **Gletscherschlucht** *(Glacier Gorge).* There you can walk along a trail through tunnels and over bridges about 1 km (½ mi) into the gorge itself. Although you can't see the glacier itself while walking along the edges of the spectacular gorge it sculpted, you'll get a powerful sense of its slow-motion, inexorable force. ⊠7 *SF* ☺*Late May–mid-Oct.*

Perhaps the greatest attraction in Grindelwald is the **Firstbahn,** a 30-minute gondola ride that is one of Europe's longest lifts and offers lovely views of the **First** ski area (7,095 feet). A garden flourishes within easy walking distance (it's even wheelchair accessible). Here you can see early summer flowers such as gentians, edelweiss, anemones, and Alpine asters.

SKIING

An ideal base for the Jungfrau ski area, **Grindelwald** provides access to the varied trails of Grindelwald First and Kleine Scheidegg–Männlichen. Grindelwald has eight funicular railways, three cable cars, 22 lifts, and 165 km (103 mi) of downhill runs. Some long runs go right down to the village; there are special areas for snowboarders and beginning skiers. One-day lift tickets for Kleine Scheidegg–Männlichen and First each cost 57 SF. A two-day pass costs 107 SF.

> **ALL IN A DAY'S CLIMB**
>
> With the Eiger taunting all climbers within sight, get up close and personal by taking the dandy one-day hike offered by **GrindelwaldSports** (☎ *033/8541290* ⊕ *www.grindelwaldsports.ch*). After a train ride from Grindelwald to Eigergletscher, you'll hike along the foot of the Eiger's fabled north face, with the guide providing stories of "sheer" excitement. The group then returns to Alpiglen for grilled-cheese sandwiches and back to Grindelwald by train. Contact the tourist office at Grindelwald's Sportszentrum on Hauptstrasse for info.

WHERE TO EAT

$–$$ ╳ **Memory Bistro.** A no-fuss, family-style bistro restaurant, this welcoming place is known for its youthful, smiley staff. It has a relaxed English pub ambience with a well-stocked bar, varied menu, and street-side tables for watching the world go by. Italian, Mexican, and American food are served alongside more traditional Swiss dishes of cheese and potato. These extend beyond seven kinds of Rösti to include gratins with meat and potato-garlic soup. A kid's menu is also on offer for up to 10 SF and Burrito or Burger Days are a weekly institution. This joint is open all year round. ⊠ *Eiger Hotel* ☎ *033/8543131* ▭ *AE, DC, MC, V* ☺ *Closed Wed. mid-Oct–mid-Dec.*
ECLECTIC

$–$$ ╳ **Onkel Tom's Hütte.** This tiny pizza parlor, set in a rustic A-frame cabin on the main drag, is as cozy as they come. Rough wooden floors accommodate ski boots, and eight wooden tables share space with a huge iron cook stove, where the young owner produces fresh pizzas in three sizes (the smallest of which is more than enough). There are also generous salads, freshly baked desserts, and a surprisingly large international wine list. Its popularity outstrips its size; so enjoy the delicious smells while you wait. ⊠ *Hauptstr. (across from Firstbahn cable-car station)* ☎ *033/8535239* ▭ *MC, V* ☺ *Closed Mon., and Nov. and June.*
PIZZA
★

WHERE TO STAY

$$–$$$ ⬚ **Hotel Alpenhof.** Wooden trellis balconies flaunt their jaw-dropping views of the Eiger's north face at this imposing chalet hotel. Happily, inside, past the geranium-bedecked façade, things are small and cozy and come with a warm welcome from the Kaufmann family. While only 200 meters from the train station, the Alpenhof is set directly on the ski slopes, so this is a haven for hikers, bikers, and skiers (who love the free private ski *bus*). The pine-paneled guest rooms accent the chalet theme, with their traditional checkered curtains and low-hanging lamps.

10

The restaurant is noted for its organic and locally sourced dishes. **Pros:** great Eiger views; friendly and helpful family business; good packages for skiing and hiking. **Cons:** nice outdoor Whirlpool, but perhaps better if it were not next to the car park. ☒ *Grindelwald* ☎*033/8535270* ⊕*www.alpenhof.ch* ⬎*17 rooms.* ⟐*In-room: no a/c, safe, refrigerator, Wi-Fi (free). In-hotel: restaurant, bar, sauna, public Wi-Fi (free), parking (free), some pets allowed (fee)* ▤*AE, DC, MC, V* ☒*Closed Nov. and Apr.* ⦿|*BP, MAP.*

$$$$ ⊞ **Hotel Belvedere.** As you wind your way into Grindelwald, this large,
★   pink structure, precariously perched above the road, comes into view. Suites are tastefully designed: the Salon Louis Philippe, for instance, has period 19th-century furniture and wood-inlay games tables. Regular guest rooms suffer a drop in decor, but there are great views of the Eiger and surrounding peaks from almost every chamber. The staff and management radiate genuine warmth and absolute professionalism; the owner takes groups of guests skiing, hiking, and golfing weekly. The bright and glossy restaurant ($$–$$$) has a fresh and creative menu, while the Spycher eatery opens only in winter to feature fondues and raclettes. **Pros:** excellent facilities and cuisine; astounding views in peaceful surroundings; nothing is too much trouble for the helpful staff. **Cons:** not cheap, but worth every penny; food is so good it may be hard to leave the hotel environs and venture out further afield! ☒ *Grindelwald* ☎*033/8545757* ⊕*www.belvedere-grindelwald.ch* ⬎*57 rooms* ⟐*In-room: no a/c, safe, refrigerator, Ethernet (fee), Wi-Fi (fee). In-hotel: 2 restaurants, bar, pool, spa, bicycles, public Internet (free for 30 mins), Wi-Fi (fee), parking (free), garage (fee), some pets allowed (fee)* ▤*DC, MC, V* ☒*Closed mid-Oct.–mid-Dec.* ⦿|*BP, MAP.*

$ ⊞ **Hotel-Restaurant Wetterhorn.** Overlooking the magnificent ice-blue upper glacier—as well as the sprawling parking lot where hikers leave their cars—this pretty, wood-trimmed inn offers generous lunches outdoors, with full glacier views, and good regional dining inside its comfortable restaurant. The adjoining Gletscherstübli attracts locals as well as the hordes of tourists and hikers who come to marvel at its namesake. Up the creaky old stairs are simple, tidy, aged-pine rooms—some have glacier views—with sink and shared bath. Dormitories with 30 beds are also available. **Pros:** perfect base location for skiing, mountaineering, and hiking; popular wholesome food stop for locals and tourists; rooms with a view and some.... **Cons:** masses of tourists passing through to savor the sights; low on amenities. ☒*Am Oberen Gletscher* ☎*033/8531218* ⊕*www.hotel-wetterhorn.ch* ⬎*10 rooms, 3 dormitories* ⟐*In-room: no a/c. In-hotel: restaurant, parking (free), some pets allowed (free)* ▤*AE, DC, MC, V* ⦿|*BP.*

$$–$$$ ⊞ **Gletschergarten Chalet-Hotel.** Built in archetypal chalet architecture—though writ so large it seems to have grown like topsy—this hotel has been in the same family for three generations. Fittingly, the interior radiates welcome, from heirloom furniture and paintings (by the grandfather) to tea roses cut from the owner's garden. There's heraldry in the leaded-glass windows, a ceramic stove with built-in seat warmer, and a cozy lounge paneled in wood taken from an old Grindelwald farmhouse. All rooms have balconies, some with glacier views, others overlooking the emerald-green hills. Ask for a corner room, as the angle views are especially pleasing. **Pros:** homey feel in traditional Swiss abode; friendly family as hosts; magnificent views over glacier. **Cons:** rooms are fairly dated with '70s vibe; breakfast could benefit from being expanded to match array offered in similar standard hotels. ⊠ *Grindelwald* 🕾*033/8531721* ⊕*www.hotel-gletschergarten.ch* ⮌*26 rooms* ⌂*In-room: no a/c, safe. In-hotel: restaurant, bar, sauna, public Internet (fee), public Wi-Fi (free), parking (free)* ▤*AE, DC, MC, V* ⦿❘*BP.*

🏨 **Mountain Hostel.** This welcoming hostel sits at the foot of the Eiger in Grund, 2 km (1½ mi) from Grindelwald. The beds, offered with or without linens, are set up in bunk-bed rooms for two to six people. Showers and toilets are down the hall. The owners take groups out on hikes, and there are outdoor barbecues in summer. Breakfast is provided, and use of a communal kitchen is available for evening meals. It's just a couple of minutes on foot from the Grund train station. As a guest here you have free and reduced access to local sporting and cultural activities—ask reception for details. **Pros:** practical, clean accommodation for bargain basement prices; peaceful spot not too far from village center; staff is excellent. **Cons:** if privacy is essential, this is not for you; big hill to the village, so get ready for some exertion even if you're not a hiker or skier. ⊠ *Grindelwald* 🕾*033/8543838* ⊕*www. mountainhostel.ch* ⮌*20 rooms* ⌂*In-room: no a/c, no phone, no TV. In-hotel: kitchen, public Internet (free), public Wi-Fi (free), parking (free)* ▤*MC, V* ⦿❘*BP* ⊗*Closed Nov.*

$$$$ 🏨 **Romantik Hotel Schweizerhof.** Behind a dark-wood, red-shuttered
★ Victorian-chalet facade dating from 1892, this big, comfortable hotel attracts a loyal clientele. Wing chairs and bookcases in the lobby lounge and dining rooms are inviting on rainy days. Guest rooms are decorated in carved pine and have tile baths. Service is attentive, unhurried, flexible, and extremely friendly. The Schmitte restaurant, aglow with decorative wall paintings and lilac hues ($$–$$$) serves nouvelle Swiss cuisine—try duck breast with oyster mushrooms and shallots, or something from their vegetarian selections. For more casual fare, repair to the sweet *Heidi*-worthy Gaststübli. Breakfasts are generous and are offered until 11:30 AM (a rarity in these parts). Extra touches: a bowling alley and free sledges and ski shoes during winter. **Pros:** nothing is rushed here, allowing you to truly relax and find a new pace; small library has books in seven languages; large garden. **Cons:** a weak point seems to be the totting up of final bills (keep your eyes open for errors while checking out); do not be surprised if the public salons are better dressed than your room. ⊠ *Grindelwald* 🕾*033/8545858* ⊕*www. hotel-schweizerhof.com* ⮌*41 rooms, 16 suites* ⌂*In-room: no a/c, safe, refrigerator, Ethernet (free). In-hotel: 2 restaurants, room service, bar, pool, spa, bicycles, laundry service, public Internet (free), Wi-Fi (free), garage (fee), no-smoking rooms.* ▤*AE, MC, V* ⊗*Closed Easter–late May and Oct.–mid-Dec.* ⦿❘*BP, MAP.*

$–$$$ ✕🏨 **Fiescherblick.** A multistory, flower-box-crazy "chalet," this is the
★ place to eat in Grindelwald, whether as a hotel guest or day-tripper: the same outstanding chef oversees the serious cuisine in the intimate restaurant and the more casual bistro ($–$$$). The seasonal menu might

10

include roast scallops in pepper sauce and black risotto, or guinea fowl in an herb glaze with basmati rice. As for rooms, try to nab one of the "superior" ones, which are bright and spacious, if more expensive. While standard rooms tend to be on the unexciting functional-brown-decor side, guests have called it a "great place to relax after a hard day's skiing." ☒ *Grindelwald* ☎*033/8545353* ⊕*www.fiescherblick. ch* ⟳*25 rooms* ⬧*In-room: no a/c, safe, refrigerator, no TV (some), dial-up. In-hotel: 2 restaurants* ▭*AE, DC, MC, V* ⊘*Closed Easter– mid-May and mid-Oct.–mid-Dec. No lunch.* ⎮⌷*BP.*

NIGHTLIFE & THE ARTS

DANCING **Challi** (☒*Hotel Kreuz* ☎*033/8545492*) has a DJ who is happy to play requests. **Gepsi** (☒*Eiger Hotel* ☎*033/8543131*) is open late; there's a fun crowd and weekly live music. A self-styled "ethno disco" (decorated with cows and alphorns), the **Plaza Club** (☒*Sunstar Hotel* ☎*033/8547777*) plays music that is strictly modern (no yodeling here). **Regina** (☒*Grand Hotel Regina* ☎*033/8548600*) offers live music nightly. Dance it up to the early morning hours at **Mescalero** (☒*Hotel Spinne* ☎*033/8548888*); occasionally there are live concerts and events here as well.

BRIENZERSEE

Reputedly the cleanest lake in Switzerland—which surely means one of the cleanest in the world—this magnificent bowl of crystal-clear water mirrors the mountain-scape and forests, cliffs, and waterfalls that surround it. Along the lake shore are some top attractions: the wood-carving center of Brienz, the wonderful open-air museum village of Freilichtmuseum Ballenberg—Switzerland's Williamsburg—and Meiringen, where Sherlock Holmes met his untimely end at the Reichenbachfälle falls. You can cruise alongside Lake Brienz at high speed on the A8 freeway or crawl along its edge on secondary waterfront roads, or you can cut a wake across it on a steamer, exploring each stop on foot, before cruising to your next destination.

ISELTWALD

9 km (6 mi) northeast of Interlaken.

Set on a lovely and picturesque peninsula jutting out into the quiet waters of the lake, Iseltwald has a bevy of cafés, rental chalets, and hotels (including the noted 19th-cenutry extravaganza the Grand Hotel Giessbach) clustered at the water's edge. Every restaurant prides itself on its fish dishes, of course.

From the village edge you may want to take off on foot; an idyllic forest walk of about 1½ hours brings you to the falls of the **Giessbach,** which tumble in several stages down rocky cliffs to the lake. You can also get to the falls by taking the Brienzersee steamer, a classic lake excursion, which departs from the landing in Brienz. By land, the most scenic route to Iseltwald from Interlaken is via the south-shore road; follow the

Brienzersee

black-and-white ISELTWALD signs. You can also take the A8 expressway, following the autoroute signs for Meiringen.

WHERE TO STAY

$$–$$$
Fodor's Choice
★

🏨 **Grandhotel Giessbach.** Overlooking the famed Giessbach Falls, across the lake from Brienz, this turreted, 19th-century Belle Epoque haven offers lovely scenic views from almost any vantage point. The lobby has high, chandeliered ceilings and period furnishings in golds, yellows, and soft pinks—stucco angels, full-length oil portraits of Swiss beauties, and other Proustian touches all cast their spell and will have you feeling like an off-duty H.R.H. in no time. Guest rooms are comfortable and spacious. The Park restaurant ($$–$$$) has a glorious "orangerie" overlooking the falls, while Chez Florent is a serious gourmand affair. Note that the official address for this hotel is Brienz. **Pros:** stunning location; old-world funicular and boathouse; all-round experience is one of utter relaxation in a unique setting. **Cons:** day-trippers dine at the restaurant terrace for lunch, so it can become crowded; isolated lakeside perch; leaving is a hard thing to do! ⊠ *Am Brienzersee* ☎ *033/9522525* ⊕ *www.giessbach.ch* ⇆ *66 rooms, 5 suites* ♿ *In-room: no a/c. In-hotel: 2 restaurants, bar, tennis court, pool, laundry service, Internet (free), Wi-Fi (free), some pets allowed (fee), no-smoking rooms.* ⊟ *AE, DC, MC, V* ☾ *Closed mid-Oct.–late Apr.*

10

BRIENZ

★ *12 km (7 mi) northeast of Iseltwald, 21 km (13 mi) northeast of Interlaken.*

GETTING HERE
Brienz is on the direct rail line with Interlaken, with very frequent train connections. Brienz is 12 km (7 mi) northeast of Iseltwald, 21 km (13 mi) northeast of Interlaken.

Visitor Information (⊠ *CH-3855* ☎ *033/9528080* ⊕ *www.alpenregion.ch*).

EXPLORING

The romantic waterfront village of Brienz, world renowned as a wood-carving center, is a favorite stop for people traveling by boat as well as by car. Several artisan shops display the local wares, which range in quality from the ubiquitous, winningly simple figures of cows to finely modeled nativity figures and Hümmel-like portraits of Wilhelm Tell. Brienz is also a showcase of traditional Oberland architecture, with some of its loveliest houses (at the west end of town, near the church) dating from the 17th century. Once an important stage stop, Brienz hosted Goethe and Byron at its 17th-century, landmark Hotel Weisses Kreuz; their names are proudly displayed on the gable.

Switzerland's last steam-driven cogwheel train runs from the center of Brienz, at the waterfront, up to the summit of **Brienzer-Rothorn,** 7,700 feet above the town. The ride takes one hour. Trains depart at least once an hour, but to avoid long waits at peak times, purchase your ticket for a particular train in advance on the day you will make the trip; they do not accept reservations. ☎ *033/9522222* ⊕*www.brienz-rothorn-bahn. ch* ⧉*74 SF round-trip* ⊗*End-May–end-Oct., daily; 1st train up Mon.– Sat. 8:37, Sun. 7:37; last train up 3:45, last train down 4:50.*

Fodor'sChoice Just east of Brienz, a small road leads to the magnificent **Freilichtmuseum**
★ **Ballenberg.** Time-channeling centuries gone by, Switzerland's Williamsburg (although Old Sturbridge Village may be more like it), this outdoor museum village is adorned with 80 characteristic Swiss houses from 18 cantons. Dotting the meadows are 19th-century barns, gorgeous pastel-shuttered houses, antique lace-making shops, old Swiss haberdashers, and plenty of lovely old chalets. Most have been carefully reconstructed. Even the gardens and farm animals are true to type. Old handicrafts and trades like spinning, forging, and lace making are demonstrated using original tools, and many of the "re-enactors" are in period costume. The settlement—found between the villages of Hofstetten and Brienzwiler—ranges over many acres and you can easily spend a half-day here. On the other hand, it's not often you come across such a collection of magnificent old relics and abodes, so spend the day at what visitors have called "the perfect family outing." Via public transport, train to the Brienz station and then transfer to municipal bus. ☎*033/9521030* ⊕*www. ballenberg.ch* ⧉*18 SF* ⊗*Mid-Apr.–end of Oct., daily 10–5.*

At Brienz you may want to try your hand at **wood carving.** During a two-hour lesson at the atelier of Paul Fuchs you can learn to carve the typical Brienzer cow. Make a reservation through the tourist office in Brienz or directly with Mr. Fuchs. You'll be placed in a class of a dozen or more. His workshop is in Hofstetten, between Brienz and Ballenberg. ✉*Scheidweg 19D, Hofstetten* ☎*033/9511418* 💳*25 SF* 🕐*Apr.–Oct.*

WHERE TO EAT & STAY

$–$$ ✕**Steinbock Brienz.** After being almost completely destroyed by a mud-
SWISS slide in 2005, this carved-wooden chalet dating from 1787 was recon-
★ structed from the ground up; it's old-style, but all new. Sit out on the broad flower-lined terrace and try to choose from no fewer than 11 interpretations of Lake Brienz whitefish and perch. The menu also has a range of veal classics. There are nine guest rooms; all are fitted with modern amenities with a bright and cheery feel. ✉*Hauptstr. 123* ☎*033/9514055* 🌐*www.steinbock-brienz.ch* 🚫*AE, DC, MC, V* 🕐*Closed Tues. and Feb.*

$–$$ ✕**Weisses Kreuz.** Generic modern improvements have erased some of
SWISS the fine origins of this structure, built in 1688 and host to Goethe and Byron, but the idea of its antiquity and the hallowed names on the gable may be allure enough. The pine-lined restaurant offers omelets and *Käseschnitte* (cheese and bread baked in its own whey) as well as lake fish, steaks, and strudel. The sunny lake-view terrace café draws locals and tourists fresh off the boat. On first appearance this spot may be lacking in charm, but the dishes and the views are well worth stopping for. ✉*Hauptstr. 143* ☎*033/9522020* 🚫*AE, DC, MC, V.*

$–$$ 🏨**Hotel Lindenhof.** In a 1787 lodge high above the lakefront, families
🕙 settle in for a week or two of evenings by the immense stone fireplace,
★ in the panoramic winter garden, or on the spectacular terrace. The grounds are vast and beautifully manicured, the atmosphere familial and formal at once. Guest rooms are quirkily and individually decorated by themes; haystack, forest, flowers, meadow, Alp hut, and more. Children would love these hideaways, the playground, and the fact that at the hotel's popular restaurant families with small ones can dine together by the fire, apart from other guests. **Pros:** family-welcoming; manicured gardens; quirky room decor. **Cons:** standard rooms are fairly small; the hotel's special brand of individuality may be too cutesy for those with little imagination or sense of fun. ✉*Lindenhofweg 15* ☎*033/9522030* 🌐*www.hotel-lindenhof.ch* 🛏*39 rooms* 🔧*In-room: no a/c, kitchen (some), Ethernet (free), Wi-Fi (free). In-hotel: 3 restaurants, room service, bar, pool, spa, bicycles, laundry service, Wi-Fi (free), parking (free), some pets allowed (fee), no-smoking rooms.* 🚫*AE, MC, V* 🕐*Closed Jan. and Feb.* 🍴*BP.*

SHOPPING

Brienz is the place for good selections of local wood carvings—everything from cows to plates to Nativity figures. The wood carvings at **H. Huggler-Wyss** (✉*Brunng. 17* ☎*033/9521000*) make it worth stopping by. For mountain crystals, fossils, and stone jewelry, go to **Bergkristalle** (✉*Hauptstr. 25* ☎*033/9512625*).

10

A Meiringer By Any Other Name

According to local legend, meringues were invented in 1720 in the Bernese Oberland town of Meiringen by a Swiss confectioner named Gasparini. The popularity of the fluffy deserts was so great that they soon spread to neighboring France, where Marie Antoinette apparently was so taken with them that she was said to actually make them herself regularly at the Trianon. From the palaces of France the dish spread to the rest of the world, and it is the French angle that led to the name change: from the original meiringer to the more common meringue. Melt-in-your-mouth meringues are still a local specialty in Meiringen, where they are sold in dozens of pastry shops. To make them yourself, whip two parts egg whites together with one part sugar until the mass is light and fluffy. Bake for three hours at low heat, then let cool. Serve with a generous dollop of fresh whipped cream. Afterward, you might want to make an appointment with your personal trainer.

MEIRINGEN–HASLIBERG

12 km (7 mi) northeast of Iseltwald, 21 km (13 mi) northeast of Interlaken.

GETTING HERE

Frequent trains run the 45-minute route between Meiringen and Interlaken.

Visitor Information (⊠ *Bahnhofstr. 22CH-3860, Meiringen* ☎ *033/9725050* ⊕ *www.alpenregion.ch*).

EXPLORING

Set apart from the twin lakes and saddled between the roads to the Sustenpass and the Brünigpass, Meiringen is a resort town with 300 km (186 mi) of marked hiking trails and 60 km (37 mi) of ski slopes at the Hasliberg ski region. Historically, its main claim to fame is as the place where meringue was invented—it seems the resident chef had too many egg whites left over and decided to do something different for visiting celeb Napoléon. But there is little history left here and, today Meiringen is merely a pleasant town, whose main street is lined with shops proffering all sorts of kitschy Swiss merchandise (don't laugh—this stuff is hard to find in many parts of the country).

Meiringen's one showstopper is the famous **Reichenbachfälle** *(Reichenbach Falls)*, where Sir Arthur Conan Doyle's fictional detective Sherlock Holmes and his archenemy, Professor Moriarty, plunged into the "cauldron of swirling water and seething foam in that bottomless abyss above Meiringen" at the climax of the "last" Holmes story, *The Final Problem* (the uproar over the detective's untimely end was such that Doyle was forced to resurrect his hero for further fictional adventures). The falls, set 2,730 feet up a mountain a little way outside of town can be visited via a funicular. ☎ *033/9714048* 🎫 *7 SF* ⏱ *Funicular: every 10 min daily, 8:30–11:45, 1–6.*

Buffs of the famous detective will delight in the **Sherlock Holmes Museum** in the center of town. Housed in a small chapel, it contains an "authentic" replica of the fictional sleuth's front room at 221B Baker Street. ✉ *Bahnhofstr. 26* ☎ *033/9714141* ⊕ *www.sherlockholmes.ch* ✉ *4 SF* ⊙ *May–Sept., Tues.–Sun. 1:30–6; Oct.–Apr., Wed., Sun. 4:30–6.*

SPORTS & THE OUTDOORS

HIKING A private, 20-km (12½-mi) road to Grindelwald prohibits cars but provides a beautiful, seven-hour Alpine hike. To obtain maps of other local hiking trails, visit the tourist office.

> ### THE PLOT THICKENS
>
> While Sherlock Holmes met his destiny at the Reichenbach Falls, the faithful will also remember that it was at nearby Rosenlaui that Holmes spent the night before his fateful struggle with Dr. Moriarty. Certain historians have put forward the theory that Conan Doyle modeled Moriarty on the famous, but somewhat sinister, German philosopher Nietzsche. Part of the evidence comes from the hotel register at Rosenlaui, which shows that Nietzsche had a holiday there in 1877, and that Doyle visited the hotel when he came to the falls a few years later.

THUNERSEE

If you like your mountains as a picturesque backdrop and prefer a relaxing waterfront sojourn, take a drive around the Thunersee (Lake Thun) or crisscross it on a leisurely cruise boat. More populous than Lake Brienz, its allures include the marina town of Spiez and the large market town of Thun, spread at the feet of the spectacular Schloss Zähringen (Zähringen Castle). There are other castles along the lake, and yet another high-altitude excursion above the waterfront to take in Alpine panoramas—a trip up the Niederhorn.

SPIEZ

19 km (11¾ mi) west of Interlaken.

GETTING HERE

A rail line connects Spiez, Thun, and Interlaken.

Visitor Information (✉ *Village CenterCH-3700* ☎ *033/6542020* ⊕ *www.spiez.ch*).

EXPLORING

Spiez is a summer lake resort with marinas for water-sports enthusiasts. The town's enormous waterfront castle, **Schloss Spiez,** was home to the family Strättligen and, in the 13th century, its great troubadour, Heinrich. The structure spans four architectural epochs, starting with the 11th-century tower; its halls contain beautiful period furnishings, some from as long ago as Gothic times. The early Norman church on the grounds is more than 1,000 years old. ☎ *033/6541506* ⊕ *www.schloss-spiez.ch* ✉ *7 SF* ⊙ *Easter–June and Sept.–mid-Oct., Mon. 2–5, Tues.–Sun. 10–5; July and Aug., Mon. 2–6, Tues.–Sun. 10–6.*

10

Thunersee & Simmental

SWITZERLAND

TO BERN

Münsingen

Schwarzenburg

Sense

Mühlethurnen

Kiesen

Schwarzenegg

Seftigen

Heimberg

A6

Thun

TO FRIBOURG

Plaffeien

Hilterfingen

Zollhaus

BERN

Oberhofen

Gunten

Oberstocken

Gwatt

Thunersee

6

FRIBOURG

A6

Spiez

Gypsera

Wimmis

TO INTERLAKEN

Schwarzseebad

SIMMENTAL VALLEY

A11

Aeschi

Bunshsen

Oberwil

TO GRUYÈRES

Boltigen

Reichenbach

Reidenbach

Frutigen

Kander

Zweisimmen

Blausee

Saanenmöser

St. Stephan

Schönried

Oeschinensee

TO CHÂTEAU-
D'OEX

Saanen

Kandersteg

Adelboden

Gstaad

Lenk

Sirine

Saane

Lötschenberg Tunnel

Lauenen

TO
FEUTERSOEY, GSTEIG,
DIABLERETS GLACIER

0   4 mi

0   4 km

Wildstrubel ▲

VALAIS

KEY

⊢ *Rail lines*

🎿 *Ski Resorts*

WHERE TO STAY

$–$$ **Hotel Seegarten Marina.** With a marble-columned pizzeria in one wing and two dining rooms that stretch comfortably along the marina front, this is a pleasant, modern family restaurant. The lake fish specialties are excellent, but there is a huge range of dishes covering pasta, meat, vegetarian, and salads, plus a children's menu—you will be spoiled for choice. Guest rooms upstairs are spare and modern, yet a nice retreat should you have a few too many cocktails in the Pirate bar after your tasty meal. **Pros:** Spiez Castle is directly behind the hotel. **Cons:** unfortunately, Spiez Castle is also out of sight. ⌧*Schachenstr. 3* ☎*033/6556767* ⊕*www.seegarten-marina.ch* ▱*AE, DC, MC, V.*

$$$–$$$$ ⌶ **Strandhotel Belvédère.** This graceful old mansion has beautiful lawns and gardens, and its manicured waterfront, a five-minute walk away down the hill, offers secluded swimming. Rooms are done in blue and rose, with homey touches such as canopy beds. Corner and lakeside rooms are worth the higher price. On the restaurant's excellent seasonal menu, look for pumpkin ravioli or succulent local chicken, then sit back and enjoy the lake vista view. The wine cellar has the finest selection of wines in the region (and is a retailer—buy a memento to take home). Note that guests have free access to the town's heated outdoor pool. **Pros:** fine, elegant dining; lakeside location and rooms with views. **Cons:** be wary of the tour-group and business-center traffic that can dissolve the peace and tranquillity; some interiors may be getting a little worn. ⌧*Schachenstr. 39* ☎*033/6556666* ⊕*www.belvedere-spiez.ch* ▭*33 rooms* ⌂*In-room: no a/c, safe, dial-up. In-hotel: restaurant, bar, gym, spa, laundry service, public Wi-Fi (fee), some pets allowed (fee)* ▱*AE, DC, MC, V* ⊘*Closed Feb* ⓧ*BP.*

THUN

10 km (6 mi) north of Spiez, 29 km (18 mi) northwest of Interlaken.

GETTING HERE
A rail line connects Thun, Spiez, and Interlaken.

Visitor Information (⌧*Bahnhof* ☎*033/2259000* ⊕*www.thuntourismus.ch*).

10

EXPLORING
Built on an island in the River Aare as it flows from Lake Thun, this picturesque market town is laced with rushing streams crossed by wooden bridges, and its streets are lined with arcades. On the Old Town's main shopping thoroughfare pedestrians stroll along flowered terrace sidewalks built on the roofs of the stores' first floors and climb down stone stairs to visit the "sunken" street-level shops.

★   From the charming medieval Rathausplatz (Town Hall Square), a covered stairway leads up to the great **Schloss Thun** *(Thun Castle)*, its broad donjon cornered by four stout turrets. Built in 1191 by Berchtold V, Duke of Zähringen, it houses the fine **Schlossmuseum Thun** (Thun Castle Museum) and provides magnificent views from its towers. The Knights' Hall has a grand fireplace, an intimidating assortment of medieval weapons, and tapestries, one from the tent of Charles the

Bold; the Hall is often the imposing venue for concerts. Other floors display local Steffisburg and Heimberg ceramics, 19th-century uniforms and arms, and Swiss household objects, including charming Victorian toys. ⊠*Schlossberg 1* ☎*033/2232001* ⊕*www.schlossthun.ch* ☜*7 SF* ⊗*Apr.–Oct., daily 10–5; Nov.–Dec. 24 and Jan. 3–end of Jan., Sun. 1–4; Dec. 25–Jan. 2, daily 1–4; Feb. and Mar., daily 1–4.*

The **Vaporama Swiss Steam Engine Museum** has gotten under way in the lakeside neighborhood of Schadau. Among a comprehensive collection of stationary steam engines is the cruising star exhibit, the completely restored 1906 steamer *Blümlisalp*. Call ahead for hours. ⊠*Seestr. 34/38* ☎*033/2232324.*

WHERE TO STAY

$$–$$$ ☷**Krone.** Positioned directly on the lovely Town Hall Square, this landmark hotel has some fine river views. Although the exterior is classic, the airy interior is stylistically modern, except for the two lovely tower rooms—round, with bay windows and marble and gilt-edged decor—that are worth requesting. There are three eateries on the premises; particularly worthy of note are the one serving a broad range of Chinese dishes and the upscale gourmet Bistro ($$–$$$) that whips up chic versions of regional specialties. **Pros:** historic character and central location; bountiful breakfast buffet. **Cons:** parking can be a problem, as it's limited and not free; despite being a quiet riverside town, it can be noisy in the center during peak season, festivals, and weekends. ⊠*Obere Hauptg. 2* ☎*033/2278888* ⊕*www.krone-thun.ch* ⮫*27 rooms* ⌂*In-room: no a/c, safe, refrigerator, Wi-Fi (fee). In-hotel: 3 restaurants, public Wi-Fi (fee), parking (fee), some pets allowed (fee)* ▭*AE, MC, V.*

$ ☷**Zu Metzgern.** At the base of the castle hill, this shuttered and arcaded *Zunfthaus* (guildhall) overlooks the Town Hall Square. The grand old building has clean, comfortable guest rooms (bathrooms down the hall)—they are straightforward in design and offered without breakfast included. There's atmospheric, traditional Swiss dining, too, whether in the wood-and-linen restaurant or on the intimate little terrace, tucked behind an ivy-covered trellis. In summer months this terrace is usually packed, creating a convivial atmosphere enjoyed by locals and guests alike. **Pros:** simple pleasures of life are to be indulged here—food, laughter, conversation; central location in the Old Town. **Cons:** parking is awkward, as there is none available on-site; honest simplicity is not always savored—if you want high style, seek it out elsewhere. ⊠*Untere Hauptg. 2* ☎*033/2222141* ⊕*www.zumetzgern.ch* ⮫*10 rooms* ⌂*In-room: no a/c. In-hotel: restaurant, no-smoking rooms* ▭*MC, V.*

SHOPPING

A good spot for traditional pottery in Thun is **Töpferhaus** (⊠*Obere Hauptg. 3* ☎*033/2227065*).

HILTERFINGEN

★ *5 km (3 mi) southeast of Thun.*

Lake Thun is famous for its waterside castles, and Hilterfingen and Oberhofen, a little farther along the shore, have two of the best. Hilterfingen's castle, **Schloss Hünegg,** was built in 1861 and furnished over the years with a bent toward Jugendstil and Art Nouveau. The stunning interiors have remained unchanged since 1900. Outside is an idyllic parkland. ⊠*Staatsstr. 52* ☎*033/2431982* ⊕*www.schlosshuenegg.ch/* ✉*8 SF* ⊘*Mid-May–mid-Oct., Mon.–Sat., 2–5, Sun. 11–noon, 2–5.*

> **YOU NEVER KNOW**
>
> In the Seetürmchen—a small tower on the lake—of the Schloss Oberhofen is a lovely, candlelit chamber where all eyes are drawn to an extraordinary carved-wood Mermaid chandelier, one of the best examples of a kind that became quite common in the 18th century. Those in the know touch the mermaid's belly for good luck.

OBERHOFEN

★ *2 km (4 mi) southeast of Hilterfingen.*

Even Walt Disney would have a hard time topping **Schloss Oberhofen** for sheer storybook, fairy-tale splendor. The jewel in the crown of Oberhofen village, this is a delightful hodgepodge of towers and spires on the waterfront. Begun during the 12th century, it was repeatedly altered over a span of 700 years. Inside, a history museum has a display of the lifestyles of Bernese nobility, along with salons done up in the plushest 19th-century style, plus a Turkish "smoking room," a display of magical medieval stained glass, and a 13th-century chapel with noted Romanesque frescoes. ☎*033/2431235* ⊕*www.oberhofen.ch* ✉*7 SF* ⊘*Mid-May–mid-Oct. 15, Mon. 2–5, Tues.–Sun. 11–5.*

SIMMENTAL & GSTAAD

10

Separate in spirit and terrain from the rest of the Berner Oberland, this craggy forest gorge follows the Lower Simme into the Saanenland, a region as closely allied with French-speaking Vaud as it is with its Germanic brothers. Here the world-famous resort of Gstaad has linked up with a handful of neighboring village resorts to create the almost limitless outdoor opportunities of the Gstaad "Super-Ski" region. From Gstaad it's an easy day trip into the contrasting culture of Lake Geneva and the waterfront towns of Montreux and Lausanne. From Interlaken, take A8 toward Spiez, then cut west on A11 toward Gstaad. The forest gorges of the Simmental Valley lead you through Zweisimmen to the Saanenland and Gstaad.

GSTAAD

49 km (30 mi) southwest of Spiez, 67 km (42 mi) southwest of Inter-laken, 68 km (43 mi) northwest of Montreux.

GETTING HERE

If you're not flying in on a private helicopter, there are twice-hourly (mornings and afternoons) and hourly train connections from Bern; change in Spiez and Zweisimmen (38 SF one-way). There's also a narrow-gauge train from Montreux every hour that costs 23 SF one-way.

Visitor Information (⊠ *Village Center* ☎ *033/7488181* ⊕ *www.gstaad.ch*).

EXPLORING

The four fingerlike valleys of the Saanenland find their palm at Gstaad, the Berner Oberland's most glamorous resort. Linking the Berner Oberland with the French-speaking territory of the Pays-d'Enhaut of Canton Vaud, the holiday region of Gstaad blends the two regions' natural beauty and their cultures as well, upholding Pays-d'Enhaut folk-art traditions such as *papier découpage* (paper silhouette cutouts) as well as decidedly Germanic ones (cowbells, wood carvings, and alphorns). Even Rösti and fondue cohabit comfortably.

However, in Gstaad neither culture wins the upper hand. During high season the folksy *Gemütlichkeit* (homeyness) of the region gives way to jet-set international style. Although weathered-wood chalets are the norm (even the two tiny supermarkets are encased in chalet-style structures), the main street is lined with designer boutiques. Prince Rainier of Monaco, Roger Moore, and Elizabeth Taylor have all owned chalets in Gstaad (Liz still does), as well as the late Yehudi Menuhin, who founded his annual summer music festival here. (The Menuhin festival takes place from mid-July through early September, and hotels fill quickly then—as they do for the Swiss Open tennis tournament, held every July.)

Gstaad is a see-and-be-seen spot, with equal attention given to its plentiful skiing and its glamorous gatherings—après-ski, après-concert, après-match. The Christmas–New Year's season brings a stampede of glittering socialites to rounds of elite soirees. But you can escape the social scene. There are several unpretentious inns, hotels, and vacation apartments, and dozens of farmhouses that rent rooms, either in Gstaad itself or in one of the nearby Saanenland hamlets (Gsteig, Feutersoey, Lauenen, Turbach, Schönried, Saanenmöser, Saanen). What paradoxically defies and maintains Gstaad's socialite status is its setting: richly forested slopes, scenic year-round trails, working dairy farms, and, for the most part, stubbornly authentic chalet architecture keep it firmly anchored in tradition. The center of Gstaad is reserved for pedestrians. You can leave your car at the parking facilities at either end of the main street.

The oldest building in the region, the **Saanen Church** was built between the 10th and 11th centuries. Just off Saanen's main street, the church is open daily for visits unless a service is being held. This Romanesque structure was renovated in the 20th century to reveal portions of medieval frescoes on the interior walls.

On Saanen's main street next to and behind the Heimatwerk (handcrafts shop), the tiny **Museum der Landschaft Saanen** *(Saanenland Museum)* traces the history of the area through tools, transport, costumes, furniture, and decorative pieces. ☎033/7447988 ⊕*www.museum-saanen.ch* ▣6 SF ☉*Mid-May–mid-Oct. and mid-Dec.–Easter, Tues.–Sun. 2–5. Closed mid-Oct.–mid-Dec.*

SKIING

Gstaad-Saanenland does not hesitate to call itself a "Super-Ski" region, and the claim is not far from the truth. With the building of the one-track railroad from Montreux at the beginning of the 19th century, this holiday region of Gstaad is increasingly popular, both for its ideal location at the confluence of several valleys and for the sunny mildness of its slopes, which, starting at 3,608 feet and soaring to 7,217 feet, stay relatively toasty compared with those of other resorts (except for the Diablerets Glacier).

Skiing in Gstaad-Saanenland is, in terms of numbers, the equivalent of Zermatt: 62 lifts can transport more than 50,000 skiers per hour to its network of 250 km (155 mi) of marked runs. In fact, these lifts are spread across an immense territory, 20 km (12 mi) as the crow flies, from Zweisimmen and St-Stefan in the east to Château-d'Oex in the west, and 20 km (12 mi) to the Diablerets Glacier in the south.

Gstaad's expansive area means that most of its lifts are not reachable on foot, and since parking is in short supply, public transport, either by the train or the postauto, is the best option. The flip side is that except in very high seasons (Christmas and February) and in certain places, such as the lift for the Diablerets, waits for lifts are tolerable. A one-day ticket costs between 29 SF and 55 SF, depending on the sector; a six-day pass costs 299 SF. The **Gstaad Ski School** (☎033/7441865) gives lessons in downhill, snowboarding, and cross-country skiing (there are more than 50 km [30 mi] of well-groomed cross-country trails).

WHERE TO EAT & STAY

$$$–$$$$ ✕**Die Chesery.** Lobster cappuccino, Brie stuffed with truffles, le pigeon
MODERN FRENCH "royal": with such showstoppers as these, award-winning chef Robert
Fodor'sChoice Speth scales the summits of culinary excellence. He masterfully mar-
★ ries exotic flavors with *cuisine de marché* local ingredients, and his results have foodies and millionaires fighting for reservations; book way ahead in high season. Set in a decorator-perfect chalet (originally built by Prince Sadruddin Aga Khan), this has been a Gstaad landmark ever since it opened in December 1962. Have your dessert—perhaps the signature hot chocolate cake with kumquats—in the piano bar, which lends the place a lively late-night dining scene. An elegant little casino in the cellar adds that James Bond touch. ⊠*Lauenenstr.* ☎033/7442451 ⊕*www.chesery.ch* ▭*AE, DC, MC, V* ☉*Closed Mon. and Tues.*

$$$$ ▥**Grand Hotel Park.** A little bit of Vail comes to the Alps in this enor-
★ mous modern hotel, which opened in May 1990 and seems bent on helping wealthy Americans make a seamless transition between two

10

cultures. Its 1910 predecessor on the site destroyed, this all-new structure refers to the old style in its deep mansard roofs and rows of arched windows, but there the homage ends: the interiors are all new, and the look is an opulent mix of chalet-modern and Spanish grandee, with a lot of flowered wallpaper, waxed wooden furniture, and wardrobes painted with Swiss folk-art scenes mixed in. The impression is opulent yet cheerful. The Park offers some of the best health facilities in the Saanenland, including an antistress program, aerobics and gymnastic classes, and an indoor saltwater pool. Treatment weeks offer an irresistible mix of glamor and virtue. **Pros:** truly top-notch wellness program and facilities; modern luxe combined with a wood-cabin-cum-chalet abode works wonders on the soul! **Cons:** you may never want to leave (which could break the bank as this is a fairly costly hideout). ⊠ *Wispilestr.* ☎*033/7489800* ⊕*www.grandhotelpark.ch* ⌁*88 rooms, 11 suites, 2 apartments* ⌂*In-room: no a/c, safe, refrigerator, Wi-Fi (fee). In-hotel: 3 restaurants, bar, tennis court, 2 pools, gym, spa, public Internet (free), public Wi-Fi (fee), some pets allowed (fee)* ⊟*AE, DC, MC, V* ⊙*Closed mid-Sept.–mid-Dec. and end of Mar.–early June* ⦿*MAP.*

$$$–$$$$ ⛼ **Le Grand Chalet.** On a hill just a 10-minute walk from the center of Gstaad, Le Grand Chalet commands a spectacular view of the surrounding mountains and village below. The spacious, comfortable rooms exude an informal elegance, with pale wood and fresh white curtains throughout. An open central fireplace separates the cozy lounge from La Bagatelle ($$–$$$$), the hotel's popular restaurant favored for its nouvelle Swiss cuisine. Try the pepper steak, baby chicken with tarragon, game in season, and marvelous local cheeses. Easy walking trails depart from the hotel's doorstep. **Pros:** fine food in the gourmet restaurant; amazing views. **Cons:** housekeeping is not the most attentive; bathrooms could be improved. ⊠*Neueretstr.* ☎*033/7487676* ⊕*www.grandchalet.ch* ⌁*20 rooms, 4 suites* ⌂*In-room: no a/c, safe, refrigerator, Ethernet (fee). In-hotel: restaurant, bar, pool, sauna, public Internet (free), parking (free), some pets allowed (fee)* ⊟*AE, DC, MC, V* ⊙*Closed mid-Oct.–mid-Dec. and Apr.–early June* ⦿*BP.*

$$$$ ⛼ **Olden.** At the eastern end of the main thoroughfare, this charming
★ Victorian-style inn has an elaborately painted facade and intricately carved woodwork in every interior niche. Guest rooms are folksy and atmospheric, but have such modern details as lighted closets. The places to see and be seen are the hotel's bar and restaurant. Offerings at the elegant establishment might include lobster bisque or lamb in an olive crust. A more economic way of scoping the Gstaad scene is to sip a coffee on the Olden's sidewalk terrace. Travelers on Fodor's Talk Forum consider this venue "definitely worth a detour." **Pros:** unique traditional hotel inn. **Cons:** there is no elevator; no spa. ⊠ *Gstaad* ☎*033/7484950* ⊕*www.hotelolden.com* ⌁*16 rooms* ⌂*In-room: no a/c, safe, refrigerator, Wi-Fi (free). In-hotel: 3 restaurants, bar, public Internet (free), Wi-Fi (free), some pets allowed (fee)* ⊟*AE, DC, MC, V* ⊙*Closed mid-Apr.–early June and end of Oct.–early Dec.* ⦿*BP.*

$$$$ ⛼ **Palace.** Towering over tiny Gstaad like Mad Ludwig's castle, this fan-
Fodor'sChoice tasyland burlesque packs a wallet-wallop. Although it cozily refers to
★ itself as a family "pension" (albeit the largest in Switzerland), it has an

indoor swimming pool with underwater music and water-jet massage, chauffeured Rolls-Royces, and oxygen cures, among other amenities. An indoor-outdoor swimming pool (with a glass floor placed on top for dancing on winter nights), tennis weeks in summer, and an elaborate health club are but a few of many compelling amenities. Conscientious travelers worried about missing out on the local experience, rest assured: the guest rooms are lavished with appropriately rustic touches, though you could play hockey in the sprawling tiled baths. The kitchen serves four lavish restaurants ($$$$), with renowned guest chefs conducting weeks of special cuisines from around the world. Be prepared for the steep 15-minute walk uphill. **Pros:** total hedonism throughout; plethora of amenities—many unique to this establishment (free laptops!). **Cons:** so expensive it hurts; steep hill to maneuver unless, of course, you are chauffered in one of the hotel's Rolls-Royces! ✉ *Palacestr.* ☎ *033/7485000, 800/745–8883 in U.S.* ⊕ *www.palace.ch* 🛏 *71 rooms, 6 suites, 1 apartment* ⚒ *In-room: no a/c, safe, refrigerator, Wi-Fi (fee). In-hotel: 5 restaurants, bar, 2 tennis courts, squash, 2 pools, gym, spa, doctor, children's programs, public Internet (free), public Wi-Fi (fee), parking (free), garage (fee), some pets allowed (fee)* ▭ *AE, DC, MC, V* ⊙ *Closed late Mar.–mid-June and mid-Sept.–mid-Dec.* ¶◎ *MAP.*

$$–$$$ ⊡ **Posthotel Rössli.** This comfortable inn, dating back to 1845, is the
★ oldest in town, combining down-home knotty-pine decor with soigné style. Blissfully in the heart of Gstaad's traffic-free zone, you are assured peace and tranquillity. Despite the mountain-cabin look, the clientele is young and chic, and the café, a local-landmark watering hole, draws crowds. The owner is an enthusiastic ski instructor, mountain guide, and hunter, and can offer many tips on local adventures (they even have their own hunting cabin in the nearby mountains). The restaurant, full of linens and candlelight, serves good Swiss fare at reasonable prices. **Pros:** low-key traditional hotel, a refreshing escape from nearby grottoes of glory; great atmosphere. **Cons:** parking available but limited; no bar area. ✉ *Promenade* ☎ *033/7484242* ⊕ *www.posthotelroessli.ch* 🛏 *18 rooms* ⚒ *In-room: no a/c, refrigerator (some), Wi-Fi (fee). In-hotel: 2 restaurants, public Wi-Fi (fee), parking (free), garage (fee), some pets allowed (fee), no elevator.* ▭ *MC, V* ¶◎ *BP.*

NIGHTLIFE & THE ARTS

BARS **Pinte** (☎ *033/7443444*), in the Hotel Olden, is where people gather after a day on the slopes. Belly up to the beautiful wooden bar or huddle around the stone fireplace.

CONCERTS The **Menuhin Festival Gstaad** (✉ *Postfach 65,* ☎ *033/7488338* 🖷 *033/7488339* ⊕ *www.menuhinfestival.com*) hosts a series of world-class concerts from mid-July to early September. **Les Sommets Musicaux de Gstaad** (✉ *36 rue de Montchoisy, case postale 1207, Geneva* ☎ *022/7386675* 🖷 *022/7368505* ⊕ *www.sommets-musicaux.com*) presents two weeks of classical music from late February to early March. Information for the festivals is available several months in advance, direct or from the Gstaad tourist bureau.

10

DANCING   **Club 95** (☎ *033/7484422*), in the Sporthotel Victoria, is popular with a younger crowd. **GreenGo** (☎ *033/7485000*), a disco in the Palace Hotel, is open only in winter. There are two crowded bars, but the focal point is the massive dance floor fitted over the hotel's pool.

SPORTS & THE OUTDOORS

MOUNTAIN   Great treks and climbs are a stone's throw from Gstaad. **Alpinzen-**
CLIMBING   **trum Gstaad** (☎ *033/7484161* ⊕ *www.alpinzentrum.ch*) can supply you with mountain guides and snow-sports teachers. **Beat's Adventures** (☎ *033/7441521 or 079/4182953*) aims its tough sports excursions at very fit people. **Experience** (☎ *033/7448800*) is the place to go for guides for off-trail skiing, ice climbing, and snowshoe trekking.

Valais

CRANS-MONTANA, VERBIER, LEUKERBAD, ZERMATT & THE MATTERHORN

Matterhorn

WORD OF MOUTH

"Remember that Zermatt is down in a 'hole.' Yes, the Matterhorn can be seen from its streets but it is a long way away. For a block-buster vista, take the short train ride to the Gornergrat viewing station. There stand Monte Rosa to the south, with its huge glaciers and massive visage, and to the west, the Matterhorn towers seemingly alone."

—brookwood

WELCOME TO VALAIS

TOP REASONS TO GO

★ **The Matterhorn:** Shutter-snap this glorious enigma from all angles, be it a luxury hotel room at its base or the sky-high Gornegrat–Monte Rosa Bahn.

★ **Be a downhill racer:** Get to know your snow at fabled ski resorts like Crans-Montana and Verbier (and the nearby lovely lift villages).

★ **Cantonal capital:** Presided over by the castle of Tourbillon, Sion is a fortified link in the giant web of precipitous passes.

★ **Going to the dogs:** Credited with saving so many lives, the revered St. Bernards still accept thanks at their Col du Grand St-Bernard hospice.

★ **Zermatt:** Worship the cult of the Matterhorn from this posh resort, where chic boutiques and raclette restaurants keynote the "high" life.

1 Val d'Entremont. If you have to pick one Valais wild valley to explore, this one also allures with the civilizing pleasures of the St-Maurice abbey and Martigny's ancient Roman treasure trove. Head east to Verbier, second to none for its ski facilities, or make a great exit south at the famous Col du Grand St-Bernard pass.

2 Sion. The canton's capital is marked by two rocky hills that materialize in front of you like a fairy-tale landscape, one crowned by the Tourbillon castle. The town has been a bishopric for 1,500 years and has a wealth of architectural delights from a Gothic cathedral to a 17th-century town hall.

11

Eiger
Mönch
Jungfrau
Gletsch
Münster
Aletschhorn
Eggishorn
Fiesch
LÖTSCHENTAL
Bietschhorn
Brig
Visp
Turtmann
ITALY
MATTERTAL
VISPERTAL
SAASTAL
Längfluh
Weisshorn
Alphübel
Piz
d'Andolla
Allalinhorn
Alphübel
rmatt
Unterrothorn
terhorn
478m
Gornergrat
Trockener Steg
Breithorn
Dufourspitze
Monte Rosa
4,634m
orn

0   10 mi
0   10 km

GETTING ORIENTED

Born in the heights above the Gletsch Glacier, the mighty River Rhône dominates this region of southern Switzerland. Its silty torrent carves out the valley of the upper Rhône, around which chic ski resorts like Zermatt and Crans-Montana are groomed into gnarls of stone and ice.

3 Conversion de la Vallée. The adjoining modern ski resorts of Crans-Montana are attractively perched 5,000 feet up on a sunny plateau among woods, grasslands, and small lakes. In nearby Val d'Anniviers, tiny villages are noted for their folkloric mazots (small wooden barns balanced on stone disks and columns).

4 Alpine Zentrum. Feast your eyes on the Matterhorn (and your belly on some great fondue) in glamorous Zermatt, where you can catch your breath strolling the car-less streets before taking a lift or train to even higher elevations. Allow half a day to get here and back, enjoying spectacular views from the train en route. Nearby is Saas-Fee, famed for its glacier skiing.

VALAIS PLANNER

How's the Weather?

The Valais is at its sunny best in high summer and midwinter; foggy dampness overwhelms in late autumn and spring. Mountain weather is impetuous, embracing with its warmth one day and obliterating views and trails the next. Take your cues from local forecasts and mountain operators who have an experienced sense about shifting patterns. Cloud layers and storms move up and down elevations hovering atop cool valley floors, following the flow of riverbeds, and are sometimes snagged on mountain ridges. Misty banks move away in short order opening up the path or vista for those who are patient.

Some of the best skiing and hiking can be had in March and September when crowds are the lightest and the sun is at the perfect arc. Because of its radiant orientation, the Valais is a particularly favored destination for Swiss and other Europeans who vacation here year after year and for weeks at a time. And remember: May and June plus November to mid-December are renovation, repair, and getaway times for locals. Facilities rotate closing periods, so you will always find a fluffy bed and good meal.

Loosen Those Belts

For Valaisans, the midday meal remains the mainstay. Locals gather at a bistro for a hearty *plat chaud* (warm meal) that includes meat, vegetable or pasta, and salad for under 20 SF.

Baskets of crusty *pain* freshly cut from thick loaves, never presliced, circulate around the table.

The evening meal is lighter, perhaps comprising an *assiette* (platter) of cheese and cold cuts shared by the table, accompanied by another bread basket and fruit.

For the time-pressed, sandwiches and quick meals can be picked up at a corner boulangerie or supermarket (Manor, Migros, or Coop), where food halls have buffets and inexpensive sit-down options.

Dress and atmosphere are understated even at top-dollar restaurants, which eschew worn jeans but seldom require a jacket.

Keep in mind that most eateries do not offer continuous service; lunch winds down around 2 and dinner does not begin before 6.

Unless a host greets you or you have a reservation, it is fine to take a seat at an open table.

Multiple dining options can share the same entrance and kitchen. A brasserie, or Stübli, is the homey casual section just inside the doorway, with paper place mats, straightforward dishes, and lively conversation.

The quieter *salle à manger* (dining room) has tables dressed in linen and a *carte* (menu) of multicourse meals and more complicated preparations.

If cheese specialties are served, a *carnotzet,* a cozy space in the cellar or a corner away from main dining, is designated to confine the aroma and foster conviviality.

Wine is a standard companion whether *vin ouvert* (open wine) poured from small pitchers or bottles selected from cellar holdings.

The pace of eating is leisurely, and the server will not bring a check until you request it.

11

Finding a Place to Stay

The most appealing hotels in Valais seem to be old. That is, historic sites have maintained their fine Victorian ambience; postwar inns, their lodgelike feel.

Most of those built after about 1960 popped up in generic, concrete-slab, balconied rows to accommodate the 1960s ski boom. They are solid enough but, for the most part, anonymous, depending on the personality of their owners.

Valais is home to some of Switzerland's most famous resorts, and prices vary widely between top-level Zermatt lodgings and simple auberges (inns) in humbler towns.

The price categories below have been equally applied, so the standards in a $$$-rated hotel in expensive Zermatt may be moderate compared with those in nonresort towns, and even the best hotels do not have air-conditioning.

Often included in the price, demipension (half-board)—also called Modified American Plan (MAP)—includes breakfast and either lunch or dinner; rates may be listed per person.

There are sometimes enormous differences between high- and low-season prices but, although some places offer low-season savings, others simply close their doors.

Remember that many resorts shut down during the lulls in May and from November to mid-December.

Big Schlock Candy Mountain

You'll feel unsated if you miss Switzerland's most photographed icon, the Matterhorn, so head to Zermatt first. Allow a half day to get there, enjoying spectacular views from the train en route (the town is pedestrian-only). Hustle to the end of the crowded village to see the mountain, then take lifts or trains to obtain less obstructed vistas.

WHAT IT COSTS IN SWISS FRANCS

¢	$	$$	$$$	$$$$
RESTAURANTS				
under 15 SF	15 SF–25 SF	25 SF–40 SF	40 SF–60 SF	over 60 SF
HOTELS				
under 100 SF	100 SF–175 SF	175 SF–250 SF	250 SF–350 SF	over 350 SF

Restaurant prices are per person for a main course at dinner. Hotel prices are for two people in a standard double room in high season, including tax and service.

Transportation Basics

An exceptional network of rail and bus services links even the most remote Valais hamlets.

Main highways are easy to navigate, but it takes skill and courage to tackle the twisted and graded (sometimes single-track and without guardrail) roads that spur off them.

Many travelers prefer to cover these distances by train or on one of the bright yellow postal buses.

These same comfortable coaches pick you up at designated roadside stops or post offices and are a good option when the hiking trail terminates or your legs are too weary to carry you farther.

Martigny, Sion, Brig, and Visp are main rail transfer hubs. Schedules are synchronized so that you step off one transport onto the other by walking from platform to parking lot.

If you must travel by car, check with the destination, as resorts like Zermatt and Saas-Fee require that you leave your vehicle in a garage or lot on the outside of town, adding parking fees to vacation costs.

And guess what? Some hotels reserve space for your car along with your bed.

VALAIS PLANNER

By Air

For international arrivals, you can choose between two airports when flying to Valais: Geneva Cointrin or Unique Zürich. Geneva Cointrin receives few international flights directly from the United States, but connecting service through London and Paris makes it preferable for those heading to the west (French) end of Valais; it's about two hours away by train or car. Unique Zürich brings passengers closer to the east (German) side, but the Alps are in the way; you must connect by rail tunnel or drive over one of the passes, which will take two to three hours. Commuter and private jet service is available into Sion.

Cointrin Airport (☎022/7177111 ⊕www.gva.ch).
Unique Airport (☎043/8162211 ⊕www.zurich-airport.com).
Aéroport de Sion (☎027/3290600 ⊕www.sion.ch).

Visitor Information

The main tourist office for the entire Valais region is located in Sion.

Valais Main Cantonal Tourist Office (✉6 rue Pré-Fleuri, Sion ☎027/3273570 ⊕www.valaistourism.ch).

By Bus

As in other parts of the country, an efficient network of postal buses covers the region, even to the most remote hamlets, at least once a day.

The bright yellow coaches pick up and deliver passengers at main rail stations like Martigny, Sion, Sierre, Visp, and Brig and transport them to higher destinations.

Many travelers prefer the convenience of being dropped off in car-less resorts and not having to navigate narrow, torturous roadways especially in icy and snowy conditions, not to mention paying additional parking fees at lots and garages.

Schedules are available online and at all tourist offices. The buses are easily hailed at their regular stops, marked with signage along the roadway or at village post offices.

They are also a convenient way to return to starting points from long-distance hikes.

Resorts like Verbier, Crans-Montana, and Saas-Fee, with its contingent valleys, have free shuttles that loop a circuit for skiers and snowboarders, as well as for summer guests.

In Sierre, in addition to the 12-minute funicular connecting the town with Crans-Montana, there is bus service on the **SMC (Sierre Mollens Crans-Montana)** that winds its way through villages on east and west routes from the train station. It will add a half hour to your arrival.

Access to St-Luc and Grimentz is made via Sierre by switching to the postbus at the station.

A similar train-bus transfer takes place in the valley station of Leuk to get to the thermal village of Leukerbad. The **LLB (Leuk Leukerbad)** schedule is synchronized with SBB arrivals and departures and takes about a half hour.

The fares and schedules for all of these connections are available through the SBB.

PostBus (☎0900/800800 [within Switzerland only, 1.19 SF per min] ⊕www.swisspost.ch).
SMC (☎027/4813355 ⊕www.cie-smc.ch). **LLB** (☎027/4702052 ⊕www.llbreisen.ch).

By Train

There are straightforward rail connections to the region by way of Geneva/Lausanne to the west and Brig/Brigue to the east. The two are connected by one clean rail sweep that runs the length of the valley. In winter a special extension of the high-speed train from France, TGV Neige, terminates in Brig. The run to main connections mid-valley takes about two hours. Add on another hour to arrive at mountain destinations. Routes into smaller tributary valleys are limited, although most resorts are served by cheap and reliable postbuses running directly from train stations. The Mont Blanc/St. Bernard Express, with its signature red and white cars, passes through Le Châble for connections to Verbier on its way from Martigny to Chamonix. In Le Châble, take the cableway or bus for the 10- to 20-minute ride. To travel to the Grand St-Bernard Pass, you will have to switch to the company's bus line in Orsières for an hour's drive to the pass or through the tunnel to Aosta, Italy. The Matterhorn Gottard Bahn ferries passengers from Brig and Visp to Zermatt, and operates frequent shuttle service from Täsch to the village on a private railway system. It also connects with the famous panoramic Glacier Express that runs between Zermatt and St. Moritz. Once in Zermatt, another arm of the network, the Gornergrat Bahn takes over to sweep skiers and day-trippers to the Gornergrat. The SBB provides 24-hour information about all rail service; consult local schedules for commuter services.

SBB Information (☎0900/300300 ⊕www.rail.ch). **Matterhorn Gottard Bahn** (☎027/9277474 ⊕www.mgbahn.ch). **Gornergrat Bahn** (☎027/9214711 ⊕www.gornergrat.ch). **Mont Blanc/St. Bernard Express** (☎027/7216840 ⊕www.tmrsa.ch).

Over Hill, Over Dale

As skiing is to winter, hiking is to summer in Valais, and the valleys that radiate north and south of the Rhône provide almost infinite possibilities. Sociable hikers can join the crowds on trails out of Saas-Fee and Zermatt, but don't overlook alternatives in the less-developed Val d'Anniviers. Skilled trekkers opt for multiday hut-to-hut excursions into the higher elevations, skirting mountains that fail to recognize official borders with France and Italy. Wine enthusiasts can explore pathways connecting vineyards between Martigny and Visp, like the well-defined trail between Sierre and Salgesch. Good maps and suggested itineraries are available.

By Car

Valais is something of a dead end by nature: a fine expressway (A9) carries you in from Lac Léman, but to exit—or enter—from the east end, you must park your car on a train and ride through the Furka Pass tunnel to go north or take the train through the tunnel under the Simplon Pass to go southeast. (The serpentine roads over these passes are open in summer; weather permitting; the Simplon road stays open all year.) You also may cut through from or to Kandersteg in the Berner Oberland by taking a car train to Goppenstein or Brig. A summer-only road twists over the Grimsel Pass as well, heading toward Meiringen and the Berner Oberland or, over the Brünig Pass, to Luzern.

If you want to see the tiny back roads you'll need a car. The A9/9 expressway from Lausanne turns into a well-maintained highway at Sierre that continues on to Brig. Additional tunnels and expanded lanes are being carved out of existing highways. Distances in the north and south valleys can be deceptive: apparently short jogs are full of painfully slow switchbacks and distractingly beautiful views. Both Zermatt and Saas-Fee are car-free resorts, though you can drive all the way to a parking lot at the edge of Saas-Fee's main street. Zermatt must be approached by rail from Täsch, the end of the line for cars (there's a central rail terminal and garage).

Updated by
Alexis Munier

THIS IS THE BROAD UPPER VALLEY of the mighty Rhône, a river born in the heights above Gletsch (Glacier), channeled into a broad westward stream between the Bernese and the Valaisan Alps, lost in the depths of Lac Léman (Lake Geneva), and then diverted into France, where it ultimately dissolves in the marshes of the Camargue. The region is still wild, remote, beautiful, and slightly unruly. Its *raccards* (typical little Valaisan barns balanced on stone disks and columns to keep mice out of winter food stores) are romantically tumbledown, its highest slopes peopled by nimble farmers who live at vertiginous angles. More than 500 km (310 mi) of mountains and glaciers span the Bietschhorn, Aletsch, and Jungfrau summits. In 2001, UNESCO named this area a World Heritage Site, joining such other natural wonders as the Galapagos Islands, Yellowstone National Park, and the Serengeti Desert.

The birthplace of Christianity in Switzerland, Valais was never reformed by Calvin or Zwingli, nor conquered by the ubiquitous Bernese—one reason, perhaps, that the west end of Valais seems the most intensely French of the regions of the Suisse Romande.

Its romance appeals to the Swiss. Longing for rustic atmosphere, they build nostalgic Valais-style huts in their modern city centers so they can eat raclette (melted cheese with potatoes and pickles) under mounted pitchforks, pewter pitchers, and grape pickers' baskets. For vacations, the Swiss come here to escape, to hike, and, above all, to ski. The renowned resorts of Zermatt, Saas-Fee, Crans-Montana, Verbier, and Leukerbad are all in Valais, some within yodeling distance of villages barely touched by modern technology.

Of course, you'll feel unsated as long as you miss Switzerland's most photographed icon, the Matterhorn, so strike out on the most direct route to Zermatt. Allow a half day to get there and back, enjoying spectacular views from the train en route (you can't drive to the town of Zermatt itself). If the weather is clear when you arrive, hustle to the end of the village to see the mountain. Then split your day of exploring between taking a lift or the train to higher elevations and strolling the narrow streets and shops, being sure to stop at one of the local restaurants for raclette.

To experience Valais, happily, it's not necessary to explore every wild valley that ribs out from the Rhône; better to choose one region and spend a few days hiking, driving, or skiing. Enter from Lac Léman and visit the Gianadda museum in Martigny. Spend the night and next day exploring the citadel and Old Town of Sion. Other Alpine resort options-Saas-Fee, Verbier, and Crans-Montana-are also magnificently sited. For the prettiest scenery, whenever time and road conditions permit, opt for the slow switchback crawl over the mountain passes rather than the more efficient tunnels.

EXPLORING VALAIS

Valais is an L-shaped valley with Martigny at its angle. Its long (eastern) leg, a wide, fertile riverbed flanked by bluffs, is the most characteristic and imposing. It's fed from the north and south by remote, narrow valleys that snake into the mountains and peter out in Alpine wilderness or lead to the region's most famous landmarks—including that Swiss superstar, the Matterhorn. Not all of Valais covers Alpine terrain, however. The western stretch—between Martigny and Sierre—comprises one of the two chief sources of wine in Switzerland (the other is in Vaud, along Lac Léman). Valaisan wines come from vineyards that stripe the hillsides flanking the Rhône.

The Val d'Entremont leads southward up an ancient route from key Roman crossroads at Martigny to the Col du Grand St-Bernard (Great St. Bernard Pass). Up the Rhône Valley, past the isolated eagle's-nest village of Isérables, two magnificent castle-churches loom above the historic Old Town at Sion. Val d'Anniviers, the valley winding south from Sierre, leads to tiny, isolated skiing and hiking resorts such as St-Luc and Grimentz. The most famous southbound valley, the Mattertal, leads from Visp to the stellar resort of Zermatt and its mascot mountain, the Matterhorn. A fork off that same valley leads to spectacular Saas-Fee, another car-free resort in a magnificent glacier bowl. From Brig, back at the Rhône, a valley mounts southward to the Simplon Pass and Italy.

BAS VALAIS & SION

At Villeneuve the Rhône broadens deltalike into a flat valley that pours into Lac Léman. But head upriver (south), crossing from the canton of Vaud into Valais, and the valley and the river change character as you move into the Bas Valais (Lower Valais). The mountains—the Dents du Midi to the west and the Dents de Morcles to the east—begin to crowd in. The Rhône no longer flows placidly but gives a taste of the mountain torrent it will become as you approach its source. And at the Martigny elbow, the most ancient of Alpine routes leaves the Rhône and ascends due south to 8,098 feet at the Col du Grand St-Bernard before descending into Italy's Valle d'Aosta. The Rhône Valley is most fertile just east of Martigny, its flatlands thick with orchards and vegetable gardens, its south-facing slopes quilted with vineyards. This patch of Valais demonstrates the region's dramatic contrasts. Over the fertile farmlands looms the great medieval stronghold of Sion, its fortress towers protecting the gateway to the Alps.

ST-MAURICE

46 km (28 mi) west of Sion, 56 km (35 mi) southeast of Lausanne.

GETTING HERE

For departure times and prices for trains and buses for most destinations in this chapter, check with www.sbbb.ch—the main Swiss public transportation Web site—or call 0900/300300 (1.19 SF per min).

Remember, if you have a Swiss Pass or another rail-discount card, it also applies to the buses.

Visitor Information (✉ *1 ave. des Terreaux* ☎ *024/4854040* ⊕ *www.st-maurice.ch*).

EXPLORING

Pushed up against a stern, gray rock face, this village is quiet and peaceful, with patrician homes lining its Grand-Rue. Once a customs station along the Roman route over the Col du Grand St-Bernard, in the 3rd century it witnessed the massacre of a band of Christian soldiers, the Theban Legion, and their chief, Maurice, who had refused to worship the Roman deities.

★ At the end of the 4th century the first bishop of the Valais built a sanctuary over Maurice's tomb, and in 515 the **Abbaye de Saint-Maurice** *(St. Maurice Abbey)* was founded. Its treasury contains a stellar collection of religious offerings, with precious Romanesque and Gothic objects given in honor of the martyrs. Contemplate both sides of the stunning bronze doors with inscriptions honoring martyrs from around the world. Excavations near the Baroque **église abbatiale** (abbey church) have revealed the foundations of the original building. ☎ *024/4860404* ⊕ *www.abbaye-stmaurice.ch* ☜ *Church free; guided tour 10 SF* ☉ *Guided tours May–June, Sept.,*

and Oct., Tues.–Sat. at 10:30, 3,
4:30, Sun. at 3 and 4:30; July and
Aug., Tues.–Sat. at 10:30, 2, 3:15,
4:30, Sun. at 2, 3:15, 4:30; Nov.–
Apr., Tues.–Sun. at 3 (if visiting on
a Tues., Wed, or Thurs. during these
months, reservations are necessary
two days in advance).

> **DOUBLE IDENTITY**
>
> You may spot posters for concerts
> by international classical stars
> such as Cecilia Bartoli or Itzhak
> Perlman at the Fondation Pierre
> Gianadda—it doubles as a
> concert hall.

WHERE TO EAT

$$$ ╳ **Le St-Christophe.** Just before enter-
SWISS   ing the Valais, stop at this stone *relais* (inn), hewn of boulders from the
gorge that separates Bex and St-Maurice. It's an unlikely location for a
gourmet kitchen ($$–$$$; closed Wednesday), but the place has been
operating successfully for decades. In the open dining room contem-
porary paintings soften the walls and enliven the atmosphere. Updated
classics and grilled specialties use ideas as refreshing as the art—think
tender beef ribsteak with creamy Béarnaise sauce studded with freshly
picked morels. Reserve one of the upper-level guest rooms and you
can stay put after dinner. ✉ *Rte. de Lavey (exit Bex, direction Lavey)*
☎ *024/4852977* 🛏 *12 rooms* ⚒ *In-room: safe, refrigerator. In-hotel:
restaurant, parking (no fee)* ▤ *AE, DC, MC, V* ⧀ *CP.*

MARTIGNY

17 km (11 mi) south of St-Maurice, 23 km (14 mi) southwest of Sion.

GETTING HERE

Martigny is the transportation hub for the Lower Valais. Trains often
stop at its rail station on the line running between Lausanne (50 min,
23 SF) and Brig (1 hr, 25 SF). Postbuses connect all the towns of the
Lower Valais. Inquire about special bus passes for the region, including
the Martigny Pass and the Valais Central Pass through the auspices of
TMRSA (Transports de Martigny et Régions) at www.tmrsa.ch.

Visitor Information (✉ *6 ave. de la Gare,* ☎ *027/7204949* ⊕ *www.martigny.ch*).

EXPLORING

At the foot of the Col du Grand St-Bernard, Martigny has long been a commercial
crossroads. Testimony to this past are the Gallo-Roman ruins discovered in 1976
by engineer Leonard Gianadda. When Gianadda's brother Pierre died in a plane
crash, Leonard created a cultural center in his memory.

Fodor'sChoice   The **Fondation Pierre Gianadda** now rises in bold geometric shapes around
★   the ruins. Inside are three separate collections, and the foundation itself
sponsors high-profile, themed art exhibits. Recent temporary exhibi-
tions have spotlighted works by Balthus, Claudel, Rodin, and Henri
Cartier-Bresson. Its permanent holdings include works by Van Gogh,
Cézanne, and Picasso. The newly renovated **Musée Gallo-Romain** dis-
plays Gallo-Roman relics excavated from a 1st-century temple: strik-
ing bronzes, statuary, pottery, and coins. A marked path leads through

the antique village, baths, drainage systems, and foundations to the fully restored 5,000-seat amphitheater, which dates from the 2nd century. In the gracefully landscaped garden surrounding the foundation, a wonderful **Parc de Sculpture** displays works by Rodin, Brancusi, Miró, Arman, Moore, Dubuffet, and Max Ernst. There's also a sizable **Musée de l'Automobile,** which contains some 50 antique cars, all in working order. They include an 1897 Benz, the Delauneay-Belleville of Czar Nicholas II of Russia, and a handful of Swiss-made models. ⌂*59 rue de Forum* ☎*027/7223978* ⊕*www.gianadda.ch* ⌸*15–25 SF* ☼*June– Nov., daily 9–7; Dec.–May, daily 10–6.*

⟳ Storyboards and films at the **Musée et Chiens du St-Bernard à Martigny** praise the lifesaving work of a breed of dog that has come to symbolize the Alpine zone straddling Switzerland and Italy. Tended for centuries by the monks of the Order of St. Augustine, who live in service on the Col du Grand St-Bernard, care has shifted to a private foundation. The animals are no longer used for rescue in the desolate reaches that surround the hospice, so they are brought down in autumn to the **Chenil à Martigny (kennel at Martigny),** located in a restored arsenal adjacent to the Roman amphitheater, where they are groomed for visitations. Exercised, trained, and sired to keep the blood line perpetuated, these cuddly, brave canines return to their mountain home in summer *(see Col du Grand St-Bernard, below),* except for eight who live year-round in Martigny. Le Collier d'Or (Gold Collar), a terraced café and gift shop expand the museum services. ⌂*34 rte. du Levant* ☎*027/7204920* ⊕*www.musee-saint-bernard.ch* ⌸*10 SF* ☼*Museum daily 10–6.*

WHERE TO EAT & STAY

$$–$$$ ✕ **L'Olivier.** If you're famished after a visit to the Fondation Pierre Gia-
ECLECTIC   nadda, stop in for better-than-average vittles at L'Olivier. The top-rated chef oversees two separate dining rooms in the same restaurant, one of which serves gourmet cuisine and the other casual, much less expensive brasserie-type fare. The menu's temptations could include crayfish gazpacho and pigeon with an arabica-infused sauce. It is located in the Hôtel du Forum, where there are 29 comfortable, pine-decorated guest rooms should you wish to spend the night. Take Bus No. 13 from the railway station to the Martigny Bourg stop. ⌂*74 av. de Grand-St- Bernard* ☎*027/7221841* 🛏*29 rooms* ⚐*In-room: safe, Wi-Fi. In-hotel: restaurant* ▭*AE, DC, MC, V* ⏹|*CP.*

VERBIER

28 km (18 mi) east of Martigny (exit at Sembrancher), 58 km (36 mi) southwest of Sion.

GETTING HERE

Verbier is a compact resort with excellent shuttle service between hotels, chalets, and the lifts. In high season, unless there is parking space at your lodging a car will be an additional expense and nuisance. From Martigny, take the St. Bernard Express train bound for Orsières, its bright red rail cars emblazoned with the region's famous mascot. Change in Le Châble, where a connecting bus takes you up the steep, winding road to the post office in the center of Verbier. If you are traveling light, there is a gondola cable-car that departs from this base station. In all, the trip from Martigny will take an hour and cost 16 SF (train, bus) or 20 SF (train, gondola). Another option is to drive to La Châble and leave the car in the large parking lot, then transfer to the resort using the bus or cableway. For departure times and prices for trains and buses for most destinations in this chapter, check with www.sbb.ch—the main Swiss public transportation Web site—or call 0900/300300 (1.19 SF per min). Remember, if you have a Swiss Pass or another rail-discount card, it also applies to the buses.

Visitor Information Verbier (⊠ *Pl. Centrale* ☎ *027/7753888* ⊕ *www.verbier.ch*).

EXPLORING

It's the skiing on sunny slopes that draws committed sports lovers to Verbier, a high-tech, state-of-the-art sports complex that links Quatre Vallées (four valleys) and multiple ski areas, including Thyon, Veysonnaz, Nendaz, and La Tzoumaz. Verbier has a huge aerial cableway, with a cabin that accommodates 150, plus 89 smaller transportation installations. There is plenty of vertical drop, to which the extreme ski and snowboard competitions can attest. Summer sports are equally serious: hiking, mountain biking, and hang gliding and its variations compete with golf as the principal sports. Perched on a sunny shelf high above the Val de Bagnes, with wraparound views and the 10,923-foot Mont-Fort towering above, Verbier is protective of its picturesque wooden chalet architecture, yet stays current with modern amenities and comforts. Thanks to its compact layout and easygoing locals, the town has a friendlier feel than the traffic-snarled sprawl of Crans-Montana or hotel-packed Zermatt. Rail and cable-car connections from Le Châble are an alternative to driving switchback roads to the resort. Once here, you can easily navigate the village on foot or by shuttle bus, and all hotels are clearly signposted.

Les Musées du Val de Bagnes is a collection of six installations, some within easy walking distance of each other, in the villages and hamlets of La Châble, Villette, Champsec, Lourtier, Sarreyer, and Le Hameau. Most open their doors only in July and August for a historical perspective of life in this isolated area. A restored home, blacksmith forge, grain and logging mill, soapstone masonry, alpine memorabilia, and contemporary art gallery make up the eclectic displays. Open days and hours vary; check the brochure available from the tourist office. ☎ *027/7761525* ⊕ *www.museedebagnes.ch*.

SKIING

At 4,921 feet, Verbier is the center of Switzerland's famous transit network, **Téléverbier** (⊕ *www.televerbier.ch*)—which consists of 12 gondolas, five cable cars, 32 chairlifts, and 44 other ski lifts giving access to 410 km (253 mi) of marked pistes. From this hub an immense complex of resorts has developed—some more modest, others more exclusive—covering four valleys in an extended ski area whose extremities are 15 km (9 mi) or so apart as the crow flies and several dozen kilometers apart by way of winding mountain roads.

Les Ruinettes gives access to Verbier's entire upper ski area, which culminates at **Mont-Fort,** at 10,923 feet. This is reached by an aerial tram, *Le Jumbo,* equipped with a cab that accommodates 150. La Chaux Express, a chondola (combination chair lift and gondola on the same cable) sweeps skiers to the upper station. You decide whether to keep your skis or snowboard on for the chair, or take them off to enter the gondola. This entire sector is crisscrossed by a dense network of astonishingly varied pistes. There are several strategic passes, including **Les Attelas, Chassoure, Col des Gentianes,** and **Tortin.** Swiss freestyle snowboarder Alex Zillio assisted with the design of the jumps, rails, and pipes at **1936 Neipark** at La Chaux. One-day lift tickets for all four valleys cost 64 SF; six-day passes, 331 SF. If you ski only Verbier, Bruson, or Savoleyres/La Tzoumaz, expect to save 12% to 35%. Automated ski passes streamline the lift check-in process; free tickets and discounts for children are available.

If you're looking for a private instructor to fine-tune your ski or snowboard technique, stop in at the **Ecole Suisse de Ski** (☎*027/7753363* ⊕*www. verbiersportplus.ch*) or at one of the two **Adrenaline** (☎*027/7717459* ⊕*www.adrenaline-verbier.ch*) locations in the **Hardcore** and **Ski Adventure** stores. For a different alpine experience, rent a sled at any of the village sports outlets and take a run down the 10 km (6 mi) track from Savoleyres to La Tzoumaz.

WHERE TO EAT

$$–$$$ ✕ **L'Ecurie.** Locals and chalet dwellers in-the-know gather at this cen-
SWISS tral, no-smoking restaurant beneath the Ermitage hotel. The eccentric owner Jean-Marc, known as Babouin (baboon) gives a hearty, if slightly drunken, welcome. Choose between the no-frills, rough-wood-tables corner, and the linen-and-candelight section set off by amber glass panels. Wood-fire grill specialties and homemade pasta are staples, but there are always a few daily specials that are equally tempting. In a region where chicken is difficult to find, the poussin with fries is a treat. ✉*Pl. Centrale* ☎*027/7712760* ▭*AE, MC, V.*

$$$ ✕ **La Grange/La Pinte.** To eat cheese or not to eat cheese will be the ques-
SWISS tion at this two-restaurant combination. In keeping with the traditional decor, you can sample regional specialties, such as fondue or dried beef in the brasserie La Pinte. On the other side of the room the prices are much less gentle but the tables more luxuriously chic at La Grange. Here you can go for more lofty epicurean choices such as liver pâté with plum sauce or Asian-inspired turbot with saffron and vegetable pearls. The wine list includes an excellent selection of local vintages to be savored in this entirely smoke-free environment. ☎*027/7716431* ▭*AE, DC, MC, V* ☉*Closed May–June.*

$$$ ✕ **Le Millénium/El Toro Negro.** Bask in the sun on the summer terrace dur-
STEAK ing lunch at Le Millénium while enjoying the fresh prawn salad with ginger sauce or the brochettes of teriyaki beef with Asian vegetables. If savory steaks and tender cutlets are more your style, squeeze into a cozy booth in the winter-only El Toro Negro grill house downstairs. It's unique for two reasons: El Toro Negro is the only place in town that serves "gaucho" style—frying pans set directly on your table, and

A WINE & CHEESE PARTY

11

Though the French influence in the western portion of this region means a steady diet of cuisine bourgeoise, leading newcomers to think entrecôte with peppercorn sauce is a native dish, the elemental cuisine of Valais is much simpler. In a word: cheese.

The most popular way to enjoy this regional product is in raclette, an exclusive invention of this mountain canton (though the French of Haute-Savoie embrace it as their own).

Ideally, the fresh-cut face of a half wheel of Orsières (a mild cheese produced in the high pastures near Martigny) is melted before an open wood fire, the softened cheese scraped onto a plate and eaten with potatoes (always in their skins, you peel them yourself—with a knife of course!), pickled onions, and tiny gherkins.

Nowadays even mountain carnotzets with roaring fires depend on electric raclette heaters that grip the cheese in a vise before toasterlike elements.

Fondue is omnipresent, and although typically made with a blend of Gruyère and Vacherin, the Valaisanne version may feature a blend of the local Bagnes, Goms, and Orsières.

Its consumption is generally held to the cold months, although locals casually request raclette *à discrétion* (as much as you want) on a cool summer's eve.

The beverage of choice to accompany your raclette is a crisp, bubbly, fruity Fendant (a local white wine), but there are other regional favorites.

Appellations and vintner names aren't as prominent in the Valais; it's the name of the grape that holds the spotlight.

Winemakers welcome tasting guests most times of the year except during harvest (late September through early October).

A true Valaisan wouldn't enjoy a fine meal without a ruby-red Dôle (pinot noir and gamay blend) swirled in a stemmed *ballon* (glass) or a sparkling white Fendant poured into a shot-size glass.

On your way through the region, follow custom and give a toast: *Santé*.

Cheese isn't the region's only culinary treasure, however. Valais rivals Graubünden in its production of *viande séchée* (air-dried beef), a block of meat marinated in herbs, pressed between planks until it takes on its signature bricklike form, and then dried in the open air. Shaved into thin, translucent slices, it can be as tender as a good prosciutto *crudo*—or as tough as leather. The flavor is concentrated, the flesh virtually fat-free.

---

where else can you find kangaroo and ostrich grilled to perfection? ⊠ *Carrefour Centrale* ☎ 027/7719900 ▤ MC, V.

WHERE TO STAY

$$$–$$$$ ▦ **Central Hotel Verbier.** Finding this hotel is easy; you'll see exterior signage on the honey-colored building standing on Verbier's traffic circle. Locating the upstairs side entrance, however, is more difficult; especially when it's obscured by vacationers filling TBar, the downstairs indoor-outdoor hot spot for light meals and drinks. In the guest rooms,

chocolate color woods and leather seating contrast with stark white walls accented with chrome lighting. Draped windows buffer the noise from the animated crowd circulating below, but don't count on sound-proofing. **Pros:** Jacuzzi tubs and plasma TVs in every room; perfect central location. **Cons:** noise can be disruptive; no in-hotel restaurant. ⊠*Pl. Central* ☎*027/7715007* ⊕*www.verbiercentralhotel.com* ⤴*8 rooms* ⌂*In-room: safe, refrigerator.* ▤*AE, DC, MC, V* ⦿*CP.*

$$$$ 🏨 **Chalet d'Adrien.** Named for the owner's grandfather, a baron who ★ discovered the village in the early 1900s, this luxury inn is packed with antiques and collectibles from old farmhouses and châteaux. Guest rooms, outfitted with hand-carved headboards and richly textured fabrics, are named for wildflowers. To work out those après-ski kinks, visit the spa's infinity pool that boasts a breathtaking view of the Alps. The epicurean Italian menu at La Table d'Adrien ($$$$) has imaginative dishes like lamb with a ratatouille cannelloni, while the more classic Grenier ($$–$$$) serves warming stews and cheese dishes. **Pros:** private ski-mansion feel; friendly, personalized service. **Cons:** 15-minute walk uphill from village; teddy-bear collection in lobby may prove too cutesy for some. ⊠*Rte. des Creux* ☎*027/7716200* ⊕*www.chalet-adrien.com* ⤴*20 rooms, 8 suites, 1 apt* ⌂*In-room: safe, refrigerator, Wi-Fi. In-hotel: 2 restaurants, bar, pool, gym, wellness center, parking (no fee).* ▤*AE, DC, MC, V* ⊙*Closed late Apr.–early July and late Sept.–early Dec.*

$$–$$$ 🏨 **Ermitage.** Centrally located, this traditional mainstay features compact guest rooms with south-facing balconies that offer views of the Combin mountains (and be sure to request one, because rooms on the north side look out at the slow crawl of cars and people along the main street). A hospitable family member welcomes you in a lobby filled with plush cushioned furniture and a Wi-Fi Internet corner—a gathering place for guests, as there is no seating en chambre. **Pros:** one of the best deals in town; well-known restaurant L'Ecurie is just downstairs. **Cons:** depressing dark green carpet throughout hotel; small rooms. ⊠*18 Carrefour Central* ☎*027/7716477* ⊕*www.ermitage-verbier. ch* ⤴*25 rooms, 1 apt* ⌂*In-room: safe, refrigerator. In-hotel: restaurant, bar, public Wi-Fi, parking (no fee), minibar* ▤*AE, DC, MC, V* ⊙*Closed mid-Sept.–mid-Oct. and mid-Apr.–mid-May* ⦿*CP.*

$$$$ 🏨 **Hotel Montpelier.** Ringed by flower-decked wood balconies, this classy, chalet-style lodge sits apart from the town hub. The lobby and restaurant are welcoming, if a bit overstuffed with "decor"—farm carts, antique stove ovens, and a player-piano. Upstairs, generously sized guest rooms are brightened with honey-colored wood and charming blue-stenciled folk decorations. The half board is far from a hardship, as the cuisine is excellent; if you'd like a change of scenery, though, the staff will recommend another restaurant in the upper village. **Pros:** covered swimming pool with view of Alps; free shuttle service to lifts. **Cons:** far from town center and lifts; Wi-Fi in lobby only. ⊠*37 rue de Centre Sportif* ☎*027/7716131* ⊕*www.hotelmontpelier.ch* ⤴*46 rooms, 24 suites, 1 apartment* ⌂*In-room: dial-up, refrigerator. In-hotel: 2 restaurants, bar, public Wi-Fi, pool, sauna, bicycles, parking (fee)* ▤*AE, DC, MC, V* ⊙*Closed May and Nov.* ⦿*MAP.*

NIGHTLIFE & THE ARTS

DANCING The popular **Crok No Name** (⊠ *Rte. des Creux* ☎ *027/7716934*) has live music or DJs nightly. If you don't plan to hit the slopes early, you can party into the wee hours at Moroccan-themed **Casbah** (⊠ *Hôtel Farinet, Pl. Centrale* ☎ *027/7716626*). The **Farm Club** (⊠ *King's Parc Hotel, Rue de Verbier Station* ☎ *027/7716121*) is the place to be seen in Verbier. Apparently it's not fashionable to turn up before 1 AM. If you're looking for someplace unpretentious, head to **IceBox** (⊠ *Rue de la Poste* ☎ *079/4489790*), where the music doesn't stop until 4 AM.

> **ON THE CALENDAR**
>
> For more than two weeks overlapping July and August, the **Verbier Festival & Academy** (☎ *027/7718282* 🖷 *027/9259068* ⊕ *www.verbierfestival.com*) hosts an impressive classical music festival of performances and master classes. Musical director James Levine assembles youth performers and celebrated guests such as Maxim Vengerov, Evgeny Kissin, and Martha Argerich to play together under a sprawling tent.

SPORTS & THE OUTDOORS

Verbier offers a variety of summer and winter high-altitude sports, ranging from rock and ice climbing to rafting and snow tubing, all led by specialist outfitters.

BICYCLING Trails and routes (250 km [188 mi]) for the enthusiast range from difficult distance rides across the passes to simpler runs closer to town. **Médran Sports** (☎ *027/7716048*), on the other side of the village, offers a choice of equipment and gear at competitive rates. Twice a week, free guided tours depart from the tourist office and there is a bike park with jumps and ramps plus a variety of training camps to improve technique.

The pros at **No Bounds** (☎ *027/7715556*) will help you plan your entire outing, plus rent standard or high-performance bikes, helmets, and shells.

HIKING & CLIMBING Randonnées and trails thread from ridgeline to valley floor in 400 km (300 mi) of pathways that cross nature reserves, highland streams, and historic villages. Sign up at **La Fantastique** (☎ *027/7714141* ⊕ *www. lafantastique.com*) or **Verbier Sport** (☎ *027/7753363* ⊕ *www.verbier-sportplus.ch*) for hut-to-hut trekking tours of the Mont Blanc region or technical rock climbing and rappelling sessions. Closer to town, **Sentier Suspendu,** an outdoor climbing wall and network of rope bridges operated by Verbier Sport, gives beginners an introduction.

SPORTS CENTERS Verbier's **Centre Sportif** (☎ *027/7716601*) is a hub for the active, with indoor skating, swimming, curling, climbing, beach volleyball, tennis, and squash; as well as whirlpools, saunas, and a solarium. There's even a backpackers' dorm and Internet café.

COL DU GRAND ST-BERNARD

40 km (25 mi) south of Martigny, 69 km (43 mi) southwest of Sion.

GETTING HERE

The opening of the Col du Grand St-Bernard, the pass connecting Switzerland and Italy, is weather dependent. This high-mountain crossing is closed during the winter months, while the tunnel remains open year-round. Don't be deceived: the roadway can be shut down in summer due to random snowfalls. On a clear day the drive on narrow twisting roads that thread in and out of avalanche breaks is unforgettable. The traffic on the approach to the pass dramatically reduces once vehicles driving through to Aosta (Italy) leave the highway at the tunnel entrance. During summer, public transport to the Hospice St-Bernard is available from Martigny. The journey starts with train service to the village of Orsières, terminus of the rail line, and then switches to coach. It's a one hour drive by car; add an additional half-hour for the rail-bus connection.

EXPLORING

★ **Col du Grand St-Bernard.** Breasting the formidable barrier of the Alps at 8,101 feet, this pass is the oldest and most famous of the great Alpine crossings, and the first to join Rome and Byzantium to the wilds of the north. Used for centuries before the birth of Christ, it has witnessed an endless stream of emperors, knights, and simple travelers—think of Umberto Eco's *The Name of the Rose,* with its two friars crossing on donkey back in howling winter winds. Napoléon took an army of 40,000 across it en route to Marengo, where he defeated the Austrians in 1800.

You'll have an easier time crossing today. If you simply want to get to Italy quickly, take the tunnel, which opens on the other side above the Valle d'Aosta. But by skipping the tiny winding road over the top, you'll miss the awe-inspiring, windswept moonscape at the summit and the hospice that honors its namesake. In 1038, the story goes, Bernard of Menthon, bishop of Aosta, came to clear the pass of brigands. When he reached the top, he found a pagan temple, which he covered with his chasuble. The shrine immediately crumbled to dust, and, by the same power the brigands were defeated. Bernard established his hospice there.

L'Hospice du Grand St. Bernard served international travelers throughout the Middle Ages. Kings and princes rewarded the hospice by showering estates upon the order. Today a dwindling number of residents—Augustinian canons—still train as mountain guides and ski instructors and host seasonal retreats that include outdoor excursions. Within the hospice there is a multilevel museum with exhibits about the history of the pass and the devoted monks of the Order of St. Augustine who have lived here. Displays of church treasures—chalices, crosses, and altar clothes in gold, silver, and jewels—are on view in another wing. The fresco-bedecked chapel remains open for daily prayers. Behind the hospice is **Chenil au Col du Grand St-Bernard,** a kennel full of the landmark's enormous, furry namesakes: the famous St. Bernard dogs who for centuries helped the monks find travelers lost in the snow. They supposedly came to Switzerland with silk caravans from central Asia and were used by Romans as war dogs; today they're kept more for sentimental than functional reasons. In winter the dogs are boarded in Martigny (*see* Musée et Chiens du St-Bernard à Martigny *above*). The most famous was Barry, who saved more than 40 people in the 19th century and today stands stuffed in Bern's Naturhistorisches Museum (Museum of Natural History). Souvenir stands sell plush versions of St. Bernards, and there are a handful of dining options on either side of the pass. ☎027/7871236 ⊕*www.gsbernard.ch* ▭*Museum and kennel 8 SF* ⊙*June and Sept., daily 9–12 and 1–6; July and Aug., daily 9–6:30.*

SION

6 km (10 mi) northeast of Verbier.

GETTING HERE

Sion is a main stop on the railway running between Lausanne (1 hr, 29 SF) and Brig (40 min, 18 SF); many postbuses threading the region stop at the train station.

Visitor Information (✉*Pl. de la Planta* ☎*027/3277727* ⊕*www.siontourism.ch*).

EXPLORING

Rearing up in the otherwise deltalike flatlands of the western Valais, two otherworldly twin hills flank the ancient city of Sion. The two hills together are a powerful emblem of the city's 1,500-year history as a bishopric and a Christian stronghold. From the top of either hill are dramatic views of the surrounding flatlands and the mountains flanking the valley. The town itself can be comfortably explored on foot in an afternoon, unless you lose yourself in one of its museums or labyrinthine antiques shops. In summer a trolley called Le P'tit Sédunois shuttles between the train station, main plaza, and elevated sights.

Sion folk are fiercely proud and independent, as reflected in the fanatical support for their soccer team and their dogged attempts to host the Winter Olympics. (There was bitter disappointment when they lost the bid for the 2006 games to rivals across the border in Turin, Italy.) A shortage of high-quality hotels gives the impression that the town is not as hospitable to travelers as the tourist-oriented ski resorts, but don't be deterred; there are ample reasons to spend time here. For example, the city walking tour offered in summer includes a wine tasting.

★ Crowning Tourbillon, the higher of Sion's hills, the ruined **Tourbillon château** was built as a bishop's residence at the end of the 13th century and destroyed by fire in 1788. If you take the rugged walk uphill, try to time it for a visit to the tiny chapel with its ancient, layered frescoes. ▭*Free* ⊙*Oct.–May, daily 11–5; June–Sept., daily 11–6.*

★ On Valère, Sion's lower hill, the **Église-Forteresse de Valère** (*Church-Fortress of Valère*) is a striking example of sacred and secular power combined—reflective of the Church's heyday, when it often subjugated rather than served its parishioners. Built on Roman foundations, the massive stone walls enclose both the **château** and the 11th-century **Église Notre-Dame de Valère** (Church of Our Lady of Valère). This structure stands in a relatively raw form, rare in Switzerland, where monu-

WORTH THE EFFORT

To reach the Musée Cantonal d'Histoire, you'll have to trek up uneven stone walkways and steep staircases, but you won't regret it.

ments are often restored to perfection. Over the engaging Romanesque carvings, 16th-century fresco fragments, and 17th-century stalls painted with scenes of the Passion, there hangs a rare **organ,** its cabinet painted with two fine medieval Christian scenes. Dating from the 14th century, it's the oldest playable organ in the world, and an annual organ festival celebrates its musical virtues.

The château complex also houses the **Musée Cantonal d'Histoire** (History Museum), renovated in 2008, which displays a wide array of medieval sacristy chests and religious artifacts. Expanded exhibits trace daily life and advances in the canton from these early centuries to the present day, including soccer championships. Explanations are in three languages, including English. Guided tours are conducted from March through October at a quarter past the hour. ☎027/6064715 ✉*Church 3 SF; museum 6 SF* ☉*Church June–Sept., Mon–Sat. 10–6, Sun. 2–6; Oct.–May, Tues.–Sat. 10–5, Sun. 2–5. Museum June–Sept., daily 10–6; Oct.–May, Tues.–Sat. 10–5, Sun. 2–5.*

The **Old Town,** up Rue de Lausanne (take a left when leaving the tourist office on the Place de la Planta), is a blend of shuttered 16th-century houses, modern shops, and a host of sights worth seeing.

The grand old **Maison Supersaxo** *(House of Supersaxo),* tucked into a passageway off Rue Supersaxo, was built in 1505 by Georges Supersaxo, the local governor, to put his rivals to shame. This extravagantly decorated building includes a Gothic staircase and a grand hall whose painted wood ceiling is a dazzling work of decorative art. ✉*Passage Supersaxo* ✉*Free* ☉*Weekdays 8–12, 1:30–6.*

The imposing **Hôtel de Ville** *(Town Hall)* has extraordinary historic roots: though it was built in the 1650s, it has transplanted stones in the entrance bearing Roman inscriptions, including a Christian symbol from the year AD 377. The 17th-century doors are richly carved wood, and the tower displays an astronomical clock. Upstairs, the **Salle du Conseil** *(Council Hall)* is also adorned with ornate woodwork. The only way to visit the Hôtel de Ville is by taking a guided walking tour of the town, which costs 10 SF and leaves from the Sion tourist office. Tours are held from July to the end of August on Tuesday, Thursday, and Saturday mornings plus Wednesday afternoons. ✉*Rue de Conthey and Rue du Grand-Pont* ✉*Free with walking tour.*

NEED A BREAK? It's a tight squeeze to get into Old Town's popular *vinotek* (wine store–tasting room) **Le Verre à Pied** (✉*29 rue du Grand-Pont* ☎*027/3211380*), where 150 regional vintages are poured seven days a week. For a few francs you can join winemakers and enthusiasts who swill and sip (often while taking advantage of their free Wi-Fi connection).

The **Musée Cantonal d'Archéologie** *(Museum of Archaeology)* displays a collection of excavated pieces, including fine Roman works found in Valais. The narrow, cobbled Rue des Châteaux, which leads up toward the twin fortifications, passes graceful old patrician houses, among them the museum. ⊠*12 rue des Châteaux* ☎*027/6064700* ⊠*4 SF* ⊙*June–Sept., Tues.–Sun. 1–6; Oct.–May, Tues.–Sun. 1–5.*

The cathedral, **Notre-Dame du Glarier** *(Our Lady of Glarier)*, is dominated by its Romanesque tower, built in the Lombard, or Italian, style and dating from the 12th century. The rest of the church is late Gothic in style. ⊠*Rue de la Cathédrale.*

Just across from the cathedral, the **Tour des Sorciers** *(Sorcerers' Tower)* is the last remnant of the walls that once ringed the town. ⊠*Rue de la Tour.*

High up in the bluffs and valleys to the south of Sion are scores of isolated eagle's-nest towns, including **Isérables.** The latter, set on a precarious slope that drops 3,280 feet into the lowlands, has narrow streets that weave between crooked old stone-shingle mazots. Since the arrival of the cable car, Isérables has prospered and modernized itself. Yet the inhabitants of this village still carry the curious nickname *Bedjuis.* Some say it's derived from "Bedouins" and that the people are descended from the Saracen hordes who, after the battle of Poitiers in 732, overran some of the high Alpine valleys. Excursions to the sights and villages of this *haute vallée* (high valley) can be accomplished in a day, with a little time to hike and explore before returning to the city.

WHERE TO EAT

$$
SWISS
✕Au Cheval Blanc. Set on one of Sion's Old Town cobblestone streets, this congenial bistro is bustling around noon, when locals take their midday meal accompanied by a glass of gamay or bière valaisanne. Top billing on the menu goes to such dishes as *Entrecôte avec frites* (steak and fries) and *moules à la marinière* (mussels in white wine and parsley butter) along with traditional dishes such as *civet de chevreuil* with spaetzle (venison stew served with dumplings). ⊠*23 rue du Grand-Pont* ☎*027/3221867* ⊟*AE, DC, MC, V* ⊙*Closed Sun.–Mon. and last 2 wks of Dec.*

$$
SWISS
✕L'Enclos de Valère. If you've worked up an appetite climbing Sion's Tourbillon, you may want to stop in this Old Town eatery on your way back down. Unfussy service, fine French cuisine, and a rustic-cottage setting make it a sentimental favorite. Seasonal items—mushrooms, asparagus, shellfish, and game—lend variety to the upscale menu. When it's not mealtime, drop in for a coffee or a bottle of regional wine. ⊠*18 rue des Châteaux* ☎*027/3233230* ⌂*Reservations essential* ⊟*AE, DC, MC, V* ⊙*Closed Sun. evening and Mon. May–Sept. and Sun.–Mon. Oct.–Apr.*

WHERE TO STAY

$$ ⚇ **Hôtel des Vignes.** For a hotel with character, head a few kilometers east of Sion to the village of Uvrier to find this sienna-color palazzo flanked by vineyards. The welcoming lobby has a central fireplace and a fountain; guest rooms are done in warm peach. **Pros:** surrounded by a gloriously landscaped park; unusual amenities include an indoor driving range. **Cons:** set in a small village a 10-minute drive from Sion; restaurant can be disappointing, and there aren't many other dining options nearby. ⊠ *9 rue du Pont, Uvrier* ☎ *027/2031671* ⊕ *www.hoteldes vignes.ch* ⤳ *33 rooms, 10 suites* ᠔ *In-room: safe, refrigerator. In-hotel: restaurant, bar, public Wi-fi, sauna (fee), 2 tennis courts, pool, parking (no fee)* ⊟ *AE, DC, MC, V* ⊘ *Closed end of Dec.–mid-Jan.* ⦿ *BP.*

$ ⚇ **L'Hôtel Du Rhône.** The reception area of this cinder-block property has a dated feel, with brown furniture and tired accents. The guest rooms are livelier, done in red, green, and blue with exhibition posters from the Fondation Pierre Gianadda. Operating under the Best Western flag, the lodging is located at the edge of Sion's Old Town. **Pros:** comfortable, no-frills base; handy location to the castle walks. **Cons:** no hotel amenities; only two no-smoking rooms available—the others bear the stink of decades of lighting up. ⊠ *10 rue de Scex* ☎ *027/3228291* ⊕ *www. bestwestern.com* ⤳ *45 rooms* ᠔ *In-room: safe, Wi-Fi. In-hotel: restaurant, bar, parking (fee)* ⊟ *AE, DC, MC, V* ⦿ *BP.*

NIGHTLIFE & THE ARTS

Sion attracts world-class musicians and scholars to its festivals celebrating the medieval organ in its church-fortress. The **Festival International de l'Orgue Ancien Valère** (*International Festival of the Ancient Valère Organ* ☎ *027/3235767*) takes place from mid-July through late August.

CONVERSION DE LA VALLÉE

Secured above the plateau north of Sierre and Leuk are the ski towns of Crans and Montana and the hot springs resort of Leukerbad, each with a different personality. Crans-Montana offers expansive skiing, pricey boutiques, and clubby restaurants. Though Leukerbad also has first-class hotels and ski runs (albeit fewer), it is the restorative pools and spas and authentic Alpine village that attract visitors here. Along this stretch of the Rhône, the switchback of language and culture begins. Valais, as it is referred to by French speakers, is called Wallis by locals with Germanic ties. To the south the remote Val d'Anniviers offers a glimpse of a simpler life before high-speed lifts and Internet cafés.

CRANS-MONTANA

12 km (7 mi) northwest of Sierre, 19 km (11¾ mi) northeast of Sion.

GETTING HERE

Operators of SMC (Sierre Mollens Crans-Montana), the funicular and bus service that connects the city of Sierre with the famous ski and golf villages of Crans-Montana, make it a snap to find the funicular departure point for a speedy ascent to the sunny communities. Once outside

11

the rail station, cross the street and look for the red lines designating the pathway. Follow the red line on the five-minute walk through the central business district to the funi. The ride (12 minutes) in roomy red-and-white cabins delivers passengers to the Montana side of town, where free shuttle buses disperse guests to hotels and chalets. If this transfer seems too cumbersome, board the SMC motor coaches waiting in the parking area adjacent to the station for a half-hour switchback ride through vineyards and forest (12 SF). Log on to www.cie-smc.ch for funicular and bus schedules.

Visitor Information (✉ *Village Center* ☎ *027/4850404* ⊕ *www.crans-montana.ch*).

EXPLORING

This well-known twin sports center rises above the valley on a steep, sheltered shelf at 4,904 feet. It commands a broad view across the Rhône Valley to the peaks of the Valaisan Alps, and its grassy and wooded plateau gets the benefit of Sierre's sunshine. Behind the towns, the **Rohrbachstein** (9,686 feet), the **Gletscherhorn** (9,653 feet), and the **Wildstrubel** (10,637 feet) combine to create a complex of challenging ski slopes. The most direct route to Crans-Montana is from Sierre, just southeast, either by car, postbus, or funicular.

The resort towns themselves are highly developed and uncaptivating, lacking the regional color and grace of Zermatt. The streets are lined with designer boutiques and hotels. Car traffic is almost always heavy, so it's best to get around on foot or shuttle bus. As in other resorts, signs point the way to the hotels. The crowds are young, wealthy, and international, roving in cocoons of the fit, fun-loving, and fashionable.

SKIING

The pearl of the region is the **Plaine Morte,** a flat glacier 5 km–6 km (3 mi–3½ mi) long, which is perched like a pancake at an elevation of 9,840 feet and has snow year-round. A cross-country ski trail (watch out for your lungs at this altitude) of 10 km–12 km (6 mi–7½ mi) is open and maintained here seven months of the year. The ascent on the gondola from **Violettes Plaines-Morte,** virtually under assault by crowds during the high season and in good weather, will in itself justify your stay in Crans-Montana. Expert skiers may prefer the **Piste Nationale,** site of previous world championships. The incredibly steep-pitched **La Toula** is a challenge for pros. The eastern section of the ski area connects to Aminona, where a park for snowboarders and a bobsled run drop from **Petit Bonvin,** at 7,874 feet. A one-day lift ticket costs 63 SF; a six-day pass costs 307 SF, permitting access to 160 km (100 mi) of runs and more than 30 ways to ride to the top. There are several classic cross-country ski circuits atop the golf courses and around the village lakes.

WHERE TO EAT

$$ ✗ **Le Mayen.** On the Montana shopping promenade, this traditional res-
SWISS taurant trimmed in dark wood and stone slabs holds one of the village's favorite spots for specialty fondues and steak tartare. It's so popular with locals that it doesn't close between seasons. All is not cheesy, as

Sion and Conversion de la Vallée

KEY
- ···→ Cable Car/ Funicular
- ─── Rail lines
- 🎿 Ski Resorts

SWITZERLAND

Lauenen
Wildstrubel ▲
Gletscherhorn ▲
GLACIER DE LA PLAINE-MORTE
Leukerbad
Les Diablerets
Crans-Montana
Vermala
Leuk
Gampel
Anzère
Salgesch
Sierre
Turtmann
RIVER
A9
Sion
Ardon
Vex
Val d'Anniviers
Stalden
Nendaz
Veysonnaz
VALAIS
Riddes
Thyon
Pyramides d'Euseigne
Grimentz
Grächen
Isérables
Ayer
St. Niklaus
Saxon
La Tzoumaz (Mayens-de-Riddes)
Zinal
Rhône
Le Hameau
▲ Mt. Gelé
Évolène
MATTERTAL
Villette
Verbier
Mt. Fort
Barrage de la Grande Dixence
Les Haudères
Weisshorn ▲
Täsch
Le Châble
Les Ruinettes
Lac des Dix
Alphübel ▲
Längflu
Bruson
Sarreyer
Dent Blanche ▲
▲ Unterrothorn
Champsec
Lourtier
Arolla
Zmutt
Zermatt

the grill turns out exceptional meat and fish dishes. ⊠ *Rue Louis-Antille* ☎ *027/4812985* 🖃 *AE, DC, MC, V.*

$
ASIAN FUSION
★

× **New Haven.** While oddly named for the classic New England town (note the GANT clothing store just next store), this fusion lounge serves up Asian-inspired fare as well as exotic seafood tapas like moules marinières with vanilla. Jazzy music, deer-horn chandeliers, and photos of retro ships give this newly opened hot spot a swanky, yet funky, touch. If they aren't already taken, grab a seat in the comfy, overstuffed brown leather chairs near the entrance. Don't be afraid to have more than one of their signature martinis, as the sleek, modern bathrooms merit a visit in themselves. ⊠ *64 rue Centrale Crans* ☎ *027/4814439* 🖃 *MC, V.*

$$$$
CONTEMPORARY
Fodor'sChoice
★

× **Restaurant Didier de Courten.** Travelers bound for the uphill resorts detour to chef-hotelier Didier de Courten's contemporary hot spot in Sierre's historical Hotel Le Terminus. One of the country's highest-rated chefs fills the tables of his gourmet restaurant and upscale brasserie with food and wine enthusiasts who admire his creativity in dishes like peppered venison medallions with red cabbage and spiced pear marmalade. Sleek design elements from the restaurant are repeated behind the red-door guest rooms outfitted with crisp white-on-white linens and colorful leather seating. L'Ampelos, the wine bar, offers an extensive sampling of top Swiss and international vintages. Reserve a table and one of their dozen or so simple hotel rooms in advance; this is a popular stand-alone destination. ✉*1 rue du Bourg Sierre* ☎*027/4551351* ⊕*www. hotel-terminus.ch* ⊗*Closed Sun.–Mon; hotel closed late June–mid-July, Christmas–mid-Jan.*

¢–$
PASTRY SHOP

✕**Taillens.** Regardless of which side of town you're on, these overflowing sibling coffee shops with exquisite pastries are a must-stop before or after an activity-packed day. Run today by the third generation of the Taillens family, this local legend is beloved by locals and visitors alike. Light meals—salads, soups, and sandwiches—keep service clipping along at a fast pace. Toss aside the calorie counter and peruse the dessert cases for a decadent concoction of chocolate, sugar, and whipped cream. ✉*Ave. de la Gare, Montana* ☎*027/4817361* ✉*Grand Pl., Crans* ☎*027/4854082* ▭*MC, V.*

WHERE TO STAY

$$$–$$$$
ITALIAN

🖼 **Aïda-Castel.** This welcoming complex has kept pace with the times. Public areas have carved or aged wood, stone, and stucco; the guest rooms, sturdy Alpine furniture, wrought iron, and stenciling. South-facing balconies are filled with afternoon sun worshippers. A unique touch is the indoor Christmas market (Nov./Dec.), where you can buy traditional Swiss tchotchkes like hand-painted cowbells. Warning: the hotel's labyrinthine layout is a perfect spot for hide and seek but may leave you wondering exactly where your room is. If you find yourself at the Wellness Center, you might opt for a massage. **Pros:** enormous, clearly lit bathrooms; live piano bar in winter. **Cons:** isolated position requires a shuttle or uphill walk to activities; in summer the hotel reserves a wing for exchange students—hence the twentysomethings who take over the common areas. ✉*Rue du Béthania, Montana* ☎*027/4854111* ⊕*www.aida-castel.ch* ⏎*56 rooms, 4 suites* ♿*In-room: safe, refrigerator, Wi-Fi. In-hotel: 2 restaurants, bar, pool, gym, parking (no fee)* ▭*AE, DC, MC, V* |◎|*MAP.*

$$–$$$

🖼 **Hôtel de l'Etrier.** A sweeping roofline, stone entry, and larch trim have an appropriately Alpine feel. Inside, the butterscotch-colored walls and raised hearth fireplace warm the lobby, which boasts floor-to-ceiling windows that frame golf course greens and southern mountains. **Pros:** multiple dining options are shared with the property's stylish sister hotel Pas de l'Ours; amenities include a treatment-filled spa, wellness center, and sizable indoor-outdoor pool. **Cons:** large rooms are uninspired, furnished with traditional heavy furniture and white duvets; some say the dining room could be better for the price. ✉*Rte. Pas de l'Ours, Crans* ☎*027/4854400* ⊕*www.hoteletrier.ch* ⏎*50 rooms, 9 suites* ♿*In-room: no a/c, safe, refrigerator, Wi-Fi. In-hotel: 3 restaurants, bar, pool, spa, gym, parking (no fee)* ▭*AE, DC, MC, V* |◎|*CP.*

$$$$
Fodor'sChoice
★

🖼 **L'Hostellerie du Pas de l'Ours.** In a town known for blocklike towers, this petite Relais et Chateaux-listed auberge with its preserved wooden facade stands out. The roomy suite-apartments have polished wood floors, stucco walls, balconies, fireplaces, and Jacuzzis. The restaurant ($$$–$$$$) draws a chic crowd, thanks to superb French cuisine such as almond-roasted lamb with apricot reduction; book well in advance for a table. Spa L'Alpage is a prime spot to rejuvenate after a day of skiing or hiking the trails. **Pros:** plush rooms rich with amenities; magnificent wellness center with indoor-outdoor pool.

Cons: somewhat of a walk into the town center; we won't ruin the surprise, but look left as you enter the lobby. ⊠*41 rue du Pas de l'Ours, Crans* ☎*027/4859333* ⊕*www.pasdelours.ch* ⌐*9 suites* ⌂*In-room: safe, refrigerator, Wi-Fi. In-hotel: Restaurant, bar, pool, gym, spa, parking (no fee)* ⊟*AE, DC, MC, V* ⊘*Closed mid-April–mid-May and mid-Oct.–mid-Nov.* ⊠*CP.*

$$ ⊡**Le Mont-Paisible.** One of the hotel directors, an architect, lent his design expertise and eye for interiors to this lookout lodge, which takes in the sweep of Valaisan mountains—indeed, the south-facing guest rooms are blessed with panoramic views all the way to the Matterhorn on a clear day. Slate floors, colorful stenciled furniture, and a raised-hearth fireplace set a sophisticated yet rustic mood. The terrific location is away from the village hubbub but near the Violettes cable-car station. **Pros:** elegant veranda serves a comprehensive continental buffet breakfast. **Cons:** hallways, often filled with dingy silk flowers in dated vases, need updating; no pool or spa, but plans are in the works in near future. ⊠*Chemin du Mont-Paisible, Montana* ☎*027/4802161* ⊟*027/4817792* ⊕*www.montpaisible.ch* ⌐*40 rooms* ⌂*In-room: safe, Wi-fi, refrigerator. In-hotel: restaurant, bar, tennis court, sauna, live music much of the year, parking (no fee)* ⊟*AE, DC, MC, V* ⊠*BP.*

NIGHTLIFE

BARS & DANCING   If you've ever wondered what Salvador Dalí would have produced if he'd illustrated a vodka ad, then head for poster-filled **The Xellent Club** (☎*027/4814439* ⊕*www.xellentclub.ch*), a Crans nightclub where martini-swilling and swaying don't get started until after 11 PM. Book a table online. The dance floor buzzes at **Le Barocke** (☎*079/2211635*), around the corner from Xellent Club. If music, videos, and shots à Gogo interest you, **Monk'is** (☎*079/4093285*), in Crans, is a hot, primate-theme venue with noshes. Up in Montana, the small but convivial **Amadeus** (☎*027/4812985*), beneath the Olympic Hotel, is a popular après-ski venue. **Le Tirbouchon** (☎*027/4802608*) is a chummy little blue-and-gold trimmed wine bar in Montana where you can imbibe from a selection of more than 250 regional vintages.

CASINO   Roulette, blackjack, poker, and an abundance of slot machines are among the games you can play at the high-stakes **Casino Crans-Montana** (☎*027/4859040*), in Montana. You can also just stop in for a drink or dinner, as there is no pressure to play. The casino is open Sunday–Thursday 10 AM–4 AM and Friday–Saturday 10 AM–5 AM; you'll need your passport for admission.

SPORTS & THE OUTDOORS

BICYCLING   The Tour de Suisse and other top-name bike competitions pass through the streets during racing season. Serious amateur mountain bikers can test the obstacle course set up in the parking lot of the Crans-Cry-d'Err cable car or the downhill practice run. Cycling enthusiasts find a full range of clothing and bike rentals at **Avalanche Pro Shop** (⊠*Montana* ☎*027/4802424*). **Crans-Montana Freeride Shop** (⊠*Crans* ☎*027/4803030*) is a convenient shop, providing bikes for rent and information about the 16 marked trails that radiate from the resort. They can also tell you which lifts to use to gain altitude without pedaling.

BOATING **Lac Grenon and Lac Moubra,** two crystalline lakes near the connected villages, are filled with pedal boats and Windsurfers on long summer days. Rentals are available at shoreside kiosks. Wakeboarding and waterskiing services are available on **Etang Long.**

HIKING Networks of well-marked trails (280 km [215 mi]) branch out from both villages, sometimes intersecting but more often leading in opposite directions. Unless you want to scale higher peaks, all that is needed is a good pair of boots and a map to guide you to signed pathways through open terrain, forests, or along the bisses (irrigation channels). Keep an eye out for fast-paced nordic walkers (power hikers using ski poles). If it's an extreme challenge you're looking for, contact the pros at **Bureau Officiel des Guides** (☎027/4811480) for gear and guidance.

SHOPPING

At times the streets of stylish Crans can feel like a fashion runway, with the leather and fur-trimmed crowd hidden behind logo sunglasses and cashmere hats. This tiny village has assembled the most high-end shops and designer boutiques in the entire region—many only open in season. Don't be deceived by its name; at **Alex Sports** (✉*Rue du Prado* ☎*0274814061*) you'll find labels such as Bogner, Escada, Ralph Lauren, and Zegna. And, yes, you can buy a down jacket or rent a pair of skis. Around the corner **Attitude** (✉*Rue Central* ☎*027/4810280*), a women's specialty shop, houses equally notable names including Burberry, Gucci, and Prada. If it's jewelry or watches you're looking for, you'll find them in the storefronts of Rue du Prado, tucked in between Hermès, Chanel, and Louis Vuitton.

VAL D'ANNIVIERS

25 km (16 mi) south of Sierre.

Visitor Information (☎*027/4558535* ⊕*www.sierre-salgesch.ch*).

EXPLORING

If you drive east of Sierre and south of the Rhône, following signs for Vissoie, you enter a wild and craggy valley called Val d'Anniviers. The name is said to come from its curious and famous (among anthropologists, at least) nomads, known in Latin as *anni viatores* (year-round travelers).

If you don't have time to follow the lengthy gorge to its end, climb the switchback road to the tiny village of **St-Luc** for a taste of rural life and celestial viewing at the observatory.

In summer you can continue down a narrow forest road to **Grimentz,** with the Weisshorn dominating the views. With a population of 370, this ancient 13th-century village has preserved its weathered-wood houses and mazots in its tiny center.

Zinal, farther into the valley, is another isolated mountaineering center with well-preserved wood houses and mazots. A stopover in any one of these windswept mountain hideouts to walk, climb, ski, or relax by the fire is a reward. In late September, when the herds are brought down from the mountains, there is a seasonal celebration and sporting event featuring fighting cows.

WHERE TO EAT & STAY

$$$
SWISS
★

Bella Tola. Stepping stones lead to the wrought-iron entry of this stately, multistory mansion perched above the main road. A mountain retreat since the late 1800s, the designer setting mixes antiques and collectibles with sepia photos, rippled mirrors, orchids, and fur pillows—the handiwork of the wife of the genial hotelier team. Floors creak and window frames sigh in cozy guest quarters that have hung on to their character through various updates. Gourmet dining is part of the top-drawer ambience, as is an ultramodern, grottolike pool and spa. **Pros:** feels like staying with an old friend; beautiful location with stunning views. **Cons:** some say the haute cuisine falls flat; many rooms are no bigger than a breadbasket. ⊠*St-Luc* ☎*027/4751444* ⊕*www. bellatola.ch* ⤵*32 rooms* ⚄*In-room: dial-up. In-hotel: 2 restaurants, bar, pool, no-smoking rooms.* ⊟*AE, DC, MC, V* ⓧ*MAP* ⊙*Closed mid-Apr.–mid-June and mid-Oct.–mid–Dec.*

$
SWISS

De Moiry. This family-run country inn is draped in a profusion of geraniums in summertime and bundled in snowbanks in winter. Guest rooms are walled in pine and larch, with carved furniture and mounds of white linen on the beds. Hikers and skiers gather on the porch or near the stone hearth in the dining room ($–$$) for raclette bubbling off the open fire. Ask the owner, who's an experienced mountain guide and photographer, to show you some of his work; it will leave you breathless. **Pros:** Swiss kitsch at its best—dig the handpainted murals of fighting cows in the restaurant. **Cons:** no Internet in the two annex rooms; high season requires mandatory half board. ⊠*Grimentz* ☎*027/4751144* ⊕*www.hoteldemoiry.ch* ⤵*17 rooms* ⚄*In-room: safe, Wi-Fi. In-hotel: restaurant* ⊟*AE, DC, MC, V* ⓧ*CP.*

HIKING
☼

Walk through the universe on an astronomically themed 6 km (4 mi) trail called **Le Chemin des Planètes.** Integrity in size and distance has been maintained in planetary stations set along a pathway that begins at the base of the **Observatoire François-Xavier Bangoud** (☎*027/4755808* ⊕*www.ofxb.ch*). Explanations about scientific elements and planet relationships are in French. The Tignousa funicular delivers you to the starting point at 2,200 meters (7,218 feet). Allow two hours to make the ascent from there, past the Hotel Weishorn. Celestial viewing using the reflecting and refracting telescopes plus camera is provided at the mountaintop observatory.

LEUKERBAD

11

21 km (13 mi) northeast of Sierre.

Visitor Information (✉ *Village Center* ☎ *027/4727171* ⊕ *www.leukerbad.ch*).

EXPLORING

At 4,628 feet, Leukerbad is Europe's highest spa village; travelers have been ascending to this Alpine retreat for centuries to take the curative waters and fill their lungs with cleansing mountain air. With 90 km (43 mi) of downhill and cross-country runs of varying difficulty, including some used for World Cup training and testing, Leukerbad is a pleasant alternative to the larger resorts, and its rejuvenating hot mineral pools are soothing for après-ski. The Torrent gondola whisks skiers to slopes; a one-day ski pass including a visit to one of the public spas is 68 SF; a six-day pass is 336 SF. Without the spa visit, ski passes cost 49 SF and 245 SF, respectively.

Summer brings hikers who love the combination of trekking and soaking. High-altitude crossings via the Gemmi Pass go back to 500 BC. The ancient connection between the Valais and the Berner Oberland can be traversed easily in a day.

Calcium sulphite hot springs flow beneath the village, filling stone troughs with warm vapor, keeping thoroughfares free of snow, and circulating to private tubs and public pools daily. In the late 1960s an arthritis and rheumatism treatment facility was established, but it has since been overshadowed by upscale wellness hotels and sports clinics. The two largest bath facilities in Leukerbad are Burgerbad and Alpentherme. Both have pools, fountains, whirlpools, jets, and sprays of thermal waters at a temperature of 35°C (100°F). Towels and robes can be rented at the reception desk.

The multilevel **Burgerbad,** with both indoor and outdoor pools, resembles an aqua park and is often packed with families clad in multicolor swim gear. The facility also has exercise rooms, a sauna, solarium, and snack bar. ✉ *Rathausstr.* ☎ *027/4722020* ⊕ *www.burgerbad.ch* 🎫 *19 SF* ⊙ *Daily 8–8.*

★ Sporting expansive Palladian windows set in marble, the **Lindner Alpentherme** looks like a temple perched on the hill. It has facilities similar to the Burgerbad but in a more sophisticated setting. Annexes contain a Clarins beauty center, medical complex, and shopping arcade that includes a pharmacy specializing in natural remedies, *confiserie* (pastry shop), and juice bar. The unique spa treatment here is the Bain Romano-Irlandais (Roman-Irish bath), a two-hour succession of hot and cold soaks and vapor treatments. Massage, herbal wraps, scrubs, and medical consultations are also on the menu. Children under six aren't allowed at this spa. ✉ *Dorfpl.* ☎ *027/4721010* ⊕ *www.alpentherme.ch* 🎫 *20 SF* ⊙ *Daily 8–8, Fridays 8–10.*

WHERE TO STAY

$$$–$$$$ **Lindner Hotels and Alpentherme Leukerbad.** Adjacent to each other in one vast complex, and set under a stunning mountain range, three hotels—Maison Blanche, Grands Bains, and the Hotel de France—are

merged under one banner. The regal Maison Blanche has contemporary wheat and sage guest rooms to create a soothing mood, while Grands Bains boasts first-class luxury with minimalist touches. The de France is the oldest and has the classiest exterior—too bad its gingham check decor is getting worn. Alpentherme, the village's posh bath and spa complex, is under the same ownership, and an underground walkway permits you to tread to your appointment in robe and slippers. Restaurants follow the ambience of each location: glitzy dining room Fin Bec ($$$–$$$$) and convivial à la carte restaurant, Sacré Bon ($$). **Pros:** private spa for guests only; packages include Alpentherme admission and treatments. **Cons:** rooms in the Hotel de France are in desperate need of a good sprucing up; some say the staff can be arrogant. ⊠ *Dorfpl.* ☎ *027/4721000* ⊕ *www.lindnerhotels.ch* ⬎ *135 rooms, 16 suites* ♿ *In-room: safe, refrigerator, Wi-Fi. In-hotel: 3 restaurants, bar, 2 tennis courts, pool, gym, spa, parking (fee)* ▤ *MC, V* ⦿ *CP.*

> **DRINK TO YOUR HEALTH**
>
> Don't forget to drink a glass of water from the tap in Leukerbad—it's touted to have added health benefits.

$$ ☷ **Waldhaus Grichting.** This is the prototypical *relais de campagne* (country inn): honey-color wood, cheerful rooms, and a vivacious proprietress. Set on a forested hillside convenient to both the Alpentherme and the Torrent station, this expanded chalet seems more like a private home than a hotel. The Stübli ($–$$) attracts locals for raclette and the daily special, and hotel guests are treated to a six-course meal in the dining room ($$–$$$), included in the price of the room. Pool and spa facilities are shared with the Alpentherme until 2010, when a new wing featuring these amenities will open on-site. **Pros:** excellent staff; child-friendly atmosphere. **Cons:** children at play in lobby; no in-hotel spa or thermal baths. ⊠ *On Promenade* ☎ *027/4703232* ⊕ *www.grichting-hotels.ch* ⬎ *16 rooms* ♿ *In-Room: safe, Wi-Fi. In-hotel: restaurant, bar, parking (fee)* ▤ *MC, V* ⦿ *MAP.*

ALPINE ZENTRUM

Immediately east of Sierre you'll notice a sharp change: *vals* become *Tals,* and the sounds you overhear at your next pit stop are no longer the mellifluous tones of the Suisse Romande but the lilting, guttural Swiss-German dialect called Wallisertiitsch, a local form of Schwyzerdütsch. Welcome to Wallis (*vahl*-is), the Germanic end of Valais. This sharp demographic frontier can be traced back to the 6th century, when Alemannic tribes poured over the Grimsel Pass and penetrated as far as Sierre. Here the middle-class cuisine changes from steak frites to veal and *Rösti* (hash brown potatoes).

ZERMATT

Fodor'sChoice *28 km (18 mi) south of Visp, plus a 10 km (6 mi) train ride from Täsch.*
★

GETTING HERE

Zermatt, the world's most famous car-free Alpine village, requires that residents and guests leave their vehicles in the village of Täsch. Shuttle service (12 mins, 16 SF round-trip) is provided by train via a state-of-the-art station with adjacent decks of covered parking. Access to the commuter trains that run every 20 minutes is eased with ramps and luggage carts that roll onto the passenger cars. Five-star hotels like those in the Seiler group have separate valet terminals plus private transfer that can be booked with your room reservation. In addition, there are open lots where the rates are less expensive, but plan to add 8–14 SF per day to your vacation expenses. If you don't want to make the half-hour drive on mountain roads into the Matter Valley, use rail service that connects through Visp. The scenic ride will take about an hour; a first-class ticket costs 52 SF.

Visitor Information (✉ *Village Center* ☎ *027/9668100* ⊕ *www.zermatt.ch*).

EXPLORING

Despite its fame—which stems from that mythic mountain, the Matterhorn, and from its excellent ski facilities—Zermatt is a resort with its feet on the ground. It protects its regional quirks along with its wildlife and its tumbledown mazots, which crowd between glass-and-concrete chalets like old tenements between skyscrapers. Streets twist past weathered-wood walls, flower boxes, and haphazard stone roofs until they break into open country that slopes, inevitably, uphill. Despite the crowds, you're never far from the wild roar of the silty river and the peace of a mountain path.

In the mid-19th century Zermatt was virtually unheard of; the few visitors who came to town stayed at the vicarage. The vicar and a chaplain named Joseph Seiler persuaded Seiler's little brother Alexander to start an inn. Opened in 1854 and named the Hotel Monte Rosa, it's still one of five Seiler hotels in Zermatt. In 1891 the cog railway between Visp and Zermatt took its first summer run and began disgorging tourists with profitable regularity—though it didn't plow through in wintertime until 1927. Today the town remains a car-free resort (there's a reason for those carriages). If you're traveling primarily by car, you can park it in the multistory terminal connected to the station in Täsch, where you catch the train into Zermatt.

Fodor'sChoice Hordes of package-tour sightseers push shoulder to shoulder to get yet
★ another shot of the **Matterhorn** (14,685 feet). Called one of the wonders of the Western world, the mountain deserves the title, though it has become an almost self-parodying icon, like the Eiffel Tower or the Empire State Building. Its peculiar snaggletooth form, free from competition from other peaks on all sides, rears up over the village, larger than life and genuinely awe-inspiring. As you leave the train station and weave through pedestrian crowds, aggressive electric taxi carts, and

aromatic horse-drawn carriages along the main street, Bahnhofstrasse, you're assaulted on all sides by Matterhorn images—on postcards, sweatshirts, calendars, beer steins, and candy wrappers—though not by the original, which is obscured by resort buildings (except from the windows of pricier hotel rooms). But break past the shops and hotels onto the main road into the hills, and you'll reach a slightly elevated spot where you'll probably stop dead in your tracks. There it is at last, its twist of snowy rock blinding in the sun, weathered mazots scattered romantically at its base. Surely more pictures are taken from this spot than from anywhere else in Switzerland.

It was Edward Whymper's spectacular—and catastrophic—conquest of the Matterhorn, on July 14, 1865, that made Zermatt a household word. Whymper stayed at the Hotel Monte Rosa before his departure and there named his party of seven for the historic climb: Michel Croz, a French guide; old Peter Taugwalder and his son, young Peter, local guides; Lord Francis Douglas, a 19-year-old Englishman; Douglas Hadow; the Reverend Charles Hudson; and Whymper himself. They climbed together, pairing "tourists," as Whymper called the Englishmen, with experienced locals. They camped at 11,000 feet and by 10 AM had reached the base of the mountain's famous hook. Wrote Whymper of the final moments:

The higher we rose the more intense became the excitement. The slope eased off, at length we could be detached, and Croz and I, dashing away, ran a neck-and-neck race, which ended in a dead heat. At 1:40 PM, the world was at our feet, and the Matterhorn was conquered!

Croz pulled off his shirt and tied it to a stick as a flag, one that was seen in Zermatt below. They stayed at the summit one hour, then prepared for the descent, tying themselves together in an order agreed on by all. Croz led, then Hadow, Hudson, Lord Douglas, the elder Taugwalder, then the younger, and Whymper, who lingered to sketch the summit and leave their names in a bottle.

I suggested to Hudson that we should attach a rope to the rocks on our arrival at the difficult bit, and hold it as we descended, as an additional protection. He approved the idea, but it was not definitely decided that it should be done.

They headed off, "one man moving at a time; when he was firmly planted the next advanced," Whymper recalled.

Croz…was in the act of turning around to go down a step or two himself; at this moment Mr. Hadow slipped, fell against him, and knocked him over. I heard one startled exclamation from Croz, then saw him and Mr. Hadow flying downward; in another moment Hudson was dragged from his steps, and Lord Douglas immediately after him. All this was the work of a moment. Immediately we heard Croz's exclamation, old Peter and I planted ourselves as firmly as the rocks would permit; the rope was taut between us, and the jerk came on us both as on one man. We held; but the rope broke midway between Taugwalder and Lord Francis Douglas. For a few seconds we saw our unfortunate companions sliding downward on their backs, and spreading out their hands, endeavoring to save themselves. They passed from our sight uninjured, disappeared one by one, and fell from precipice to precipice on to the Matterhorn glacier below, a distance of nearly 4,000 feet in height. From the moment the rope broke it was impossible to help them. So perished our comrades!

A "sharp-eyed lad" ran into the Hotel Monte Rosa to report an avalanche fallen from the Matterhorn summit; he had witnessed the deaths of the four mountaineers. The body of young Lord Douglas was never recovered, but the others lie in little cemeteries behind the park near the village church, surrounded by scores of other failed mountaineers, including an American whose tomb bears the simple epitaph I CHOSE TO CLIMB.

In summer the streets of Zermatt fill with sturdy, weathered climbers, state-of-the-art ropes and picks hanging at their hips. They continue to tackle the peaks, and climbers have mastered the Matterhorn literally thousands of times since Whymper's disastrous victory.

It's quite simple to gain the broader perspective of high altitudes without risking life or limb. A train trip on the **Gornergrat–Monte Rose Bahn** functions as an excursion as well as ski transport. Part of its rail system was completed in 1898, and it's the highest open-air rail system in

Europe (the tracks to the Jungfrau-joch, though higher, bore through the face of the Eiger). It connects out of the main Zermatt train station and heads sharply left, at a right angle to the track that brings you into town. Its stop at the **Riffel-berg**, at 8,469 feet, offers wide-open views of the Matterhorn. Farther on, from **Rotenboden**, at 9,246 feet, a short downhill walk leads to the **Riffelsee**, which obligingly provides photographers with a postcard-perfect reflection of the famous

> **DID YOU KNOW?**
>
> Zermatt lies in a hollow of meadows and trees ringed by mountains—among them the broad **Monte Rosa** and its tallest peak, the **Dufourspitze** (at 15,200 feet, the highest point in Switzerland)—plus 36 others that tower above 13,000 feet—of which visitors hear relatively little, so all-consuming is the cult of the Matterhorn.

peak. At the end of the 9-km (5½-mi) line, the train stops at the summit station of **Gornergrat** (10,266 feet), and passengers pour onto the observation terraces to take in the majestic views of the Matterhorn, Monte Rosa, Gorner Glacier, and an expanse of scores of peaks and 24 other glaciers. Make sure to bring warm clothes, sunglasses, and sturdy shoes, especially if you plan to ski or hike down. ⊠ *Zermatt station* ☎ *027/9214711* 🎫 *76 SF round-trip, 38 SF one-way* ⊙ *Departures daily every 24 min, 7–7.*

☯ To get a sense of life in this high-altitude region and climber's risks, visit the **Matterhorn Museum,** a sunken village of chalets, mazots, and dwellings depicted as an archaeological site, which visitors walk through, experiencing different periods of time along the way. The personal accounts of local docents liven up the displays of antiquated equipment, clothing, and historical documents about those who lived and climbed here. There is a farmer's cottage, hotel, and church interior, plus stuffed and mounted animals. A multimedia film takes you atop the Matterhorn for dramatic climate changes; an Internet center enables you to research questions on your own. ☎ *027/9674100* 🎫 *10 SF* ⊙ *Easter–June, Oct., daily 2–6; July–Sept., daily 11–6; Nov.–mid-Dec., closed; mid-Dec.–Easter, daily 3–7.*

Climb the winding pathway behind the ski and snowboard school to the white church on the hill, **St. Peter's** *(The English Church)*. Anglican services are still held in the tiny sanctuary established by the British who ignited a climbing fervor to conquer the Matterhorn and other towering peaks in the region. Take time to pause in the cemetery that holds the graves of those who were not fortunate enough to return safely and others who remained in this beloved community to live out their lives.

SKIING

Zermatt's skiable terrain lives up to its reputation: the 63 lift installations, 73 lifts, and mountain railways are capable of moving well above 50,000 skiers per hour to reach its approximately 313 km (194 mi) of marked pistes—if you count those of Cervinia in Italy. Among the lifts are the cable car that carries skiers up to an elevation of 12,746 feet on the Matterhorn Glacier Paradise (previously known as Klein Matterhorn), the small Gornergratbahn that creeps up to the Gornergrat, and a subway through an underground tunnel that gives more pleasure to ecologists than it does to sun-loving skiers.

The skiable territory on this royal plateau was once separated into three separate sectors, but the installation of a gondola to Riffelberg has linked the three together. The first sector is **Sunegga-Blauherd-Rothorn,** which culminates at an elevation of 10,170 feet. **Gornergrat-Stockhorn** (11,155 feet) is the second. The third is the region dominated by the **Matterhorn Glacier Paradise (MGP),** which goes to Italy. The best way to prioritize your ski day is still to concentrate on one or two areas, especially during high season. Thanks to snowmaking machines and the eternal snows of the Klein Matterhorn Glacier, Zermatt is said to guarantee skiers 7,216 feet of vertical drop no matter what the snowfall—an impressive claim. Gravity Park, a snowboarding center on Theodul glacier below the MGP, has pipes, kickers, and rails to thrill. A one-day lift ticket costs 71 SF; a six-day pass costs 350 SF; if you want to ski to Italy it costs 80 SF and 394 SF. Ask for the hands-free "Smart Card" or "Swatch Access Key" with computer chip gate activation and billing. A **ski and snowboard school** (⊠*Skischulbüro, Bahnhofstr.* ☎*027/9662466)* operates seven ski schools from mid-December until April and in July and August.

WHERE TO EAT

$$ ⨯**Elsie's Bar.** This tiny log cabin of a ski haunt, directly across from the
SWISS Zermatt church, draws an international crowd as soon as it opens its doors at 4 o'clock. They come to select from an extensive list of aged scotches and mixed cocktails. Light meals include cheese dishes, oysters, escargots, and would you believe spaghetti with caviar and crème fraîche? ⊠*Kirchepl. 16* ☎*027/9672431* ⊟*AE, DC, MC, V* ☉*Closed May and mid-Oct to Dec.*

$$ ⨯**Findlerhof.** This mountain restaurant is ideal for long lunches between
SWISS sessions on the slopes or for a panoramic break on an all-day hike.
Fodor'sChoice It's perched in tiny Findeln, between the Sunnegga and Blauherd ski
★ areas; the Matterhorn views are astonishing. The food is decidedly fresh and creative. Franz and Heidi Schwery tend their own Alpine garden to provide lettuce for their salads and berries for vinaigrettes and hot desserts. The fluffy *Matterkuchen,* a bacon and leek quiche, will fortify you for the 30- to 40-minute walk down to the village. ⊠*Findeln* ☎*027/9672588* ⊟*MC, V* ☉*Closed May–mid-June and mid-Oct.–Nov.*

$$ ⨯**Grill-Room Stockhorn.** The moment you step across the threshold
SWISS into this low-slung, two-story restaurant decked with mountaineering memorabilia, tantalizing aromas of cheese melting should sharpen your appetite. Downstairs you can watch your meat roasting on the open grill while enjoying the chalet-style decor. Upstairs a mélange of Mediterranean tiles and traditional Valaisan exposed dark-wood beams creates a romantic atmosphere. This is a great place for regional dishes and meat specialties like juicy Chateaubriand grilled to perfection dripping with a creamy Béarnaise sauce, served by lively staff. ⊠*Hotel Stockhorn, Riedstr. 22* ☎*027/9671747* ⊟*AE, MC, V* ☉*Closed mid-May–mid-June and Oct.*

$$ ✕**Whymperstube.** At this little restaurant in the Hotel Monte Rosa,
SWISS   plates of melted raclette and bubbling pots of fondue are delivered to
★   tightly packed tables by an agile waitstaff. Be sure to try the unusual
variations on cheese dishes like the fresh mushroom or pear-laced fon-
due. The restaurant is named for Edward Whymper, the first man to
reach the Matterhorn summit—imagine the climbers' stories that must
have echoed within these walls. In the winter season the place stays
open until 1 AM. ⊠*Bahnhofstr. 80* ☎*027/9672296* ⚍*Reservations
essential* ⊟*AE, DC, MC, V.*

$$ ✕**Zum See.** In a hamlet (little more than a cluster of mazots) of the same
SWISS   name, this restaurant turns out inventive meals that merit acclaim. A half
★   hour's walk from Zermatt, it overflows until late afternoon with diners
sunning on the terrace or packed into the 400-year-old log house. (The
quickest way to get here is to walk or ski down from Furi.) Hosts Max
and Greti Mennig masterfully prepare such daily specials as venison
salad with wild mushrooms and handmade tortelloni with nettle-ricotta
filling. The selection of wines and brandies sets skiers aglow. ⊠*Zum
See* ☎*027/9672045* ⚍*Reservations essential* ⊟*MC, V* ☉*Closed mid-
Apr.–mid-June and mid-Oct.–mid-Dec. No dinner.*

WHERE TO STAY

Many Zermatt hotels, especially larger ones, decide on a year-by-year
basis to close during low season, which lasts from "melt-down" (anywhere from late April to mid-June) until "pre-season" (November
through mid-December). If you plan to travel during the low season,
be sure to call ahead. That noted, the summer "low season" can prove
more popular than the winter ski season, with rates and availability
to match.

¢–$ 🏨**Alpenhotel.** If steep resort prices don't suit your budget, stay downhill
in the village of Täsch. Train connections to Zermatt are easy, though
you'll have to compete with guests required to leave their cars in nearby
lots. This Best Western standard has tidy rooms with blond modular
furniture and tile showers, plus an on-premises bakery and wellness center. **Pros:** tasty, fresh breakfast pastries; free Wi-Fi connection throughout hotel. **Cons:** schlepping your skis on the train to Zermatt; this
"parking" city doesn't specialize in nightlife. ⊠*Täsch* ☎*027/9662644*
⊕*www.bestwestern.ch/alpenhof* ⌑*29 rooms* ⚷*In-room: refrigerator,
Wi-Fi. In-hotel: restaurant, bar, gym* ⊟*AE, DC, MC, V* ⦿*CP.*

$$$$ 🏨**Apartmenthotel Zurbriggen.** Sleeping under the roof of Olympic medal-
ist Pirmin Zurbriggen's six-unit apartment house may not make you a
better skier, but the view will elicit dreams of starting gates and downhill races. Flexible configurations with fully stocked kitchenettes can
sleep a couple or expand to include a pack of friends. Near the cable
car to Matterhorn Glacier Paradise, this ultramodern glass structure
has plenty of tech-amenities: flat-screen TV, Wi-Fi, CD players, and so
on. **Pros:** convenient ski location; personalized service. **Cons:** long walk
from the town center; breakfast only—no restaurant. ⊠*Schulhmattstr.
68* ☎*027/9663838* ⊕*www.zurbriggen.ch* ⌑*4 apartments, 2 suites*
⚷*In-room: safe, kitchen, Wi-Fi. In-hotel: pool, spa* ⊟*MC, V* ⦿*CP.*

$ **Hotel Admiral.** An easygoing anglophone owner makes it a snap to check in at this fastidious lodging along Zermatt's river promenade. Guest rooms are simple yet spacious, with mountain views. The Sunnegga cableway is just across the way, so access to the slopes couldn't be easier. Skiers warm themselves at the raised-hearth fireplace in the lobby lounge and gather on the outdoor deck. **Pros:** convivial clientele; laidback atmosphere makes it easy for solo travelers to meet new friends. **Cons:** phony chalet exterior; odd blue carpeting throughout the hotel; "garni" means only breakfast served. ✉ *Matterstr. 23* ☎ *027/9669000* ⊕ *www.hotel-admiral.ch* ⤶ *24 rooms, 1 suite* ᗉ *In-room: safe, refrigerator, Wi-Fi. In-hotel: restaurant, bar, spa* ⊟ *AE, DC, MC, V* ◎ *CP.*

$$$$ **Hotel Mirabeau.** The best of old and new merge at this two-part hotel with a traditional building and contemporary new addition. Guest rooms in the main building are smartly furnished, but it's the newer addition that is the attention-getter, with elements of old chalets combined with sleek bedding and open Jacuzzi baths. An epicurean restaurant, Corbeau d'Or ($$$), attracts outsiders for refined, fresh cuisine. The spa center and Josef's, a popular wine lounge, are bonuses in a location set apart from the hub of the village. **Pros:** personable personnel; winning mix of old and new; light-filled rooms. **Cons:** mixed reviews for the kitchen; spa facilities a far cry from those of other nearby hotels. ✉ *Untere Mattenrstr. 12–14* ☎ *027/9662660* ⊕ *www.hotel-mirabeau.ch* ⤶ *44 rooms, 18 suites* ᗉ *In-room: safe, refrigerator, Wi-Fi. In-hotel: 2 restaurants, bar, pool, spa* ⊟ *AE, DC, MC, V* ◎ *MAP.*

$$$$ **Hotel Monte Rosa.** Alexander Seiler founded his first hotel in the core of this historic building, expanding it over the years to its current size. (This was the home base of Edward Whymper when he conquered the Matterhorn in 1865.) Behind its graceful, shuttered facade you'll find an ideal balance between modern convenience and history in the original ceiling moldings, fireplaces, and Victorian dining hall. Recently renovated rooms boast impeccable, soft-toned decor; southern views go quickly and cost more. The bar is an après-ski must. The pool and health facilities are shared with sister-hotel Mont Cervin, and guests can take advantage of the hotel group's dine-around plan. **Pros:** smack dab on the main pedestrian drag near all the entertainment hotspots; historical significance sets a unique, inspiring mood…you'll feel like conquering the Matterhorn yourself. **Cons:** no in-hotel pool or spa facilities; though trendy, the bar is narrow and uncomfortably cramped. ✉ *Bahnhofstr. 80* ☎ *027/9660333* 📠 *027/9660330* ⊕ *www.seilerhotels.ch* ⤶ *43 rooms, 3 suites* ᗉ *In-room: safe, refrigerator, Wi-Fi. In-hotel: restaurant, bar* ⊟ *AE, DC, MC, V* ⊘ *Closed mid-Apr.–mid-June and late Oct.–mid-Dec.* ◎ *MAP.*

$$$$ **Mont Cervin Hotel Palace.** Part of the Seiler dynasty, this Leading Hotels of
Fodor'sChoice   the World property is luxurious, genteel, and one of Zermatt's grandes
★   dames. The main lounge has a soaring three-story sash-window view of the town and Matterhorn that is to die for. Guest rooms are decorated with tasteful stripes and plaids in primary colors, while suites have luxe rustic touches and fabrics; most rooms have Matterhorn views. The Residence, across the street, offers spacious apartments. The main restaurant ($$$) has a light, modern ambience with dishes to

match, including sea bass with white tomato mousse on lemon risotto. There's also a more casual dining option in-hotel ($–$$), and others at the hotel's sister properties. The hotel will reserve covered parking and transportation from Täsch. **Pros:** station pick-up in a red antique horse-drawn carriage; wellness and spa facilities that are tops. **Cons:** big-city luxury removes you somewhat from the village atmosphere. ⊠ *Bahnhofstr. 31* ☎ *027/9668888* ⊕ *www.seilerhotels.ch* ⬅ *87 rooms, 31 suites, 15 apartments* ⚿ *In-room: safe, refrigerator, Wi-Fi. In-hotel: 2 restaurants, bar, pool, gym, spa* ⊟ *AE, DC, MC, V* ⊘ *Closed May–mid-June, Oct. and mid-Nov.* ⦿ *MAP.*

$$$$ **The Omnia.** A super-sophisticated glass-and-steel tower juts out of
★   the hillside above Zermatt's church square, its only concession to local architecture the wooden panels that cap each end. Part engineering marvel, the rest 21st-century chic, this hotel is literally a standout in a village of traditional hoteliers. A private tunnel leads to the secure elevator where you are whisked to the contemporary lobby with stone firebox and van der Rohe–like furnishings. Often replete with great Matterhorn vistas, guest rooms are lettered not numbered, a tip of the hat to personalization. The restaurant and bar are equally sleek places to sip and dine; the wellness area with multiple steam applications and a contoured tile relaxation room adds solitude. **Pros:** Bose sound-systems and designer toiletries; jaw-dropping Matterhorn views from decks and balconies. **Cons:** set apart high above the village; staggered level arrangement can be confusing. ⊠ *Auf dem Fels* ☎ *027/9667171* ⊕ *www.the-omnia.ch* ⬅ *18 rooms, 12 suites* ⚿ *In-room: safe, refrigerator, Wi-Fi. In-hotel: restaurant, bar, pool, gym* ⊟ *AE, DC, MC, V* ⊘ *Closed late Apr.–late May, Oct. and Nov.* ⦿ *CP.*

$$–$$$ **Pollux.** Despite its hideous 1960s exterior, this newly remodeled hotel displays modern elegance, with guest rooms trimmed in pine, stone walls, and artistic tile and wood flooring. Though few of its windows look onto the Matterhorn, its position directly on the main street puts you in the heart of town. The restaurant ($$) is based around a central fountain; an old-fashioned *pinte* ($–$$) draws locals for its low-price lunches, snacks, and Valaisan cheese dishes. Its popular T-Bar disco is always packed. **Pros:** sparkling clean; après-ski cocktails at the fireside bar. **Cons:** street below can be noisy; no view from the wellness zone. ⊠ *Bahnhofstr. 28* ☎ *027/9664000* ⊕ *www.hotelpollux.ch* ⬅ *35 rooms* ⚿ *In-room: safe, refrigerator, Wi-Fi. In-hotel: 2 restaurants, bar, spa* ⊟ *AE, DC, MC, V* ⦿ *CP.*

$$$$ **Riffelalp Resort 2222m.** Accessed by the little Gornergrat railway and
Fodor'sChoice   enjoying a stunning location, this hotel is a winner in many respects. Set
★   at 7,288 feet amid fields and Alpine forests, this mountaintop option offers both direct views of the Matterhorn—especially breathtaking in the orange glow of early morning—and enchantingly stylish decor. Guest rooms are storybook in ambience, with Heidi-esque woodwork, couture fabrics, sumptuous sofas, Jacuzzi tubs, and Bose sound systems. Dining ranges from pizza to plush: the Alexandre restaurant has elegant wood paneling, the Walliser Keller is a cut-stone tavern, while the Al Bosco sun terrace is just the place to enjoy a "Matterhorn pizza." Bliss out with chilling footbaths and organic saunas in the spa center,

which is crowned by an indoor pool that is a whirlpool extravaganza and an outdoor pool that is no less than Europe's highest—wow. Even transit is made memorable, as you can ride a private restored tram to and from the train station. **Pros:** far from the village hubbub; no better skiing location in Zermatt. **Cons:** no train service from the village after 11:30 PM; location means dining is limited to the hotel's three options. ☒ *Riffelalp CH-3920* ☎*027/9660555* ⊕*http://www.zermatt. ch/riffelalp/e/* ☞*65 rooms, 5 suites, 2 apartments* ♿*In-room: safe, refrigerator, Wi-Fi. In-hotel: 3 restaurants, bar, 2 pools* ▤*AE, DC, MC, V* ☾*Closed mid-Apr.–late June and mid-Oct.–mid-Dec.* ⦿*MAP.*

$-$$ ▦**Romantica.** Among the scores of anonymously modern hotels along the Zermatt plain, this modest structure offers an exceptional location directly above the town center, a block up a narrow, mazot-lined lane. Its tidy, bright gardens, game trophies, and granite stove give it personality. You can also stay in one of the two *Walliserstadel*, charming, 200-year-old huts in the garden. Keep in mind that this is a *garni* hotel (no restaurant), so only breakfast is served. **Pros:** quiet, yet only a stone's throw from the trendiest nightlife; big balconies and windows. **Cons:** overly kitschy murals in lobby; most double beds are two twins side by side—leaving lovebirds divided. ☒*Churm 21* ☎*027/9662650* ⊕*www.reconline.ch/romantica* ☞*13 rooms, 1 apartment, 2 cabins* ♿*In-hotel: bar* ▤*AE, DC, MC, V* ⦿*CP.*

$-$$ ▦**Touring.** Reassuringly traditional architecture, sunny guest rooms full of pine, and an elevated position apart from town with excellent Matterhorn views make this an appealing, informal alternative to the chic downtown scene. Hearty daily menus are served to pension guests in the cozy dining room (the same menu is available in the Stübli). **Pros:** excellent rapport quality/price; delicious, comprehensive breakfast buffet includes local specialties. **Cons:** lacking modern amenities—no elevator, no Wi-Fi. ☒*Riedstr. 45* ☎*027/9671177* ⊕*www.touring.buz.ch* ☞*20 rooms* ♿*In-hotel: restaurant, bar, public Internet, no elevator* ▤*MC, V* ⦿*CP.*

NIGHTLIFE

GramPi's Bar (☎*027/9677788*), located on the Bahnhofstrasse in what locals call the Bermuda Triangle because of the concentration of nightspots, is a lively bar, where you can get into the mood for dancing downstairs with a Lady Matterhorn cocktail. Across the cobblestones is the multifaceted **Postli** (☎*027/9671931*), with **The Pink,** a live concert hall (open only in winter); **Loft Club,** where a DJ spins tunes for late-night revelers; **Broken Bar,** a grotto dance floor with a different beat; and **Papa Caesar Lounge,** for those who prefer to sit and sip whiskey and smoke a cigar. Venues rotate openings depending on the season. Marking one of the points in the Bermuda Triangle trefoil is the **Hexen Bar** (☎*027/9675533*), which is decorated in witch memorabilia and serves cocktails and cognacs into the wee hours.

At **Vernissage** (☎*027/9676636*) you can see old and current films in the screening room, have a drink at the bar, or check out the art scene at the gallery. For an excellent choice in wines served with a modern flair head down the pathway beside the Hotel Mirabeau to **Josef's Wine Lounge**

(☎027/9662560). A double dose of folklore song and dance can be had at the **Schwyzer Stübli** (☎027/9660000), in the Hotel Schweizerhof; be prepared for rowdy sing-alongs and accordion music.

SPORTS & THE OUTDOORS

HIKING   With 400 km (248 mi) of marked trails available, you'll have plenty of options for exploring the mountains on foot. Outfitted with scarred boots, rucksacks, and walking sticks, trekkers strike out in all directions for daylong excursions ranging from easy to exhausting. Maps and route guides are available at the tourist office. Be sure to pack rain gear and a warm jacket along with sunscreen, as the weather changes quickly. Multiday lift passes will ease the way up and leave some change in your pocket for an after-hike beer.

MOUNTAIN BIKING   Mountain biking is closely monitored by Zermatt authorities to prevent interference with hiking on trails. To keep pace with other resorts, about 25 km (15 mi) have been set aside for dedicated downhill tracks with challenging features. A map is available at the tourist office. Bikes can be rented at **Slalom Sport** (☎027/9662366).

MOUNTAIN CLIMBING   The Matterhorn is one of the world's most awe-inspiring peaks, and many visitors get the urge to climb it. However, this climb must be taken seriously; you have to be in top physical condition and have climbing experience to attempt the summit. You also need to spend 7–10 days acclimatizing once in the area. Less-experienced climbers have plenty of alternatives, though, such as a one-day climb of the Riffelhorn (9,774 feet) or a half traverse of the Breithorn (13,661 feet). For those wanting a challenge without such extreme altitudes, try a guided trip across the rugged Gorner gorge. For detailed information, advice, instruction, and climbing guides, contact the **Zermatt Alpin Center** (✉*Bahnhofstr. 58* ☎*027/9662460* ⊕*www.alpincenter-zermatt.ch*).

SHOPPING

Zermatt may be Switzerland's souvenir capital, offering a broad variety of watches, knives, logo clothing, and Matterhorn-in-a-box stones. Popular folk crafts and traditional products include large grotesque masks of carved wood, and lidded *channes* in pewter or tin, molded in graduated sizes; they're sold everywhere, even in grocery stores.

You'll see lots of stores offering state-of-the-art sports equipment and apparel, from collapsible grappling hooks for climbers to lightweight hiking boots in brilliant colors to walking sticks—pairs of lightweight, spiked ski poles for hikers to add a bit of upper-body workout to their climb. **Bayard** (✉*Bahnhofpl. 2* ☎*027/9664950* ✉*Bahnhofstr. 35* ☎*027/9664960*) has sporting-goods shops scattered throughout the village, including these two main branches. **Glacier Sport** (✉*Bahnhofstr. 19* ☎*027/9681300*) specializes in ski and climbing equipment and accessories.

SAAS-FEE

36 km (22 mi) south of Visp.

GETTING HERE

Car-free Saas-Fee is on a bus line connection with Brig (1 hr, 18 SF) and Visp (45 mins, 15.80 SF); take the train here from Brig by transferring at Visp or connect with Zermatt by rail with a transfer at Stalden-Saas.

Visitor Information (✉ *Village Center* ☎ *027/9581858* ⊕ *www.saas-fee.ch*).

EXPLORING

At the end of the switchback road from Saas-Grund lies a parking garage where visitors must abandon their cars for the length of their stay in Saas-Fee. But even by the garage you'll be amazed, for the view on arriving at this lofty (5,871 feet) plateau is humbling. (In true Swiss-efficient fashion, you can drop off your bags curbside and call an electric shuttle that will arrive to fetch you in the time it takes to park your car.)

Saas-Fee is at the heart of a circle of mountains called the Mischabel, 13 of which tower to more than 13,120 feet, among them the **Dom** (14,908 feet), the highest mountain entirely on Swiss soil.

The town lies in a deep valley that leaves no doubt about its source: it seems to pour from the vast, intimidating **Fee Glacier,** which oozes like icy lava from the broad spread of peaks above. *Fee* can be translated as "fairy," and although Saas-Fee itself is a tourist-saturated resort, the landscape could illustrate a fairy tale.

★ Carved into the deep ice of the Fee Glacier at 11,482 feet, an **Eis Pavillon** *(ice cave),* considered the largest in the world, combines fascinating construction with a dash of kitsch. Twenty-six feet below the ice pack, the cavernous facility provides an impressive view of the surreal, frozen environment inside glacial formations. There are ice sculptures, exhibits on glaciology and crevasse rescue, and even a chapel-like room for meditation, concerts, and art shows. A special collaboration with global adventurer Mike Horn simulates elements of his polar expedition in film and interactive displays. The ticket for the cable car and underground funicular is pricey, but if you are up on the mountain, spring for the entrance fee and have a look below the frozen surface of the earth. ✉ *Mittelallalin* ☎ *027/9573560* 💰 *5 SF* ⊕ *Daily 8:30 or 9–approx. 4, depending on the season (when the last cable car leaves).*

SKIING

The first glacier to be used for skiing here was the **Längfluh** (9,414 feet), accessed by gondola, then cable car. The run is magnificent, sometimes physically demanding, and always varied. From the Längfluh you can take a lift to reach *the* ski area of Saas-Fee, the **Felskinn-Mittelallalin** sector (9,840–11,480 feet). Felskinn harbors its own surprise: in order to preserve the land and landscape, the Valaisans have constructed a subterranean funicular, the Métro Alpin, which climbs through the heart of the mountain to Mittelallalin, that is, halfway up the Allalinhorn (13,210 feet). Tourists debark in a rotating restaurant noted more for the austere grandeur of its natural surroundings than for its food. Felskinn-Mittelallalin's exceptional site, its high elevation, its runs (15 km [9 mi]), and its ample facilities (cable car, funicular, and three ski lifts) have made Saas-Fee the number one summer-skiing resort in Switzerland. It's also one of two official European snowboard centers sanctioned by the International Snowboard Federation. Lifts don't connect with other resorts in the valley—Saas-Almagell, Saas-Balen, or Saas-Grund. However, good days of skiing can be found a bus ride away, and hiking trails open in winter and summer link all four valleys. A one-day lift ticket costs 69 SF; a six-day pass costs 372 SF and includes ski bus to valley lifts. A special excursion plan to Zermatt is available, as is a savings program for parents who buy six-day passes, which allows discounted skiing for children under 16.

WHERE TO EAT

¢–$ ✕**Restaurant Skihütte.** During the winter high season you'll have to be
SWISS quick in order to snag a table on the sun-filled deck of this traditional restaurant on the main drag. A great location at the bottom of the lift is perfect for a cold after-ski brewski or tummy-warming Williamine pear schnapps. Inexpensive yet well-prepared Walliser favorites and tasty snacks hold you for another drink and a few more rays. ☎027/9589280 ▤AE, MC, V.

$$$$ ✕**Restaurant-Vinothek Fletschhorn.** Gault-Millau's 2007 chef-of-the-year
SWISS Markus Neff presides over this gourmand's paradise, located in the Wald-
Fodor's Choice hotel Fletschhorn. The vibe is innovative, the flavoring superb, and the
★ dishes rotate seasonally and are based on local products. Among the winners are pan-fried duck foie gras on sautéed mango or the roasted Alpine lamb chops with rye bread crust and creamy potato gratin. Lunch is a great time to sample the gourmet team's talents at a more favorable price. The expansive vinothek stocks more than 40,000 bottles that match the cuisine's high style. ⊠ *Waldhotel FletschhornCH-3906* ☎*027/9572131* ⊕*www.fletschhorn.ch* ⌖*Reservations essential* ▤*AE, DC, MC, V* ☾*Closed late Apr.–early June and mid-Oct.–early Dec.*

WHERE TO STAY

$$$$ ⊟**Beau-Site.** Surrounded on three sides by glorious mountains, this elegant hotel is presided over by the super-attentive and friendly Urs and Marie-Jeanne Zurbriggen-Roosen—a proud family with unyielding standards. Interiors of glossy wood, stacked stone, and leaded glass give the look of a respected manor house. Guest rooms (most have balconies) have baths with modern fixtures; furnishings tastefully mix antiques with the more modern. The refined main restaurant ($$–$$$) rates as one of the most romantic around. Intimate dining of a different type can be found at La Ferme ($–$$), a low-slung, elegantly rustic restaurant with a central woodstove and farmhouse detail. **Pros:** friendly, dirndl-clad female staff work the reception desk; fluffy sheepskins cover the patio furniture. **Cons:** price of half-board is a bit high for what you get. ⊠ *Saas-Fee* ☎*027/9581560* ⊕*www.beausite.org* ⤶*15 rooms, 3 suites, 16 apartments* ⌂*In-room: safe, refrigerator. In-hotel: 3 restaurants, bar, pool, spa, minibar* ▤*DC, MC, V* ☉*MAP.*

$$$$ ⊡ **Ferienart Resort & Spa.** Located in the center of town, this wood-chalet
Fodor'sChoice   hotel offers some of the best views around. Guest rooms have enticing,
★   lovely decors—the best offer an intoxicating blend of chandeliers, rustic
woods, and cozy furnishings. As for amenities, they can be mixed—
generous seating areas in some, tight built-in nooks in others; whirlpool
baths versus standard tubs—so quiz the reservationist to ensure you
get the room you want. The array of restaurants is dee-scrumptious,
with decors nearly more tempting than the food; they range from the
folkloric, painted-wood extravaganza that is Cäsar Ritz to a Tuscan-
style trattoria and an Asian-fusion spot. Their three-quarter pension
plan includes a light lunch or afternoon sweets along with morning and
evening meals. The wellness area with mock grotto pool and waterfall
has a "textile-free" zone with unique steam and spa treatments. **Pros:**
top-of-the-line wellness facilities, including extensive beauty treatments;
babysitting and daycare center a plus for families; gorgeous restaurants.
Cons: rooms vary drastically in style, comfort, and quality; inconsistent
service. ⊠ *Saas-Fee* ☎*027/9581900* ⊕*www.ferienart.ch* ⇆*83 rooms,
5 suites, 4 apartments* ⌂*In-room: safe, refrigerator, Wi-Fi. In-hotel: 4
restaurants, bar, pool, gym, spa* ▤*AE, DC, MC, V* ﺗﻌﻠﻢ*MAP.*

$$$$ ⊡ **Hotel du Glacier.** Flaunting the most elegant facade in town, this is
↻   one of the original hotels in the village. Happily, this veteran shows no
signs of its age: a new management team has added its own distinctive flair and made it a welcoming, kid-friendly hot spot—parents will
enjoy the babysitting service. The little ones will even go for the interior decor: guest rooms have modular furniture and are accented with
primary colors (even the spotless baths). The downstairs restaurant,
Feeloch ($$–$$$), is a popular spot for grill and cheese dishes. The
eclectic menu includes red-pesto chicken, T-bone steaks, raclette, and
fondue. And the Ice Box Bar is a great spot to reboot after a day on
the mountain. **Pros:** half-board included in the rates; certain packages
include use of sister hotel Ferienart's comprehensive spa and wellness
center. **Cons:** roaring with the thunder, not pitter-patter, of little feet;
some feel the hotel merits three-star, rather than four-star, status. ⊠
Saas-Fee ☎*027/9581600* ⊕*www.duglacier.ch* ⇆*36 rooms, 4 suites*
⌂*In-room: safe, Ethernet. In-hotel: 2 restaurants, bar, spa, children's
programs* ▤*AE, DC, MC, V* ﺗﻌﻠﻢ*MAP.*

$$–$$$ ⊡ **Unique Dom Hotel.** Follow the snowboarders who flock to Popcorn,
the wildly popular on-site bar and gear boutique, to find this contemporary hotel—a place where a traditional exterior belies a funky interior. Modern furnishings in vibrant colors and unusual shapes fill the
lobby lounge. The amply sized rooms with modular furniture all have
TV-stereo combinations loaded with Sony PlayStations. **Pros:** laid-back,
chilled atmosphere; the hotel's bars are legendary party spots. **Cons:** if
you weren't born in the 1980s (or 1990s!), you'll be older than most;
some say the nighttime noise levels can be a problem, so bring earplugs.
⊠ *Saas-Fee* ☎*027/9587700* ⊕*www.uniquedom.com* ⇆*40 rooms*
⌂*In-room: Wi-Fi. In-hotel: restaurant, 2 bars, public Internet* ▤*AE,
DC, MC, V* ﺗﻌﻠﻢ*CP.*

$$$$ ⊡ **Waldhotel Fletschhorn.** Once a customhouse, this quiet, sophisticated
★   *Landgasthof* (country inn) is set apart from the resort at the end of a
forested lane. Pine paneling, antiques, and serene views mellow the

rooms' ultramodern fittings and rotating contemporary art exhibits. Not a detail goes unnoticed—even the floors are pampered, with colorful, exotic rugs to cushion your every step. The hotel's restaurant is a culinary delight. **Pros:** staff will pick you up in an electric car at the station, half-board is a steal at only 95 SF per person. **Cons:** 25-minute walk from the village; not amenity-heavy; this Relais & Châteaux property is so lovely you may not want to ever leave; does this setting need jazzy modern art? ⊠ *Saas-Fee* ☎*027/9572131* ⊕*www.fletschhorn. ch* ⌂*13 rooms, 2 suites* ⚿*In-room: Wi-Fi. In-hotel: restaurant, steam room* ▤*AE, DC, MC, V* ☼*Closed late Apr.–early June and mid-Oct.– early Dec.* ⎮◎⎮*CP.*

$$ ⛰ **Wellness Hotel Pirmin Zurbriggen.** Move into the valley without compromising quality at this upscale guesthouse owned and run by a local world champion and his equally athletic wife. Tucked back on a country lane across from the Saas-Almagell lift, the lodge mixes ultra-modern public and spa areas with traditional guest rooms. Enjoy an aperitif in front of the trophy-laden glass case while pondering your next downhill run. The restaurant is the showpiece here—a vast, glowing, wood-trimmed, cathedral-ceiling space warmed up by antiques and good food. **Pros:** pool with built-in cinema makes for incredible movie nights; 1,000-square-meter spa. **Cons:** children two years old or more pay half the adult price; isolated location requires a walk to town. ⊠*Saas-Almagell* ☎*027/9572301* ⊕*www.zurbriggen.ch* ⌂*24 rooms, 2 suites, 2 apartments* ⚿*In-room: safe, refrigerator, Ethernet. In-hotel: restaurant, bar, pool* ▤*AE, DC, MC, V* ⎮◎⎮*MAP.*

NIGHTLIFE & THE ARTS

BARS &   A popular dance zone, **Vernissage** (☎*027/9581904*) is located at the
DANCING   Ferienart Walliserhof hotel. The **Metropol Hotel** (☎*027/9571001*) hosts late-night revelers with mixed music sets at **Crazy Night Disco** and offers spirits at **John's Pub.** People often squeeze into **Nesti's** (☎*027/9574112*), a perennial après-ski favorite. Snowboarders and a younger crowd congregate for brews at **Popcorn** (☎*027/9587706*) at the Unique Hotel Dom. **The Living Room Bar** (☎*027/9587700*) is another hot spot at the Unique Hotel Dom.

MUSIC   Like other resorts, Saas-Fee is not without echoes of symphonies and chorus groups during its summer months. The **International Alpine Music Festival** and **Summer Festival** please audiences in July and August with orchestral performances and chamber music concerts. Bookings and ticket information are available through the tourist office.

SPORTS & THE OUTDOORS

HIKING   Larch forests, flower and herb-filled meadows, and glacial zones offer a huge variety of trails (350 km [218 mi]) at all levels of difficulty. Historic routes cross passes into Italy and extend outbound along ridgelines toward the Rhône River. Bus and lift services make it easy to return to the village in time for dinner. Most hotels will pack a lunch for the outing, or you can stop at buvettes (snack bars) scattered along the trails. **Sentier des Chapelles (Trail of the Chapels)** is a time-worn pilgrimage route from Saas-Fee to Saas-Grund featuring 15 shrines with costumed wooden statues strung along the path like beads on a rosary.

MOUNTAIN
CLIMBING

The **Bergfürerbüro** (☏027/9574464) conducts daily guided forays year-round; you can rent season-appropriate equipment. Another popular activity is gorge crossing, which uses safety cables and pulleys to traverse the valley's deep divide. There are also a few *via ferrata* (ironway), preset routes with ladders and cables secured in place to challenge climbers at all stages of competence.

SLEDDING
☽

Your stay won't be complete without a few runs on the **Feeblitz** (☏027/9573111), the curved and looped track of the *Rodelbobbahn* (bobsled) near the Alpin Express cable-car station.

SPORTS
CENTER

The **Bielen Recreation Center** (☏027/9572475) has a four-lane swimming pool, children's pool, whirlpools, steam baths, sauna, solarium, table tennis, billiards, badminton, and two indoor-tennis courts.

BRIG & THE ALPINE PASSES

This region is the Grand Central Station of the Alps. All mountain passes lead to or through Brig, as traffic and rail lines pour in from Italy, the Ticino, central Switzerland, and the Berner Oberland. It is also a transit link for Paris, Brussels, London, and Rome. The Simplon, Nufenen, Grimsel, and Furka passes provide exit options and stunning vistas dependent on destination. Northeast of this critical junction the spectacular Aletsch Glacier, the largest in Europe, straddles the cantons of Valais and Bern. The Rhône River becomes increasingly wild and silty until you arrive at its source in Gletsch, at the end of the valley called Goms.

BRIG

19 km (12 mi) southeast of Leukerbad.

GETTING HERE

Car-free Saas-Fee is on a bus-line connection with Brig (1 hr, 18 SF) and Visp (45 mins, 15.80 SF); take the train here from Brig by transferring at Visp or connect with Zermatt by rail with a transfer at Stalden-Saas.

Visitor Information (✉ *Train station* ☏027/9216030 ⊕ *www.brig.ch/tourismus*).

EXPLORING

A rail and road junction joining four cantons, this small but vital town has for centuries been a center of trade with Italy. Often overlooked as merely a transit point, the town has a legacy that can be appreciated in a couple of hours: a restored core with cobblestone streets, shops, cafés, and the main attraction, the fairy tale–worthy merchant's castle.

Fodor's Choice
★

The fantastical **Stockalperschloss,** a massive Baroque castle, was built between 1658 and 1678 by Prince Kaspar Jodok von Stockalper und Thurm (1609-91), a Swiss tycoon who made his fortune in Italian trade over the Simplon Pass. Soaring spectacularly with three towers topped with gilt onion domes and containing a courtyard lined by elegant Italianate arcades, it was once Switzerland's largest private home and is now restored. Inside are libraries, archives, and some Baroque period rooms. Group tours in English are available upon request. To get here from the station, walk up Bahnhofstrasse to Sebastienplatz; then turn left onto Alte Simplonstrasse. ⊠ *Alte Simplonstr. 28* ☎ *027/9216030* 🕾 *7 SF* ⊙ *May–Sept., Tues.–Sun., guided tours at 9:30, 10:30, 1:30, 2:30, 3:30, and 4:30. May and Oct. no tour at 4:30.*

> ### VIEWS OF THE PAST
>
> From the summit of Simplon Pass you can still see parts of the old road used by traders and Napoléon, and it's easy to imagine the hardships travelers faced at these heights. Look north toward the Bernese Alps to see a portion of the massive Aletsch Glacier.

SIMPLON PASS

23 km (14 mi) southeast of Brig.

Beginning just outside Brig, this historic road meanders through deep gorges and wide, barren, rock-strewn pastures to offer increasingly beautiful views back toward Brig. At the summit (6,593 feet), the **Hotel Bellevue Simplon-Kulm** shares the high meadow with the **Simplon Hospitz** (Simplon Hospice), built 150 years ago at Napoléon's request and now owned by the monks of St. Bernard. Just beyond stands the bell-towered **Alt Spital**, a lodging built in the 17th century. Beyond the pass, the road continues through Italy, and it's possible to cut across the Italian upthrust and reenter Switzerland in the Ticino, near Ascona.

OFF THE BEATEN PATH

Simplon Tunnel. If you'd rather ride than drive, you can hop aboard (or load your car on) the train through this tunnel, which starts above the eastern outskirts of Brig and runs nearly 20 km (12 mi) before ending in Italian daylight. The first of the twin tunnels—once the world's longest railway tunnels—was started in 1898 and took six years to complete.

ALETSCH

★ *13 km (8 mi) north of Brig.*

GETTING HERE

Car-free Alpine villages are often at the terminus of a rail line. Rierdalp's transportation link to the Rhône Valley is a giant gondola that lifts passengers from the village of Mörel to the hamlet above. Commuters with shopping bags, workmen lugging tool boxes, and travelers with wheeled-suitcases and skis fill the cabin, which holds 80. The Aletsch Riederalp Bergbahn is located across the street from the Mörel train station, a stop on the Matterhorn Gornergrat line. The 16-minute ride covers nearly 2,000 meters, stopping at the middle station for a handful of residents who board using a silolike elevator. Electric carts from hotels meet the half-hourly arrivals and departures. The round-trip fare is 28 SF. More transfer information can be found at www.riederalpbahnen.ch.

CLOSE UP

Europe's Longest Glacier—But for How Long?

11

Aletsch's famous glacier—24 km (15 mi)—was at its longest 150 years ago, but now recedes 100–165 feet a year. Concern about the recession of the earth's ice formations has made preserving the Aletsch Glacier internationally significant. So UNESCO designated a 250-square-km (97-square-mi) area around the glacier, shared between the cantons of Valais (77%) and Bern (23%), as a protected site. Generations ago the Swiss sensed the need to safeguard the area and began placing parts in conservationist hands.

The glacier's starting point, Concordia Platz, is the confluence of three ice masses that move down from the Bernese Alps. Here the ice has been measured as deep as 2,952 feet— over twice the height of the Empire State Building. Another magnificent formation, the Mäjelensee is a lake with icebergs floating on top, carved into the glacier field with walls of ice and stone. As the glacier's ice recedes, nature reclaims the land,

first with moss and small plants, then forest. Pro Natura, the conservation organization that oversees the region, describes the process as "forest emerging from ice." Though some of the area's pine and larch are 600–700 years old, extreme conditions keep them short. Animals thought to be extinct thrive here; chamois, marten, badgers, lizards, and birds have adapted to the elevation and temperature.

Cable cars ferry tourists to ridge tops above Ried and Fiesch, where 360-degree views of the sweep of ice are framed by extraordinary peaks. You can see the Bernese Alps, including the Sphinx station on the Jungfraujoch called the "Top of Europe"; the Valaisan Alps; and even into Italy and France. Hiking trails lead to the glacier's edge, and guides take trekkers across parts of the ice field. All around are places to admire nature's grandeur and be grateful for its protection.

EXPLORING

Ice-capped peaks with small mountain resorts staggered up their spines rim the Aletsch, a glacier that shares its name with the area surrounding it, paralleling the valley floor. A variety of ecological zones—from deep, frozen expanses in the center to forests emerging at the fringes—are part of a wilderness region that is now firmly in the hands of conservationists, protected as a UNESCO international nature site. In contrast to these extreme expanses, sunny south-facing slopes are active with skiers and hikers staying in the villages of Riederalp, Bettmeralp, and Fiescheralp.

Villa Cassel, a turn-of-the-20th-century mansion, was considered a wealthy Englishman's folly when the Tudor-style structure was installed on the rugged pass above the village of Ried. It has weathered time well and is now the headquarters for **Pro Natura Zentrum Aletsch,** an environmental education center. The naturalist organization offers guided tours, glacier walks, and expeditions to spot marmots and eagles. In addition, the center offers self-directed paths, an Alpine garden, a tearoom, and even dorm and private rooms for overnight stays. Some information is available in English; prices vary according to the activity.

To access the facility, take the cable car from Morel to Riederalp. From the village station it's a 30-minute walk, but more appealing and challenging is the hike from Moosfluh (an additional gondola ride) where you can catch views of the glacier rimmed by its old-growth Alpine forest. ⌂ *Riederalp* ☎ *027/9286220* ⊕ *www.pronatura.ch/aletsch* ⌐ *8 SF* ⊙ *Mid-June–mid-Oct., daily 9–6.*

SKIING

The three resorts of **Riederalp, Bettmeralp,** and **Fiescheralp** are connected by trails, lifts, and shuttle buses. There are 33 lifts and 83 km (52 mi) of runs, a quarter of which are expert and peak at 9,415 feet. A one-day lift ticket for access to the whole Aletsch ski area costs 56 SF; a six-day pass costs 294 SF. All of the essentials are in place in these picture-book villages, but don't expect lots of amenities, varied dining choices, or glitzy nightlife. Riederalp is best known as the home of Art Furrer, who became famous in the United States as one of the pioneers of free-style skiing. His ski school, the **Skischule Forum Alpin** (☎ *027/9284488* ⊕ *www.artfurrer.ch*) is still up and running. You will see his name on everything from hotel placards to the weather Web cam.

WHERE TO STAY

$$–$$$$ 🏨 **Wellness Resort Alpenrose.** Ski legend Art Furrer returned to his village and became the recreational and hospitality backbone of the community; this hotel is the most upscale in his portfolio. Perched on a ledge with views shared by Swiss and Italians, the multibuilding complex combines a traditional hotel with newer structures connected by covered walkways. Dining areas satisfy demi-pension and à la carte diners. **Pros:** the pizzeria is a popular draw for oven-fired pies; the spa—with pool, sauna, and massage options—shares spectacular vistas. **Cons:** standard rooms above the lobby and busy dining venues show their age; uninspired decor. ⌂ *Riederalp* ☎ *027/9284545* ⊕ *www.artfurrer.ch* ⌐ *35 rooms, 18 suites* ⌂ *In-room: safe, refrigerator, Wi-Fi. In-hotel: 3 restaurants (1 only in summer), bar, spa* ⊟ *AE, DC, MC, V* ⊙ *Closed Easter–mid-June and mid-Oct.–mid-Dec.* ⊡ *CP.*

EN ROUTE   If the day is clear, grab the chance for a spectacular ride to the top of one of the lofty peaks that shadow the roadway by taking the **Fiesch cable car** (☎ *027/9712700*) up to Eggishorn (9,303 feet). The panoramic views of Alps and glaciers will leave you breathless. As the cable car rotates 360 degrees, you can tick off famous Bernese and Valaisan peaks. The Jungfrau, Eiger, Matterhorn, and Dom are clearly visible, as are peaks that lie across the border in Italy and France.

Vaud

LAUSANNE, ROUTE DU VIGNOBLE, MONTREUX,
VEVEY, LES ALPES VAUDOISES

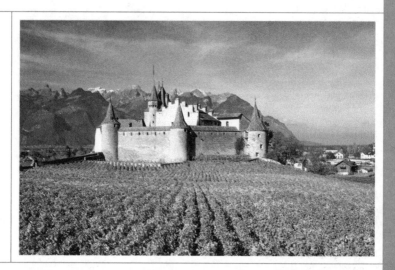

Chateau d'Aigle

WORD OF MOUTH

"If the weather is fine, the following easy walk rewards you with
an incredible view. Take a train from Geneva to Vevey, train it
to Puisdoux-chexbres, and walk down the steep vineyard to the
lakeshore—here, the wine village of St-Saphorin offers breathtaking vistas of Lac Léman and the French Savoie Alps."

—Kappa

WELCOME TO VAUD

TOP REASONS TO GO

★ **Montreux's Promenade du Lac:** Walk three magical miles along Lac Léman to the Château de Chillon, Switzerland's most beautiful castle.

★ **Tramping with Charlie Chaplin:** Vevey commemorates its celebrated citizen in bronze at its lake rose garden and is designing a museum in his honor in Corsier.

★ **Lausanne's table for two:** Acolyte of superchef Fredy Girardet, Philippe Rochat is now a master culinary king in his own right.

★ **The grape escape:** From La Côte to Chablais, vineyards and wine cellars allow you to sip vintages that seldom make it beyond the border.

★ **Palatial pursuits:** Grandes dames of luxury, the Beau Rivage Palace and Montreux Palace hotels even synchronize their gilded awnings to the sun's daily tour over the lake.

1 La Côte. Studded with wine villages, this region is famed for its châteaux—Coppet's housed Madame de Staël, Pragins displays Swiss history, and Morges has 10,000 miniature lead soldiers in residence. But don't miss waterside Nyon, founded by Julius Caesar.

12

GETTING ORIENTED

From Lord Byron to Audrey Hepburn, beauty lovers have always been attracted to the crescent-shaped, glacier-fed Lac Léman (aka Lake Geneva). Beyond its dockside villages and vineyards, more urban desires can be sated by Lausanne's cathedral architecture, modern art, and fine dining.

3 Lavaux Vignobles & Riviera. Set amid wine villages, the gorgeously picturesque Corniche de la Vaud heads toward Vevey, home to Nestlé food giant. Globetrotters have always loved this romantic town— Rousseau, Henry James, and Hemingway are just a few who loved taking walks here. More modern is Montreux: spilling down the hill to a sunny bay, this usually tranquil city goes hot-cool when the Jazz Festival takes over in July.

2 Lausanne. Not quite the city it was when Voltaire, Rousseau, and Victor Hugo waxed passionate about its beauty, Lausanne is largely a modern maze, but here and there you'll enjoy a burnt-orange jumble of medieval rooftops, shuttered windows with flower boxes, and misty Lac Léman and the Alps. Happily, the art and nightlife scenes are lively.

VAUD PLANNER

How's the Weather?

The lake sparkles and clouds lift from Mont Blanc from spring to fall; November tends to be drizzly gray, and then winter brightens things up above the plain (as they call the flatter terrain surrounding the lake).

Crowds monopolize Montreux and Chillon year-round, but overwhelm them in July (jazz festival time) and August (Europe-wide vacations).

It's worth aiming for concert and dance season in Lausanne: from September through May.

Remember that at these latitudes summer daylight extends until 9 PM, allowing you to pack a lot into one day; the reverse is true in winter.

In Search of the Perfect Lunch

Because of its sunny, scenic position, the Lac Léman shore draws weekenders and car tourists who speed along the waterfront highway, careening through cobbled wine towns in search of the perfect meal.

As in all great wine regions, *dégustation* (wine tasting) and *haute gastronomie* (refined cuisine) go hand in hand.

In inns and auberges throughout La Côte and Lavaux (the two stretches of vineyard-lined shore) you'll dine beside ascoted oenophiles who lower their half lenses to study a label. They then go on to order a multicourse feast to complement their extensive tastings.

To experience Vaud's best cuisine, look for *déjeuners d'affaires* (business lunches), plats du jour, and prix-fixe menus, which can offer considerable savings over à la carte dining.

Of course, you will be spoiled for choice by the quality of Lausanne's restaurants.

Prices—like quality—can be high, but if you wander through the backstreets you will see that the less affluent in Lausanne eat well, too.

Happy surpise: even some department stores have excellent inexpensive restaurants and cafés.

WHAT IT COSTS IN SWISS FRANCS				
¢	$	$$	$$$	$$$$
RESTAURANTS				
under 15 SF	15 SF–25 SF	25 SF–40 SF	40 SF–60 SF	over 60 SF
HOTELS				
under 100 SF	100 SF–175 SF	175 SF–250 SF	250 SF–350 SF	over 350 SF

Restaurant prices are per person for a main course at dinner. Hotel prices are for two people in a standard double room in high season, including tax and service.

Finding a Place to Stay

It's a pleasure unique to Vaud to wake up, part floor-length sheers, and look out over Lac Léman to Mont Blanc. A series of 19th-century grand hotels with banks of balconied lakeview rooms were created to offer this luxury to such grand-tourists as Strauss, Twain, Stravinsky, and Henry James. Yet there's no shortage of charming inns offering similar views on an intimate scale. The hotels of Lausanne and Montreux are long on luxury and grace, and low prices are not easy to find. Especially at peak periods— Christmas–New Year's and June–August—it's important to book ahead. These days, in-room Internet connections, safes, and business centers are the rule rather than the exception. Small auberges in the villages along the lake, and the vineyards offer traditional dishes and simple comforts. At the cantonal tourist office Web site, www.lake-geneva-region.ch, you can scan hotel facilities and rates, then click to reserve.

Making the Most of Your Time

To experience the highlights of lake and mountain, reserve five days. Spend two savoring Lausanne and its Old Town, museums, and hyperactive waterfront. Dine at one of the region's top restaurants; lunch will leave more funds in your travel budget than an evening meal. The Corniche route winds its way through the vineyards and hamlets of the Lavaux. Pull-offs are strategically interspersed for photo-ops and to steady the nerves of drivers not used to narrow, cantilevered roadways. Get out and walk a section of the wine trail and definitely taste a glass of white wine. A few hours in the harbor-front town of Vevey, especially its older section and the glitzy, Riviera-like city of Montreux will suffice. A visit to the region would be incomplete without a tour of Chillon—the fabled fortress that inspired Lord Byron to pen his famous poem "Prisoner of Chillon." For a good night's sleep in the brisk mountain air, hop a train from Montreux or take the winding drive to Villars-sur-Ollon, where chalet architecture contrasts dramatically with contemporary museums and estate homes of the lowlands. Break in the new day with an Alpine walk before doubling back down the steep canyon for connections to Nyon for a dose of Roman history. Extra days enable you to explore a *vignoble* (vineyard) and surrounding wine village like Lutry or Aigle, shop village markets, or cruise the lake on one of those red-and-white steamers you have seen crisscrossing the waterfront.

Visitor Information

The main regional tourist office is located in Lausanne.

Office du Tourisme du Canton de Vaud (⊠ *60 ave. d'Ouchy, Lausanne* ☎ *021/6132626* ⊕ *www.lake-geneva-region.ch*).

Transportation Basics

Excellent rail and bus service links towns, depositing commuters and travelers at clean, well-lit stations in the heart of everything.

If driving, rent the smallest car your physique and luggage will allow, as narrow lanes in wine villages and parking in cities are headaches.

To access wineries in La Côte and Chablais and to traverse the Corniche road of the Lavaux, a car is essential.

Intercity trains stopping in Nyon, Morges, Lausanne, Vevey, and Montreux dovetail their schedules for transfers to local S-trains and buses.

You'll discover that the best of the region—either city or countryside—can easily be experienced on foot.

Supplement your travels with an occasional taxi or public transit when the grade becomes too steep or your legs too weary.

GETTING AROUND

By Car

There are two major arteries leading to Lac Léman, one entering from the north via Bern and Fribourg (A12), the other arcing over the north shore of Lac Léman from Geneva to Lausanne (A1), then to Montreux and on south through the Alpes Vaudoises toward the Col du Grand St-Bernard (A9) in Canton Valais. They are swift and often scenic expressways, and the north-shore artery (A1 and A9) traces a route that has been followed since before Roman times.

Secondary highways parallel the expressways, but this is one case where, as the larger road sits higher on the lakeside slopes, the views from the expressway are often better than those from the highway. Be sure, however, to detour for the Corniche road views between Lausanne and Vevey.

Parking within cities and major towns is difficult and zone restricted. Although expensive, opt for public garages that are clearly signed whenever possible. Take the ticket with you after entry, as payment is made via automated machines at the pedestrian entrance; many locations accept credit cards. The ticket returned after payment is your access card to exit.

By Bus

A useful network of postbus routes covers the region for the resourceful traveler (with plenty of time) who desires connections to outlying villages and hamlets; some routes are covered only once or twice a day.

The signature yellow buses pick up at rail stations and drop off at rural post offices, harking back to the day when they were the main source of mail delivery. Schedules are available from tourist offices and rail stations; in smaller towns at the post office.

Lausanne has an excellent city bus network called the *tl* (Transports Publics de la région Lausannoise) that includes the Metro (m2–a subway that runs uphill through the city from the port of Ouchy), and commuter rail lines that bring passengers in from near suburbs.

Fares depend on how many zones you transit—tickets start at 2.60 SF for single trip or 7.60 SF all day; *Mobilis*, a pass that combines all rail and bus services, starts at 7.60 SF. The Lausanne Transport Card provided to all hotel guests is free, and so are your rides on local buses, trains and the Metro. If you plan to stay out late club hopping, a *pajama service* runs on most lines until 2 AM.

Throughout the Riviera, bus service is provided by *VMCV* (Vevey-Montreux-Chillon-Villeneuve). The Line 1 trolley bus parallels the lakefront and is the most heavily used. Spur routes to the villages of Corsier, Blonay, and others are part of the network, while separately operated funiculars from Vevey and Territet take passengers to the hill towns of Mt. Pelerin and Glion.

Tickets on all transportation lines are purchased at automated machines either located at the stop or once on board (at the rear, not from the driver).

Hotel guests receive a Riviera Card that allows gratis rides on buses and reduced fares on other modes of transportation, and if you have a Swiss Pass you can travel free on city buses and funiculars in the country and access all national museums.

PostBus (☎084/8888888 ⊕www.swisspost.ch).
tl (☎090/0564900 toll call ⊕www.t-l.ch). **VMCV** (☎021/9891818 ⊕www.vmcv.ch).

By Train

Lausanne lies on a major train route between Bern and Geneva, with express trains connecting from Basel and Zürich. From Geneva, trains take about 30 minutes and arrive in Lausanne up to four times an hour; from Bern they take a little more than an hour and arrive twice an hour. TGVs (high-speed trains) run to and from Paris in about four hours and have 10 schedule options. The Cisalpino train to Milan and to Venice has at least four daily departures, plus connecting service via Brig. There is also a Euronuit (night sleeper) connection to Italian cities.

Regional trains along the waterfront, connecting major lake towns, are frequent and swift unless you board one of the S-trains that stops at every village. Travel time between centers like Geneva and Nyon, or Lausanne and Vevey is about 15 minutes; count on doubling that on an S-train.

There are no conductors on the local lines to check tickets, but be assured there are random audits and stiff fines for those who board without paying. Tickets for all rail services can be purchased at automated machines on the station platforms.

There are also several private rail systems leading into small villages and rural regions, including the Montreux–Oberland–Bernois (MOB) Railroad's Golden Pass, which climbs sharply behind Montreux and cuts straight over the pre-Alps toward Château-d'Oex and the Berner Oberland. Reserve space in one of their glass-dome, panoramic cars and take in the countryside with food and beverage service brought to your seat.

The historic Blonay–Chamby Railroad has steam-powered seasonal excursions, as does the Rochers-de-Naye line. From Nyon, the red-and-orange cars of the Nyon–St-Cergue-Morez Railroad deliver passengers to St-Cergue in 30 minutes, before going on to the border town of La Cure and into France.

The Swiss Pass is accepted on these private lines, but there may be an additional fee for panoramic excursions. Inquire at local tourist offices or train stations about a regional pass that combines rail, boat, bus, and cable-car excursions on these private transports at a reduced fee.

Blonay–Chamby Railroad (☎021/9432121 ⊕www.blonay-chamby.ch). **Montreux–Oberland–Bernois Railroad** (MOB ☎021/9898181 ⊕www.mob.ch). **SBB** (☎090/0300300 (toll call) ⊕www.rail.ch).

By Boat & Ferry

Like all fair-size Swiss lakes, Lac Léman is crisscrossed with comfortable and reasonably swift steamers, here run by the Compagnie Générale de Navigation. In summer they sometimes run more often than the trains that parallel their routes. With a Swiss Pass you travel free. You can embark and disembark freely at ports along the way. The trip from one end of the lake to the other will take the better part of a day, as routes are designed to serve a third of the lake per circuit, connecting towns on both the French and Swiss sides. Shorter trips like the one from Lausanne to Vevey will take an hour.

Compagnie Générale de Navigation (☎084/8811848 ⊕www.cgn.ch).

By Air

Geneva's Cointrin is the second-busiest international airport in Switzerland. From Cointrin, Swiss connects to other airports throughout the country. Low-cost carrier easyJet also serves a number of European destinations. Both Zürich's Kloten and Geneva's Cointrin have rail stations connected by sky bridges in adjacent terminals making it a snap to transit to all major towns in the region.

Cointrin Airport (✉60 km [38 mi] southwest of Lausanne ☎022/7177111 ⊕www.gva.ch).

Updated
by Kay
Winzenried

IN JUST ONE REGION, you can experience a complete cultural, gastronomic, and scenic sweep of Switzerland. Vaud (pronounced Voh) has a stunning Gothic cathedral (Lausanne) and one of Europe's most evocative châteaux (Chillon), palatial hotels and weathered-wood chalets, sophisticated culture and ancient folk traditions, snowy Alpine slopes and balmy lake resorts, simple fondue, and the finesse of some of the world's great chefs. Everywhere there are the roadside vineyards with luxurious rows of vines and rich, black loam.

This is the region of Lac Léman (Lake Geneva), a grand body of water graced by Lausanne and Montreux. The lake's romance—Savoy Alps looming across the horizon, steamers fanning across its surface, palm trees rustling along its shores—made it a focal point of the budding 19th-century tourist industry and an inspiration to the arts. In a Henry James novella the imprudent Daisy Miller made waves when she crossed its waters unchaperoned to visit Chillon; Byron's Bonivard languished in chains in the fortress's dungeons. In their homes outside Montreux, Stravinsky wrote *The Rite of Spring* and Strauss his transcendent *Four Last Songs*. And perhaps going from the sublime to the ridiculous, film fans of James Bond will remember Sean Connery's car chase through the hillsides around Lac Léman in hot pursuit of Auric Goldfinger's Rolls as it swept its way to the villain's Swiss factory, neatly tucked in the mountains north of the lake.

Throughout the canton French is spoken, and the temperament the Vaudoise inherited from the Romans and Burgundians sets them apart from their Swiss-German fellow citizens. It's evident in their humor, their style, and—above all—their love of their own good wine.

EXPLORING VAUD

Lac Léman is a graceful swelling in the Rhône River, which passes through the northern hook of the Valais and channels between the French and Vaudoise Alps before breaking into the open at Bouveret, west of Villeneuve. The lake is shared by three of Switzerland's great French cities, grandes dames of the Suisse Romande: Lausanne, Montreux, and Geneva. Though the lake's southern shore lies in France's Haute-Savoie, the green hillsides of the north portion and the cluster of nearby Alps that looms over its east end are all part of the canton of Vaud.

LA CÔTE

Just northeast of Geneva, La Côte (the shore) of Lac Léman has been settled since Roman times, with its south-facing slopes cultivated for wine. It is thus peppered with ancient waterfront and hillside towns, castles, and Roman remnants. Train and bus service connects most towns and villages, but a car is a must if you want to wind through tiny wine villages. Do get out and walk—if only to hear the trickling of any number of Romanesque trough fountains and to saunter along a lakefront promenade. Be willing to traverse a few times from the slopes

La Côte

VAUD

Chéserex

A1
A9

1

Bière

Vufflens-
le-Château

St-Sulpice

A9

Pully

Bussy

Aubonne

A1

Morges

Lutry

Route du Vignoble

Lausanne
see detail
map

St-Cergue

Bursins

Rolle

Allaman

Luins

Lac Léman

Gingins

Gland

Cheseaux

Prangins

Evian-les-
Bains

FRANCE

Nyon

Divonne-
les-Bains

Céligny

La Dranse

Coppet

FRANCE

Mies

A1

Versoix

KEY

Rail lines

Vésenaz

GENÈVE

0   6 mi

SWITZERLAND

Genève

0   6 km

A1a

to the waterfront and back if you're determined to cover all the region's
charms; sticking exclusively to either the diminutive Route du Vignoble
or the shore road deprives you of some wonderful sights.

COPPET

9 km (6 mi) south of Nyon, 46 km (28 mi) southwest of Lausanne.

GETTING HERE

Coppet is but the first of many towns that rim Lac Léman and are
strung along a main rail line in synchronized links approximately 20
minutes apart. Main stations like Morges, Nyon, Lausanne, Vevey, and
Montreux are served by all trains (regional and inter-regional) allowing
multiple arrivals and departures every hour; Coppet, Rolle, Lutry, Cully,
St-Saphorin by the local S-trains every half hour. Ticket prices vary with
short runs costing 3–5 SF and longer ones 10–15 SF. For departure times
and prices for trains and buses for most destinations in this chapter,
check with www.sbb.ch—the main Swiss public transportation Web
site—or call 0900/300300 (toll call). Remember, if you have a Swiss
Pass or another rail-discount card, it also applies to the buses.

EXPLORING

Its pretty, arcaded main street, with occasional peeks through to the jettied waterfront, makes Coppet a pleasant stop for a stroll.

★ But it's the **Château de Coppet** that puts this lake village on the map. Enclosed within vast iron gates, the château has been kept in its original 18th-century form, with luxurious Louis XVI furnishings arranged in a convincingly lived-in manner; its grounds, which harbor grand old trees, hidden courtyards, and stone stairs, are equally evocative.

Built in the 1300s, the château was restored when purchased in 1784 by Jacques Necker, a Genevan banker who served as financial minister to France's Louis XVI. The turmoil of the French Revolution and Necker's opposition to Napoléon forced him into exile in this splendid structure, where his remarkable daughter, Madame de Staël, created the most intriguing salon in Europe. Her intellectual sparkle and concern for the fiery issues of the day attracted the giants of the early Romantic period: Lord Byron, the Swiss historian Jean-Charles Sismondi, the German writer August Wilhelm von Schlegel, and British historian Edward Gibbon. Part of the château is still occupied by family descendants, but you can see the interior on a guided tour. The language of the commentary is generally chosen according to the language of the tour participants. Tours in English are not always available. ⊠*3 chemin des Murs, uphill from waterfront highway* ☎*022/7761028* ⊕*www.swisscastles. ch* 🎟*10 SF* ☉*Apr.–Oct., daily 2–6.*

WHERE TO STAY

$$$ 🏨**Hôtel du Lac.** First ranked as a *grand logis* in 1628 to distinguish it from a common roadhouse, this historic inn still feels like an exclusive men's club, catering to power-lunchers and well-heeled travelers. It fronts on the main road and is accessible by boat, with a sycamore-shaded terrace and rooms with exposed beams, niches, and antiques. Its inventive restaurant draws a regular clientele for its exquisite open-grill specialties. Reservations for the restaurant are essential. **Pros:** a step back in time with subtle modern links; old-style restaurant is a regional draw. **Cons:** located in a tiny village with little to do; weekend family celebrations dominate the terrace and dining room. ⊠*51 Grand-Rue* ☎*022/9608000* 🖨*022/9608001* ⊕*www.hoteldulac.ch* 🛏*12 rooms, 4 suites, 3 apartments* ♿*In-room: refrigerator, kitchen (some), Wi-Fi. In-hotel: restaurant, bar, parking (no fee)* ☰*AE, DC, MC, V* ⍾*CP.*

EN ROUTE With its lakefront setting, small port, lawns for sunbathing, and pier, the endearing village of **Céligny** provides the best swimming opportunities for miles around. The enclave, 6 km (4 mi) north of Coppet, is wholly charming: rows of vineyards, a historic (but private) château and church, and a village square adorned with flowers and a stone fountain. Richard Burton made his home here during the last years of his life. You can visit the village cemetery, where you'll find Burton's simple grave in the smaller area, hugging the edge of the forest.

12

Tour Options

Walking tours led by local historians in Lausanne, Vevey, and Montreux are increasingly popular. They are organized by the towns' tourist offices and are given daily between April and September. English-speaking guides are often available, but you should call in advance to check. Most local tourist offices offer daily general tours in summer to Gruyères, to Chamonix and Mont Blanc, to the Alps by coach, and to Les Avants and Château-d'Oex by the Montreux–Oberland–Bernois railroad line's panoramic train. There is also a chocolate excursion to the Nestlé factory in Broc. To ensure a tour with English commentary, reserve in advance.

The two drop-by branches of the Lausanne tourist office (in the Gare Centrale at 9 pl. de la Gare) run a daily two-hour coach trip into the Old Town, including a visit to the cathedral and an extended city coach tour that takes in the Lavaux vineyards.

NYON

10 km (6 mi) north of Coppet, 27 km (17 mi) southwest of Lausanne.

GETTING HERE

Nyon is one of the main stations of the main rail line that goes along the shore of Lac Léman, served by all trains (regional and inter-regional), allowing multiple arrivals and departures every hour.

Visitor Information (⊠*8 ave. Viollier* ☎*022/3656600* ⊕*www.nyon.ch*).

EXPLORING

Lovely Nyon, with its waterfront drive, shops, museums, and a castle dominating its cliff-top Old Town, was founded by Julius Caesar around 45 BC as a camp for war veterans. The Romans called it Noviodunum and developed the entire region for miles around. Lovely views can be had from the château-museum's terrace and the town's waterfront promenade, where boats and swans bob in the waves.

★ Flanked by a statue of Caesar, the **Musée Romain** *(Roman Museum)* contains an attractively mounted collection of sumptuously detailed architectural stonework, fresco fragments, statuary, mosaics, and earthenware. Closed for renovation January to July 2009, the museum was built atop foundations of a 1st-century AD basilica; a pristine miniature model inside and an excellent trompe l'oeil palace on an outside wall evoke the remarkable original structure. A complete listing of the exhibits in English is available upon request, as are guided tours. ⊠*Rue Maupertuis* ☎*022/3617591* ⊕*www.mrn.ch* ✉*8 SF includes Musée du Léman and Château de Nyon* ⊗*Apr.–Oct., Tues.–Sun. 10–5; Nov.–Mar., Tues.–Sun. 2–5.*

Dominating Nyon's hilltop over the waterfront is **Le Château de Nyon**, a magnificent 12th-century multispire fortress with a terrace that takes in sweeping views of the lake and Mont Blanc. Its spacious rooms hold the collection of the **Musée Histo-rique,** which traces the history of the castle inhabitants from residence by the Dukes of Savoy (1293–1536) through occupation by the Bernese (1536–1798) to reclamation by the canton following the Vaud revolution. The upper floors held prisioners until 1979, while the city council and courts met in chambers here until 1999. Exhibits throughout highlight the city's position as a renowned porcelain center. Modern-day conversions include a marriage salon and a *caveau des vignerons* (wine cellar) featuring wines of local growers. ⊠ *Pl. du Château* ☎ *022/3638351* ⊕ *www. chateaudenyon.ch* 🎫 *8 SF includes Musée du Léman and Musée Romain* ⊙ *Apr.–Oct., Tues.–Sun. 10–5; Nov.–Mar., Tues.–Sun. 2–5.*

> ### CHÂTEAU COUNTRY
>
> Home to magnificently restored Château de Chillon, Vaud offers a variety of smaller draws as well, including Nyon, Coppet, Prangins, Rolle, Allaman, Aubonne, and Aigle. But the most legendary house was the Villa Diodati, still standing in the Geneva suburb of Cologny. Here, on one stormy night in the summer of 1816, Byron, Shelley, and Shelley's wife, Mary Wollstonecraft Shelley, all competed to think of the most terrifying horror story: Mrs. Shelley's *Frankenstein* took the prize. Scandalously, the municipality auctioned off the villa decor years ago and the house is now private.

♻ Nestled in a charming floral park that parallels the water, the **Musée du Léman** has interactive exhibits about the fragile ecosystems of the lake, recreational boating activities, and coast guard rescue techniques, as well as a sizable lake-water aquarium, housed in a shuttered 18th-century hospital. ⊠ *8 quai Louis-Bonnard* ☎ *022/3610949* ⊕ *www. museeduleman.ch* 🎫 *8 SF includes Musée Romain and Le Château de Nyon* ⊙ *Apr.–Oct., Tues.–Sun. 10–5; Nov.–Mar., Tues–Sun. 2–5.*

WHERE TO EAT

$ ✕ **Auberge du Château.** This traditional restaurant, just steps from Nyon's
SWISS   château, serves straightforward Swiss fare, well-priced plats du jour, and specialty items like shrimp and vegetables on a pillow of saffron cream. In fall the menu expands to include an assortment of game. A big terrace lets diners study the château; in winter broad windows take in the comings and goings on the municipal plaza. ⊠ *8 pl. du Château* ☎ *022/3616312* ⊟ *AE, DC, MC, V.*

$$ ✕ **Café du Marché.** Away from the activity of the castle plaza, this delight-
ITALIAN   ful eatery near the market square has umbrella-shaded tables that spill out onto the cobblestones. Inside, the compact rooms hidden behind lace curtains fill with business associates taking their main meal or entertaining clients. Italian influences accent pasta, lake fish, and produce that may have been plucked from one of the nearby open-air stalls. ⊠ *3 rue du Marché* ☎ *022/3623500* ⊟ *MC, V* ⊙ *Closed Sun.*

WHERE TO STAY

$$$ ⊡ **Hôtel Ambassador.** Terra-cotta stucco and peaked dormers set off this petite hotel on Nyon's main thoroughfare. Request one of the "under the roof" rooms; these have hand-hewn dark wooden beams, floral bedding, and compact modern baths. The quiet garden terrace with its view of

the castle (which is illuminated at night) is an exquisite spot for a glass of wine or a light meal. **Pros:** in upper part of town, which provides best access to sights and shopping; easy parking across the street. **Cons:** older building allows for small layouts; standard fare at the restaurant. ⊠*26 rue St-Jean* ☎*022/9944848* ⊕*www.hotel-ambassador-nyon.ch* ⬅*19 rooms* ⚹*In-room: no a/c, refrigerator, Wi-Fi. In-hotel: restaurant, bar* ⊟*AE, DC, MC, V* ❙⊙❙*CP.*

PRANGINS

3 km (2 mi) northeast of Nyon.

GETTING HERE

Take a train to the Nyon station and switch to local bus service that picks up passengers outside the main entrance. The ride takes seven minutes to the village stop and will cost 3 SF: from there it is a three-minute walk to the château.

EXPLORING

You'll see the elegant hillside château that's home to the national museum before you reach this little commune, where the pace of life moves gently between the boulangerie, post office, and café.

★ The 18th-century **Château de Prangins** is the Suisse Romande branch of the **Musée National Suisse** *(Swiss National Museum).* The castle estate once had land holdings that stretched all the way to Rolle. Its four floors detail (in four languages, including English) Swiss life and history in the 18th and 19th centuries. Surrounded by parks and gardens (take note of the extensive culinary plantings set according to ancient documents), the museum is also a major venue for cultural events and regional celebrations. A café with terrace is open for lunch and refreshments. ☎*022/9948890* ⊕*www.musee-suisse.com* ⊠*7 SF* ⊙*Tues.–Sun. 11–5.*

NEED A BREAK?

After strolling the galleries and gardens of the National Museum, head to **Rapp Chocolatier** (⊠*6 rue des Alpes* ☎*022/3617914* ⊙*Closed Sun.*), a petite chocolate shop in the heart of town. Here handmade confections are stacked in perfect pyramids, and a school and demonstration kitchen are adjacent, so if your timing is right you'll see artisans shaping molten cocoa and plying their forms with heavenly fillings.

WHERE TO STAY

$$$$ 🖼 **La Barcarolle.** Hidden in a parklike setting off the lake road, this mustard-color complex is a modern *relais* (inn) amid historic châteaux and country homes. The hotel's name and musical theme reflect its owner's fondness for great classical composers. Guest rooms with lawn and lake views contain painted furniture and floral furnishings in red and gold. Spacious baths have granite countertops, separate tub and shower, and towel warmers. The bright breakfast room and fine dining area spill onto a wide terrace. French cuisine dominates the menu, which ranges from fish specialties to mint-infused duck on date cinnamon risotto. **Pros:** secluded idyllic retreat; grand rooms

with lots of amenities. **Cons:** must have a car to cover the distance to other villages and activities; restaurant very good, but no other dining choices. ✉*Rte. de Promenthoux* ☎*022/3657878* ⊕*www.labarca-rolle.ch* ⤶*36 rooms, 3 suites* ♿*In-room: refrigerator, Wi-Fi. In-hotel: restaurant, bar, pool, parking (no fee)* ▭*DC, MC, V* ⃝*CP.*

EN ROUTE Twelve kilometers (7 mi) northeast of Nyon, the lakefront village of **Rolle** merits a detour for a look at its dramatic 13th-century **château,** built at the water's edge by a Savoyard prince. While in town you can visit the Moinat Antiques and Decoration shop for a sample of what it takes to furnish a grand country home.

LOCAL TREATS

The villages of Vinzel and Bursins are the best sources for a very local specialty, the *malakoff.* These rich, steamy cheese-and-egg beignets have always been a favorite of the Vaudois, but after the Crimean Wars they were renamed after a beloved officer who led his army of Vaud-born mercenaries to victory in the siege of Sebastopol.

ROUTE DU VIGNOBLE

36 km (22 mi) between Nyon and Lausanne.

Parallel to the waterfront highway, threading through the steep-sloping vineyards between Nyon and Lausanne, the Route du Vignoble (Vineyard Road) unfolds a rolling green landscape high above the lake, punctuated by noble manors and vineyards.

Luins, home of the flinty, fruity white wine of the same name, is a typical pretty village.

Just up the road, the village of **Vinzel** develops its own white wines on sunny slopes and sells them from the *vin-celliers* (wine cellars) that inspired its name.

The route continues through **Bursins,** home of an 11th-century Romanesque church, and goes all the way to Morges. The road is clearly signposted throughout.

NEED A BREAK? While driving the Route du Vignoble you can sample the local wine and munch a few rich *malakoffs* (egg-and-Gruyère fritters) at **L'Union** (✉*Bursinsl* ☎*021/8241204*).

In Luins there is the **Auberge de Luins** (✉*Luins* ☎*021/8241159*)—usually there is a cluster of villagers gathered at the community table debating the quality of the latest vintage or regional politics.

Wild About Wine

As one of the main wine-producing regions in Switzerland, Vaud is best savored when sampling the local vintages.

If you're only tangentially interested, check the blackboard listings in any café for local names of *vins ouvert* (open wines), sold by the deciliter: the fruity whites of Épesses and St-Saphorin of Lavaux (between Lausanne and Montreux); the flinty Luins, Vinzel, and other La Côte variations (between Lausanne and Geneva); or the flowery Yvorne and Aigle, the best-known names from Le Chablais (between Villeneuve and Bex). You'll be tasting the previous season's harvest (local vintages are not aged).

If time allows, drive down narrow, fountain-studded stone streets in tiny wine villages, where inns and *vignobles* (vineyards) offer tastings. Keep an eye peeled for hand-painted signs announcing CAVEAU OUVERT or DÉGUSTATION; this indicates that a cellar owner or cooperative is pouring wine. (Do designate a driver; laws are strict.)

Local vintners welcome visitors year-round, except during harvest, which is usually in October. Some vineyards have sophisticated tasting rooms; at others a family member gathers guests around a tasting barrel within the working cellar. You may share a barrel top or slot at the bar with locals, as these are communal gathering spots.

If there is a particular winemaker you want to visit, phone ahead for an appointment. Most cellars charge for tasting, and if you occupy the winemaker's time beyond a casual pour, it is appropriate to buy a bottle unless you find the label not to your liking.

In July and August you can head for a Saturday market in Vevey, where, for the price of a commemorative glass, winemakers and tasters move from booth to booth. To boost your knowledge of wine cultivation, processing, and labeling, go to the Château d'Aigle's Musée de la Vigne et du Vin.

Interconnected hiking trails (signposted in several languages, including English, and full of informative tidbits) span the length of the shore from Ouchy to Chillon, traversing vineyards and traffic arteries from the lakefront to hillside villages. Walking the entire 32-km (19-mi) *parcours viticole* (wine route) takes about 8½ hours, but you can also break it into smaller segments, allowing time for wine tastings and meals at local restaurants.

Tourist offices can provide a copy of the specialized map that identifies the route and cellars open for tastings. (If you're doing a portion of the trail, you can easily catch a train back to your starting point, as there are hourly stops in every village along the lakefront.)

Speaking of trains, if the distance and grade of the trails seem too much, you can take the bright yellow coaches of the Train des Vignes (vineyard train) through the rows of pinot noir, gamay, and chasselas vines. The train starts from Vevey's station, near the waterfront, and ends more than 2,000 feet above sea level in the village of Puidoux-Chexbres; its timetable is part of the regular CFF schedule.

12

MORGES

23 km (14 mi) northeast of Prangins, 8 km (5 mi) west of Lausanne.

Visitor Information (✉ *2 rue du Château* ☎ 021/8013233 ⊕ www.morges.ch).

EXPLORING

On the waterfront just west of the urban sprawl of Lausanne, Morges is a pleasant lake town favored by sailors and devotees of its **Fête de la Tulipe** *(Tulip Festival)*, held annually in April and May.

The town's castle, built by the duke of Savoy around 1286 as a defense against the bishop-princes of Lausanne, now houses the **Musée du Château,** which combines three collections: weapons, military uniforms, and 10,000 miniature lead soldiers. In the Salle Général Henri Guisan, you'll find memorabilia of this World War II general, much honored for keeping both sides happy enough to leave Switzerland safely alone. ☎ 021/3160990 ⊕ www.chateau-morges.ch ☑ 10 SF ⊗ Feb.–June and Sept.–mid-Dec., weekdays 10–noon, 1:30–5, weekends 1:30–5; July and Aug., Tues.–Sun. 10–5.

In the heart of town, a 16th-century courtyard-centered mansion, once home to renowned engraver Alexis Forel, displays the holdings of the **Musée Alexis Forel.** Although most of Forel's exceptional engravings are in the Musée Jenisch, in Vevey, here you can experience his home surroundings. Thick-beamed salons filled with high-back chairs, stern portraits, and delicate china remain as they were in the 1920s, when musicians and writers such as Stravinsky, Paderewski, and Rolland gathered for lively discussions and private concerts. An attic room has a selection of 18th-century puppets and porcelain dolls. ✉ *54 Grand-Rue* ☎ 021/8012647 ⊕ www.museeforel.ch ☑ 8 SF ⊗ Apr.–early Dec., Wed.–Sun. 2–6.

⟳ The oar-powered warships of the Greeks, Romans, and Phoenicians once crossed the waters of Lac Léman. Now you can follow in their wake on *La Liberté,* a reconstruction of a 17th-century galley. This brainchild of historian Jean-Pierre Hirt is part public works project, part historical re-creation. Unemployed workers helped handcraft the 183-foot vessel. Christened in 2001, the ship sails the lake twice a day mid-May to mid-October; the 1½-hour tour costs 27 SF, the two-hour 38 SF. You must book space in advance. ✉ *45 rue de Lausanne* ☎ 021/8035031 ⊕ www.galere.ch.

OFF THE BEATEN PATH

Vufflens-le-Château. This village, 2 km (1 mi) northwest of Morges, is known for its namesake château, a 15th-century Savoyard palace with a massive donjon and four lesser towers, all trimmed in fine Piedmont-style brickwork. It's privately owned, but the grounds are open to the public.

WHERE TO EAT & STAY

$$$$

FRENCH

★

✕ **L'Ermitage des Ravets.** A multicourse gastronomic treat awaits at the restaurant in this 17th-century farmhouse, set beneath old, draping trees. Chef Bernard Ravet and his family serve the classics with modern twists. Son Guy, who trained at top addresses in France and the U.S., is prepping to step into his father's shoes, while daughter Nathalie, sommelier-of-the-year (2007), pours carefully paired vintages. Pastry magic is in the hands of another daughter, as the chef's wife presides over the dining room. Artistry on the plate includes four styles of duck and goose foie gras or saddle of venison with truffles and chanterelles. Reservations are essential and the business lunch a gem. Chic guest rooms beg a stay for the night. ✉ *26 rte. du Village, Vufflens-le-Château* ☎ *021/8046868* 🟰 *AE, MC, V* ⊘ *Closed Sun. and Mon., late Dec. and Aug.*

12

$$$ 🏨 **Hotel Fleur du Lac.** As the draperies are pulled back from south-facing windows, sun-splashed Mont Blanc comes into direct view. This lakefront retreat, just outside town on the main route to Lausanne, is surrounded by abundant seasonal plantings and stately old trees. Guest rooms are filled with a mix of antique and modern furniture. Updates keep appearances refreshed (though not consistent throughout). The terrace and dining room are the big draws. Book well in advance, as the guest return rate is unusually high. **Pros:** resort "campus" feeling, with private dock and lake access; connected to town by lakefront pathway. **Cons:** repeat guests tend to be graying; not close to the train station. ✉ *70 rue de Lausanne* ☎ *021/8815811* ⊕ *www.fleur-du-lac.ch* 🛏 *31 rooms, 7 suites* ♿ *In-room: no a/c, safe, refrigerator, Wi-Fi. In-hotel: restaurant, bar, public Wi-Fi, parking (no fee)* 🟰 *AE, DC, MC, V.*

LAUSANNE

66 km (41 mi) northeast of Geneva, 108 km (67 mi) southwest of Bern.

GETTING HERE & AROUND

You will exhaust yourself if you attempt to walk the hillsides of Lausanne from Ouchy (at the lakefront) to Old Town. So do what the locals do and use the "tl" (Transports Publics de la région Lausannoise), a subway, rail, and bus network. The Métro (m2) subway is the quickest vertical ride from lake to suburbs with stops at the main train station, trendy Flon, and Bessières (cathedral) before terminating in Epalinges. The automated ticket machines can be confusing, as they list all routes. Short runs will get you anywhere you want to go in the heart of the city in 10 minutes, and should cost about 2.50 SF. For schedules and fares, go to www.t-l.ch. Lausanne serves as gateway to the region and connector for the east-west routes across the Alps to Milan (3 hrs) and the TGV to Paris or Avignon (4 hours). Trains coming from the north (Zürich-Bern) make an eastern turn stopping in Lausanne, before continuing to Morges, Nyon, and Geneva; to travel west (Vevey, Montreux) a switch, often on the adjacent platform, is necessary.

Visitor Information (✉ *2 ave. de Rhodanie* ☎ *021/6137373* ⊕ *www.lausanne-tourisme.ch* ✉ *Gare Centrale, 9 pl. de la Gare* ✉ *Ouchy, pl. de la Navigation*).

EXPLORING

"Lausanne is a block of picturesque houses, spilling over two or three gorges, which spread from the same central knot, and are crowned by a cathedral like a tiara.... On the esplanade of the church...I saw the lake over the roofs, the mountains over the lake, clouds over the mountains, and stars over the clouds. It was like a staircase where my thoughts climbed step by step and broadened at each new height." Such was Victor Hugo's impression of this grand and graceful tiered city. Voltaire, Rousseau, Byron, and Cocteau all waxed equally passionate about Lausanne—and not only for its visual beauty. It has been a cultural center for centuries, the world drawn first to its magnificent Gothic cathedral and the powers it represented, then to its university, and during the 18th and 19th centuries to its vibrant intellectual and social life. Today the Swiss consider Lausanne a most desirable city in which to live.

Lausanne's importance today stems from its several disparate roles in national and world affairs. Politically, it is the site of the Tribunal Fédéral, the highest court of appeals in Switzerland. Commercially, although it is by no means in the same league as Zürich or Bern, it figures as the headquarters for many multinational organizations, corporations, and sports federations. On a major international rail route and at a vital national junction 66 km (41 mi) northeast of Geneva, Lausanne serves as a trade center for most of the surrounding agricultural regions and the expanding industrial towns of Vaud. This prosperity spills over into the arts; there's a surprising concentration of dance companies—including that of Maurice Béjart—as well as several theaters, jazz cellars, and a pair of excellent orchestras. Thousands of students come for the top-notch universities, private academies, and technology centers. Lausanne is also the world's Olympic capital; the International Olympic Committee has been based here since 1915 (its founder, Baron Pierre de Coubertin, is buried nearby at Montoie Cemetery).

The balance of old and new has not always been kept. The first 20 years after World War II saw an immense building boom, with old buildings and whole neighborhoods pulled down to make way for shining contemporary office and apartment buildings—an architectural exuberance that has given Lausanne a rather lopsided air.

EXPLORING LAUSANNE

Rising in tiers from the lakeside at Ouchy (1,181 feet) to more than 2,000 feet, the city covers three hills, which are separated by gorges that once channeled rivers. The rivers have been built over, and huge bridges span the gaps across the hilltops. On one hill in particular, modern skyscrapers contrast brutally with the beautiful proportions of the cathedral rising majestically from its crest. Atmospheric alleys and narrow streets have mostly been demolished, yet the Old Town clustered around the cathedral has been painstakingly restored.

Below the Old Town spreads the commercial city center, and in the bottom of the hollow between Avenue Jules Gonin and Rue de Genève is the Flon, a neighborhood with plenty of nightspots. Still farther south, along the lake, is the separate township of Ouchy, an animated resort area dominated by the Château d'Ouchy, with a tower dating from the Middle Ages.

MAIN ATTRACTIONS

⑤ Cathédrale de Notre-Dame *(Cathedral of Our Lady)*. A Burgundian Gothic architectural treasure, this cathedral, also called the Cathédrale de Lausanne, is Switzerland's largest church—and probably its finest. Begun in the 12th century by Italian, Flemish, and French architects, it was completed in 1275. Pope Gregory X came expressly to perform the historic consecration ceremony—of double importance, as it also served as a coronation service for Rudolf of Habsburg as the new Holy Roman Emperor. Rudolf brought his wife, eight children, seven cardinals, five archbishops, 17 bishops, four dukes, 15 counts, and a multitude of lesser lords to watch in the church's exquisitely proportioned nave.

Fodor'sChoice ★

Viollet-le-Duc, a renowned restorer who worked on the cathedrals of Chartres and Notre-Dame-de-Paris, brought portions of the building to Victorian Gothic perfection in the 19th century. His repairs are visible as paler stone contrasting with the weathered local sandstone.

Streamlined to the extreme, without radiating chapels or the excesses of later Gothic trim, the cathedral wasn't always so spare; in fact, there was brilliant painting. Zealous Reformers plastered over the florid colors, but in so doing they unwittingly preserved them, and now you can see portions of these splendid shades restored in the right transept. The dark and delicate choir contains the 14th-century tomb of the crusader Otto I of Grandson and exceptionally fine 13th-century choir stalls, unusual for their age alone, not to mention their beauty. The church's masterpiece, the 13th-century painted portal, is considered one of Europe's most magnificent. A tribute to 21st-century technology, the 7,000-pipe Fisk (American-made) organ fills the sanctuary with swells of sacred music. Constant repairs and renovations often shroud parts of the structure in scaffolding.

Protestant services (the cathedral was reformed in the 16th century) exclude nonworshipping visitors on Sunday at 10 AM and 8 PM. You may want to come instead for the evening concerts given on an almost weekly basis in spring and autumn; call ahead for a precise schedule. Guided tours are given July to mid-September. ⊠*Pl. de la Cathédrale, Old Town* ☎*021/3167161* ☉*Mar.–Oct., weekdays 7–7, weekends 8–7; Nov.–Feb., weekdays 7–5:30, weekends 8–5:30.*

⑥ Château St-Maire. The fortresslike elements of this 15th-century stone cylinder certainly came into play. The castle was built for the bishops of Lausanne; during the 16th century the citizens wearied of ecclesiastical power and allied themselves with Bern and Fribourg against the bishops protected within. Before long, however, Bern itself marched on Lausanne, put a bailiff in this bishops' castle, and stripped the city fathers of their power. The Bernese imposed Protestantism on the Lausannois, and their Catholic churches and cathedral were ransacked to fill the coffers of Bern. Today the Château St-Maire is the seat of the cantonal government. ⊠*Pl. du Château, Old Town.*

12

Lausanne

KEY
- ⊢→⊣ Rail lines
- ═══ Tramway

R. de la Pontaise

R. de la Borde

La Borde

Avenue Louis Vulliemin

10

Avenue Jomini

Avenue Davel

9

Av. Gindroz

Avenue Bergières

R. du Maupas

Avenue de Beaulieu

Chemin des Cèdres

Avenue Vinet

R. Pré-du-Marché

R. du Vallon

Pl. du Tunnel

Avenue de l'Université

R. du Tunnel

6

Pl. du Château

R. Cité-Devant

R. Cité-Derrière

R. Dr César

Pl. Chauderon

R. de l'Ale

R. des Terreaux

Pl. de la Riponne

R. Madeleine

Pl. de la Cathédrale

8

R. St-Laurent

R. Haldimand

R. de Genève

Place Bel-Air

Pl. St-Laurent

Pl. de la Palud

7

5

R. St-Étienne

R. St-Martin

Pl. Chauderon-Montbenon

R. Pichard

R. Grand St-Jean

Escaliers du Marché

3 **4**

Pont Bessières

R. Caroline

Avenue Jules Gonin

R. Centrale

Avenue Louis Ruchonnet

Rue du Grand-Chêne

R. Pépinet

1

2 R. de Bourg

Pl. St-François

R. Marterey

R. du Petit-Chêne

Rue du Midi

Av. du Théâtre

Place de la Gare

Avenue W. Fraisse

Gare Centrale

Avenue de la Gare

14 ←

R. du Simplon

11 **12**

13

0 �000 200 yards

0 �000 200 meters

A GOOD WALK: LAUSANNE

Begin in the commercial hub of the city, the **Place St-François** (nicknamed Sainfe by the Lausannois), where you'll see the former Franciscan Église St-François. Behind the church, take a near hairpin turn right onto the fashionable main shopping street, the ancient **Rue de Bourg.** At the top of Rue de Bourg, Rue Caroline leads you left and left again over the Pont Bessières, where you can see the city's peculiar design spanning gorges and covered rivers.

Crossing the bridge and bearing right brings you up into the Old Town. On your left, the imposing palace of the Old Bishopric now houses the **Musée Historique de Lausanne.**

Adjacent is the **Musée de Design et d'Arts Appliqués Contemporains,** known as the "Mudac" to locals. Straight ahead, at the top of Rue St-Étienne, towers the tremendous **Cathédrale de Notre-Dame,** which is on par with some of Europe's finest churches.

With the cathedral on your left, walk up the narrow passage of Rue Cité-Derrière to the Place du Château and its eponymous monument, the **Château St-Maire.** As you face the château, turn left and walk down the Rue Cité-Devant.

As you pass the cathedral again, veer right toward a flight of wooden steps that leads down to the dramatic Escaliers du Marché, a wood-roof medieval staircase and the Place de la Palud and the **Hôtel de Ville,** the seat of the municipal and communal councils. Turning right, just up Rue Madeleine, you will come upon the Place de la Riponne and the imposing **Palais de Rumine.**

A long hike up Avenue Vinet, northwest of the Old Town, will take you to the **Collection de l'Art Brut,** an unusual museum of fringe art across from the Beaulieu convention center. To view the works of more classical, well-known painters, visit the **Fondation de l'Hermitage,** a 15-minute bus ride from the Old Town. Take Bus No. 3 from the Gare Centrale (central train station) or Bus No. 16 from Place St-François.

South of the Old Town, Ouchy's **Débarcadère** has typical quayside attractions—vendors and people strolling on a promenade. It can be easily reached by the steep subway Métro; there are stations across from the Gare Centrale and under the Rue du Grand-Chêne in the Flon. (There's also a large underground parking garage, a boon in this space-pressed city.)

Just east of Ouchy, on a hillside overlooking the lake, the dramatic **Musée Olympique** tells about the history and sports of the Olympic Games. It's less than half a mile from the Débarcadère along the Quai de Belgique, which turns into the Quai d'Ouchy.

Uphill and connected by garden pathways, the **Musée de l'Elysée** is a photography museum housed in a restored 18th-century *campagne* (country manor home). West of Ouchy at Vidy is the **Musée Romain de Lausanne–Vidy,** where you can see a reconstructed private Roman home. Like the Musée Olympique, this is easy to get to on foot or by bus; it's just under a mile from the Débarcadère.

12

Cimitère du Bois-de-Vaux. Always adorned with white flowers as was her signature style, the grave of Coco Chanel lies within a large wooded cemetery park on the western edge of the city that memorializes other luminaries like Baron Pierre Coubertin, founder of the International Olympic Committee.

> **BEHIND THE SCENES**
>
> A self-portrait of Viollet-le-Duc, renowned restorer of the Cathédrale de Notre-Dame, appears in the face of King David, harp and scroll in hand, to the right of the main portal.

Urban legend has it that Madame Chanel's beloved companion, her dog, is buried not far away in the pet cemetery on the grounds of the stately Beau-Rivage Palace. ⊠*2 rte. de Chavannes ⊙ Open daily dawn to dusk ☞ Accessible by No. 2 Bus to Bourdonnette or No. 4 and 1 Maladière to Bois-de-Vaux stop.*

❾ Collection de l'Art Brut. This singular museum focuses on the genre of
★ fringe or "psychopathological" art, dubbed *l'art brut* (raw art) in the 1940s by French artist Jean Dubuffet. His own collection forms the base of this ensemble of raw material from untrained minds—prisoners, schizophrenics, or the merely obsessed. Strangely enough, the collection is housed in the Château de Beaulieu, a former mansion of Madame de Staël, she of the sophisticated salons. The exhibits range from intricate yarn and textile pieces to a wall full of whimsical seashell masks. One of the most affecting works is a panel of rough carvings made by an asylum patient in solitary confinement; it was shaped with a broken spoon and a chamber-pot handle. You can get here by walking up Avenue Vinet or by taking Bus No. 2 from Place St-Laurent in the direction of Le Désert. ⊠*11 ave. des Bergières, Beaulieu* ☎*021/3152570* ⊕*www.artbrut.ch* 💶*10 SF, free the first Sat. of month* ⊙*July and Aug., daily 11–1 and 2–6; Sept.–June, Tues.–Sun. 11–1, 2–6.*

⓫ Débarcadère *(Wharf).* In fine weather the waterfront buzzes day and
ↈ night—strollers, diners, concertgoers, in-line skaters, artisans selling their wares—while the white steamers that land here add to the traffic. It's as if sedate Lausanne lifts her skirts a bit at the shoreline. ⊠*Pl. du Port, Ouchy.*

❿ Fondation de l'Hermitage. A 15-minute bus ride from the Old Town takes
★ you to this beautifully set 19th-century country home. The estate is now an impressive art gallery with a fine permanent collection of Vaudois artists and headline-grabbing, yet seriously presented, blockbuster shows. Exhibits have included the works of Picasso, Giacometti, and the American Impressionists. Details of the elegant villa have been preserved, including intricate moldings, carved fireplaces, and multipatterned parquet floors. Allow time for a walk on the grounds and a coffee or light meal at **L'esquisse,** the café backdropped by the outlying orangerie. Call ahead to check the museum's hours, since it shuts down during transition periods between exhibits and for private events. To get here, take Bus No. 3 from Gare Centrale to the Motte stop or Bus No. 16 from Place St-François to Hermitage. ⊠*2 rte. du Signal, Sauvabelin* ☎*021/3125013* ⊕*www.fondation-hermitage.ch* 💶*15 SF* ⊙*Tues., Wed., and Fri.–Sun. 10–6, Thurs. 10–9.*

12

❼ Hôtel de Ville *(Town Hall).* Constructed between the 15th and 17th centuries, this is the seat of municipal and communal councils. A painted, medieval **Fontaine de la Justice** (Justice Fountain) draws strollers to lounge on its heavy rim. Across the street you can watch the

> **TO MARKET, TO MARKET**
>
> On Wednesday and Saturday a fresh-produce market sets up on Rue de Bourg.

modern **animated clock,** donated to the city by local merchants; moving figures appear every hour on the hour. A street market is held in the square every Wednesday and Saturday morning. ✉*2 pl. de la Palud, city center* ☎*021/3152525* ✉*Free.*

❸ Musée Historique de Lausanne *(Lausanne History Museum).* The Ancien-Évêché (Old Bishopric) holds a wealth of both temporary and permanent historical exhibits about the city. Don't miss the 250-square-foot scale model of 17th-century Lausanne, with its commentary illuminating the neighborhoods' histories. Also look for the re-created 19th-century shop windows. ✉*4 pl. de la Cathédrale, Old Town* ☎*021/3154101* ⊕*www.lausanne.ch/MHL* ✉*8 SF* ☉*July and Aug., daily 11–6; Sept.– June, Tues.–Thurs. 11–6, Fri.–Sun. 11–5.*

❶ Place St-François *(St. Francis Square).* The stone-paved square is dominated by the massive post office and the former Franciscan **Église St-François** (Church of St. Francis), built during the 13th and 14th centuries. From 1783 to 1793, Gibbon lived in a house on the site of the post office and there finished his work on *The Decline and Fall of the Roman Empire.* In those days the square, now reserved for pedestrians, was a popular riding circuit. ✉*St-François.*

NEED A BREAK?

Le Saint François (✉*5 pl. St-François* ☎*021/3202751*), a see-and-be-seen gathering spot opposite the church, serves decadent pastries and inventive light meals in a sleek blond-wood setting or outside on the plaza. Just behind the restaurant is an epicurean boutique chock-full of gourmet items, including private-label products from regional gastronomic star Philippe Rochat.

❷ Rue de Bourg. Once a separate village isolated on a natural ridge, this is now Lausanne's fashionable main shopping street. Narrow and cobblestoned, it's lined with platinum-card stores such as Hermès and Louis Vuitton, plus home-furnishing emporiums and jewelry salons. Boutiques have been built into the centuries-old buildings, though some have added fittingly modern facades. ✉*St-François.*

ALSO WORTH SEEING

❹ Musée de Design et d'Arts Appliqués Contemporains *(Museum of Contemporary Design and Applied Arts).* A museum of contemporary design seems amiss in this ancient quarter of the city and in the restored Maison Gaudard, yet it demonstrates the passion for art in everyday life. Temporary and permanent installations feature glassworks, textiles, and graphics. Creative and performing arts merge in multimedia shows. ✉*6 pl. de la Cathédrale, Old Town* ☎*021/3152530* ⊕*www.mudac.ch* ✉*6 SF* ☉*Tues.–Sun. 11–6.*

🔞 **Musée de l'Elysée.** Stark white walls and parquet floors form an invit-
☙ ing backdrop for the changing array of contemporary photography
assembled by this museum in an 18th-century country manor. Recent
shows have included "Edward Steichen–Lives in Photo" and "Con-
troversies: A Legal and Ethical History of Photography." Wander the
rooms, cellar, and attic spaces to view multiple exhibitions—some interactive and designed especially for children. The park surrounding the
estate is a quiet place to find a shaded bench and critique the current
show. ✉ *18 ave. de l'Elysée, Ouchy* ☎ *021/3169911* ⊕ *www.elysee.ch*
🎫 *8 SF* ☉ *Tues.–Sun 11–6.*

⑫ **Musée Olympique** *(Olympic Museum).* With high-tech presentation and
☙ touching mementos, this complex pays tribute to the athletic tradition
in ancient Greece, to the development of the modern Games, to the
evolution of the individual sports, to Paralympic competitions, and to
the athletes themselves. There are art objects—an Etruscan torch from
the 6th century BC, Rodin's *American Athlete*—as well as archival films
and videos, interactive displays, photographs, coins and stamps, and
medals from various eras throughout Olympic history. A museum shop,
a lovely café overlooking the lake and sculpture park, and occasional
Sunday-afternoon classical concerts complete this ambitious, world-
class endeavor. Brochures and guided tours are available in English.
✉ *1 quai d'Ouchy, Ouchy* ☎ *021/6216511* ⊕ *www.museum.olympic.
org* 🎫 *15 SF* ☉ *Apr.–Oct., daily 9–6; Nov.–Mar., Tues.–Sun. 9–6.*

⑭ **Musée Romain de Lausanne–Vidy** *(Lausanne-Vidy Roman Museum).* Two
Roman communities, Lousonna and Vidy, flourished near the lakefront
from 15 BC into the 4th century; excavations of their ruins have brought
these ancient settlements to light. A reconstructed private home serves
as the museum's headquarters, where displays include a small trove
of coins, votive figures, mosaics, and objects from daily life—carved
combs, toga pins, jewelry. On request, you can get guided tours in
English of the museum and the vast archaeological sites. The museum
is west of Ouchy, just off the Lausanne-Maladière exit from E25/A1.
Bus No. 1 stops at Maladière. ✉ *24 chemin du Bois-de-Vaux, Vidy*
☎ *021/3154185* ⊕ *www.lausanne.ch/MRV* 🎫 *8 SF* ☉ *July and Aug,
daily 11–6, Sept.–June, Tues.–Sun. 11–6.*

⑧ **Palais de Rumine.** Built at the turn of the last century, this enormous neo-
☙ Renaissance structure houses several museums, all with a local spin. The
Musée Cantonal de Géologie *(Cantonal Geology Museum* ☎ *021/6924470*
🎫 *6 SF* ☉ *Tues.–Thurs. 11–6, Fri.–Sun. 11–5)* has an excellent fos-
sil collection, including a mammoth skeleton. Besides its collection
of regional fauna, the **Musée Cantonal de Zoologie** *(Cantonal Zoology
Museum* ☎ *021/3163460* 🎫 *6 SF* ☉ *Tues.–Thurs. 11–6, Fri.–Sun.
11–5)* has a rare collection of comparative anatomy. The top exhibit
at the **Musée Cantonal d'Archéologie et d'Histoire** *(Cantonal Archaeology
and History Museum* ☎ *021/3163430* ⊕ *www.musees-vd.ch/fr/musee-
darcheologie-et-dhistoire* 🎫 *6 SF* ☉ *Tues.–Thurs. 11–6, Fri.–Sun. 11–5)*
is the gold bust of Marcus Aurelius discovered at nearby Avenches in
1939. The **Musée Cantonal des Beaux-Arts** *(Cantonal Museum of Fine Arts*
☎ *021/3163445* ⊕ *www.musees-vd.ch/fr/musee-des-beaux-arts* 🎫 *10SF*

🕑*Tues. and Wed. 11–6, Thurs. 11–8, Fri.–Sun. 11–5)* has an enlightening collection of Swiss art, not only by the Germanic Hodler and Anker but also by Vaud artists—especially Bocion, whose local landscapes are well worth study during a visit to this region. Each museum has some descriptions or an abbreviated guide in English. There are no combination entrance tickets, but all museums offer free admission the first Sunday of each month. ✉*6 pl. de la Riponne, City Center.*

12

WHERE TO EAT

$$$ ✕**À la Pomme de Pin.** Behind the cathedral, this winsome *pinte* (wine
SWISS pub)—one of Lausanne's oldest—produces an eclectic menu ranging from French to Italian to Swiss (rabbit and Rösti, anyone?), along with reasonable plats du jour, served both in the casual café and the adjoining linen-decked restaurant. The glass-panel door is often left ajar by neighbors dropping in for a glass of wine or espresso and a quick round of gossip. ✉*11–13 rue Cité-Derrière, Old Town* ☎*021/3234656* ▤*AE, MC, V* 🕑*Closed Sun. No lunch Sat.*

$$ ✕**Bleu Lézard.** A cross section of Lausanne urbanites—hip artists, yup-
ECLECTIC pies, shoppers, university students—fights for tables at this stylish res-
★ taurant. Dishes such as yakitori chicken brochette or duck with figs, plus an array of vegetarian offerings are available at remarkably low prices. A tongue-in-cheek decor of found-object art and easygoing waiters dressed in whatever they found near the bed that morning add to the laid-back ambience. Mixed drinks and live music draw a nocturnal clientele downstairs. ✉*10 rue Enning, City Center* ☎*021/3123830* ▤*AE, MC, V.*

$$$ ✕**Café Beau-Rivage.** As if turning its back on Michelin-starred sibling,
MODERN SWISS La Rotonde, and the aristocratic Beau-Rivage Palace, which shelters
★ both, this young, lively brasserie-café faces the lake and the Ouchy waterfront scene. Its flashy brass-and-Biedermeier dining area and bar fill with smart Lausannois and internationals enjoying trendy cuisine du marché. Despite the brasserie atmosphere, there are no paper place mats: linen, silver, and monogrammed damask set the tone. In summer the pillared terrazzo terrace (protected from embarcadero traffic by rose gardens) is the place go; dine on lamb tajine with apricot coriander compote or sea bream with Niçoise potatoes. ✉*17–19 pl. du Port, Ouchy* ☎*021/6133330* ⌖*Reservations essential* ▤*AE, DC, MC, V.*

$$ ✕**Café Restaurant du Théâtre.** Locals come here for smoky, oven-fired
ITALIAN individual-size pizza, but the home-style pasta and risotto are also robust and flavorful. The stucco-walled dining room is tight and toasty in winter; in summer there is nothing more delightful than sitting under the garden's sprawling trees and umbrellas. Entrances connect to a theater complex, making it a natural for pre- and postperformance dining. ✉*12 ave. du Théâtre, City Center* ☎*021/3515115* ▤*AE, MC, V* 🕑*Closed Sun. and Mon. evening.*

$$ ✕**Café Romand.** All the customers seem to know each other at this vast,
SWISS smoky dining institution, where shared wooden tables and clattering
★ china create the perfect ambience for fondue feasts, mussels, *choucroûte* (sauerkraut), or a sausage plate. Prominent members of Lausanne's arts

community swarm here after rehearsals and concerts, as service continues until 11 PM—late by Swiss standards. The not obvious entrance is set back in a passage, and the dining room sits above the kinetic church plaza. ✉*2 pl. St-François, St-François* ☎*021/3126375* ▤*MC, V* ◷*Closed Sun.*

$ ✕**Manora.** If you're fed up with heavy Vaud cheese dishes and local
FAST FOOD sausage, this cheery self-service outpost on the top floor of the city's popular Manor department store offers startlingly inexpensive options. Stir-fries sizzle in huge woks under silent no-smoke hoods; there are also iced pitchers of fresh-squeezed fruit juices, assemble-your-own salads, a fruit bar, a pasta station, and a dessert buffet. No one dish costs more than 20 SF, and the no-smoking dining section is a lifesaver in this city of chain-smokers. It's also a great place for morning coffee and a croissant, plus the free newspaper. ✉*7 rue St-Laurent, City Center* ☎*021/3213699* ⌀*Reservations not accepted* ▤*No credit cards.*

$$$$ ✕**Restaurant de l'Hôtel de Ville–Philippe Rochat.** Secure in his position as
FRENCH heir to the legendary chef Fredy Girardet, Philippe Rochat reigns as
Fodor'sChoice culinary don of the region. It's a quick drive west from Lausanne to
★ his understated manse. Service is spectacular and the food is absolutely stellar. His style is superluxe French, and he is famed for his imaginative combinations of flavors plus stunningly refined presentations on the plate. For these finely orchestrated prix-fixe menus the ingredients are key—lamb raised in the Pyrenees, cardoons (an artichokelike vegetable) grown in the village. Pace yourself, reserving time and room for selections from the immense cheese cart or celestial desserts. Make reservations as far ahead as possible—lunch may be your only option. ✉*1 rue d'Yverdon, Crissier* ✛*7 km (4 mi) west of Lausanne* ☎*021/6340505* ⌀*Reservations essential* ▤*AE, MC, V* ◷*Closed Sun. and Mon. and late July–mid-Aug, end Dec–early Jan.*

WHERE TO STAY

$$$ ▦**Alpha Palmiers.** Behind this historic facade you'll find a courtyard hotel of modern proportions. Filled with light from the atrium, the streamlined rooms have ample work spaces and safes large enough to hold a laptop. A bamboo garden and palm trees add freshness to the active reception-restaurant areas. Though the hotel is close to the train station, the walk uphill is a bit of a challenge with luggage. The Thai kitchen overseen by imported chefs attracts locals for the most authentic Asian food around. **Pros:** family-run modern operation eschews chain feel; garage parking a godsend in this hilly city. **Cons:** access on a one-way pedestrian thoroughfare tricky to navigate; popular for group meetings. ✉*34 rue du Petit-Chêne* ☎*021/5555599* ⊕*www.fhotels.ch* ⬖*210 rooms* ♿*In-room: safe, refrigerator, Ethernet. In-hotel: 2 restaurants, bar, gym, parking (fee)* ▤*AE, DC, MC, V.*

$$$$ ▦**Beau-Rivage Palace.** Of the scores of luxury hotels in Switzerland, this
Fodor'sChoice gleaming grande dame stands apart, its neoclassical structure seamlessly
★ restored to period opulence, its vast waterfront grounds manicured like a country estate. Every inch of marble, crystal, and polished mahogany sparkles like new. Guest rooms have many modern touches—remote

light controls, towel heaters, wireless connections. The hotel has a trio of top notch restaurants: the romantic La Rotonde (Michelin-starred and jacket required) and the Café Beau-Rivage and the Miyako sushi bar. The über-restorative spa, Cinq Mondes, umbrella canopied terraces, footpaths, and a hovering staff make it easy to understand why some guests stay the season. **Pros:** ultimate in old-world elegance with modern flair; park setting with lake views is incomparable. **Cons:** pack the designer labels or you will feel dowdy and underdressed; staff formality adds to upper-crust ambience. ⊠ *17–19 pl. du Port, Ouchy* ☎ *021/6133333* ⊕ *www.brp.ch* ⏎ *155 rooms, 20 suites* ⌂ *In-room: safe, refrigerator, Wi-Fi. In-hotel: 3 restaurants, 2 bars, 2 tennis courts, pool, gym, spa, parking (fee)* ⊟ *AE, DC, MC, V.*

$$$$
Fodor's Choice
★
Hôtel Angleterre & Résidence. Within four graceful 18th- and 19th-century villas and a historic hotel near the waterfront, this small complex has been modernized without ruffling its gentility or disturbing its graceful stone arches, marble floors, or discreet gardens. The hotel, where Lord Byron penned *The Prisoner of Chillon,* anchors the compound. A private courtyard with glass pavilion receives guests and dispenses them to quarters furnished in styles ranging from contemporary historical to garden-party floral. A meal taken on the terrace of L'Accademia, the quay-facing Italian bistro, provides a glimpse of lakefront lifestyle. It's the best of both worlds: small-hotel attentiveness plus access to the facilities of the grand Beau-Rivage Palace next door. **Pros:** hip urban feel steeped in history; part of energetic lakefront scene. **Cons:** alley entrance to garage and reception difficult to find; hard to snag a table on the patio for lunch or a sunset cocktail. ⊠ *11 pl. du Port, Ouchy* ☎ *021/6133434* ⊕ *www.angleterre-residence.ch* ⏎ *63 rooms, 12 suites* ⌂ *In-room: safe, refrigerator, Ethernet. In-hotel: 2 restaurants, bar, pool, parking (fee)* ⊟ *AE, DC, MC, V* ⍽ *EP.*

$$$
Hôtel Regina Garni. Owners at this friendly lodging spent more than a decade in the United States, so the language barrier is nonexistent. Guest rooms are neatly squared away with color-coordinated carpets and upholstery, most with shower-baths. Some have panoramic views of the cathedral, while others look out onto red-tile rooflines. Guest rooms on the top floor are modern multilevel spaces with bleached-plank ceilings and cherrywood furniture. The hotel is well situated in a pedestrian zone with parking access. Note that there is no restaurant, only a breakfast room. **Pros:** sights and shopping just outside the front door; well-priced in an expensive lodging city. **Cons:** functional, unfussy interiors; not able to drive up to entrance. ⊠ *18 rue Grand-St-Jean, City Center* ☎ *021/3202441* ⊕ *www.hotel-regina.ch* ⏎ *36 rooms* ⌂ *In-room: no a/c, safe, refrigerator, Wi-Fi. In-hotel: parking (no fee), public Internet* ⊟ *AE, MC, V* ⍽ *CP.*

$
Lausanne Guest House. This tidy 19th-century town house not far from the train station is run by a brother-and-sister team. Guest rooms are spread over five floors—some private with baths, others dorm-style with shared showers and toilets. You can prepare meals in the community kitchen or on the outdoor grill, or get caught up at the Internet corner with multiple terminals. The guest house is ecologically conscious, using solar heating and a special ventilation system, which makes smoking

off-limits. **Pros:** super-clean and tidy with helpful staff; shared house atmosphere. **Cons:** front desk not manned around the clock; adjacent to rail line, where soundproof windows shut out noise except when you want a breath of fresh air. ⊠*4 Epinettes* ☎*021/6018000* ⊕*www. lausanne-guesthouse.ch* ⊲*25 rooms, 6 with bath* △*In-room: no a/c, no phone, no TV. In-hotel: bicycles, laundry facilities, parking (fee), public Internet* ⊟*AE, DC, MC, V* ℐℴ*EP.*

$$$$ ▦ **Lausanne Palace & Spa.** This Edwardian landmark, distinctly urbane in
★ setting and style, stands on a hill high over the lake, with layers of city scenery draped behind. It faces a city street, so to take advantage of its views you need a back room. Rooms have Empire reproduction decor with period details such as inlaid wood and dramatic art deco baths. The sleek, calming Ayurveda spa offers a wide array of treatments and classes. You are likely to spot International Olympic Committee officials exiting the meeting areas, as the city's influential professionals often entertain clients at the assortment of dining venues and bars. **Pros:** top-drawer address sure to impress; easy access to nightlife of the Flon and all levels of shopping. **Cons:** dramatic interior can feel weighty; doorman and concierge are quick to size you up. ⊠*7–9 rue du Grand-Chêne, City Center* ☎*021/3313131* ⊕*www.lausanne-palace. ch* ⊲*121 rooms, 31 suites* △*In-room: safe, refrigerator, Ethernet. In-hotel: 3 restaurants, bars, pool, gym, spa, public Wi-Fi, parking (fee)* ⊟*AE, DC, MC, V.*

$$$ ▦ **Nash Carlton.** A quiet tree-lined street in one of Lausanne's nicest neighborhoods masks this lodging's close proximity to the train station. Rococo-style architecture is emphasized by embossed wallpapers, textured upholstery, and sweeping draperies in guest rooms and dining areas. The marble lobby and guest-room baths are polished to a high gloss; other aspects of inkeeping are equally as bright. Relax with a glass of wine in the French-influenced Nash Bar, knowing you are minutes from the Métro and the lakefront promenade. **Pros:** residential setting is a respite; well-priced neighborhood eateries within easy walking distance. **Cons:** in-between location neither lakefront (no views) nor commercial; uninspired breakfast buffet. ⊠*4 ave. de Cour* ☎*021/6130707* ⊕*www.nashotels.com* ⊲*38 rooms, 6 suites* △*In-room: safe, refrigerator, Ethernet. In-hotel: restaurant, bar, parking (no fee)* ⊟*AE, MC, V* ℐℴ*EP.*

NIGHTLIFE & THE ARTS

NIGHTLIFE

BARS   One of the city's choicest and liveliest gathering spots is **Le Bar** (⊠*Beau-Rivage Palace, Ouchy* ☎*021/6133333*). There's a sophisticated armchair-filled lounge and a tiny wine bar inside the hotel's lower lobby entrance, where you can sip your favorite cocktail or wine. Upstairs sibling **Bar Anglais** offers spectacular lake views from its clubby setting and terrace chaises. The Lausanne Palace serves the after-hours crowd in the stately **Bar du Palace** (⊠*City Center* ☎*021/3313131*); the hotel's stylish, pared-down **LP Bar** is just a corridor away. In a city with its own jazz music school, look for a range of styles at

Le Chorus (✉*3 ave. Mon Repos, City Center* ☎*021/3232233*), where the renowned jazz cellar serves food and drinks. To explore the vintages of the country, drop in at the **Swiss Wine Bar** (✉*9 rue St-Laurent, Old Town* ☎*021/3230133*) where they pour more than 400 different wines and host tasting events.

DANCING Since most nighttime activity is centered on the Flon and Place St-François areas, it's easy to sample several hot spots. Things don't get going until midnight, and rock on until 5 AM. If you pass a crowded club where the music is to your taste, duck in. It may be one of the happening locations too new or ephemeral to list here. On the west side of town, **Amnesia Club** (✉*9 ave. E. Jacques-Dalcroze, Vidy* ☎*021/6190650*) fills four levels with themes ranging from beach party to R&B Soul. A 20 SF cover for nonmembers puts a damper on the party mood. Latin and tropical music dominate, but funk, rock, and disco fill **Atelier Volant** (✉*12 rue des Côtes-de-Montbenon, Flon* ☎*021/6248428*). Inside a converted cinema at **D! Club** (✉*Pl. Centrale, city center* ☎*021/3515140*) there's a mix of film, fashion, and music. Special-effect lighting and video screens lend tech appeal at **Loft Electroclub** (✉*1 pl. de Bel-Air, Flon* ☎*021/3116463*), whose multiple floors and bars come to life Wednesday through Saturday. Clubbers come from as far away as Zürich and Basel for playlists by their favorite touring DJ's and live performances at **MAD** (✉*23 rue de Genève, Flon* ☎*021/3406969*). On Sunday night the club hosts a gay crowd.

THE ARTS

Lausanne is one of Switzerland's arts capitals. Event seasons generally run from September to May, though summer brings outdoor concerts and more casual events. A listing of free and ticketed offerings can be found in *Allons-y*, while monthly updates appear in *Reg'art* (in French). Check out the daily newspaper *24 Heures* for listings as well. Tickets for many performances can be purchased through **Ticket Corner** (☎*090 0800800 toll call* ⊕*www.ticketcorner.ch*). Or look online at **Billetnet** (⊕*www.billetnet.ch*).

The Opéra de Lausanne shares the stage at **Salle Métropole** (✉*1 pl. Bel-Air, City Center* ☎*021/3450025*) with the riveting experiments of the **Maurice Béjart** ballet company. The hall is also home to the **Orchestre de Chambre de Lausanne.** The **Théâtre de Beaulieu** (✉*10 ave. des Bergières, Beaulieu* ☎*021/6432110*), right across from the Collection de l'Art Brut, hosts full-scale musical performances like those of the **Orchestre de la Suisse Romande,** which Lausanne shares with Geneva. For a variety of French-language theater old and new head to **Théâtre Kléber-Méleau** (✉*9 chemin de l'Usine-à-Gaz, Rennes-Malley* ☎*021/6258429*) or **Théâtre Vidy-Lausanne** (✉*5 ave. Émile-Jacques-Dalcroze, Vidy* ☎*021/6194545*).

SPORTS & THE OUTDOORS

BICYCLING

Gare CFF de Lausanne (*train station* ⊠*5a pl. de la Gare, City Center* ☎*051/2242162*) rents bikes. You must make a reservation at least one day in advance; in summer three days is recommended. For a lakefront ride, check out a set of wheels at **Guy Delessert** (⊠*4 pl. du Vieux Port, Ouchy* ☎*021/6170928*).

SWIMMING

Bellerive (⊠*23 ave. de Rhodanie, Ouchy* ☎*021/3154860*) has access to the lake and three pools, one Olympic-size, plus generous lawns and a self-service restaurant. The indoor pool at **Mon-Repos** (⊠*4 ave. du Tribunal-Fédéral, City Center* ☎*021/3154888*) stays open from late August through June. The pool at **Piscine de Montchoisi** (⊠*30 ave. du Servan, outside City Center* ☎*021/3154962*) makes artificial waves; it's open from May through August.

SHOPPING

High-end designer names and funky boutiques are found on **Place St-François, Rue St-François, Rue de Bourg,** and **Rue du Grand-Pont.** Less expensive shopping is along **Rue St-Laurent** and **Rue de l'Ale.** Generally, store hours are weekdays 9:30–7, 9:30–6 on Saturday, closed Sunday.

BOOKS

For magazines, travel guides and other books, and music, **FNAC** (⊠*6 rue Genève, Flon* ☎*021/2138585*) is *the* superstore and a nice exception to Sunday closings; it even has a hyperactive coffee bar and ticket kiosk.

DEPARTMENT STORES

Bon Génie (⊠*10 pl. St-François, St-François* ☎*021/3452727*) has clusters of designer areas on several levels. **Globus** (⊠*Rue Centrale at Rue du Pont, City Center* ☎*021/3429090*) is a large upscale department store with a splendid basement food hall. Value-priced **Manor** (⊠*7 rue St-Laurent, City Center* ☎*021/3213699*) stocks a full range of merchandise, including logo items and souvenirs. It has bountiful food offerings, too.

MARKETS

There are fruit and vegetable markets in Lausanne along **Rue de l'Ale, Rue de Bourg,** and **Place de la Riponne** every Wednesday and Saturday (8–2:30). **Place de la Palud** adds a flea market to its Wednesday and Saturday produce markets and is the site of a handicrafts market the first Friday of the month from March through December. A weekly flea market sets up on Thursdays on **Place Chauderon.** Seasonal additions include summer produce found Sunday along the **Allée Bacounis** in Ouchy, and the Marché Noel (Christmas Market) in December on the transformed **Place St-François** and **Place de la Ripon.**

WATCHES

Most watch shops specialize in brands and are clustered in the St-François neighborhood.

Bucherer (✉ *1 rue de Bourg* ☎ *021/3123612*) sells Rolex, Tag Heuer, and Baume & Mercier.

Boutique Tourbillon (✉ *8 pl. St-François* ☎ *021/3235145*) sells Blancpain and Omega. If you are searching for Ebel, go across town to **Guillard** (✉ *1 pl. du Palud* ☎ *021/3126886*). Large Swatch boutiques are located in the Globus and Manor department stores (above).

12

LAVAUX VIGNOBLES & RIVIERA

To the east of Lausanne stretches the Lavaux, a UNESCO-designated World Heritage Site with remarkably beautiful vineyards that rise up the hillsides all the way from Pully, on the outskirts of Lausanne, to Montreux—a distance of 24 km (15 mi)—and then beyond to the fortress-crowned town of Aigle. Brown-roof stone villages in the Savoy style, old defense towers, and small baronial castles stud the green-and-black landscape. The vineyards, enclosed within low stone walls, slope so steeply that all the work has to be done by hand. Top soil, fungicides, and manure are carried in containers strapped to workers' backs. In early October pickers harvest the fruit, carrying the loads to the nearest road and driving them by tractor to the nearest press. Some Lavaux vintages are excellent and in great demand, but unfortunately, as with so much of Switzerland's wine, the yield is small, and the product is rarely exported. Throughout the year, especially on weekends, wine-growers' cellars and some of the private châteaux-vignobles open for tastings (and, of course, sales). A listing of cave open hours, festivals, and eateries can be found at ⊕ *www.lavaux.ch*.

Fodor'sChoice ★ The scenic **Corniche de la Vaud** stretches some 17 km (10 mi) through Lavaux, threading above the waterfront from Lausanne to Vevey, between the autoroute and the lakeside Route 9. This is Switzerland at its most Franco-European, reminiscent in its small-scale way of the Riviera or the hill towns of Alsace. You'll careen around hairpin turns on narrow cobbled streets, with the Savoy Alps glowing across the sparkling lake and the Dents du Midi looming ahead. Stop to gaze at the scenery from roadside overlooks or wander down a side lane into the fields of Riex, Épesses, Rivaz, or the Dézaley, the sources of some of Switzerland's loveliest white wines and typically magical little Vaudois villages.

LUTRY

5 km (3 mi) southeast of Lausanne.

GETTING HERE

Many of the wine villages within the Lavaux Vignobles region are accessible by the local train that runs between Lausanne and Villeneuve every half hour. There is no bus service to hamlets that lie up hill from these stations, but locals find the uphill walk quite pleasant and part of their daily routine. For those not in shape, consult a map or the brochure *A la découverte des terrasses de Lavaux* before setting out. Some of the

KEY

↜—↜ Rail lines

⛷ Ski Resorts

treks take 15 to 20 minutes on rather steep terrain. By car the villages
are accessible from the A9 or the main lakefront highway via a network
of narrow curvy roads.

EXPLORING

From its origins as a simple fishing village, this medieval town on the
skirt hem of Lausanne expanded in the 11th century with the installation of the Benedictine monks from Savigny-en-Lyonnais. The religious order is credited with taming the wild hillsides, terracing them,
and expanding the cultivation of wine grapes—a tradition that thrives
today. Celebrated at the end of September, the **Fete des Vendages** (harvest
festival) is but one of the lively events that brings families and tourists
to the plaza for food, wine, and entertainment.

In the sweep of the Reformation, the monastic order was closed and
the church converted from its modest configuration to a more elaborate
center of worship. The **Église de Lutry** is worth a stop for its stained-glass
windows and 16th-century Flemish paintings, which cover the nave and
choir. Lutry eschews becoming an urban annex, its character preserved
in narrow streets that follow the contour of the land, dropping from
estate vineyards to the waterfront, twisting in and out of rugged walls
that were once protective fortifications. Follow your instincts in exploring back alleys and crooked passageways. You're likely to discover a

jewelry studio or tearoom hidden in a nook or bend. For a history lesson, pause to read the multilanguage panels. For a different perspective, take in the shoreline aboard one of the steamers that pulls up to the dock, or head uphill for a view from a vineyard aerie. On summer weekends a miniature train connecting Lutry and Cully travels along grape-growers' paths through the heart of these appellations

12

ST-SAPHORIN

★ *5½ 5 km (3 mi) southeast of Lausanne.*

At the end of the Cornich Road, just west of Vevey, St-Saphorin is perched above the water. With its impossibly narrow, steep cobbled streets and ancient winemakers' houses crowded around fountains and crooked alleys, this is a village that merits a stop. It lies along the ancient Roman highway, and its small church sits atop Roman foundations. There's a tiny **museum** of Roman artifacts (including a sizable millstone) in the church. Go through the low door near the altar; you can see the museum whenever the church is unlocked and services are not being held. The explanations are all in French, but it's easy to chart the church's expansion through its ruins.

For additional vineyard explorations accompanied by jaw-dropping vistas, take the vertical grade uphill—on foot or by car—to Chexbres. Be attentive, as the close, walled-street relies on tight pull-offs to pass oncoming vehicles. The reward is a different orientation on the working wine village, complete with rail connections to whisk you back down to the active waterfront via Vevey.

WHERE TO STAY & EAT

$$–$$$
MODERN SWISS
★
✕ **L'Auberge de l'Onde.** Once the main *relais* (stagecoach stop) between the Simplon Pass and Geneva, this vineyard stop is out of central casting, groaning with history and heady with atmosphere: Igor Stravinsky and Charlie Chaplin were among the artists loyal to its charms. The tiny wood-paneled pinte (café), where winemakers come to read the daily papers with a pitcher of St-Saph, as they call it, and devour the upscale plat du jour, is enticing, as are the adjacent, white-tablecloth salons and upstairs attic beamed grill room. The staff hovers while day-tripping connoisseurs and repeat faithfuls sniff and roll perfumed wine over their tongues and savor exquisite dishes from its top-notch kitchen. ⊠ *Centre Ville* ☎ *021/9254900* ⊕ *www.aubergedelonde.ch* ⊟ *MC, V* ☉ *Closed Mon. and Tues.*

$$$
CONTINENTAL
★
🏨 **L'Hôtel Baron Tavernier.** Lodging high up on the Corniche Road yields superlative views with elegant comfort. The inn is named after 17th-century author and adventurer Jean-Baptiste Tavernier, and its entry is stocked with stained glass, porcelain, and metal works similar to the trove brought back from his travels to Persia, Africa, and the Orient. Guest rooms assume a modern appearance, clad in honey and green with marbled bathrooms and private balconies. Le Deck, an expansive terrace bar and alfresco eatery connected by a crosswalk, is tethered above the lake like a hot air balloon. **Pros:** jaw-dropping views of lake, vineyards, and mountains; solitude adjacent to wine trails and

cellar doors. **Cons:** overflow crowds drawn to outdoor restaurant on weekends; complicated to access without a car. ✉*Rte. de la Corniche, Chexbres* ☎*021/9266000* ⊕*www.barontavernier.ch* ⌂*11 rooms, 7 suites* ♿*In-room: no a/c, refrigerator, Ethernet. In-hotel: restaurant, bar, parking (no fee)* ⊟*AE, DC, MC, V* �*CP.*

VEVEY

13.5 km (8.5 mi) east of Lutry, 19 km (12 mi) east of Lausanne.

GETTING HERE

The 7-minute regional and local S-trains linking the adjacent cities Vevey-Montreux have departures every 10 to 15 minutes, but the trolley bus that snakes along the lake road is more scenic—its route extends from Villenuve to the Vevey Funicular and is the best way (other than by car) to reach Château de Chillon. Depending on how many zones you cross, the fare is about 3 SF. There is a map and fare chart on the automated ticket machine located in the back of the bus or you can find them on www.vmcv.ch.

Visitor Information (✉*29 Grand-Pl.* ⊕*www.montreux-vevey.com*).

EXPLORING

This soigné waterfront town was the setting for Anita Brookner's evocative 1985 novel *Hotel du Lac,* about a woman retreating to a lake resort to write; her heroine was attracted to the site, in part, because of its slightly stuffy 19th-century ways. In the 1870s Henry James captured this mood of prim grace while writing (and setting) *Daisy Miller* in the Hôtel des Trois Couronnes. Indeed, despite its virtual twinning with glamorous Montreux, Vevey retains its air of isolation and old-world gentility. Loyal visitors have been returning for generations to gaze at the Dent d'Oche (7,288 feet), across the water in France, and make sedate steamer excursions into Montreux and Lausanne. Today there are some who come just to see the bronze statue of Charlie Chaplin, in a rose garden on the lakefront quay, and to take the funicular or mountain train up to Mont Pèlerin. Vevey is also a great walking town, with more character in its shuttered Old Town; better museums, landmarks, and shops; and more native activity in its wine market than cosmopolitan Montreux can muster. By following an excellent brochure-map published by the tourist office, you can travel "On the Trail of Hemingway"—and to the homes and haunts of some 40 other luminaries.

★ Le Corbusier's **Villa le Lac,** a single-story white house built directly on the Vevey waterfront, was constructed for his parents in 1923. It remains unaltered, with his original furnishings and details preserved within. Shingled in corrugated sheet metal, with a white-metal railed balcony looking over the water and a "birdhouse" chimney in molded concrete, it is typically sculptural and, in a modest way, visionary. ✉*21 rte. de Lavaux, Corseaux* ☎*021/9254011* ⌂*5 SF* ⏱*Self-guided tours Apr.– Oct., Wed. 1:30–5:30.*

12

The Nestlé Foundation, a dynamic force in the region, sponsors an unconventional museum, the **Alimentarium**. A sculpture of an apple at the entrance of the 19th-century lakefront mansion symbolizes the museum's purpose: the celebration and study of food. In a stainless-steel kitchen chefs demonstrate their skills, and displays on food preparation cover everything from the campfire to futuristic equipment. Other sections focus on merchants, supermarkets, food presentation, and marketing; you can also stroll

CELEBRITY SIGHTINGS

Among the notables who have been drawn to Vevey are Graham Greene, Victor Hugo, Jean-Jacques Rousseau (who set much of his *Julie, ou la Nouvelle Héloïse* here), Fyodor Dostoyevsky, Gustave Courbet, Oskar Kokoschka, Charlie and Oona Chaplin (buried in the cemetery at Corsier), and Swiss native Édouard Jeanneret, known as Le Corbusier.

through herb and vegetable gardens. The exhibits have material in English; some are interactive. ⌧*Quai Perdonnet* ☎*021/9244111* ⊕*www.alimentarium.ch* ⌲*10 SF* ☽*Tues.–Sun. 10–6.*

The **Musée Historique du Vieux Vevey** *(Historical Museum of Old Vevey)* occupies a grand 16th-century manor house, briefly home to Charlotte de Lengefeld, wife of Friedrich von Schiller. It retains some original furnishings as well as collections of arms, art, keys, and winemaking paraphernalia. The first floor serves as headquarters for the Brotherhood of Winegrowers, the organization that stages the mammoth Fêtes des Vignerons (Winegrowers' Festival). The festival is held roughly every 25 years; you can get a taste of the most recent celebration (1999) from the costumes, photographs, and memorabilia on display. ⌧*2 rue du Château* ☎*021/9210722* ⊕*www.museehistoriquevevey.ch* ⌲*Free* ☽*Apr.–Oct., Tues.–Sat. 11–5; Nov.–Mar., Tues.–Sat. 2–5.*

The **Musée Suisse de l'Appareil Photographique** *(Swiss Camera Museum)* displays an impressive collection of cameras, photographic equipment, and mounted work. It also hosts "Images," a biennial multimedia show held in the fall of even-numbered years. ⌧*99 Grande-Pl.* ☎*021/9252140* ⊕*www.cameramuseum.ch* ⌲*8 SF* ☽*Tues.–Sun. 11–5:30.*

NEED A BREAK?

Pause for a glass of a local or imported vintage at the storefront wine bar **Les Dix Vins** (⌧*24 rue des Deux-Marchés* ☎*021/9223033*), on a side street between market plazas. The owner's friendly enthusiasm adds to the pleasure of time spent toasting, chatting, or people-watching.

If sweets are more your mood, pick a luscious assortment of hand-crafted chocolates from the case at **Poyet** (⌧*8 rue du Théâtre* ☎*021/9213737*), on the pedestrian walkway near the tourist office, or join the ladies for a light lunch in the adjacent dining room.

Just east of town, the **Musée Suisse du Jeu** *(Game and Toy Museum)* fills a 13th-century castle. Games of strategy and chance, ranging from dice to video games, are represented in displays spanning centuries. Its excellent

Fond of Fondue

Though fondue is de rigueur in any Alpine setting, Vaud is a fanatical stronghold. In the Pays-d'Enhaut (Highlands), cattle head uphill in summer, and production of local cheeses—the firm, fragrant Gruyère and L'Etivaz—soars. They are sold at various stages: young and mild, ripe and savory, or aged to a heady tang. Take a guided hike from Chateaux-d'Oex to the highland pastures to see all aspects of cheese making and then share a bubbly pot of perfection.

Fondue is simply cheese melted together with white wine, garlic, and a dash of kirsch. Aficionados debate the perfect blend of cheeses and whether to include mushrooms, tomatoes, and even chunks of potatoes. Most restaurants serve a blend of Gruyère, Emmental, and Appenzeller; others have their own recipe. The especially popular *moite-moite* (half and half) is half Gruyère and half bold l'Etivaz or creamy Vacherin.

Diners dip chunks of bread on long forks into the bubbling mixture. Many restaurants serve fondue in an adjoining *carnotzet* or *Stübli* (French and German versions of a cozy pub)—both to re-create a rustic Alpine experience and to spare fellow diners the fierce aromas of cheese, garlic, and the fuel that keeps the fondue melted. It's a dish best suited to winter.

Appropriate accompaniments are a fruity white wine or plain black tea—never red wine, beer, or cola—and the traditional *coup du milieu* (shot in the middle), a reviving midmeal shot of kirsch. The salty cheese will make you yearn for water; go light and never with ice. Custom dictates that if you lose your bread in the caquelon, women must kiss the host or nearest man, while men buy another round.

gift shop is stocked with Legos, puzzles, and board games. Tours and notes are available in English. The courtyard eatery, Domino, a former gardener's cottage, serves snacks and light meals. ⊠*1½ km (1 mi) east of Vevey on Rte. 9, Au Château, La Tour-de-Peilz* ☎*021/9772300* ⊕*www.museedujeu.com* ⊠*8 SF* ☉*Tues.–Sun. 11–5:30.*

OFF THE
BEATEN
PATH

Blonay–Chamby Railroad. From Vevey and Montreux, a number of railways climb into the heights, which in late spring are carpeted with an extravagance of wild narcissi. If you like model railroads, you will especially enjoy a trip on the Blonay–Chamby Railroad, whose real steam-driven trains alternate with electric trains. You can depart from either end (parking is more plentiful in Blonay); trains make a stop at a small museum of railroad history in between. The trip takes about 20 minutes each way, not including a browse in the museum. ⊠*Case Postale 366, Lausanne* ☎*021/9432121* ⊕*www.blonay-chamby.ch* ⊠*Round-trip ticket 18 SF* ☉*May–Oct., weekends 10–6:30.*

WHERE TO EAT

CONTEMPORARY ✕**Charly's Café.** Enter the multilevel casual eatery from the lakefront or cobblestone plaza near the main marketplace. Upstairs seating catches the breeze; lower-level tables spill out on to the fountain-filled pedestrian zone and in summer an outpost is set up across the street on the lakeside promenade. Friendly servers deliver mugs of steaming latte with crusty croissants to the morning crowd hunched over free daily newspapers including the *Herald Tribune*. Neatly stacked club sandwiches surrounded by a heap of fries served late into the evening are popular with expats and revelers, while pleasing and well-priced plated specials of fresh fish or pasta appeal to the early crowd. ⊠*45 rue du Lac* ☎*021/9215006* ▤*MC, V* ⊘*Closed Dec.–Feb.*

$$
SWISS ✕**Le Mazot.** Offerings at this tiny pinte are limited. Regulars favor the tender steak—entrecôte of beef or *cheval* (horse)—accompanied by an overflowing plate of fries or a half-moon of crispy Rösti. After years of overseeing bubbling pots of fondue, the other popular draw, hand-painted murals and mirrors set in dark frames have a smoky patina. The narrow room is crowded with scarred booths and bare tables, which can be moved together in long chains. It's a casual neighborhood place where local wines are poured from pewter pitchers and the people at the next table eavesdrop. ⊠*7 rue du Conseil* ☎*021/9217822* ▤*MC, V* ⊘*Closed Wed. No lunch Sun.*

$$$
FRENCH ✕**Le Montagne.** This elegant, intimate restaurant is set in a restored home in the wine village of Chardonne. Perched on a sunny shelf high above the Nestlé corporate complex, it offers a view of the lake (from part of the dining room) that is worthy of a champagne toast. Traditional French preparations like beef medallions and rack of lamb are straightforward, smartly garnished, and paired with fresh herbs and vegetables. A well-composed wine list of Swiss and international selections offers breadth to match. Those who like a stroll before and after dinner can take the mostly flat five-minute walk to the funicular, an easy way to access these upper reaches. ⊠*21 rue du Village, Chardonne* ☎*021/9212930* ▤*AE, DC, MC, V* ⊘*Closed Sun. and Mon. and three (varying) weeks in Sept. and Dec.*

$$
SWISS ✕**National.** The crowd is mixed across ages at this popular west side location. A frequently changing menu combines fresh ingredients with a twist on standards like lake fish grilled with Cajun spicies instead of fried or a bowl of penne topped with Thai ingredients (instead of Bolognese). The casual vibe overflows onto the patio, with seating under the twinkling lights—a respite from the serious smoking crowd. A thriving bar with extended service hours and proximity to the cinema attracts late diners. ⊠*9 rue du Torrent* ☎*021/9237625* ▤*MC, V.*

WHERE TO STAY

$$$–$$$$ ⊞**Astra Hotel.** Offering the best of old and new, this hotel contains 1920s frescoes of a winegrowers' festival on the ceiling of La Brasserie, the old-fashioned restaurant, as well as a modern annex of guest rooms wired with up-to-the-minute technology. Colors are strong—plaid spreads and geometric-print draperies in bold orange and red with carpets dominated by dark green or blue. Adjacent to the train station, the congenial family-run place has an outdoor café and coffee bar, both convenient rendezvous points. An underground garage uses an elevator to lower cars from the narrow alley entrance to parking spaces beneath the building. **Pros:** immediate access to the rail station; family-friendly management team. **Cons:** noise from busy intersection rises through open windows; tough to get a reservation, as business travelers dominate during the week. ⊠*4 pl. de la Gare* ☎*021/9250404*

⌂021/9250400 ⊕www.astra-hotel.ch ⇶88 rooms, 8 suites, ♿In-room: safe, refrigerator, Ethernet, Wi-Fi. In-hotel: 3 restaurants, bar, gym, parking (fee) ▤AE, DC, MC, V ⏐○⏐CP.

$$$$ ▦ **Grand Hôtel du Lac.** Anita Brookner set her novel *Hotel du Lac* in this
★ lakefront doyenne where readers find an abundance of refinement and global sophistication proffered beneath the Relais & Châteaux banner. Dramatic Oriental decor in the lobby and lounge are a sharp contrast to soothing pastels and honey creams that outfit luxe guest rooms. The veranda takes on a garden-party air at Sunday brunch, when fortunately hat and gloves are no longer de rigueur. An intimate spa and the only outdoor pool in town add to the attraction for today's discerning sojourners. **Pros:** historically elegant; pool and garden plus harbor access are sensational in summer. **Cons:** at the outer edge of town; lakefront festivals and neighborhood block parties can engulf. ✉1 *rue d'Italie* ☎021/9250606 ⌂021/9250607 ⊕www.grandhoteldulac.ch ⇶41 *rooms. 9 suites* ♿In-room: safe, refrigerator, Ethernet. In-hotel: res-taurant, bar, pool, gym, spa, parking (fee) ▤AE, DC, MC, V ⏐○⏐CP.

$-$$ ▦ **Hostellerie Bon Rivage.** This hotel blends right in with the estates fac-ing the lake on the main road between Vevey and Montreux. Its breezy rooms with blond modular furniture overlook a small marina and the turrets of the village castle. The building was once home to the Order of St. Joseph; the nuns still maintain a small chapel on the main floor. Request a lakefront room, not only for the superb view, but also to avoid street noise. Keep an eye out for l'Olivier's chef harvesting herbs and vegetables for Provençal-inspired dishes from the walled garden below. **Pros:** price/value relationship is tops; picturesque marina setting on the main transportation line. **Cons:** no a/c necessitates closed shutters against the afternoon sun; most guest rooms have only a shower bath. ✉18 *rue de St-Maurice, La Tour-de-Peilz* ☎021/9770707 ⊕www. bon-rivage.ch ⇶50 *rooms* ♿In-room: no a/c, Ethernet. In-hotel: res-taurant, bar, public Wi-Fi, parking (no fee), some pets allowed ▤AE, MC, V ⏐○⏐CP.

$$$$ ▦ **Hôtel des Trois Couronnes.** Honeycombed by dramatic atrium stairwells
★ that look down on marble columns and gleaming floors inlaid with golden coronets, this regal landmark was Henry James's home base when he wrote (and set here) the novella *Daisy Miller*. A vast lakefront terrace overlooks the pollards, the promenade, and the steamers plying the lake. Burgundy brocade with floral swags and coverlets contrast boldly with neutral striped wallpaper in generously sized guest rooms. The spa, called Puressens (Pure Senses), offers a full range of restorative services that are a relaxing extension to time spent in the lower-level pool. **Pros:** from valet to spa attendant, the staff is superb; perfect balance of modern refinement and history. **Cons:** noise wafts up into rooms from terrace parties; even the best face-lifts show a few age lines. ✉49 *rue d'Italie* ☎021/9233200 ⊕www.hoteldestroiscouronnes.com ⇶45 *rooms, 10 suites* ♿In-room: safe, refrigerator, Ethernet. In-hotel: restaurant, bar, pool, gym, spa, public Wi-Fi, parking (no fee) ▤AE, DC, MC, V.

NIGHTLIFE

Despite its quiet, small-town appearance, Vevey has gathering spots where the music is loud and revelers dance until dawn. At **Epsylon Club** (✉30 ave. *General Guisan* ☎021/9212196), people warble karaoke daily, with full-throttle clubbing on the weekend. Gays and straights gather for music and cocktails plus imaginative theme parties at **Il Baretto** (✉3 *rue du Theâ* ☎021/9212281), an enclave near the town theater. Across the Place du Marché, **National** (✉9 *rue du Torrent* ☎021/9237625) combines music and late food.

SPORTS & THE OUTDOORS

As you drive along the highway, you will see sunbathers lounging on rocks jutting out into the lake and swimmers playing on the stony beaches. It's difficult to tell if they are on private property or have public access. There *are* swimming areas open to everyone that include a mix of facilities—toilets, showers, changing cabins, and snack bars—but lifeguards are only at the pools, so be careful. Slippery rocks, drop-offs, and water traffic on the lake require special attention. **Jardin Doret** (✉*Off Pl. du Marché* ☎021/6178131) provides access to the lake, a generous lawn with play area, and a snack bar. The indoor pool at **Basin de Natation** (✉13 *pl. des Anciens-Fossés, La Tour-de-Peilz* ☎021/9770307) is open most of the year; there's also a beach at the port. The **Vevey/Corseaux Plage** (✉19 *ave. de Lavaux, Corseaux* ☎021/9212368), west of Nestlé headquarters, has both lake swimming and two large pools (indoor and outdoor).

SHOPPING

Boutiques and galleries in the Old Town east of Place du Marché deserve attentive shopping. **L'Air du Temps** (✉25 *rue des Deux-Marchés* ☎021/9222303) carries gifts for the home plus wine accessories. Next door is the town's best cheese shop, **La Grenette** (✉27 *rue des Deux-Marchés* ☎021/9212345).

Saint-Antoine (✉1 *ave. Général-Guisan*), a modern, multilevel complex diagonally across from the train station, clusters large and small retailers within its glass panels. An extra bonus: its underground parking is a smart alternative to the cramped, restricted parking in the Old Town.

Tuesday and Saturday bring neighbors, politicians, and foodies to the center of Old Town for the **Vevey Open-Air Bazaar** open-air bazaar where wagons circle and stalls fill tidy rows; each piled high with produce from nearby farms, meats cut to order, or seafood netted at dawn. Handicrafts, flower stands, and assorted wares round out the mix and add to the convivial atmosphere of friendly banter and vendor exchanges. As Vevey is a marketing center for regional wines, the local white is sold in summer at the Saturday market, adding to the spirit of a folkloric festival; you buy your own glass and taste *à volonté* (at will).

EATING WELL IN THE VAUD

The marvelous culinary delights of the region range from the *cuisine marché* (cuisine based on fresh market produce) of top-drawer chefs to the simplest fare: *papet Vaudois* (a straightforward stew of leeks, potatoes, and cream served with superb local sausages), delicate *filets de perche* (local perch fillets, sautéed or fried), and even *malakoffs* (egg-and-Gruyère fritters), which hark back to the days when the soldiers of La Côte fought in the Crimean Wars. Fondue, the Swiss national dish, can be ordered in any season, but locals prefer chillier months or cooler climes before gathering around a *caquelon* (earthen pot) of bubbling cheese.

A generation of acolytes from the kitchen of renowned chef Fredy Girardet are now master performers in their own right, showcasing their culinary talents in villages scattered along the lake. Season after season, they fill their high-end dining rooms with scores of obsessed restaurant habitués and locals celebrating milestone events. Eating well does not mean you have to raise your credit card limit or book a table months in advance. There is hardly a village without a white-tablecloth dining area. It could be a nook of half a dozen tables or a carefully orchestrated salon, the space and the menu set apart. Your host has stocked the cellar with top-quality vintages from neighboring wineries as well as global selections, and the staff is amply qualified to pair them with the *menu du jour.*

Be adventurous and stop when you see a sign or lace-curtained window you find inviting. There is probably an exceptional meal to be had—one that is in harmony with the character of the wines produced down the lane and appreciative of each head of sun-sweetened lettuce.

MONTREUX

4 km (2 mi) southeast of Vevey, 21 km (13 mi) southeast of Lausanne.

GETTING HERE

Montreux is accessible via the main rail line that runs from Lausanne to the Valais. It is a 20- or 30-minute ride from Lausanne depending on whether you use a regional or local train. Service arrives every 15 minutes during rush hour and every 20 minutes throughout the rest of the day. By car it takes approximately half an hour on the A9 motorway; Exit 19 from the elevated roadway winds down to the lakefront road and into the center of town.

Visitor Information (✉ *5 rue du Théâtre* ☎ *084/8868484* ⊕ *www.montreux-vevey. com* ✉ *Pl. de l'Eurovision, Montreux*).

EXPLORING

Montreux could be called the Cannes of Lac Léman—though it might raise an eyebrow at the slur. Spilling down steep hillsides into a sunny south-facing bay, its waterfront thick with magnolias, cypresses, and palm trees, the historic resort earns its reputation as the capital—if

12

not the pearl—of the Swiss Riviera. Unlike the French Riviera, it has managed, despite overwhelming crowds of conventioneers, to keep up appearances. Its Edwardian-French deportment has survived considerable development, and though there are plenty of harsh modern high-rises with parking-garage aesthetics, its mansarded landmarks still unfurl yellow awnings to shield millionaires from the sun.

Famed for the nearby lakeside Château de Chillon, Montreux is where Stravinsky composed *Petrouchka* and *Le Sacre du Printemps*, and where Vladimir Nabokov resided in splendor. Indeed, Montreux and its suburbs have attracted artists and literati for 200 years: Byron, Shelley, Tolstoy, Hans Christian Andersen, and Flaubert were drawn to its lush shoreline. When its casino opened in 1883, tourism began in earnest. Even rock star Freddie Mercury came under the resort's spell; a statue of the late Queen singer stands on the quay. But the resort is best known for its annual jazz festival, which lately has strayed from its original focus to include rock, R&B, Latin, and hip-hop. Each July Montreux's usually composed promenade explodes in a street festival of food tents, vendor kiosks, and open band shells, which complement standing-room-only concert hall venues.

Above the train station a complex of 17th-century homes once belonging to the town's successful winemakers is now the **Musée de Montreux** *(Museum of Old Montreux).* This historical museum traces regional development from the time when Roman coins were used as tender, focusing on agricultural life and the shift to tourism. Profiles of famous residents and visitors who lived and worked in the area are highlighted. The museum's cellar restaurant is a good place to sample typical cuisine. ✉ *40 rue de la Gare* ☎ *021/9631353* ⊕ *www.museemontreux.ch* 🔒 *6 SF* ⊙ *Apr.–Nov., daily 10–noon, 2–5.*

Montreux's cultural center, the **Maison Visinand,** is housed in a restored mansion in the Old Town. Its calendar of events mixes exhibitions and performances with classes and studios for painting, photography, and dance. ✉ *32 rue du Pont* ☎ *021/9630726* ⊕ *www.maisonvisinand.ch* 🔒 *Free* ⊙ *Wed.–Sun. 3–6.*

NEED A BREAK?

The lunch-and-tearoom set (ladies with poodles, Brits in tweeds, fashion plates in Gucci) regularly descends on **Zurcher** (✉ *45 ave. du Casino* ☎ *021/9635963*), the irresistible confiserie on Montreux's main drag. A green salad, the *potage du jour* (soup of the day), and a chocolate-striated torte make a great quick meal. The café is closed on Monday.

Fodor's Choice ★ Certainly the greatest attraction at Montreux and one of Switzerland's must-sees is the **Château de Chillon,** the awe-inspiringly picturesque 12th-century castle that rears out of the water at Veytaux, down the road from and within sight of Montreux. Chillon was built on Roman foundations under the direction of Duke Peter of Savoy with the help of military architects from Plantagenet England. For a long period it served as a state prison, and one of its shackled guests was François Bonivard, who supported the Reformation and enraged the Savoyards.

He spent six years in this prison, chained most of the time to a pillar in the dungeon, before being released by the Bernese in 1536.

While living near Montreux, Lord Byron visited Chillon and was so transported by its atmosphere and by Bonivard's grim sojourn that he was inspired to write his famous poem "The Prisoner of Chillon." He charts the prisoner's despair and brief moments of hope, culminating in the realization on release that "these heavy walls to me had grown/A hermitage—and all my own!/...So much a long communion tends/To make us what we are:—even I/Regain'd my freedom with a sigh." Like a true tourist, Byron carved his name on a pillar in Bonivard's still-damp and chilly dungeon; his graffito is now protected under a plaque.

In high season visitors to Chillon must now file placidly from restored chamber to restored turret, often waiting at doorways for entire bus-loads of fellow tourists to pass. Yet the 19th-century Romantic-era restoration is so evocative and so convincing, with its tapestries, carved fireplaces, period ceramics and pewter, and elaborate wooden ceilings, that even the jaded castle hound may become as carried away as Byron was. While you're waiting your turn, you can gaze out the narrow windows over the sparkling, lapping water and remember Mark Twain, who thought Bonivard didn't have it half bad. Proceeds from the purchase of a bottle of Clos de Chillon, the white wine from estate vineyards, goes to restoration activities. ⊠ *Veytaux* ✛ *less than 3 km (2 mi) south of Montreux* ☎ *021/9668910* ⊕ *www.chillon.ch* 🎟 *10 SF* ⊗ *Mar. and Oct., daily 9:30–5; Apr.–Sept., daily 9–6; Nov.–Feb., daily 10–4.*

OFF THE BEATEN PATH

Les Avants. The Montreux–Oberland–Bernois (MOB) railroad leads to the resort village of Les Avants (3,181 feet) and then on to Château-d'Oex, Gstaad, and the Simmental. Noël Coward bought his dream home in Les Avants, at 8 route de Sonloup. Ernest Hemingway wrote to his family and friends of the village's fields of daffodils—and, more in character, of its bobsled track.

WHERE TO EAT

$$$$
CONTEMPORARY
★

✕ **L'Ermitage.** Freestanding on its own waterfront-garden grounds, this genteel, intimate retreat offers top-drawer haute gastronomie and a few luxurious rooms upstairs. Chef Étienne Krebs's exceptional menu may include duckling with quinoa and foie gras or spice-roasted lamb with a chickpea pancake. You won't go wrong with suggested wine pairings, many from select Swiss vineyards. On-cue service overseen by the chef's wife is calm and elegant. A bit less formal than the dining room is the canopied terrace, open daily in summer for alfresco dining. ⊠ *75 rue du Lac, Clarens* ☎ *021/9644411* ⊕ *www.ermitage-montreux.com* 🖃 *AE, DC, MC, V* ⊗ *Closed Mon. in Sept.–May, plus late Dec.–late Jan.*

$$
THAI

✕ **Mai Thai.** Weary of regional cuisine? Freshly made spring rolls, satays, and spicy dishes from this storefront eatery on the edge of Clarens will lighten up the program. Traditional pad thai, multicolor curries, and seafood preparations are superb. A longtime resident of the neighborhood draws locals to the Asian-accented dining room, but at the first hint of warmth they scurry to tables on the deck across the street with superior views of the lake and gardens. It's not an inexpensive meal, but one that will leave you feeling a continental shift. ✉*40* ▾ Clarens ☎*021/9642536* ▭*MC, V* ⊘*Closed Mon.*

$$$$
MODERN FRENCH
Fodor'sChoice
★

✕ **Le Pont de Brent.** Tucked on a hillside next to its namesake bri... suburb of Brent, this small but elegant establishment ties with Rochat's restaurant for the honor of best table in the region. Who would guess that the pale stone exterior of this unassuming building screens showstopping cuisine? Norman chef Gérard Rabaey performs alchemy with local ingredients to turn out dishes almost too pretty to eat, such as Breton lobster and crayfish with lemongrass or veal kidneys with black truffles. All is warm here, from the ocher walls to the welcome and service. The four-course business lunch is a well-priced sampler of the chef's talents. ✉*4 rte. de Blonay, 7 km (4½ mi) northwest of Montreux, Brent* ☎*021/9645230* ⊕*www.lepontdebrent.com* ⌂*Reservations essential* ▭*MC, V* ⊘*Closed Sun. and Mon., last 3 wks of July, and late Dec.–early Jan.*

$$
ITALIAN

✕ **La Rouvenaz.** If it's an oven-fired pizza or plate of pasta you have been pining for, there's no place more convivial or convenient than this trattoria on the main drag. The atmosphere is warmed by terra-cotta walls with bold blue accents and endless pitchers of wine. Seafood is fresh and a specialty of the house, whether atop a pie crust or a mound of linguine. There is a satellite location serving light fare and desserts across the street on the lakefront promenade. ✉*1 rue du Marché* ☎*021/9632736* ▭*MC, V* ⊘*Closed Mon.*

$$$
SWISS

✕ **La Vieille Ferme.** Follow the winding road into the village of Chailly. Past the fountain and across the street, you'll see the stone facade of a 14th-century farmhouse restored to rustic elegance and said to be the oldest in the region. Dining rooms that were once stalls and family quarters have stucco and wooden beams. The owner's philosophy—A BON MANGER, BON BOIRE (good food and good drink)—is carved above the raised fireplace that doubles as a grill. The cuisine is true to the heritage of the homestead: beef Stroganoff, chicken simmered in honey and lemon. If it's a fondue or raclette you prefer, a separate carnotzet serves these cheese specialties. ✉*40 rue de Bourg, Chailly-sur-Montreux* ☎*021/9646465* ▭*AE, MC, V* ⊘*Closed Mon. and Tues.*

WHERE TO STAY

$$$$
Fodor'sChoice
★

🏨 **Fairmont Le Montreux Palace.** Silver mansards and yellow awnings flag this vast institution as a landmark, though its aristocratic interiors are now filled with cell-phone-chatting travelers. This colossal Belle Epoque folly of stained glass, frescoes, and flamboyant molded stucco opened in 1906 and counts Vladimir Nabokov among its notable residents (a bronze of the author stands in the lakeside gardens). Updated facilities do not compromise the allure of this grand hotel. You can be cyber-connected from any corner or secluded in a massage suite at the Willow Stream Spa. Guest rooms have fruitwood furniture, bold accessories, and Jacuzzis trimmed in granite and marble. If you are homesick for an American cocktail or sandwich, Harry's Bar sates. Ah, the good life. **Pros:** halls and salons are replete with history and decorative architecture; discreet staff can handle any request. **Cons:** easy to feel lost in the shuffle of high-end conferences and incentive group meetings; prices are steep for basics like breakfast and parking. ✉*100 Grand-Rue*

12

☎021/9621212 ⊕*www.fairmont.com* ⤴*185 rooms, 50 suites* ⬧*In-room: safe, refrigerator, Ethernet. In-hotel: 4 restaurants, 2 bars, 2 pools, gym, spa, parking (fee)* ⊟*AE, DC, MC, V.*

$$$ ⛺**Masson.** If you enjoy being away from the downtown resort scene, look up this demure little inn on a hillside in Veytaux, between Chillon and Montreux. Since it was built in 1829, it has had only four owners, and the current family takes pride in its genteel period decor and the personalized attention that attracts repeat guests season after season. You'll find floral prints, brass beds, pristine linens, buffed parquet, and expansive lake views from the numerous balconies. The breakfast buffet is generous, with homemade breads and jams. **Pros:** serene old family-estate feel; genial hostess is an accomplished innkeeper. **Cons:** need a car unless you want to trek uphill from the bus stop; no other restaurants nearby. ⌂*5 rue Bonivard, Veytaux* ☎*021/9660044* ⊕*www.hotelmasson.ch* ⤴*33 rooms* ⬧*In-room: no a/c, safe, refrigerator. In-hotel: restaurant, parking (no fee)* ⊟*AE, MC, V* ⊗*Closed Oct.–Apr.* ⦿|*CP.*

$–$$ ⛺**Tralala Hotel.** In a town of world-renowned musical heritage the rooms of this small modern inn tucked in the sharp curve of an Old Town thoroughfare are themed for jazz, rock, and blues stars. The black, white, and red interiors are far from kitschy in their sleek minimalism. The top floor has views over the city's rooftops, with postage-stamp balconies and contemporary shower-baths. An active wine bar doubles as the morning breakfast nook. **Pros:** refreshing contrast to the town's stately hotel scene; attracts a well-heeled thirtysomething crowd. **Cons:** limited kitchen requires that you dine elsewhere; public street or pay garage parking can be a headache and costly. ⌂*2 rue du Temple 2* ☎*021/9634973* ⊕*www.tralalahotel.ch* ⤴*32 rooms, 4 suites* ⬧*In-room: safe, Wi-fi. In-hotel: bar, bicycles* ⊟*AE, MC, V* ⦿|*CP.*

NIGHTLIFE & THE ARTS

Montreux's famous festivals and arts events are listed in a seasonal booklet published by the tourist office; tickets are sold from its booth at the waterfront. The renowned **Montreux Jazz Festival** takes place every July in the ultramodern **Auditorium Stravinski** (⌂*95 Grand-Rue*) and other lakeside venues. For tickets to these popular events, it's easiest to monitor the schedule (not released until late April or May) on the Web site ⊕*www.montreuxjazz.com.* Popular events sell out in hours, so be ready to purchase online. The **Ticket Corner** (☎*090/0800800 toll call* ⊕*www.ticketcorner.com*) also sells tickets. In summer Montreux offers a variety of free outdoor concerts from its bandstand on the waterfront near the landing stage.

BARS   The swank **Harry's New York Bar** (⌂*100 Grand-Rue* ☎*021/9621200*), at the Montreux Palace, has a pianist after 5. Adjacent to a popular Italian restaurant (La Rouvenaz), the eclectic **La Vinoteca** (⌂*1 rue du Marché* ☎*021/9632736*) is the smallest bar in town. An urbane, designer-clad crowd flocks to the **Mayfair Café** (⌂*52 Grand-Rue* ☎*021/9667978*) to take in the afternoon sun and make plans for the evening.

CASINO   The **Casino Barrière** (⌂*9 rue du Théâtre* ☎*021/9628383*) has dancing, slot machines, table games, and multiple dining venues. Revised gambling regulations have upped the betting limits, making it a major

gaming center. Be sure to bring your passport, as no other ID w[
you in. Table games don't begin until 4 PM. The casino is open fro[
AM to 3 AM, Friday and Saturday to 5 AM.

DANCING   A DJ oversees the playlist at the **Imperia Club Cat** (✉*100 Grand-Rue*
☎*021/9630404*), the Montreux Palace's hot spot with exotic Hindu
temple decor and dancing. Techno and Latin sounds accompanied by
colorful lighting pulse at **Black Pearl** (✉*92 Grand-Rue* ☎*021/9635288*),
where weekend partying goes until 5 AM.

SPORTS & THE OUTDOORS

BOATING   Water sports are popular along Montreux-Vevey's waterfront. Lessons
and rentals are available at locations in marinas and from docks that
rim the lake. **Ecole de Voile de Montreux** (✉*Clarens* ☎*021/4691338*), the
local sailing club, gives sailing lessons. **Nautic Loisirs** (✉*Quai du Casino*
☎*078/6061588*) rents all types of equipment, from paddle to motor
boats, kayaks to windsurfers.

SWIMMING   **La Maladaire** (✉*Clarens* ☎*021/9645703*) has an Olympic-size indoor
pool. The **Casino Barrière** (✉*9 rue du Théâtre* ☎*021/9628383*) has a
pool on an outdoor terrace with a bar.

SHOPPING

Souvenir shops, tony boutiques, and jewelry stores are interspersed
randomly along the Grand-Rue.

The **Forum** (✉*6 pl. du Marché*), a modern complex, is anchored by
grocery giant Migros and topped with shops, restaurants, and expensive condominiums. Underground parking is connected to the **Place du
Marché,** a large covered pavilion where the weekly open-air food market
is held every Friday morning. The pavilion also doubles as the hub for
festivals, concerts, and the famous Marché Noël (Christmas Market).

LES ALPES VAUDOISES

At the eastern tip of Lac Léman, the Alps on the French and Swiss sides
close in on the Rhône, and the lakefront highways begin a gradual,
ear-popping ascent as the scenery looms larger and the mountains rise
around you. The high-altitude Alpine resorts of Villars and Les Diablerets have their respective charms for winter-sports fans and summer
hikers, but sightseers plain and simple head to two other destinations:
Aigle, famed for its storybook chateau, and Château-d'Oex, a moun-
tain-aerie favorite of hot-air balloonists. Here you are in the midst of
the Pays-d'Enhaut, a rustic, lower-altitude region surrounded by rocky
ridges and velvet hillsides sprinkled with ancient carved-wood chalets.
You can make a beeline from one to another, but rail connections are
cumbersome and driving often challenging; you'd do well to choose one
dreamy spot and stay put—by the fireplace or on the balcony—for as
many days as your itinerary allows.

AIGLE

17 km (10 mi) south of Montreux, 38 km (24 mi) southeast of Lausanne.

GETTING HERE

Connections to the ski and hiking resorts of Les Diablerets and Villars-sur-Ollon radiate from the town of Aigle. Most regional trains departing from Lausanne stop at this transfer station, but not all. Brightly painted coaches with only second-class seating wind their way to mountain villages, arriving in one and a half hours. The fastest way to get to Villars is to switch to the regional bus, but you can use train service available from Bex, the next stop on the line. As at Aigle, not all trains service this station. Round-trip tickets will cost approximately 50 SF.

Visitor Information (⊠ *5 rue Colomb* ☎ *024/4663000* ⊕ *www.aigle.ch*).

EXPLORING

On a smooth plain flanked by the sloping vineyards of the region of Le Chablais, Aigle is a scenic wine center. Its **Château de Savoie**, originally built in the 13th century, was almost completely destroyed—and then rebuilt—by the 15th-century Bernese.

★ On sabbatical from a fairy-tale storybook, the 15th-century, spired-and-turreted **Château d'Aigle** allows both the novice and wine aficionado to get a close-up look at wine-making history and promotion. First peruse display casks, bottles, presses, and winemakers' tools in the wood-beamed chambers of the **Musée Vaudois de la Vigne et du Vin et de L'Etiquette** (Vine, Wine, and Wine Label Museum of Vaud), in the chateau. Some living quarters are reproduced, and there's even a collection of costumes worn over the centuries at the local Fête des Vignerons. The separate **Musée de l'Étiquette** (Museum of Wine Labels), in a timbered attic in an adjacent warehouse called the Maison de la Dîme, chronicles the history of prestigious vintages through a collection of labels representing more than 50 countries and dating back 200 years. Pay an additional 6 SF for a tasting of the local vintages and take the souvenir glass with you. ☎ *024/4662130* ⊕ *www.chateauaigle.ch* 🖾 *9 SF* ⊙ *Apr.–June, Sept., and Oct., Tues.–Sun. 11–6; July and Aug., daily 11–6; Nov.–Mar., tours by appointment.*

VILLARS-SUR-OLLON

15 km (9 mi) southeast of Aigle, 53 km (33 mi) southeast of Lausanne.

Visitor Information (⊠ *Rue Centrale* ☎ *024/4953232* ⊕ *www.villars.ch*).

EXPLORING

At 4,264 feet, this welcoming ski center spreads comfortably along a sunny terrace, the craggy peaks of Les Diablerets (10,528 feet) behind it and before it a sweeping view over the Rhône Valley all the way to Mont Blanc. Balanced along its ridge and open to the vast space below, the busy little downtown—sports shops, cafés, resort hotels—tapers off quickly into open country. Though it's thriving with new construction, Villars retains a sense of coziness and tradition, and some of its family-

12

owned hotels have preserved the feel of mountain lodges that's rare these days in Switzerland. What Villars lacks in glitz, it amply compensates for with unpretentious good cheer. A network of lifts connecting with Les Diablerets makes this a good choice for skiers or hikers who want to experience Suisse Romande relatively unspoiled. The boarding schools headquartered in the area keep the town animated with teen adrenaline, backing sports such as snowboarding, mountain biking, in-line skating, and rock climbing.

SKIING

Villars nicely balances sophistication and Alpine isolation, thanks to a compact village, 36 lifts, and 100 km (67 mi) of downhill runs. The main ski area above the village can be reached easily either by cable car to **Roc d'Orsay** (6,560 feet) or by cog railway from the center to **Bretaye** (5,925 feet); either site allows access to the lifts that fan out over a sunny bowl riddled with intermediate runs and off-trail challenges. From Bretaye you can also take lifts up to **Grand Chamossaire** (6,954 feet) for gentle, open runs. Trails from Chaux Ronde are easy enough for beginners, but the more advanced can find jumps and trees enough to keep them more than alert. Just beyond Villars, the linking resort of **Gryon,** with runs that pitch off Les Chaux, presents a few more options and a change of scenery, again with trails for all levels of skill. For serious skiers, the link to **Les Diablerets Glacier** provides stepped-up challenges in vertical territory that is used for training professionals. One-day lift tickets without glacier access cost 49 SF. If you are going to ski for six days, purchase the region's all-inclusive pass for 277 SF, which provides access to Glacier 3000 at Les Diablerets and Les Mosses. There are also 50 km (31 mi) of cross-country trails plus sledding and snowshoeing.

WHERE TO EAT

$ ✕ **Le Refuge de Frience.** Detour off the scenic route from Villars to Gryon
SWISS   at Barboleuse to get to this 18th-century Heidi-esque chalet in the highland pastures. It combines the grist of Alpine legend with good, honest food. Three cheery rooms glowing with log fires under low, beamed ceilings give way to unfettered views of the mountains. You won't see many tourists here; it's a word-of-mouth place that packs in locals and weekend expats in the know. They go for the fondue and raclette, river trout, and plates of fresh regional mushrooms—and wine spouting from an old *fontaine,* a wrought-iron contraption rarely seen in restaurants. ⊠ *4½ km (3 mi) from Villars, Alpe des Chaux* ☎ 024/4981426 ⊟MC, V ☉ *Closed Tues., Apr.–May, and mid-Nov.–mid-Dec.*

SKI, FLOAT, AND SURF ALL IN ONE DAY

The Alpes Vaudoises allow you to experience all levels of skiing difficulty. Summer opens trails and high-altitude passes for hikers and mountain bikers. Well-marked paths in every direction give proof that the Swiss adore an outing, especially with the requisite rest stop at a *buvette* (snack bar). You can also take on a more unusual activity, such as strenuous river-gorge expeditions, breathtaking paragliding and hot-air ballooning, and even mountain surfing (zipping downhill on a skateboardlike scooter with handlebars).

WHERE TO STAY

$$$$ 🛏️ **Grand Hôtel du Park.** You can't sleep any closer to the slopes than at this upscale lodge at the base of the mountain, which has been run by the same family for generations. Its park setting is enjoyable in all seasons, and the honey-colored wood interior says ski chalet. South-facing, generously sized balcony rooms are warmed by the afternoon sun and come with exceptional Alpine views. Themed culinary weeks feature round-the-world cuisine, a delightful change from regional dishes. **Pros:** garden that surrounds feels like a private estate; aging gracefully. **Cons:** ski groups and families can dominate; the short walk to the village for services and other dining venues seems far, especially in bad weather. ✉️ *Rte. du Col de la Croix* ☎️ *024/4962828* ⊕ *www. parcvillars.ch* ⇢ *55 rooms* 🛎️ *In-room: no a/c, refrigerator, Wi-Fi. In-hotel: 4 restaurants, bar, pool, gym, 2 tennis courts* ▭ *AE, DC, MC, V* ☺ *Closed Nov.* ❘⊙❘ *CP.*

SPORTS & THE OUTDOORS

HIKING   There are 300 km (186 mi) of hiking trails in the region. Most only require a map (pick one up at the tourist office) and a good pair of hiking shoes. If you would like to tackle more difficult routes or add mountaineering to your outing, **Villars Experience** (✉️ *Rue Centrale* ☎️ *024/4954138* ⊕ *www.villars-experience.ch*) has guides and equipment.

SPORTS   The **Centre des Sports** (✉️ *Chemin de la Gare* ☎️ *024/4951221* ⊕ *www.*
CENTERS   *cds-villars.ch* ✉️ *Rte. du Col de la Croix* ☎️ *024/4953030*) has two locations. One has an indoor skating rink (skates available for rent) and an indoor pool, whereas the other offers an extensive range of activities—from badminton to wall climbing—as well as an outdoor pool.

LES DIABLERETS

19 km (12 mi) northeast of Aigle, 59 km (37 mi) southeast of Lausanne.

Visitor Information (✉️ *Village Center* ☎️ *024/4923358* ⊕ *www.lesdiablerets.ch*).

EXPLORING

This small resort (3,806 feet) lies at the base of the 10,525-foot peak of the same name—which sheds the dramatic namesake 9,840-foot glacier. The village was named after a folklore tale of devils who played skittles among the desolate glacier peaks. A compact handful of hotels, shops, and steep-roof chalets are strung along a winding road. The valley brightens only when sun finds its way over crags and crests, which may be why skiing is guaranteed year-round and the Swiss team trains here in summer. To get here from Villars during those warm months, car travelers can cut along spectacular heights on a tiny 13%-grade road over the Col de la Croix (5,832 feet). Keep an eye out for packs of mountain bikers pushing their way across the pass.

Fodor's Choice   The ride on **Glacier 3000,** an aerial cableway strung from its station at
★   Col du Pillon 7 km (4 mi) outside the resort village to a shelf at Scex-Rouge, is a thrill and well worth the steep fare. Vistas of Alpine peaks,

vast meadows, and clusters of sloping-roof farmhouses extend to Lac Léman and the Jura Mountains. The 20-minute ascent is done in two segments, ending at the metallic, jewel box–shaped restaurant designed by world-famous architect Mario Botta. In warm weather, skiers share the glacial zone with snowcat (motorized vehicle), dogsled tours, and alpine coasters. ☎024/4923377 ⊕*www.glacier3000.ch* ⊠*57 SF* ⊙*May–Aug., daily 9–4:50; mid-Sept.–April, daily 9–4:30.*

SKIING

The connection of Les Diablerets' ski facilities with those of Villars adds considerably to ski options—including summer skiing on the glacier itself. The lift to **Meilleret** (6,394 feet), the peak that lies directly above the village of **Les Diablerets** (3,806 feet), serves as the aerial linchpin with Villars. A cable car from another station in the village lifts skiers to **Isenau,** which has intermediate and expert runs cascading from the peak of **Floriettaz** (6,956 feet). But it is the glacier—and the dramatic peak-top pistes at **Quille du Diable** and **Scex-Rouge** that many come to ski. Take a bus to Col du Pillon, where a series of gondolas ascends along the sheer wall to mountaintop ski stations. From Scex-Rouge, a popular run carries you around the top of the **Oldenhorn** and down to **Oldenegg,** a wide-open intermediate run through a sheltered valley. For an additional adrenaline rush, there's one gravity-defying expert slope, directly under the gondola, from **Pierre-Pointes** back to the valley.

Before purchasing your tickets, study ski maps carefully and assess your stamina and skill level. Lift rates are often priced in combinations. A one-day pass for Les Diablerets/Villars is 49 SF; Isenau is 42 SF. Adding Glacier 3000 takes the cost up to 58 SF, but you will have 74 lifts and 200 km (137 mi) of runs from which to choose. (Reduced family prices are available.)

Cross-country skiers can explore 45 km (27 mi) of trails, some tracking through woods and meadows. There are also runs specifically designed for sledding and snow tubing.

WHERE TO EAT & STAY

$ ✕**Auberge de la Poste.** The Pichard family, keepers of this weathered
SWISS centuries-old chalet, holds dear the inn's heritage of feeding and lodging stagecoach passengers and Alpine enthusiasts. The rustic structure has carved eaves with hand-painted designs, creaky floors, and old, rippled, handblown-glass windows. In summer the front patio hugging the main street fills with boot-clad hikers reaching across platters of air-dried meats and mountain cheeses sided with baskets of crusty dark bread. The change of seasons brings the crowd inside to sit on heavy wooden furniture eager to swirl ragged cubes of bread in fondue caquelons or scrap raclette and potatoes together on their plates. The menu also includes salads, meat dishes, and rösti, but don't expect any fussy preparations. ⊠*Rue de la Gare* ☎024/4923124 ⊕*www. aubergedelaposte.ch* ⊟*MC, V* ⊙*Closed Nov.*

$$$$ **Eurotel Victoria.** Sharing the same name as its sister hotel in Villars, this resort lodging holds true to regional decor with carved blond-wood furniture accented by bold-colored fabrics much like those worn by the outdoors enthusiasts who tramp through the lobby and fill the bar after a day on the mountain. Service is polished and housekeeping tidies rooms with precision, lining up bath amenities like toy soldiers. The lively restaurant refuels the active crowd, many of whom opt for the half-board program based on quality and variety. ✉Chemin du Vernex ☎024/4923721 ⊕www.eurotel-victoria.ch ➤110 rooms, 13 suites ⚑In-room: no a/c. Internet. In-hotel: restaurant, bar, pool, gym, refrigerator ▤AE, DC, MC, V ⊙Closed late Apr.–June, Oct., and Nov. ⏼CP.

SPORTS & THE OUTDOORS

You can satisfy your taste for adventure with activities ranging from leisurely to extreme. **Centre ParAdventure** (✉Rue de la Gare ☎024/4922382) can take you hang gliding, canyoning, sledding, dirt biking, and zorbing (rolling down the mountainside in a huge plastic ball). **Mountain Evasion** (✉Pl. de la Gare ☎024/4921232 ⊕www. mountain-evasion.ch) organizes luge, snowshoeing, canyoning, rock climbing, and dirt-biking excursions, among others. Both have English-speaking guides. **Parc des Sports** (✉Centre Ville ☎024/4923988) is the hub of summer and indoor athletics from archery to tennis, swimming to wall climbing.

For a real tobogganing experience, try the 7-km (4.5-mi) run from **Vioz-Mazots**, accessible from the Meilleret lift, at night. You can rent sleds at any of the village sports stores; the ticket to the top costs 12 SF. Alternatively, you can book an all-inclusive excursion (transportation, equipment, and hot cider après sled run) with Mountain Evasion or Center ParAdventure. Evening outings start with a delicious fondue dinner followed by a torchlit race to the bottom.

CHÂTEAU-D'OEX

33 km (20 mi) northeast of Aigle, 64 km (40 mi) east of Lausanne.

GETTING HERE

In any season the train trip to the Alpine village of Château-d'Oex is one of the most picturesque in the country. Board the standard rail cars of the MOB (Montreux Oberland Bernois) or pay 15 SF extra for reserved seats on the luxurious Golden Pass coaches (discounted with a Swiss Pass). There is a separate MOB ticket office and platform on the upper level of the Montreux station. A one-way, first-class ticket will cost 30 SF. The switchback ride climbs into the vineyards above the city with 180-degree views of the lake and mountains. Once your visit is complete, continue into the Berner Oberland on the same line that passes through Gstaad or backtrack to the lake. The MOB Web site is www.mob.ch.

Visitor Information (✉La Place ☎026/9242525 ⊕www.chateau-doex.ch).

EXPLORING

At the crossroads between the Col des Mosses highway to Aigle and the Valais and the route to the Berner Oberland lies Château-d'Oex (pronounced *day*), a popular sports resort that connects with the greater

Gstaad ski region. Its perhaps even greater claim to fame these days is ballooning, with hot-air-balloon competitions that draw mobs of international enthusiasts and fill hotels throughout the region. In spring 1999 the Breitling *Orbiter 3* balloon launched from the valley floor for its record-breaking nonstop trip around the world. The town itself is a mix of Edwardian architecture with weathered-wood chalets, spreading over a green forest-top hillside above the highway. It heads the French end of the valley of the Sarine River.

12

Separated from the high-altitude Alpine resorts by the modest Col des Mosses (4,740 feet), the Pays-d'Enhaut (Highlands) hereabouts offers an entirely different culture from that of its Vaud cousins. Here the architecture begins to resemble that of the Berner Oberland, which it borders. Deep-eaved wooden chalets replace the Edwardian structures of the lake lands, and the atmosphere takes on a mountain-farm air. A stone's throw up the valley you cross the Sarine/Saanen and the so-called Rösti Border, where the culture and language switch to Bernese German.

This is still Gruyère cheese country. A style known as L'Etivaz is made from milk drawn exclusively from cows grazed on pastures at elevations between 3,280 feet and 7,216 feet. The sweet, late-blooming flowers they eat impart a flavor that lowland cheeses can't approach. Visitors passing through the eponymous village after crossing the Col des Mosses can stop at the Caves à Fromages (a cheese-makers' cooperative), where a worker in rubber boots will be happy to sell you brick-size chunks of both young and aged cheeses at prices well below those at resort groceries.

The highlands are also the source of one of Switzerland's most familiar decorative arts: *papier découpé,* delicate, symmetrical paper cutouts. They are cut in black, often with simple imagery of cattle and farmers, and fixed on white paper for contrast. The real thing is a refined craft and is priced accordingly, but attractive prints reproducing the look are on sale at reduced prices throughout the region.

★ In Château-d'Oex's small center, the **Musée Artisanal du Vieux Pays-d'Enhaut** *(Artisan and Folklore Museum of the Old Highlands)* shows the intracies of découpage and gives insight into life in these isolated parts. Complete interiors layered in an old farmhouse reproduce interiors from a farmer's home, a cheese-maker's cottage, and a carpenter's studio. ⊠ *Grand-Rue* ☎ *026/9246520* 🎫 *8 SF* 🕐 *Tues.–Sun. 2–5. Closed Nov.*

The technical and sporting elements of hot-air ballooning that put this tiny village on the world map are highlighted at **Espace Ballon,** a museum and exhibition space run by professional pilots. Permanent and changing shows follow the history of avionics, challenges shared by flying enthusiasts, and flight records that have been broken by adventurers like Bertrand Piccard and Brian Jones, whose Breitling *Orbiter* set off from a nearby meadow. In addition, there are 3-D movies that take the viewer along for a ride, or you can schedule your own voyage into the thermals. ⊠ *La Place* ☎ *026/9242222* ⊕ *www.espaceballon.ch*

⊠8 SF ⊙ *Mid-Dec.–mid Mar and July–mid-Sept., daily, 10–12 and 2–6; mid-Mar.–June and mid-Sept.–mid-Nov., daily 2–6.*

WHERE TO EAT & STAY

¢–$ ✕**Le Chalet.** A reproduction of a mountain cheese-makers home doubles
SWISS   as a demonstration kitchen where hot milk is stirred in a vast copper vat on an open fire in the afternoon (1:30–5). The region's piquant tasting specialty is melted in fondues and raclettes, served on *croûtes* (open-face toasted-cheese sandwiches), and mixed with macaroni or potatoes. Expect large groups at one of the main attractions in town, with a gift shop that sells regional crafts and dairy products. ☎026/9246677 ⊟MC, V ⊙*Closed Mon. in June–Feb., Mon.–Tues. in Mar.–May.*

$$ ▦**Bon Accueil.** In beautifully proportioned 18th-century weathered-wood farmhouses on the outskirts of town, this is the quintessential French-Swiss country inn. Guest rooms mix aged pine planking, painted furniture, and antiques, and under the old low-beam ceilings the floors creak agreeably. Up-to-date amenities, immaculate appointments, and fresh flowers—inside and out—keep standards well above rustic. The restaurant is even more civilized, and on winter nights there's a firelit stone cellar bar with low-key jazz. **Pros:** peaceful surroundings; unexpected top-notch kitchen. **Cons:** a hike to village shops, restaurants, and the train station; rooms in the main house more appealing. ⊠ *Château-d'Oex* ☎026/9246320 ⊕*www.bonaccueil.ch* ⇆*18 rooms* ⌂*In-room: no a/c. In-hotel: restaurant, bar, parking (no fee)* ⊟AE, DC, MC, V ⊙*Closed mid-Nov.–mid-Dec.* ⎜⎜⎜CP.

SPORTS & THE OUTDOORS

BALLOONING   The annual hot-air ballooning festival gets off the ground in late January in a spectacle featuring over a hundred vibrant balloons. On Friday night a *night glow* is held. Scramble to the top of the hill that has the church (look for the steeple) for a stunning view of brilliantly colored, backlit balloons choreographed to music. A lively village fair follows. If you'd like to get up in the air yourself, you can arrange for an accompanied flight year-round through **Ballon Château-d'Oex** (⊠ *Château-d'Oex* ☎026/9242533 ⊕*www.ballonchateaudoex.ch*).

Geneva

The Bol d'Or Rolex regatta on Lake Geneva

WORD OF MOUTH

"A short stroll from our hotel is Geneva's tremendous fountain, the Jet D'Eau, rising 450 feet at 125 mph and visible from all over the town. Lake Geneva is unbelievably clear—the bottom can be seen nine feet below us. Using the floating bridge, we stroll to the town center. Even atop the cathedral bell tower, the fountain still reaches above us. Amazing."

—stumblebum

WELCOME TO GENEVA

TOP REASONS TO GO

★ **Falling water:** The feathery Jet d'Eau, Geneva's iconic harbor fountain and the ultimate public shower, is visible for tens of miles in every direction.

★ **Time on your hands:** Chances are good you'll leave this city of watchmakers with a new timepiece— for glorious old ones, visit the Patek Philippe Museum.

★ **City of God:** The Protestant Reformation moved through Geneva like a hurricane almost five centuries ago; the city's churches still bear scars.

★ **Block party!:** The Fêtes de Genève gives everyone a mid-summer break by turning the Rade into a 10-day smorgasbord of international foods.

★ **Exclusive baubles:** To wander the Rue du Rhône is to take a roll call of the world's finest jewelers–only here they're homegrown.

1 The Waterfront. La Rade, the 3-mile-long necklace along which Geneva is strung, is woven of parkland, tree-lined promenades, harbor traffic, and working marinas. Mont Blanc hovers over the Left Bank.

2 The Vieille Ville. The pre-Roman Celts who settled this strategically perfect hill could not have imagined it would grow into a renegade religious fortress, a center of government, or the gentrified soul of a large city. Today it is also home to many of Geneva's museums.

GETTING ORIENTED

13

Well-groomed and graceful, crowned with a cathedral and draped around the southwestern tip of Lac Léman, Geneva is a postcard waiting to happen. Headquarters of the 16th-century Calvinist Reformation and an independent crossroads of people and trade from the beginning, the Vieille Ville harbors three millennia of history; today the city also hosts the United Nations and shares most of its borders with France.

3 Plainpalais. A newcomer and a workhorse, Plainpalais is also a shape-shifting free spirit. Contemporary art has colonized one-time factories along Rue des Bains; university students amble to class at Uni Mail, and the Swiss National Circus sets up shop on the Plaine de Plainpalais.

4 International Area. United Nations security may give these broad, leafy avenues a sense of danger, but the Red Cross Museum and the Palais des Nations never lack visitors. The villas and diplomatic compounds around them house a community with its finger firmly attached to the world's pulse.

GENEVA PLANNER

How's the Weather?

Hot and sunny with a slight breeze in summer, crisp and clear in spring and autumn, rainbow-prone in June—Geneva's weather, when it's good, is spectacular.

The Alps glow pink and the Jura fades to silhouette at the end of the day; restaurants set tables outside from March through October.

There are other days—whole weeks of them in winter—when stratus clouds coagulate between the mountains and grey out everything in sight.

But relief comes from La Bise, the often bitingly cold north wind that blows in off the lake, clears away *la grisaille*, and reveals sparkling snow-covered peaks.

Transportation Basics

The Rhône River divides Geneva into two parts: the Rive Gauche (Left Bank) and the Rive Droite (Right Bank). The Rive Gauche, to the south, comprises the Vielle Ville (Old Town), Eaux-Vives, most of the city's shopping and major museums, and Plainpalais. The Rive Droite includes the *quartier international* (International Area), the train station, the airport, Les Pâquis, and the luxury waterfront hotels. Pont du Mont-Blanc, the city's heavily traveled main bridge, connects the two sides of the river.

Geneva has an extensive public transportation system, but you won't need it to see most sights. Pedestrians have an almost sacred right of way here—crossing the street in designated places can bring four lanes of traffic to a screeching halt—and walking is by far the most (cost-) effective way to discover quayside promenades, parks, shopping areas, and car-free cobblestone alleys. Street parking demand outstrips supply, meter maids are zealous, and taxis expensive; canton-wide public transport, meaning buses, trams, trains, and shuttle boats, is clean, punctual, ubiquitous, and cheap. (In fact, it's free for visitors, campers, hostellers or palace dwellers. Ask for your Geneva Transportation Card at the desk; it's valid for the length of your stay.) Count on 20 minutes on foot from the Gare Cornavin—the main train station, between Place de Cornavin and Rue de Montbrilliant—to either Place du Bourg-de-Four or Place Neuve.

Visitor Information

Genève Tourisme (✉ *18 rue du Mont-Blanc, Les Pâquis, Case Postale 1602, Genève 1* ☎ *022/9097070* 🖷 *022/9097075* ⊕ *www.geneve-tourisme.ch*) is head-quartered inside the large post office building halfway between the Pont du Mont-Blanc and the Gare Cornavin. Additional information booths serve the airport and, from June through September, the train station. The Arcade d'information de la Ville de Genève, run by the city on the Pont de la Machine, is another excellent, multilingual source of information about all things Geneva.

Making the Most of Your Time

A curious tension exists in Geneva between dour intellectual concepts and breathtaking physical beauty, and you will probably find yourself torn between the urge to wander the quays and the sense that you ought to hit the museum trail. Don't choose: try to divide whatever time you have in the city equally between an extended stroll along the waterfront and a thorough exploration of the Vieille Ville.

Make time for the International Area if it interests you—never mind if it doesn't. Do not, however, skip Carouge, the creative, convivial warren of craftspeople and artists to the south of the city. Do try to see some specialist collections (the Fondation Bodmer and the Patek Philippe Museum are stars), do check out the Rues-Basses shopping scene, and make sure that you go somewhere—Port Noir, the tip of the Jet d'Eau jetty, the cathedral towers, La Perle du Lac, Cologny—where you can see distance: Geneva genuinely does look equally good from up close and far away.

With that in mind, here's a sample itinerary that hits all the bases in three days. Spend your first morning exploring the downtown waterfront, with its boats, swans, 16-foot-wide flowered clock face, and feathery Jet d'Eau.

Then window-shop your way along the Rues-Basses and up into the Vieille Ville. Have lunch on Place du Bourg-de-Four, and investigate the Espace St-Pierre, an umbrella term for the starkly beautiful Cathédrale St-Pierre, Musée International de la Réforme, and underground Site Archéologique. Don't forget the contemplative Auditoire de Calvin (if it's open); the Monument de la Réformation sums it all up.

The next day head for the International Area. Spend the morning at the Palais des Nations and the Musée International de la Croix-Rouge, have lunch at the Château de Penthes, and spend the afternoon wandering the Jardin Botanique. Then head over to Carouge for a late-afternoon stroll through galleries and craftshops.

On your third morning, head back to the Vieille Ville and work steadily through the Maison Tavel, Musée Barbier-Mueller, and Musée Rath. Eat lunch near Place Neuve, and then explore watchmaking at the Patek Philippe Museum, watch history unfold at the Fondation Bodmer, or take a break and spend the afternoon cruising Lac Léman with its wide-open, nice-day views of the mountains or chugging along the Rhône River past surprisingly untamed and silent shores atangle with flora and fauna.

Shop-till-You-Drop Alert

Goldsmiths and enamelers set up shop in Geneva during the Reformation, forging alliances with watchmakers, who had also arrived as refugees. Spectacularly, this was the beginning of a beautiful friendship.

Today teams of expert craftsmen toil steadily behind chic shop walls, windows glitter with baubles of every shape, size, and color.

Result? The world over, Geneva-based heavyweights like Patek Philippe and Vacheron Constantin are rightfully known for unparalleled excellence.

But great shopping is not confined to timepieces and jewelry. Handmade chocolates are an art form here. Along with such dee-scrumptious goodies, you'll find many other boutique delights.

Stores just off the beaten path can be extraordinarily vibrant, department stores amply reward those willing to wander multiple floors, and the Vieille Ville has no shortage of antiques shops.

And don't forget that Geneva is also a city of markets; chatty fruit and vegetable vendors, taciturn flea-market regulars, and craftspeople clustered in designated squares continue the legacy of the medieval trade fairs.

13

GETTING AROUND

By Air

British Airways, easyJet, and Swiss fly direct between London and Geneva; Swiss and Continental operate direct service from New York.

Swiss also schedules frequent connections to its hub in Zürich.

Cointrin International Airport, Switzerland's second-largest, lies 5 km (3 mi) northwest of downtown Geneva.

As for airport transfers to the city, the No. 10 bus runs regularly between the airport departure level and downtown Geneva.

The ride takes about 20 minutes and the fare is 3 SF.

Taxis are plentiful but expensive: expect to pay 35 SF or more to reach the city center, plus 1.50 SF per bag.

Trains run about every 15 minutes between Cointrin and the Gare Cornavin, Geneva's main train station, from 6:18 to 12:48 AM; the six-minute trip costs 3 SF.

Return trips free with Geneva Transport Card.

Airport Information Cointrin (☎ *022/7177111* ⊕ *www. gva.ch*).

By Bike

Bike lanes, indicated by a yellow line and a yellow bicycle symbol on the pavement, are ubiquitous downtown. Yellow signs indicate routes elsewhere in the canton. Genèv'Roule "lends" bicycles from May to October in all of their locations; Les Grottes stays open year-round. Pay a deposit of 20 SF and the bike is yours for four hours and must be returned the same day.

Bike Rentals Genèv'Roule (✉ *17 pl. Montbrillant, Les Grottes* ☎ *022/7401343* ⊕ *www.geneveroule.ch* ✉ *Bains des Pâquis, Les Pâquis* ✉ *Pl. du Rhône, Centre Ville* ✉ *Plaine de Plainpalais, Plainpalais* ✉ *Pl. de l'Octroi, Carouge*).

By Boat & Ferry

The Compagnie Générale de Navigation operates steamship connections between Geneva and Nyon, Lausanne, Vevey, and Montreux. They also service assorted smaller lake towns in Switzerland, as well as Yvoire, Thonon-les-Bains, and Evian-les-Bains, in France. Swiss Pass holders travel free; those with a Swiss Boat Pass pay half price. Smaller-scale lake travel, including a shuttle service across Geneva's harbor, is entrusted to the Mouettes Genevoises. These M1-4 lines are covered by the standard 3 SF city-bus fare, and are free with the Geneva Transport Card.

Boat & Ferry Information Compagnie Générale de Navigation (*CGN* ☎ *0848/811848* ⊕ *www.cgn.ch*).

Mouettes Genevoises (✉ *4 quai du Mont-Blanc, Les Pâquis* ☎ *022/7322944* ⊕ *www.mouettesgenevoises.ch*).

By Taxi

Taxis are clean and drivers are polite, but be prepared to pay a 6.30 SF minimum charge plus 3.20 SF per km (about ½ mi) traveled. In the evening and on Sunday the rate climbs to 3.80 SF per km. Cabs won't stop if you hail them; go to a designated taxi stand (marked on the pavement in yellow) or call.

Taxis Taxi-Phone (☎ *022/3314133* ⊕ *www.taxi-phone.ch*).

By Bus & Tram

The Gare Routière de Genève, Geneva's central bus station, lies hidden behind the English Church off Rue du Mont-Blanc and handles buses arriving from or departing for points across Europe. Local buses and trams operate every few minutes on all city routes from 5 AM to midnight, when, on Friday and Saturday, the Noctambus night-bus service kicks in. Buy a 3 SF ticket from the UNIRESO vending machine at the stop before you board (instructions are given in English) and use the system, transferring at will between buses, trams, airport-bound trains, and the Mouettes Genevoises harbor shuttles, for one hour.

Day passes, known as *cartes journalières*, are available from vending machines, Unireso sales points, and the Transports Publics Genevois (TPG) booths at the train station and rond-point de Rive. Unlimited city-center travel between 9 AM and midnight costs 7 SF; 10 SF will buy you a 24-hour period that begins when the ticket is purchased and allows two people to travel for the price of one on weekends. The Geneva Transport Card costs nothing for anyone staying at a campsite, hostel, or hotel; ask at the desk, the card gives you free access to the whole city and canton for the length of your stay. Holders of the Swiss Pass, in any case, travel free.

Bus & Tram Information Gare Routière de Genève (✉ pl. Dorcière, Les Pâquis ☎ 0900/320230 ⊕ www.gare-routiere.ch). **Transports Publics Genevois** (TPG; ☎ 0900/022021 ⊕ www.tpg.ch and www.unireso.com).

By Train

Express trains from most Swiss cities arrive at and depart from the Right Bank Gare Cornavin every hour.

Bern is about two hours away, Zürich and Basel roughly three.

The French TGV leaves up to seven times a day for Paris, including weekends, and arrives 3½ hours later; the Cisalpino makes the four- to five-hour journey to Milan three times each morning.

Regional trains leave every 15 minutes en route to Nyon and Lausanne.

Touch-screen consoles (in English) in the main ticket hall sell tickets for any destination in Switzerland.

Train Information Gare Cornavin (✉ 7 pl. Cornavin ☎ 0900/300300 ⊕ www.cff.ch).

By Car

Geneva's long border with France makes for easy access from all points French. Paris (to the northwest) is six hours away; Dijon (to the north), Lyon (to the southwest), Grenoble (to the south), and Chamonix (to the southeast) are all within two hours' drive on the French A40 expressway (l'Autoroute Blanche). The French south shore of Lac Léman gives access to the Valais via Evian-les-Bains.

The Swiss A1 expressway, along the north shore, connects Geneva to the rest of Switzerland by way of Lausanne. Traffic along the quays clogs easily, and parking in town is both restricted and expensive; look for electric signs on major incoming roads that note the whereabouts of (immaculate) municipal parking garages and their current number of empty spaces.

Updated by
Gail
Mangold-Vine

TODAY THE WORLD'S LARGEST CENTER for multilateral diplomacy and a hotbed of luxury shopping, Geneva was a postcard-perfect city known for enlightened tolerance long before Henry Dunant founded the International Red Cross here (1864), the League of Nations moved in (1919), the World Health Organization (WHO) set up shop after World War II, or the World Wide Web was invented here at CERN, the European Center for Nuclear Research. Once a place of refuge for the religious reformers Jean Calvin and John Knox, it has sheltered Voltaire, Victor Hugo, Alexandre Dumas, Lord Byron, and Mary Shelley, offered safe haven to Richard Wagner and Franz Liszt, and expelled its native son Jean-Jacques Rousseau for being liberal way before his time.

Today a whopping 40% of the city's 187,000 inhabitants are not Swiss, but the more than 150 countries that maintain permanent missions to the United Nations Office in Geneva represent merely the most recent group of foreigners to descend on the city. Four hundred years ago it was wave after wave of Protestant refugees: the English fled Bloody Mary, Protestant Italians the wrath of the pope, Spaniards the Inquisition, French Huguenots the oppressive French monarchy—and Geneva flourished, under the iron yoke of its 16th-century reformer, as a multilingual stronghold of Protestant (specifically Calvinist) reform.

The city's history as a crossroads stretches back farther still. The Genevois controlled the only bridge over the Rhône north of Lyon when Julius Caesar breezed through in 58 BC; the early Burgundians and bishop-princes who succeeded the Romans were careful to maintain this control. The strategically placed (and wealthy) city-state fell to the French in 1798, then made overtures to Bern as Napoléon's star waned. Geneva finally joined the Swiss Confederation as a canton in 1815. But don't get too carried away with Swiss stereotypes here—they are as foreign to the Genevois as risotto or gnocchi might be to a resident of Bern.

Geneva's museums have drawn particular benefit from the city's unique perspective on history and cultural exchange: you can visit a military exhibit up the hill from the Red Cross's examination of the horrors of war; weigh the extremes of ancient and contemporary ceramics; browse archaeological finds from Egypt and the Far East; compare pre-Christian primitive art with its modern incarnation; relive the Reformation; or explore the fruits of human thought and creativity as expressed on paper, in science, and inside the case of a tiny pocket watch. The Palais des Nations forms the ultimate living (and working) museum of 20th-century history.

The early December celebration of the Escalade, a 17th century military victory that marked a turning point in Geneva's history, offers a unique peek at the city's core character; the early-August Fête de Genève showcases a different, more easily accessible modern identity and culminates in a fireworks extravaganza set to music that perfectly exploits the beauty of Geneva's physical setting. Mary Shelley conceived of Frankenstein's monster during a dark and stormy night in Geneva, letting him escape over the cliff-face of the Salève, to the south-east of the city. But on a beautiful summer night with an ice cream in hand, the Alps glowing pink in the sunset, and the harbor lights ablaze, it's hard to imagine anything but bliss.

EXPLORING GENEVA

The *République et Canton de Genève* (Republic and Canton of Geneva) commands sweeping views of the French Alps and the French Jura from its fortuitous position at the southwestern tip of *Lac Léman* (Lake Geneva). The water flows straight through the city center and into the River Rhône en route to Lyon and the Mediterranean, leaving museums, shops, restaurants, and parks to jostle for space on its history-laden south shore, known as *Rive Gauche* (Left Bank). Busy shopping streets underline the hilltop *Vieille Ville* (Old Town), the Plaine de Plainpalais lies to its west, and Eaux-Vives stretches along the quays to the east. The *quartier international* (International Area), the *Gare Cornavin* (main train station), and sumptuous waterfront hotels dominate the north shore, or *Rive Droite* (Right Bank). St-Gervais, just north of the ponts de l'Ile, was once a watchmaking quarter. Les Pâquis, an unruly mix of artists, ethnic communities, and scrappy pleasure-seekers, extends north from the Pont du Mont-Blanc. The International Area, on the outer edge of the city, is a short tram ride from the station; all other neighborhoods are easily toured on foot.

Numbers in the text correspond to numbers in the margin and on the Geneva map.

AN OPEN INVITATION

Nothing is too insignificant, it would seem, to be feted in Geneva: it enthusiastically supports a stream of celebrations, including wine-harvest, jazz, and cinema-arts festivals. The three-day Fête de la Musique marks the summer solstice with more than 500 open-air concerts; the Fête de l'Escalade rolls back the clock to 1602 each December. The flamboyantly raunchy Lake Parade grinds its way along the quays in July. The 10-day Fêtes de Genève fill the waterfront each August with Ferris wheels, open-air discos, international foods, and a massive display of fireworks set to music.

13

THE WATERFRONT

Geneva is centered on water. The city's quays line the downtown area, link the well-groomed Right and Left Banks, and form a horseshoe-shape continuum of scrupulously tended parkland, historical sites, grand hotels, monuments, and breathtaking views.

MAIN ATTRACTIONS

3 **Beau-Rivage.** Jean-Jacques Mayer's descendants still own and operate the hotel he built in 1865. It has discreetly witnessed the birth of a nation (Czechoslovakia, in 1918), the death of an empress (Empress Elisabeth of Austria, in 1898), the sale of royal treasure (the Duchess of Windsor's jewels, in 1987), and the passage of crowned heads from around the world. Sotheby's commandeers its conference rooms for

A GOOD WALK

Discounting its final uphill loop through Cologny, this walk covers 5 km (3 mi) of largely flat, paved promenade—the perfect way to spend a leisurely day following the sun. Wear sunscreen and comfortable shoes, bring a book and binoculars if you have them, and give yourself at least a few hours to stroll and linger—there are always boats coming in, swans to feed, benches to rest on, and people to watch.

From Gare Cornavin, take Bus No. 1 to the Sécheron stop and walk through the gate labeled RESTAURANT LA PERLE DU LAC. The second paved path to your left after the parking lot leads to the Villa Bartholoni, home of the **Musée d'Histoire des Sciences,** housed in an elegant neoclassical mansion.

Turn right as you exit the museum, and make your way down to the water. On a clear day **Mont Blanc** floats above the hills on the far side of the lake like a sugar-dusted meringue. Keep the water to your left as you head past the Mouettes Genevoises landing dock, La Perle du Lac, and spectacular seasonal flower beds.

Continue straight along Quai Wilson as the traffic curls down to meet you. The stately **Palais Wilson,** on your right, housed the League of Nations from its creation after World War I until 1936. Pass the Hotel President Wilson, and follow the manicured lawns and ornate buildings around a sharp curve to the right. The Bains des Pâquis, hugely popular public baths with protected space to swim and sunbathe, occupy most of the jetty extending to your left. The Grand Hotel Kempinski, a bit farther along to your right,

continues the Right Bank parade of grand hotels.

Keep walking past the Port des Mouettes and the Hotel d'Angleterre. The slender statue of Sissi, Empress Elisabeth of Austria, on your left, was erected in 1998 to mark the centennial of her death; she was stabbed as she left the **Beau-Rivage** to board one of the paddle steamers docked alongside the quay. Make a brief detour to your left for a close-up view of the boats and the city center. Then cross the street in front of the Beau-Rivage and angle left to the elaborate **Monument Brunswick.**

Cross back to the quay at the far end of the block, head right past the plaque marking the spot where Sissi was stabbed, and take the last staircase before the Pont du Mont-Blanc down to the left. Continue straight under the bridge. When you surface in front of the Four Seasons des Bergues, make two lefts onto the pedestrians-only Pont des Bergues. The **Ile Rousseau,** halfway across, harbors a statue of its locally contentious namesake. The **Temple de la Fusterie,** on the far side of the bridge, was Geneva's first custom-built Calvinist church.

Turn left when you reach dry land, and follow the quay under the Pont du Mont-Blanc a second time. Head straight at the top of the ramp, then right toward the statue commemorating the union of Geneva and the Swiss Confederation on September 12, 1814. With the statue on your right, follow the path as it arcs to the right, and keep walking until the **Horloge Fleurie** comes into view on the left.

13

Continue past the floral clock face and through the Jardin Anglais, toward its graceful 19th-century fountain. Keep going straight when you get back on the lakeside path, past the bust of Gustave Ador on your right.

Take care on the steps down and angle left toward *La Neptune*, the only original boat of its kind still in service on Lac Léman. Sticking out of the water to its right are the Pierres du Niton, two glacial erratics deposited during the last Ice Age. Geneva's Guillaume-Henri Dufour designated the larger one as the base reference point (1,222 feet above sea level) for all altitude measurements taken during the 19th-century land survey that produced the first map of Switzerland.

Return to the upper promenade by the next set of stairs, continue to your left past more flower beds, and veer back to the lower level where Rue du 31-Décembre meets Quai Gustave-Ador. The **Jet d'Eau,** Europe's tallest fountain, gushes straight up from the lake halfway along the stone jetty before you; it also produces spray that feels like the mother of all sprinklers. The lighthouse at the end of the jetty has an unmatched view of the Centre Ville. Return to the quay and continue to the left past the city's main marina. Look back for a great view of the cathedral just before you reach the statue of *La Bise* (the North Wind). Then turn right when the asphalt ends and cross the street opposite **Parc La Grange.** Have a peek at the park and return to the quay, or wander through the rose garden on the left inside the gates, make your way into the

neighboring Parc des Eaux-Vives, and return to the quay farther down the road. Regardless of which park exit you use, cross the street and continue to the right past parallel beds of roses and terrific Jura, lake, and city views. At Port Noir, where the formal quay ends, a simple nautical monument commemorates the June 1, 1814, landing of Swiss troops sent to guarantee Geneva's safety in the aftermath of Napoléon's rule.

If you're feeling energetic and time permits, continue past Port Noir, cross the street at the traffic light, and follow the steep, leafy Rampe de Cologny about 1 km (½ mi) up to the hilltop village of Cologny, where Byron's guest Mary Shelley wrote *Frankenstein* at the Villa Diodati (private). Continue straight through the small traffic circle and head left to the end of the Auberge du Lion d'Or parking lot for sweeping views of the Palais des Nations, lake, and Jura; turn right at the traffic circle toward the **Fondation Martin Bodmer** if the sweeping vista of human thought is more your style.

Retrace your steps or take the peaceful pedestrian Chemin du Righi, just below the museum, back down the hill, then head left to Port Noir past Genève Plage, a public beach, and the posh, private boating club, Le Nautique. If the sun is setting, stay awhile and watch the city lights flicker on; in July and August, opt for an open-air film at Cinélac. When you're ready to head home, cross the street and take Bus No. 6 (direction Vernier-Village) to the Métropole stop. From there you can take Bus No. 8 (direction OMS) or walk across the Pont du Mont-Blanc to the train station.

jewelry auctions twice a year. ✉*13 quai du Mont-Blanc, Les Pâquis* ☎*022/7166666* ⊕*www.beau-rivage.ch.*

⑪ **Fondation Martin Bodmer** *(Martin Bodmer Foundation).* The library that
Fodor'sChoice sources this humbling exhibition of original texts—from cuneiform
★ tablets, papyrus scrolls, and parchment to a dizzying array of first editions—maps the history of human thought. Dramatic displays of bas-
reliefs and dimly lit Egyptian books of the dead give way to Homer's
Iliad; handwritten Gospels according to Matthew and John; multiple,
exquisite, copies of the Koran; Dante; a perfectly preserved Gutenberg
Bible; Shakespeare (the complete works, published in 1623); an auto-
graph score by Mozart; *Oliver Twist;* the *Communist Manifesto;* and
Alice in Wonderland. A comprehensive printed guide is available in
English. The collection is displayed in a subterranean space designed by
Mario Botta; hilltop views from the terrace above are superb. ✉*19–21
route du Guignard, Cologny* ☎*022/7074433* ⊕*www.fondationbod-
mer.org* 🎟*15 SF* ⊙*Tues.–Sun. 2–6.*

⑦ **Horloge Fleurie** *(Flower Clock).* The city first planted this gigantic, and
accurate, floral timepiece in 1955 to highlight Geneva's seminal role in
the Swiss watchmaking industry. Some 6,500 plants are required each
spring and fall to cover its 16-foot-wide surface. ✉*Corner Quai du
Général-Guisan and Pont du Mont-Blanc, Centre Ville.*

⑨ **Jet d'Eau** *(Water Jet).* The direct descendant of a late-19th-century
⟳ hydroelectric safety valve, Europe's tallest fountain shoots 132 gallons
Fodor'sChoice of water 390 feet into the air every second at 120 mph (wind conditions
★ permitting). The water is aerated on the way up by a special nozzle,
making it white. ✉*Off quai Gustave-Ador, Eaux-Vives.*

**NEED A
BREAK?** The ice-cream maestros at **Gelateria Arlecchino** (✉*1 rue du 31-Décembre,
Eaux-Vives* ☎*022/7367060* ⊕*www.larlecchino.ch*), across the street from
the Jet d'Eau, crank out more than 40 homemade flavors, including ginger-
lime, tiramisu, *pannacotta* (cream custard), fig, green tea, licorice, and three
options for diabetics.

★ **Mont Blanc.** At 15,767 feet, Mont Blanc is the highest mountain in
Europe and the crown jewel of the French Alps. Geneva's Right Bank—
particularly its waterfront parkland—has a front-row view framed by
three less-lofty acolytes: Les Voirons, to the left; Le Môle, in the center;
and Le Salève, to the right.

① **Musée d'Histoire des Sciences** *(Museum of the History of Science).* Walk-
★ around glass cases display age-old sundials and astrolabes, microscopes
and telescopes, barometers, and ornate globes that collectively document (in English) the evolution of modern science; there's a small room
full of harrowing medical implements upstairs. The neoclassical Italianate jewel that houses the collection, the Villa Bartholoni, dates from
1830. ✉*128 rue de Lausanne, International Area* ☎*022/4185060*
⊕*mah.ville-ge.ch/culture/mhs* 🎟*Free* ⊙*Wed.–Mon. 10–5.*

② **Palais Wilson.** Inaugurated in 1875 as the Hotel National, the largest of
Geneva's grand palaces, this dignified structure leapt to international

GENEVA'S TOURING OPTIONS

BOAT TOURS

The Compagnie Générale de Navigation boards passengers on both sides of the Pont du Mont-Blanc and serves multicourse meals aboard special Belle Epoque steamship cruises. Separate, hour-long CGN loops of the lower lake point out local sights. Swissboat and the Mouettes Genevoises jointly operate smaller-scale guided tours that take in castles, famous homes, ports, and parkland along the lake every day from April to October. Trips last anywhere from 40 minutes to two hours; recorded commentary is in English. The boats leave from two spots on the Quai du Mont-Blanc—opposite the Monument Brunswick (Swissboat) and opposite the Grand Hotel Kempinski (Mouettes Genevoises)—as well as from the Eaux-Vives waterfront between the Jet d'Eau and the Jardin Anglais. The Mouettes Genevoises also operate nearly three-hour natural-history tours of the Rhône. Live commentary is in English, and the boats depart from Place de l'Ile.

Fees & Schedules Compagnie Générale de Navigation (*CGN* ☎ *0848/811848* ⊕ *www.cgn.ch*). **Mouettes Genevoises** (✉ *4–8 quai du Mont-Blanc, Les Pâquis* ☎ *022/7322944* ⊕ *www.mouettes genevoises.ch*). **Swissboat** (✉ *4–8 quai du Mont-Blanc, Les Pâquis* ☎ *022/7324747* ⊕ *www.swissboat.com*).

BUS TOURS

Key Tours conducts two-hour bus-and-minitrain tours of the International Area and the Vieille Ville, leaving from Place Dorcière daily at 1:30 PM as well as at 10:30 AM May–October. The circuit costs 45 SF, and recorded commentary is in English. Between March and December you can also opt to catch the minitrain (independent of the bus tour) at Place du Rhône for a trip around the Vieille Ville. A second minitrain leaves from the Quai du Mont-Blanc for a tour of the International Area and Right Bank and Left parks. From march to October, a third minitrain departs from the Quai du Mont-Blanc for a ride to the Botanical Gardens and back. Each loop lasts between 35 and 75 minutes; the cost is 9–23 SF. Afternoon bus tours of the Geneva countryside are also available May–October.

Fees & Schedules Key Tours (✉ *7 rue des Alpes, Les Pâquis* ☎ *022/7314140* ⊕ *www.keytours.ch*).

WALKING TOURS

English-speaking guides linked to Genève Tourisme lead a two-hour walk through the Vieille Ville every Saturday at 10 AM. Additional weekday circuits at 10 AM, as well as 6:30 PM outings on Tuesday and Thursday, take place between June and late September. The cost is 15 SF. English-language audio guides to the Vieille Ville last 2½ hours and cost 10 SF plus a 50 SF deposit. The CD and player must be returned within four hours. You can price and arrange tailor-made thematic tours that trace the history of watchmaking, Jean Calvin's legacy, or any one of 17 other subjects, by calling one of the numbers below.

Fees & Schedules Genève Tourisme (✉ *18 rue du Mont-Blanc, Les Pâquis* ☎ *022/9097000*). **Service des Guides** (✉ *18 rue du Mont-Blanc, Les Pâquis* ☎ *022/9097030*).

13

prominence on April 28, 1919, when the peace negotiators in Paris chose Geneva to host the newborn League of Nations. Hotel rooms were converted to offices, 700 international civil servants began work here in November 1920, and the building was renamed in honor of U.S. President Woodrow Wilson in 1924. By 1936 the faltering League had run out of space and moved to the custom-built Palais des Nations. Ten years later it was dismantled. The Palais Wilson was gutted by fire in 1987, meticulously restored in 1998, and now houses the headquarters of the United Nations High Commissioner for Human Rights (HCHR). It is not open to the public. ✉ *51 rue des Pâquis, Les Pâquis.*

NEED A BREAK?   The crowded and casual cafeteria at **Bains des Pâquis** (✉ *30 quai du Mont-Blanc, Les Pâquis* ☎ *022/7322974* ⊕ *www.bains-des-paquis.ch*) serves hearty lunchtime *plats du jour* by the water in summer; look for champagne fondue with a harbor backdrop on winter evenings.

ALSO WORTH SEEING

5 **Ile Rousseau.** Jean-Jacques Rousseau, the son of a Genevois watchmaker, is known to history as a liberal *French* philosopher in part because Geneva's conservative government so thoroughly rejected his views. His statue on this former city bastion, erected reluctantly in 1835 (57 years after his death), was surrounded by trees and deliberately hidden from view until the 1862 construction of the pont du Mont-Blanc gave Rousseau the last laugh. ✉ *Off Pont des Bergues, Centre Ville.*

8 **La Neptune.** Old photos of Geneva show scores of black masts and graceful, cream-color lateen sails crowding the lake. Now La Neptune, the only authentic traditional barge still in existence is hired out for day sails. Built in 1904 and restored twice, in 1976 and 2005, she hauled stone and sand between far-flung construction sites until 1968. ✉ *Off Quai Gustave-Ador, Eaux-Vives* ☎ *022/7322944.*

4 **Monument Brunswick.** Charles d'Este-Guelph, the famously eccentric (and deposed) duke of Brunswick, died in Geneva in 1873 and left his vast fortune to the city on condition that his tomb, a replica of the 14th-century Scaligeri mausoleum in Verona, be given prominence. No one is sure why his sarcophagus faces inland. ✉ *Bounded by Rue des Alpes, Quai du Mont-Blanc, and Rue Adhémar-Fabri, Les Pâquis.*

10 **Parc La Grange.** The Orangerie and the Théâtre de Verdure stage performances and open-air concerts through the summer months; new varieties of roses compete for prizes each June; and the remnants of a first-century Roman villa crown the hillside in this gracious, sun-dappled park, once the private grounds of an 18th-century villa overlooking the lake. William Favre's bequest of his family's domain to the city in 1917 stipulated that the park be made available to the public during the day and closed at night. It is still the only green space in Geneva to be locked when the sun goes down. ✉ *Quai Gustave-Ador, Eaux-Vives.*

6 **Temple de la Fusterie.** Designed by Huguenot refugee Jean Vennes and completed in 1715, Geneva's first specifically Calvinist church was built to accommodate the flood of French Protestants that followed the 1685 revocation of the Edict of Nantes. The plain, Baroque facade blended into the secular landscape around it; the well-lighted and whitewashed galleries within allowed 750 people to hear every word the minister said. ⊠ *Pl. de la Fusterie, Centre Ville.*

VIEILLE VILLE

Geneva's Old Town (Vieille Ville), a tight cluster of museums, boutiques, historical sites, and sidewalk cafés capped by the cathedral, represents the city's core. The cantonal government's executive, legislative, and judicial branches operate within its walls; the Left Bank radiates out from its slopes.

13

MAIN ATTRACTIONS

㉑ **Auditoire de Calvin** *(Calvin's Lecture Hall).* Reformed services in English, Italian, Spanish, Dutch, and German made this simple Gothic structure, built in the 15th century on the site of two prior churches and originally called the New Church of Our Lady, a potent international gathering place for 16th-century Protestant refugees. The Scots reformer John Knox preached here from 1556 to 1559 while he translated the Bible into English; Calvin and his successors used the space to teach theology and train missionaries into the 18th century. Today the Auditoire hosts the Church of Scotland, the Dutch Reformed Community, and the Waldensian Church of Italy; the Church of Scotland welcomes visitors to its Sunday-morning service at 11. ⊠ *1 pl. de la Taconnerie, Vieille Ville* ⊠ *Free* ⊙ *Variable.*

⑲ **Cathédrale St-Pierre** *(St. Peter's Cathedral).* A stylistic hybrid scarred
★ by centuries of religious upheaval and political turmoil, this imposing cathedral somehow survived the ages with its dignity intact. The massive neoclassical facade was an 18th-century addition meant to shore up 12th-century Romanesque-Gothic walls; stained-glass windows, the Duke of Rohan's tomb, a few choir stalls, and the 15th-century **Chapel of the Maccabees** hint at lavish alternatives to Calvin's plain chair. Fifteenth-century bells and bird's-eye city views reward those who climb the **north tower.** ⊠ *Cour St-Pierre, Vieille Ville* ☎ *022/3117575* ⊕ *www.saintpierre-geneve.ch* ⊠ *North tower 4 SF* ⊙ *June–Sept., Mon.–Sat. 9:30–6:30, Sun. noon–6:30; Oct.–May, Mon.–Sat. 10–5:30, Sun. noon–5:30.*

㉔ **Fondation Baur** *(Baur Foundation).* Alfred Baur's lovingly preserved collection of Far East Asian art, Switzerland's largest, packs more than 10 centuries of Chinese ceramics and jade, Japanese smoking paraphernalia, prints, netsuke, lacquerware, and sword fittings into a tranquil 19th-century townhouse on the edge of the Vieille Ville. Thematic temporary exhibits occupy the basement; general texts in English introduce each room. ⊠ *8 rue Munier-Romilly, Centre Ville* ☎ *022/7043282* ⊕ *www.collections-baur.ch* ⊠ *10 SF* ⊙ *Tues.–Sun. 2–6.*

⑬ **Hôtel de Ville** *(City Hall).* Sixteen countries signed the first Geneva Convention in the ground-floor **Alabama Hall** on August 22, 1864, making it the birthplace of the International Red Cross, and the League of Nations convened its first assembly here on November 15, 1920.

Geneva (Genève)

KEY

🚢 Ferry lines

ℹ️ Tourist Information

⸺ Tram lines

Gare de Cornavin

Pl. de Cornavin

Rue Sismondi

Rue Rossi

Rue des Pâquis

R. Adhémar

Rue Pradier

Square Pradier

Rue Chaponnière

Rue de Berne

Rue des Alpes

Place des Alpes

Basilique Notre Dame

Rue du Mont-Blanc

Sq. de Chantepoulet

Hôtel des Postes ℹ️

Place Dorcière

Rue Voltaire

Rue Jean-Dassier

Rue de Malatrex

Place des 22 Cantons

R. de Chantepoulet

Holy Trinity English Church

Rue Ami-Lévrier

Square du Mont-Blanc

4

Blvd. James-Fazy

Rue du Mandement

Rue Necker

Rue deCornavin

Rue J.-J.-Rousseau

Rue du Cendrier

Rue Kléberg

Place des Bergues

Quai du Mont-Blanc

Rue du Temple

Rue des Terreaux-du-Temple

R. des Corps Saints

Rue de Coutance

R. Grenus

Place Grenus

Rue des Etuves

Bergues

Pont du Mont-Blanc

R. Vallin

Pl. de St. Gervais

Quai des Bergues

Île Rousseau

5

Rhône

Pl. de la Couloureniére

26

Pont de la Machine

Pont des Bergues

ℹ️

33

Quai des Forces - Motrices

Pl. des Volontaires

Quai de la Poste

Pl. de Bel-Air

Rue du Commerce

Rhône

Quai du Général-Guisan

Pl. du Rhône

Rue du Rhône

Rue du Stand

Pl. de la Poste

Rue du Stand

Rue de la Confédération

Rue de la Cité

R. de la

6

R. du Marché

Pl. du Molard

R. Neuve du-Molard

Rue des Rois

Rue de l'Arquebuse

Rue Jean-Petitot

Synagogue

Blvd. Georges-Favon

Rue de Hesse

Blvd. du Théâtre

Rue François-Diday

Rue de la Corraterie

R. de la Terrasse

Rue de la Rôtisserie

Rue de la Croix-d'Or

32

Grand Théâtre

R. Bovy-Lysberg

Pl. du Cirque

Pl. Bela-Bartok

Rue Calame

Rue du Général-Dufour

Grand. Rue

R. J.- Calvin

Temple de la Madeleine

28

Pl. Neuve

Rue des Granges

17

15

18

R. du Puits St-Pierre

Conservatoire de Musique

27

Rampe de la Treille

16

14

20

19

13

R. de l'Hôtel - de-Ville

21

Rue des Bains

Rue du Vieux-Billard

Rue Bartholoni

Blvd. de St.-Georges

Rue des Savoises

Av. du Mail

Blvd. Georges-Favon

Skate Park

Pl. de la Taconnerie

22

Rue René - Louis Piachaud

Rue Étienne

12

Rue de la Croix-Rouge

Promenade des Bastions

Rue Gourgas

MAMCO Centre d' Art Contemporain

31

30

Plaine de Plainpalais

Université de Genève

Rue du Conseil- Général

Rue De-Candolle

Université

Rue de l'Athénée

R. de l'Athénée

Rue des Vieux-Grenadiers

29

Parc des Bastions

Rue St.-Léger

Cours des Bastions

Rond-point de Plainpalais

Sq. de la Comédie

Blvd. des Philos- ophes

Rue St.-Ours

0 ____ 220 yards

0 ____ 200 meters

Area of Inset

Les Bains des Pâquis

Lac Léman

Fabri

Jetée des Eaux-Vives

Lac Léman

Promenade du Lac

Jardin Anglais

Pl. Longemalle

Rue du Rhône

Pl. des Eaux Vives

Rond-point de Rive

Carrefour de Rive

Pl. Franz-List

Église Russe

Place Émile-Guyénot

13

The canton's executive and legislative bodies meet here; until 1958 city functionaries lived here. But the history of this elegant vaulted compound begins in 1455, when the city built a large fortified tower, the **Tour Baudet**, to house the State Council Chamber. Its circular ramp, an architectural anomaly added during the Reformation, was used by at least one lawmaker to reach the second-floor meeting place without dismounting his horse. ⊠ *2 rue de l'Hôtel-de-Ville, Vieille Ville* ☎ *022/3272118* ⊕ *www.geneve.ch* ⊠ *Free* ⊙ *Daily; information booth weekdays 9–noon, 2–5.*

⑮ Maison Tavel *(Tavel House).* Vaulted cellars and ground-floor kitchens display medieval graffiti, local coins, 15th-century tiles, and a guillotine in Geneva's oldest house, now a museum focused on life in the city from 1334 to the 1800's. Seventeenth-century ironwork, doors, and other fragments of long-demolished houses fill the first floor; a bourgeois home complete with 18th-century wallpaper is re-created on the second. The enormous Magnin Model (which depicts Geneva as it looked before its elaborate defense walls came down in 1850) is housed in the attic; temporary exhibits rotate through the basement. ⊠ *6 rue du Puits-St-Pierre, Vieille Ville* ☎ *022/4183700* ⊕ *mah.ville-ge. ch* ⊠ *Free* ⊙ *Tues.–Sun. 10–5.*

㉓ Musée d'Art et d'Histoire *(Museum of Art and History).* The city has based its huge archaeology, fine art, and applied art collections in this custom-built museum since 1910. They include, notably, Switzerland's largest concentration of Egyptian art, Escalade-era weapons, Alpine landscapes from both ends of the 19th century, and substantial contemporary art. The 15th-century *Miracle of the Fishes,* in which Christ paces the waters of Lac Léman, keeps things focused locally; temporary exhibits range much farther afield. ⊠ *2 rue Charles-Galland, Vieille Ville* ☎ *022/4182600* ⊕ *mah.ville-ge.ch* ⊠ *Free* ⊙ *Tues.–Sun. 10–5.*

⑱ Musée International de la Réforme *(International Museum of the Reformation).* Engaging audiovisuals, period artifacts, and carefully preserved documents explain the logic behind the Protestant Reformation, explore its impact as a religious, cultural, and philosophical phenomenon, and trace its roots from the early 16th century through today in this sophisticated, modern, and remarkably friendly museum. The sparkling 18th-century premises, on the site where Geneva voted to adopt the Reform, connect by underground passage to the *Site Archéologique;* all signage and audioguide material is in English. ⊠ *4 rue du Cloître, Vieille Ville* ☎ *022/3102431* ⊕ *www.musee-reforme.ch* ⊠ *10 SF, 16 SF with cathedral towers and Site Archéologique* ⊙ *Tues.–Sun. 10–5.*

Fodor'sChoice
★

ALSO WORTH SEEING

⑭ Ancien Arsenal *(Old Arsenal).* Designed as a granary on the site of a Roman marketplace and converted to a gunpowder depot after l'Escalade, this municipal storage space has sustained Geneva through the ages. The current 1636 structure stocks history: murals on the inner wall and frescoes along the outer rim of the arcade tell the town's story from Julius Caesar to 1848; records in the State Archives date back to 1387. Scholars and officials use this institution, not the general public.

✉ *Intersection of Rue de l'Hôtel-de-Ville and Rue du Puits-Saint-Pierre, Vieille Ville.*

⑯ Eglise Saint-Germain *(Saint-Germain Church).* The second chapel on the left maps a structural lineage that began in AD 400, and the steeple dates from the 14th century; the rest of this pristine 15th-century sanctuary served as a Protestant temple, a butcher's warehouse, a foundry, and a government meeting hall before Napoléon's troops returned it to Catholicism in 1803. Allocated to the Old Catholics since 1873, its whitewashed walls, strategic lighting, and 20th-century stained glass frame weekly classical music concerts in summer. Attending a concert or a service—there's one on Sunday at 10—is usually your only chance to see the inside. ✉ *9 rue des Granges, Vieille Ville* ⊕ *www. concerts-st-germain.ch.*

⑫ Monument de la Réformation *(Wall of the Reformers).* Conceived on a grand scale and erected between 1909 and 1917, this solemn 325- by 30-foot swath of granite pays homage to the 16th-century religious movement spearheaded by Guillaume Farel, Jean Calvin, Théodore de Bèze, and John Knox. Smaller statues of major Protestant figures, bas-reliefs, and inscriptions connected with the Reformation flank the lifelike giants as they hover over Bern, Geneva, and Edinburgh's coats of arms; Oliver Cromwell is surrounded by Pilgrims praying on the deck of the *Mayflower* and the 1689 presentation of the Bill of Rights to King William and Queen Mary by the English Houses of Parliament. The Reformation's—and Geneva's—motto, *Post Tenebras Lux* (After Darkness, Light), spreads over the whole. ✉ *Parc des Bastions, Centre Ville.*

Fodor'sChoice
★

⑰ Musée Barbier-Mueller. Josef Mueller began acquiring fine primitive art from Africa, Oceania, Southeast Asia, and the Americas in 1907. Today his family's vast, inspired collection of sculpture, masks, shields, textiles, and ornaments spans six continents and seven millennia. A small selection is on view at any given time, displayed like jewels in warm, spotlighted vaults of scrubbed stone. Basement galleries focus consistently on pre-Columbian America, Africa, and Southeast Asia. ✉ *10 rue Jean-Calvin, Vieille Ville* ☏ *022/3120270* ⊕ *www.barbier-mueller. ch* 🎟 *8 SF* ⊘ *Daily 11–5.*

★

㉕ Muséum d'Histoire Naturelle *(Museum of Natural History).* Large, evocative wildlife dioramas complete with sound effects cover most major animal types; large quantities of fossils and a multimedia display on plate tectonics lead to human evolution, gigantic crystals, precious stones, exotic birds, coral reefs, and a case full of polyhedrons in this spacious museum swarming with local school groups. Swiss geology, the history of the solar system, and thematic temporary exhibits round out the collection; most labels are in French. ✉ *1 rte. de Malagnou* ☏ *022/4186300* ⊕ *www.ville-ge.ch/mhng/* 🎟 *Free* ⊘ *Tues.–Sun. 10–5.*

🅒

㉒ Place du Bourg-de-Four. Ancient roads met in this layered Vieille Ville square before heading south to Annecy and Lyon, east to Italy and the Chablais, north to the Rues-Basses, and west through the center of town to the bridge. Once a Roman cattle market, later flooded with refugees,

★

it's still the quintessential Genevois crossroads, where shoppers, lawyers, workers, and students all meet for drinks around an 18th-century fountain. ⊠ *Intersection of Rue de la Fontaine, Rue Verdaine, Rue des Chaudronniers, Rue Etienne-Dumont, Rue Saint-Léger, and Rue de l'Hôtel-de-Ville, Vieille Ville.*

㉒ **Site Archéologique.** Archaeologists found multiple layers of history
☺ underneath the Cathédrale St-Pierre when its foundations began to fal-
Fodor'sChoice ter in 1976. Excavations have so far yielded remnants of two 4th-cen-
★ tury Christian sanctuaries, mosaic floors from the late Roman Empire, three early churches, and an 11th-century crypt. The first Romanesque cathedral on the site was built in 1000; today audio guides in English and careful lighting help navigate the (reinforced) underground maze that remains. ⊠ *6 cour St-Pierre, Vieille Ville* ☎ *022/3117574* ⊕ *www. site-archeologique.ch* ⊠ *8 SF* ⊗ *Tues.–Sun. 10–5.*

PLAINPALAIS

Reclaimed from the swamps that formed the confluence of the Rhône and Arve rivers as recently as 1850, the area centered on the diamond-shaped Plaine de Plainpalais is now home to contemporary art galleries, traveling circuses, weekly markets, local and regional media, the sprawling Université de Genève, and remnants of a late-19th-century industrial past.

MAIN ATTRACTIONS

㉚ **Centre d'Art Contemporain** *(Center for Contemporary Art)*. Andy Warhol, Cindy Sherman, Nan Goldin, Pippilotti Rist, Thomas Scheibitz, and Shirana Shabhaz are some of the pioneering Swiss and international artists who have presented work here since 1974, when Geneva's answer to the Germanic Kunsthalle began showing the art of tomorrow today. The Centre's seven annual exhibits tend to be transdisciplinary and shocking in their quest to examine the practice of art in a cultural context. ⊠ *10 rue des Vieux-Grenadiers, Plainpalais* ☎ *022/3291842* ⊕ *www. centre.ch* ⊠ *5 SF* ⊗ *Tues.–Sun. 11–6.*

㉙ **Patek Philippe Museum.** Geneva's renown as a center for watchmaking
Fodor'sChoice and enameling, sustained since the 16th century, finds full justification
★ in this breathtaking private collection of delicate gold watch cases, complicated watch innards, lifelike portrait miniatures, and softly lighted enameled fans, pens, pocket knives, snuffboxes, telescopes, and vanity pistols that shoot singing birds. Most of the objects displayed in this former watchmaking workshop are hundreds of years old; many were created in Geneva by Patek Philippe, one of the city's most venerable watchmaking companies. Meticulously restored workbenches, audio-visual displays, classical music, and a horological library complete the picture; the 2½-hour guided tour (in English at 2:30 on Saturday) puts it all in context. All signage is in English. ⊠ *7 rue des Vieux-Grenadiers, Plainpalais* ☎ *022/8070910* ⊕ *www.patekmuseum.com* ⊠ *10 SF (tour 15 SF)* ⊗ *Tues.–Fri. 2–6, Sat. 10–6.*

㉗ Place Neuve. Aristocratic town houses now overlook Geneva's opera house, the Musée Rath, the Conservatoire de Musique, and the gilded wrought-iron entrance to the Parc des Bastions, but until 1850 this wide-open space was the city's heavily fortified main southern gate. The equestrian statue at the center of the square honors Guillaume-Henri Dufour, the first general of Switzerland's federal army and the first person to map the country. The large bust of Henry Dunant, founder of the International Red Cross, marks the spot where public executions once took place. ⊠*Intersection of Blvd. du Théâtre, Rue de la Corraterie, Rue de la Croix-Rouge, and Rue Bartholoni, Centre Ville.*

13

ALSO WORTH SEEING

㉝ Bâtiment des Forces Motrices *(Power Station).* A fine example of 19th-century industrial architecture moored in the middle of the river, Geneva's second opera house was built in 1886 by engineer Théodore Turrettini to supply drinking water, harness the river's energy for local industry, and keep the lake level steady. Restored and converted to a 985-seat theater in 1997, it now hosts the overflow from the Grand Théâtre as well as classical concerts by the Orchestre de la Suisse Romande and traveling productions. The cavernous L-shaped lobby has retained two of its original 18 turbines. ⊠*2 pl. des Volontaires, Plainpalais* ☎*022/3221220* ⊕*www.bfm.ch.*

㉜ Cimetière de Plainpalais *(Plainpalais Cemetery).* Originally part of a 15th-century hospital complex built on dry land outside the city to isolate victims of the plague, these verdant 7 acres bordering the city's tax office hold the mortal remains of Jean Calvin, Simon Rath, Guillaume-Henri Dufour, William Favre, Jorge Luis Borges, and Sergio Vieira de Mello (the United Nations Special Representative killed in Iraq in 2003), as well as many of the people whose names grace street signs all over town. The relative paucity of tombstones reflects a turbulent history of flooding, overcrowding, and neglect; funeral monuments were introduced in the 19th century. ⊠*10 rue des Rois, Plainpalais* ⊕*www.cimetieredesrois.ch* ☜*Free* ⊘*Daily 8–5:30.*

㉛ Mamco (Musée d'Art Moderne et Contemporain) *(Museum of Modern and Contemporary Art).* Concrete floors and fluorescent lighting set the tone for this gritty collection of stark, mind-stretching, post-1960 art that shares its former factory compound with separate centers for contemporary photography and publishing. The industrial surroundings help juxtapose aesthetic approaches; temporary exhibits add current artists to the mix. ⊠*10 rue des Vieux-Grenadiers, Plainpalais* ☎*022/3206122* ⊕*www.mamco.ch* ☜*8 SF* ⊘*Tues.–Fri. noon–6, weekends 11–6.*

㉘ Musée Rath. Switzerland's original fine arts museum, inaugurated in 1826 and named for its late benefactor, Simon Rath, housed Geneva's growing collections of art and archaeology until they overflowed to the Musée d'Art et d'Histoire in 1910. Now the Rath hosts two major temporary exhibitions each year; they range in focus from archaeology to contemporary art. ⊠*Pl. Neuve, Centre Ville* ☎*022/4183340* ⊕*mah.ville-ge.ch* ☜*9 SF* ⊘*Tues. and Thurs.–Sun. 10–5, Wed. noon–9.*

A GOOD WALK

Begin at Place Neuve, Geneva's musical hub, and walk through the gates of the Parc des Bastions. The Université de Genève, on your right, is descended from Calvin's groundbreaking Academy; the enormous **Monument de la Réformation** spreads 150 years of Protestant history along the park wall to your left. Climb the steps and ramp to the right of the Monument, cross Rue de la Croix-Rouge, and zigzag up to the mercifully flat promenade de la Treille.

Catch your breath on the world's longest bench by the *Marronnier Officiel* (Official Chestnut Tree), then turn to the **Hôtel de Ville**, seat of Geneva's cantonal government; its Alabama Hall overlooks the terrace, stained-glass windows on the floor above indicate the Grand Council Chamber, and the fortress-like segment on the far left is the 15th-century Tour Baudet. Follow the promenade to the statue of Charles Pictet de Rochemont, Geneva's and ultimately Switzerland's delegate to the Congress of Vienna, and head right through the 18th-century portico. Turn to the right into No. 2 rue de l'Hôtel-de-Ville to see the arcaded inside of the government complex.

Exit through either door and cross the street to the city's 17th-century **Ancien Arsenal,** now home to the State Archives. The **Maison Tavel,** on the far side of the arcade, has a huge scale model of Geneva in 1850, before the city walls came down.

Turn right when you leave the museum, right again at the top of the hill, and head into the Grand-Rue. The Espace Jean-Jacques Rousseau, a 25-minute audiovisual overview (in English) of the philosopher's life, occupies his birthplace at No. 40; Swiss painter *par excellence* Ferdinand Hodler kept a studio across the street at No. 33.

By No. 28, former residence of writer Jorge Luis Borges, turn left into Ruelle du Sautier, which feeds out by the quietly soulful **Eglise Saint-Germain.** Duck inside the church if it's open, then follow Rue des Granges down past the back of the 18th-century facades overlooking Place Neuve. Albert Gallatin, the Geneva native who was Thomas Jefferson's Treasury Secretary, was born at No. 7. The Fondation Zoubov has recreated a sumptuous 18th-century salon at No. 2.

Continue through Place du Grand-Mézel, Geneva's medieval meat market and 15th-century Jewish ghetto. Detour briefly to the left; Rue de la Cité connects the Old Town with its ancient river crossing. The ornate sides of the Grand Théâtre loom over Rue de la Tertasse.

Head back up the Grand-Rue past No. 11 and turn left down Rue de la Pélisserie, which curves past a plaque noting George Eliot's visit to the city and becomes Rue Jean-Calvin. The **Musée Barbier-Mueller** presents thematic exhibits of primitive art across from No. 11; Calvin and his family lived on this site from 1543 until his death in 1564.

Turn right at the fountain, then left into Rue Otto-Barblan. The Cour de Saint-Pierre, home to the Espace Saint-Pierre—an umbrella term for the **Musée International de la Réforme,** the **Cathédrale St-Pierre,** and the underground **Site Archéologique**—has been Geneva's

13

spiritual center since the time of Celtic goddesses. You can tour the Espace in any order; what follows is the scenic route.

Head straight into Rue du Cloître, past the spot where Geneva made its single biggest collective decision, and follow it to the museum. Turn left upon leaving with a full appreciation of the Reformation's legacy and make a right into Rue de l'Evêché. This becomes Rue Guillaume-Farel when you reach the back of the cathedral; the sober, contemplative chapel straight ahead is the **Auditoire de Calvin.** Peek inside if the doors are open, then continue straight back to the Cour de Saint-Pierre. The entrance to the Site Archéologique is the wrought-iron gate to your immediate right; finish with the view from the cathedral towers.

Now return to Rue Guillaume-Farel and either go down the steep, covered Passage des Degrés-de-Poules behind the cathedral or take Rue des Barrières farther along to the right. Ascend the stairs, past mythical mosaics of the Rhône, the Arve, and Neptune; from the edge of the Terrasse Agrippa-d'Aubigné, look back for a terrific view of the cathedral; the 15th-century Temple de la Madeleine and a contemporary flea market with merry-go-round frame a vista straight ahead that extends past the Rues-Basses to the lake and Bains des Pâquis.

Follow the terrace wall to the right and down the ramp to rue de la Fontaine, then head right past the Lutheran Church and the bottom of the Passage des Degrés-de-Poules to **Place du Bourg-de-Four.** Continue past the Palais de Justice to

the crest of the hill, then dip straight down the other side to Rue Etienne-Dumont.

Continue straight to Place Franz-Liszt—the composer lived in the corner house on the right—and turn left onto Promenade de Saint-Antoine. Descend the steps marked *Saint Antoine parking & Site Archéologique* for a stroll through the massive remains of Geneva's defense walls, then ride the elevator back up and cross the bridge on your right to the wide-ranging **Musée d'Art et d'Histoire.**

Exiting the museum, turn right and head for the Eglise Russe; you can't miss the six gleaming gilt cupolas crowning this 19th-century church filled with gold and silver icons. Take either street marked Rue François-Le-Fort away from the church, cross Rue Charles-Galland, and head left a block later on Rue Munier-Romilly. The **Fondation Baur,** a serene private museum of Asian ceramics, jade, and lacquerware, is the last door on the right.

From here, take any of the streets linking Rue du Mont-de-Sion with Boulevard des Tranchées, and turn left. The **Muséum d'Histoire Naturelle** is the modern black-and-white building shrouded by trees on the far side of Route de Malagnou. Bus No. 8 (direction OMS) leaves from here for the Right Bank; Rive and the waterfront are a short walk down the hill.

Remember: wear good walking shoes and let bookstores and cafés temper the steady stream of history. This route can easily fill a day (most museums are closed Mondays).

㉖ Tour de l'Ile. The lone surviving fragment of a 13th-century castle built by Bishop Aymon de Grandson to protect Geneva from attack via the bridge and demolished in 1677, this carefully preserved lookout tower now houses the Banque Safdié. It is not open to the public. ✉ *Rue de la Tour-de-l'Ile, Centre Ville.*

INTERNATIONAL AREA

The Palais des Nations, 10 minutes north of the Gare Cornavin by tram, is the focal point of Geneva's humanitarian and diplomatic zone. Modern structures housing UN agencies dominate streets leading to it; embassies, 19th-century villas full of nongovernmental organizations, and museums surround them.

> **TRIP TIP**
>
> Entrance fees at seven of Geneva's private collections are substantially reduced for holders of the Passeport Musées, a little booklet that, when stamped at the door like a passport, allows one free entrance each to the Fondation Baur, Fondation Martin Bodmer, Musée des Suisses dans le Monde, Musée Barbier-Mueller, Musée International de la Croix-Rouge et du Croissant-Rouge, Musée International de la Réforme, and Patek Philippe Museum. Tourist information booths, many hotels, and the museums themselves sell the booklets; they are valid for three months, cost 20 SF, and can be handed off to a friend.

To get to this sector, take Tram No. 13 or No. 15 from the Gare Cornavin to the end of the line (Nations), and disembark onto the recently renovated pedestrian Promenade des Nations. Towering over the 84 computer-managed water-fountains is Swiss artist Daniel Berset's *Broken Chair,* a memorial to land-mine victims. To your left are the world headquarters of the International Telecommunications Union (ITU) and the World Intellectual Property Organization (WIPO); to your right, past an honor guard of flags from member countries, sits the rarely used ceremonial entrance to the famed Palais des Nations.

MAIN ATTRACTIONS

㊉ Jardin Botanique *(Botanical Garden).* Sixty-nine peaceful acres of winding paths and streams, mountain views, and Alpine rock gardens bear witness to Geneva's early-19th-century fascination with botany. They also include tropical and Mediterranean hothouses, beds of irises, classic rose gardens, an aviary, a deer park, a garden of scent and touch, a living catalog of economically useful and medicinal plants, a seed bank, and a formidable research institute. Several of the trees predate 1700. ✉ *1 chemin de l'Impératrice, International Area* ☎ *022/4185100* ⊕ *www.ville-ge.ch/cjb* 💲 *Free* ☉ *Apr.–Sept., daily 8–7:30; Oct.–Mar., daily 9:30–5.*

㉟ Musée Ariana. An architectural anachronism when it was completed in 1887 and stocked with Gustave Revilliod's immense collection of ceramics, sculpture, furniture, textiles, coins, books, and silverware, this serene Italianate structure ceded its parkland to the Palais des Nations in 1928 and now houses the **Musée Suisse de la Céramique et du Verre** (Swiss Museum of Ceramics and Glass). Stoneware, earthenware, porcelain, and glass covering 700 years of East-West exchange populate the upper floors; contemporary work rotates through the basement. ✉*10 av. de la Paix, International Area* ☎*022/4185450* ⊕*mah.ville-ge.ch* ⛶*Free* ⊗*Wed.–Mon. 10–5.*

36 **Musée International de la Croix-Rouge et du Croissant-Rouge** *(International*
Fodor'sChoice *Red Cross and Red Crescent Museum).* Powerful mute statues speak
★ to the need for human kindness in the face of disaster, and balanced but often grim exhibits trace the history of the struggle to provide it in this carefully nonjudgmental museum buried in the hillside beneath the world headquarters of the International Committee of the Red Cross.

13

Audiovisuals show the post-battle horrors at Solferino that moved Henry Dunant to form the Red Cross; endless aisles of file boxes hold 7 million records of World War I prisoners. Good deeds are dramatized, from the proverbial Samaritan's to Clara Barton's. There's a replica of a 6½-foot by 6½-foot concrete cell in which Red Cross workers discovered 17 political prisoners; the **Mur du Temps** (Wall of Time), a simple timeline punctuated by armed conflicts and natural disasters in which more than 10,000 people died, puts the overall story into sobering perspective. Good news, in the form of disaster-relief kits and snapshots used to reunite Rwandan families after the 1994 genocide, is also on display, however; signage and audio guides are in English. ✉*17 av. de la Paix, International Area* ☎*022/7489525* ⊕*www.micr.org* ⛶*10 SF* ⊗*Wed.–Mon. 10–5.*

34 **Palais des Nations** *(Palace of Nations).* Built between 1929 and 1936
★ for the League of Nations, this monumental compound became the European office of the United Nations in 1946 and quickly evolved into the largest center for multilateral diplomacy in the world. Today it hosts some 9,000 conferences and 25,000 delegates each year; it is also the largest nexus for United Nations operational activities after New York.

Security is tight: be prepared to show your passport and join a tour to see the interior. Points of particular interest include the **Assembly Hall,** the largest of 34 conference rooms, where the UN General Assembly and scores of world leaders have met, and the ornate **Council Chamber,** home to the Conference on Disarmament, which glows with allegorical murals. Tours last about an hour and are conducted in English. There are no set starting times. ✉*14 av. de la Paix, International Area* ☎*022/9174896* ⊕*www.unog.ch* ⛶*10 SF* ⊗*Jan.–Mar. and Nov.–mid-Dec., weekdays 10–noon, 2–4; Apr.–June, Sept., and Oct., daily 10–noon, 2–4; July and Aug., daily 10–5.*

ALSO WORTH SEEING

37 **Musée des Suisses à l'Etranger** *(Museum of the Swiss Abroad).* Books, audio guides in English, and 19th-century rooms full of models, paintings, documents, and objects highlight the considerable achievements of Swiss people outside Switzerland in this dense little museum surrounded by parkland. Swiss Guards and military men give way to artists, bankers, explorers, doctors, writers, archaeologists, chocolatiers, and inventors as the centuries progress; many, like Albert Gallatin, were surprisingly prominent.

✉18 chemin de l'Impératrice, International Area ☎022/7349021 ⊕www.chateau-de-penthes.ch. 🎫5 SF ⊘Jan.–Mar., Wed.–Fri. 2–5, weekends 10–noon, 2–5; Apr.–Dec., Tues.–Sun. 10–noon, 1–5.

㊳ Musée Militaire Genevois (*Geneva Military Museum*). The humble setting adds authenticity to this detailed look at a neutral but thoroughly competent military force. Uniformed models, weapons, prints, and documents proceed in chronological order through the eventful history of la Garde Genevoise from 1814 to the present, including a Napoleonic officer's outfit, Guillaume-Henri Dufour's personal effects, and a full-scale recreation of a Genevois border post during World War II. ✉18 chemin de l'Impératrice, International Area ☎022/7344875 ⊕http://musee militaire.tripod.com 🎫Free ⊘Early Feb.–mid Dec., Tues.–Sat. 2–5, Sun. 10–noon, 2–5.

> **PEACOCKS & ART DECO**
>
> The design of the Palais des Nations was determined by architectural competition in 1926; the building is a superb example of the severe blend of Art Deco and stylized classicism that characterized much of European architecture in the late '20s and '30s. Its details—bronze torchères, gleaming marble—and many of its decorations (including huge allegorical murals by Catalan artist José Maria Sert) have been preserved practically untouched. And why do peacocks roam outside? A stipulation in the will of the man who originally owned the land!

WHERE TO EAT

THE SCENE

Relatively few restaurants focus on a see-and-be-seen angle for targeted age groups; what unites diners at the best ones, whether simple cafés or gastronomic havens, is an appreciation for good food (read "slow food"—the noted food movement born in Italy a few decades ago which puts emphasis on locally sourced ingredients, regional tastes, and authentic preparations). So, people-wise, you can expect to see a little of everything in Geneva restaurants, which still basically follow traditional lines: cafés, bistros, brasseries, and restaurants.

Increasingly, there's a trendy "non-French" spin, and, as with hotels, a big facelifting drive is on as regards decor. Also note the rise of tapas "grazing" menus; places that offer both light menus (club sandwiches) and five-course meals; and signature restaurants—Vineet Bhatia (Rasoi) and Paul Bocuse (Brasserie) at the Mandarin Oriental, the Pourcel brothers (EastWest and Tiffany), and Alain Senderens at Cité du Temps (run by chic Arthur's Rive Gauche) on Pont de la Machine. At the other end of the scale, fast food usually runs to salad creations, fresh sandwiches, and warm quiche to go; lunchtime *plats du jour* and bakeries with tearooms are delicious budget options.

While dress-code days are gone, casual elegant is rule of thumb, and hours for meals generally remain noon to two PM and seven to nine-thirty or ten PM; open-late pubs, bars, and clubs satisfy night owls. And yes, after the stores close on Saturday afternoon Geneva's city center is virtually dormant—and most but by no means all restaurants close. That's because the Genevois spend their weekends eating at country inns and village cafés, which are mostly open weekends.

These days, Geneva restaurants (and bars and clubs) are all no-smoking. Some are now charging for the *carafe d'eau* (tap water). Since it is not local custom to take small children to better restaurants, infrastructure (and welcome) may be poor if you arrive babies in tow. Tipping? Local diners may leave the change as a gesture when they leave, but tipping for exceptional service is up to the customer and is still the (great) exception, not the rule.

13

WHAT IT COSTS IN SWISS FRANCS					
	¢	$	$$	$$$	$$$$
AT DINNER	under 15 SF	15 SF–25 SF	25 SF–45 SF	45 SF–65 SF	over 65 SF

Prices are per person for a main course at dinner.

$$ ✕**Au Pied-de-Cochon.** Low ceilings, whitewashed beams, white tile, and a
FRENCH worn zinc bar give context to simple regional dishes like cassoulet, *longeole* sausage, sauerkraut, *émincé de veau* (veal strips in a cream sauc), *filets de perches,* and the namesake pigs' feet (served grilled or stuffed). The crowd can be noisy, and table service can occasionally be a tad gruff, but local folk and tourists keep streaming in not least because it's one of the few places in town that serves meals straight through from noon to 10 PM. The terrace is great for people-watching. ⊠*4 pl. du Bourg-de-Four, Vieille Ville* ☎*022/3104797* ⊕*www.pied-de-cochon.ch* ▤*AE, DC, MC, V.*

$$–$$$ ✕**Bistrot du Boeuf Rouge.** The Belle Epoque dining room is gently clut-
FRENCH tered with Art Nouveau posters, smoked glass, and figurines; waiters
Fodor'sChoice soften absolute correctness with a local sense of humor; and the rich,
★ true-blue menu draws hordes of foreign as well as local Lyonnaise cognoscenti to this cozy downtown bistro mere blocks from the major hotels. Many of the house specialties—*boudin noir,rillettes,* foie gras, terrine, *andouillettes,* pistachio-filled sausage—are made on-site; the *quenelles de brochet* (pike), gratin *dauphinois* (baked cream, potatoes and cheese) are to die for; and the tender *filet de bœuf* barely requires a knife. And save space for dessert—the silky *flan au caramel* may be the best in town. ⊠*17 rue Alfred-Vincent, Les Pâquis* ☎*022/7327537* ⊕*www.boeufrouge.ch* ▤*AE, MC, V* ⊘*Closed weekends.*

$$–$$$ ✕**Bistrot du Boucher.** Aperitifs are on the house, steak tartare is mixed to
STEAK your taste, and waiters wear long aprons and solemn expressions as they
★ bring out the *côte de boeuf* (rib-steak) to be viewed before it's carved. Cheeky cow posters, figurines, and paintings add a sly hilarity to the Art Nouveau woodwork and stained-glass ceiling; the homemade chocolate-pear tart is decadently serious. ⊠*15 av. Pictet-de-Rochemont, Eaux-Vives* ☎*022/7365636* ▤*AE, MC, V* ⊘*Closed Sun. No lunch Wed. and Sat.*

$$–$$$ ✕ **Brasserie Lipp.** The "Années Folles" decor—green-and-white tiles,
FRENCH   mustard-yellow ceilings, warm wood—and busy waiters in ankle-length
★   aprons channel Paris as Genevois diners of all stripes tuck into hearty
portions of *choucroute* (sauerkraut) with pork and potatoes, sausage
with lentils, vegetable couscous, tartares of beef or fish, and heaping
platters of seafood. Or maybe a pound of steak—at 98.50 SF by far the
most expensive thing on the menu. The dining room expands onto a
delightful summer terrace at the foot of the Vieille Ville, and, unusually
for Geneva, this place serves late: the kitchen stays open until 12:30
AM. ✉ *Confédération-Centre, 8 rue de la Confédération, Centre Ville*
☎ *022/3111011* ⊕ *www.brasserie-lipp.com* ▭ *AE, DC, MC, V.*

$$–$$$ ✕ **Café des Bains.** Right across from MAMCO (Geneva's museum of
ECLECTIC   contemporary art), in an arty neighborhood that has come to be known
Fodor'sChoice   as QuARTier des Bains, this trendy-chic eatery-cum-bar that spills out
★   onto a sidewalk terrace during the summer months mixes a classic
French café look with contemporary touches (featuring large-scale
prints by star Swiss artist-photographer Balthasar Burkhard). Chefs
Christopher Brocard and Fabien Kuczkowska inject world flavors into
a basically French seasonal repertoire, although one thing that's always
on the dessert menu is American-style cheesecake. Good wines are on
offer, many sold by the glass. The café also has a fun lifestyle shop
a few doors down. ✉ *26 rue des Bains, Plainpalais* ☎ *022/3215798*
⊕ *www.cafedesbains.com* ⌂ *Reservations essential* ▭ *AE, DC, MC,
V* ⊘ *Closed Sun. and Mon.*

$$ ✕ **Café des Négociants.** A mix of traditional French café furniture and
FRENCH   contemporary design, this upscale spot remains very popular, one rea-
Fodor'sChoice   son being the terrace allowing diners to enjoy the highly picturesque
★   streets of Carouge during the summer months. Wine is taken seriously
here, and there is a handsome cellar where the sommeliers are more than
happy to help you make your selection—you can even arrange ahead to
eat at the cellier's refectory table. Chef Thierry Minguez's lunch offer-
ings tend to focus on a *plat* (18 SF) or *menu* (29 SF) *du jour,* while din-
ner is more á la carte, with menus changing every two months. Either
way, the cooking has a sunny, southern French feel to it. ✉ *29 rue de la
Filature, Carouge* ☎ *022/3003130* ⊕ *www.negociants.ch* ⌂ *Reserva-
tions essential* ▭ *AE, DC, MC, V* ⊘ *Closed Sat. and Sun.*

$–$$ ✕ **Café Léo.** Trendy locals descend for lunch, then linger over coffee at
ITALIAN   this atmospherically tiny, sunny corner bistro whose highlights include
★   avocado and Roquefort salad, homemade ravioli, veal *piccata* with
mustard sauce, and a noteworthy *tarte au citron* (lemon tart). Before
and after lunch you can join the old-timers inside drinking small cups
of strong coffee and perusing local newspapers mounted onto anti-theft
wooden sticks, or sit outside in season watching the streams of people
walking by—Rive is one of Geneva's Left Bank hubs. ✉ *9 cours de Rive,
Centre Ville* ☎ *022/3115307* ⊕ *www.cafeleo.com* ▭ *MC, V* ⊘ *Closed
Sun. No dinner Sat.*

$–$$ ✕ **Café Lyrique.** Black-and-white floor tiles offset warm yellow walls, high
FRENCH   wedding-cake ceilings, and portraits of Beethoven, Verdi, Strauss, and
Liszt; the menu starts with soups and salads, moves on to pasta, lake
fish, and sirloin with the special house butter, and ends with desserts

that taste as good as they look. Solid comfort food is what you get at this relaxed corner brasserie opposite the Grand Théâtre. Time your arrival carefully, as it's bursting with business folk at lunch, and pre- and postopera crowds sweep through at night; an alternative is afternoon tea. Try and sit in the brasserie, or on the terrace; the dining room can have less of a buzz. ⊠ *12 blvd. du Théâtre, Centre Ville* ☎ *022/3280095* ⊕ *www.cafe-lyrique.ch* ☐ *AE, MC, V* ⊘ *Closed weekends.*

$$$$
FRENCH
Fodor'sChoice
★

✕ **Domaine de Châteauvieux.** Philippe Chevrier's expansive kitchen, out in the heart of Geneva's wine country, draws inspiration and the culinary equivalent of spun gold from local and regional foods (many of which are sold on-site in a little *épicerie*). The restaurant is the focal point of a 16th century *domaine*, or château complex, that was once attacked by the Genevois; these days they come in peace to find antique winepresses, kitchen gardens, weathered stone, ancient beams, a leafy summer terrace with sweeping hilltop views, and a gastronomic experience that can stretch to seven courses and cost 300 SF per person. Exquisite seasonal dishes rarely repeat from year to year but reliably transform asparagus in spring, game come October, and truffles in winter; the Menu Surprise, at 270 SF, is an invitation to sit back, relax, and let the kitchen sing. The cellar houses top Swiss and French wines, and there's a humidor off the bar; take a boat up the Rhône to Peney or drive 20 minutes—about 16 km (10 mi)—from Geneva. Café de Peney down the hill also belongs to Chevrier; it is much less pricey, and it's open seven days a week. ⊠ *16 chemin de Châteauvieux, Peney-Dessus, Satigny* ☎ *022/7531511* ⊕ *www.chateauvieux.ch* ⚷ *Reservations essential* ☐ *AE, DC, MC, V* ⊘ *Closed Sun. and Mon.*

$$$–$$$$
ITALIAN
★

✕ **Il Lago.** Risotto with lobster and basil, risotto with calamari and champagne, and tortelli with cheese, lemon, and mint are some of the northern Italian creations Carrara native and unabashed lover of pasta Marco Garfagnini has road-tested on diners and then added to his menu. Set in the Four Seasons des Bergues hotel, the green- and blue-tinted dining room, split in half by gilt French doors, is decorated with brocades, chandeliers, and sweeping hand-painted scenery—if seared scallops with wild mushrooms in a shellfish reduction or braised veal cheek with semolina gnocchi and asparagus were served at Versailles, this is what it might be like. In season, there's a gorgeous sidewalk terrace complete with olive trees and aromatic herbs. ⊠ *Four Seasons des Bergues, 33 quai des Bergues, Centre Ville* ☎ *022/9087110* ⊕ *www. fourseasons.com/geneva* ☐ *AE, DC, MC, V* ⚷ *Reservations essential.*

$–$$
PAN-ASIAN

✕ **Jeck's Place.** Even by Genevois standards, this unassuming little restaurant near the train station presents a staggering mix of cultures. Jeck Tan, a native of Singapore, a graduate of Switzerland's top hotel school, and the establishment's namesake, left behind a staff well-versed in English, a menu written in Malay, Chinese, Thai, and French, and a devoted following of Asian ex-pats. The food—whether smooth, deep-fried bean curd with peanut sauce, chicken in green curry, spicy noodle dishes, or roast duck *au diable*—is delicious in any language, and priced just right, with only Peking duck (at 95 SF) going out of the twenty-to-thirty franc range for a main course. ⊠ *14 rue de Neuchâtel, Les Pâquis* ☎ *022/7313303* ⊕ *www.jecksplace.ch* ☐ *AE, DC, MC, V* ⊘ *No lunch weekends.*

$$–$$$ ✕ **L'Auberge d'Hermance.** Each of the three eating spaces—the fire-lit din-
FRENCH   ing room, winter garden, and terrace—has a burnished fairy-tale charm;
Fodor'sChoice   not for nothing is this village inn part of the Romantik collection. The
★   look is chic and cozy, replete with twig chandeliers, Hansel-and-Gretel
wainscoting, framed paintings, and sumptuous wood carvings. The
storybook-worthy lakeside village itself, a national heritage site, is eminently worth a stroll, and it's just a bus ride away, about 16 km (10 mi)
from Left Bank city center. (In season you can come by boat and return
by bus). The auberge's big specialty is rock-salt-encrusted roast chicken
(for two—40 SF a person), but perch fillets (44 SF) are always in high
demand. The inn also has some gloriously stylish guest rooms; doubles
run 260 SF. ⊠ *12 rue du Midi, Hermance* ☎ *022/7511368* ⊕ *www.*
hotel-hermance.ch ⌖ *Reservations essential* ▭ *AE, DC, MC, V.*

$$–$$$ ✕ **L'Hôtel-de-Ville.** It's hard to get more Genevois than this: *filets de*
FRENCH   *perches, longeole* sausage, game in season. Choose the five-course *Gene-*
vois Goûtez Moi set-menu for a guided culinary tour; each course is
paired with a glass of different local wine. This place does a brisk trade,
clients include Genevese and tourists alike, and the location at the political heart of the Vieille Ville guarantees a loyal crowd of civil servants
during the week. Service can be somewhat frank, but it's all part of the
brasserie-style ambience. The dining room transfers to the sidewalk in
summer, and the kitchen closes late for Geneva—at 11:30 PM. ⊠ *39*
Grand-Rue, Vieille Ville ☎ *022/3117030* ▭ *AE, DC, MC, V.*

$–$$ ✕ **L'Opéra Bouffe.** The mood is casual-chic and friendly, with rows of
FRENCH   wine bottles on floor-to-ceiling shelving, large framed mirrors and opera
posters on the walls, and classical music in the background. The Syrian
chef rolls out subtle updates of traditional French bistro fare imbued
with his own flair: fresh figs with bacon, honey, and cumin, or spicy
lamb with chickpea purée. He overhauls the menu once a month, but
there would be a riot if he stopped including warm *tarte Tatin* with Gruyère cream. ⊠ *5 av. de Frontenex, Eaux-Vives* ☎ *022/7366300* ⊕ *www.*
operabouffe.ch ▭ *AE, DC, MC, V* ⊘ *Closed Sun. No lunch Sat.*

$$–$$$ ✕ **La Favola.** Lace curtains, embroidered tablecloths, antique silver, col-
ITALIAN   lections of teapots and Murano glass, a sponge-painted ceiling, and
a vertiginous spiral staircase strike a delicate balance between rustic
and fussy in this wood-paneled dollhouse located on the street where
Jean Calvin, the Protestant reformer, used to live. The food echoes
the decor: part country-simple, part city-chic. Homemade pastas come
drizzled with herbs, the carpaccio is paper-thin, the tiramisu divine;
seasonal risottos, creamy polenta, and regional wines reflect the Ticinese chef's roots in Ascona, near Locarno. ⊠ *15 rue Jean-Calvin, Vieille*
Ville ☎ *022/3117437* ⊕ *www.lafavola.com* ▭ *No credit cards* ⌖ *Res-*
ervations essential ⊘ *Closed weekends June–Aug., Sat. lunch and Sun.*
Sept.–May.

$$–$$$ ✕ **La Perle du Lac.** Built in 1827 as the guesthouse for the nearby Villa
FRENCH   Bartholoni, this sprawling lakeside chalet set amid public parkland
stays open from February to December and comes dramatically into
its own in summer. Pink tablecloths and hanging geraniums frame an
unobstructed view of Mont Blanc, the Mouettes Genevoises water taxis
dock directly out front, and the glassed-in Orangerie is a rainy-day

alternative to the covered terrace; the wine list is exhaustive and the French-accented seasonal menu highlights seafood, like lobster ravioli or scallops with pear and smoked breast of duck, but also fish: marlin tartare, and grilled salmon, or sea bass. ⊠ *126 rue de Lausanne, International Area* ☎*022/9091020* ⊕*www.laperledulac.ch* ☰*AE, DC, MC, V* ⊘*Closed Mon. and Jan.*

$$$–$$$$

FRENCH

Fodor'sChoice

★

✕**Le Buffet de la Gare des Eaux-Vives.** It's a bit of a surprise to find one of Geneva's best restaurants set in an unprepossessing yellow pavilion replete with corrugated iron roofing and adjacent to the train station that connects commuters with Savoy (France). While softened by focal flora in the dining room and potted bamboo and olive trees outside, the decor is heavily into industrial design, so the view out back onto warehousing, spray-can graffiti, and weedy abandoned railroad tracks somehow all makes sense. The focus here, though, is on the kitchen, and Serge Labrosse's Mediterranean-French cooking is seriously skilled, creative both in terms of ingredients and presentation. It is also seasonal, another good sign, which means that the menu changes frequently. The wine list highlights Geneva wines. ⊠*Ave. de la Gare des Eaux-Vives, Eaux-Vives* ☎*022/8404430* ⊕*www.lebuffetdelagare.ch* ✍*Reservations essential* ☰*AE, MC, V* ⊘*Closed Sat. and Sun.*

$$$–$$$$

FRENCH

★

✕**Le Chat Botté.** The dining room of the Beau-Rivage's elegant hotel restaurant has just a hint of the library about it—bookcases, framed prints, reading lamps—and is generally used only when the weather's cold. Between May and September service is moved to the flower-filled terrace upstairs with its majestic harbor views. The menu also evolves with the seasons: chef Dominique Gauthier tweaks the details of his line-up every few months, and highlights range from classics like the fillets of Austrian venison with quince and cinnamon compote or the roast Scottish woodcock served up with sweet chestnuts and cepes from the Voirons to the nouvelle—one winner are the scampis roasted in Kadaïf, citrus vinaigrette, and basil chiffonade. That noted, French classics like foie gras, salt- and freshwater fish, roasted rack of lamb, and lobster put in regular appearances. Vegetarians will always find something here; the wine cellar, Geneva's largest, has 40,000 hand-picked bottles. ⊠*Beau-Rivage Hotel, 13 quai du Mont-Blanc, Les Pâquis* ☎*022/7166920* ⊕*www.beau-rivage.ch* ✍*Reservations essential* ☰*AE, DC, MC, V.*

$$$$

FRENCH

★

✕**Le Lion d'Or.** The hilltop village of Cologny is Geneva's Beverly Hills with a view, and this sleek, Zen, urban-sophisticate takes full advantage of its real estate. Burnished-silk walls and picture windows frame the sun setting over the lake and Jura Mountains in the main dining room; the first-floor lounge-bar looks south toward the city; strategically placed orchids soften the enormous portrait in the lobby; and the shaded outdoor patio-terrace floats under a blue sky and above the herb garden. Seasonal cuisine by local celebrity chefs Gilles Dupont and Tommy Byrne is modern, light, full of Asian accents, and artfully presented. The bistro next door shares the restaurant's kitchen, but not its prices. ⊠*5 pl. Pierre-Gautier, Cologny* ☎*022/7364432* ⊕*www.liondor.ch* ✍*Reservations essential* ☰*AE, DC, MC, V* ⊘*Closed weekends.*

13

Where to Stay and Eat in Geneva

Lac Léman

Jetée des Eaux-Vives

Lac Léman

Promenade du Lac

Jardin Anglais

Quai du Général-Guisan

Pl. Longemalle

Quai Gustave-Ador

Rue du Rhône

Rue de Rive

Rue du

Cours de

Rond-point de Rive

Rive

Carrefour de Rive

Rue de la Terrassière

Pl. des Eaux Vives

Av. Pictet-de-Rochemont

Av. de Frontenex

Rue des Eaux-Vives

R. des Eaux-Vives

Rue du Lac

Rue Muzy

Rue Versonnex

R. de la Scie

Rue du 31 Décembre

Rue de Villereuse

Rue Verdaine

Vieux-Collège

R. Théodore-de-Bèze

Rue des Chaudronniers

Ferdinand Hodler

R. des Glacis-de-Rive

R.-A. Lachenal

Promenade de St-Antoine

Bলvd. Jaques-Dalcroze

Rue Charles-Galland

Rue Töpffer

Église Russe

R. Sturm

Pl. Franz-List

Promenade du Pin

Blvd. Helvétique

R. F. Lefort

R. F. Gourd

R. F. Lefort

R. Munier-Romilly

Rue de St-Victor

Blvd. des Tranchées

Rue Plantamour

Rue de Rive

Fontaine

Rue de la

Rue d'Italie

Rue P. Fatio

Blvd. Helvétique

Fabri

KEY

- 🚢 Ferry lines
- ① Hotels
- ❶ Restaurants
- 🛈 Tourist information
- ▬ Tram lines

13

$$ ✕ **Le Relais de l'Entrecôte.** It is rare to find a line of people waiting for a
STEAK table anywhere in Geneva, so the fact that it's commonplace outside
Fodor'sChoice this bustling wood-paneled Parisian import means the tender strips of
★ grilled steak drenched in herb-based *sauce maison* (house sauce) are a
true cut above. A crisp green salad sprinkled with walnuts, robust house
wine, and thin, golden fries complete the only option on the menu; but
don't worry, there's a second portion on the way, and desserts—like
the flower bouquets adorning the restaurant—remain fabulous. ✉️*49
rue du Rhône, Centre Ville* ☎️*022/3106004* ⊕*www.relaisentrecote.fr*
△*Reservations not accepted* ▭*MC, V* ☾*Closed July.*

¢ ✕ **Le Thé.** Almost everything on the menu in this microscopic piece of
CHINESE China, whether succulent rice-flour crepes stuffed with shrimp, dim
★ sum, steamed bread, wobbly cubes of tapioca cake, or rare, scented,
and little-known teas, is steamed. The delicate red-clay teapots lining
the walls are for sale, and the front door is easy to miss, and the nine tiny
tables fill up fast—call ahead or drop by after 1:30 for lunch. For a
fine selection of teas, and an off-the-beaten track buying experience,
venture into their atmospheric emporium, Dragon Art, at nearby 5 rue
des Savoises. ✉️*65 rue des Bains, Plainpalais* ☎️*079/4367718* ▭*No
credit cards* ☾*Closed Sun.*

$–$$ ✕ **Les Armures.** A robust Swiss menu has made this Vieille Ville insti-
SWISS tution a magnet for local street sweepers, foreign heads of state, and
everyone in between. Before tucking into a fondue or raclette (melted
cheese served with small potatoes in their skins, pickled pearl onions,
and cornichons), order a plate of air-dried meat cut paper thin—a specialty of the canton of Grisons—for starters. Other specialties include
Schübling (sausage), and veal strips in cream sauce: both come with
sinfully delicious *Rösti*, a buttery cake of grated potatoes. The kitchen
serves until 11:30 PM (11 on Sunday) and in season you can sit outdoors and soak up the Old Town's historic vibe. ✉️*1 rue du Puits-
St-Pierre, Vieille Ville* ☎️*022/3103442* ⊕*www.hotel-les-armures.ch*
▭*AE, DC, MC, V.*

$$$$ ✕ **Restaurant Hôtel Parc des Eaux Vives.** Located in a renovated old château
FRENCH surrounded by a manicured park with lake and Jura views, this is one of
Fodor'sChoice Geneva's top foodie meccas. Chef Olivier Samson's style is very French
★ (albeit with world references) and it's seasonal—which means the menu
changes frequently. The decor has a vaguely Art Deco flair, with sleek
ebony chairs, gilded mirrors, and mottled silvered walls. The many-
course set menus will run you between 145 SF and 260 SF, but here's
a tip: weekdays there's a Business Lunch for 79 SF, and on sunny days
you can sit outside and soak up those magic vistas. The establishment
also has a bar, a substantially cheaper brasserie with terrace, and even
a few rooms (doubles are 460 SF to 875 SF). ✉️*82 quai Gustave-Ador,
Eaux-Vives* ☎️*022/8497575* ⊕*www.parcdeseauxvives.ch* △*Reservations essential* ▭*AE, DC, MC, V* ☾*Closed Sun. and Mon.*

$$–$$$ ✕ **Roberto.** Roberto Carugati, still spry in his nineties, attempts to "stay
ITALIAN out of the way" these days and let his daughter, Marietta, oversee the
red-gold dining room he opened in 1945, but don't be surprised to see
him drop in. The easy formality he perfected continues to lure lawyers,
bankers, politicians, and fashionable Italians for melt-in-the-mouth

EATING WELL IN GENEVA

Geneva's many restaurants teem with innovative, experimental menus and chefs with lofty pedigrees, but its traditional cooking is simple, earthy, full of flavor, and solidly middle class. *Cardon* (cardoon, a locally grown vegetable related to the artichoke and available in winter) is baked with cream and Gruyère cheese. Lac Léman yields abundant fish—perch, trout, *féra* (whitefish), and *omble* (char)—in summer. *La chasse* (wild game) turns up on menus between late September and mid-December. The culinary influence of Lyon, 150 km (94 mi) to the southwest, can be felt year-round in dishes such as *pieds de cochon* (pigs' feet), *longeole* (unsmoked pork sausage stuffed with cabbage and fennel), *petit salé* (salt pork), *fricassée de porc* (simmered pork), *abats* (organ meats), *andouillettes* (chitterling sausages), and *boudin noir* (rich, rosy-brown blood sausage, best eaten in cold weather). Potatoes (often served au gratin) are a favorite side dish. Pears, in the form of a spiced compote, a delicate tart, or a light eau-de-vie, have a well-established role come dessert.

Think local when choosing your wine. The Romans planted vines in Geneva; by now area vintners produce red, white, and sparkling wines that consistently earn high marks. (Bartholie, a boutique sparkling wine, has been known to trump French champagnes in international competition.) Small, ancient Chasselas grapes lead the charge of whites; the round, generous taste of Gamay dominates the reds. There are also excellent local bottles of Chardonnay, Pinot Blanc, Pinot Gris, Gewürztraminer, Aligoté, Pinot Noir, Gamaret, and Cabernet Sauvignon. The hilly area around Satigny, Dardagny, and Russin (known for its annual harvest festival) is by far the canton's most productive.

gnocchi with butter and sage, grilled sole, vitello tonnato, and risotto with saffron served from shining copper and silver pots. Unusual and rare Italian wines keep conversation flowing into the night. ⊠*10 rue Pierre-Fatio, Centre Ville* ☎*022/3118033* ⊟*AE, MC, V* ⊙*Closed Sun. No dinner Sat.*

¢–$ ✕**Taverne de la Madeleine.** The sunny, elevated stone terrace looks across
FRENCH at the 15th-century Temple de la Madeleine, homemade fruit tarts sell for 3.50 SF per slice between 3 PM and 6 PM, and the lunch-only kitchen in this big, plain, friendly canteen serves wholesome *plats du jour*— reasonably priced lunch specials served by most Geneva restaurants on weekdays—but must-trys include the *filets de perches* (a dish that is ubiquitous in the French-speaking part of Switzerland), chocolate mousse, and lemon pie. The city's temperance league owns and operates the Taverne, so it serves no wine or beer. ⊠*20 rue Toutes-Âmes, Vieille Ville* ☎*022/3106070* ⊟*AE, DC, MC, V* ⊙*Closed Sun. No dinner.*

WHERE TO STAY

THE SCENE

Despite a few new hotels at all levels—including some creative takes on essentially traditional concepts (thankfully, no pods yet)—the palace image continues to be the defining one. There is something quintessentially Geneva about the wealth these places ooze, and the waterfront ones on the Right Bank give you sweeping summary of the city's other iconic features: the Jet d'Eau, Old Town, La Rade (the harbor), river, lake, and mountains. They're also near parks—another of the city's points of pride—for that early morning jog as the sun rises across the water.

Overall, the hospitality sector has seen an overhaul in Geneva these past years, as owners recognize that Decor Matters and that updates (and upkeep) are essential. Getting connected—Internet, Wi-Fi—are buzzwords (few establishments now are without facilities, even if Wi-Fi especially is mostly still on a pay basis), while palaces continue to open spas at a fast clip. Courtesy Matters, too. In the past, hotel sniffiness was a problem in this conference- and convention-driven town. Genuinely gracious, go-the-extra-mile-with-a-smile service remains vexingly confined to the professionally trained top and family-run bottom of the rate structure, but the good news is that the concept of gracious service is making across-the-board inroads!

Geneva hotels do err on the expensive side, which is in large part due to the fact that the dollar that used to get you two, three, even four Swiss francs now only gets you around one, but also because the practice of massively hiking up rates during events like the annual car show in March persists. Speaking of which, large events can suddenly fill entire hotels, so book as early as you can.

As for breakfast (if not included), you won't readily find places outside the big hotels that do bacon and eggs, but if you're happy with croissants and coffee, head for the nearest café. As for practicalities, many places accept children up to a certain age for free, or another bed can be put in your room for a low extra. More and more hotels take pets, but rules can be complicated, so deal with this ahead to avoid surprises (also as regards the charge, which can be hefty).

WHAT IT COSTS IN SWISS FRANCS				
¢	$	$$	$$$	$$$$
FOR TWO PEOPLE	under 100 SF	100 SF–200 SF	200 SF–300 SF	300 SF–500 SF	over 500 SF

Prices are for two people in a standard double room, including tax and service.

$$$–$$$$ 🏨 **Ambassador.** With superb top-floor views of the Vieille Ville, just steps from the Four Seasons des Bergues (and one of Geneva's four Starbucks), this Rhône-side hotel is undergoing renovation—working its way down all seven floors and adding generous closet space, flat-screen TVs, and a contemporary aesthetic to guest rooms that have double-paned windows, attractive white-tile bathrooms, and lots of natural light. Many of the huge doubles would be called suites elsewhere. Now if they could only do something about that airport-lounge lobby. **Pros:** ideal location; thumbs up for the unusually attractive decor in renovated rooms. **Cons:** when you walk in, you think "uh-oh"—the lobby and restaurant, though soigné, need some serious refurbishing; the single elevator is overworked. ✉ *21 quai des Bergues, St-Gervais* ☎ *022/9080530* ⊕ *www.hotel-ambassador.ch* 🛏 *66 rooms* ♻ *In-room: safe, refrigerator, pay Wi-Fi. In-hotel: restaurant, bar, laundry service, Wi-Fi (fee), parking (fee), no-smoking rooms* ⊟ *AE, DC, MC, V.*

$$$$ 🏨 **Beau-Rivage.** While luxuriously contemporary where it counts, and
★ with that all-important crisp feel, guest rooms of this gracious, history-rich landmark hotel are awash in swathes of tasseled drape and Louis Something furniture; standard rooms may be less *époque* but still bask in the vibe, and all rooms (and public spaces) feed off from a grand five-story atrium. Sotheby's Geneva offices are here; there's an elegant bar and world-class Thai restaurant, along with Le Chat Botté, the French restaurant that moves to an upstairs terrace in summer. Savoring a meal on its awning-shaded balcony with cascades of flowers in planters—not to mention lake, mountain, and Jet d'Eau views to die for—continues to be a Best of Geneva experience. **Pros:** family-owned; not to worry that there's no spa on-site—if you feel the need for extra pampering, they have a deal with the Spatio day spa. **Cons:** the plants and the incongruously dated "modern" furniture surrounding the burbling lobby fountain could use a little feng shui. ✉ *13 quai du Mont-Blanc, Les Pâquis* ☎ *022/7166666* ⊕ *www.beau-rivage.ch* 🛏 *82 rooms, 11 suites* ♻ *In-room: safe, refrigerator, Wi-Fi. In-hotel: 2 restaurants, room service, bar, gym, laundry service, public Internet (fee), Wi-Fi (free), parking (fee), no-smoking rooms* ⊟ *AE, DC, MC, V.*

$ 🏨 **Bel'Espérance.** Rooftop views of Lake Geneva, bright yellow-and-blue
Fodor'sChoice rooms, tile baths, impeccable upkeep, and a graceful Louis-Philippe–
★ style salon and breakfast room put this Salvation Army–run former *foyer pour dames* (ladies' boarding house) on a par with much pricier hotels. (Don't let the tiny area just inside the entrance fool you: the reception desk and public rooms are up the flight of stairs.) Large doubles connect to form "suites" for parents and children, the communal kitchen has a fridge with lockers, the whole hotel is off limits to smokers, and Place du Bourg-de-Four is right up the hill. **Pros:** sitting on the roof terrace, soaking up spectacular views; the clean, airy vibe. **Cons:** street entrance could use a spiff-up; neither access nor pay-parking favor those arriving by car. ✉ *1 rue de la Vallée, Vieille Ville* ☎ *022/8183737* ⊕ *www.hotel-bel-esperance.ch* 🛏 *37 rooms, 3 studios* ♻ *In-room: no a/c, kitchen (studios only), Wi-Fi. In-hotel: safe at reception desk, laundry facilities, public Internet and Wi-Fi (free), all rooms are no-smoking, parking (fee)* ⊟ *AE, DC, MC, V* 🍴 *BP.*

$ 🏨 **Central.** Warm Indonesian wood, intense pastel greens and blues,
★ sponge-painted terra-cotta, and exotic flowers reflect the Gangsted family's ties to Bali in this friendly, low-cost hotel. Wedged into the top of a Left Bank shopping street, it actually occupies the top floors of an office building. Flexible sleeping configurations include budget rooms with

a bunk bed and shower, expansive apartments for six, and everything in between. Most guest rooms have balcony views, about half are air-conditioned, and all come with movies, free wireless access, and—there being no breakfast room—breakfast delivered to your door. **Pros:** the warm reception; upper range of accommodations is exceptionally spacious. **Cons:** tiny elevator; bathrooms in the lower price range are tight; if you're driving, pay parking will add a tidy slice to costs. ⊠*2 rue de la Rôtisserie, Centre Ville* ☎*022/8188100* ⊕*www.hotelcentral.ch* ⊲*28 rooms, 1 suite, 8 apartments* ⚒*In-room: no a/c (some), kitchen (some), DVD (some), VCR (some), Wi-Fi. In-hotel: room service, Wi-Fi (free).* ⊟*AE, DC, MC, V* ⊺⚬⎮*BP.*

$$$ ⌕**Cornavin.** The comic-book character Tintin made this hotel famous with *L'Affaire Tournesol* (*The Calculus Affair*) in 1956. Now the nine-story clock pendulum in the lobby, the deft manipulation of frosted glass and natural light on the top two floors, the spectacular glassed-in breakfast hall, and panoramic views compete for attention. Fourteen large triples and six interconnecting doubles easily accommodate families; double-glazed windows keep things quiet. This hotel is exceptionally well located: practically joined at the hip to the train station, it also has easy access to the international and main business quarters, as well as the airport. **Pros:** those views; that neat ride in the glassed-walled elevator past what has to be Geneva's tallest clock. **Cons:** a certain blandness and impersonality can occasionally make itself felt. ⊠*Gare de Cornavin, Centre Ville* ☎*022/7161212* ⊕*www.fhotels. ch* ⊲*160 rooms, 4 suites* ⚒*In-room: safe, Wi-Fi (fee). In-hotel: bar, public Internet and Wi-Fi (free), laundry service, no-smoking rooms* ⊟*AE, DC, MC, V.*

$$$$ ⌕**D'Angleterre.** Impeccable taste, total discretion, and a tangible passion for detail mark this stylish boutique hotel where thematic decoration stretches from African to Baroque, desks are equipped with office supplies, breakfast can be tailored to your needs, and room service includes afternoon tea. Guest rooms are done in beige on brown and give off a masculine and sophisticated vibe: the opulent suites go the Louis Seize route and are breathtakingly pretty. Downstairs, the Leopard Room bar has a working fireplace and live music Tuesday through Saturday; Windows, the quayside winter-garden restaurant, serves creative French cuisine with a front-row view of the Jet d'Eau and Mont Blanc. **Pros:** one of the best examples of a luxurious boutique hotel you'll find anywhere, beautifully maintained, and with smiling, friendly service. **Cons:** it's hard to think of any—cramped elevator? ⊠*17 quai du Mont-Blanc, Les Pâquis* ☎*022/9065555* ⊕*www.dangleterrehotel.com* ⊲*39 rooms, 6 suites* ⚒*In-room: safe, refrigerator, Wi-Fi (free). In-hotel: restaurant, room service, bar, gym, laundry service, Wi-Fi (free), parking (fee), no-smoking rooms* ⊟*AE, DC, MC, V.*

$ ⌕**De Genève.** A small hotel, this spot has its own brand of charm and
★   exceptionally caring staffers. Rustic stone, carved wood, and a thoroughly cozy chalet-style lobby give way to cheery rooms full of eclectic modern and antique furnishings, original art, and delicate stenciling in this family-run establishment housed in a block-long Belle Epoque building. Corner doubles with bay windows and parquet floors face

the 15th-century Temple de Saint-Gervais, double-glazing ensures silence, and breakfast comes with a backdrop of plane trees. **Pros:** very personal, original decor; they take pride in good service. **Cons:** chalet lobby-cum-breakfast area can get very crowded; need for pay parking makes it less of an option for drivers. ✉*1 pl. Isaac-Mercier, St-Gervais* ☎*022/7323264* ⊕*www.hotel-de-geneve.ch* ↪*39 rooms* ⚿*In-room: no a/c, Wi-Fi (fee). In-hotel: bar, laundry facilities, laundry service, public Internet and Wi-Fi (fee), no-smoking rooms* ▤*AE, DC, MC, V* ⦿|*BP.*

13

¢–$

Fodor'sChoice

★

De la Cloche. Head up one flight of stairs and enter a realm of flocked wallpaper, creaky parquet floors, chandeliers, fireplaces, and ornate ceilings that serve as reminders that this kindly bed-and-breakfast was once a plush private apartment. Right across the street from the entrance of the Grand Hotel Kempinski and one block from the lake, this has a prime location. Some of the eight guest rooms have Jet d'Eau views, while others overlook a quiet courtyard; all have light yellow walls and light blue duvets. Breakfast is served in your room. Owner Christian Chabbey doubles as informal concierge. **Pros:** that location; you get an authentic feel for genteel, Olde Worlde, Genevois living that exists to this day. **Cons:** the usual pay parking situation; no elevator; mostly shared bathroom facilities. ✉*6 rue de la Cloche, Les Pâquis* ☎*022/7329481* ⊕*www.geneva-hotel.ch/cloche* ↪*8 rooms, 5 with shower* ⚿*In-room: No a/c, Wi-Fi* ▤*AE, DC, MC, V* ⦿|*BP.*

$$–$$$

Fodor'sChoice

★

Domaine de Châteauvieux. A whole different Geneva experience can be yours once you take a Rhône meander out here and wind up in the heart of the Geneva wine country. Surrounded by flowers, vineyards, and rolling green mountain views, this sturdy stone manor offers interesting bike-riding countryside right outside the gates (reserve the hotel's bicycles ahead). Inside, delicate stenciling, marble sinks, and bright calico reflect a happy marriage of good taste and warm country spirit—the decor is as relaxing as the *chambre romantique*'s hot tub. Most guest rooms are nicely spacious, often dramatically accented with rough-hewn stone walls. Last but not least, the breakfast includes homemade bread and pastries, local honey, and jams made in-house from local fruit—only fitting thanks to the famed stone-and-wood-beam restaurant onsite. **Pros:** lovely wine-country setting; fabulous restaurants. **Cons:** staying here doesn't guarantee you a place in the restaurant (reserve your table when you reserve your room); no elevator; a cab to or from the airport or city center can run up to 80 SF. ✉*16 chemin de Châteauvieux, Peney-Dessus, Satigny* ☎*022/7531511* ⊕*www.chateauvieux.ch* ↪*12 rooms, 1 suite* ⚿*In-room: safe, refrigerator, Wi-Fi (fee). In-hotel: restaurant, room service, bar, laundry service, public Internet and Wi-Fi (fee), parking (free), no-smoking rooms* ▤*AE, DC, MC, V* ⦿|*BP.*

$$$–$$$$

EastWest. Take a small hotel and convert it into a townhouse-y bijou with a world-traveler feel. Add a signature restaurant and "tapas" bar driven by globe-trotting three-star Michelin chefs (the Pourcel brothers) and you have something unique—a Geneva first. The contemporary taste, and mix of art and design objects in guest and public rooms alike, is exquisite here; so is the food at Sens, the restaurant part of which overlooks a lovely small court where bamboo riffles in the breeze against a water wall. The "tapas" bar has nothing to do with hearty Spanish nibbles but rather with rarefied gourmet delights that take their references from all over. **Pros:** aesthetics, sophistication, luxurious sensuality. **Cons:** space (closets et al.) can be a little tight; this place is definitely not for the "I know what I like" meat-and-potatoes type. " ✉6 rue des Pâquis, Les Pâquis ☎022/7081717 ⊕www.eastwesthotel.ch ⤴37 rooms, 4 suites ⚲In-room: safe, refrigerator, Wi-Fi (free). In-hotel: restaurant, room service, bar, gym, public Internet and Wi-Fi (free), laundry service, parking (fee), no-smoking rooms ▤AE, DC, MC, V.

$$$$ 　🏨 **Four Seasons des Bergues.** Unpretentious service gives the first Four
FodorsChoice 　Seasons in Switzerland and the oldest (1834), least self-conscious, of
★ 　Geneva's grand hotels an inner glow. Louis-Philippe opulence, ornamental stucco, and Portuguese marble mesh seamlessly with perfect maintenance and modern comforts like flat-screen TVs that turn toward you, luxuriously thick mattresses, in-room spa treatments, and breakfast menus that stretch from Asia to the Alps. Guest rooms booked for children have pint-sized bathrobes and slippers, milk and cookies, and a smorgasbord of toys. Not to mention that the views—Jet d'Eau, Old Town—from this swooningly impressive, yet so personal hotel are superb. Or that the restaurant, Il Lago, features northern Italian cuisine that many say is the best in Geneva. **Pros:** what can you say about perfection? **Cons:** even the issue of "no spa" is temporary, as a full Four Seasons spa with large pool is scheduled for 2010. ✉33 quai des Bergues, Centre Ville ☎022/9087000 ⊕www.fourseasons.com/Geneva ⤴68 rooms, 35 suites ⚲In-room: safe, refrigerator, Wi-Fi (fee). In-hotel: restaurant, room service, bar, gym, laundry service, Wi-Fi (fee), parking (fee), no-smoking rooms. ▤AE, DC, MC, V.

$$$$ 　🏨 **Grand Hotel Kempinski.** Ask for a renovated room lakeside, and it is top standard—a little same-y, but you can't beat the view from the large windows. This Grand Central of a place continues to be a favorite of businessmen, who hold meetings in the lobby, off which some serious jewelry shops and what connoisseurs say is Geneva's finest purveyor of cigars, Gérard, feed. Floor Two, a favorite with young professional expats, has a huge bar-lounge-eatery space with terraces court and lakeside; Le Grill, one of Geneva's best (and priciest) Chinese restaurants, and its jet-settiest club, the Java, are all in the building. Clothing shops, drugstore, hairdresser, spa facilities, and pool complete this self-contained world. **Pros:** big-city buzz; Le Grill's fabulous views and striking dinner atmosphere (torches aflame outside picture windows). **Cons:** a certain anonymity; un-refurbished rooms, while impeccable, are dated. ✉19 quai du Mont-Blanc, Les Pâquis ☎022/9089081 ⊕www.kempinski-geneva.com ⤴398 rooms, 25 suites ⚲In-room: safe, refrigerator, Wi-Fi (fee). In-hotel: 3 restaurants, room service, bar, pool, gym, spa, laundry service, free Internet terminal, Wi-Fi (fee), parking (fee), no-smoking rooms ▤AE, DC, MC, V.

$ 　🏨 **Ibis.** This cheerful chain hotel is ultraconvenient if you're arriving late or departing early: breakfast starts at 4 AM (on request), the reception desk is staffed 24/7, and the train station is just 10 minutes away on foot. Smooth wood and apricot accents add warmth to green pinstripes in the bright, well-appointed, and spotless guest rooms, and the bathrooms get high marks for plentiful hot water. **Pros:** nicely conceived hotel; great value for money. **Cons:** not in a pretty location; space is at a premium; breakfast for two adds about 20% to the tab. ⊠*10 rue Voltaire, St-Gervais* ☎*022/3382020* ⊕*www.ibishotel.com* ⤷*64 rooms* ⟲*In-room: pay Wi-Fi (some). In-hotel: bar, Wi-Fi (fee), parking (fee), all rooms are no-smoking.* ⊟*AE, DC, MC, V.*

$–$$ ⛫**International et Terminus.** The leafy outdoor terrace, soft yellow facade, and peach-paneled lobby impose civility on this modest hotel's central but chaotic location on a busy street opposite the Gare Cornavin. Guest rooms have marbled tile bathrooms, sleek wood furniture, double-glazed windows, and restful rose, green, and raspberry color schemes. The multilingual, uniformed staff is on duty round the clock. La Véranda, the restaurant where breakfast is served, also offers reasonably priced lunches and dinners, including the ubiquitous Geneva *plat du jour* (weekday lunch special) for a modest 15 SF. **Pros:** a more-than-correct deal for the money; restaurant terrace is an oasis in a noisy area. **Cons:** car access is awkward, and parking fees add to costs. ⊠*20 rue des Alpes, Les Pâquis* ☎*022/9069777* ⊕*www.international-terminus.ch* ⤷*60 rooms* ⟲*In-room: no a/c, safe, refrigerator, Wi-Fi (fee). In-hotel: restaurant, laundry service, parking (fee)* ⊟*AE, DC, MC, V* ⦿*BP.*

$$–$$$ ⛫**Le Montbrillant.** Exposed stone walls and massive wooden beams channel mountain huts in the lobby of this busy family-run hotel behind the Gare Cornavin. Studios have kitchenettes, dormer windows, cathedral ceilings, and monthly rates. Guest rooms have clean lines, rosy wallpaper, white-satin duvets, blue-gray trim, flat-screen TVs, and double-glazed windows; those facing forward also have a terrific view of the TGV high-speed train as it arrives from Paris (for anyone traveling by TGV, this is the place to stay: the hotel entrance is a few steps from the boarding area). **Pros:** friendly desk staff; good value for money. **Cons:** hard to access by car; for some a bit too close to the station (and one of the restaurants—Café de la Gare—doubles as a watering hole for train travelers). ⊠*2 rue de Montbrillant, Les Grottes* ☎*022/7337784* ⊕*www.montbrillant.ch* ⤷*58 rooms, 24 studios* ⟲*In-room: safe, refrigerator, Wi-Fi (fee). In-hotel: 2 restaurants, room service, bar, laundry service, public Internet (free), Wi-Fi (fee), parking (free), no-smoking rooms* ⊟*AE, DC, MC, V* ⦿*BP.*

$$$$ ⛫**Le Richemond.** Some say the soul departed from this landmark hotel when Rocco Forte took over and asked designer John Stefanidis to revamp it. The latter's take on the old crimson and crystal grandeur is hit-and-miss—but stay in a deluxe suite (3,500 SF) overlooking the Monument Brunswick and the ultra-chic pied-à-terre vibe is likely to win you over. The new bar, and Sapori, the Italian eatery, both have see-and-be-seen terraces, and the basement boasts a labyrinthine, candle-lit spa with a water wall for some serious chilling. **Pros:** retains the luxe home-away-from-home-feel for which it has always been known—and love that chill-out zone, which also has a his-and-hers massage therapy room for relaxing *à deux.* **Cons:** corporate-style decor and florals in the public spaces can be incongruous, lacking flow. ⊠*Jardin Brunswick,*

13

Les Pâquis ☎022/7157000 ⊕*www.roccofortecollection.com* ⇗83
rooms, 26 suites ◐*In-room: safe, refrigerator, Wi-Fi (fee). In-hotel:*
restaurant, room service, bar, gym, spa, laundry service, Wi-Fi (fee),
parking (fee), no-smoking rooms ▤*AE, DC, MC, V.*

$$$$ ⊞ **Les Armures.** Original 17th-century stonework, frescoes, painted
beams, and tapestries adorn the lobby and some rooms in this low-key
luxury hotel near the cathedral; others have clean modern lines and
restful deep-brown accents. Cobblestone views, a sense of peace, and
surprising amounts of natural light frame glowing glass-and-tile baths,
fresh flowers, thick bathrobes, and flat-screen TVs throughout; two very
quiet rooms give onto a tiny inner courtyard. The hotel's restaurant is
one of the city's most popular venues for Swiss specialties—raclette,
fondue, et al. Even (as a discreet plaque by the door announces) Bill
Clinton, when U.S. president, came here to sample them. **Pros:** at the
heart of Geneva's historic quarter; continental breakfast is included in
the room rate. **Cons:** not a lot of infrastructure (no gym, etc.) and too
quiet for some. ✉*1 rue du Puits-St-Pierre, Vieille Ville* ☎*022/3109172*
⊕*www.hotel-les-armures.ch* ⇗*27 rooms, 5 suites* ◐*In-room: safe,*
refrigerator, Wi-Fi (fee). In-hotel: restaurant, room service, bar, laun-
dry service, public Internet (free), pay Wi-Fi, parking (fee), no-smoking
rooms ▤*AE, DC, MC, V* ⦿*CP.*

$$$$ ⊞ **Mandarin Oriental du Rhône.** Don't let that boring facade fool you—
inside there's a feng shui-ed (clean energy) feel, and the recent redesign
of the public rooms harmonizes beautifully with guest rooms. Not to
mention the hotel's alluring mix of original Art Deco–influenced furniture, contemporary all-you-could-wish-for amenities, and fabulous
Rhône views on the river side. Smiling staff wearing elegant flowing
uniforms, lush flower displays, and a deliciously perfumed lobby greet
you when you walk in, and besides the MO bar there are not one but
two signature restaurants (Paul Bocuse Brasserie, Rasoi by Vineet Bhatia, the latter serving "evolved"—and deluxe—Indian cuisine), plus
the full spa with large pool due to open in 2009. **Pros:** a natural easy
vibe to the service; the luxury of spaciousness; Geneva's first upscale
Indian restaurant. **Cons:** at these prices, there should be no charge
for Wi-Fi. ✉*1 quai Turrettini, St-Gervais* ☎*022/9090000* ⊕*www.*
mandarinoriental.com/geneva ⇗*197 rooms, 31 suites* ◐*In-room:*
safe, refrigerator, Wi-Fi (fee). In-hotel: 2 restaurants, room service,
bar, gym, laundry service, public Internet (free), Wi-Fi (fee), parking
(fee), no-smoking rooms ▤*AE, DC, MC, V.*

$$$$ ⊞ **President Wilson.** No-thrills modern outside, but one step inside and
you'll be seduced by the wafting scents of votive candles and the high-
glitter-cum-slice-of-nature lobby and public salons. Swarovski crystals
pressed into marble flooring, onyx, cut glass, platinum mosaics, and
gold leaf are all mixed in with artist Jae-Ho Lee's nature statements.
The striking results—stay here only if you like modern minimalism done
with a sumptuous Baroque touch—suggest the water and mountains
the hotel has fabulous views of. Top Lebanese eating at Arabesque
and world-influenced French cuisine at Spice's, the sophisticated new
lounge space called Glow, bar, boutique, hairdresser, and a spa and
outdoor pool with restaurant (dig the sexy night-lighting) add to the

appeal of the impeccably appointed guest rooms. **Pros:** loads of polished eat-and-drink options; you can reserve the spa's Jacuzzi, sauna, and chill-out room for yourself, with or without significant other. **Cons:** the unequivocal opulence may seem a bit flashy to some, and the rooms, while fully up to snuff, a bit same-y. ⊠*47 quai Wilson, Les Pâquis* ☎*022/9066666* ⊕*www.hotelpwilson.com* ✒*174 rooms, 54 suites* ⚒*In-room: safe, refrigerator, Wi-Fi (fee). In-hotel: 3 restaurants (1 seasonal), room service, bar, pool, gym, spa, laundry service, Wi-Fi (fee), parking (fee), no-smoking rooms* ▤*AE, DC, MC, V.*

13

$ 🏨**St-Gervais.** Red tartan carpeting and clean white linens warm some of the garretlike rooms in this old Right Bank inn; others have transitioned to blue walls and accents, parquet floors, and modular wooden desks. Fluffy white towels, hair dryers on request, and friendly service are common to all. A quality breakfast that includes orange juice, fruit yogurt, whole bread, fresh croissants, butter, honey, and choice of jams and hot beverage is served from 6:30 AM to 9 AM in the wood-paneled bar-café on the ground floor. **Pros:** easy train-station access; a caring vibe; good value for money. **Cons:** some find the café/lobby a bit dark; mostly shared bathroom facilities; not ideal for drivers. ⊠*20 rue des Corps-Saints, St-Gervais* ☎*022/7324572* ⊕*www.stgervais-geneva.ch* ✒*26 rooms, 2 with bath* ⚒*In-room: no a/c, Wi-Fi (fee). In-hotel: bar, Wi-Fi (fee)* ▤*AE, DC, MC, V* ◉*BP.*

$$$$ 🏨**Swissôtel Métropole.** Massive scrubbed-stone arches, swirled wrought-iron sconces, brass accents, warm colors, lush carpets, and the immediate proximity of high-voltage rue du Rhône shopping give this 1854 Left Bank palace an air of urban gentility and center-city bustle. Guest rooms have triple-glazed windows; they are decorated in what the hotel calls a "contemporary yet cozy Italian" style and come equipped with espresso machines. The newly refurbished Grand Quai restaurant has lost its 19th century-style grandeur in favor of a more streamlined contemporary look in browns and silver—attending one of its theme dinners periodically organized on the roof terrace is worth it for the wraparound view of Geneva alone. **Pros:** central Left Bank location; crimson Mirror Bar (with pianist) has winning cocoon feel. **Cons:** limited space for cabs and other vehicles to stop, so arrivals and departures can be stressful—and some complain that rooms, although renovated, don't reflect the absolute latest in five-star decor. ⊠*34 quai du Général-Guisan, Centre Ville* ☎*022/3183200* ⊕*www.geneva.swissotel.com* ✒*111 rooms, 16 suites* ⚒*In-room: safe, refrigerator, Wi-Fi (fee). In-hotel: 2 restaurants, room service, bar, gym, laundry service, public Internet (free), Wi-Fi (fee), parking (fee), no-smoking rooms* ▤*AE, DC, MC, V.*

$$$ 🏨**Tiffany.** Adjacent to the banking and theater districts, this hotel and ★ its restaurant are favorites with artists and bankers alike. It's not hard to see why: the pretty Art Nouveau decor is one-of-a-kind, and the whole place has recently been given a face-lift that embraces its 19th century originality but gives it a contemporary edge. Since the hotel is owned by the same family as the EastWest, the renovation included bringing in the French Pourcel brothers to inject a light, Mediterranean note into popular chef Alban Mestre's excellent French cuisine. With a sidewalk terrace, bar, library/business room, and small gym, this appealing,

tasteful and friendly hotel is real value for the money. **Pros:** an exceptionally convenient property with a great restaurant. **Cons:** standard bathrooms with their Art Nouveau–style tiling have been spiffed up but not replaced—so don't look for up-to-the-minute-design in that department. ⊠*20 rue de l'Arquebuse, Plainpalais* ☎*022/7081616* ⊕*www. tiffanyhotel.ch* 🛏*43 rooms, 3 suites* ⚿*In-room: safe, refrigerator, Wi-Fi (fee). In-hotel: restaurant, room service, bar, laundry service, public Internet (free), Wi-Fi (fee), parking (fee), no-smoking rooms* ⊟*AE, DC, MC, V.*

NIGHTLIFE & THE ARTS

Genève Agenda publishes monthly English and French listings of concerts, performances, temporary exhibits, restaurants, and clubs. A popular guide, it is also called the *Monthly Guide of Geneva*—free copies are available from tourist information booths and hotels, and the publication can also be downloaded from the Web site (⊕*www. le-guide.ch*)

NIGHTLIFE

A successful night out in Geneva—whether exclusive, trendy, or pub-based—can hinge on understanding that you are not in a major metropolis. Though bars and clubs have lots of life, much of it English-speaking, it may not be possible to party till dawn.

BARS

For a sophisticated vibe, **Arthur's Rive Gauche** (⊠*7–9 rue du Rhône, Centre Ville* ☎*022/8103260* ⊕*www.arthurs.ch*) is a top option. **Senso Le Lobby** (⊠*56 bis rue du Rhône, Centre Ville* ☎*022/3103990* ⊕*www. senso-living.ch*)is a sleek and soigné bar (with restaurant). When it comes to wine bars, **Boulevard du Vin** (⊠*3 blvd. Georges-Favon, Plainpalais* ☎*022/3109190* ⊕*www.boulevard-du-vin.ch*) tops a lot of lists. In season, sit outside at quintessentially Genevese **La Clémence** (⊠*20 pl. du Bourg-de-Four, Vieille Ville* ☎*022/3122498* ⊕*www.laclemence.ch*). Big with English-speakers is **Mr. Pickwick Pub** (⊠*80 rue de Lausanne, Les Pâquis* ☎*022/7316797* ⊕*www.mrpickwick.ch*). The Guinness is on tap and the accents are robustly Irish at **Mulligan's** (⊠*14 rue Grenus, St-Gervais* ☎*022/7328576* ⊕*www.ireland.ch*). The **Roi Ubu** (⊠*30 Grand-Rue, Vieille Ville* ☎*022/3107398*) draws a lively, young international crowd. Classic pub comfort, American bartenders, and large-screen TVs draw crowds to the **Spring Bros. Irish Pub** (⊠*23 Grand-rue, Vieille Ville* ☎*022/3101024*).

CLUBS

DJs, R&B, and house fuel a trendy vibe at **Platinum Glam Club** (⊠*18 quai du Seujet, St. Jean* ☎*022/7389091* ⊕*www.platinum-club.ch*) from 11 PM to 5 AM, daily in July and August. **Bypass** (⊠*1 carrefour de l'Etoile, Acacias* ☎*022/3006565* ⊕*www.bypass-geneve.ch*) lures cosmopolitan twenty- and thirtysomethings to the outer edge of Carouge. Up-and-coming musicians from around the world perform live at the

La Cité Sarde

Geneva's Greenwich Village, Carouge (from *quadruvium*) began life in the Roman era as a crossroads next to a bridge over the river Arve. It remained a mere hamlet until 1754, when the Duke of Savoy, by then also King of Sardinia, annexed it with intent to create a rival commercial hub for Geneva. That never happened, courtesy of the French Revolution, but the town grew so fast that the royal planners in Turin drew up five separate development plans between 1772 and 1783; their harmonious architecture, plazas, and courtyard gardens still recall Mediterranean ways unheard of in Geneva. Colorful shop windows, sidewalk cafés, friendly restaurants, hole-in-the-wall galleries, tree-lined fruit-and-vegetable markets (on Wednesday and Saturday), open doors, and working artists infuse Rue St-Joseph, Rue Ancienne, Rue St-Victor, and Place du Marché with vibrant creative energy; don't miss the outdoor street fairs on the last weekend in August and mid-December.

small, relaxed, and affordable **Chat Noir** (✉ *13 rue Vautier, Carouge* ☎ *022/3434998* ⊕ *www.chatnoir.ch*). One of the coolest bar/discos, on two floors and open Thursday though Saturday till five, is Soul Influenced Product, or **La SIP** (✉ *8–10 rue des Vieux-Grenadiers, Plainpalais* ☎ *no phone* ⊕ *www.lasip.ch*). Local fashionistas and a genuine big-city vibe make **Javaclub** (✉ *Grand Hôtel Kempinski Genève, 19 quai du Mont-Blanc, Les Pâquis* ☎ *022/9089088* ⊕ *www.javaclub.ch*) the place to see and be seen. **Moa Club** (✉ *22 chemin des Batailles, Vernier* ⊕ *www.moaclub.com*) has a popular vibe and a dance-party schedule loaded with techno. The cocktails are potent and the dance hits current at **Shakers** (✉ *4 rue Arnold-Winkelried, Centre Ville* ☎ *022/3105598* ⊕ *www.shakers.ch*).

THE ARTS

Geneva's legacy as a cultural crossroads has produced an unusually rich arts scene for a city of its size: most performance spaces in town are roadhouses, through which flow a steady stream of foreign as well as Swiss artists. Tickets remain on sale from theater box offices up to the day of performance, but it's wise to book ahead. The Service Billetterie at **FNAC Rive** (✉ *16 rue de Rive, Centre Ville* ☎ *022/8161256* ⊕ *www.fnac.ch*) manages sales for a huge, ever-changing list of events. The third-floor ticket booth at **Globus** (✉ *48 rue du Rhône, Centre Ville* ☎ *022/3195583*) handles concerts and theatrical performances throughout Switzerland; note that it does not accept credit cards.

FILM

English-language films are always screened undubbed somewhere in town—check local newspaper listings for the initials *v.o.*, short for *version originale* (original version). The **CAC Voltaire** (✉ *16 rue du Général-Dufour, Centre Ville* ☎ *022/3207878* ⊕ *www.ville-ge.ch/ culture/grutli*) organizes ongoing, undubbed classic film mini-festivals in the basement of the Grütli Arts Center. **Cinélac** (✉ *Port-Noir, Cologny*

☎022/3196111 ⊕*www.orangecinema.ch*) screens a different film outside by the lake every night from July through August.

MUSIC & DANCE

Classical music, opera, contemporary dance, and the occasional film
festival cycle through the **Bâtiment des Forces Motrices** (✉*2 pl. des Volontaires, Plainpalais* ☎022/3221220 ⊕*www.bfm.ch*). The **Grand Théâtre**
(✉*pl. Neuve, Centre Ville* ☎022/4183130 ⊕*www.geneveopera.
ch*) stages a total of some 18 operas, ballets, and recitals each season
(September to June). **Victoria Hall** (✉*14 rue du Général-Dufour, Centre Ville* ☎022/4183500 ⊕*www.ville-ge.ch/vh/*), Geneva's classical
concert venue, is home to the venerable **Orchestre de la Suisse Romande**
(☎022/8070000 ⊕*www.osr.ch*). The AMR musical association
stocks the program at **Sud des Alpes** (✉*10 rue des Alpes, Les Pâquis*
☎022/7165630 ⊕*www.amr-geneve.ch*) with nervy improvisation and
contemporary jazz.

THEATER

The creative, colorful children's theater **Am Stram Gram** (✉*56 rte. de
Frontenex, Eaux-Vives* ☎022/7357924 ⊕*www.amstramgram.ch*)
draws inspiration from myth, folktales, lyric poetry, Shakespeare, and
contemporary writing. Anne Bisang's **Comédie de Genève** (✉*6 blvd. des
Philosophes, Plainpalais* ☎022/3205001 ⊕*www.comedie.ch*) stages
modern drama and international classics. The experimental **Théâtre
du Grütli** (✉*16 rue du Général-Dufour, Centre Ville* ☎022/3289868
⊕*www.grutli.ch*) fills its spare, flexible space with contemporary Swiss
and foreign plays. All three theaters' productions are in French.

SPORTS & THE OUTDOORS

SKIING

Geneva is surrounded by terrific downhill skiing, most of it in the
French Alps. Buses to Chamonix, Courchevel, Megève, and Morzine-
Avoriaz—to name but a few desirable options—depart from the **Gare
Routière de Genève** (✉*pl. Dorcière, Les Pâquis* ☎0900/320230 ⊕*www.
gare-routiere.com*) throughout the season (generally early December to
mid-April). Trips take 1½–2 hours. Check whether the 65–90 SF to-
and-from fare includes a ski-lift pass.

SWIMMING

The Genevois love their beaches, which open in May and stay crowded
through September. Lac Léman water quality is closely monitored by
the **État de Genève** (⊕*www.geneve.ch/plages*) and regularly recertified
clean and safe for swimmers. A laid-back and popular concrete sunbathing area surrounds a protected mid-harbor swim zone and casual
restaurant at **Bains des Pâquis** (✉*30 quai du Mont-Blanc, Les Pâquis*
☎022/7322974 ⊕*www.bains-des-paquis.ch*). **Genève-Plage** (✉*Port
Noir, Cologny* ☎022/7362482 ⊕*www.geneve-plage.ch*) has green
lawns, an Olympic outdoor pool, lake access, multilevel diving boards,
basketball and volleyball courts, Ping-Pong tables, a canteen, and a
water slide.

SHOPPING

Official store hours are Monday to Wednesday from 9 to 7, Thursday from 9 to 9, Friday from 9 to 7:30, and Saturday from 9 to 6. Shops may, however, open later Monday, close earlier Thursday and Saturday, or close for lunch.

AUCTIONS

13

As a jewelry capital rivaled only by New York, and an international center for Swiss watchmakers, Geneva regularly hosts high-profile auctions by the major houses. **Antiquorum** (⊠*2 rue du Mont-Blanc, Centre Ville* ☎*022/9092850*) focuses on collector timepieces. **Christie's** (⊠*8 pl. de la Taconnerie, Vieille Ville* ☎*022/3191766*) auctions off wine as well as exclusive jewelry and watches twice a year. **Sotheby's** (⊠*13 quai du Mont-Blanc, Les Pâquis* ☎*022/9084800*) displays exquisite lots of jewelry and watches in May and November before they are sold.

DEPARTMENT STORES

Bon Génie (⊠*34 rue du Marché, Centre Ville* ☎*022/8181111*) stocks floor after hushed floor with designer clothing and cosmetics. **Globus** (⊠*48 rue du Rhône, Centre Ville* ☎*022/3195050*) forms a physical link between the Left Bank shopping arteries and excels at home accessories, kitchen paraphernalia, hosiery, men's and women's clothing, and food.

MARKETS

Halle de Rive (⊠*17 rue Pierre-Fatio/29 blvd. Helvétique, Centre Ville* ⊕*www.halle-de-rive.com*) sells fresh cheeses, meats, pasta, fish, flowers, wine, and chocolate all day Monday through Saturday. A vibrant seasonal fruit-and-vegetable market fills **Boulevard Helvétique** on Wednesday and Saturday mornings. Arts-and-crafts vendors crowd **Place de la Fusterie** every Thursday. Flea market stalls move into position around the **Plaine de Plainpalais** on Wednesday and Saturday, replacing the Tuesday and Friday morning fruit-and-vegetable stands.

SHOPPING STREETS

Geneva's principal shopping streets, known collectively as the **Rues-Basses** (Low Streets), run parallel along the Left Bank. **Rue du Rhône,** closest to the river, marks the epicenter of luxury shopping. One block in is the more popular thoroughfare known variously as **Rue de la Confédération, Rue du Marché, Rue de la Croix-d'Or,** and **Rue de Rive.** Galleries, antiques shops, home-accessories emporia, and chic boutiques line the **Grand-Rue,** as well as streets radiating out from **Place du Bourg-de-Four. Rue du Mont-Blanc** represents the frenetic hub of Right Bank shopping.

SPECIALTY STORES

ANTIQUES

Antiquités Scientifiques (⌧*19 rue du Perron, Vieille Ville* ☎*022/3100706*) buys, sells, and assesses telescopes, barometers, microscopes, binoculars, sundials, and cameras. Head to **Librairie Ancienne** (⌧*20 Grand-Rue, Vieille Ville* ☎*022/3102050*) for leather-bound and gilt first editions (not in English). **Montparnasse** (⌧*40 Grand-Rue, Vieille Ville* ☎*022/3116719*) deals in pristine original prints of Geneva, maps, and paintings from the 18th- and early-20th century École Suisse. Well-polished English furniture fills the **Regency House** (⌧*3 rue de l'Hôtel-de-Ville, Vieille Ville* ☎*022/3103540*). **Rue des Belles Filles** (⌧*8 rue Etienne-Dumont, Vieille Ville* ☎*022/3103131*) buys and sells vintage jewelry, clothing, linens, crystal, silver, china, and paintings.

WORD OF MOUTH

"I am not a big shopper, but do like wandering the shops around Geneva's Eaux-Vives area. Shops are usually closed on Sundays other than in train stations and airports, so do your shopping on Saturday. Evenings? There may be symphony, opera and ballet on offer. The Grand Théâtre is a beautiful venue to see any performance in. There are often free classical concerts in churches (check with your hotel) or the website for the Office du Tourisme de Genève: www.geneve-tourisme.ch." —Cicerone

BOOKS

French giant **FNAC** (⌧*16 rue de Rive, Centre Ville* ☎*022/8161220*) holds readings and devotes its block-length upper floor to current French (and a few English) titles. **Librairie Archigraphy** (⌧*1 pl. de l'Ile, Centre Ville* ☎*022/3116008*) sells art, design, and architecture books in a setting worthy of its subjects. **Librairie Bernard Letu** (⌧*2 rue Jean-Calvin, Vieille Ville* ☎*022/3104757*) carries an inspired range of multilingual art and photography titles. French-language books about Geneva form the tip of the proverbial (and dusty) iceberg at the venerable old **Librairie Jullien** (⌧*32 pl. du Bourg-de-Four, Vieille Ville* ☎*022/3103670*). **Off the Shelf** (⌧*15 blvd. Georges-Favon, Plainpalais* ☎*022/3111090*) lures English-speaking browsers with a sunny space and a hand-picked selection. The English section within the commercial chain **Payot** (⌧*5 rue de Chantepoulet, Les Pâquis* ☎*022/7318950*) keeps abreast of current U.S. and U.K. trends.

CHOCOLATE

Silky, handmade white-chocolate truffles top the winter selection at **Arn** (⌧*12 pl. du Bourg-de-Four, Vieille Ville* ☎*022/3104094*). Local cobblestones inspired Henri Auer's *pavés glacés,* creamy bite-size delicacies that have become Genevois classics; his descendants at **Auer** (⌧*4 rue de Rive, Centre Ville* ☎*022/3114286*) maintain the tradition. **Du Rhône** (⌧*3 rue de la Confédération, Centre Ville* ☎*022/3115614*) has sold bittersweet hot chocolate since 1875. **Merkur** (⌧*32 rue du Marché, Centre Ville* ☎*022/3102221* ⌧*Galerie marchande de Cornavin, Les Pâquis* ☎*022/7324182*) stocks Swiss-theme gift boxes, individual bars, and huge champagne truffles. **Rohr** (⌧*3 pl. du Molard, Centre*

Ville ☎*022/3116303* ✉*4 rue de l'Enfer, Centre Ville* ☎*022/3116876)* models its smooth, rich signature truffles after old Geneva garbage cans. Don't be fooled; it's the best chocolate in town.

GIFTS & SOUVENIRS

Mercerie Catherine B (✉*17 rue de la Cité, Vieille Ville* ☎*022/3107779)* sells Swiss-themed samplers—hearts, flowers, chalets, cows—framed or that you can embroider yourself. Crafts, including carved wooden toys, make **Epsetera** (✉*29 rue Saint-Joseph, Carouge* ☎*022/3432950)* fun for all ages. And where would we be without the Swiss army knife? Consider the vast choice at **Riethmüller** (✉*19 pl. Longemalle, Centre Ville* ☎*022/3124052)*.

JEWELRY

Bucherer (✉*45 rue du Rhône, Centre Ville* ☎*022/3196266* ✉*22 rue du Mont-Blanc, Les Pâquis* ☎*022/7327216)* sells luminous pearls and diamonds of all sizes. **Bulgari** (✉*30 rue du Rhône, Centre Ville* ☎*022/3177070)* favors heavy gold necklaces and rings crusted with jewels. **Cartier** (✉*35 rue du Rhône, Centre Ville* ☎*022/8185454)* famously renders feline grace in diamonds, rubies, and emeralds. **Chopard** (✉*8 rue de la Confédération, Centre Ville* ☎*022/3113728* ✉*27 rue du Rhône, Centre Ville* ☎*022/3107050)* creates icelike necklaces out of inlaid diamonds. **Gilbert Albert** (✉*24 rue de la Corraterie, Centre Ville* ☎*022/3114833)* lets nature inspire interchangeable stones wrapped in curvaceous, coral-like gold.

PAPER GOODS

Clean lines and vibrant color define the writing paper and fabric-bound photo albums at **Bookbinders** (✉*15 rue de la Fontaine, Vieille Ville* ☎*022/3016450)*. **Brachard** (✉*10 rue de la Corraterie, Centre Ville* ☎*022/8170555)* has wonderful papers, cards, pens, exquisite notebooks—and don't miss Brachard Contemporary across the street to the right, up the stairs at No. 7, then upstairs again in the passageway. Spiral and perfect-bound notebooks, photo albums, and monochromatic cards form tall swathes of color at **Ordning & Reda** (✉*20 rue de Rive, Centre Ville* ☎*022/8101020)*.

WATCHES

Bucherer (✉*45 rue du Rhône, Centre Ville* ☎*022/3196266* ✉*22 rue du Mont-Blanc, Les Pâquis* ☎*022/7327216)* is Geneva's one-stop shop for prestigious, indestructible Rolex models. **Franck Muller** (✉*1 rue de la Tour-de-l'Ile, Centre Ville* ☎*022/8180030)* creates complicated modern timepieces. **Patek Philippe** (✉*41 rue du Rhône, Centre Ville* ☎*022/8095050)* occupies the 1839 building where Antoine Norbert de Patek invented the winding mechanism inside all watches. **Piaget** (✉*40 rue du Rhône, Centre Ville* ☎*022/8170200)* wraps its ultraflat tourbillons in sleek white gold. **Vacheron Constantin** (✉*7 quai de l'Ile, Centre Ville* ☎*022/3161740)*, the oldest watch company in Geneva, sold its first sober design in 1755.

VOCABULARY

	English	French	French Pronunciation
Basics			
	Yes/no	Oui/non	wee/no
	Please	S'il vous plaît	seel voo **play**
	Thank you	Merci	mare-**see**
	You're welcome	De rien	deh ree-**enh**
	Excuse me	Pardon	pahr-**doan**
	Hello	Bonjour	bohn-**zhoor**
	Goodbye	Au revoir	o ruh-**vwahr**
Numbers			
	One	Un	un
	Two	Deux	deuh
	Three	Trois	twa
	Four	Quatre	**cat**-ruh
	Five	Cinq	sank
	Six	Six	seess
	Seven	Sept	set
	Eight	Huit	weat
	Nine	Neuf	nuf
	Ten	Dix	deess
Days			
	Today	Aujourd'hui	o-zhoor-**dwee**
	Tomorrow	Demain	deh-**menh**
	Yesterday	Hier	yair
	Morning	Matin	ma-**tenh**
	Afternoon	Après-midi	ah-pray-mee-**dee**
	Night	Nuit	nwee
	Monday	Lundi	**lahn**-dee
	Tuesday	Mardi	**mahr**-dee
	Wednesday	Mercredi	**mare**-kruh-dee
	Thursday	Jeudi	**juh**-dee
	Friday	Vendredi	**vawn**-dra-dee
	Saturday	Samedi	**sam**-dee
	Sunday	Dimanche	**dee**-mawnsh

*Prevalent Swiss-German dialect

German	German Pronunciation	Italian	Italian Pronunciation
Ja/nein	yah/nine	Sí/No	see/no
Bitte	**bit**-uh	Per favore	pear fa-**voh**-reh
Danke	**dahn**-kuh	Grazie	**grah**-tsee-ay
Bitte schön	**bit**-uh **shern**	Prego	**pray**-go
Entschuldigen Sie *Äxgüsi	ent-**shool**-de-gen-zee **ax**-scu-see	Scusi	**skoo**-zee
Guten Tag *Grüezi *Grüss Gott	**goot**-en **tahk** **grit**-zee groos got	Buon giorno	bwohn **jyohr**-noh
Auf Widersehen *Ufwiederluege *Tschüss (*familiar*)	Auf **vee-der**-zane oof-**vee-der**-lawgah choohs	Arrivederci	a-ree-vah-**dare**-chee
Eins	eints	Uno	**oo**-no
Zwei	tsvai	Due	**doo**-ay
Drei	dry	Tre	tray
Vier	fear	Quattro	**kwah**-troh
Fünf	fumph	Cinque	**cheen**-kway
Sechs	zex	Sei	say
Sieben	**zee**-ben	Sette	**set**-ay
Acht	ahkt	Otto	**oh**-to
Neun	noyn	Nove	**no**-vay
Zehn	tsane	Dieci	dee-**eh**-chee
Huete	**hoi**-tah	Oggi	**oh**-jee
Morgen	**more**-gehn	Domani	do-**mah**-nee
Gestern	geh-**shtairn**	Ieri	ee-veh-ree
Morgen	**more**-gehn	Mattina	ma-**tee**-na
Nachmittag	nahkt-**mit**-ahk	Pomeriggio	po-mer-**ee**-jo
Nacht	nahkt	Notte	Noh-teh
Montag	**mohn**-tahk	Lunedì	**loo**-neh-dee
Dienstag	**deens**-tahk	Martedì	**mahr**-teh-dee
Mittwoch	**mit**-vohk	Mercoledì	**mare**-co-leh-dee
Donnerstag	**doe**-ners-tahk	Giovedì	**jo**-veh-dee
Freitag	**fry**-tahk	Venerdì	**ven**-air-dee
Samstag	**zahm**-stahk	Sabato	**sah**-ba-toe
Sonntag	**zon**-tahk	La Domenica	lah doe-**men**-ee-ca

English	French	French Pronunciation

Useful Phrases

English	French	French Pronunciation
Do you speak English?	Parlez-vous anglais?	par-lay-vooz awng-**gleh**
I don't speak French/German/Italian.	Je ne parle pas français.	juh nuh parl pah fraun-**seh**
I don't understand.	Je ne comprends pas.	juh nuh kohm-prawhn **pah**
I don't know.	Je ne sais pas.	juh nuh say **pah**
I am American/British.	Je suis américain/anglais	jhu sweez a-may-ree-**can**/awn-**glay**
I am sick.	Je suis malade.	juh swee ma-**lahd**
Please call a doctor.	Appelez un docteur s'il vous plâit.	a-pe-lay uhn dohk-**tore** seel voo **play**
Have you any rooms?	Est-ce que vous avez une chambre?	Ehskuh vooz ah-vay-oon **shahm**-br
How much does it cost?	C'est combien?	say comb-bee-**enh**
Do you accept . . . (credit card)	Est-ce que vous acceptez . . .	Ehskuh voo zahksehptay . . .
Too expensive	Trop cher	troh **shehr**
It's beautiful.	C'est très beau.	say tray boh
Help!	Au secours!	o say-**koor**
Stop!	Arrêtez!	a-ruh-**tay**

Getting Around

English	French	French Pronunciation
Where is . . .	C'est où . . .	say oo
The train station?	la gare?	la gahr
The post office?	la poste?	la pohst
The hospital?	l'hôpital?	lo-pee-**tahl**
Where are the rest rooms?	Où sont les toilettes?	oo sohn lay **twah**-let
Left	A gauche	a **gohsh**
Right	À droite	a **drwat**
Straight ahead	Tout droit	**too drwat**

Dining Out

English	French	French Pronunciation
Waiter/Waitress	Monsieur/Mademoiselle	muh-**syuh**/mad-mwa-**zel**
Please give me . . .	S'il vous plait, donnez-moi . . .	see voo **play** doh nay **mwah**

*Prevalent Swiss-German dialect

German	German Pronunciation	Italian	Italian Pronunciation
Sprechen Sie Englisch?	Shprek-hun zee **eng**-glish	Parla inglese?	**par**-la een **glay**-zay
Ich sprech kein Deutsch.	ihkh **shprek**-uh kine doych	Non parlo italiano.	non **par**-lo ee-tal-**yah**-no
Ich verstehe nicht.	ihkh fehr-**stay**-eh nikht	Non capisco.	non ka-**peess**-ko
Ich habe keine Ahnung.	ihkh hah-beh kine-eh **ah**-nung	Non lo so.	non lo **so**
Ich bin Amerikaner(in). Engländer(in).	ihkh bin a-mer-i **kah**-ner(in)/**eng**-glan-der(in)	Sono americano(a)/ Sono inglese.	**so**-no a-may-ree-**kah**-no(a)/**so**-no een-**glay**-zay
Ich bin krank.	ihkh bin **krahnk**	Sto male.	sto **ma**-lay
Bitte rufen einen Arzt.	**bit**-uh **roof**-en ine-en **ahrtst**	Chiami un dottore per favore.	kee-**ah**-mee oon doe-**toe**-ray pear fah-**voh**-reh
Haben sie ein Zimmer?	**Ha**-ben zee ine **tsimmer**	C'e una camera libera?	chay **oo**-nah **cam**-er-ah **lee**-ber-eh
Wieviel kostet das?	**vee**-feel **cost**-et dahs	Quanto costa?	**kwahn**-toe-**coast**-a
Nehmen Sie . . .	**nay**-men zee . . .	Posso pagare . . .	**pohs**-soh pah-**gah**-reh . . .
Es kostet zu viel.	es **cost**-et tsu feel	Troppo caro	**troh**-poh **cah**-roh
Das ist schön.	dahs is **shern**	É bello(a).	eh **bell**-oh
Hilfe!	**hilf**-uh	Aiuto!	a-**yoo**-toe
Halt!	hahlt	Alt!	ahlt
Wo ist . . .	**vo** ist	Dov'è . . .	doe-**veh**
Der Bahnhof?	dare **bahn**-hof	la stazione?	la sta-tsee-**oh**-nay
Die Post?	dee **post**	l'ufficio postale?	loo-**fee**-cho po-**sta**-lay
Das Krankenhaus? *Das Spital?	dahs **krahnk**-en-house dahs shpee-**tahl**	l'ospedale?	lo-spay-**dah**-lay
Wo ist die Toilette?	vo ist dee twah-**let**-uh	Dov'è il bagno?	doe-**vay** eel**bahn**-yo
Links	links	a sinistra	a see-**neess**-tra
Rechts	rechts	a destra	a-**des**-tra
geradeaus	geh-**rod**-uh ouse	Avanti dritto	a-**vahn**-tee **dree**-to
Herr Ober/ Fräulein	hehr **oh**-ber **froy**-line	Cameriere(a)	kah-meh-**ryeh**-reh(rah)
Bitte geben sie mir . . .	**bit**-uh gay behn zee-**meer**	Mi dia pear-fah-**voh**-reh . . .	mee **dee**-a

English	French	French Pronunciation
The menu	La carte	la cart
The bill/check	L'addition	la-dee-see-**ohn**
A fork	Une fourchette	ewn four-**shet**
A knife	Un couteau	uhn koo-**toe**
A spoon	Une cuillère	ewn kwee-**air**
A napkin	Une serviette	ewn sair-vee-**et**
Bread	Du pain	due penh
Butter	Du beurre	due bur
Milk	Du lait	due lay
Pepper	Du poivre	due **pwah**-vruh
Salt	Du sel	due sell
Sugar	Du sucre	due **sook**-ruh
Coffee	Un café	uhn kahfay
Tea	Un thé	uhn tay
Mineral water *carbonated/still*	De l'eau minéral *gazeuse/non gazeuse*	duh loh meenehrahl gahzuhz/noh(n) gahzuhz
Wine	Vin	venh
Cheers!	A votre santé!	ah vo-truh sahn-**tay**

*Prevalent Swiss-German dialect

German	German Pronunciation	Italian	Italian Pronunciation
Die speisekarte	dee **shpie**-zeh-car-tuh	Il menù	eel may-**noo**
Die Rechnung	dee **rekh**-nung	Il conto	eel **cone**-toe
Eine Gabel	**ine**-eh-**gah**-buhl	Una forchetta	oona for-**ket**-a
Ein messer	I-nuh-**mess**-ehr	Un coltello	oon kol-**tel**-o
Einen Löffel	I-nen **ler**-fuhl	Un cucchiaio	oon koo-kee-**ah**-yo
Die Serviette	dee zair-vee-**eh**-tuh	Il tovagliolo	eel toe-va-lee-**oh-lo**
Brot	broht	Il pane	eel **pa**-nay
Butter	**boo**-tehr	Il burro	eel **boo**-roh
Milch	meelch	Il latte	eel **lot**-ay
Pfeffer	**fef**-fehr	Il pepe	eel **pay**-pay
Salz	zahlts	Il sale	eel **sah**-lay
Zucker	**tsoo**-kher	Lo zucchero	loh **tsoo**-ker-o
eine Kaffee	**ine**-eh **kah**-feh	un caffè	oon kahf-**feh**
einen Tee	**ine**-en tay	un tè	oon teh
Mineral wasser *mit gas/ohne gas*	mi-neh-**raal**-**vahs**-sehr mit gahz/**oh**-nuh gahz	L'acqua minerale *gassata/naturale*	l'ah kwa mee-neh-**rah**-leh gahs-**sah**-tah/nah-too-**rah**-leh
Wein	vine	Il vino	eel **vee**-noh
Zum Wohl! *Proscht	zoom vole prosht	Salute!	sah-**loo**-teh

Travel Smart Switzerland

WORD OF MOUTH

"While renting a car to drive the famous Swiss mountain passes is an option, I know you are on a budget and this may not be within it; however Swiss Post Bus run on all these passes, and this would be a quite thrilling and inexpensive way to go up and over one or more of these routes, IMO. The passes are twisting and fun and the way the big buses manage to manoeuvre them is amazing. The scenery above the treeline is like a moonscape!"

—cicerone

GETTING HERE & AROUND

Switzerland offers perhaps the best transit network in Europe: impeccable expressways studded with emergency phones; trams and buses snaking through city streets; steamers crisscrossing blue lakes; and, of course, the famous trains, whose wheels roll to a stop under the station clock just as the second hand sweeps to 12.

Once at the station, a web of transportation options gets you even closer to those spectacular views: cogwheel trains grind up 45-degree slopes, lifts and gondolas sail silently to vantage points, tiny Alpine Metros bore through granite up to green tundra above 8,000 feet.

Traveling by car is the surest way to penetrate the Swiss landscape, but if you invest in a rail pass, you will not feel cut off. Most Swiss trains intersect with private excursion networks and allow for comfortable sightseeing itineraries without huge layovers. And there's always a sturdy yellow postbus, following its appointed rounds at minimal cost; connections to obscure villages and trails are free to holders of the Swiss Pass.

Happily and conveniently, you can get the full scoop on public transportation to many Swiss cities, towns, and villages just by going to the special "Getting Around" section near the front of every regional chapter in this book. In addition, under many towns and cities, you will find a detailed "Getting Here" paragraph, replete with routes and rates.

▌ BY AIR

The entire country of Switzerland is smaller in area than the state of West Virginia, so flying from one region to another is a luxury that, considering how efficient the trains are, few travelers require—unless there's a convenient connection from your intercontinental arrival point (Geneva, Zürich) to a smaller airport (Basel, Bern, Lugano, and Sion).

In Switzerland you will not usually need to check in more than an hour before boarding. If you are catching a connecting flight, make sure you have at least an hour to transfer, especially on Sunday in Zürich, where delays are frequent. To avoid delays at airport-security checkpoints, try not to wear any metal. Jewelry, belt and other buckles, steel-toe shoes, barrettes, and underwire bras are among the items that can set off detectors. Be sure to check your airline's limit on checked and carry-on luggage; Swiss and other airlines often accept one carry-on item.

For 20 SF per bag round-trip, passengers on Swiss and partner airlines with tickets on Swiss Federal Railways can forward their luggage to their final destination, allowing them to travel unencumbered. Baggage check-in and airline boarding passes can be arranged at more than 50 train stations around Switzerland, but must be done 24 hours in advance. An English-language "Fly-Rail Baggage" brochure is available free of charge from the Swiss Federal Railways.

Note that Swiss and many budget airlines such as easyJet charge for food and drink during flights.

Swiss, which does not allow smoking, stocks Nicorette gum.

Flying time to Geneva or Zürich is just under 2 hours from London, 7 hours from New York, 10 hours from Chicago, 14 hours from Los Angeles, and 23 to 25 hours from Sydney.

In Switzerland there is no longer a need to reconfirm your flight, though it won't hurt to do so. Swiss and other airlines now send electronic delay messages to passengers who provide cell phone numbers.

Airline Security Issues Transportation Security Administration (⊕ *www.tsa.gov*) has answers for almost every question that might come up.

AIRPORTS

The major gateways are the Unique Zürich Airport (ZRH) and Geneva's Cointrin Airport (GVA). Most Swiss flights will fly via Zürich Airport, the airline's hub. Be sure to allot yourself at least an hour to transfer to your connecting flight. Delays are especially common on Sunday. The EuroAirport near Basel is used by many airlines as a stopover. Its proximity to Basel and Zürich makes it very convenient.

International Airports Geneva: **Cointrin Airport** (☎ *022/7177111* ⊕ *www.gva.ch*). Zürich: **Unique Zürich Airport** (☎ *043/8162211* ⊕ *www.flughafen-zuerich.ch*). Basel: **EuroAirport Freiburg-Basel-Mulhouse** (*MLH* ☎ *0761/1200–3111 from Switzerland 061/3253111* ⊕ *www.euroairport.com*).

Regional Airports Basel: **EuroAirport** (☎ *061/3253111* ⊕ *www.euroairport.com*). Bern: **Belp** (☎ *031/9602111* ⊕ *www.alpar.ch*). Lugano: **Aeroporto Lugano-Agno** (☎ *091/6101111* ⊕ *www.lugano-airport.ch*). Sion: **Aéroport de Sion** (☎ *027/3290600* ⊕ *www.sionairport.ch*).

Upper Engadine: **Engadine Airport** (✉ *Samedan* ☎ *081/8510851*).

FLIGHTS

Swiss Air Lines, the national carrier more commonly known as Swiss, flies from Boston, Chicago, Los Angeles, Miami, and New York to Zürich, as well as from New York to Geneva. Continental flies from Newark to Geneva and Zürich. Qatar Airways is the third and last company that rallies New York and Geneva. Swiss flies from London to Geneva and Zürich, as does British Airways. From Australia and New Zealand, connections to Switzerland are available via Frankfurt or Bangkok. Air Canada connects major Canadian cities to Basel, Geneva, and Zürich via Frankfurt or Munich.

American and Delta fly from New York, Miami, and Los Angeles to Zürich.

Low-cost airlines flying into Geneva include bmi Baby (from Birmingham and other cities in the United Kingdom), easyJet (from London and other European cities), fly Baboo (from Lugano, Florence, Venice, Prague), flybe (from Southampton), Hapag Lloyd Express (from Cologne-Bonn), and Jet 2 (from Leeds-Bradford). If you're headed to Zürich, Helvetic (from London) and Belair (from Mediterranean islands as well as Dubrovnik and other cities) are among the low-cost carriers.

Airline Contacts Aer Lingus (☎ *0870/8765000 in U.K., 0818/365000 in Ireland, 044/2869933 in Switzerland* ⊕ *www.aerlingus.com*).

Air Canada (☎ *888/247–2262* ⊕ *www.aircanada.com*).

American Airlines (☎ *800/433–7300* ⊕ *www.aa.com*).

British Airways (☎ *0870/850–9850 in U.K., 0848/847847 in Switzerland* ⊕ *www.britishairways.com*).

Continental Airlines (☎ *800/523–3273 for U.S. and Mexico reservations, 800/231–0856 for international reservations, 043/8009214 in Switzerland* ⊕ *www.continental.com*).

Delta Airlines (☎ *800/221–1212 for U.S. reservations, 800/241–4141 for international reservations* ⊕ *www.delta.com*) to Zürich.

Northwest Airlines (☎ *800/225–2525* ⊕ *www.nwa.com*).

Swiss (Swiss International Air Lines) (☎ *877/359–7947, 0848/852000 in Switzerland* ⊕ *www.swiss.com*).

United Airlines (☎ *800/864–8331 for U.S. reservations, 800/538–2929 for international reservations* ⊕ *www.united.com*).

USAirways (☎ *800/428–4322 for U.S. and Canada reservations, 800/622–1015 for international reservations* ⊕ *www.usairways.com*).

Low-Cost Carriers Belair (☎ 043/2118120 in Switzerland ⊕ www.belair-airlines.com). **easyJet** (☎ 0870/600–0000 in U.K. ⊕ www. easyjet.com). **fly Baboo** (☎ 0848/445445 in Switzerland, 0800/4454–4545 in Europe ⊕ www.flybaboo.com). **flybe** (☎ 0871/700–0535 in U.K. ⊕ www.flybe. com). **Helvetic** (☎ 0207/026–3464 in the U.K., 043/5579099 in Switzerland ⊕ www.helvetic.com).

AIR PASSES

EuropebyAir offers passes for travel that connect Basel, Geneva, and Zürich to other European destinations. For one (variable) sum, you can buy up to 20 flight segments, which make each one only $99–125 each, not including fuel surcharge and taxes. Unless you plan to make many trips to major cities outside of Switzerland, this type of pass may not prove a value.

Contact EuropebyAir (☎ 888/321–4737 ⊕ www.europebyair.com).

I BY BOAT

All of Switzerland's larger lakes are criss-crossed by elegant steamers, some of them restored paddle steamers. Their café-restaurants serve drinks, snacks, and hot food at standard mealtimes; toilet facilities are provided. Service continues year-round but is greatly reduced in winter. Unlimited travel is free to holders of the Swiss Pass. The Swiss Card and the Flexipass (⇨ By Train) may also be used for boat travel. For some travel such as night cruises, you may have to pay a fee. The Swiss Card doesn't give you any discount on Lake Maggiore.

Tickets can be purchased at ticket booths near the docks before departure; for some shorter boat rides tickets are also sold at a counter on board before departure. Tourism offices usually have the latest schedules, though it may be better to check with the boat companies. Credit cards are generally accepted, as are Swiss francs and euros.

The Compagnie Générale de Navigation offers excursion boat rides on Lake Geneva for about 20 SF to 68 SF, depending on the distances covered. In the Ticino, the Navigazione Lago di Lugano and Navigazione Lago Maggiore-Bacino Svizzero run frequent daily boat trips. In Zürich, boat rides of 1½ to 7 hours are available in summer. In winter, the number of boat rides dwindles.

Information Compagnie Générale de Navigation (✉ Rhodanie 17, Lausanne ☎ 0848/811848 ⊕ www.cgn.ch). **Navigazione Lago di Lugano** (✉ Casella Postale 65, Lugano ☎ 091/9715223 ⊕ www.lakelugano. ch). **Navigazione Lago Maggiore-Bacino Svizzero** (✉ Lungolago Motta, Locarno ☎ 091/7511865 ⊕ www.navigazionelaghi.it).

I BY BUS

Switzerland's famous yellow postbuses (called *Postautos* or *cars postaux*), with their stentorian tritone horns, link main cities with villages off the beaten track and even crawl over the highest mountain passes. Both postbuses and city buses follow posted schedules to the minute: you can set your watch by them. You can pick up a free schedule for a particular route in most postbuses; full schedules are included in train schedule books. You can also check the Swiss Post Web site. Watch for the yellow sign with the picture of a bus. Postbuses cater to hikers: walking itineraries are available at some postbus stops.

There's also a special scenic postbus route, the *Palm Express*. This route goes from St. Moritz to Lugano via the Maloja Pass. The buses run daily from mid-June through mid-October and from late December through the first week of January. Postbuses run only from Friday to Sunday from the second week of January to the first week of June and from late October to mid-December. Reservations can be made at any train station or tourist office. The Swiss Pass (⇨ By Train) gives unlimited travel on the postbuses. You may have to pay a supplement of 5 SF to 20 SF on some of the Alpine routes; check the timetables or ask the staff.

Be sure to ask whether reservations are required, as is the case for some Alpine pass routes.

Note that information about prices and schedules on the Swiss Post bus system are almost more readily available logging on to the main Swiss train Web site, www. sbb.ch (which covers both national train and bus routes), than to the less comprehensive Swiss Post Web site listed below.

Bus Information Swiss Post
(☎ *0900/800800, 1.19 SF per min* ⊕ *www.postbus.ch*).

▌ BY CAR

CAR RENTALS

If booked from overseas, rates in Zürich and Geneva begin at around $50 a day and $200 a week for an economy car with air-conditioning, a manual transmission, and unlimited mileage. This does not include the 7.6% tax on car rentals. Try to arrange for a rental before you go; rentals booked in Switzerland are considerably more expensive. European companies like Europcar and Sixt often have better deals.

Eurailpass and Europass *(⇨ By Train)* both offer discount passes combining rail travel and car rental.

Your own driver's license is acceptable in Switzerland, but an International Driving Permit (IDP)—available from the American and Canadian automobile associations and, in the United Kingdom, from the Automobile Association and Royal Automobile Club—is a good idea in case of emergency. In certain European countries you may not be able to rent a car without an International Driving Permit, which can be used only in conjunction with a valid driver's license and which translates your license into 10 languages.

Check the AAA web site for more info as well as for IDPs ($10) themselves. The minimum age is generally 20, and you must have possessed a valid driver's license for at least one year. Note that some agencies do not allow you to drive cars into Italy. In Switzerland some rental agencies charge daily fees of about 25 SF for drivers under 25. If you wish to pay cash, agencies may request a deposit.

CAR RENTAL RESOURCES

Local Agencies Europcar (☎ *0848/808099* ⊕ *www.europcar.ch*). **Sixt** (☎ *0848/884444* ⊕ *www.sixt.ch*).

Major Agencies Alamo (☎ *800/522-9696* ⊕ *www.alamo.com*).

Avis (☎ *800/331-1084* ⊕ *www.avis.com*).

Budget (☎ *800/472-3325* ⊕ *www. budget.com*).

Hertz (☎ *800/654-3001* ⊕ *www.hertz.com*).

National Car Rental (☎ *800/227-7368* ⊕ *www.nationalcar.com*).

Wholesalers Auto Europe (☎ *888/223-5555* ⊕ *www.autoeurope.com*).

Europe by Car (☎ *212/581-3040 in New York, 800/223-1516* ⊕ *www.europebycar.com*).

Eurovacations (☎ *877/471-3876* ⊕ *www. eurovacations.com*).

Kemwel (☎ *877/820-0668* ⊕ *www. kemwel.com*).

GASOLINE

If there's one thing that's generally cheaper in Switzerland than elsewhere in Western Europe, it's gasoline. If you are crossing borders, try to fill the tank in Switzerland unless you happen to be driving a diesel, which is cheaper in Austria, France, and Germany, but not Italy. Regular unleaded (*bleifrei* in German, *sans plomb* in French) gas costs just over 1.85 SF per liter. Leaded fuel is no longer available. Prices are slightly higher in mountain areas. Have some 10 SF and 20 SF notes available, as many gas stations (especially in the mountains) have vending-machine pumps that operate even when they're closed. Simply slide in a bill and fill your tank. Many of these machines also accept major credit cards with precoded PIN numbers. You can request a receipt (*Quittung* in German, *quittance* in French) from the machine.

PARKING

Parking areas are clearly marked. In blue or red zones a *disque* (provided in rental cars or available free from banks, tourist offices, or police stations) must be placed clearly in the front window noting the time of arrival. These zones are slowly being replaced by metered-parking white zones. Each city sets its own time allotments for parking; the limits are posted. Metered parking is often paid for at communal machines that vary from city to city. Some machines simply accept coins and dispense tickets. At others you'll need to punch in your parking space or license plate number, then add coins. The ticket for parking may or may not have to be placed in your car window; this information is noted on the machine or ticket. Parking in public lots normally costs 2 SF for the first hour, increasing by 1 SF every half hour thereafter.

ROAD CONDITIONS

Swiss roads are well surfaced, but when you are dealing with mountains they do wind a lot, so don't plan on achieving high average speeds. When estimating likely travel times, look carefully at the map: there may be only 32 km (20 mi) between one point and another—but there may be an Alpine pass in the way. There is a well-developed expressway network, though some notable gaps still exist in the south along an east–west line, roughly between Lugano and Sion. In addition, tunnels—notably the St. Gotthard—are at times closed for either repairs or weather conditions, or they become bottlenecks in times of heavy traffic. Road signs throughout the country use a color-coding system, with the official route numbers in white against a colored background. Expressway

signs are green, and highway signs are blue (unlike in the rest of Europe, where expressway signs are blue and highway signs are green). Signs for smaller roads are white with black lettering. All signage indicates the names of upcoming towns as well, and it is generally easiest to use these names for navigating. A combination of steep or winding routes and hazardous weather means some roads will be closed in winter. Signs are posted at the beginning of the climb.

To find out about road conditions, traffic jams, itineraries, and so forth, you can turn to two places: the Swiss Automobile Club has operators standing by on weekdays from 8 to 5 to provide information in all languages. Dues-paying members of the Touring Club of Switzerland may contact the organization for similar information. Note that neither of these numbers gets you breakdown service. For frequent and precise information in Swiss languages, you can dial 163, or tune in to local radio stations.

Automobile Associations Swiss Automobile Club (☎ *031/3283111*). **Touring Club of Switzerland** (☎ *022/4172424*). U.S.: **American Automobile Association** (*AAA* ☎ *315/797–5000* ⊕ *www.aaa.com*); most contact with the organization is through state and regional members.

ROADSIDE EMERGENCIES

All road breakdowns should be called in to the central Switzerland-wide emergency number, 117 or 140. If you are on an expressway, pull over to the shoulder and look for arrows pointing you to the nearest orange radio-telephone, called Bornes SOS; use these phones instead of a mobile phone because they allow police to find you instantly and send help. There are SOS phones every kilometer (½ mi), on alternate sides of the expressway.

Emergency Services Police (☎ *117*).

Touring Club Suisse (Swiss equivalent of AAA) (☎ *140*).

RULES OF THE ROAD

As in most of the rest of Europe, driving is on the right. Vehicles on main roads have priority over those on smaller roads. At intersections, priority is given to the driver on the right except when merging into traffic circles, when priority is given to the drivers coming from the left. In residential areas in some places—notably Geneva—traffic coming from the right has the right of way. In urban areas the speed limit is 50 kph (30 mph); on main highways, it's 80 kph (50 mph); on semi-expressways, the limit is 100 kph (60 mph), and on expressways, the limit is 120 kph (75 mph). On expressways the left lane is only for passing other cars; you must merge right as soon as possible. It is illegal to make a right-hand turn on a red light. The blood-alcohol limit is 0.05.

▌ BY TRAIN

The Swiss Federal Railways, or SBB/ CFF/FFS, boasts one of the world's densest transportation networks; trains and stations are clean and, as you'd expect, service is extremely prompt. The cleanliness extends to restrooms—in some countries these are grim affairs, but in Switzerland's large city stations look for "McClean" restrooms. They have nothing to do with the red-and-yellow hamburger chain; instead, they're immaculate, sleekly designed spaces, with bathrooms, changing stations, showers, and a toiletries kiosk. Entrance is about 1 SF or 2 SF (showers 12 SF) depending on the extent of your use.

Trains described as Inter-City or Express are the fastest, stopping only in principal towns. *Regionalzug/Train Régional* means a local train. If you're planning to use the trains extensively, get the official timetable ("Kursbuch" or "Horaire") for 16 SF. The Swiss Federal Railways also has an excellent Web site allowing you to work out itineraries online, including suburban trains and buses.

REMEMBER

In spite of its laid-back image, Switzerland suffers the bug of aggressive driving as well. Tailgating, though illegal, is a common problem, as is speeding. If you are being tailgated on the expressway, just move into the right lane and ignore any high-beam flashing and visible signs of road rage behind you. If you are driving extra slowly, let the people behind you pass you.

Children under age seven are not permitted to sit in the front seat. Use headlights in heavy rain, in poor visibility, or in tunnels—they are compulsory. Always carry your valid license and car-registration papers; there are occasional roadblocks to check them. Wear seat belts in the front- and backseats—they are mandatory.

To use the semi-expressways and expressways, you must display a sticker, or *vignette*, on the top-center or lower corner of the windshield. You can buy one at the border or in post offices, gas stations, and garages. A vignette costs 40 SF or € 27. Driving without a vignette puts you at risk for getting a 100 SF fine. Cars rented within Switzerland already have these stickers; if you rent a car elsewhere in Europe, ask if the rental company will provide the vignette for you.

Traffic going up a mountain has priority except for postbuses coming down. A sign with a yellow post horn on a blue background means that postbuses have priority. On winding mountain roads, a brief honk as you approach a curve is a good way of warning any oncoming traffic. In winter be sure your car has snow tires and snow chains. The latter are mandatory in some areas and advisable in most. Snow-chain service stations have signs marked SERVICE DE CHAÎNES À NEIGE or SCHNEEKETTENDIENST; snow chains are available for rent.

In addition to the federal rail lines there are some private rail lines, such as the Montreux-Oberland-Bernois line and the Rhätische Bahn. Most private lines generally accept discount rail passé sor accord a reduction on the price.

If your itinerary requires changing trains, bear in mind that the average connection time is six to ten minutes.

TRAIN TIPS

If you happen to suffer from motion sickness, note that the Swiss ICN trains—and the German ICE, the French TGV, and the Italian Cisalpino—all use "tilt technology" for a less jerky ride. One side-effect, however, is that some passengers might get literally seasick, especially if the track is curvy (as between Biel/Bienne and Geneva). An over-the-counter drug for motion sickness should help. Also close the shades and avoid looking out the window.

Consider a first-class ticket only if the extra comfort is worth the price. The principal difference between first and second class is more space, as the first-class cars are less crowded. Seat size is the same, upholstery fancier, and you usually will be delivered to the track position closest to the station.

RAIL PASSES

You can rely on the Swiss rail service to provide clean, timely service in both first and second class. If you are eager to read or get some work done on the train, try the Quiet Area compartments available in first and second class on a number of routes in Switzerland. Travelers are asked not to use cell phones, listen to music, or engage in loud conversation. The upper decks of some first-class cars also offer business compartments or seats; they are designated with the laptop icon and are equipped with power outlets.

If Switzerland is your only destination in Europe, there are numerous passes available for visitors. The Swiss Pass is the best value, offering unlimited travel on Swiss Federal Railways, postbuses, Swiss lake steamers, and the local bus and tram services of 38 cities. It also gives reductions on many privately owned railways, cable cars, and funiculars. And it gives you access to about 450 museums in the country.

Available from Switzerland Tourism and from travel agents outside Switzerland including Rail Europe and Europe On Rail, the card is valid for four days (260 SF second class; 390 SF first class); eight days (376 SF second class; 564 SF first class); 15 days (455 SF second class; 683 SF first class), 22 days (525 SF second class; 788 SF first class); or one month (578 SF second class; 867 SF first class). There's also the **Flexipass** offering the same for three to six days in a 30-day period at the user's convenience (249 SF–397 SF second class; 374 SF–596 SF first class). There's an approximately 15% discount on the Swiss Pass and the Flexipass for two or more people. The **STS Family Card** is issued at no cost to nonresidents of Switzerland and Liechtenstein, upon request. Children up to 16 accompanied by a parent travel for free.

Within some popular tourist areas **Regional Holiday Season Tickets** are available. Their discount offers vary; prices vary widely, too, depending on the region and period of validity. Passes are available from Switzerland Tourism and local tourist boards, as well as the train stations, but to be on the safe side inquire well in advance.

The **Swiss Card**, which can be purchased in the United States through Rail Europe, Europe On Rail, and at train stations at the Zürich and Geneva airports and in Basel, is valid for 30 days and grants full round-trip travel from your arrival point to any destination in the country, plus a half-price reduction on any further excursions during your stay (182 SF second class; 285 SF first class). For more information about train travel in Switzerland, get the free "Swiss Travel System" or

"Discover Switzerland" brochures from Switzerland Tourism.

Switzerland is one of 17 countries in which you can use Eurailpasses, which provide unlimited first-class rail travel, in all of the participating countries, for the duration of the pass. If you plan to rack up the miles, get a standard pass. These are available for 15 days (€ 580), 21 days (€ 754), one month (€ 936), two months (€ 1328), and three months (€ 1,634). If your plans call for only limited train travel, look into a Eurail Selectpass, which costs less money than a Eurailpass. Unlike with Eurailpasses, however, you get a limited number of travel days, in a limited number of countries, during a specified time period. For example, a two-month pass allows between 5 and 15 days of rail travel; costs range between € 368 and € 816. Keep in mind that the basic Eurail Selectpass is good only in France, Germany, Italy, Spain, and Switzerland, though you have the option of adding two "associate countries" (Austria, Hungary, the Netherlands, Belgium, Luxembourg, Greece, or Portugal). There are numerous other options available, however, especially if you have planned your itinerary carefully—these depend on how many countries you care to visit, and so on. In addition to standard Eurailpasses, ask about special rail-pass plans. Among these are the Eurail Youthpass (for those under age 26), the Eurail and Europass Saverpasses (which give a discount for two or more people traveling together), the Euraildrive Pass and the Europass Drive (which combine travel by train and rental car).

Many travelers assume that rail passes guarantee them seats on the trains they wish to ride. Not so. You need to book seats ahead even if you are using a rail pass; seat reservations are required on some European trains, particularly high-speed trains, and are a good idea on trains that may be crowded—particularly in summer on popular routes. You will also need a reservation if you purchase sleeping accommodations. Whichever pass you choose, remember that you must purchase your pass before you leave for Europe. The Swiss Federal Railways has a user-friendly site that lets you check fares and schedules. You can also call its hotline, which has information in English. Most rail stations let you purchase tickets from machines that accept cash and major credit cards.

Make seat reservations for trips during rush hours and in high season, especially on international trains.

CHANNEL TUNNEL
With the Channel Tunnel completing a seamless route, you can leave London around noon on the Eurostar and (thanks to connections via Paris–Lyon on the French *train à grande vitesse*) have a late supper in Geneva. Note that the TGV tracks connecting Geneva and Paris are a bit bumpy, which can be unsettling for sensitive passengers. Also note that the *Venice–Simplon–Orient Express* stops in Luzern between London and Venice–information is available from the tour company Abercrombie & Kent.

Train Contacts **Europe On Rail** (☎877/667-2457 ⊕www.europeonrail.com). **Jungfraubahnen** (☎033 828 71 11 ⊕www.jungfraubahn.ch).

Matterhorn Gotthard Bahn (☎0900/300300 1.19 SF per min ⊕www.mg-bahn.ch).

Montreux Oberland Bernois (☎021/9898181 ⊕www.mob.ch).

Rail Europe (☎914/682-5172 or 800/438-7245 Ontario ☎800/361-7245 ⊕www.raileurope.com). **Rhätische Bahn** (☎081 288 43 40 ⊕www.rhb.ch).

Swiss Federal Railways (☎0900/300300 1.19 SF per min ⊕www.rail.ch).

SCENIC ROUTES
Switzerland makes the most of its Alpine rail engineering, which cuts through the icy granite landscape above 6,560 feet,

by offering special trains that cross over spectacular passes with panoramic cars. The *Glacier Express,* for example, connects the two glamorous resorts of Zermatt and St. Moritz, crawling over the Oberalp Pass and serving lunch in a burnished-wood period dining car; the *Wilhelm Tell Express* combines a rail crossing of the Saint Gotthard Pass with a cruise down the length of Lake Luzern. The *Golden Pass/Panoramic Express* climbs from the balmy waterfront of Montreux into the Alpine terrain through Gstaad to Interlaken and rolls on to Luzern via the Brünig Pass. (Note this involves several train changes.) The *Bernina Express* ascends from Chur to St. Moritz, then climbs over the magnificent Bernina Pass into Italy, where visitors can connect by postbus to Lugano. Throughout Graubünden, the famous "Panorama" rail cars of the Rhätibahn thread through glorious peaks and valleys—see Chapter 4 for details. Most of the sightseeing itineraries listed above take 4–11 hours' travel time. For information on these and other scenic routes, contact Swiss Federal Railways or Railtour Suisse, Switzerland's largest train-tour company.

Scenic Tour Information **Railtour Suisse** (✉ *Chutzenstr. 24, Bern* ☎ *031/3780101* ⎙ *031/3780222* ⊕ *www.railtour.ch*). **Swiss Federal Railways** (☎ *0900/300300 1.19 SF per min* ⊕ *www.rail.ch*).

ESSENTIALS

■ ACCOMMODATIONS

Switzerland is as famous for its hotels as it is for its mountains, watches, and chocolates; its standards in hospitality are extremely high. Rooms are impeccably clean and well maintained, and they are furnished with comforts ranging from the simplest to the most deluxe. Prices are accordingly high: you will pay more for minimal comforts here than in any other European country. Americans accustomed to spacious motels with two double beds, a color TV, and a bath-shower combination may be disappointed in their first venture into the legendary Swiss hotel: spaces are small, bathtubs cost extra, and single rooms may have single beds. What you're paying for is service, reliability, cleanliness, and a complex hierarchy of amenities you may not even know you need.

Where no address is provided in the hotel listings, none is necessary: in smaller towns and villages, a postal code is all you need. To find the hotel on arrival, watch for the official street signs pointing the way to every hotel that belongs to the local tourist association.

Some things to bear in mind when you check in: the standard double room in Switzerland has two prim beds built together, with separate linens and, sometimes, sheets tucked firmly down the middle. If you prefer more sociable arrangements, ask for a "French bed," or *lit matrimonial*—that will get you a double mattress. Some hotels may offer extra beds—for example, to expand a double room to a triple. Also note that air-conditioning is not as prevalent as in the United States; evenings are generally cool, so Alpine air often stands in for air-conditioning. Unfortunately, global warming has had a real impact in Europe and you may discover that even early October can prove hot and sticky in Switzerland; if this poses a major problem for you, spend the extra money to book at a hotel that offers air-conditioning (and, ipso facto, also be sure it will be functioning during the time you are at the hotel).

Most hotels in Switzerland allow children under a certain age to stay in their parents' room at no extra charge, but others charge for them as extra adults; be sure to find out the cutoff age for children's discounts. The Swiss Hotel Association (⇨ *Hotels, below*) has listings of family-friendly hotels throughout the country. Supervised playrooms are available in some of the better hotels, and many winter resorts provide lists of reliable babysitters. For recommended local sitters, check with your hotel.

Particularly in ski resorts or in hotels where you'll be staying for three days or more, you may be quoted a room price per person including *demi pension* (half board). This means you've opted for breakfast included and to eat either lunch or dinner in the hotel, selecting from a limited, fixed menu. Unless you're holding out for gastronomic adventure, your best bet is to take half board. Most hotels will be flexible if you come in from the slopes craving a steaming pot of fondue, and they will then subtract the day's pension supplement from your room price, charging you à la carte instead.

Price charts are based on the cost of a standard double room during high season, including tax, service, and breakfast only. Note that a hotel's prices may vary widely during the rest of the year and that the half board available at many hotels, for only slightly more than our listed room cost, significantly increases the value of these hotel stays. When comparing lodging options, check the hotels' low season rates and meal plans.

■TIP→Assume that hotels operate on the European Plan (EP, no meals) unless we specify that they use the Breakfast Plan (BP,

LOCAL DO'S & TABOOS

GREETINGS

In Switzerland it's polite to say hello and good-bye (*bonjour, au revoir; grüezi, auf Wiedersehen; buongiorno, arrivederci*) to everyone you speak to, from police officers to cashiers. The standard gesture for each is a simple handshake. In the French- and Italian-speaking cantons it is standard for friends to greet each other with three kisses on the cheek. In the German-speaking areas kissing is much less common, as is hugging.

LANGUAGE

One of the best ways to avoid being an Ugly American is to learn a little of the local language. You need not strive for fluency; even just mastering a few basic words and terms is bound to make chatting with the locals more rewarding.

Nearly 70% of the population of Switzerland speaks one dialect or another of German; Swiss German can be a far cry from High German, although standard German is generally understood. French is spoken in the southwest, around Lake Geneva, and in the cantons of Fribourg, Neuchâtel, Jura, Vaud, in parts of Bern, and in most of Valais. Italian is spoken in Ticino and parts of Graubünden. In the Upper and Lower Engadines, in the canton of Graubünden, the last gasp of a Romance language called Romansh is still in daily use. In the areas most frequented by English-speaking tourists—Zermatt, the Berner Oberland, the Engadine, Luzern—people in the tourist industry usually speak English. See the vocabulary section in this book for helpful words and phrases.

Fodor's French for Travelers, Fodor's German for Travelers, and Fodor's Italian for Travelers (available at bookstores everywhere) are excellent.

with full breakfast), Continental Plan (**CP**, continental breakfast), Full American Plan (**FAP**, all meals), or Modified American Plan (**MAP**, breakfast and dinner), or are **all-inclusive** (**AI**, all meals and most activities).

BED & BREAKFASTS

You can order brochures and get information about B&Bs from the user-friendly site of Bed & Breakfast Switzerland, ⊕*www.bnb.ch*. You can make reservations online through the site.

FARM STAYS

An unusual option for families seeking the local experience: stay on a farm with a Swiss family, complete with children, animals, and the option to work in the fields. Participating farm families register with the Schweizerischer Bauernverband (Swiss Farmers Association), listing the birth dates of their children, rooms and facilities, and types of animals your children can see. Prices are often considerably lower than those of hotels and vacation flats. You should be reasonably fluent in French or German, depending on the region of your stay. More information is available through Switzerland Tourism.

Contacts Schweizerischer Bauernverband (*Swiss Farmers Association* ✉ *Laurstr. 10, Brugg* ☎ *056/4625111* 🖷 *056/4415348* ⊕ *www.sbv-usp.ch*). Verein Ferien auf dem Bauernhof (*Swiss Holiday Farms Association* ✉ *Feierlenhof, Altnau* ☎ *071/6952372* 🖷 *071/6952367* ⊕ *www.bauernhof-ferien.ch*).

HOTELS

When selecting a place to stay, an important resource can be the Swiss Hotel Association (SHA), a rigorous and demanding organization that maintains a specific rating system for lodging standards. Four out of five Swiss hotels belong to this group and take their stars seriously. In contrast to more casual European countries, stars in Switzerland have precise meaning: a five-star hotel is required to have a specific staff–guest ratio, a daily change of bed linens, and extended hours for room service. In contrast, a two-star hotel must have telephones in the rooms, soap in the bathrooms, and fabric tablecloths in the restaurant. But the SHA standards cannot control the quality of the decor and the grace of service. Thus you may find a five-star hotel that meets the technical requirements but has shabby appointments, leaky plumbing, or a rude concierge, or a good, family-run two-star pension that makes you feel like royalty.

Some rules of thumb: if you are looking for American-style chain-motel comfort—a big bed, color TV, minibar, safe—you will probably be happiest in four-star business-class hotels. A number of four-star hotels in Switzerland are part of the Best Western chain. If you are looking for regional atmosphere, family ownership (and the pride and care for details that implies), and moderate prices but don't care about a TV or minibar, look for three stars: nearly all such rooms have showers and toilets. Two stars will get you tidy, minimal comfort, with about a third of the rooms having private toilet and bathing facilities. One-star properties are rare: they have only shared facilities and no phone available in-house and generally fall below the demanding Swiss national standard. Several hotels in the SHA are specially rated *Landgasthof* or *relais de campagne,* meaning "country inn." These generally are rustic-style lodgings typical of the region, but they may range from spare to luxurious and are rarely set apart in deep country; some are in the midst of small market towns or resorts. The SHA distinguishes them as offering especially high-quality service, personal attention, and parking.

Many hotels close for a short period during their region's off-season. Closing dates often vary from year to year, so be sure to call ahead and check.

A few useful phrases in French, German, and Italian: a room with a bath (*une chambre avec salle de bain, ein Zimmer mit Bad, una camera con bagno*); a room with a view (*une chambre avec vue, ein Zimmer mit Aussicht, una camera con vista*); a quiet room (*une chambre calme, ein ruhiges Zimmer, una camera tranquilla*).

Contacts Swiss Hotel Association (✉ *Monbijoustr. 130, Bern* ☎ *031/3704111* ⊕ *www.swisshotels.ch*).

INNS

Travelers on a budget can find help from the *Check-in E & G Hotels* guide (E & G stands for *einfach und gemütlich*: roughly, "simple and cozy"), available through Switzerland Tourism. These comfortable little hotels have banded together to dispel Switzerland's intimidating image as an elite, overpriced vacation spot and offer simple two-star standards in usually very atmospheric inns.

Other organizations can help you find unusual properties: the Relais & Châteaux group seeks out manor houses, historic buildings, and generally atmospheric luxury, with most of its properties falling into the $$$ or $$$$ range. A similar group, Romantik Hotels and Restaurants, combines architectural interest, historic atmosphere, and fine regional food. Relais du Silence hotels are usually isolated in a peaceful, natural setting, with first-class comforts.

Contacts Relais & Châteaux (✉ *15 rue Galvani, Paris, France* ☎ *33/1/45–72–90–00* ⊕ *www.relaischateaux.ch*). **Relais du Silence** (✉ *17 rue d'Ouessant, Paris, France* ☎ *+33/1/44–49–79–00* ⊕ *www.silencehotel.com*). **Romantik Hotels and Restaurants** (☎ *49/69/661–2340* ⊕ *www.romantikhotels.com*).

▮ COMMUNICATIONS

INTERNET

Many hotels now have in-room wireless Internet; ask about rates before you plug in (just make sure your computer is Wi-Fi-enabled—if you are using your own computer, you will need an adapter plug and should use a surge protector). You will also find Internet terminals in airports and train stations in many cities and towns. Many hotels and public places have now been turned into Wi-Fi (in Europe: WLAN) "hot spots." Usually you must pay a fee to log on, though some hotels will provide the service for free. Cost is 5 SF for a half-hour, or 19 SF for two hours. Unused portions of your time will not be stored for you. Some cities provide Wi-Fi service for free.

Contacts Cybercafes (⊕*www.cybercafes. com*) lists more than 4,000 Internet cafés worldwide.

PHONES
The good news is that you can now make a direct-dial telephone call from virtually any point on earth. The bad news? You can't always do so cheaply. Calling from a hotel is almost always the most expensive option; hotels usually add huge surcharges to all calls, particularly international ones. In some countries you can phone from call centers or even the post office. Calling cards usually keep costs to a minimum, but only if you purchase them locally. And then there are mobile phones *(⇨below)*, which are sometimes more prevalent—particularly in the developing world—than land lines; as expensive as mobile phone calls can be, they are still usually a much cheaper option than calling from your hotel.

The country code for Switzerland is 41. When dialing a Swiss number from abroad, drop the initial 0 from the local area code. The country code is 1 for the United States and Canada, 61 for Australia, 64 for New Zealand, and 44 for the United Kingdom.

CALLING WITHIN SWITZERLAND
Dial 1811 or 1818 for information within Switzerland (1.60 SF for the initial connection, 0.25 to 0.70 SF the first minute and around 0.20 SF thereafter) 24 hours a day. All telephone operators speak English, and instructions are printed in English in all telephone booths.

WORD OF MOUTH

Did the resort look as good in real life as it did in the photos? Did you sleep like a baby, or were the walls paper thin? Did you get your money's worth? Rate hotels and write your own reviews in Travel Ratings or start a discussion about your favorite places in Travel Talk on www.fodors.com. Your comments might even appear in our books. Yes, you, too, can be a correspondent!

Dial the local area code (including the 0) when calling any local number.

There's direct dialing to everywhere in Switzerland. For local area codes, consult the pink pages, and for international country and city codes, consult the green-banded pages at the front of the telephone book. Include the area code preceded by 0 when dialing anywhere within Switzerland.

To make a local call on a pay phone, pick up the receiver, insert a phone card, and dial the number. A local call costs 0.50 SF plus 0.10 SF for each additional unit. Toll-free numbers begin with 0800. Swisscom phone cards are available in 5 SF, 10 SF, or 20 SF units; they're sold at post offices, train stations, airports, and kiosks. Slip a card into an adapted public phone, and a continual readout will tell you how much money is left on the card. The cost of the call will be counted against the card, with any remaining value still good for the next time you use it. If you drain the card and still need to talk, the readout will warn you: you can either pop in a new card or make up the difference with coins, although very few phones still accept coins. Many phone booths now also accept Visa, MasterCard, and American Express cards, but be sure to have a four-digit PIN code.

CALLING OUTSIDE SWITZERLAND
The country code for the United States is 1.

Language Regions
of Switzerland

GERMANY

FRANCE

Basel

Zürich

AUSTRIA

GERMAN

LIECHTEN-
STEIN

Bern

Fribourg

FRENCH

ROMANSH

St. Moritz

ITALIAN

Bellinzona

Geneva

Sierre

ITALY

0   60 miles

0   90 km

You can dial most international numbers direct from Switzerland, adding 00 before the country code. If you want a number that cannot be reached directly, or if you need an international phone number, dial 1811 or 1818 for a connection. It's cheapest to use the booths in train stations and post offices: calls made from your hotel cost a great deal more. For precise information on the cost of any call, dial 0800/868788. Current rates for calls to the United States, United Kingdom, and Canada are 0.12 SF per minute weekdays and 0.10 SF per minute on weekends and Swiss holidays. Calls to Australia and New Zealand cost 0.25 SF a minute weekdays and 0.20 SF per minute on weekends and Swiss holidays.

Access Codes AT&T Direct (☎ *0800/890011*). **MCI WorldPhone** (☎ *800/444-4141*). **Sprint**

International Access (☎ *800/877-4646 for other areas*).

CALLING CARDS
A variety of international phone cards in denominations of 10 to 50 SF are available in newspaper shops. They often offer the cheapest rates. You can use the code on the card until you run out of units.

MOBILE PHONES
If you have a multiband phone (some countries use different frequencies than what are used in the United States) and your service provider uses the world-standard GSM network (as do T-Mobile, Cingular, and Verizon), you can probably use your phone abroad. Roaming fees can be steep, however: 99¢ a minute is considered reasonable. And overseas you normally pay the toll charges for incoming calls. It's almost always cheaper to send a text message than to make a call,

since text messages have a very low set fee (often less than 5¢).

If you just want to make local calls, consider buying a new SIM card (note that your provider may have to unlock your phone for you to use a different SIM card) and a prepaid service plan in the destination. You'll then have a local number and can make local calls at local rates. If your trip is extensive, you could also simply buy a new cell phone in your destination, as the initial cost will be offset over time.

■TIP→ If you travel internationally frequently, save one of your old mobile phones or buy a cheap one on the Internet; ask your cell phone company to unlock it for you, and take it with you as a travel phone, buying a new SIM card with pay-as-you-go service in each destination.

Cellular phones (*natels*) may be rented at either the Geneva or Zürich airport from Rent@phone. You can arrange for a rental on a daily, weekly, or monthly basis. The Rent@phone desks are clearly indicated in each airport.

Contacts Cellular Abroad (☎ 800/287–5072 ⊕ www.cellularabroad.com) rents and sells GMS phones and sells SIM cards that work in many countries.

Mobal (☎ 888/888–9162 ⊕ www.mobalrental. com) rents mobiles and sells GSM phones (starting at $49) that will operate in 140 countries. Per-call rates vary throughout the world.

Planet Fone (☎ 888/988–4777 ⊕ www. planetfone.com) rents cell phones, but the per-minute rates are expensive.

Rent@phone (☎ 022/7178263 in Geneva, 043/8165063 in Zürich ⊕ www.rentaphone.ch).

■ CUSTOMS & DUTIES

Entering Switzerland, a visitor who is 17 years or older and is arriving from Europe may bring in 200 cigarettes or 50 cigars or 250 grams of tobacco; 2 liters of alcohol up to 15 proof and 1 liter over 15 proof.

Visitors over 17 may bring gifts valued at up to 300 SF duty-free. Medicine, such as insulin, is allowed for personal use only.

Information in Switzerland Federal Customs Administration (⊕ www.ezv.admin.ch/index.html).

U.S. Information U.S. Customs and Border Protection (⊕ www.cbp.gov).

■ EATING OUT

The restaurants we list are the cream of the crop in each price category. Price charts appear in the dining subsection of the Planner section, which is found near the beginning of each regional chapter. In chapters devoted to a single city, price charts appear in the introductions to the dining section. Please note that the price charts reflect the cost of only the main dish at dinner, and that two- and three-course menus are offered in many restaurants, representing a better value than the à la carte price charts would indicate.

MEALS

Breakfast in Switzerland tends to be little more than coffee with bread, butter, and marmalade. If you prefer a lot of milk in your coffee, ask for a *renversé* in French (literally, *upside-down*) or a *Milchkaffee* in German. Increasingly popular in German-speaking Switzerland is the *latte macchiato,* steamed milk with espresso but very little foam, or cappuccino, lots of steamed and foamy milk with espresso. The signature Bircher muesli—invented by Dr. Maximilian Oskar Bircher-Benner at his diet clinic at the end of the 19th century—is available in most supermarkets (such as Migros and Coop) and can make a hearty lunch, especially when served with plain or fruit yogurt instead of milk.

Many restaurants close after lunch (as of 3 PM) and reopen for dinner (about 6 PM). In remote regions it may prove difficult to find kitchens open past 9 or 10 PM, so plan ahead. Many restaurants are closed on Sunday and many close for the month of August or even longer. Bars often close at 1 or 2 AM, although clubs continue serving into the wee hours.

For lunch or dinner, most regions offer cheese specialties. Remember when eating these tasty dishes, that you tend to be full before your brain registers the fact, and the fatty cheeses can result in difficult digestion. Fondue (literally, "melted" in French) originated in the western part of Switzerland and comes in regional varieties, of which the fondue moitié-moitié is the most famous (combining equal portions of Gruyère and Vacherin). Bits of white bread are skewered on long, thin forks and twirled in the melted cheese. Anyone losing his or her piece of bread has to perform some small activity as "penance," like singing a song, or paying for the next round. The grilled cheese remaining in the *caquelon* is known as the *religieuse* ("the nun") and is a favorite. The other big cheese specialty is *raclette* from the canton of Valais. Traditionally, the cut surface of half a cheese wheel is exposed to a fire and the melted cheese is consistently scraped off (*racler* means "to scrape") and eaten with baked potatoes, pickled white onions, and other condiments. Another cheesy dish is a *Malakoff*, a chunk of Gruyère that is pressed onto a piece of toast and then deep-fried. You may order only one Malakoff at a time (which may be a blessing in disguise to those who tend to bite off more than they can chew).

A crisp wine as you dine or a shot of kirsch after a meal can help soothe your overtaxed stomach. Some fondue experts recommend washing these heavy cheese dishes down with hot black tea and not drinking too much while eating.

There are other fondues that are not so "cheesy." *Fondue bourguignonne* involves dipping bits of meat (veal, beef, chicken, or even horse) in hot oil. The lighter "Chinese" variation (*fondue chinoise*) features meat, fish, and vegetables in bouillon. The boiled or fried tidbits are dipped in condiments. There is even a sweet fondue version, with fruits dipped in hot chocolate sauce.

On a lighter touch, the French-speaking cantons pride themselves on *filets de perche* (fried perch fillets), possibly the most popular dish in the region. A few variations on the theme exist—some with herbs or cognac sauce—but the traditional version is served with lemon and french fries on the side. German-speaking Switzerland made its mark in culinary history with the ubiquitous *Rösti,* a grated potato pancake—often spruced up with herbs, bacon, or cheese—that is served with nearly any meat. Competing with Rösti for most popular side dish, *Spätzli* (egg-flour dumplings) continue to be fashioned according to age-old local traditions (though toss-in-boiling-water-and-serve packets have a strong following). The Ticino, to the south, has preserved its penchant for Italian cuisine with a simple touch that reflects the erstwhile poverty of the region: risotto, gnocchi, polenta, and pasta dishes appear on most menus. Graubünden has its own set of specialties, also harking back to its regional history as a canton cut off from the world during the winter months. For descriptions of *capons, maluns,* and *pizzocheri,* see the chapter on the region.

Besides these staples, you are likely to encounter a variety of stews, organ meats, and sausages. Classics such as *truite meunière* (trout rolled in flour, fried in butter, and served with lemon and parsley) are also standard fare.

Children's menus are available in many restaurants around Switzerland; otherwise, you can usually request a child-size portion and the prices will be adjusted accordingly.

Unless otherwise noted, the restaurants listed in this guide are open daily for lunch and dinner.

PAYING

Credit cards are widely accepted, and euros often accepted, especially in areas that border on the European Union. Note that service is included unless indicated on the menu. It is customary to leave a small tip in cash (up to 10% depending on how pleased you are with the service).

For guidelines on tipping see Tipping below.

RESERVATIONS & DRESS

Regardless of where you are, it's a good idea to make a reservation if you can. We only mention them specifically when reservations are essential (there's no other way you'll ever get a table) or when they are not accepted. For famed restaurants, book as far ahead as you can (often 30 days), and reconfirm as soon as you arrive. (Large parties should always call ahead to check the reservations policy.) We mention dress only when men are required to wear a jacket or a jacket and tie.

WINES, BEER & SPIRITS

Quality and diversity are the hallmarks of Swiss wine, celebrated in annual festivals where everyone samples the year's harvest. They may not be widely exported, but Swiss wines are generally available in restaurants, and you can also get to know them in wine cellars (often with delicious local cheese). All of Switzerland's 23 cantons produce wines, but six areas outdo the rest: the Valais, Vaud, Geneva, the Three Lakes region in western Switzerland, the German-speaking region of eastern Switzerland, and the Ticino. The Chasselas is by far the most successful among white grapes, and pinot noir among the reds. Other top white grape varieties include Müller-Thurgau and Sylvaner; reds feature gamay and merlot. You can get more information from the Swiss Wine Exporters' Association (⊕ *www.swisswine.ch*).

Switzerland counts more than 120 official active breweries that regularly produce *Lager, Spezialbier* (slightly stronger and a touch more bitter than the lager), and *Festbier* (strong, dark holiday beer produced at Easter and Christmas and sometimes sold as *Bockbier* or *Märzenbier*). Specialty beer includes the amber *Altbier,* the corn-infused *Maisbier,* and *Weizenbier* (wheat beer). A bit of trivia: the strongest beer ever brewed is said to have been the now-retired Samichlaus brand from the Feldschlösschen Brewery; with a whopping 14% alcohol content, it had no head and an aroma akin to molasses.

Switzerland is brimming with spirits—most notably, *kirsch* (cherry spirit) from Zug and the Lake Luzern region has gained worldwide recognition. Plums are used to make *Zwetschgenwasser.* The tiny damassine plum, reportedly brought back from Damascus by a crusading knight, is distilled into the delightfully fragrant *Damassine,* available in Saignelégier. The many apple spirits include *Träsch* and *Gravensteiner;* pears from the Valais give their spirit to the redolent *Williamine.* A unique variety of grappas is up for grabs in the grottoes of the Ticino; this potent firewater gets its name and taste from the skins of the grape. Now that vodka is gaining popularity among consumers around the globe, the Swiss have begun to promote their own designer spirit: Xellent, which entered the market in its sleek red bottle in 2003.

▌ ELECTRICITY

The electrical current in Switzerland is 220 volts, 50 cycles alternating current (AC); wall outlets take plugs that have two or three round prongs. The two-pronged continental-type plugs can be used throughout the country.

Consider making a small investment in a universal adapter, which has several types of plugs in one lightweight, compact unit. Most laptops and mobile phone chargers are dual voltage (i.e., they operate equally well on 110 and 220 volts), so require only an adapter. These days the same is true of small appliances such as hairdryers. Always check labels and manufacturer instructions to be sure. Don't use 110-volt outlets marked FOR SHAVERS ONLY for high-wattage appliances such as hairdryers.

Contacts Steve Kropla's Help for World Traveler's (⊕ *www.kropla.com*) has information on electrical and telephone plugs around the world.

Walkabout Travel Gear (⊕ *www.walk aboutravelgear.com*) has a good coverage of electricity under "adapters."

▌ EMERGENCIES

Foreign Embassies American Embassy (⊠ *Jubiläumsstr. 93, Bern* ☎ *031/3577011, 031/3577344 24-hour emergency hotline*). **Consular agency** (⊠ *Rue Versonnex 7* ☏ *Geneva* ☎ *022/8405160*). **Consular agency** (⊠ *Dufourstr. 101* ☏ *Zürich* ☎ *043/4992960*).

General Emergency Contacts Ambulance (☎ *144*). **Fire** (☎ *118*). **Police** (☎ *117*).

▌ HEALTH

SPECIFIC ISSUES IN SWITZERLAND

Switzerland's reputation for impeccable standards of cleanliness is well earned. But even at the foot of an icy-pure 6,500-foot glacier, you'll find the locals drinking bottled mineral water; you'll have to insist a little if you want tap water with your meal. This is as much a result of the tradition of expecting beverages in a café to be paid for as it is a response to health questions. If you're traveling with a child under two years old, you may be advised by locals not to carry him or her on excursions above 6,500 feet; check with your pediatrician before leaving home. Adults should limit strenuous excursions on the first day at extra-high-altitude resorts, those at 5,248 feet and above. Adults with heart problems may want to avoid all excursions above 6,500 feet.

WORD OF MOUTH

Was the service stellar or not up to snuff? Did the food give you shivers of delight or leave you cold? Did the prices and portions make you happy or sad? Rate restaurants and write your own reviews in Travel Ratings or start a discussion about your favorite places in Travel Talk on www.fodors.com. Your comments might even appear in our books. Yes, you, too, can be a correspondent!

When hiking or skiing in the mountains, be aware of the dangers of altitude sickness, as well as other afflictions such as heat stroke, dehydration, sunstroke, frostbite, and snow blindness. Wear sunglasses with side shields or goggles to avoid snow blindness, especially if you have light-colored eyes. Symptoms of altitude sickness, which occurs in some individuals who ascend rapidly to high altitudes, include numbness, tingling, nausea, drowsiness, headaches, and vision problems. If you experience discomfort, return to a lower altitude as soon as possible. You should wear sunscreen all through the year; many different brands are available at ski shops near the slopes. If you plan to spend extended periods in rural areas, take precautions against ticks, especially in spring and summer. Wear long sleeves, long pants, and boots, and apply insect repellent containing the powerful repellent DEET. Two vaccines against tick-borne infections are available in Europe: TicoVac (also known as FSME Immun) and Encepur, but neither has been approved in the United States. Remove ticks with tweezers, grasping the insect by the head.

OVER-THE-COUNTER REMEDIES
Basic over-the-counter medicines are available from pharmacies (*pharmacie, Apotheke, farmacia*), which are recognizable from afar thanks to signs with green crosses.

▮ HOURS OF OPERATION

Most businesses still close for lunch in Switzerland, generally from noon or 12:30 to 1:30 or 2, but this is changing, especially in larger cities, and especially in the German-speaking part of the country. All remain closed on Sunday. Banks are open weekdays from 8:30 to 4:30 or 5. Post offices are generally open limited hours on Saturday.

Gas station kiosks are usually open daily from 6:30 AM until 9 PM. Automatic pumps, which accept major credit cards and Swiss bank notes, are in service 24 hours a day.

Museums generally close on Monday. There is, however, an increasing trend toward staying open late one night a week, usually on Thursday or Friday evening.

Pharmacies are generally open weekdays from 9 to 1 and 2 to 6, and Saturday 9 to 1. In cities, they tend to stay open through the lunch hour. To find out which pharmacy is covering the late-night shift, check listings posted near or on the window of any pharmacy.

Shops are generally open every day except Sunday. They usually close early (4 or 5 PM) on Saturday except in larger cities, where they stay open until 6 on Saturday and often stay open until 8 or 9 one day a week. Smaller stores close for an hour or two for lunch. Stores in train stations in larger cities often open on Sunday (until 9 PM); in the Geneva and Zürich airports, shops are open on Sunday.

HOLIDAYS

National holidays include January 1 (New Year), Good Friday (March or April), Easter Sunday and Monday (March or April), May 1 only in some regions (Labor Day), Ascension Day (May), Whitsunday and Whitmonday (May), August 1 (Swiss National Holiday), and December 25–26 (Christmas and Boxing Day).

▮ MAIL

Mail rates are divided into first-class "A" (airmail) and second-class "B" (surface). Letters and postcards to North America weighing up to 20 grams (about .70 oz) cost 1.80 SF and 1.40 SF; to the United Kingdom, 1.30 SF and 1.20 SF.

Airmail letters and postcards generally take two to three business days to reach the United Kingdom from Switzerland when sent first class and four to seven days in second class. Letters take three to seven business days to reach the United States when mailed first class and seven to fifteen in second-class, four to five days in first class and from eight to fifteen days in second class to reach Australia and New Zealand.

If you're uncertain where you'll be staying, you can have your mail, marked *poste restante* or *postlagernd,* sent to any post office in Switzerland. It needs the sender's name and address on the back, and you'll need proof of identity to collect it. You can also have your mail sent to American Express for a small fee; if you are a cardholder or have American Express traveler's checks, the service is free. Postal codes precede the names of cities and towns in Swiss addresses.

SHIPPING PACKAGES

FedEx and UPS operate out of Basel, Bern, Geneva, Lugano, and Zürich, although overnight service is guaranteed only to selected European destinations. An envelope weighing up to 1.1 lb will cost about 70 SF to the United States and Canada, 87 SF to the United Kingdom, 90 SF to Australia and New Zealand.

▮ MONEY

Despite increased competition across Europe, the recent decrease in the Swiss franc's value against other currencies, and the negligible inflation rate over the past several years, Switzerland remains one of the most expensive countries on the continent for travelers, and you may find yourself shocked by the price of a light lunch or a generic hotel room. If you are traveling on a tight budget, avoid staying in well-known resorts and the most sophisticated cities; Geneva, Zürich, Zermatt, Gstaad, and St. Moritz are especially expensive. One sure way of saving some pennies: in those cities (and others) you can often find a good meal at the cafeterias of the local Migros or Coop supermarket chains, or at the Manor department stores. If you are traveling by car, you have the luxury of seeking out small family hotels in villages, where costs are relatively low. Unless you work hard at finding budget accommodations, you will average more than 150 SF a night for two—more if you stay in business-class hotels.

A cup of coffee or a beer costs about 3.50 SF in a simple restaurant; ordinary open wines, sold by the deciliter ("deci"), start at about 3.80 SF. All three beverages cost sometimes double that in resorts, city hotels, and fine restaurants. A plain, one-plate daily lunch special averages 14–18 SF. A city bus ride costs between 1.80 SF and 3 SF, a short cab ride 18 SF.

Prices throughout this guide are given for adults. Substantially reduced fees are almost always available for children, students, and senior citizens.

ATMS & BANKS

Your own bank will probably charge a fee for using ATMs abroad; the foreign bank you use may also charge a fee. Nevertheless, you'll usually get a better rate of exchange at an ATM than you will at a currency-exchange office or even when changing money in a bank. And extracting funds as you need them is a safer option than carrying around a large amount of cash.

■ TIP→ PINs with more than four digits are not recognized at ATMs in many countries. If yours has five or more, remember to change it before you leave.

You can withdraw money from ATMs in Switzerland as long as your card is properly programmed with your personal identification number (PIN). For use in Switzerland, your PIN must be four digits long. If your PIN is longer than four digits, you may want to change it before leaving home. Banks offer good wholesale exchange rates.

CREDIT CARDS

Throughout this guide, the following abbreviations are used: **AE**, American Express; **DC**, Diners Club; **MC**, MasterCard; and **V**, Visa.

If you plan to use your credit card for cash advances, you'll need to apply for a PIN at least two weeks before your trip. Although it's usually cheaper (and safer) to use a credit card abroad for large purchases (so you can cancel payments or be reimbursed if there's a problem), note that some credit-card companies *and* the banks that issue them add substantial percentages to all foreign transactions, whether they're in a foreign currency or not. Check on these fees before leaving home, so there won't be any surprises when you get the bill.

■ TIP→ Before you charge something, ask the merchant whether or not he or she plans to do a dynamic currency conversion (DCC). In such a transaction the credit-card *processor* (shop, restaurant, or hotel, not Visa or MasterCard) converts the currency and charges you in dollars. In most cases you'll pay the merchant a 3% fee for this service in addition to any credit-card company and issuing-bank foreign-transaction surcharges.

Dynamic currency conversion (DCC) programs are becoming increasingly widespread. Merchants who participate in them are supposed to ask whether you want to be charged in dollars or the local currency, but they don't always do so. And even if they do offer you a choice, they may well avoid mentioning the additional surcharges. The good news is that you *do* have a choice. And if this practice really gets your goat, you can avoid it entirely thanks to American Express; with its cards, DCC simply isn't an option.

Reporting Lost Cards American Express (☎ 800/992–3404 in the U.S., 336/393–1111 collect from abroad ⊕ www.americanexpress.com).

Diners Club (☎ 800/234–6377 in the U.S., 303/799–1504 collect from abroad ⊕ www.dinersclub.com).

MasterCard (☎ 800/622–7747 in the U.S., 636/722–7111 collect from abroad ⊕ www.mastercard.com).

Visa (☎ 800/847–2911 in the U.S., 410/581–9994 collect from abroad ⊕ www.visa.com).

CURRENCY & EXCHANGE

■ TIP➔ Even if a currency-exchange booth has a sign promising no commission, rest assured that there's some kind of huge, hidden fee. (Oh…that's right. The sign didn't say no *fee*). And as for rates, you're almost always better off getting foreign currency at an ATM or exchanging money at a bank.

The unit of currency in Switzerland is the Swiss franc (SF), available in notes of 10, 20, 50, 100, 200, and 1,000. Francs are divided into centimes (in Suisse Romande) or Rappen (in German Switzerland). There are coins for 5, 10, 20, and 50 centimes or Rappen. Larger coins are the 1-, 2-, and 5-franc pieces.

At press time (winter 2008) the Swiss franc stood at 1.12 to the U.S. dollar, 1.05 to the Canadian dollar, and 1.98 to the pound sterling.

In terms of convenience, train stations have the edge; more than 300 stations have currency exchange offices that are open daily, including lunch hours, when many banks are closed. These booths swap currency, buy and sell traveler's checks in various currencies, and cash Eurocheques.

Currency Conversion Google (⊕ www.google.com).

Oanda.com (⊕ www.oanda.com). **XE.com** (⊕ www.xe.com).

■ PACKING

In most of Switzerland dress is casual. City dress is more formal. Men would be wise to pack a jacket and tie if dining in some of the expensive restaurants, even in mountain resorts; otherwise, a tie and sweater are standard at night. Women wear skirts more frequently here than in the United States, though anything fashionable is fine. Except at the chicest hotels in international resorts, you won't need formal evening dress.

Even in July and August the evening air grows chilly in the mountains, so bring a warm sweater. And bring along a hat or sunscreen, as the atmosphere is thinner at high altitudes. Glaciers can be blinding in the sun, so be sure to bring sunglasses, which should have side shields especially for high-altitude hiking or skiing. Good walking shoes or hiking boots are a must, whether you're tackling medieval cobblestones or mountain trails.

To ensure comfort, budget travelers should bring their own washcloth and soap, not always standard in one- and two-star-rated Swiss hotels. If you're planning on shopping and cooking, a tote bag will come in handy: most groceries do not provide bags, but sturdy, reusable plastic totes can be bought at checkout. Coin-operated laundries are rare, so laundry soap is useful for hand washing.

■ PASSPORTS

Australian, British, Canadian, New Zealand, and U.S. citizens need only a valid passport to enter Switzerland for stays of up to 90 days.

▌ RESTROOMS

Restroom standards are high even for public toilets, such as those run by McClean in train stations, where you have to pay a 1 to 2 SF fee. It is appropriate to buy a drink in a bar when you want to use the facilities. Basel has made waves with its public toilets with one-way glass—no one can see you when you're inside, but you have a view of the entire street.

Find a Loo **The Bathroom Diaries** (⊕ *www. thebathroomdiaries.com*) is flush with unsanitized info on restrooms the world over—each one located, reviewed, and rated.

▌ SPORTS & THE OUTDOORS

HIKING

The Swiss Alps are riddled with hiking trails; yellow trail indicators are standard all over the country. Hiking is an especially popular pastime in the German-speaking areas, such as the Berner Oberland. For suggested hiking itineraries, including lists of huts for overnight stays, contact regional tourist offices or the Fédération Suisse de Tourisme Pédestre (Swiss Hiking Federation); many newspaper stands, kiosks, train stations, and bookstores also carry detailed topographical maps with marked trails.

Contacts **Fédération Suisse de Tourisme Pédestre** (*Swiss Hiking Federation* ✉ *Im Hirshalm 49, Riehen* ☎ *061/6069340* ⊕ *www. swisshiking.ch*).

SKIING

Switzerland's legendary phenomenal ski slopes are bolstered by excellent transportation networks, plentiful vacation packages, and visitor facilities.

Slope difficulty levels are indicated with color codes. A black slope is the most difficult; red indicates intermediate levels; blue is for beginners. A daily bulletin of ski and weather conditions throughout Switzerland is available by calling ☎ 0900/162333 (0.86 SF per min); reports are in the local language.

Serious skiers may want to join the Swiss Alpine Club. Applications should be addressed to the Sektion Zermatt branch. Remember to include a passport-size photo. Excursions involve much climbing. It's not necessary to be fluent in German. For a booklet of mountain-club refuges, contact the Swiss Alpine Club in Bern. A refuge directory called "Hütten der Schweizer Alpen," complete with color photos, can be ordered for 44 SF from the club's office.

Contacts **Swiss Alpine Club** (✉ *Sektion Zermatt, Haus Dolomit, Zermatt* ☎ *027/9676002* ✉ *Monbijoustr. 61, Postfach, Bern* ☎ *031/3701880* 🖶 *031/3701890* ⊕ *www.sac-cas.ch or www.sac-verlag.ch*).

▌ TAXES

What you see is what you pay in Switzerland: restaurant checks and hotel bills include all taxes.

If your purchases in a shop amount to 400 SF and the goods are exported within 30 days of the purchase date, you may reclaim the V.A.T. (7.6% in Switzerland). This tax is included in the sales price of most items.

When making a purchase, ask for a V.A.T. refund form and find out whether the merchant gives refunds—not all stores do, nor are they required to. Have the form stamped like any customs form by customs officials when you leave the country or, if you're visiting several European Union countries, when you leave the EU. After you're through passport control, take the form to a refund-service counter for an on-the-spot refund (which is usually the quickest and easiest option), or mail it to the address on the form (or the envelope with it) after you arrive home. You receive the total refund stated on the form, but the processing time can be long, especially if you request a credit-card adjustment.

Global Refund is a Europe-wide service with 225,000 affiliated stores and more than 700 refund counters at major airports and border crossings. Its refund form, called a Tax Free Check, is the most common across the European continent. The service issues refunds in the form of cash, check, or credit-card adjustment.

V.A.T. Refunds Global Refund
(☎ 800/566–9828 ⊕ www.globalrefund.com).

■ TIME

Switzerland is six hours ahead of New York, nine hours ahead of Los Angeles, one hour ahead of London, and nine hours behind Sydney. Since new daylight savings protocols took effect in 2007, the U.S. benefits from an extra month of DST, during which time one hour must be subtracted to the above time differences with Switzerland.

Time Zones Timeanddate.com (⊕ www.timeanddate.com/worldclock).

■ TIPPING

Despite all protests to the contrary and menus marked *service compris,* the Swiss *do* tip at restaurants, giving quantities anywhere from the change from the nearest franc to 10 SF or more for a world-class meal that has been exquisitely served. Unlike American-style tipping, calculated by a percentage, usually between 10% and 20%, a tip is still a tip here: a nod of approval for a job well done. If, in a café, the waitress settles the bill at the table, fishing the change from her leather purse, give her the change on the spot—or calculate the total, including tip, and tell her the full sum before she counts it onto the tabletop. If you need to take more time to calculate, leave it on the table, though this isn't common practice in outdoor cafés. If you're paying for a meal with a credit card, try to tip with cash instead of filling in the tip slot on the slip: not all managers are good about doling out the waiters' tips in cash. Bartenders are also tipped along these lines. Tipping porters and doormen is easier: 2 SF per bag is adequate in good hotels, 1 SF per trip in humbler lodgings (unless you travel heavy). A fixed rate of 5 SF per bag applies to porter fees at the Geneva and Zürich airports. Tip taxi drivers the change or an extra couple of francs, depending on the length of the drive and whether they've helped with your bags. To tip other hotel personnel, you can leave an appropriate amount with the concierge or, for cleaning staff, with a note of thanks in your room.

■ VISITOR INFORMATION

Contacts U.S. (nationwide)
(☎ 212/757–5944 📠 212/262–6116 ⊕ www.myswitzerland.com). **AngloPhone** (☎ 0900/576444) is an English-language information service giving details on hotels, restaurants, museums, nightlife, skiing, what to do in an emergency, and more. Lines are open weekdays 9–noon and 2–7. Calls cost 3.13 SF per minute.

ONLINE TRAVEL TOOLS

The Switzerland Tourism Web site (⊕ *www. myswitzerland.com*) allows travelers to customize a vacation in Switzerland and even to book it through an interactive travel planner.

All About Switzerland Go Ski (⊕ www.goski. com). **Great Outdoor Recreation Pages** (*GORP* ⊕ www.gorp.com). **Pro Helvetia** (⊕ www.pro-helvetia.ch). **Swiss Broadcasting Corporation** (⊕ www.swissinfo.org). **Swissart Network** (⊕ www.swissart.ch). **Swissworld** (⊕ www.swissworld.org).

Weather Accuweather.com (⊕ www. accuweather.com).

Weather.com (⊕ www.weather.com).

INDEX

Photo Credits: **Chapter 1: Experience Switzerland:** 7, *Klosters Tourismus/swiss-image.ch.* 8, *Christof Sonderegger/Switzerland Tourism/swiss-image.ch.* 9 (left), *Bruno Meier/Switzerland Tourism/swiss-image.ch.* 9 (right), *Peter Rüegger/SGV Luzern/swiss-image.ch.* 10, *Basel Tourismus/swiss-image.ch.* 11 (left), *Terence du Fresne/Bern Tourismus/swiss-image.ch.* 11 (right), *Grindelwald Tourismus/swiss-image.ch.* 15 (left), *Christof Sonderegger/Switzerland Tourism/swiss-image.ch.* 15 (right), *Lookat/swiss-image.ch.* 18 (top left), *Patrick Frischknecht/age fotostock.* 18 (bottom left), *Trevor Payne/Alamy.* 18 (top center), *Doris Brawand/Switzerland Tourism.* 18 (right), Swiss Cities/Christof Sonderegger/Switzerland Tourism/swiss-image.ch. 19 (left), *Peter Adams/age fotostock.* 19 (top center), *Max Schmid//Switzerland Tourism/swiss-image.ch.* 19 (bottom center), *Grant Farquhar/Alamy.* 19 (right), *StockShot/Alamy.* 20, *JTB Photo Communications, Inc./Alamy.* 21, *SuperStock/age fotostock.* 22, *Valais Tourism/Switzerland Tourism/swiss-image.ch.* 23 (left), *Christof Sonderegger/Switzerland Tourism/swiss-image.ch.* 23 (right), *Lucia Degonda/Switzerland Tourism/swiss-image.ch.* 25 (left and right), *Christof Sonderegger/Switzerland Tourism/swiss-image.ch.* **Chapter 2: Zurich:** 29, *Visual & Written SL/Alamy.* 30 (top), *Switzerland Tourism/swiss-image.ch.* 30 (bottom), *Samuel Mizrachi/Switzerland Tourism/swiss-image.ch.* 31, *Zuerich Tourismus/swiss-image.ch.* **Chapter 3: Eastern Switzerland & Liechtenstein:** 69, *Ch. Perret/Heidiland Tourism/Switzerland Tourism/swiss-image.ch.* 70, *Schaffhausen Tourismus/swiss-image.ch.* 71 (top), *S. Boegli/Switzerland Tourism/swiss-image.ch.* 71 (bottom), *R. Giger/Switzerland Tourism/swiss-image.ch.* **Chapter 4: Graubünden:** 103, *Danilo Donadoni/age fotostock.* 104 (top), *Raphael Koch/Davos Tourismus/swiss-image.ch.* 104 (bottom), *Daniel Kalberer/Ferienregion Heidiland/swiss-image.ch.* 105 (top), *Christian Perret/Davos Tourismus/swiss-image.ch.* 105 (bottom), Davos Tourismus/swiss-image.ch. 106, *Klosters Tourismus/swiss-image.ch.* **Chapter 5: The Ticino:** 153, *Loetscher Chlaus/Alamy.* 154 (top), *Remy Steinegger/Swissminiatur/swiss-image.ch.* 154 (bottom), *Stephan Engler/Switzerland Tourism/swiss-image.ch.* 155, *Stephan Engler/Switzerland Tourism/swiss-image.ch.* 156, *Remy Steinegger/Ticino Turismo/swiss-image.ch.* **Chapter 6: Luzern & Central Switzerland:** 189, *Heinz Schwab/Switzerland Tourism/swiss-image.ch.* 190 (top), *Luzern Tourismus/Switzerland Tourism/swiss-image.ch.* 190 (bottom), *Max Schmid/Switzerland Tourism.* 191, *Christof Sonderegger/Switzerland Tourism/swiss-image.ch.* 193, *D. Brawand/Switzerland Tourism/swiss-image.ch.* **Chapter 7: Basel:** 225, *Niklaus Buergin/Basel Tourismus/swiss-image.ch.* 226, *Basel Tourismus/swiss-image.ch.* 227 (top), *Stephan Engler/Switzerland Tourism/swiss-image.ch.* 227 (bottom), *Basel Tourismus/swiss-image.ch.* 229, *Dominik Pluess/Basel Tourismus/swiss-image.ch.* **Chapter 8: Fribourg & Neuchâtel:** 257, *Philipp Giegel/Switzerland Tourism/swiss-image.ch.* 258 (top and bottom), *Franck Auberson/UFT/swiss-image.ch.* 259 (left), *Christof Sonderegger/Switzerland Tourism/swiss-image.ch.* 259 (right), *Franck Auberson/UFT/swiss-image.ch.* 260, *Franck Auberson/UFT/swiss-image.ch.* **Chapter 9: Bern:** 291, *Stephan Engler/Switzerland Tourism/swiss-image.ch.* 292 (top), *Bern Tourismus/swiss-image.ch.* 292 (bottom), *Christof Sonderegger/Switzerland Tourism/swiss-image.ch.* 293 (top and bottom), *Terence du Fresne/Bern Tourismus/swiss-image.ch.* 295, *Stephan Engler/Switzerland Tourism/swiss-image.ch.* **Chapter 10: Berner Oberland:** 321, *Jon Arnold/age fotostock.* 322 (top), *Robert Boesch/Switzerland Tourism/swiss-image.ch.* 322 (bottom), *Christof Sonderegger/Switzerland Tourism/swiss-image.ch.* 323 (top), *Christof Sonderegger/Switzerland Tourism/swiss-image.ch.* 323 (bottom), Grindelwald Tourismus/swiss-image.ch. 326, *Jungfrau Railways/swiss-image.ch.* **Chapter 11: Valais:** 369, *Worldwide Picture Library/Alamy.* 370 (top), *Emanuel Ammon/Crans-Montana Tourisme/swiss-image.ch.* 370 (bottom), *Christof Sonderegger/Switzerland Tourism/swiss-image.ch.* 371 (top), *Emanuel Ammon/Crans-Montana Tourisme/swiss-image.ch.* 371 (bottom), *Thomas Andenmatten/Bettmeralp Tourismus/swiss-image.ch.* **Chapter 12: Vaud:** 417, *BL Images Ltd/Alamy.* 418 (top), *Stephan Engler/Switzerland Tourism/swiss-image.ch.* 418 (bottom), *Lucia Degonda/Switzerland Tourism/swiss-image.ch.* 419 (top), *Robert Boesch/Switzerland Tourism/swiss-image.ch.* 419 (bottom), *Christof Sonderegger/Switzerland Tourism/swiss-image.ch.* 420, *Peter Maurer/Switzerland Tourism/swiss-image.ch.* **Chapter 13: Geneva:** 469, *Christof Sonderegger/Switzerland Tourism/swiss-image.ch.* 470 (top), *Danita Delimont/Alamy.* 470 (bottom), *Samuel Mizrachi/Switzerland Tourism/swiss-image.ch.* 471, *Hemis/Alamy.* 472 and 475, *Christof Schuerpf/Switzerland Tourism/swiss-image.ch.*

ABOUT OUR WRITERS

Fodor's success in showing you every corner of Switzerland is a credit to our hardworking writers. Many editions ago, this guide was originally authored by Nancy Coons. Since then, our Switzerland-based authors have added much to the book. Although there's no substitute for travel advice from a good friend who knows your style, our contributors are the next best thing—the kind of people you would poll for travel advice if you knew them.

Katrin Gygax was born in Zürich. Her family moved to California when she was four and moved to Vancouver when she was six, and then she didn't stop traveling for the next 28 years. Now based in Zürich with her own translating business, she writes movie reviews, mystery novels, and sings whenever possible. For this edition, she updated the chapters on Zürich, Eastern Switzerland, Luzern and Central Switzerland, and Bern.

Suzanne Hégelé grew up in the United Kingdom after being born in New Zealand. She is now settled in Zürich with her Swiss husband and children yet continues to follow her passions of traveling the globe for both work and personal satisfaction. Having worked in broadcasting over the last ten years (specializing in documentaries and travel shows), she has many a tale to share. For this edition, she updated the chapters on Berner Oberland, Fribourg and Neuchâtel, and Graubünden.

Gail Mangold-Vine is Swiss by marriage. Daughter of a U.S. diplomat, she grew up all over the world, conveniently learning fluent French, German, and Italian—Switzerland's official languages—along the way. After having lived in Zürich for 15 years, she now owns a content creation company in Geneva, and writes regularly about travel, art, and food and wine for the Swiss and world media. Her book about Geneva, *Touring Geneva Wine Country*, is in its second edition. For this edition, she updated the chapter on Geneva.

Alexis Munier sold everything she owned and relocated to Europe six years ago. The author of the newly published *Talk Dirty: French* and *Talk Dirty: Italian*, this opera singer-turned-polyglot lived and worked in Russia, Slovenia, and Italy before settling down in Lausanne with her Swiss husband. Despite running after a baby in diapers, Munier still finds time to be a writer, English teacher, and translator. For this edition, she updated our Valais, Ticino, and Travel Smart chapters.

Sharon-Anne Wilcox has worked as a journalist and editor for a wide range of popular magazines in the United Kingdom and Europe. A Londoner by birth, she enjoys reporting on city life throughout the world. Now settled in Zürich, she's become an aficionado of Switzerland's wonderful mountains and valleys. For this edition, she updated the chapter on Basel.

Kay Winzenried made her first visit to Switzerland from the United States in 1980 and has returned every year since. Now a dual citizen, she has lived in both the French- and German-speaking regions. She uses the centrally located country as a base for travels throughout Europe and gateway to other parts of the world. Hiking with friends and family, exploring vineyards, and dining—be it rustic or haute cuisine—are her pleasures. For this edition, she updated the Vaud chapter, the region where she pursues her culinary and wine passions.

We'd also like to thank the staff of the Swiss regional tourist offices, as well as the Switzerland Tourism office in New York City, for their help with questions big and small.